THE VOICE IS ALL

THE VOICE IS ALL

The Lonely Victory of
JACK KEROUAC

Joyce Johnson

VIKING

VIKING
Published by the Penguin Group
Penguin Group (USA) Inc., 375 Hudson Street, New York, New York 10014, U.S.A. • Penguin Group (Canada), 90 Eglin-
ton Avenue East, Suite 700, Toronto, Ontario, Canada M4P 2Y3 (a division of Pearson Penguin Canada Inc.) • Penguin
Books Ltd, 80 Strand, London WC2R 0RL, England • Penguin Ireland, 25 St. Stephen's Green, Dublin 2, Ireland (a divi-
sion of Penguin Books Ltd) • Penguin Books Australia Ltd, 250 Camberwell Road, Camberwell, Victoria 3124, Australia
(a division of Pearson Australia Group Pty Ltd) • Penguin Books India Pvt Ltd, 11 Community Centre, Panchsheel Park,
New Delhi – 110 017, India • Penguin Group (NZ), 67 Apollo Drive, Rosedale, Auckland 0632, New Zealand (a division of
Pearson New Zealand Ltd) • Penguin Books (South Africa) (Pty) Ltd, 24 Sturdee Avenue, Rosebank, Johannesburg 2196,
South Africa

Penguin Books Ltd, Registered Offices: 80 Strand, London WC2R 0RL, England

First published in 2012 by Viking Penguin, a member of Penguin Group (USA) Inc.

10 9 8 7 6 5 4 3 2 1

Grateful acknowledgment is made for permission to reprint excerpts from *Windblown World: The Journals of Jack Kerouac, 1947–1954*, edited by Douglas Brinkley. Copyright © The Estate of Stella Kerouac, John Sampas, Literary Represen-
tative, 2004. Used by permission of Viking Penguin, a member of Penguin Group (USA) Inc.

LIBRARY OF CONGRESS CATALOGING IN PUBLICATION DATA
Johnson, Joyce, date.
    The voice is all : the lonely victory of Jack Kerouac / Joyce Johnson.
        p.   cm.
    Includes bibliographical references and index.
    ISBN 978-0-670-02510-7
    1. Kerouac, Jack, 1922–1969. 2. Authors, American—20th century—Biography. 3. Beat generation—Biography.
I. Title.
    PS3521.E735Z733 2012
    818'.54—dc23
    [B]   2012000603

Printed in the United States of America

ALWAYS LEARNING   PEARSON

For Hettie Jones, whom I met just the other day in 1957,

and for Lily Pinchbeck, my favorite book lover

CONTENTS

Am I concerned with happiness? I am concerned with my work.

—Friedrich Nietzsche, *Thus Spake Zarathustra*

Home I'll never be.

—Jack Kerouac, *On the Road*

Well, anyway, all those sons of bitches had turned into angels without my noticing! Whole clouds full of angels, including some very far-out and disreputable ones, all over the place. Roaming around, high over the city!

—Louis-Ferdinand Céline, *Journey to the End of the Night*

INTRODUCTION

Precariously balanced between conflicting selves, between two cultures and two different languages, between ambition and self-immolation, Jack Kerouac rose suddenly to fame in 1957 with a label that only half fitted him: "King of the Beats." With a novel set at the end of the postwar period about two rootless young men engaged in a quest for connection, ecstacy, and enlightenment, Kerouac found himself elected the outlaw voice of the generation sociologists too confidently called "Silent" and at the center of a ferocious culture war that is being fought bitterly to this day. *On the Road* would eloquently define for young Americans that nagging secret itch they felt for a fuller, more meaningful, much freer life and send many of them out in search of that elusive "It" right in their own country, while the author of the book that had inspired them, and stripped him of his anonymity, retreated into alcoholic seclusion in the suburban house he'd bought for his mother. The label "Beat" will probably always be affixed to Kerouac, yet it obscures another important side of him that has so far been poorly understood—the deeply traditional Jean-Louis Kerouac, who had been raised in a French-speaking, Catholic, Franco-American family in Lowell, Massachusetts. The hidden Jean-Louis side of Kerouac was always there and always felt and it would become dominant again in the last sad decade of his life.

No one was more aware of Kerouac's dualities and contradictions than he was, and it was his genius to find a voice that would contain them when he was only twenty-nine. In fact, it is partly the constant flux of shading and mood which makes the music of that voice so vibrantly alive. According to the legend that congealed around Jack—to which he contributed himself—the writing of *On the Road* was a completely spontaneous act, a flood of words so unstoppable that it had to be typed on a scroll during the twenty days it took to get it all down in the spring of 1951. But this too obscures the real story as well as the full appreciation of Kerouac's achievement. His mastery did not come suddenly or effortlessly. Choosing English as the language he would use to express himself in his writing, he set himself the task of acquiring it when he was only a boy, coming home from the Lowell Public Library with armloads of books. By the time he was nineteen he had dedicated his life to his work—a choice beyond the comprehension of his family. He would spend the next ten years writing stories, poems, entire novels, working toward the point when he would find the courage to cast off the artifices of conventional plot-driven fiction and, finally, the American mask that concealed his ethnic identity. The process of discovering a way to capture the movements of his mind without self-censorship or second thoughts began with *On the Road,* but would find its fullest expression in the much more radical novel he began shortly afterward. With *Visions of Cody,* Jack would make his own singular contribution to the great stream-of-consciousness experiments of twentieth-century literature.

On the Road came out too late for Jack. He had barely survived the despair and near destitution of the six grim years after he finished it. But he had managed to produce eleven more books—all of them written in very short concentrated bursts of creative energy, and published, as Allen Ginsberg wrote in his preface to *Howl,* "in heaven." This body of work, as John Clellon Holmes would astutely observe, is "not so much concerned with events as it is with consciousness, in which the ultimate events are images." In his own way, Jack was a perfectionist with an aesthetic no one without his extraordinary gifts could live up to. Each paragraph had to be a "poem," each sentence "a breath separation of the mind." In 1952, after driving himself to complete *The Subterraneans* in only three days, he looked in the mirror and did not recognize the gaunt white face he saw there. Two years later, he began to wonder whether he had written himself out. Jack's voice was his center; outside that center was chaos. He told me once that he had written all his books so that he would have something to read in his old age, but he would die in 1969 at the age of forty-seven, with the book that meant the most to him, *Visions of Cody,* still unpublished in its entirety.

For many years, I waited for a definitive biography of Kerouac to appear. But I have come to wonder, especially in the process of writing this book, whether there can be such a thing as a *definitive* biography. Even our own lives cannot be entirely defined despite our knowledge of "the facts," which is why some writers—and Kerouac was one of them—are drawn toward the ceaseless examination of the self. Our perceptions change, as well as what we remember, as the passage of time alters our angle of vision.

"Poor Leecie," Jack wrote in *Desolation Angels*, the novel in which I appear as a character, "she never understood Goyeshe me." If I had written this biography in my fifties, when there was so much less reliable information available, mistaken assumptions would undoubtedly have led me down some wrong paths. If I had attempted to write about Jack in my twenties, when my memories of my own relationship with him between 1957 and 1958 were still fresh, I would not have had the objectivity I brought to my memoir, *Minor Characters*, when I began it in 1981.

There are many ways to tell the story of Jack Kerouac, depending upon the biographer's point of view or agenda. One can emphasize the Beat aspect, while treating the ways Kerouac does not seem Beat at all as puzzling inconsistencies. One can speculate on the nature of Kerouac's sexuality; present a relentless chronicle of his drinking and dysfunctional behavior; call him a saint or a manic depressive; visit all the places he lived or to which he traveled and attempt to show that everything in *On the Road* or his subsequent "true life" novels was true. One could, until fairly recently, go out with a tape recorder and conduct interviews with many of the people he knew or even track down those who had run into him a few times in Florida, New York, or San Francisco and were convinced they knew all about him. Such recollections, reliable and not, were by default the bases of many of the biographies that preceded this one, and it is good that so much valuable and colorful material was collected before it could evaporate. But I have been interviewed myself and have often been troubled afterward by distortions that changed the meaning of what I said and even by invented anecdotes other writers have added to the accounts I gave them. I can only imagine how many distortions, misrememberings, and outright fabrications there must be in the huge accumulation of Kerouac oral history.

In doing the research for this book, I have relied instead upon Jack's own written words as well as the letters, journals, and books of his closest friends, especially Allen Ginsberg, Neal Cassady, and John Clellon

Holmes. The papers of these remarkable men recapture the past in the most authentic way—not as a frozen entity but as something still volatile, quivering with life, passion, contradiction.

If one were to try to reconstruct Jack purely from what people have said about him, one would have to leave out a good part of his most important relationship—the one he had with his work. Although Kerouac's life was at times so crowded with dramatic events and intense, complicated friendships that one month in it could seem like a year, he spent far less time than most people in the company of others. What has always especially interested me, in fact, is the Kerouac no one ever saw, the man alone in a room writing. As a boy Jack thought he was only playing as he put the stories he imagined down on paper in the English he was determined to master. I am interested in the way that play grew into the kind of need that could consume a man's entire existence, endangering his ability to survive, making him seem "indolent" or selfish in the unsympathetic eyes of most of society. I am interested in the epiphanies that came to him when it seemed impossible to move his work forward. I am interested, in short, in the unlikely miracle of the development of a great artist—something I can only shed some light upon but do not presume to entirely account for.

This book would have been impossible to write if I had not had access to the vast carefully preserved Kerouac Archive that was deposited in the Berg Collection of the New York Public Library in 2002 after being closed to scholars for three decades. While full permission to quote from Jack's unpublished papers remains restricted to writers whose projects have been sanctioned by the Kerouac estate, an exciting new era of Kerouac scholarship has opened up. Now that the Kerouac papers can be read, Kerouac's life can finally be traced with a depth and accuracy that were inconceivable before.

I have chosen to tell only a portion of Jack's story, ending this book in November 1951 as he creates the opening sections of *Visions of Cody*. The bleak details of his decline can be found in other books, but to me what is important is Jack's triumph in arriving at the voice that matched his vision—the reason we will continue to read him. His works live on, while the Beat Generation has not existed for a very long time.

THE VOICE IS ALL

PART ONE

FRANCO-AMERICAN GHOSTS

THE LOST BROTHER

There's a dead child buried in the pages of Jack Kerouac's first novel, *The Town and the City*. A boy named Julian, still a live presence for his mother, who insists, "He's still taking care of us, even though we don't see him—he's still here." But the omniscient narrator swiftly moves on—it's Julian's brothers and sisters, characters who will "burn savagely across days and nights of living," whose lives will be followed in the hundreds of pages that follow, and Julian is not *here* for them. Caught up in the tumult of their stories, the reader can easily forget the dead boy. He's survived by a twin named Francis, an odd duck intellectual who stands aloof from those around him, but nothing more is explicitly made of Julian himself. It's as if the writer had tentatively touched a smoldering ember.

The novel, published in 1949, is about the Martins, a large Catholic New England family, half Irish, half French Canadian. There are eight Martin children—five boys and three girls—packed into a warm lower-middle-class household bursting with life until the impact of the war scatters them. I read *The Town and the City* when I was twenty-one in the fall of 1956, hardly able to tear myself away until I'd finished it. I remember feeling that Jack Kerouac knew everything about the anguished but necessary process of leaving home.

When I met Jack only a few months later, in January 1957, I was surprised to learn that he had grown up with only one sister. In fact, compared to most French Canadians, Jack's parents, Leo and Gabrielle, had had an unusually small family. It turned out, though, that he actually did have a dead brother in his past named Gerard. Gerard had suffered from rheumatic fever; his heart had given out when he was nine and Jack was four. That was about all Jack ever told me about his brother, although he intimated that in some way this family tragedy explained him.

He was thirty-four and deeply weary. A cloud of melancholy—*ennui* was his word for it—hung over his exuberance. In the midst of Manhattan, he'd talk longingly of the mountaintop in Washington where he had spent sixty-three days in unbroken solitude the previous summer. "I'm just an old hermit," he'd remind me, warning me not to count on him: "Do what you want." The publication of *On the Road* loomed ahead of him, less than a year in the future.

I romanticized Jack at first. With his gleaming black hair, tender blue eyes, and ruddy complexion, I could hardly help it. He looked like a man who had walked straight out of the American wilderness. I thought I'd never met anyone who'd lived with more absolute freedom. No job, no money, no address for the last half dozen years. A need to keep moving, as if whenever he stayed anywhere too long, he exhausted the present by soaking it in too intensely. Even those first weeks he spent with me were a prelude to another journey. He told me about Tangiers, where he was headed next, as if he had already walked through the Casbah, heard the whanging music in the hot narrow streets. Little that he found in his travels would ever match his expectations.

Today many would call Jack's way of life homelessness. But behind its seeming aimlessness was a fierce, often self-punishing, discipline. He let me know that everything he did was in the service of his writing. Unfailingly generous to other writers, he urged me to follow his example and expose myself to a broad range of risk and experience, so that I could someday write "a big novel" myself.

Shortly before Jack's path crossed mine, he had gone down to Orlando, Florida, to see his mother. It had been a Christmas visit—nothing that suggested to me how fatally and inextricably he was bound to her in a mutual dependence that had its convoluted roots in his earliest memories. Like Jack's other friends, I knew him and didn't know him. He could be open in a charismatic way that drew out other people's secrets, but he held on to his own.

In the letters Jack wrote to certain people he revealed his obsession with Gerard, but he never revealed it to me during the periods we lived together. Still, the clues were there, if only I'd recognized them. In a curious way, I think he felt "at home" with me. "I had me a companion there," he'd later write in *Desolation Angels*. I wasn't his type, really, not a girl with whom he was in danger of getting into deep water. He let me know right away that he usually went for dark women—women who looked "fellaheen," as if they had Indian blood like his mother. It took him about a year to say he loved me, but we immediately hit it off as friends. He liked it that I was a writer and quiet the way he was. And he appreciated my efforts to make food for him that reminded him of his mother's cooking—I made him many pots of Lipton's pea soup, to which, at his suggestion, I added the Franco-American touch of bacon or salt pork.

In those days I had a big gray cat. Jack soon took it over, giving it the name Ti Gris. For some reason he didn't go into, he was very devoted to cats. He would feed Ti Gris in a way that never failed to charm me. Like a small boy, he'd lie flat on his belly with his chin pressed against the rim of the cat's bowl, murmuring encouraging words half in French, half in English. Many years later, I was startled when the eerie significance of those little scenes dawned on me for the first time as I read *Visions of Gerard*:

> When the little kitty is given his milk, I imitate Gerard and get down on my stomach . . . "You happy, Ti Pou?—your nice lala—"

I realized then that without knowing it I had witnessed a secret sacrament, heard Jack Kerouac calling up his dead brother.

One thing I noticed immediately was Jack's astonishing ability to remember just the kinds of things most people would have forgotten. I have never known anyone whose past seemed so available to them. With an extraordinary rush of detail, Jack could recall a conversation with a stranger in a barroom; a high school football game in Lowell, Massachusetts; a diner where he'd stopped for a cup of coffee in one of the godforsaken towns he'd passed through out west. I can still remember his way of "digging" someone he'd just met, the hunch of his shoulders when he'd lean forward as if every word he was hearing were valuable—something to be saved up in the vast, roomy warehouse of his memory.

He told me that the kids he'd grown up with in Lowell had called him "Memory Babe."

Uniquely equipped to work directly from life, Jack had resisted doing so all through his apprenticeship years in his twenties, when he was determined to master the art of creating imaginative fiction. The year 1950 found him struggling with increasing frustration to follow up *The Town and the City* with a big-canvas novel set in the West, written in a style heavily influenced by Thomas Wolfe and Herman Melville. But on December 28, in the first of four installments of a remarkable piece of confessional writing addressed to his friend Neal Cassady, he unleashed the stunning first-person voice that had been bottled up inside him. Two months earlier, in the midst of a period of deep frustration with his work, Jack had made a discovery he considered crucial: "the voice is all." Now, as he vowed to renounce both "fiction and fear," he felt so intoxicated by new power and fluency that he could not resist making the claim that he remembered the very day he was born, coming into the world on March 12, 1922, on a late afternoon in Lowell, Massachusetts, "red as fire." But the long-held-back memories that had prompted his breakthrough pressed upon him. Quickly he got down to what he called "the agonized cock of the matter"—"My brother was a saint and that explains all"— and his opening bravado faded. In fact, he apologized for briefly giving in to the temptation to depart from the absolute truth.

Having set himself the task of writing a truthful and unguarded confession to the friend he regarded as a surrogate brother, Jack had to acknowledge at the outset that much of what he was about to write about Gerard would have to be drawn from what he'd been told by others, particularly his mother. Though he insisted his heart told him otherwise, he allowed that Gabrielle Kerouac had probably exaggerated at times. Nonetheless, as if he were still a child, he was not about to refute anything his mother had told him. After all, she had always kept her eye on everything in her household and could even have listened behind the door to catch every utterance of his "little saint-brother." But Jack's voice was infused with the urgency of a man struggling to disentangle his adult sense of what was real and what was not from the image of this saintly Gerard he could barely recall. There are very few places in Kerouac's writing where he ever feels at a loss—it is only when it comes to his brother that his memory fails him.

From his mother's grief a hagiography had been born. And Gabrielle Kerouac had evidently been a very compelling narrator. The touchingly detailed anecdotes she told her impressionable surviving son evoked a Gerard whose goodness and tenderness had been otherworldly, a boy who had fed the flocks of little birds that were drawn to his windowsill and disappeared mysteriously after his death, a boy who had wept over a dead mouse he had rescued from a trap, sternly scolding the family cat for slaughtering it. Gabrielle recalled her older son drawing angels; lying in the grass in the backyard, he had told her he was watching heaven—a place so real to him he was able to describe it to her and to the nuns in his parochial school as if he had been granted a vision. Gerard's unusually close relationship with his four-year-old brother, Ti Jean, had also been a dominant feature of her stories. Her two little boys had been inseparable and Gerard had taught Ti Jean everything he knew—from how to draw to how to be good. Lovingly admiring Ti Jean's rosy cheeks and the small body that was so much sturdier than his own, Gerard had called him "Ti Pousse," or "Little Thumb." "I know now I imitated him through life," Jack told Neal reverently in one of the abrupt shifts of feeling that animated his new voice. He noted that in photographs he and Gerard had looked very much alike when they were small and regretted that he could not remember the expression in his brother's eyes or anything he had said to him.

In fact, the only Gerard Jack's memory could summon up was quite different from the one he told Neal he'd always imitated. By all accounts, Gerard had been a sensitive, gifted, empathetic child, with an imagination very much heightened by the teachings of the Catholic Church, but in reality, he had not always been the gentlest of brothers. Confined to the house during the last months of his life, deprived of playmates his own age and often in agony from his swollen limbs, he had sometimes run out of patience with Jack and treated him with a severity that was very frightening to a four-year-old. In fact, Jack's last memory of Gerard was the slap across the face that had been his punishment for knocking over an elaborate crane Gerard had been carefully building with his Erector set. What particularly disturbed him, even as a man of twenty-eight, was a hazy memory like a waking dream of "a gaunt and ragged phantom" standing over his crib in the middle of the night "intent on me with hate."

As Jack continued his confession, a memory came to him of watching his increasingly frail brother sledding with other children one winter afternoon and having a premonition then that Gerard was going to die. He had always felt guilty of being "the knower" of his brother's death—a guilt that extended to the death of anyone he knew.

Although Jack had forgotten so much about Gerard, all the emotions of his childhood—sorrow, guilt, anger, a sense of abandonment— churned inside him as he worked on the first three installments of the confession. The truth was, he had resented Gerard for becoming the focus of all their mother's attention. He could recall yelling for her when she was just across the room, oblivious to his needs as she nursed his older brother. During one crisis in Gerard's illness, Jack had sat forlornly on the porch steps, locked out of his home. His father—groaning with pain from rheumatism in an upstairs bedroom, worrying about being unable to go to work and grieving over the impending loss of his oldest child—had also been less available to him during this chaotic and frightening time. As young as he was, Jack had had an acute awareness of what he called "a conspiracy between my mother and brother against my father and me," that somehow did not include his seven-year-old sister, Caroline.

This configuration would shift after Gerard's death when Jack would take his brother's place and win back the attention of his mother. "But my triumph was my loss," Jack wrote Neal in a third letter on January 9. The bitter clarity of this insight, however, did nothing to free him from the grip of his childish logic: If, according to his mother, Gerard was Jesus, "Judas was me." That deadly equation made Jack the betrayer of his brother: "He was an angel, I was a mortal; what he could have brought into the world, I destroyed by my mere presence."

Death-haunted childhoods ran in Jack's family. Born in 1889, shortly before his family's departure from Canada, Leo Kerouac had lost five of his fifteen siblings by the time he was six. Nashua, New Hampshire, with epidemics raging through its immigrant neighborhoods, had proved to be an unhealthy place for the Kerouac children. In 1892, Leo's six-year-old sister succumbed to tubercular meningitis; over the next three years three babies died of cholera one after another. The last fatality, in 1896, was a fourteen-year-old girl.

The deaths had unhinged Leo's hardworking father, Jean Baptiste Kerouac. In Canada, Jean Baptiste had been an itinerant farm manager. He had moved his growing family to nine different locations; sometimes they had lived in the area around Jean Baptiste's birthplace, Rivière-du-Loup, on the northern edge of Quebec, sometimes farther south on the outskirts of Montreal. But in Nashua, where the Kerouacs arrived in 1890 when thousands of other French Canadians were also abandoning their failing farms and migrating to New England, Jean Baptiste had been quickly able to establish himself as a carpenter and build a two-story frame house for his wife and children; there Leo's three younger siblings had been born. One more proof that the nomadic days of the Kerouacs were finally over was Jean Baptiste's purchase of two adjoining family plots in the Nashua cemetery. But as the plots filled with the coffins of his children, Jean Baptiste set about destroying himself with drink. In the midst of thunderstorms, he would terrify his family by standing outside the house he had built, shaking a kerosene lantern at lightning bolts and daring God to strike him down. He dropped dead in the midst of a violent argument with a relative when Leo was fifteen. Within a year his exhausted wife, Clementine, followed him into the graveyard.

Gabrielle Kerouac, whom everyone called Gabe, had a low opinion of her husband's people, whom she considered a crazy bunch and compared to "a snarling pack of cubs," Leo being the notable exception. Gabe clung to her husband and children; although she enjoyed socializing, she had a tendency that increased with time to view people outside her immediate family with contempt and suspicion. Born in St.-Pacôme, Quebec, but raised in Nashua like Leo, she had lost her mother when she was two and had no memories of her. Two of her father's sisters had had a hand in raising her; Gabe would brag about the genteel ways of the Lévesques, then bitterly complain that her relatives had treated her like a housemaid. She had felt close to the woman Louis Lévesque married when she was eight, whom she called Ti Ma, and to her two half-siblings. But by the time her father died of a sudden heart attack, in 1911, his second wife had become estranged from him and had moved to Brooklyn with her children. With no one in her father's family stepping forward to take her in, Gabe found herself alone in the world at sixteen. Jack's older sister, Caroline, would later ascribe their mother's suffocating need to control her children's lives and her jealousy of their other relationships to her "inborn terror" of abandonment.

Louis Lévesque had been born in Quebec to a half-Iroquois mother, an ancestry Jack was later proud of. At seventeen, he had come to Nashua as a laborer. When he died twenty years later, he was the owner of a tavern, but left his daughter unprovided for. Gabe had to go to work in a shoe factory, standing over a moving blade all day long skiving leather. Her fingertips turned permanently brown from the acid used for tanning. For the next four years, she lived in a boarding house with other workers. Then Leo Kerouac rescued her from the lonely existence of a factory girl. He took her away from Nashua, the scene of all their terrible memories, and gave her a home of her own in Centralville, the most up-and-coming French Canadian neighborhood in Lowell, Massachusetts, where some of his older siblings were living. He even bought his bride an old twenty-five-dollar piano, which would later accompany the Kerouacs wherever they moved. Gabe loved to sing for her children and accompany herself; in her lost girlhood there had been piano lessons. She took fanatical care of the small, spotless world Leo had given her, as if evil could be warded off with a dishcloth. It was the marriage of two orphans determined to start a new, unshadowed life. But within a year Gabe gave birth to a baby with a weak heart.

Whenever he looked at old photographs of his brother's thin, sad-eyed, pallid face, Jack could see Gerard's cruel fate plainly spelled out: "Never for once," he told Neal, "did all his angels and lambs come to his aid when he needed them most."

Gerard's death was one too many for Leo and Gabrielle. It did not strengthen the bond between them. Instead they retreated from each other. Leo would go more and more his own way, burying his grief by immersing himself in the small printing business he had recently established; in his spare time, he would obsessively follow the horse races and escape into the masculine world of gambling and hard drinking. When Leo came home late at night after a poker game, he would often find that his two small children, Ti Jean and Ti Nin, had taken his place in bed. Gerard's agonizing death caused Leo to lose his faith and stop going to church, but his wife became increasingly devout.

Gabe came apart when Gerard died, so worn out from her ordeal that she lost all her teeth. During the long weeks when she nursed Gerard day and night, she must have known how futile her efforts would be, though she prayed for a miracle. It was Gerard's second bout of rheumatic fever and his heart could not withstand it. There was no medicine that could cure him, and God did not intervene. Crazed with grief on the day of Gerard's wake, Gabe secluded herself from the relatives and neighbors who streamed into the house. The unbearable thought that her good little boy had never had a chance consumed her. Her own faith was threatened. The only way she could accept Gerard's death was to convince herself that he had been taken from her for a reason known only to God.

In *Jack Kerouac: a chicken-essay*, Victor-Lévy Beaulieu, the first writer to go into the implications of Jack's French Canadian background, which he understood as a Québécois on a visceral level, suggests that the example of Marie Rose Ferron, the young "visionary-invalid" of Woonsocket, Rhode Island, revered throughout New England in the 1920s for her saying "Death is only a passage that leads to life," may have given Jack's mother a way to find solace in the belief that her son had also been a victim soul. "Little Rose" had died very recently in 1925—the same year a far more widely worshipped "visionary-invalid," Therese de Lisieux, had been canonized.

Like the ancestors of the Kerouacs, Therese had been born in Brittany. She had dedicated herself to God at the age of two, entered a Carmelite convent when she was only fifteen, and died there nine years later of consumption. Deathly ill when she was ten, she had been saved by a miracle, which she attributed to the Blessed Virgin. Her famed posthumous autobiography, *The Story of a Soul*, was filled with childlike imagery in which she portrayed her soul in diminutive terms, as a "little ball," a "little boat," a "little flower," and, perhaps most poignantly for Gabrielle Kerouac, a "little bird," so weak that it is unable to fly and can only feebly raise its wings. Like Gabe's own child, Therese had died without medication—in her case, refusing to alleviate her suffering, which she regarded as her offering. Humbly she had given herself up to God as an intercessor for others. It is likely that the parish priest or the nuns who came to the Kerouac house tried to comfort Gabe by showing her the analogies between Gerard's sufferings and the sufferings endured by the Little Flower as well as by Little Rose Ferron. But Gabe may well have recognized them herself.

Despite Jack's bitter awareness of how his own life had been impacted by the "mysticism" of the Catholic Church, his childhood faith never lost its hold on him and he prayed to Ste. Therese throughout his life. In fact, his devotion to her was silently woven into the fabric of *The Town and the City*, for Therese's family name was Martin and she'd been one of nine children.

At first Gerard's death had seemed a thrilling event to four-year-old Jack because of its novelty. He ran up to his father on the street with the news, *"Gerard est mort!"*—one more thing he would feel guilty about for the rest of his life.

The small boy was certain that great changes were about to occur. "Rumors of exciting preparations were in the air. We would all go away to Canada with Gerard." His excitement lasted through Gerard's wake and funeral. Jack recalled the nuns entering his house like "a wave of dark light," the overpowering fragrance of incense, candle wax, and lilies inside the church, the black cars waiting outside, and how he had wondered on the way to the cemetery in Nashua why everyone was crying, since Gerard was surely coming back.

He had felt his first doubts as he watched the shovels of dirt fall upon his brother's coffin, but he continued to wait for Gerard to return in the days after the funeral. Meanwhile his mother remained inconsolable; every room and corner in their Beaulieu Street house reminded her of her loss. Leo, quickly realizing that they could no longer live there, soon arranged to move his family to a larger house on Hildreth Street in a different part of Centralville. It was then that Jack first began to understand that Gerard was gone and not in Canada, that his brother's death had a terrifying finality despite all the talk of heaven. He was far too young for this lesson, but it couldn't be unlearned. For the rest of his life he would wrestle with a pervasive awareness of mortality that would make human effort and even love seem meaningless and futile. At times he would sense the presence of God, but his books celebrate life in the shadow of the only certainty—that death is inevitable. His mission, as he saw it by the time he wrote *On the Road*, was to "moan for man."

In the Kerouacs' new home, Gabe set a small statue of Ste. Therese upon a shelf. Jack could remember suddenly becoming afraid of it, suggesting that something had made him associate the gentle Little Flower with Gerard. Perhaps very soon after his brother's death his mother had told him that Gerard was now his very own intercessor, who had died "to save me, as it were, for my mother's arms." He was later told that around the time they moved he had become a "thin, sallow, weary child," very different from the robust Ti Pousse he'd been.

Jack's outpouring to Neal was very Catholic—an attempt to confess his way out of the toils of the past, as if the act of telling could release him from a lifelong feeling of guilty inauthenticity that came from having to live in the shadow of his saint-brother. He believed the repercussions of Gerard's death had turned him into "the subtle and dishonest soul I am today," a kind of "orphan" within his own family. (Perhaps this early damage to his self-image, this feeling of being ashamed to be alive, was at the root of the shyness he never conquered, which he would try to overcome with alcohol.) With his memories and insights, Jack built up a powerful indictment of his mother. In the end, though, it offered him no deliverance, since he was as incapable of bringing himself to judge Gabe as he was to let go of the intercessor she had created for him. One of the saddest and most revealing lines Jack ever wrote was this: "I bow . . . to the mystery of my loneliness for Gerard that I have never been able to remember."

As he worked on his confession, he and his second wife were living with his mother. After Gabe learned he had been writing about Gerard, she immediately intruded, telling him many things he had apparently forgotten or never known, "having to do with all, all." Despite the energy and confidence that had propelled it forward, Jack's memoir writing ended abruptly in early January. He would not delve into the subject of his relationship with his brother until 1956, when he wrote the luminous novel *Visions of Gerard*. In it Jack used Gabe's stories; but the Gerard he created in his own image was a Buddhist saint as well as a Catholic one, whose vision of heaven was replaced by an empty blue sky with "nothing there."

JEAN-LOUIS KEROUAC

To renounce "fiction and fear," the vow Jack made to Neal and himself in the winter of 1950, meant in part that he intended to write about his life from now on without shame and without resorting to fictional disguises. In *The Town and the City*, his aim had been to write "a universal American story," and he had deliberately avoided emphasizing the Martin family's ethnic background and their devout Catholicism. Lamely defending himself in response to the objections of a Franco-American critic who had raised questions about these issues, he pointed out that he was hardly the only person of their background "to hide their real sources," because unlike other minorities, such as Jews or Italians, Franco-Americans could pass as "Anglo-Saxon."

A fiction writer today, in our multicultural-minded era, would make the most of his hyphenated background and in fact would consider it an asset. But sixty years ago, the label "Franco-American" would have been a liability for an ambitious novelist. Franco-Americans had been stereotyped as backward and primitive people and most educated middle-class readers had little interest in them. Sociologists referred to them as "the silent minority." Grace Metalious, the author of the 1956 best seller *Peyton Place*, concealed her Franco-American heritage behind her Greek married name.

The fiction Jack wrote immediately after completing *The Town and the City* in 1948 was a series of abortive attempts at road novels whose all-American western protagonists were usually given American names like Ray Smith, Chad Gavin, Red Moultrie. But Jack began to find the issue of obscuring his ethnic identity increasingly tormenting. In a May 19, 1950, journal entry, the guilt he had not previously acknowledged fully rose to the surface. He had smoked a good deal of marijuana, and in that free-floating, associative state of mind he had a vision that he recorded in his notebook—a visitation from a "French Canadian older brother" who scolded him for trying to "defrench" himself: "He hinted I should go to Lowell, or Canada, or France, and become a Frenchman again and write in French and shut up. He keeps telling me to shut up. When I can't sleep because my mind is ringing with gongs of English thought & sentences, he says, '*Pense en Français*,' knowing I will calm down and go to sleep in

simplicity." Jack did not see this older brother as Gerard, but as "my original self returning after all the years since I was a child trying to become
'un Anglais' in Lowell from shame of being a Canuck." He wrote that it
was actually the first time he understood that he "had undergone the
same feelings any Jew, Greek, Negro or Italian feels in America, so cleverly had I concealed them, even from myself, so cleverly and with such
talented, sullen aplomb for a kid."

When Jack finally wrote *On the Road* as a "true life" novel in the famous scroll draft of April 1951, he was ready to give his protagonist/nar-
rator his own name—providing a clue to that character's ethnicity. He
also indicated that "Jack" had a working-class background, came from a
New England mill town, and felt a deep connection to people with Indian
blood. By the time the novel was published, however, in 1957, "Jack" had
become the symbolically named "Sal(vatore) Paradise." Due to intense
pressure from the legal department of his publisher, Jack had reluctantly
disguised not only the names and identities of all the other characters in
the book but his own as well, going so far as to turn his mother into an
aunt. But he did not stoop to putting in details that would have authenti-
cated Sal's identity as an Italian—there is not even a reference to pasta in
the novel.

On the Road has come to be the book most closely identified with Kerouac. The very name Kerouac has entered the vernacular, become a word
signifying youthful restlessness and rebellion. The novel is now accepted
as an American classic—as iconically American as *The Adventures of
Huckleberry Finn*, a work it has often been compared to. It is celebrated
for its sweeping portrayal of the American melting pot and Jack is credited with being ahead of his time in writing about black people and Mexican migrant workers, groups that, like the French Canadians, were
usually left out of the fiction of other white American writers during the
fifties. Jack himself is still generally perceived as "all American," although more and more scholars have become interested in exploring his
French background. But most of *On the Road*'s enthusiastic readers—
especially those who have not read Kerouac's Lowell novels, *Dr. Sax, Visions of Gerard*, and *Maggie Cassidy*, or his later books, *Big Sur, Vanity
of Duluoz*, and *Satori in Paris*—would be startled to learn that French

Canadians both in Quebec and in the United States have for a long time claimed Kerouac as their own. To them, everything about Jack's books—from *The Town and the City* to *Satori in Paris*—is French, including Jack's way of using English. "To the end," observed the Franco-American scholar Armand Chartier, Kerouac remained faithful to "the culture of the past: his own past, that of his family, and that of his Canadian ancestors."

In his memoir *American Ghosts*, the Franco-American novelist David Plante, although not one of Kerouac's greatest fans, stated unequivocally that Kerouac's novels "including *On the Road*, in which he identifies himself as entirely American, are deeply Franco-American." Victor-Lévy Beaulieu found reflections of his own childhood in the pages of *Dr. Sax*, which he called "the best documentation we possess on Franco-American life in the 1920s and 1930s." Impelled to write his book-length essay shortly after Jack's death in 1969, Beaulieu was overwhelmed by the emotional power of his feeling of connection to Kerouac:

> . . . it was enough for him, for old Jack, to have just a few facts which would mark him profoundly so that all the rest of his life turned around them (those great black flies of anguish, confusion and despair)—(and Lowell, the nesting-place, with its crowds of beings who had started off on the wrong foot, unhealthy people speaking a bizarre tongue, shattered, expressing only the opposite of speech: stomach noises, onomatopoeia, verbs turned into subjects, and subjects becoming objects, and expressing nothing but social misery, moral decay, death . . .

When I read this for the first time in the 1980s, I immediately felt that Beaulieu, who had never known Jack, grasped something essential about him that had eluded Kerouac's American biographers as well as most of those who thought they knew Jack well, including me. Yet, when I searched my own memory, I couldn't remember one time when Jack had ever spoken about his ethnicity as if it were an issue that in any way caused him problems or set him apart. In fact, he talked about it very little (no more than I, the child of assimilated parents, talked about being Jewish) and when he did his allusions tended to be casual, anecdotal, nostalgic, and often culinary. But he did make a point of telling me—several times, in fact—that his baptismal name was Jean-Louis Lebris de Kerouac and that he was the descendant of a Breton baron on his father's side who had emigrated to Quebec in the eighteenth century.

In the spring of 1957, while passing through London, Jack went to the library of the British Museum to look up the Kerouac coat of arms and found the motto *"Aimer, travailler, souffrir,"* which he felt summed his life up perfectly. In 1965, four years before his death, he used half of his two-thousand-dollar advance for *Desolation Angels* to finance a trip to France to trace his genealogy and search for living descendants of his Breton ancestors. Poor by then and barely able to function, he found only an old man in Brest, who, like many others in the local phone book, had the name Lebris.

I remember how one of Jack's old friends, Lucien Carr, had a way of mischievously needling Jack that often made me uncomfortable. "You dumb Canuck," Lucien would say, gratuitously repeating this several times in a single conversation. I'd look over apprehensively at Jack, but I never saw him wince. His face would be absolutely impassive. Years later, however, when I first read Victor-Lévy Beaulieu, something struck me: I remembered that sometimes when Jack was feeling wounded or angry, he'd sign his letters Ti Jean. In his darkest states of mind he'd use the name Jean-Louis, as if he had retreated into a different, remote persona, sternly reminding outsiders like me that we did not know him at all.

In *Maria Chapdelaine*, Louis Hémon's classic novel of French life, first published in 1921, there is a character who reminds me of Jack—a handsome, vigorous young man, brimming with vitality, who, in contrast to the long-suffering *habitant* farmers eking out a living from the stony soil of northern Quebec, has chosen to live more freely as a *coureur du bois*. Rather than struggling to wrest potato fields from the forest and staying on his father's farm ("I would not have been able to stick to that," he says. "I would have felt like a cow tethered to a stake"—an attitude strikingly similar to the way Jack at nineteen expressed his own feelings about factory labor: "If I should stay in here, I would just as soon get rid of my brains and transfer them to a plow-horse on the farm"), Hémon's young outsider lives in camps deep in the woods for months at a time, traps furs with the Indians, and does a certain amount of drinking and swearing—all of which he is ready to give up once he falls in love with the beautiful young heroine of the novel. Returning to see her at Christmastime, he gets lost in a blizzard. Despite his knowledge of how to survive in the forest, he makes the fatal mistake of turning northward, which takes him only deeper into the wilderness—his body is never found. (An unsentimental reader might infer from this that, ironically, it's his temptation to settle down that kills him.) The name of this character, interestingly enough, is François Paradis.

Although I have no proof that Jack ever read *Maria Chapdelaine*, it was a best seller in the United States and Canada all through the 1920s and into the next decade, and people like Leo Kerouac in the French Canadian communities of New England would have been well aware of it, since books that reflected their experience were rare. The tragic story of the young author, Louis Hémon, was recounted in the introduction to the book in the Modern Library edition of 1934. I wonder whether Jack came across it in his "Saturday avidities of reading" at the Lowell public library.

Louis Hémon was a romantic figure, remembered by a friend as "a silent man who fled from the world and loved solitude and meditation." Born in 1880, he was a Breton who lived in Paris and London at the turn of the century, often depending upon the humiliating support of his mother and sister as he worked on several novels, only one of which was published in his lifetime. After fathering an illegitimate child, whose mother died in an insane asylum, Hémon decided to change his life and embarked for Quebec in 1912, embracing a vagabond-like existence that prefigured Jack's four decades later. Hémon wandered westward into the rugged Lake St. John country, where he worked for the railroad and then became a farmhand on a remote homestead. In sharing the hard life of the *habitants*, he seemed to find the spiritual renewal he had been looking for as well as the subject of the novel he wrote in his spare time. In 1913, he mailed the manuscript of *Maria Chapdelaine* from Montreal to a publisher in Paris, then took off for the Canadian wilderness again on foot. While walking along the tracks of the Canadian Pacific railroad in Northern Ontario, he and another man were struck by a train and killed. Perhaps they had been drinking. In the silence of the wilderness, they did not hear the oncoming train as it rounded the bend.

Maria Chapdelaine, a naturalistic novel in the tradition of Knut Hamsun, is a testament to the somber spiritual beauty Hémon saw in the *habitants'* way of life. One reads it today with double vision, moved by the Chapdelaines' struggle for survival, by their sense of duty, by the religious beliefs that make their hard labor sacramental and sustain them through lean times and tragedy. But looked at another way, the Chapdelaines' existence is grim and hopeless. Completely cut off from the rest of the world, they live in primitive conditions as if there has been little progress since the first French settlers came to Quebec. Their few social contacts are confined to their tiny parish and every aspect of their lives is ruled by their church. The heroine's mother is often melancholy because the family is so isolated, but she never complains—one does not question the will of God. Introspection is a luxury the *habitants* cannot afford. It is even considered selfish to grieve too much. François Paradis dies despite all of Maria's prayers for him, but the parish priest tells her she is distressing herself "beyond what is reasonable and right" or "pleasing in the sight of God." She must put her sadness aside to marry another man and bear his children, to work in the fields beside him, and she will probably remain as poor and isolated as her mother. But her reward will be in heaven, a much better place than earth. Her obligation is not to seek personal happiness but to perpetuate the life she has known, with all its traditions, for the cultural survival of her own people and their blind faith.

"Country folk do not die for love," wrote Hémon, defining the fatalism and passivity of the *habitants,* "nor spend the rest of their days nursing a wound. They are too near nature and know too well the stern laws that rule their lives. Thus it is, perhaps, that they are sparing of high-sounding words; choosing to say 'liking' rather than 'loving,' 'ennui' rather than 'grief,' so that the joys and sorrows of the heart may bear a fit proportion to those more anxious concerns of life which have to do with their daily toil, the yield of their hands, provision for the future."

Although Hémon was criticized by Canadian critics in the 1920s for not showing the "lighter side" of the *habitants*—"the irrepressible gaiety, the mercurial swiftness of change from the heavy and brooding to the lightsome and sunny, and above all, utter joy of living and superb carelessness"—the novel encapsulated much of the powerful mystique that the *habitants* brought with them when hundreds of thousands of them, like Jack's grandparents, abandoned the worn-out potato fields that could no longer feed their large families for life in the textile-mill towns of New England—an emigration that began after the Civil War and peaked in the 1880s and 1890s.

In the novel a young man named Lorenzo Suprenant returns from Lowell to revisit his old parish with money in his pockets. He offers Maria a chance to escape to Massachusetts with him, promising there will be a fine job for her in the mills, and talking of the shops, the electric cars, the endless amusements to be found in a "vast American city." She is tempted to go, but then realizes she would be leaving not only her family but, most painful of all, her language, *joual*—a language the *habitants* considered sacred, since it was inextricably woven into their religious observance. Foreign speech would surround her and her own children would forget how to sing the hymns she has sung all her life. After that realization, she decides to marry a hardworking young man on a neighboring farm who immediately promises to clear a field for her. Her duty is outlined for her in a mystical epiphany: "to abide in that Province where our fathers dwelt, living as they have lived, so to obey the unwritten command that once shaped itself in their hearts, that passed to ours, which we in turn must hand on to descendants innumerable."

Victor-Lévy Beaulieu takes a far less exalted view than Louis Hémon of the lives of the *habitants*: "it was a time of great poverty and black misery; the time of the rural province—old houses covered with tarpaper or shingles and mangy old dogs sleeping on the doorstep—and a proliferation of blackflies and the flock of snot-nosed children wearing rubber boots, looking at the dusty road, their bellies hollow and cobwebs in their hair."

The memoirist Harding Lemay, one of the few Franco-American writers of Jack's generation, grew up on a subsistence farm in Quebec but ran away to New York in 1939 when he was seventeen. He had nineteen siblings, only eleven of whom survived. His parents were illiterate and both were alcoholics; so were his older brothers. In *Inside, Looking Out*, Lemay writes of feeling so ashamed of his background that he concealed it from all his American friends for years by constructing an entirely new story of his life.

Despite their bitter memories of conditions in Quebec, many French Canadian emigrants kept in the back of their minds the hope that someday they would return to their ancestral lands with the riches they had accumulated in America. Looking backward from the perspective of exiles adapting with difficulty to an alien culture, they idealized Canada, which they thought of as "the land of miracles." No wonder four-year-old Jack had the notion that Gerard had gone there to be brought back to a greater life. "Canada brooded in the air and haunted me," Jack wrote. "Canada was my bosom of God."

In the backwoods communities of Quebec, the *habitants* had existed in a time warp, their isolation preserving the ancient ways of life and ingrained suspicion of the outside world their seventeenth- and eighteenth-century ancestors had brought with them, emigrating at a time when much of France Profonde, including Brittany, was an unmapped wilderness. When they packed up their few possessions in the 1890s and loaded their children onto farm wagons or trains, the *habitants* hoped to establish in the towns of New England a kind of lower Quebec, where their culture would be essentially unchanged, apart from their adjustment to tending factory machines rather than fields and cattle and clustering in crowded communities rather than living on isolated farms. Believing that factory jobs would have more dignity than farm labor, the first French Canadians to work in the mills wore their Sunday clothes to work.

If Maria Chapdelaine had followed Lorenzo Suprenant to Lowell, she would have found herself in a completely different kind of novel—this one by a writer like Emile Zola or Frank Norris rather than the impressionable Louis Hémon, who had fallen in love with her people and needed so badly to find a new meaning in life. In this alternate fate for Maria Chapdelaine, the backdrop of her father's fields and the dark, endless forest stretching out behind them fades away, replaced by enormous red-brick mill buildings that line both sides of a broad, swift-moving river and narrow back streets filled with three-story wooden tenements. On rickety upstairs porches, precariously attached to the buildings, women hang their laundry and crowds of children play, spilling out of apartments too small to contain them. The smell of raw sewage drifts up from the alleys where the privies are. Maria's job is the most menial one in the textile mill, where she works twelve-hour days, shut away from fresh air and sunlight in a loft where the windows are boarded up so that there will be enough humidity to keep the cotton thread flexible. The deafening noise of the looms, the howling sound they make, is maddening. The air she breathes in is full of white lint, settling on her clothing, her hair, infiltrating her lungs so that she coughs all the time like the other factory women and the girls in their early teens who are also working there. François Paradis would scarcely recognize her.

In 1912, ten years before Jack was born, there were historic strikes in the New England mill towns. Anarchist organizers from the IWW appeared in Lowell and in the neighboring city of Lawrence just across the Merrimack to unionize the textile workers, most of whom were immigrants. Thousands of people of different nationalities—the Irish, the Italians, the Greeks, the Poles, the Armenians, the Jews—collectively walked off their jobs. In Lawrence, they marched in the streets for six weeks, demanding "Bread and Roses." The army and a volunteer militia of Harvard men were brought in to keep order. Police arrested a trainload of children who were being sent away to New York because their parents were unable to feed them. Only the French Canadians, in their fatalistic stoicism, kept on working. They believed striking was sinful. Their church and their newspapers were on the side of management.

The French Canadians were despised by workers of other nationalities because they were willing to take the worst jobs, the ones no one else wanted, and to work for the lowest wages. The Massachusetts Department of Labor called them "the Chinese of America." New Englanders had other names for them—frogs, pea-soupers, dumb Canucks, white niggers. Because they kept to themselves and showed so little desire to assimilate, it was believed they were a backward people. Reviled by other groups, they had their own prejudices—particularly a primitive hatred of Jews that had been inculcated in them by their church.

They clustered in the mill towns where the trains brought them and created enclaves where no English needed to be spoken—self-contained *"petits Canadas"* like certain neighborhoods in Lowell, where they had their own churches, parish schools, shops, social clubs, and funeral parlors. Every Franco-American community had its own newspapers. It was not only the virulent prejudice against them that made them choose to be walled off, it was their cultural pride, which they called *"la survivance."* In Canada they had held out against the English foreigners who had taken their country from them in the eigthteenth century. It was now their duty to endure, surrounded by the foreigners of America. In the words of the inspiring voice that reminded Maria Chapdelaine of her solemn duty, "many centuries hence the world will look upon us and say:—These people are of a race that knows not how to perish. . . . We are a testimony."

La survivance depended upon the stubborn preservation, at all costs, of *famille, foi, et langue* (family, faith, and language), all of which were under threat in the mill towns of the United States. By the 1920s thousands of French Canadians had given up the lives they had tried to establish in New England and returned to Quebec, where conditions had improved somewhat, and to the cultural purity that meant so much to them. The families who stayed in New England still chose to live apart in their closed communities, but gradually, over the next forty years, their children, exposed to American public education and the big dreams of success inspired by mass culture, began to leave the *petits Canadas* of their parents, a journey Jack made much earlier than most. Many of those second- and third-generation children promised not to change—to keep speaking French and never to lose their faith, to above all remain closely bound to their families—but change they did. For Jack, whose attachment to his heritage was as strong as it was anguished, the process of becoming American would never be completed, and it would prove to be particularly wrenching.

PART TWO

A HALF-AMERICAN BOYHOOD

LA SALLE DE MORT

Just like his father, Jean Baptiste, Leo Kerouac kept moving his family around. The second-floor apartment on Hildreth Street was the fourth place in the Centralville neighborhood where Jack had lived since he was born. By the time Jack was seventeen, he had lived at eleven different locations. Did the Kerouacs move so frequently in order to find better quarters? After 1929, they definitely needed increasingly cheaper ones as Leo Kerouac's fortunes sharply declined. But were they also driven by some internal restlessness, some unhappiness that pursued them from place to place, making them start packing again not long after they had settled down somewhere for a while? In Gabrielle Kerouac's old age, when Jack could finally afford to buy an entire house for her, no living situation would content her; from 1958 to 1968, they would pull up stakes six times in Long Island, Florida, and Massachusetts, three times futilely returning to parts of the East Coast they had already given up on.

Lupine Road, Burnaby Street, Beaulieu Street, Hildreth Street, West Street, Moody Street, Sarah Avenue, Gershon Avenue, Phoebe Avenue . . . In *The Town and the City*, Jack wrote that for children to be uprooted from a home they had lived in amounted to "a catastrophe of their hearts. What dreams children have of walls and doors and ceilings that they always knew, what terror they have on waking up at night in strange new rooms, disarrayed and unarranged, all frightful and unknown."

"Our house is our corner of the world," wrote the philosopher Gaston Bachelard. "As has often been said, it is our first universe, in every sense of the word." In his view, "We comfort ourselves by reliving memories of protection. Something closed must retain our memories while leaving them their original value as images."

When Vladimir Nabokov and his family had to leave Russia, Nabokov suffered the physical loss of Vyra, the much loved country estate that had been the scene of his childhood and the birthplace of his creativity. He never saw Vyra again, but even after he was in exile it remained his in memory and was a source of strength—he called it his "unreal estate." But Jack had no such "closed" psychic property. Instead there was a permanent sense of homesickness, all the more painful for not being attached to any one dwelling. Yet all that uprooting may have sharpened his memory, each leave-taking prompting him to hold on to certain images of "home"—images that never faded from his consciousness—before the scene changed again.

Over and over in the dreams Jack recorded from the late 1940s through the early 1960s, the family (frequently just Jack and his mother) are on the run, in flight from some nameless threat that pursues them from place to place. At different addresses the heavy, carved family furnishings, the only vestiges of stability, keep turning up. Sometimes in ominously red nightmare parlors, all that furniture, even his mother's piano, becomes oppressive. The Beaulieu Street parlor—where Gerard lay in his coffin—keeps reappearing. *"La salle de mort."* It was in a nightmare Jack had at the age of seven, after the family moved from Hildreth Street to West Street: "the horrible dream of the rattling red living room" where skeletons danced "because my brother Gerard haunted them." He dreamed he woke up screaming next to a Victrola in an adjoining room. "All dreams," he would later write, "come from visions of experience. They are released because they are already there in the mind."

In a brief autobiographical sketch written when he was nineteen, Jack described himself as a "morbid child" of six, all alone in one of those "dark and dull" parlors where sofas and chairs cast funereal black shadows. He's listening to the tick of the clock. The sky outside is overpoweringly drab. He could remember himself wondering "whether it wouldn't have been better not [to] be born."

The move to Hildreth Street in August 1926 so soon after Gerard's death seems to have been a disaster for him. At twenty-eight, he still recalled the deathly grayness hanging over everything the day the family took possession of their quarters in the house that seemed "huge" and "shrouded." Moving had meant that they were leaving Gerard behind forever, rather than waiting for him to return. As young as he was, he could sense "the deliberate beginning of forgetfulness." It didn't help that his new home was one house away from a cemetery.

On his first day there, he had reluctantly followed his mother and sister inside. As they walked down a hallway, his mother opened a closet and something white came tumbling out and whacked her on the head. *"Les morts sont dans la maison!"* she screamed, terrifying Jack, who thought Gerard's angry spirit had pursued them to their new home. But his sister Nin and his father burst out laughing because it had only been an ironing board. Perhaps the laughter helped jolt Gabe back to reality. Later that day, when Jack told her he was hungry, she immediately made him a bread and butter and sugar sandwich—something he never forgot. It was if his mother, closed off with her grief, had been blind to him, but had suddenly awakened.

Before Gerard became so ill, he had been Jack's chief playmate and to some extent his minder. When other boys came over to play with her older son, Gabe would chase them away, telling them that Gerard "belonged" to Jack. On Hildreth Street, Jack discovered "that I was alive and could do things on my own." He recalled making a dramatic speech, complete with gestures, to a mattress on the sunporch soon after the family moved in. In the void of his brother's absence, Jack's imagination became his companion, summoning up another world for him that he could enter simply by playing "March of the Tin Soldiers" or "Dardanella" over and over on the Victrola and marching up and down in the living room in time to the rhythms of the music. He would throw sofa pillows on the floor and jump onto them, wrestling the Great Vulture that had swooped down upon him, always managing to get away. Once, pretending he was trapped in the coils of a giant snake, he went out in the front yard, trussed himself up with a rope, and lay there writhing so convincingly that older boys coming home from school asked who had done that to him. As a death-haunted child, he had a need to feel invincible. Confronting the terrors he deliberately made up, he could be as self-sufficient as he would be later on in the deep, safe solitudes of his writing.

Gray colors Jack's accounts of his early years, but gradually brown begins to seep in. The brown is often associated with his mother. It was the color of the bathrobe she wore when she tended to him when he was sick. It was the brown of her kitchen, always the safe, warm place wherever

they lived, filled with the reassuring smells of vanilla and caramel pud-
dings and all the brown foods she cooked for them—oatmeal, beans, *cor-
tons*, rich stews swimming in pork fat, date pie. Gray was the color of
feeling dead or deadened. Brown was life-giving. But it is also the color of
the word *sad* that tolls through all Jack's writings—the brown of a primordial melancholy as well as the familiar, comforting brown of home.
He would try to escape that brown, but memory would always draw him
back to it. It was the color of his homesickness.

Jack's childhood coincided with the Great Depression, but economic depression had come to Lowell years before the stock market crash of 1929.
Soon after the strikes of 1912, textile mills all over New England began to
close, as the owners moved their operations south in search of a cheaper,
more docile labor force. In the tenement slums of Lowell's Little Canada,
even in Centralville, there were children who went hungry— like a small
boy Gerard once brought home from school so that Gabe could give him
something to eat.

Many of Lowell's poorer children grew up during these hard times
without having had childhoods; they were sent out to work or had to
learn to fend for themselves or to care for younger siblings. Children in
the crowded tenements still died regularly from disease. By comparison,
Jack's childhood was sheltered, even enviable. His stomach was never
empty, and he was encouraged by his parents to play and enjoy himself.
With only two children to support, Jack's parents could buy them toys
and books and send them to the movies on Saturday afternoons. They
worried about their four-year-old son, who was so fearful at night and
spent so much time alone in the world of his fantasies; Gabe continued to
reassure Ti Jean that Gerard was looking out for him in heaven. She hung
a cheerful nursery picture in his room that admonished him, "Jack be
nimble." Hoping an exciting change of scene might be all that was needed
to restore his happiness, she took him on a visit to her stepmother, who
lived in Brooklyn with her Greek second husband and Gabe's half sister.
Jack would remember riding the New York subways, the lights that glit-
tered brighter than the ones in Lowell, and the charged sense of being in
the midst of a great city. But the terrifying dreams that disturbed his
sleep kept coming.

Centralville, where the Kerouacs lived until Jack was ten, was the most pleasant French-speaking neighborhood in Lowell and a good place to raise children. Most of the families who lived there (including a few of other ethnicities) were, like Jack's parents, precariously beginning to work their way up into America's lower middle class. A trolley ran down the middle of Hildreth Street and cars passed by from time to time. But there were grass and trees all around. Nearby was an abandoned old gray stone mansion Jack came to think of as The Castle, which would play an important role in his boyhood fantasies and ultimately in his novel *Dr. Sax*. Behind the Kerouacs' house was a thicket of brush where Jack could follow a little path to a sand bank from which he could see the Merrimack River. On the opposite bank was Lowell's "mile of mills," with the crowded-together rooftops of the city in the distance.

Downtown Lowell was the domain of Jack's father, a world of men going about their important and mysterious affairs. By the time the Kerouacs lived on Beaulieu Street, Leo had managed to establish his own business, Spotlite Print, in an old wooden one-story building down near the Merrimack River behind Lowell's movie theater, the Royal. Not far from the Royal was the B. F. Keith Theater, where touring vaudeville artists appeared onstage. Leo had landed the job of printing the handbills that advertised their performances. In *Visions of Gerard,* Jack remembered his father as an energetic young businessman always alert to new money-making opportunities. "A completely honest man full of gaiety," he wrote a few years later, "soured in last years over Roosevelt and World War II." Tender to his children, who could move him to the point of tears, Leo had a mordant, bitter side as well, a tendency to feel persecuted and a deep knowledge that nothing in life worked out and that there was no promise of a Canuck heaven. "Eat or be eaten," he says to his older son in *Visions of Gerard.* "We eat now—the worms eat us." Undoubtedly, the series of deaths in his family when he was a child had left its mark upon him.

As one of the youngest of Jean Baptiste's fifteen children, Leo had had more education than his older siblings. His father, evidently recognizing how bright he was, had sent him to a private Catholic boarding school in Rhode Island for a year. Leo had completed high school, and by the age of seventeen, shortly before the death of his father, had learned English well enough to be taken on as a printer's apprentice at the *Telegraph*, Nashua's English-speaking newspaper. He graduated from his apprenticeship to a job at *L'Impartial*, a daily read by French Canadians all over New England, working as a reporter there as well as a printer until he was twenty-three, when his company sent him to Lowell to run *L'Etoile*, a struggling paper they had just acquired. Around the time he married Gabe, Leo also began selling insurance for Metropolitan Life. When he established his own business at Spotlite Print, he started his own small newspaper, the *Lowell Spotlight*, for which he wrote articles and editorials in English about entertainment and local politics.

Gabe, who had learned to write English fairly fluently, spoke it reluctantly and poorly; she stayed within the confines of the Franco-American community, socializing only with relatives and neighbors. Her husband, however, moved with unusual ease between Lowell's French- and English-speaking worlds, making friends, glad-handing, and doing business in both. He was still good-looking in his thirties before he gained a lot of weight and alcohol took its toll on his body—a cigar-smoking man who liked to stroll along Lowell's streets sporting a straw hat. With his powerful athlete's build, jet-black hair, and blue eyes, he must have looked a good deal like Jack. Leo was popular with the vaudeville artists he met in the course of his dealings with the Keith Theater and would often drink and play poker backstage with them, bringing home stories about hanging out the night before with W. C. Fields or the Marx Brothers—stories that may not have been received enthusiastically by Gabe, whom Leo often left to her own devices. He'd show up for dinner, then go off on his nocturnal adventures, gambling away money the family could not afford to lose.

Sometimes Leo would take his small son with him into the heart of Lowell, and Jack would experience some of that in-the-city quickening of the senses, even though Lowell didn't glitter like New York. If home was brown, Lowell was red, its landscape dominated by huge redbrick mills and warehouses that had been built in the nineteenth century when Lowell was in its heyday as the epicenter of the American Industrial Revolution.

In Jack's boyhood, canals still funneled water power to the mills. Narrow cobblestoned alleys, like the one behind the Keith Theater where vaudeville stars walked to the stage door, ran between the looming commercial buildings; freight trains rattled along tracks down by the Merrimack River. Because few people drove in those days, the streets were full of walkers and a mixture of different languages—Greek, Syrian, and Polish as well as French and English—could be overheard. They boarded streetcars that carried them off to their separate neighborhoods. On Saturday nights rowdy crowds with a little money to blow congregated in Kearney Square bound for the two theaters or the downtown bars or Ming's Chinese restaurant, where the proprietor was a friend of Leo's. If he was out with his parents after dark, Jack saw a different Lowell—a Lowell with the illusory glamour that red neon cast upon those redbrick walls. Redbrick and neon. An image that would stay with him. Shiny red over workaday red. The opposite of brown.

At Spotlite Print he watched Leo chomping on his ever-present cigar as he operated the linotype machine. His father would spit into the same receptacle where flying pieces of sizzling lead would also land from time to time. When Jack was allowed to bang away on the keys of Leo's big L. C. Smith typewriter, he could pretend he was setting that hot type himself. A man who worked for Leo lived in Little Canada. Evidently, Leo sometimes took his small son with him when it was necessary to stop by at the man's apartment. Everyone spoke French in Little Canada just as they did in Centralville but the language was coarser and more elemental here—"a vigorous Canuckois," the kind spoken on the abandoned farms of Quebec. Life was raw and raucous; there was desperation in the air. Inside a tenement apartment with the windows open, one could hear a cacophony of grief, rant, rage, popping firecrackers, people yelling the latest gossip, crashing dishes smashed by shrieking women. In *Visions of Gerard*, Jack imagines his father present as his employee and his wife tear away at each other. It's one of those ferocious circular arguments that solve nothing, the woman complaining about her husband's heavy drinking and the money thrown away on it, the man asserting his absolute right to drink. The language is utterly coarse. "Don't call me a cow, dog!" the wife screams.

As Jack later indicated to friends, he heard many fights over the same issues between his mother and father as Leo's drinking and gambling escalated. But in all his books, he seldom showed the bitterness between his parents. His loyalty to them would have prevented him from exposing them in that way. "I had a beautiful childhood," he wrote in 1958 when a publisher asked him for a capsule biography.

Sometimes small children have epiphanies they remember for the rest of their lives. Virginia Woolf called such experiences "moments of being" and saw them as the foundations of consciousness. In 1942, Jack recalled one that had occurred just before his seventh birthday on a February day that he considered "the day I was born." On his way home through the snow-covered streets, pulling his sled behind him, he'd "stopped to look at the sad windows of the houses. Why, why? I asked myself, aged six. Pourquoi I might of said, because I was French. At any rate, I wanted to know, and I couldn't quite make it out, and I still cannot make it out, which is in a nutshell the story of the inward war raging inside of me . . ."

He would always believe that until that moment he had been walking along "dead," or, in other words, locked inside himself. But then "with a sweep of bewilderment I began to live—a man on the earth, his relation to all things, to his fellow man, to his society, and to the universe."

A CATHOLIC EDUCATION

In 1928, dressed like Gerard in a parochial schoolboy's "little black stockings and pants," Jack was escorted by two of his aunts to St. Louis de France, already associated in his mind with "rainy funerals for little boys." In its basement, where he had sat beside his weeping parents at Gerard's funeral, wondering why everyone was crying, he would now be starting first grade. His teachers were the same nuns who had come to the house on Beaulieu Street to take down his brother's dying words.

At St. Louis de France, small children received instruction in humility, chastity, and obedience and were lectured on their general sinfulness and unworthiness. From the moment they walked in, boys were strictly separated from the little girls in their dark blue dresses with white lace collars. The children were taught to remain absolutely still, their eyes fixed on the teacher. When they broke the rules, the all-powerful nuns showed little of the mercy and kindness they preached. Jack would never forget how the mother superior whacked his friend Mike Fournier on the behind with a metal-edged ruler, and how the nuns would use a comb dipped in drip-pipe water from the *"pissoir"* to tame the unruly hair of little boys. Perhaps it was here that he first learned to distrust women.

The long school day began with morning prayers, followed by the Pledge of Allegiance to the American flag, which was said in English, and the Oath of Allegiance to the Sacred Heart flag of Quebec, which was said in French, ending with the solemn promise to always rally *"la race canadienne-française."*

First graders were confronted with three different languages, each with its own uses, its own boundaries—as distinct as the ethnic boundaries between social classes in Lowell. In the mornings, during the French half of the day, they were taught the rudiments of classical French, the language of the simply written religious texts they were given as reading materials. They would also be taught their catechism, the history of Canada, and a little art and music. But these lessons, punctuated by prayers every hour of the school day, would be conducted in the everyday language of the teachers and their students.

To say you spoke French in Massachusetts really meant you spoke *joual,* which in Lowell would be the *joual* common to Lowell, which neither Montrealers nor Parisians would consider correct. *Joual* got its name in the 1920s from the way French Canadians pronounced *cheval,* the French word for *horse.* Essentially a spoken language, it was a French without layers of subtlety and *politesse.* Powerfully direct and emotionally expressive, it had its own grammar with significant deviations from the usages of classical French, and for many of its words there were no canonical spellings. Even the spelling of someone's name could change according to the way another person spoke it. For Jack, classical French would remain a familiar but foreign language, and he would read French literature with the aid of a dictionary.

Joual had always been a wild and rich anarchic soup. Ingredients from everywhere had fallen into it—first the different *patois* of the provinces all over France from which the original ten thousand or so settlers of New France had been recruited or deported in the seventeenth and eighteenth centuries—a time when France Profonde was a veritable Babel of regional languages, some of which bore little relationship to the French spoken in Paris. Jack later believed *joual* was principally derived from the

Breton *patois* with Celtic roots spoken by his ancestors, but according to Gerard Brault, it was actually the *patois* of Île-de-France, the area around Paris, that became dominant. There were words in *joual* from the Indian tribes the settlers traded with, whose women they took as wives; words from the hated English who stole the North American territory, which should have belonged to France forever, as the children in Jack's school were taught on those French mornings. The *joual* spoken in twentieth-century New England was filled with French-inflected adaptations of Americanisms and was still continuing to evolve.

All through New England, the instruction of Franco-American children in their parochial schools followed the same model—even into the 1960s. In *American Ghosts*, David Plante, who grew up in Providence, where many immigrants from Canada had settled, recalled his feeling of being unconnected to that lost "French Continent" the nuns talked about, although it remained "an invisible presence" to him. He drew his sense of French Canadian identity mainly from learning French, which was "so much the language of our religion that my first reading book—*Mon premier livre de lecture*—made us believe that the very letters of our language" were sacred. According to this primer, "All beings here on earth, men and things, have been baptized, that is, have received a name that serves to identify them. The sounds that have been taught also have names, baptismal names." The sounds children learned from that book were not abstract symbols; each had its physical counterpart in nature: *B* was like the sound "made by a baby with his lips"; *V* "made you think of a passing wind." As Plante mastered spoken and written English, "there remained within this language the baptized letters of my French religion, letters that always promised the invisible; but as much as I tried, my English could not fulfill that promise." In absorbing English he began to lose his French and, to some extent, the faith that it embodied. Jack underwent a similar process that led to both linguistic confusion and richness. "I cannot write my native language," he admitted in 1950. At the same time he believed that the freedom and inventiveness with which he had learned to handle English came from having to "refashion it to fit French images."

The English Jack was taught to read and write in the long afternoons at St. Louis de France was secular and utilitarian—the language children would need to go about their business in America, the language spoken by Protestants and Irish Catholics who didn't worship in the proper way. In halting English the children struggled through math, American history, civics, and geography—but the hourly prayers continued to be said in French.

It all left Jack a little tongue-tied when he was growing up, contributed to his permanent shyness. At twenty-one, he still felt self-conscious about his accent and his English usage and worried about sounding illiterate. "All my knowledge rests in my 'French Canadianness,' and nowhere else," he later believed. Yet he had been born with a remarkable ear. At four, sitting outside the house where his relatives were mourning Gerard, Jack caught the doleful underlying *sound* of their lamentations— "AH BWA! AH BWAH!"—and started imitating it until a grown-up came out to silence him. On this level of the music of language, which mysteriously communicates mood and meaning beyond the manifest content of what appears on the page, he began to take in the book *Anglais* they were trying to teach him in school, alien sounds that did not seem to fit the shape of his mouth, whose music was so different from the one in which he swam in his element like a little fish.

In the Lowell public school, children were reading about the innocuous adventures of American kids like Dick and Jane, but Jack's first books were probably the somber French readers where religious illustrations accompanied moral lessons, in which first graders were advised to "endure their suffering" and not to drink or smoke. As Jack's reading proficiency increased, he graduated to texts in which the martyrdoms of saints and of the French missionaries who had converted the Indians were often described in gory graphic detail, undoubtedly giving him new material for his nightmares. During history classes, he was probably far from the only child in the room with Indian blood who had to listen as his Iroquois ancestors were portrayed in a most unfavorable light. "The earth is an Indian thing," he would later believe.

Recalling his school days in *Visions of Cody*, Jack wrote that he had been one of hundreds of "little death-haunted" Catholic schoolboys who existed in "a state of orderly terror and also boredom." He believed that the habit of confession, which had been ingrained in him early, had been carried over into his writing. But as with everything, Jack was of two minds about his Catholic education. Looking backward in 1959, he was grateful for the rigors of his schooling. "When I got to public schools and college I was already so far advanced I set new records cutting classes in order to go to the library and read all day, or to stay in my room (at college) and write plays."

"*Seigneur, Seigneur, ayez pitié pour nous,*" the six-year-olds prayed in their piping voices, kneeling on the cold floor of their basement classroom. "*Purifiez nos coeurs.*" They prayed to the all-seeing invisible presence who would come to permeate their thoughts, to a God from whom nothing was to be expected beyond pity, but who could never be blamed for not sparing them from the suffering and pain that would only end with the deaths they were already working toward. In *Visions of Gerard,* Gerard's father tells him, "*Mon pauvre ti loup,* me poor lil Wolf, you were born to suffer." The God who had been unable to help Gerard was torn apart by his inability to help men while they were on earth, but from his forgiveness of men's sins flowed the purity the children were directed to pray for and all that was best in human beings was bound up in his great pity and grief.

Man's terror of death was by no means an abstraction to Jack. But what could purity have meant to a child of six?

When he was five and as interested as most children are at that age in exploring their sexuality, he had urinated in joyful innocence under a porch in Centralville with the twin brothers who were his playmates. Writing about this years later to Neal Cassady, he recalled the "tremendous little kick" he'd felt. The little boys had been told it was wrong to do this sort of thing, but on that particular day, although the Lord saw what they were up to, "his wrath was postponed."

The comeuppance came when Jack was seven and went to his first confession. A voice from inside a box, who seemed to know his secrets, asked him whether or not he had played with his "little *gidigne.*" Scared and humiliated, he had to tell the awful truth—"*Oui, mon père*"—and do the penance of repeating the many prayers enumerated by the priest. It was the end of his innocence. From that point on, he knew that what he had guiltlessly enjoyed before was not allowed by the Lord.

Jack's four years at St. Louis de France helped perpetuate the inner torment he suffered as a small child. Remembering himself at six in *Mexico City Blues*, Jack recalled being afraid of himself as well as of everyone else. "I was the first crazy person / I'd known," was the piercing way he put it. Playing with the tiny people who lived in the toy house he got for Christmas, he'd wondered whether they felt a terror like his.

At home, the ground was about to shift under his feet again. His father's printing business was still making money, but Leo was losing so much at cards and at the races that Gabe had gone back to work in a shoe factory after twelve years of being a housewife. Early in 1929, when Jack was in third grade, it became necessary for the Kerouacs to move from Hildreth Street to cheaper quarters. In the home they moved into the following year, a small rose-covered cottage on West Street where Jack remembered feeling scared and sad, he had one of his most terrifying episodes. Under the influence of an old silent film about Ste. Therese that had been shown one day at school, he had a hallucination in which his mother's plaster statuette of the Little Flower came to life, turning its head when he passed it in the dark, just as a statue of Ste. Therese had done in the movie.

The most ordinary things made him fearful: a coat left hanging on a hook, a closed closet, his bedroom door left ajar in the middle of the night. As a grown man, he would choose to give up churchgoing "to ease my horrors," but as a child taken to services every Sunday, he had to endure the smell of flowers and candle wax that always reminded him of funerals. At eight, he still took refuge from his nightmares in the bed his mother shared with Nin. (His father slept in his own "tragic bedroom.")

As a child, Jack did not fear solitude. In fact, he often sought it out. But it had to be a safe kind of solitude, involving the knowledge that his mother was going about her routines somewhere in the house; then his imagination would be freed for the games he'd turned to after Gerard's death. By the time Jack was five, he began calling his fantasies "movies"— conscious imitations of the adventure serials he and Nin saw at Saturday children's matinees at the Royal Theater, which had introduced him to a whole new range of different Englishes whose exciting sounds as spoken by actors on the screen swiftly accrued meaning for him—from football hero *gee whizzes* and the tight-lipped utterances of cowboys like Tom

Mix who called each other "pardner" to the hissing menaces of vampires in elegant tuxedos and the nasal New Yorkese of the Marx Brothers, all of which Jack imitated as he performed the roles for himself.

"*Nosferatu* is an evil name suggesting the red letters of hell—the sinister pieces of it like 'fer' and 'eratu' and 'nos' have a red and heinous quality," he would later write, revealing how his ear translated sound. But during his childhood, the sounds of words sometimes misled him. At ten, enchanted by the beauty of the word *malodorous*, which he probably pronounced with an accent on its third syllable, he used it for the name of a benign wizard he dreamed up who lived in the abandoned mansion in Centralville. Thus, Dr. Malodorous became the forerunner of Dr. Sax. By the time Jack wrote the novel *Dr. Sax* in 1952, he had discovered the value of his "mistakes." Half of the novel portrays his boyhood, but the other half is fantasy—Jack's version of a 1930s horror movie, where malevolent, elegantly dressed characters gather and party in the Centralville mansion and plot the destruction of Lowell. Their dialogue makes very little actual sense but it is very suggestive and each character is delineated by the sounds and rhythms of its speech. It's as if Jack were trying to recapture the way he took in what he heard at the movie matinees he went to with Nin.

By third grade he became absorbed in putting his own movies down on paper. Sitting at the little green desk where Gerard had taught him how to draw, he created comic strips, inspired by ones in the funny papers sold at the candy store, which he was now able to read. The first of his comics was a very simple one called "Kuku and Koko at the Earth's Core," but, like his "movies," the narratives soon became extended and "highly developed." They must have impressed the Kerouacs' Nashua relatives, for somehow a sick little boy in that town heard about them and asked to read them and never gave them back.

At Jack's age, Gerard had been the artist of the family. Leo thought his pictures good enough to have been done by an adult. He had even shown off Gerard's gift to his friends by having him draw whatever they asked him to right in front of them. Now Jack had become the artist in Gerard's place.

Meanwhile, he was growing strong and agile, physically confident in the daylight world outdoors where the phantoms of the night could not reach him. Sundays were gloomy for him, but his Saturdays and summer holidays never seemed to last long enough. Then he was free of the dark school basement, free to roam the Dracut woods and the banks of the Merrimack as much as he wanted to. The river fascinated him. He watched its currents froth and foam, listened to the thundering sound of the falls that powered the mills. He wondered about the Merrimack's mysterious beginnings somewhere up near Canada, fascinated by the thought that as it flowed past Lowell it was on its way to the sea. For Jack and other Lowell boys it was an inexhaustible playground—their summer swimming hole, their winter ice-hockey rink, a source of endless places to explore.

Now he had a best friend—Mike Fournier, who lived nearby and whom he admired for his fearlessness. Nothing seemed to daunt Mike—not even a beating by the mother superior, which he underwent without a tear and which he claimed didn't hurt. The two of them "ransacked" the riverbanks, spied on couples making love, got yelled at by their mothers for being too wild together. Jack would always regard Mike as one of his "brothers" and remember qualities in him that reminded him of Neal Cassady. Their fathers were also close friends. But for some reason Jack felt agonizingly shy in the presence of Mr. Fournier, whom he felt considered him unworthy to be Leo's son.

One Saturday in May Jack ran away with Mike, Mike's little brother, and the Fourniers' dog. They took off and headed for New Hampshire. With every step along the wooded sand path that ran alongside the Merrimack River, Jack felt he was being torn from his mother. But he kept walking. By nightfall, they were twenty miles away from Centralville, cold, hungry and uncertain what to do next. They camped out and for the first time, Jack slept under an open sky. The following day they were found by the police and their relieved fathers.

Due to the deepening of the Depression in 1930, business at Spotlite Print had fallen off, although Leo had never been more popular in Lowell. After he ran some editorials in the *Lowell Spotlight* exposing corruption at city hall, people began suggesting that he run for mayor. At the cottage on West Street, Jack's parents started having raucous parties with their old gang, a group of couples, including Mike Fournier's parents, who called themselves The Dirty Dozen, and a louche priest who couldn't keep his hands off women. It was a revival of the good times Leo and Gabe used to have before their terrible troubles with Gerard, and for Jack, the festivities kept the ghosts away, at least temporarily. A lot of moonshine was drunk at those uproarious gatherings, which often kept up the neighbors. The guests played practical jokes and told dirty stories; the poker games in the kitchen went on till dawn, when Gabe brewed black coffee for the last hungover players. She liked to drink herself, but she didn't drink nearly as much as her husband, who was always slipping out of the house to get "a little nip" of illegal alcohol somewhere or other.

All through much of 1931, Leo kept writing his denunciatory editorials, naming the targets of his righteous criticism without caring how many enemies he was making—after all, the world was a "pisspot," as he often said. Still riding high, he bought a 1929 Model T Ford, a car he was unfortunately unable to drive because he was too short-legged to reach the gas and brake pedals. Another bad investment was his relocation of Spotlite Print to more spacious quarters, in an alley on Bridge Street close to the Keith Theater and the river, which he financed with a three-thousand-dollar loan from a friend that he would later be unable to pay back. But much of his energy was going into his new sideline—a training gym in Centralville for boxers and wrestlers.

There was a lot of the impresario in Leo, and he envisioned an exciting new career for himself as a promoter of wrestling matches, which were becoming increasingly popular in the 1930s. He introduced his eight-year-old son to this world, taking Jack to the gym to watch his stable of muscular young French Canadians pound away at punching bags. His chief boxing protégé, twenty-two-year-old Armand Gautier, who also worked for Spotlite Print, seemed like "Mister America" to Jack.

Armand became the family's chauffeur, driving Leo's Ford all the way to Montreal over the Fourth of July weekend, where Jack met some of his Canadian cousins for the first time. On another trip the Kerouacs went to visit some older sisters of Leo's who lived in the backwoods of Winchendon, Maine, probably much as they had lived in Rivière-du-Loup before they emigrated. His father had clearly climbed to far greater heights in America than these members of the Kerouac family.

In "In the Ring," an article written in 1968, Jack insisted that "capitalism" had nothing to do with Leo's motivation for running his wrestling club and that his father was, in fact, "as honest as the day pretended to be long." The same article, however, contains a vivid description of a match Armand had been directed to lose in the first round. Instead Jack saw his hero "turn red with French Canadian rage" and knock his opponent flat after the man had spat at him. He was present when his father gave Armand hell for making him lose his bet.

Jack's mother seemed to relish being brought into Leo's world. There was always a suppressed yearning in Gabe for a larger, more interesting life, as long as it did not violate her strict Catholic morality. She accompanied Jack to all the big matches of her husband's wrestlers. In one a man fell through the ropes right into her lap. "I'm sorry, Madame," he apologized. To which she gamely answered, "I don't mind as long as it's a good French man."

What excited Jack most was something beyond the matches themselves—something he would call "the poetry of it all," drenched in the smell of the cigars his father smoked. He would become a writer concerned above all with the poetry of what he remembered and perceived.

PAWTUCKETVILLE

In the summer of 1932, when Jack was ten, he left Centralville with its pervasive reminders of Gerard's death when the Kerouacs rented a house on the edge of Pawtucketville, a working-class suburb of Lowell, within walking distance of downtown. For Jack's parents, the move was a sign that their hard-won middle-class status was slipping from their grasp. But for Jack it proved to be a kind of liberation.

The Kerouacs' small white cottage was on Phoebe Avenue, a dirt road that ran through an area that had once been farmland; a neighbor's cherry trees could be seen from the parlor window and a pinewood with a brook and a pond that was a popular swimming hole was within walking distance. But only a few blocks away were rows of dilapidated four-story wooden tenements—a warning that the family had further to fall. Leo's gym had closed its doors. Badly needing a second job in order to pay off his debts and keep Spotlite Print in business, he began working nights at the Pawtucketville Social Club, where he was in charge of the bowling alley and pool table and had janitorial duties. He would preside over the poker games that started around midnight.

Pawtucketville had an abundance of street life. There were bars, penny candy shops, lunch carts, and local characters, and everywhere Jack looked there were kids, most of them from big Franco-American families, but there were Greek and Irish kids as well, boys who yelled in the tenement yards or played baseball in the field behind the Textile Institute or hung out in the Riverside Avenue park or in Destouches' candy store, which drew Jack like a magnet because of its assortment of comics and pulp magazines. One boy skated up to Jack and introduced himself three nights after the family moved to Phoebe Avenue—a boy named Zap Plouffe, who died a few months later after being run over by a milk wagon. Jack added Zap to the ghosts who haunted him, but fought back against the old humiliating fears: "I had learned to stop crying in Centralville and I was determined not to start crying in Pawtucketville."

Jack's closest new friend, George J. Apostolos, another newcomer to the neighborhood, had moved in right across the street. When Jack visited G.J. for the first time, he felt he had crossed into "the enemy camp of Thebans, Greeks, Jews, Niggers, Wops, Irishmen, Polocks"—all of whom were minorities that his parents had dark suspicions about. Before G.J. came into his life, Jack thought Greeks were "raving maniacs."

Soon Jack and G.J. got to know two French boys, Freddie Bertrand and Roland Salvas. The four kids became a regular gang who ran in and out of one another's houses, played softball together in the field behind the Textile Institute, and exchanged the facts of life. These Pawtucketville boys already smoked cigarettes (Jack was the only one who didn't) and used language that would have horrified Gabe, let alone the nuns at St. Louis de France. Smart, tough, and good-hearted, they all sensed there was something unusual about Jack. At first, they called him Jackie, and as time went on, Zagg; they were the ones who eventually came up with the nickname Memory Babe. Jackie's facility at drawing cartoons, a skill he was willing to teach, impressed them greatly, and so did his ball playing. He was as serious about that as he was about everything that interested him. If the Pawtucketville boys were aware of Jackie's vulnerability, they didn't hold it against him. "Everything hurt the guy," G. J. Apostolos recalled years later. "Just a drizzly November day would zing him." They were also aware that Jack's parents thought they were beneath their son, but didn't hold that against him either. Gabe especially disapproved of Jack's relationships with G.J. and Freddie, but he wouldn't give up his gang. Like many kids, he began to lead a double life.

He wasn't the only one in the group who'd been through a lot. G.J. had lost his father and was "Greekly tragic" about it. "My old man's in the grave," G.J. would say philosophically, "and no one's the worse for it." Freddie, a thin, handsome boy who always seemed to be smiling or excited and swore "like a son of a bitch," had spent several years in an orphanage after his parents split up, with his siblings scattered in different Massachusetts institutions. Freddie's father, a heavy drinker, had recently gone back to Freddie's mother and had reconstituted the family in one of the grim tenements on Moody Street. He outdid Freddie in cursing. The mother struck Jack as a little crazy when he heard her scream with laughter as Freddie stuck his hand up her skirt. At Freddie's, he met a neighborhood prostitute, who once exposed herself to him and his friends when they were in their early teens. (By that time, Jack had enough street knowledge to understand that his own father frequented "her purple doorways.")

A fifth boy, Scottie Beaulieu, became part of the gang after Jack spotted him pitching in a baseball game at the Textile Institute. Scottie handled himself with an imperturbable air of maturity that Jack greatly admired. His last name, Beaulieu—the name of the street where Gerard had died and where Jack had "learned to cry and be afraid of the dark"— immediately resonated with him. It was a coincidence that seemed to signify that all his *"life wasn't black."*

One great improvement in Jack's life was his new school, St. Joseph's, where he entered fifth grade in 1932. The instruction by the Marist brothers in all subjects, including English, was excellent, and there were no reminders of the past. Jack sang in the choir and was soon near the top of his class, vying for first place with a boy named Ernie Eno, who resembled Gerard. Jack developed a crush on Ernie—"it was a real love affair at eleven," he wrote in *Dr. Sax*, adding that it was before he "learned to distinguish between sexes." He prayed to a photo of Gerard to have Ernie return his love, but Gerard did not effect a miracle. The two schoolmates did play together at times, but that was as far as it went.

That year an unusual idea came to Jack for one of his "movies"—it didn't have to be about someone he made up, he realized. Why couldn't he watch *himself* as he went through an entire day, from the time he got up in the morning to go to St. Joseph's to the time he went to bed, putting in everything that happened? It was the first time he'd thought about being the hero of his own fictions. But it also seems to indicate that as young as he was, life may have already seemed a dream that was not quite real to him. In *Visions of Gerard*, Ti Jean, watching his brother's funeral, thinks, "It's a vast ethereal movie, I'm an extra and Gerard is the hero and God is directing it from Heaven." Deeply depressed in Mexico City three weeks before the publication of *On the Road*, Jack would ask in his journal why God had made the movie he was in so "cruel."

Perhaps noticing what an unusually thoughtful boy Jack was, the Marist brothers gratified Gabe by telling her that her son had the makings of a priest. She and Leo had every expectation that Jack would continue his French education until high school, which would certainly have delayed his full mastery of English. As fate had it, however, the brothers discovered that their promising student was in the wrong district for St. Joseph's and would have to transfer to Lowell's Bartlett Junior High the following year. The Kerouacs were furious but there was no other alternative. Jack took the entrance exam for Bartlett and did so well he was skipped into seventh grade.

Jack's arrival at Bartlett in the fall of 1933 was a crucial step in his long, strange journey into America. It seems metaphorically appropriate that his daily route to his "English" school involved crossing the Moody Street Bridge, which spanned a wild part of the Merrimack. One hundred feet below, fast-moving currents surged over high jagged rocks. It had been the scene of suicides; in fact, Jack had heard one of his own cousins, a young woman who yearned to become a concert pianist, tell his mother she had considered jumping off it and drowning herself. When he was going to St. Joseph's, he'd had to overcome his fear of the crossing, but the month before Jack started seventh grade, an episode on the bridge reawakened all his terror. As he walked across it one August night with his mother, after they had visited a churchyard where the Stations of the Cross were graphically depicted in a series of lurid waxen dioramas, a fat man carrying a watermelon just a few paces ahead of them on the bridge keeled over and died. Jack saw everything—how the watermelon man suddenly collapsed into a sitting position, how he urinated on himself, how his glassy eyes stared at nothing. That night Jack crawled into bed between his mother and sister. It took some time before he could bear to sleep alone.

He seems to have had a kind of breakdown. His family probably didn't recognize it as such, but they knew something was wrong. Gabe kept him inside for a week. She wasn't feeling well herself, and she and Jack spent each day in bed together. "I lay reading *The Shadow Magazine*," Jack recalled in *Dr. Sax*, "or feebly listening to the radio downstairs in my bathrobe, or blissfully sleeping one leg thrown over my mother in the night time—so secure did I become that death vanished into fantasies of life."

Each day after he had made it over the bridge, Jack's route to Bartlett Junior High took him through a neighborhood of handsome New England homes where some of his new classmates lived—the kinds of boys who, as he pictured them, always wore white in the summertime all the way down to their sneakers, as they rode around on the expensive bikes their fathers could afford to buy them. He was beginning to be acutely aware of the differences between boys like them and boys like him. At Bartlett, he felt so embarrassed by the slow way he spoke English that he hardly uttered a word in his classes. His homeroom teacher, Miss Dineen, thought Jackie Kerouac was very well behaved, but had no idea how bright he was until she discovered that his silence was hiding a surprising gift. When he wrote little stories for her class, his English was fluent and extraordinarily vivid, although he had read none of the good literature more privileged children were given. She must have wondered how that French boy came by that strong voice on the page, probably never realizing how much language Jack had picked up from sources that had nothing to do with school—from comics and pulp magazines, from the Saturday movies, from his efforts to communicate with G.J. and other boys he met. Miss Dineen suggested that Jack might enjoy poetry, and recommended Walt Whitman, John Greenleaf Whittier, and Longfellow's *Evangeline*, which she must have thought would interest him particularly since it was about the expulsion of his people from Nova Scotia. She felt he belonged in an advanced English class, taught by the school librarian, Miss Mansfield, but unfortunately, it was reserved for college-bound kids, not for those who, like Jack, had been registered by their parents as "commercial" and were being trained for the low-grade office and industrial jobs that awaited them after high school.

Miss Mansfield ran an after-school Scribblers' Club that Jack had heard about from a sixth grader named Sebastian Sampas, whom he had once protected from some school bullies. Like Jack, Sebastian was beginning to write poetry. He was small, precocious, acutely sensitive, and a great reader, unlike any other boy Jack had run into. With the newfound confidence Miss Dineen had given him, he went with Sebastian to the Scribblers' Club. When he showed Miss Mansfield a story he had written about an Irish cop, at first she couldn't believe he had written it himself, but quickly she took him under her wing and sometimes borrowed his stories to read to the English class she taught. Miss Mansfield introduced Jack to *Huckleberry Finn* and the *Iliad*. That year he joined the Lowell Public Library, where he headed every Saturday, coming home each time with an armload of books.

He read in that blind, indiscriminate way of book-hungry children, devouring popular juvenile fiction like the saccharine *Bobbsey Twins* series, *Rebecca of Sunnybrook Farm*, and *The Little Shepherd of Kingdom Come*, along with classics like *A Tale of Two Cities*, *The Last of the Mohicans*, and the works of Jack London. But he still stopped by Destouches's candy store as he was walking home from school to gaze longingly at the covers of the latest issues of *The Shadow*, *Phantom Detective*, and *Star Western*, which he had no money to buy and which the proprietor wouldn't allow him to even take off the racks. He would have to wait to borrow them from Zap Plouffe's older brothers, who had stacks of back issues in their basement. All he could afford to buy in Destouches' was penny candy, and the old man would snarl at him to go get it himself and to "bring me the penny after," as he recalled years later in a fragment of an unfinished novel called *Memory Babe*. When I read this as I sat in the Berg Collection of the New York Public Library, it explained something I'd always wondered about—why Jack had several times urged me to call my first novel *Pay Me the Penny After*. To my ears that phrase had sounded very odd, but Jack had been quite persistent about my using his "great title." Fifty years later I realized he'd been trying to give me a little piece of his past.

Jack shared his passion for what his mother exasperatedly called "those goddamn thrilling novels" with G.J. and with a boy he met at Bartlett, his first "English friend," Billy Chandler; Billy and Jack would go to each other's houses to write stories and draw cartoons. "Those dime novels . . ." Jack wrote nostalgically at nineteen, "it wasn't so much the killing in these stories that we used to feed upon, it was rather the dark and mysterious labyrinthial movement of our heroes, the sibilant hiss of their secret sanctumed laugh." But it was also the Manhattan setting of these tales that captured Jack's imagination—a city of yellow taxicabs in the rain and Fifth Avenue mansions and the wood-paneled gentleman's club, where the Shadow, after putting aside his mask, sat calmly playing chess, taking an evening off from pursuing evildoers.

The novel Jack wrote at eleven, however, entitled *Mike Explores the Merrimack*, owed far more to Mark Twain than to the creator of the Shadow. As Jack recalled it in *Visions of Cody*, it was about a boy starting off in a swamp and having a series of adventures as he floated on and on toward his final destination—the sea. Unfortunately, Nin threw it out when he was thirteen along with the rest of his earliest writing.

One provider of new material for Jack's imagination was his father, who started taking his eleven-year-old son along with him to racetracks in Rockingham, New Hampshire; Pawtucket, Rhode Island; and Boston. Sometimes the two of them would stay overnight in cheap hotels. Jack drank in the atmosphere at the tracks just as he had responded to the "poetry" of Leo's wrestling club, and began to dream about becoming a jockey. For the rest of his life he would be crazy about horses. He especially loved to see them dash through the rain, throwing up great muddy splashes with their hooves. He listened closely to the conversations around him, the complaints of the bettors, the knowing talk about owners and stables and pedigrees. Leo showed him how to read the racing papers, and sometimes consulted him for advice about which horses to bet on, but their excursions were never exactly lighthearted. For Leo the races were not a game—they had become a grim business. He was betting his survival and self-worth with every dollar.

On the outs with Gabe and suffering from bouts of rheumatism that often kept him groaning on the parlor couch, Leo needed to have by his side a young companion who looked up to him. He didn't object to having Jack hang around with him at the Pawtucketville Social Club. According to Jack's first diary, he was spending nearly every night there during January and February 1934, learning how to bowl and shoot pool. Essentially a saloon, the club was hardly an appropriate place for a twelve-year-old boy, but Leo very seldom told Jack to go home. He was at the club the night Leo was arrested for gambling on the premises. But, as Jack loyally noted in his diary, his pa ended up making five dollars anyway. In one entry, he made particular mention of seeing the movie version of *David Copperfield* in which his father's poker buddy W. C. Fields played the improvident Mr. Micawber. Perhaps Mr. Micawber reminded Jack of Leo.

In September 1934, the Kerouacs had to pack up again. The cottage they moved into on Sarah Avenue, just around the corner from Phoebe Avenue, seemed to Jack the saddest one in its row of small, rundown houses, although at least it had its own apple tree in the backyard. For a short while the Kerouacs kept a horse in that yard—a gift to Leo from the mayor of Lawrence, Massachusetts. Jack and his neighborhood friends rode around on it, but then it ran away and was never found. Oddly enough, the real horse was nowhere nearly as important to Jack as an imaginary racehorse in the form of a ball bearing named Repulsion. (One of Jack's linguistic mistakes had resulted in a very odd name for a winner.) In a game Jack had invented called The Turf, Repulsion was invariably the champion when pitted against other, lighter horses, who, unlike him, were only marbles. It was a game Jack played obsessively in his room in the new house, laying out the track on the linoleum floor with a wet mop, sending his "horses" down the steep incline of a Parcheesi board, and timing them as they crashed into the finish line—the opposite wall.

In effect, he had created an alternate universe, where he as the all-powerful Jack Lewis (the English equivalent of Jean-Louis) was not only a famous jockey and the owner of a stable of thoroughbreds but the racing commissioner and the editor of *The Turf*, the racing paper he wrote and published, sometimes setting the type for it in his father's print shop, otherwise meticulously printing it out by hand, complete with headlines, in carefully ruled columns on gray or green paper, with newspaper photos of racehorses pasted in. Jack was partial to gray paper because it reminded him of rainy days at the track, while the pale green matched the small haunted desk that had belonged to his brother and still had Gerard's chalk marks on it. The issues of *The Turf,* precursors of the fiction Jack would later write in which he brilliantly depicted physical action, from football games to Neal Cassady's driving to the moves of a saxophone player, were works of childhood genius, with more richly detailed reportage about the horses that were running, the personalities that guided their destiny, and the history of each race than the papers Leo used to handicap his bets. To make the races he recorded as real and exciting as possible, Jack added elements of time, chance, and entropy, deliberately chipping his marbles every few months, damaging some so badly that those "horses" would have to be put down.

Like the idea for a novel might come to a writer, the game had been born in Jack's mind all at once on a gray afternoon as he sat idly rolling marbles in the parlor of the house on Phoebe Avenue. Suddenly he'd experienced what he later called a moment of *"complete inspiration"* in which his "whole life's richness" swam before him "in a palpable moth-life cloud."

Jack's alter ego, Jack Lewis, had more than one enterprise. Another, which also required a newspaper to document it, was the Imaginary Baseball League, a card game Jack invented after Leo took him to Fenway Park to see the Red Sox. Jack played it for the rest of his life. But The Turf ended abruptly when he was around fourteen. As he was playing with Repulsion in his yard, this time using the ball bearing as a baseball, he hit a home run that sent it into the bushes. It rolled away from him, vanishing forever, marking the end of his "childish play."

FOOTBALL HERO

In November 1935, Leo Kerouac got one of the thrills of his life as he and a crowd of neighborhood spectators watched some kids playing a sandlot football game. The Dracut Tigers, Jack's team of thirteen-year-olds, which included G.J., Freddie Bertram, and Scottie Beaulieu, were pitted against a team of seventeen- and eighteen-year-old toughs who hung around the pool table at the Pawtucketville Social Club. These older boys, who had a grudge against Leo because he kept throwing them out for being nonpaying customers, had challenged the Tigers to a game after they had seen Jack score nine touchdowns in a game with a team of youngsters from Rosemont. The youths were out to teach Jack and his self-righteous father a lesson. No sooner had Jack caught the ball after the kickoff than the older boys piled on top of him. Yelling "Get the little Christ of a [Kerouac]!" one of them punched him in the mouth, as Leo, identifying with every move of his son's, watched in a mounting rage. On the next play, Jack got even, coming at his opponent head-on and sending him sliding across the field unconscious. (If the opposing teams were wearing the close-fitting leather football helmets that were used back then, they would have offered the boys relatively little protection against the head injuries they were in constant danger of receiving.)

"Ha ha ha," Leo yelled (and there weren't many such moments of triumph in his disappointing life), "that'll teach you to punch a thirteen-year-old boy *mon maudit crève faim.*" From that point on, he began taking an intense—in fact, an overly intense—interest in Jack's development as a future sports star. Now there was an ambition that Leo, as well as most of Lowell, could appreciate.

All that year, Jack had put himself through rigorous training to improve his game. To strengthen his legs, he had been running laps on the cinder track at the Textile Institute, and after he had become the captain of the Dracut Tigers, he had gotten the others to train with him, timing their speeds with a device he'd ingeniously rigged up when he was twelve, using the turntable of an old Victrola. In the summertime, when his team played baseball, he would use his Imaginary Baseball League cards to work out strategies with Scottie Beaulieu, bringing his fantasy and real worlds together.

With the exception of G.J., Jack's team was all Canuck. Over the next few years, almost every Saturday in the fall, the Dracut Tigers played football against a team of Greek kids in what Jack remembered as bruising "Homeric battles" that in retrospect seemed like rehearsals for the war looming directly ahead of them in which many of those same boys would be killed or wounded, with those who survived "eviscerated of 1930's innocent ambition."

But the real battles on Lowell's football fields did not replace The Turf. Jack's desire to hole up in his room and be Jack Lewis remained as powerful as ever—linked to his growing urge to put words down on paper in English and make something out of his imaginings. True writers don't *choose* to write; driven by an inexplicable hunger for the process, they can't help but do so. This need was born in Jack very early.

Oddly enough, Gabe persisted in treating her football player son as if he were unusually delicate. Having lost one boy, she indulged and babied the surviving one in every way she could. Until Jack was twelve, she even insisted on bathing him herself and was horrified, as Jack once told Allen Ginsberg, when she noticed that Ti Jean had an erection. Unwittingly, she became the enabler of the solitude that was essential for the development of Jack's writing. On the slightest pretext, she'd allow him to play hooky and stay home with her, sometimes just because it was raining. She felt a need to keep her boy close to her, and she was becoming more and more dependent on him for the affection she wasn't getting from her gloomy, irascible husband. When Jack took a break from The Turf on one of his stolen afternoons, he'd find his mother waiting with a delicious treat that must have felt like a reward for his creative activity. "There, try a nice one of vanilla, it's good for you," she says to him in *Dr. Sax*, pushing a white-frosted cupcake in his direction.

When Jack became a grown man, this still seemed an ideal setup—to be alone with his writing yet not completely alone (because in truth he couldn't handle total solitude very well), to have his mother hovering nearby, just out of sight, eternally ready to take care of his needs.

If Leo or Nin thought Gabe was pampering Jack and letting him spend too much idle time in his room, perhaps Gabe defended him the way Mrs. Martin defends her son Francis's odd self-absorption in *The Town and the City:* "If he keeps so much to himself, it's because he has a lot on his mind." But she did begin to worry that Jack was up there abusing himself and to watch for signs of that, closely examining his handkerchiefs.

In Jack's memories of his mother, she's seldom dressed to go out, but is wearing what he once wrote he'd like all his women to wear—a Depression-era cotton housedress, with an apron smeared with flour.

Blue-eyed and dark-haired, she's "smiling, nice." In life, Gabe may have been worried sick about how she was going to feed her family and would save even a quarter of an onion, but in Jack's books, her resolute cheerfulness is her dominant quality and she seldom raises her voice to her son or her husband. In a 1954 poem that begins "I keep falling in love / with my mother," Jack sentimentally describes her as a Dutch doll, always ready to serve him. In a 1944 photo, however, there's nothing in the least doll-like about her. Her face in that picture, taken when she was in her forties, is gloomy, hard, deeply lined—a face you would call formidable if you saw it on a concierge in a French movie. By his late teens, Jack would be telling G.J., "I can never be what she wants. I can't live with her." Baked into Gabe's cupcakes were chains of iron.

On March 12, 1936, Jack's fourteenth birthday, there were warnings in the *Lowell Sun* about an enormous flood upriver that was going to sweep right through the town. The peaceful Merrimack was swollen with broken ice floes and was about to become a raging monster. It had already devastated river towns in New Hampshire. By the following morning, its water was steadily rising, four inches an hour. Bartlett canceled its classes. When Jack took a walk with his mother that afternoon, they saw crowds of open-mouthed people anxiously standing on the shore near the Falls as trucks of sandbags began to arrive. He would remember the scene colored in shades of gray—"a gloomy newsreel of 1930's."

Early the next day, he and Billy Chandler, still enjoying the unexpected holiday from school, went to take a look at "the scenes of wrath and destruction that already we could hear roaring over our Wheaties." The river was brown with churned-up mud; houses and trees were being swept along by the flood as well as the entire roof of a barn, which the boys thought would have made a terrific raft for them. High on the novelty of it all, Jack dreamily took in the tremendous spectacle, with no sense of being in any danger. It was as if he had the curious sense of immunity reporters feel when they're covering a story. He became part of the action himself when he leaped onto the passing roof of a chicken coop and would have been swept away if Billy hadn't yelled to him to jump off.

It took a while before he and Billy realized that what they were witnessing was a huge disaster directly affecting people they knew. Freddie Bertram and his family had to be evacuated from the tenement where they lived; Miss Mansfield lost her Rosemont cottage to the Merrimack, and there would be no more meetings of the Scribblers' Club that year. Sebastian Sampas's house on Stevens Street was also destroyed. And so was Leo's Bridge Street print shop, which had filled with six feet of water, damaging the equipment he had recently borrowed money to buy. The ramifications of the flood would soon put him out of business, and never again would he be his own boss. The floodwaters didn't reach Sarah Avenue, but the Kerouacs had been left as poor as the people who lived in the tenements on Moody Street, which was where they had to move just before Jack started high school.

Their rundown building was right across the street from Freddie Bertram's tenement. On the ground floor was a greasy spoon called Textile Lunch. The flat was four flights up, and cockroaches owned the lavatory. Trying to make the best of things, Gabe, who'd had to return to the shoe factory, put a chair out on the rickety fourth-story porch, which looked as if it were in imminent danger of crashing to the street. On hot summer nights Jack would sleep out there. From his little corner room with its familiar green desk and toy pool table, he now looked out on crowded rooftops and a "wrinkly tar sidewalk" instead of the apple tree on Sarah Avenue.

Not long after the flood Jack stopped going to the church services he found so oppressive and funereal, though he continued to pray in his own way. One day the following fall, however, he walked into the cathedral of St. Jean Baptiste, where he had been a choirboy, looking for a priest to talk to. He told the young seminarian there that he had an unusual problem: Everyone was laughing at him because he wanted to be a writer.

Father "Spike" Morrissette would later recall that something had made him take Jack very seriously and speak to him of the great spiritual influence writers could have on their readers. He was proud that he had given Jack, who had just started high school as a commercial student, the life-changing advice to go all out for varsity football at Lowell High in the hope of winning a scholarship to a good college. He also told Jack that an aspiring writer would have to prepare himself to leave Lowell and go to New York and warned him about the many disappointments he would probably face. He remembered Jack saying he didn't mind disappointments.

There is a feeling of prophecy about this turning-point story that has made it an integral part of the Kerouac legend. But there is not one allusion to it in Jack's writings, or to Father Morrissette, who later spoke of Jack as someone who had profoundly influenced his own spiritual life.

At fourteen Jack certainly needed encouragement to pursue his dream from some respected adult. He may also have gotten some practical advice from Miss Mansfield, who remained his literary mentor even after he left Bartlett. But when he told his father he wanted to be a writer, Leo's reaction, as Jack describes it in *Visions of Gerard*, was crushing: "Artist schmartist!" Leo fancied himself an authority on literature and had boundless admiration for Victor Hugo, but in his view an artist was a no-good parasite who relied on others to support him. Although he had called Gerard a great artist, he probably would not have put such a crazy idea in his head if Gerard had not been mortally ill.

Jack's ideas of college were hazy, largely based on sports novels and movies he'd seen, but he must have imagined himself feasting on great books and understood that he was unlikely to meet many Franco-American boys like him among his fellow students. Now that he'd been convinced he couldn't become a writer without a higher education, suddenly his whole future seemed to depend upon how well he could train himself to play football. It would no longer be the game he played on Saturdays with his friends just for the fun of it. He lost a little of his boyhood innocence. It was the beginning of what he would someday bitterly call his "white ambitions."

With the Dracut Tigers, Jack remained a Pawtucketville star, but for the next year and a half, he found himself sitting out every official football game for Lowell High, no matter how hard he drove himself at practice. Since he had skipped a year of grammar school, he was younger than all the other varsity players, as well as shorter and not as strong. Looking for an edge, he joined the track team to develop his running speed.

Leo was convinced that it was "politics" and a prejudice against Canucks that made the Irish football coach keep Jack on the bench. Everywhere he looked in those days Leo saw enemies. He had not only lost Spotlite Print but was now embroiled in a nasty dispute with the friend who helped finance his business. For Leo, Lowell had turned into "Stinktown on the Merrimack." Hating his own life, he began to live through Jack's, disregarding Jack's determination to become a writer. His son was going to make a name for himself in football and he would make a comeback as his manager.

Jack's chance to show what a good player he was didn't come until his junior year, when the coach, noticing how powerful his legs were, put him in to replace another player in the first game of the season against Greenfield High. It was a classic "worm turns" scenario. The boy whom the coach had previously overlooked made two touchdowns and nearly scored a third with a thirty-yard run at the end of the game, putting everything he had into that winning run. "No one could run as hard and as strong on a straight line as Jack Kerouac," said a former teammate, Duke Chiungas. Jack won four more games for Lowell that season, but each time he was brought in only during the final minutes. Leo was outraged, but meanwhile Jack's name began to appear in Lowell and Boston newspapers, and Frank Leahy, the coach at Boston College, started to take a serious interest in him.

At sixteen, Jack wrote a seventy-seven-page segment of a football novel, set on a big campus like the ones he fantasized about. He typed the manuscript flawlessly on the L. C. Smith typewriter that used to be at Spotlite Print and passed it around to G.J., Billy Chandler, and the rest of his gang. He had gone a long way toward mastering the sports novel genre, despite the places where he reached for a literary-sounding word and faltered, coming up with a near miss such as "predaceous lion" for a "predatory" one. As Jack Lewis, he had written thousands of words by this time, and was able to describe the blow-by-blow action on the football field like a professional. Instinctively, however, he put in details that went beyond such reportage. Just before a kickoff, Jack gives his protagonist, Bill Clancy, the "huge lump in his throat" Jack must have felt before a big game. After Bill and his team win a glorious victory before a cheering crowd, the mood of the novel changes very effectively. The locker room Bill returns to is "chilly" and he "shivered as he hauled off his sticky uniform. His body gave out steam, his feet were cold. His ribs ached with exhaustion and his head felt hot and stuffy." There's a brief feeling of letdown and emptiness after the victory that adds depth to Bill's character.

Although the members of the supporting cast—Bill's coach, his girl, the rival players—are stereotypical, Bill himself is not. Like the boy who explored the Merrimack in the novel Jack wrote in junior high school, Bill is an orphan. He's the first vagabond in Jack's fiction. Since the death of his father, Bill has been "drifting along," without a trace of self-pity, preferring the life of a hobo, "hitchhiking and hopping freights" and sleeping on the lawns of professors, to staying back in Arkansas with his aunt and sisters. Bill had tried college for a year, but quit and "took to the road again." Now he has drifted onto the campus of State University, where he has decided to try out for the football team so that he can get back into school and study economics, figuring that he needs an education if he is ever to make a decent amount of money in the Machine Age. As a football player, Bill proves to be "madly determined" when he's up against his opponents, but the most interesting thing about him is that he isn't really invested in the game the way the other players are. Although he may be unstoppable on the playing field, he's always a little detached from the whole business of winning, and in one scene he's reluctant to tear himself away from a book when it's time for the game.

There's a split in Bill Clancy between the active and reflective sides of his nature, but it causes him no pain. In fact, he's the epitome of "cool," with the kind of equanimity that would always elude Jack. With no parents to breathe down Bill's neck, he's gloriously free to do whatever he wants and go wherever he chooses, without guilt.

There is no recorded date to establish exactly when in his sixteenth year Jack wrote the Bill Clancy novel, but I suspect it was around the time of the big Thanksgiving game of 1938, Lowell against Lawrence, which definitively ended his anxiety about whether or not he would be able to go on to college. Because the two teams were well matched, the game was particularly hard-fought, and after sitting through most of it, Jack won it spectacularly for Lowell with the only touchdown of the day. Lowering his head and shoulders, he ran as if his life depended on it, mowing down two Lawrence players in the last minutes of the second half as the spectators cheered wildly. Watching from the bleachers were Frank Leahy from Boston College and Lou Little, the celebrated football coach at Columbia.

When a bus took Jack's team back to Lowell, "crowds waved at them" and they were met at the high school by a throng of excited kids. Jack broke away from the celebration and walked home to Pawtucketville by himself. In *The Town and the City*, Peter, the football-playing son of the Martin family, hopes that "no one would ever notice him again." His sense of emptiness after victory is much greater than Bill Clancy's. Somehow Peter knows that what he has achieved in the stadium will separate him from those he feels closest to, as if he has betrayed them in some way "by having performed great feats that required their silence and praise."

When Jack walked into the flat on Moody Street, he was hailed as a hero by his father and learned that Frank Leahy would be joining the Kerouacs for Thanksgiving dinner. A few days later, Lou Little's representatives also came by to court him. And then Jack found himself facing a choice that would determine his whole future—whether to go to school in New York or Boston.

The choice should have been his to make, but unfortunately, his father had a stake in the outcome. Leo had desperately tried to secure a good job in Lowell, but he'd acquired a reputation for belligerent behavior, exacerbated by his heavy drinking, which undoubtedly worked against him. When he'd had his own business, he'd taken great satisfaction in throwing customers who offended him—including a Greek Orthodox priest and the manager of the Keith Theater—out the door, but now he had bosses to answer to. He had managed to get hired by a local printer after a miserable year of working in Andover as a linotypist and seeing his family only on weekends. As luck would have it, Leo's new employer, Sullivan Printers, happened to handle all the printing work for Boston College. Leahy offered to use his influence to get Leo a promotion at Sullivan if he could persuade Jack to go to Boston College, also promising Leo that when he moved to Notre Dame the following year, he would take Jack with him.

But Jack's heart was set on going to Columbia, even though he would first have to spend a year at Horace Mann prep school to make up some deficits in math and French. Surprisingly, Gabe, usually the practical one in the family, the one who scrimped and saved and performed household miracles on a few dollars, was all in favor of Jack's taking Lou Little's offer. She had been the boss of the household while Leo was out of town. As far as she was concerned, he had lost all his authority after the terrible mistakes he'd made. What did Leo know about anything? She told Jack not to listen to his father because Leo would always hold him back. Jack found himself at the center of the old household conspiracy—the one he had sensed as a child. Now it had been reconfigured, with Jack, instead of Gerard, in an alliance with his mother and his father occupying the position of odd man out.

Gabe had another motive for wanting Jack at Columbia. She had been dazzled by New York on the two visits she had made with him to her relatives—the last one had been only two years earlier. She was a woman who had spent her entire life in mill towns, and she naïvely thought of New York in terms of the neon lights of Broadway, the shows at Radio City Music Hall, with the cute Rockettes all lined up, kicking in unison on the huge stage of the Art Deco movie palace. If Jack was going to make his life in that city, she was going to be right there with her darling boy, her honeylamb, as she called him, with or without Leo.

Jack deferred his decision for months as his parents yelled at each other over the kitchen table. He had always sought Leo's approval and he must have felt that to let down his father was a terrible thing. But Boston College with its Jesuit professors didn't appeal to him—he'd had enough of a Catholic education. New York was where he felt he belonged, among all the other writers there, and he imagined a glamorous career for himself as a hard-boiled reporter like Damon Runyon covering the gritty city beat. Toward the end of the summer, after his mother took him to New York to talk to Lou Little, Jack turned down Leahy's offer, even though Sullivan Printers had been putting threatening pressure on his father to make him go to Boston. Because of Jack's choice, Leo did lose his job. "He went downtrodden to work in places out of town," Jack wrote guiltily in

Vanity of Duluoz. He knew that by going to Columbia he had sentenced his father to a bleak and embittered existence in exile from Lowell, but he counted on making it up to Leo with the brilliant college football career ahead of him.

FIRST LOVE

Since he was going to repeat his senior year at Horace Mann, Jack did not take his remaining courses very seriously. The exception that spring was English where he had an excellent teacher. Once a week he absented himself from all his classes to spend a day at the Lowell Public Library. There, he read *Les Misérables* and worked his way through the great books in the Harvard Classics. Goethe's *Faust* was a major discovery, introducing him to the concept of duality and giving him a new way to think about himself. "As for myself," Faust reflects, "there are two of me, unreconciled. The one clings to earth with its whole body sensually, while the other soars with all its might to the abodes of the blest." Fascinated by Faust's desire to experience "all that is given to humanity" and by his bargain with the devil in return for knowledge and power, Jack added *Faustian* to his growing vocabulary and began to think about dedicating himself to art.

Meanwhile, now that he had become the local football hero, Jack was suddenly getting a lot of attention from girls. Over the last two years, he had filled out and grown taller. By this time, he was a broad-shouldered young man—in fact, a devastatingly handsome one, although he was still shy and ill at ease socially. On the rare occasions he spoke in class, the last embarrassing traces of his accent could be heard. One of his classmates, Margaret Coffey, was out to make Jack her boyfriend. She was a bright, poised girl who stood out at Lowell High. Thinking beyond early marriage and beyond Lowell, Peggy was determined to become a band singer, an ambition she realized a few years later when she sang with Benny Goodman. Jack shared her passion for swing music, which was being widely broadcast on the radio.

Soon Jack started making dates to meet Peggy Coffey under the big clock on the outside of the school building. In the goldfish bowl of Lowell High, everyone was saying that she was the girl for him; even Nin, who took a great interest in her little brother's love life, thought so. But although Jack felt proud to be seen with Peggy, it wasn't love.

At sixteen the person Jack felt most deeply connected to was G. J. Apostolos—"the funniest guy in the world," as Jack later described him to John Clellon Holmes, telling him he "really *learned* things" from his "dumb Greek" friend—"style, tone, the way to look at things." Jack could talk to G.J. in ways he could talk to no other friend and even tell him some of the things another boy might have ridiculed or considered unmasculine. In a letter he wrote to G.J. that year, Jack set down his first written description of one of his dreams. In it, "my mother was sick . . . and I was hysterical and you were there to comfort me." G.J. understood Jack's passionate devotion to Gabe, and, in fact, encouraged it, since he too was a mother-dominated boy. Like Jack, he consequently had tremendous guilt about sex. After a sordid sexual encounter a couple of years later, G.J. vowed to henceforth save all his love for his mother and advised Jack to do the same.

G.J. had a tendency to become morose, which he countered by a willingness to go to absurd extremes in his comic escapades, regardless of the consequences. He had a touch of the quality Jack would later admiringly call "madness" when he found it in men like Neal Cassady or Allen Ginsberg—some extravagant, heedless abandon to the moment that could light up the world like "roman candles," as he put it in *On the Road*. It was something Jack always felt he lacked himself. Although shy and deeply introverted, he was always more than willing to be carried along by the madness of others. Jack later relished the memory of the crazy mock fights G.J. instigated with "wild witch doctor dances" in which he would have to defend himself against a "huge, moronic French" opponent named Iddyboy, as G.J. looked on with exaggerated horror. When Jack was with G.J., he would *become* G.J., just as he would later *become* Neal whenever the two of them were together, a personality change others would notice. Perhaps that troubling permeability of Jack's began with his mother, who recognized no boundaries; perhaps it began with his imitations of Gerard. Yet looked at another way, it was the form love took for him.

Although he made new friends in high school with boys of Irish and

Greek extraction, Jack's social life still revolved around the Pawtucketville gang. The teenagers ran around in a pack, just as they had done when they were twelve, indulging in the kind of wild horseplay they'd always found hysterically funny. In summer they swam naked in Pine Brook; in winter they found joy in throwing snowballs at cars as well as in playing hockey. One of their hangouts was a seedy pool hall called The Club de Paisan on the edge of Little Canada, whose proprietor they called Le Père. Some strange adventures bonded them—like the time they carried an old drunk home to his "haunted house" and he passed out on his couch, convincing them he had died. But something was different after the game that won Jack his ticket out of Lowell. The others knew Jack's life would no longer resemble theirs. Going off to college would not only lift Jack into a different social sphere, it would prolong the freedom of his adolescence. Meanwhile their boyhoods were rapidly running out. Directly ahead of G.J., Roland Salvas, and Scottie lay the grim responsibilities of working-class manhood. Looking at his friends only a year later, Jack could already see "the terror and death of early morning, of walking to the mill in the cold morning," of returning home to go "to bed, because you have to get up early to go to work."

The impending loss of Jack was particularly hard on G.J. And what made it worse for him was that Jack unexpectedly became seriously interested in an Irish girl named Mary Carney. If the boy gang had unwritten rules, one of them was that you couldn't fall in love; your first allegiance was to your buddies.

In the football novel Jack had written, Bill Clancy has a high-minded romance with a professor's daughter, undoubtedly the kind of girl Jack was hoping to meet in college, but Jack's first love was a brakeman's daughter who had dropped out of school after ninth grade. He had met her at a dance on New Year's Eve, to which she had come unescorted. "I saw her, standing in the crowd, forlorn, dissatisfied, dark, unpleasantly strange," he wrote in *Maggie Cassidy*—a sentence that captures the feeling he had then that girls were alien, somewhat frightening creatures. He had been led to Mary by a loutish youth who told him, "I tried and tried to work that chick."

Mary Carney was slender and rosy-cheeked with black curly hair and "sensuous, drowning lips, devourous lips"—the template for all the dark women Jack would get hung up on. A year older than he was, miles ahead of him in her understanding of relations between the sexes, and with a taste for intrigue, she was far more ready for sex than Jack was. But she had very accurately figured out the workings of the double standard and had a strong instinct for self-preservation. For an uneducated girl like Mary, there were pathetically few options—her goal was marriage and the sooner the better. Meanwhile her power over boys lay in her ability to hold them off. If she lost her virginity, she would be devalued. Lowell was a town where fast girls were despised and treated like sluts by Catholic working-class boys like G.J. and Scottie Beaulieu, who at the same time pressured them to have sex. G.J. looked upon girls who gave men what they wanted as "receptacles," a view that was probably shared to one degree or another by the rest of the gang.

For the next eight months, Jack and Mary, in the tangled throes of teenage lust, wrestled inconclusively on the couch in the parlor of Mary's home in South Lowell. They kissed until their mouths burned in long "futile" necking sessions that scared both of them. It was "that queer era in 20th century America, just before the girls started to chase the boys down the street," Jack would later write. "It was the time when you would boast about how long you 'necked' last night—Enough to drive anybody to 'theft' or 'suicide.'" Overwhelmed by his physical attraction to Mary but faithful to his mother, who wanted to keep him pure, and his strict Catholic upbringing, Jack was careful not to touch the forbidden parts of Mary's body. Meanwhile, ticking away in the background was his departure for New York in September and his elevation to prep school student status, which would put Mary at a social disadvantage compared to other girls he might meet.

As insurance against the impending interruption of their romance, Mary began openly seeing other boys who were more mature than Jack, while expressing her jealousy and suspicion of Peggy, whom Jack continued to date. Crazy about Jack, with whom she would be involved on and off for the next three years, Peggy didn't guard those off-limits areas of her body with as much vigilance as her rival. Meanwhile, Mary's feelings fluctuated maddeningly with her moods. She would push Jack away, then want him back, at the same time complaining that he was too young to know what to do with her. She would ignore him when he came to her house, then send notes to him at school, apologizing for being a "scatter-brain" (a word that for Lowell girls was synonymous with *flirt*) and doing things that hurt him.

Her inconsistent behavior was a torment for Jack, who was just about to turn seventeen. His feelings of humiliating rejection, his jealousy of other boys, even a couple of older high school buddies, his desire to pos-sess Mary exclusively while reserving the right to see Peggy—all these new feelings kept him in turmoil for months. Just as he had prayed for the love of Ernie Eno when he was ten, Jack "listened in the silence of my mother's house to divine how God was going to arrange the success of my love."

Mary suggested one obvious way the two of them would never have to separate. Jack could marry her and they could move into a little red cot-tage by the railroad tracks and start having babies. It worried Mary that Jack hadn't already picked out a trade, but she was sure her father could get him a job on the railroad. In Lowell, that early marriage idea wasn't at all far-fetched—many teenagers married right out of high school. (What other sanctioned way was there for them to have sex?) In fact, just the year before, Jack's eighteen-year-old sister had freed herself from her family's strict supervision by marrying Charley Morrissette, a lout a good deal older than she was, who drank at the Pawtucketville Social Club and bragged about the size of his penis. Already Nin was having regrets about marrying so soon, but Jack started mentally moving into that little red cottage with his dark-haired bride. At the same time he was stricken by the fear of losing his home "and going off into unknown sui-cides of weddings and honeymoons."

Meanwhile Gabe, terrified that she would lose her handsome son to the Irish girl and that Jack would throw away his chance to become a col-lege boy, an all-American football champion, and, eventually, a big insur-ance executive, implored him to "respect decency—listen, Ti Jean you'll never be sorry if you follow a clean life."

G.J. had yet to have a girlfriend. "Don't let no broad get you, Zagg—" he says vehemently in *Maggie Cassidy*, "love aint worth it." His remedy in the novel for the love affair that's getting Zagg down is brutal: "Screw her, then leave her, take it from an old seadog—women are no good."

Decades later, Mary Carney was still a sore point, as far as G.J. was concerned. When he was interviewed in 1978 for *Jack's Book*, an oral history biography, G.J. denied there had been any connection between the fictional Maggie Cassidy and the real Mary Carney. In fact, there had never been *anything*, he insisted, between Jack and Mary. "It was all in Jack's mind, his imagination."

Was this true? Aside from the fact that G.J.'s letters to Jack in 1940 indicate that Jack kept him fully informed about the ups and downs of the love affair, a folder of letters from Mary Carney herself, two of which Jack adapted for *Maggie Cassidy*, is filled with allusions to the vacillations, misunderstandings, and bruised feelings Jack described in the novel. On the outside of that folder is a note in Jack's handwriting saying Mary's letters should be destroyed, although he carefully preserved almost all the correspondence he received from others during his lifetime. Was he protecting Mary Carney's privacy or still feeling some residual anger over the pain she had caused him when he was young and naïve? "She was a wench, hear, and she toyed with my heart—and broke it," he wrote in 1943 to John MacDonald, a bookish, rather straitlaced friend he had known since high school and whose opinion was still important to him. Nine years later, however, the thought of Mary evoked nostalgic feelings. "How I loved her sad dark face and wanted to marry her at 16 and be a brakeman on the Boston & Maine railroad," he wrote to John Clellon Holmes in 1952.

In 1954, after a brief reunion with Mary Carney during a visit to Lowell, Jack wrote *Maggie Cassidy*. In the novel, the loss of Maggie represents much more than the loss of a high school sweetheart. The real loss seems to be the loss of the narrator's ability to love anyone after her with the same pure vulnerability and passion: "Never dreaming was I, poor Jack Duluoz, that the soul is dead. . . . That love is the heritage, and cousin to death. That the only love can only be the first love, the only death the last." Despite its broadly comic passages, the novel is an elegy of sorts, written in memory of the intensity of youthful feelings during a period when Jack was feeling numbed and empty.

Jack wasn't around to contradict G.J. or his biographer, Ellis Amburn, who in 1998 used the botched romance in *Subterranean Kerouac* as one more piece of evidence in his single-minded and strangely vengeful campaign to prove that Jack was homosexual. But Mary Carney had already had her say in *Jack's Book:* "There was something deep between Jack and me, something nobody else understood or knew about." She too had an ax to grind, although a different one from Amburn's: "Jack was so sensitive. All he wanted was a house and a job on the railroad." But of course, that completely left out Jack's desire to write, something that was never well understood by most of the women he felt attracted to as well as most of the people who had known him in Lowell.

As he went through life, Jack would often find himself in the position of wanting two irreconcilable things simultaneously—in this case, the Lowell girl he was smitten with versus the irresistible adventure of becoming an unattached young writer in the great metropolis he mostly knew about from the movies he'd seen at the Royal Theater.

At the end of the summer of 1939, a car accident in Vermont, where Jack had driven with his old friend Mike Fournier, nearly rendered his whole romantic dilemma moot. Jack suffered a head injury bad enough to require a couple of weeks of hospitalization—one more blow in addition to all the ones he'd received playing football since he was twelve. Could there have been any truth to what his mother later claimed, that he had seemed to her a very different person after the accident? Did the effects of cumulative damage to the brain over Jack's lifetime, topped off by a particularly bad beating in 1958, when he was physically attacked as he left a bar, contribute to his deepening alcoholism and depression?

By the time Jack recovered from the accident, it was Mary Carney who saved him from making up his mind. When he arrived for his farewell date with her, he found that she had seemingly forgotten all about him and was off with another boy. Shortly afterward, outfitted with a sports jacket paid for by his mother with some of the shoe factory earnings she hid in her corset, Jack went off to his all-boys school in New York City.

Gabe was triumphant. Her honeylamb was safe, for now. When G.J. dropped by to ask after Jack, she unkindly told him, "Now Jack's going to meet the people he should have grown up with." Apparently she was unaware that most of the Horace Mann students were Jews.

PART THREE

AN UPROOTING

MANHATTAN

In 1939, the train ride from Lowell to New York took half a day, but for Jack the psychic distance traveled was immense. In his time, and even up until the 1960s, relatively few young Franco-Americans would make lives for themselves far from the communities where they were born. Lowell had given Jack the only sense of belonging he would ever know. New York, where he would find no one like him, no friend he could speak to in his language, would never become home, although its "electrical vibrations" would always draw him back. "That black sweater of mine I always sleep in," he wrote me from Florida, where he was staying with his mother, in 1958, "it always crackles and bristles in New York, here it doesn't." By the time he was in his early twenties, Jack was acutely aware that there were many divisions in his soul, and he admitted that the deepest was the one between the town and the city.

On September 20, 1939, a couple of days after his arrival in New York, Jack groped for a persona in which he could take on the city. Sitting at the desk in his unfamiliar room in his stepgrandmother's house in Brooklyn, he built up his courage by telling himself he was an unknown genius named John L. Kerouac who was going to make his mark on literature. In the fat *cahier* in which he intended to document his conquest of Manhattan day by day, John L. Kerouac then reflected that using a pen instead of a typewriter put him in the hallowed tradition of those old "gladiators" and "immortal souls of journalism," Thackeray, Dickens, and Samuel Johnson.

Early the following morning he set out from Brooklyn. When he was fourteen, on his last visit to his mother's relatives, he had crossed the Brooklyn Bridge on foot—a walk he would often repeat in the future. This time he took a subway straight to Times Square, bought a ticket for the 9:45 A.M. show at the Paramount, and took a seat right in the front row so that he wouldn't miss a note of the live performance of the Glenn Miller Orchestra that followed the movie, lamenting afterward in his *cahier* that he had been surrounded by "illiterates" completely insensitive to the beauty of the music. He bought himself a few things on Forty-second Street that day and did a little shoplifting as well, then wandered into a secondhand bookstore. There he found himself among scholarly-looking types, but didn't like them any better than the ignoramuses at the Paramount who had clapped in all the wrong places. For the moment, an Olympian disdain was his chief defense against feeling like a green-horn in Manhattan.

By the next day, Jack was feeling more like himself. After reading the two previous days' entries, he correctly decided he must have been out of his mind when he wrote them. Still he compared his journal to a "castle" in which he could keep in touch with his thoughts, far removed from the antlike horde swarming below.

It was a Sunday. Enjoying his last bit of leisure in Ti Ma's sunny back-yard, Jack vowed to go on reading the Bible daily and to prepare himself for becoming a "perfect journalist" by studying Latin and four other sub-jects on his own. The following morning, he took his first two-and-a-half-hour ride to Horace Mann in Riverdale, up in the Bronx, the last stop on the IRT subway. After traveling back to Brooklyn that evening follow-ing a long day of courses and football practice, he was too tired to write more than two lines in his new *cahier* and said good-bye to it for the time being.

Horace Mann, remote in its own way from Manhattan, softened the shock of Jack's arrival in the city. Built at the top of a bluff in a leafy neighborhood of Tudor-style mansions, it provided its students with a tranquil world of ivy-covered granite buildings and manicured grounds. Once the boys walked up the long hill from the subway stop on Broad-way, they landed in a setting that reminded Jack of the way the British public school Rugby had been depicted in *Tom Brown's Schooldays*.

It was a school with excellent teachers where there wasn't much em-phasis on being athletic. The Jewish kids from well-to-do families who made up the majority of the student body concentrated on getting good marks and, unlike the boys at Lowell High, had little passion for playing sports. In fact, the football team was famous for consistently losing games. To give the team a fighting chance, high school athletes like Jack from poorer families, whom sportswriters referred to as "ringers," had been brought in on scholarship.

In a school dominated by upper-class WASPs, Jack, who was still terribly shy, might have felt intimidated. But among his new classmates, he was oddly comfortable even though he had never known any Jews before. Although he was an outsider in their world, he didn't have to feel inferior to them. Like the Canucks, they were a despised people, even the wealthy Jews. In fact, he had enough empathy for them to wonder how they felt every morning when they had to sing "Onward, Christian Soldiers." Given his French and Indian ancestry, he had his own misgivings about singing the Protestant hymn "Lord Jeffrey Amherst." Despite such fellow feeling, Jack brought to Horace Mann all the ingrained prejudice that was part of his cultural baggage, for it was not only his parents who hated Jews but most of his friends in Lowell. Even Mary Carney derisively referred to Horace Mann as "Jews Paradise."

In the years before World War II, anti-Semitism was pervasive in America. Many of the most virulent anti-Semites were people like Jack's father who had never done well and who had been hit especially hard by the Depression. Leo despised President Roosevelt, whom he believed to be in cahoots with Jewish bankers against the "little people." His hero was Charles Lindbergh, who admired Hitler. But even the literati were anti-Semitic. The novelist Thomas Wolfe, who would soon become Jack's chief literary influence, consistently referred to his mistress Aline Bernstein as "The Jew," even during the height of his passion for her. He wrecked an elegant dinner party by falling into a rage when Sherwood Anderson's wife told him it was rumored that he had some German Jewish blood. The Jewish hostess soothed Wolfe by saying she understood completely and didn't blame him a bit.

The relatives Jack was staying with in Brooklyn shared Leo's deplorable politics. His Uncle Nick, the Greek married to Ti Ma, Jack's step-grandmother, would often urge Jack to take a break from his studies and come and listen to Father Charles Coughlin, remembered today as "the Father of Hate Radio." The populist "Radio Priest" spoke out on behalf of the little people who had been hurt by the Wall Street financiers whom he blamed for the Depression, but there was a sinister fascistic and anti-Semitic side to his messages. By 1939, his weekly diatribes against "the Christ-killers and Christ-rejectors" were reaching an audience of 40 million. Perhaps Uncle Nick hoped Jack would be motivated to join Father Coughlin's Christian Front, an organization modeled upon Hitler's Brown Shirts, for which the priest was actively recruiting young street toughs.

Without repudiating the attitudes that were woven into his loyalty to his family, Jack soon found himself gravitating toward the Jewish boys in his classes. They weren't much to look at, he thought, but he got a kick out of their humor, which triggered his own. "Incunabular Milton Berles," he called them in *Vanity of Duluoz.* Their wisecracking voices got into his ear and stayed there; some Yiddish crept into his *Anglais* vocabulary. These young comedians shared his intellectual interests; he could talk to them in ways he could never talk to G.J. or Scottie. The chief wit, Eddie Gilbert, took Jack home to Flushing for several weekends; there Eddie's father, a man who had prospered in the lumber business, allowed him to examine the first hundred-dollar bill he'd ever seen. In Eddie's room, Jack looked with wonderment and envy at "the swell dresser full of clean socks and shirts the brass handles clicking significantly and softly rich, the closet full of tennis sneakers and rich golden shoe trees making me grip my breast, and the tennis racket on the wall." He would remember Eddie as a Gatsby-like figure and was not at all surprised to hear years later that Eddie had become known as a "financial wizard" before embezzling two million dollars and fleeing to Brazil.

Jack did strike up an acquaintanceship with one boy whose background his family would have approved of—an odd duck named Henri Cru, whom Jack considered a real Frenchman. Henri had gone to boarding school for a few years in Paris; his father was an eminent professor of French literature. He wasn't much of a student and was expelled later that year for selling condoms and switchblade knives to younger boys, but Henri convinced Jack that he was a French aristocrat. All through their long relationship Jack good-naturedly tolerated the ribbing he got from Henri about his crude manners. In his youth Henri was very handsome, but by the time I met him in the late 1950s, when he was working as a moving man in Greenwich Village, he weighed around three hundred pounds. I remember feeling Henri was treacherous, both weirdly possessive of Jack and eaten up with jealousy of him, something Jack didn't seem to notice.

Jack's closest friend at Horace Mann was Seymour Wyse, a Jewish seventeen-year-old English "hepcat" with an impressive knowledge of jazz, who had been sent to America with his brother to escape the possible invasion of Britain by the Nazis. Another new friend, Pete Gordon, whose father had made a fortune on Wall Street, helped wean Jack away from his current admiration for Conan Doyle and introduced him to the writings of Ernest Hemingway, whose stripped-down twentieth-century prose immediately influenced the stories Jack started publishing in the Horace Mann literary magazine.

I doubt that Pete or Seymour or Eddie Gilbert ever realized that Jack was anti-Semitic. (The thought never crossed my own mind when I was involved with him, even though I knew how prejudiced his mother was.) All through his life Jack would veer between the abstract prejudice ingrained in him and the affection he genuinely had for his Jewish friends; mixed with the affection, however, was always his silent awareness of their otherness. This was one of the darker aspects of the town-and-city split.

On the football team the players were mostly of Italian and Irish extraction, although there was one other French Canadian ringer, who didn't care to be reminded that he and Jack shared the same background. Some teammates made disparaging remarks about Jack spending so much of his time with his new Jewish pals. Jack later denied that his fellow ringers had anything against Jews; it was just that they resented the wealth of the Jewish students and the luxury they took for granted. He wrestled with such envious feelings himself every time he opened his brown paper bag in the lunchroom and took out a peanut butter sandwich as he hungrily eyed the turkey and chicken sandwiches being consumed all around him.

The wealthy boys not only began to share their sandwiches with Jack but, like Eddie Gilbert, brought him home for weekend visits. How exotic he must have seemed to them, as if he had stepped right out of a Horatio

Alger novel—the rugged, poor, compellingly handsome athlete from another world who had read more books than they had, a living advertisement for self-improvement. In Fifth Avenue and West End Avenue apartments, as luxurious as the ones he'd seen on movie screens, Jack walked on thick Oriental rugs and sat self-consciously at dinner tables before daunting arrays of highly polished silverware. Now he had to put into practice the good table manners his sister had drilled into him over the summer, using a copy of Emily Post's book of etiquette. At Pete Gordon's, a smiling black butler brought Jack his morning grapefruit, but Pete's financier father reminded him of his ringer status with a patronizing compliment. Why, Mr. Gordon asked his son at the breakfast table, wasn't Pete more like their young visitor, who combined "all the excellence of a Greek, that is, the brain of an Athenian and the brawn of a Spartan."

Jack kept G.J. informed about his glamorous New York adventures in letters that to G.J. seemed like "books." One letter of Jack's made G.J. warn him to watch what he said with a Jewish boy who could be useful to him in the future. Jews, he advised Jack, were supposed to be very sensitive.

On Armistice Day, the Horace Mann team played its third game of the season against a school from Garden City, Long Island. Leo Kerouac had come down for that long weekend. It was Jack's best game so far with a spectacular run in the first quarter and an impressive kick in the third, followed by his second pass in only a few weeks. Finally Leo had seen him playing in top form from the beginning to the end of a game, which Jack hoped made up a little for losing his job at Sullivan Printers. But even before the game, Jack had been sending home clippings from New York papers, whose reporters had noticed his impressive contributions to Horace Mann's surprising winning streak that fall.

By the time Leo returned to his dreary life in Meriden, Connecticut, where he was staying in a rooming house and working as a linotypist, he had kidded around in the locker room with Jack's victorious coaches and teammates, gone to a couple of Broadway shows, and treated his boy to a steak dinner at Jack Delaney's. With a son who he felt was now well on his way to becoming all-American, he'd had a weekend of feeling like a high roller.

Jack never missed a session of football practice that fall, but he regularly cut his academic classes, as he had done in Lowell. Manhattan became his principal area of study. He found Forty-second Street inexhaustibly fascinating with its neon signs, penny arcades, and pornographic peep shows, its cheap eating places and theaters, and the lowlife characters who stationed themselves in the cafeterias and flitted furtively through the crowds of people who had come from everywhere in search of a good time. The street seemed to him like one vast "room." Sometimes he went there to gorge himself on movies, going straight from a French classic like *The Lower Depths* with Jean Gabin at the Apollo Theater to an Alice Faye film at the Paramount, where he returned to hear Glenn Miller, admiring him much less now that his taste in jazz was becoming more discriminating. By the time he went backstage to interview Miller for the *Horace Mann Record*, the thing that struck him most was that he had actually heard Miller say the word *shit*.

Jack's daytime explorations of the city were usually solitary, but with Seymour Wyse he started going to Harlem at night to hear jazz. "Outside in the street," he wrote a few months later, "the sudden music which comes from the nitespot fills you with yearning for some intangible joy—and you feel that it can only be found within the smoky confines of the place."

In the history of jazz, 1939 was "an exceptional moment," as Ralph Ellison wrote twenty years later, "and the world was swinging with change." The two boys happened to arrive on the scene just in time for what Ellison called "a momentous modulation into a new key of musical sensibility: in brief, a revolution in culture" that in the musical world prefigured the 1950s revolution in literature of the Beat movement. The Old Guard in jazz was represented by the big swing bands that had become wildly popular with young people around 1937, when, as Jack put it in his essay "The Birth of Bop," the "Depression began to crack" and everyone, particularly the emerging American "alienated teenager," who was about to become the "hepcat" of the 1940s, had grown "tired of being poor and low and gloomy in a line." The swing bands played from well-rehearsed musical arrangements before large enthusiastic audiences in venues like the Paramount, but by 1939, brilliant, formally trained younger players were beginning to search for their individual voices in daring experiments with improvisation in after-hours jam sessions in Harlem. "Often they were quiet and of a reserve which contrasted sharply with the exuberant and outgoing lyricism of the older men," wrote Ellison. "They were concerned, they said, with art, not entertainment." The young black innovators were also trying "to create a jazz that could not be so easily imitated and exploited by white musicians" like Glenn Miller. "You only have so many notes," observed Dizzy Gillespie, one of the pioneers of Bop. "We invented our own way of getting from one place to the next."

For Seymour Wyse, jazz was and would remain an overpowering obsession, the focus of his life. That year he was wild about the Count Basie Orchestra and Jack soon caught his enthusiasm. They followed Basie to various Harlem clubs. One of them was Minton's, the epicenter of the after-hours insurgency in jazz and one of the rare places in America where blacks and whites mingled comfortably. The packed room was a fascinating cross-section of Manhattan—from high-society people and white college professors to black intellectuals and artists and pimps and their women. That fall Jack had passed through a brief period of excitement about Dixieland after Pete Gordon took him to Fifty-second Street to hear Mugsy Spanier, but he responded more powerfully to the new and wilder sounds he was hearing in Harlem as he listened to the dazzling solos of Basie's trumpet player Roy Eldridge and the tenor saxophonist Lester Young, who had become Seymour's god. When they stumbled out of Minton's still dazed and excited by the music and got on the downtown subway, Seymour would still be hearing Lester's "developing choruses" in his head.

The Count Basie Orchestra inspired Jack's first writings about jazz, which were published in the *Horace Mann Record*. In his initial piece he wrote, "Count Basie's swing arrangements are not blaring, but they contain more drive, more power and more thrill than the loudest gang of corn artists who tear their horns apart." In that sentence Jack struck exactly the right note, even though for the time being he was still checking out his opinions with Seymour and another knowledgeable boy named Donald Wolf.

By the spring of 1940, Jack's own musical taste was clearly defined. As far as he was concerned, "real jazz" was "music which has not been pre-arranged—free-for-all adlib. It is the outburst of passionate musicians, who pour all their energy into their instruments in the quest of soulful expression and super-improvisation. . . . It gets you—right down to your shoetops."

All through that year of unclouded success at Horace Mann, Lowell followed Jack to New York in letters from those he'd left behind—letters that reminded him how lucky he was, how exceptional, compared to the boys he knew back home. Roland Salvas hadn't yet made up his mind to enter high school, Freddie was looking for a job in a foundry, G.J. had switched to a college-bound track without much hope of ever going to college. In the fall, G.J. dropped out of school for a few months and went to a CCC camp in Estes Park, Colorado, where the WPA provided forestry jobs for unemployed youths.

The boys all looked up to Jack the way Jack's family did, expecting great things of him in the future, imagining a more glamorous existence than the one he actually had—canceling out those peanut butter sandwiches and those two-and-a-half-hour subway rides in which he did his physics homework standing up.

G.J.'s letters in particular may have made Jack feel he had been selected to live for everyone else. Although G.J. was having the adventure Jack longed for of being out west, he felt he was surrounded by "morons" and "degenerates" and looked back nostalgically to last summer's long nightly walks in Lowell, when he and Jack had discussed everything from philosophy to sex. Afraid that he and Jack would lose touch, he was desperately trying to emulate him—taking a typing course, writing a script for either radio or film, starting a novel inspired by a double feature of *The Hound of the Baskervilles* and *Wuthering Heights*. G.J. asked Jack what great books he should read, but Jack may have winced when he read his old friend's response to *Hamlet*. The line "To be or not to be—that is the question" had made G.J. laugh hysterically.

In early November, Jack was surprised to hear from Mary Carney. Writing in a deliberately offhand tone, she asked if he had met any debutantes he liked more than her and went into detail about whom she was dating. In one line she called him a "lunkhead"; in another she called him the love of her life. Mary had been very much on Jack's mind, but he wrote back so coolly—asking her what on earth she saw in him—that he scared her. Her next letter was 100 percent ardent. Her longing for Jack was giving her sleepless nights. She was so sick with love, she promised to turn over a new leaf and get over being jealous of the other girls who were after him. (Jack passed this letter to a classmate in study hall who congratulated him on being a real "heartbreaker.")

He hitchhiked home that Thanksgiving with Pete Gordon and another classmate, so that he could bring the "madcaps" of New York and Lowell together. It was the first of his attempts to bridge that troubling gap between the town and the city. Roland Salvas tried to impress Jack's prep school guests by breaking a shop window on Moody Street. Gabrielle and Leo evidently kept their feelings about having Jews in their house to themselves. In the midst of the holiday festivities, Jack broke away to see Mary. Crazy about her all over again after a passionate necking session, he promised they would see each other when he came back for Christmas.

When he wrote to G.J. about this development, G.J. replied that he could understand the attraction of Mary's "physical assets." But he mockingly expressed amazement that after being in New York, Jack still hadn't gotten laid. G.J., still terrified of girls himself, was determined to act like a seasoned "whoremaster" with one he'd recently met. Soon after reading the challenge in G.J.'s letter, Jack set out to prove him wrong by losing his virginity. The first woman he ever slept with was a redheaded prostitute in a hotel room near Times Square.

Undoubtedly, Jack gave G.J. all the details, but did he really give them to Mary in December as he does in *Maggie Cassidy*, prompting her to ask him to "do to me what you do to those girls in New York"? A good Catholic girl, she was, after all, still holding out for marriage. As a demonstration of his sexual ineptness, Jack's failure to take Mary to bed forthwith has been analyzed to an absurd degree by two of his biographers, Gerald Nicosia and Ellis Amburn. The bind Jack and Mary found themselves in was actually quite commonplace even in the long-term relationships of older couples. Fear, unrealistic expectations, and the possibility of dire consequences surrounded the sexual act. The quaint phrase "going all the way" says it all.

By the spring, when Mary, chaperoned by her mother, came down to

New York for Jack's senior prom, Jack had gone on to have more experiences with prostitutes—not such an unusual course of action at that time. In Harlem, he sought out black women, with whom he evidently felt less inhibited than he did with whites. He had been culturally conditioned to view women in a very limited way—either as alluring and dangerous sirens or as elemental maternal figures. For true companionship, he would turn to men, always pleasantly surprised yet wary of commitment when he met women who offered him more than his stereotypes. At eighteen, Jack was learning fast that sex could be separated from emotional content before he ever went to bed with a woman he loved. To add to his sexual confusion, he had been approached by some gay men. He confided this to G.J., who assured him it had happened only because of his "manly beauty."

What broke up Jack's relationship with Mary, however, was "town and city" anxiety. In Lowell, she'd been a prize he dreamed of winning, but she could not be transplanted to Manhattan. For both teenagers, the challenge of the prom was to prove how well they would pass in a crowd of affluent, upper-class young people. Jack was able to borrow a tuxedo, but unfortunately decided to have a sunlamp treatment to give him that carefree tan his classmates brought back from holidays in Bermuda—the result was a humiliating beet-red face. Mary confronted a sea of pastel tulle formals from Lord & Taylor and Saks Fifth Avenue in a gown she'd sewn herself and was certain all the other girls were laughing at her. The self-consciously sophisticated repartee of Jack's crowd was over her head. "Oh fer krissakes . . . get it over with!" she uncoolly interrupts the Pete Gordon character in *Maggie Cassidy* as he shows off his suave knowledge of cocktails. When Jack looked at Mary Carney that night, he saw the glaring reflection of his own "social fear." She made it clear that she didn't belong in New York and didn't care to. If Jack wanted to marry her, he would have to marry Lowell too.

When the weekend was over, Mary and her mother went home—she to her limited mill town existence, Jack to his "whirlpools of new litter and glitter."

At the Horace Mann graduation exercises in May, Jack was again reminded that he was, after all, an outsider in the world of his classmates. Despite his winning touchdowns, his 92-point average, his three stories published in the literary magazine (the latest, "Une Veille de Noel," was the talk of the whole school), he could not take part in the ceremony because he could not afford to buy himself a white suit.

Proudly pretending not to care, he lay on the grass behind the grandstand leafing through a book of Walt Whitman's poems as his classmates claimed their diplomas. Over the next ten years, most of his Horace Mann friends, with the exceptions of Henri Cru and Seymour Wyse, would drop out of his life. When he went to a reunion of his class in 1947, where he saw Eddie Gilbert for the last time, the "fantastic wits" of Horace Mann already had their sights set on careers as "formidable restaurateurs, realtors, department store tycoons," while he had not sold one word of the million he'd written.

Heading back to Lowell a day after the graduation exercises, even the sight of the old grim redbrick mills through the windows of the train looked good to Jack. He was back "where the road began," as he would write later that summer. Thinking about his months away from home, he reminded himself in emotional language that sounds directly translated from his French thoughts, "I hope, little madman, that you realize that destination is not really a tape at the end of a straight-way racing course, but that it is a tape on an oval that you must break over and over again as you race madly around."

By the time Jack graduated from Horace Mann, the Kerouacs were barely hanging on in Lowell. The Depression was on the wane, but not for them. They had moved their belongings out of Moody Street to a smaller second-floor flat in a house on Gershom Avenue. Leo was still drifting from one Connecticut printing plant to another, counting on a vague promise from the Columbia coach Lou Little that he would get him a job in New York. Gabrielle could find only part-time employment in the Lowell shoe factories. Her earnings combined with Nin's barely held everything together. Nin was working as a bookbinder at Sullivan Printers. She was back with the family now because she was divorcing her husband, who had treated her cruelly.

That summer, however, Jack was in a world of his own. It was books, not worries about the family's future, that kept him up at night, with his desk lamp turned on and swing bands softly playing on the brand-new

Emersonette radio his mother had surprised him with. Taking a tip from Jack London, whose biography he was now reading, Jack papered the walls of his Gershom Street room with lists of polysyllabic words with Latin roots that were still giving him trouble: "Ubiquitous, Surreptitious, Demonological . . ." It was usually the suffixes that tripped him up, some French/English/*joual* confusion he was determined to overcome. Meanwhile, his reading tastes were changing. He had once considered Jack London one of the greatest writers in the world, and was still ready to defend him against any criticism, but Walt Whitman, who had intensified his longing to explore America from coast to coast, and Ernest Hemingway, who had unclogged his sentences, were his current idols and he was about to find a new one.

THE SUMMER OF SEBASTIAN

If the young people of Jack's day had a Kerouac of their own, it was William Saroyan, who wrote in the preface to *The Daring Young Man on the Flying Trapeze*, the book that made him famous at twenty-four:

> A writer can have, ultimately, one of two styles: he can write in a manner that implies that death is inevitable, or he can write in a manner that death is not inevitable. . . . If you write as if you believe that ultimately you and everyone else alive will be dead, there is a chance that you will write in a pretty earnest style.

I can imagine Jack reading these words in the summer of 1940, instantly knowing which of these two writers he was going to be, as if he had received a message intended just for him. But Saroyan had other important things to teach Jack. Apparently, it was entirely possible to become a writer without a college education, for now Jack learned that no one had taught Saroyan how to write. Saroyan's parents spoke Armenian (a language even fewer Americans spoke than *joual*) and he had never even completed high school. He had simply gone ahead and thought up his own rules that knocked established masters of fiction like O. Henry off their pedestals. The precepts he offered demystified the act of writing and made it seem as natural as breathing:

1. "Do not pay any attention to the rules other people make."
2. "Forget everybody who ever wrote anything."
3. "Learn to typewrite so you can turn out stories as fast as Zane Grey."
4. "Try to be alive. You will be dead soon enough . . ."

Saroyan had been only two years older than Jack when he began to figure all this out, a literally starving writer living on bread, cigarettes, and coffee—or often just on air—in skid-row hotels, freezing windowless attics, or on the streets of San Francisco's Chinatown—the same bleak streets where Jack would someday walk himself with empty pockets, ravenously staring at the glazed ducks hanging in restaurant windows.

Saroyan was defiantly proud of his essentially situationless stories. None of them really had what most people would call a plot. They were mostly the meditations of a young writer alone in a succession of grim rooms or they depicted him wandering around skid row talking to men even worse off than he was. A couple of them were about encounters with bedraggled prostitutes, which no doubt reminded Jack of his own recent experiences. Saroyan's power over his thousands of readers came from the passion in his voice, from the fervent and innocent idealism of the 1930s—that earnestness which seems rather antiquated now. *The Daring Young Man on the Flying Trapeze* was permeated by the despair of the Great Depression, which at times in Saroyan's writing, with its complete lack of irony, seemed indistinguishable from the rich, black despair of adolescence. He was a writer who never held back his tears. His sudden moments of epiphany—brief perceptions that despite everything life was "splendid," a word he forgetfully used over and over again—undoubtedly made many weep with him.

In the journal Jack started at Columbia that fall, he would claim he had written eighty not very good stories while he was at Horace Mann, sixty of which he sold to classmates for a dollar apiece. But quite apart from that badly needed sixty bucks, all that writing had paid off.

"Une Veille de Noel," with its autobiographical elements, its skillfully sustained mood, its mixture of realism and mysticism, had been an impressive performance for a writer who had just turned eighteen. For Franco-Americans the Veille de Noel was one of the most important, sacred, and joyous holidays of the year celebrated by family feasts that began after church services and went on until dawn with drinking, singing, and dancing. In stark contrast to that tradition (an irony none of Jack's Horace Mann readers would have grasped), Jack set the story in a bar in Greenwich Village on Christmas Eve, where Mike, a sardonic graying man, reminiscent of Leo Kerouac, is glumly drinking, while snow falls outside—all portrayed vividly in short, spare sentences. The radio plays, the grinning bartender serves drinks to some tipsy students, an old vagrant sleeps in a corner. Mike's wife arrives, but Mike doesn't respond to her gesture of affection. Then a stranger walks in, a thin man with a white face and very white hands, who doesn't drink but wants to wish everyone a merry Christmas. There's a change in the atmosphere of the barroom, a sudden stillness—all evoked with great delicacy. The old man suddenly wakes up and stares at the stranger. After the stranger says he has to be on his way and walks out into the street, Mike's six-year-old son appears—every night he comes to the bar to remind his father to come home. (Did Jack think of him as Ti Jean or Gerard, or both?) To Mike's son, the snowy night is beautiful. In the mystical ending of the story, he asks his father whether he saw the angel too.

When he began the year at Horace Mann, Jack was clumsily attempting to follow in the footsteps of his nineteenth-century British "gladiators" until Hemingway led him into twentieth-century American territory. Now his writing changed again as he fell under Saroyan's spell. For the first time, he experimented with abandoning plot and began to explore the possibilities of an autobiographical, first-person voice.

He'd read *The Daring Young Man on the Flying Trapeze* upon the insistence of the Greek boy Sebastian Sampas, whom he had met at Bartlett Junior High. For eighteen-year-old Sebastian, that book had become a spiritual and political manifesto. In fact, he was rather Saroyanesque himself. In love with art and beauty, he wore his emotions on his sleeve— a great poem could move him to tears; so could an unfeeling word or an unkind act or the self-destructive behavior of a friend. Often giddily poised between exaltation and despair, Sebastian possessed a crazy kind of courage that made him seem strangely indifferent to what others thought of him. Nothing could keep him from leaping up on a table in a Moody Street barroom to declaim Byron or walking the rough streets of

Pawtucketville loudly singing "Begin the Beguine," the long black coat he'd draped over his shoulders sailing out behind him like a cape. With his "flashing dark eyes" framed by the black hair waving above his forehead, he looked to Jack like the epitome of a young romantic poet, as well as a little like the movie star Victor Mature. Soon Jack began affectionately calling Sebastian "the Prince of Crete."

Sebastian came from a very large Greek family who lived in a rambling old house across the river that Jack later gave to the Martin family in his first novel. Like Jack's mother, Sebastian's father worked in a shoe factory, but he had been able to send his oldest son, Charles, to college, and now Sebastian, following in his brother's footsteps, was about to enter Emerson College in Boston in the fall. Jack, who would marry Sebastian's gentle, self-sacrificing older sister, Stella, in 1967, two years before his death, envied Sebastian for having all those siblings and was fascinated by the histrionic atmosphere of the crowded Sampas household, where he was likely to walk in on erupting quarrels and tears and passionate reconciliations. Stella tried to take care of everyone and make peace. She was a woman who devoted her entire life to her family and was still a virgin when she became Jack's wife.

It couldn't have been easy to be Sebastian in Lowell. He had been marked as a target for bullies since Greek parochial school, where he'd disgraced himself as early as first grade by weeping when a teacher corrected his recitation of the Greek alphabet. But his classmate Charles Jarvis later remembered how once Sebastian had fiercely thrown himself into a fight to defend a smaller boy, and how in third grade, at the funeral of a little girl, Sebastian had bent over her coffin, passionately sobbing "You will go to heaven! You will go to heaven. But why did you leave us now? Why?," kissing the dead girl's forehead before being led away by the teacher. At Bartlett Junior High, Sebastian had fallen hopelessly in love with an Irish girl who kept rejecting him because he was Greek and who had found it troubling that Sebastian wouldn't give up—that was a memory that still hurt him very much. He would be similarly tenacious in his love for Jack.

It was painful to Sebastian that people stared at him and thought him weird, yet he was whole in his strangeness, not split the way Jack was. If Sebastian's strangeness was out there for all to see, Jack's had so far been largely hidden. His Lowell friends were so used to his silences, they didn't think too much about them, and he would always come out of his shell to throw himself into their wild escapades. Though there were some who interpreted Jack's silences to mean that he was arrogant and conceited, he had been regarded generally as an exemplary youth ever since the 1939 Thanksgiving football game.

But Sebastian instinctively had a deeper understanding of Jack. He came looking for him soon after Jack came home from New York, calling his name one night from the street. Although they hadn't spent any time together since the flood of 1936, when the Sampas family had to move out of their ruined house into one in a different neighborhood, Sebastian had never forgotten him and had looked up G.J. to get his address. He told Jack he had been watching him. He knew all about his determination to become a writer and had been longing for the chance to talk to him again.

Sammy Sampas was as full of big dreams as Jack was. "I want to write plays, produce, direct and act them," he says in *Vanity of Duluoz*. "I want to wear a white Russian tunic with a blood red heart sewn on the part over my heart." You can hear all his eagerness, naïveté, and vulnerability in those lines. He wanted Jack to write plays too, wanted him to read Thomas Wolfe now that he'd read Saroyan, wanted him to be part of a club he'd started for which he'd managed to round up a few other Lowell youths who seemed like kindred spirits. The club had a lofty name—The Young Prometheans (suggesting the influence of Goethe). There were a couple of other Greeks in it and a couple of Irish guys too, despite the historic antagonism in the town between those two ethnic groups. Perhaps because of his own sufferings as a kid who didn't fit in, Sebastian's goal in life was to bring about what Saroyan had called "the brotherhood of man." Saroyan didn't believe in the separations caused by governments or races and thought all men should have a common language. He claimed he had no fear of being laughed at by sophisticated cynics. Neither did Sebastian, who would talk about this idea of brotherhood to anyone who would listen.

G.J. and the rest of the Pawtucketville gang couldn't figure out what on earth Jack saw in Sebastian, though they sensed he was good-hearted— "that crazy bastart," they call him in *The Town and the City*. Jack's father meanly referred to him as "Greta Garbo." None of that made any difference to Jack, although sometimes he was embarrassed by Sebastian's public outpourings of feeling and his theatrical behavior. Sebastian was his first real soul mate—"a comrade, a confidante in the first glories of poetry and truth," he would write in his first novel. By the time he wrote *Visions of Gerard*, Jack would not only explicitly link Sebastian Sampas with his brother but also with Buddha and Jesus Christ: "Without Gerard what would have happened to Ti Jean? . . . It was only many years later when I met and understood Savas Savakis [Jack's fictional name for Sebastian] that I recalled the infinite and immortal idealism which had been imparted to me by my holy brother." He implied that if it hadn't been for Sebastian, the spiritual guide he'd been destined to find, he might have lost his faith and forgotten Gerard's "one bright truth: All is Well, practice Kindness, Heaven is Nigh."

It was a summer when heaven seemed immensely distant, when the Olympics had to be called off for the first time in history. In May, the Nazis had invaded Denmark, Norway, France, Belgium, Luxembourg, and the Netherlands; on June 14, Hitler's army entered Paris. By the third week in August, bombs were falling on London. But for Jack, it turned out to be an almost perfect time—a prewar American pastoral he would look back upon with nostalgia.

He had a small job that he found dreary, trying to sell subscriptions to the *Lowell Sun* to households that obviously couldn't afford to take the paper. But the rest of his time belonged luxuriously to him—there would be no classes, no football practice, until the fall. Reunited with his Pawtucketville gang, he would have a summer of "bareass" swimming at Pine Brook at dawn when the water was coolest and baseball games on the Dracut Tigers' field. There would also be rowdy beer fests now that he and G.J. and Scottie and the others were old enough to drink in bars. Leo had given Jack his first beers when he was sixteen, but it wasn't until his eighteenth summer that he discovered the heightening effect of a large quantity of alcohol, how having too many beers could make his mind open up to what seemed like revelatory truths and make him a full participant in the mad action at hand, even if he had to puke up everything he'd downed afterward. The first time Jack and his friends discovered the new sensation of getting intoxicated, "we were all so exhilarated we kept grabbing everybody in the street and telling them they were God." (G.J. was the one who had actually started this, finding God in a drunk he met in the lavatory of a Moody Street barroom.) During one night of drinking, they all piled into a car and went to find "Filthy Mary," a girl who worked in the Royal Theater, where Ronald Salvas was an usher, and who had sex with them one by one backstage after the show. On another occasion, "Filthy Mary" was willing to take on two carloads of boys. This time, however, Jack, G.J., and Scottie felt squeamish and decided not to wait for their turns.

Jack split himself between his riotous old friends and his intense separate relationship with Sebastian Sampas. He wrote an antiwar radio script because Sammy asked him to. "The Spirit of '14" was performed in a Pawtucketville park that June before Sammy went off to Boston to study drama at Emerson. The radio play expressed Jack's conviction that war— even against the Nazis, who were no more than "the dregs of imperfect humanity"—wasn't worth the sacrifice of the lives of young men. Sammy played a legionnnaire from World War I who commits suicide in a bar in front of some untried youths after showing them the stump where his left hand used to be. "I am war!" Sebastian roared. "I was born in the good old U.S.A. like a lot of you, but I was molded into a graceful sculptor's dream in 1914, so that I could satiate the wild creative desires of society's foppish misfits." Jack played a boy who hated the thought of throwing away his life on a battlefield after working so hard to go to college. The other five members of the newly created Variety Players Group included G.J.; Billy Chandler, who in high school had been the president of the Drama Club; and John Kouzmantelis, Sebastian's close friend, who had been on the Lowell High track team with Jack. One reads the cast list of "The Spirit of '44" with an eerie feeling. Sebastian, Billy, and John, along with some other Lowell boys Jack had grown up with, would all lose their lives in the oncoming war.

In "We Thronged," one of the Saroyan-influenced stories Jack wrote that summer, he evoked his feeling of deep communion with Sammy and Billy on a night the three of them stayed up talking about "eternity and infinity and the government and Reds and women and things and even plays." Unwilling to break the spell by going to sleep, they set out for Pine Brook at 3:30 A.M. Jack ran up a hill and "waited for the sun," feeling like "king of the world." Sammy sang "The Road to Mandalay" at the top of his lungs with the other two boys joining in just before the sun "painted things red." But since Jack had never seen Mandalay, nothing seemed more meaningful to him that dawn than the "solidity" of New England and how they had rapturously "thronged, the three of us, through the gorgeous woods to see the sunrise." The story ended, however, on a foreboding and ambiguous note, with Jack seeing two old women on their way to early morning Mass and suddenly thinking, "Fear." (He would weave a version of this story into *The Town and the City*.)

Before he left for Columbia at the end of the summer, Jack wrote nearly a dozen of these stories, sitting at his father's L. C. Smith typewriter, smoking cigarette after cigarette, enjoying the raspy throat they gave him. *The Daring Young Man on the Flying Trapeze* lay close at hand in case he needed inspiration. Under Saroyan's influence, he began to pour his emotions into what he wrote, abandoning the restraint of his Hemingwayesque style. One night he swatted a wasp that flew against his lamp—the following day he wrote about feeling like a murderer after finding the corpse (a theme he would return to in *Big Sur* twenty-two years later). He wrote about the cigarettes he smoked and his distaste for his job as a subscription salesman; he wrote about Nothing, on a night he could think of nothing to write about: "I try to think hard and imagine myself nothing, but I am too much alive to think myself nothing, so that despite the fact that I know its inevitability, I feel as if I'll always go on." Jack discovered that his past was also a subject worth exploring, now that he had lived long enough to have accumulated one. He went back to the rose-covered cottage on West Street, and stood outside recalling the dreams and nightmares he'd had there. Then he made himself walk over to the house on Beaulieu where Gerard had died: "I remembered the high snow, my sandwich, calling for my mother, weeping, all." It upset him to see a man walk into his old house, "brushing aside the past of tomorrow," but then he reminded himself to "hold the present now because someday it will be very precious."

COLUMBIA

In 1941, when no one, except perhaps Sebastian, could understand why Jack had thrown away his Columbia scholarship, he defiantly made sense of the change that had come over him in one of the Whitmanesque poems he had been writing:

> At 18, I suddenly discovered the
> delight of rebellion—and was,
> drunk with it 1½ years, not
> knowing how to wield this mad
> thing, being more or less wielded
> by it. Saroyan sparked it—
> indolent, arrogant Saroyan . . .

Since the age of fourteen, Jack had driven himself very hard, living up to his parents' expectations, working steadily toward his future. But the summer of 1940, when he was discovering the way he wanted to write, had not lasted nearly long enough for him. His rebellion began almost as soon as he arrived at Columbia and found himself confronting an exhausting schedule that included four grueling hours of daily football practice and a full load of courses, plus the nighttime dishwashing job on campus that paid for his meals. Suddenly all Jack wanted was the freedom he was being asked to surrender in return for his education.

His disaffected mood made his efforts on the football field seem pointless, particularly since Lou Little treated him exactly the way his high school football coach had, keeping him out of the first Columbia game of the season, against Rutgers, until the second half. (For the rest of his life, Jack would blame Little for robbing him of his chance to make an immediate, spectacular, Bill Clancy–like success of himself.) The *Columbia Spectator* did say he was "probably the best back on the field," but the word *probably* must have stung him. He wanted to be a hero "or nothing," as he put it in *The Town and the City*—a dangerous feeling that also applied to his real aim in life—writing.

The week after the Rutgers game, Lou Little, who had finally noticed his running, began showing some interest in him. But by now Jack could see that his studies would be going down the drain, since he could not find the time to read the great classics his Columbia professors assigned him. He fell asleep in his chair one night with *The Iliad* dropping out of his hands.

Lou Little put him into the first half of the second freshman game of the season. As he looked over his taller and heavier opponents from St. Benedict's prep school, Jack decided to show them how fast a "French boy" could run. His forward charge drew whoops from the spectators. Knocked down, he picked himself up and threw himself back into the game, leaping up to catch the ball with two St. Benedict's players grabbing at his ankles. Twisting himself free, Jack heard his right leg break with a loud crack. Although he had to be helped off the field, the coaches told him he merely had a sprain. For the next week, they kept him limping through practice until an X-ray proved that he had cracked his tibia.

The leap that had granted him his secret wish, liberating him from football, ironically made Jack the campus hero he'd longed to be. Several fraternities immediately rushed him. Each night, with his crutches beside him, he sat surrounded by admirers in the Lion's Den, the pub in the basement of Butler Hall where he had formerly washed dishes, as he wolfed down big helpings of steak and hot fudge sundaes. Only the constant stream of anxious letters from Gabe made him feel guilty about enjoying himself. She and Leo were worried sick that he would lose his scholarship.

Mon pitou, mon chéri, my honey boy, my darling honeylamb, she called him, always coming up with some new endearment, binding him to her with infinite threads of treacle. Gabe didn't hesitate to keep reminding her boy how lonely she was without him, or what an unspoken sacrifice it would be to send him the money she'd just offered him when she had so little herself. By making Jack her confidant regarding Leo, she involved him in a subtle and guilt-producing betrayal of his father. Leo was becoming "unmanageable." Leo had just lost another job in Connecticut because he couldn't stop himself from telling people what he thought of them. In her husband's personal vendetta against the unjust world, he evidently couldn't take the advice he'd given his son in the one letter he wrote him after his accident—to view his setbacks as a way of keeping himself humble.

Now that some of the necessary, seemingly idle time he'd craved had been restored to Jack—time to smoke a pipe in his room, to read and dream, to listen to Beethoven and Sibelius—he went back to the journal he'd begun in September, which he'd called "The Journal of an Egotist." Weren't artists of a "rare breed," like Saroyan (and himself), fully entitled to be egotists? he'd asked himself during his first week at Columbia. While he knew his prose wasn't as good as Dickens's, weren't all written words sacred? Six weeks later, however, Jack saw himself in a more critical way—as someone who, despite the tender care he'd received from his parents, had grown into an unfeeling aesthete, with no value in the world except for his writing. Nonetheless, his new spirit of rebellion prevailed. He vowed to defer "maturity" until his twenties, absorb as much experience as he could, and live like an "eccentric artist." He had just taken Sebastian's recommendation and read Thomas Wolfe's *Look Homeward, Angel.*

Today Thomas Wolfe has largely fallen out of fashion, but to read him in the 1940s was a rite of passage for the sensitive young person, who found in the story of Eugene Gant all the loneliness, rage, and yearning of American adolescence. To open *Look Homeward, Angel* was to plunge into an overwhelming word storm, lit by flashes of lyric lightning and pierced by lamentation: "O lost, and by the wind grieved, ghost, come back again." The magic was something beyond sense, a powerful mood communicated by the pure sound and hypnotic rhythms of Wolfe's voice. Swept along by the oceanic prose, an enraptured reader would hardly notice the repetitiousness and verbal excesses that irritated some of Wolfe's critics and even his admirers.

Two years before Jack discovered him, Wolfe had died of tuberculosis of the brain at thirty-eight, leaving a legend behind him and the romantic image of a towering, solitary figure striding across the Brooklyn Bridge in a black overcoat like the one adopted by Sebastian Sampas. Wolfe had been so tall he preferred to stand up when he wrote, and his daily output had been as outsized as he was. Jubilant the day he broke his record, he'd charged into the street with his coat flapping open, shouting, "Ten thousand words! Ten thousand words!" In contrast to modernist writers like Hemingway and Fitzgerald with their spare imagistic prose, Wolfe was so much a "putter-inner" that he never knew where to stop. Between *Look Homeward, Angel,* which immediately made him famous, and his second autobiographical novel, *The Web and the Rock,* he sequestered himself for four years in a basement apartment in Brooklyn Heights lost in intersecting webs of memories—one begetting another and another—covering the floor with thousands of pages of handwritten drafts in his Herculean attempt to "crystallize for myself . . . the whole material picture of the world around me." Though Jack would use his memory in a more selective way, Wolfe's prodigious powers of recall apparently functioned much the way Jack's did, characterized, as Wolfe described it, "in a more than ordinary degree by the intensity of its sense impressions." Summoning up an iron railing he'd once seen in Atlantic City, for example, Wolfe could "see it instantly just the way it was, the heavy iron pipe; its raw, galvanized look; the way the joints were fitted together."

Wolfe's four huge novels were, according to Maxwell Perkins, the editor at Scribner's who had discovered him, "almost literally autobiographical," but Wolfe thought of them another way, "as a life completely digested in my spirit." "Fiction is not fact," he warned the readers of his first book, "but fiction is fact selected and understood, fiction is fact arranged and charged with purpose." This would also eventually define Jack's conception of fiction.

As soon as he started reading Wolfe, Jack was certain he'd actually *seen* him with his own eyes on his own first walk across the Brooklyn Bridge in 1937. Whether or not this was the case, Wolfe would become an almost palpable presence in Jack's imagination, casting his tall, disheveled shadow over the long walks he took from one end of New York to the other and over the pages he wrote himself. He would look to Wolfe when measuring his own achievement and defend him fiercely from detractors with more modernist tastes—at the same time defending his own aesthetic.

Through Wolfe, Jack absorbed the influence of Shakespeare, for Wolfe had brought an Elizabethan richness into his language; his word-drunk lyricism also had echoes of Whitman, Melville, and Joyce. But what Wolfe opened up to Jack most of all was a way of transcending his outsider status through a passionate identification with Wolfe's majestic Whitmanesque vision of America—the feeling of the grand immensity and diversity that lay beyond the ethnic ghettoes of Lowell, Massachusetts, or the encircling mountains that isolated Wolfe's Asheville, North Carolina.

They had both grown up as brilliant, introverted boys ready to burst out of their stultifying small towns and conquer the world with their extraordinary gifts. Both had powerful alcoholic fathers, possessive infantilizing mothers, beloved lost brothers, town-and-city conflicts. But the similarities of their psyches were no less striking. Neither was ever able to find a balance between work and life and both had what Jack called "dual" natures. Both were subject to sudden mood changes and drank to excess. Both were somewhat paranoid about the motives of other people, yet also naïvely trusting. Both were attracted to women, but preferred to spend their time with men. When it came to writing, Wolfe "put in more long, sober, grueling hours than anyone on earth," according to his friend and biographer Elizabeth Nowell, but Jack's dedication to work was equally remarkable.

I believe that it was partially because of such affinities that Jack's response to Wolfe was so immediate and so deep. Encountering him in *Look Homeward, Angel* in the fictional persona of Eugene Gant, Jack discovered an alter ego—a ghostly older brother in literature whom he sought to "imitate."

On November 27, 1940, Jack consciously tried to write himself out of one of his familiar dark moods that seemed to come and go like weather. For the first time, he dealt with his emotions directly in his journal, rather than writing about himself in a more abstract, self-consciously elevated way. (He seemed to have already learned a good deal from Wolfe's renderings of Eugene Gant's inner turmoil.) He was recalling the visit he'd just had from G.J. and Scottie and wondering about his failure to enjoy it after looking forward to it for weeks. Perhaps it was a dismal barroom conversation that had brought him down—Scottie had been talking excitedly about the three of them getting New York jobs and having mistresses and going out to drink together all the time. The catch was that everything depended upon their making a good living. Scottie thought there was a future for himself in air-conditioning; G.J. was hoping to become a lawyer. Listening, Jack had felt strangely separated from his old friends, gloomily thinking to himself that it made no difference whether you died in a filthy gutter in Singapore or in a posh Park Avenue apartment.

He was beginning to rely on alcohol to deal with his moods. One of them was brought on by a date with a sixteen-year-old Barnard girl named Norma Blickfelt, a "Russian" beauty who played him classical music on the piano and was one of the first girls he'd met whom he could talk to about his intellectual interests. He would later describe Norma as having a man's mind in a woman's body—the highest praise he could give a girl but something he apparently found daunting. Jack believed himself in love with her. The tragedy was that she was too young and pure for an "older man" of eighteen. After he kissed Norma good night on December 12, Jack felt torn by love, rage, and the desire to forget this tormenting relationship altogether.

The only thing to do was to head for the West End, one of the few off-campus gathering places in the neighborhood, apart from a couple of dreary cafeterias and some lunch counters. Just down the street from a small gray church with a large illuminated sign that read THE WAGES OF SIN IS DEATH, it was a cavernous den of collegiate iniquity, permeated by odors of boiled cabbage, knockwurst, and nicotine, with a horseshoe-shaped bar where you could hardly avoid running into Columbia people you knew, from frat boys to young intellectuals, plus a hard-core group of neighborhood characters, lowlifes, and alcoholics. Six beers, ordered three at a time, put Jack into a state of ecstatic longing for symphonic music and all that life had to offer, followed by tears and the wish to be home with his mother. Afterward, as he wrote up his feelings about Norma in his dorm room, he had no idea why he'd gotten so drunk. He wondered, Was it partially because he'd wanted to write about his misery in his journal? The following morning he felt dead inside and completely disgusted with himself—a feeling he would come to know well in the future.

Now that *Look Homeward, Angel* had made Jack wonder what experiences he was missing by being in college, he hardly cared about his classes and often didn't bother to do the assignments if he preferred to be reading Wolfe or *For Whom the Bell Tolls*. (Eugene Gant had also found much of what he had to learn in college quite meaningless, though he'd kept up with his studies.) What was the point of reading about Charles II and the rise of Parliament, Jack asked himself as his first semester drew to a close, when there was fascism in the world and, most important of all, the battle going on in his stormy psyche? What could be more futile than studying chemistry, the class he hated and cut the most?

He went home for Christmas and got drunk under the Christmas tree with G.J. At a dance he ran into Mary Carney and was smitten with her again. When he returned to Columbia he seemed to stabilize, though Nin, on a visit to him in New York, noticed how much her little brother was drinking. When she mentioned this to their parents, evidently thinking it was pretty funny, Leo hit the roof.

Weeks of letters had preceded Nin's visit. Now that she was a young divorcée, Nin was rather pathetically determined to live it up and and was all in a flutter about being introduced to Jack's teammates. When they were growing up together, they had fought constantly. She'd had the burden of being the responsible older sister, walking her little brother to school, escorting him to the movies and the library, enduring his retaliations for bossing him around. But suddenly all Nin's seniority seemed to be erased. Apologizing to Jack for having turned into a "scatterbrain," she wrote to him when she returned to Lowell with a certain awed deference, anxious to know how she'd gone over with his Columbia friends—boys who were younger than she was. Perhaps Jack had been anxious about that himself during his sister's visit and had tried to drink his way past his own feelings of embarrassment. (Ten years later, Nin appeared in one of Jack's dreams, trying to impress Dinah Shore at a party where Jack feels ill at ease himself. As Jack listens "bleakly," his sister talks to Dinah in "a kind of halting Canuck-English speech," making "painful" attempts at " 'social smartness.' ")

Jack had joined the Phi Gamma Delta fraternity, which was hardly in keeping with his new self-image as an eccentric artist, but he did refuse to wear their blue beanie. After making his case, he impressed his frat brothers with how much he could drink by picking up a beer barrel and downing its dregs. What he really liked best about the frat house was its large collection of jazz records. Even Glenn Miller could still bring tears to his eyes. In fact, his closest New York friend remained Seymour Wyse, who was attending NYU and with whom Jack continued to go and listen to the pioneers of bebop up in Harlem. Although Jack was considered very popular at Columbia and at the end of that year was voted vice president of the sophomore class, most of his Columbia relationships were superficial. But he did begin to form a lasting bond with a freshman from Poughkeepsie named Jack Fitzgerald, who was as passionate about jazz and writing as he was.

Ellis Amburn makes much of an incident that spring in which, according to him, Jack went down to Greenwich Village with some members of the football team and joined them in a "brutal assault" upon a gay violinist, an act he felt guilty about for the rest of his life. But Jack had a horror of brutality—even the violence of football games seemed wrong to him—and would usually do anything to avoid a fight. He alluded to the gay-bashing incident in *The Subterraneans*, but described his part in it in a markedly different way: One member of the team "pushed a violinist a queer into a doorway and I pushed another one in, he slugged his, I glared at mine." This suggests that Jack was merely pretending to go along with the reprehensible action and didn't have his heart in it, though participating in it at all, let alone not trying to stop it, was indeed something to be ashamed about. The episode does demonstrate, in a disturbing way, how dangerous Jack's permeability could be—as if the split between the two sides of his personality, the tough small-town boy and the sensitive artist, left him with no firm center.

That spring, in a short piece called "God," Jack explored his complicated feelings about homosexuality. He described sitting on a bench on Riverside Drive and being cruised by a man with "flirtatious eyes" who kept walking back and forth in front of him: "Greedy eyes, shining in the night. Hopeful eyes. A degenerated sag in his clothing." Something held Jack there, however, listening to the rhythmic creak of the man's shoes, wondering how often he would dare to return: "I felt repugnant toward him. But then I knew that it was a sickness, deserving of pity. He cannot help it, I thought. And neither can I." Jack asked himself whether he and the man could be seeing things the same way—"this hazy heaven, the river, the lights"—then, looking at the scene around them, he decided, no. Out of pity, however, he left the remainder of his cigar for the stranger when he finally got up and left the park.

In early June, Jack hitchhiked back to Lowell with his Columbia problems seemingly resolved. He had cut a great many of his classes but had buckled down to his studies well enough to get good marks in nearly everything. Fully recovered from his injury, he had gone back to football practice and felt that Lou Little was again looking upon him with favor. The only cloud hovering over what promised to be another golden summer was the fact that he had failed chemistry and had to prepare himself to pass a makeup exam if he wanted to hold on to his scholarship.

Jack took out his chemistry books now and then, but he could never pass up an opportunity to go swimming at Pine Brook or drink beer with his friends. And the rapid progress he was making with his writing made chemistry seem so insignificant that he soon stopped bothering with it at all. He had come home with two new plays, had completed a pile of new stories (including some ghostwritten for other students), and was planning to start a novel. When he was at Horace Mann, he'd thought of himself as a journalist; now he was calling himself a poet—a prose poet, however, not a versifying one. Like Walt Whitman, he would "erect structures of thought for mankind," dedicate himself to "an eternal search for truth," try to be "timeless in a society built on time."

His latest literary influence was Albert Halper, a now-forgotten author of naturalistic novels about working-class life. In a piece about his own first years as a writer, Halper had used the expression "I've got a locomotive in my chest," which Jack seized upon as a perfect summation of his own state of mind. Like Halper he had "a million hungers and not one of them appeasable"; like Halper he was "lonely among multitudes, and does not know why." These affinities, however, made Jack worry a little about not being as much of an original as he had previously thought.

It may have been Sebastian, however, who had discovered Halper first. Bursting with excitement, intellectual curiosity, despair, and yearning, he had been feeling that unstoppable locomotive in his own chest when he'd written to Jack at the end of January. During his months at Columbia, Jack had often found himself missing Sammy. One weekend in March, he'd hitchhiked to Lowell just to show him a play he'd written, in which he'd depicted his friend in the midst of one of his poetic ecstasies running through Pine Woods as naked as a "wood nymph" as he shouted out Poe's "Bells." Apparently, Sammy made no objection to this characterization. He had become the trusted and necessary first reader to whom Jack showed his work, whose confirming reaction somehow made a piece feel finished. In the future Jack would be lucky enough to find others who could play this important role—notably Allen Ginsberg and John Clellon Holmes.

Sebastian had felt very hurt when G.J. and Scottie had visited Jack in October and April, deliberately leaving him out. The deep rapport between the two youths was at times charged with erotic feelings neither of them wanted to acknowledge. Once when Jack was drunk, Sebastian had shaken his hand and felt a strange kind of thrill. Jack had called that sensation "homoistic," but Sebastian was convinced it had been religious—the ecstasy of profound universal brotherhood. He made no apologies for not behaving in the exaggeratedly macho manner other friends of Jack's considered proof of masculinity, and didn't see the point of the swear words Jack used when he was with G.J. and Scottie. Jack didn't always appreciate having Sammy try to be his conscience, but then they'd have one of their deep, soulful exchanges that would restore him to a feeling of "substance."

According to Cornelius Murphy, Jim O'Dea, and George Constantides, three of Sebastian's Young Prometheans who were interviewed by Barry Gifford and Lawrence Lee in the late seventies, Sebastian morally disapproved of Jack's relationship with Peggy Coffey, whom Jack was seeing again that summer. In *Vanity of Duluoz*, Jack portrays them wholesomely sitting under an apple tree on Friday nights as they sing "every show tune in the book," bonded by their mutual love for popular music. But there is also the memory of a more sirenlike Peggy boldly showing up in "broad daylight" poured into a "fire engine red dress and high heels, whee." Peggy was still determined to be Jack's girl and had been trying to hang on to him by playing it cool, reminding him whenever he seemed restless that what she really wanted was to become a famous singer. All Jack's friends knew that by this time she was going to bed with him. To be having sex with an admired popular girl who wasn't a known slut—that was a huge deal in Lowell. Even the high-minded Young Prometheans took a rather prurient interest in the affair, phoning Jack every few minutes on one occasion when Sebastian told them Peggy was over at Jack's house. Unlike them, however, Sammy reportedly felt anguished because Jack had no intention of chivalrously making an honest woman of her.

In *The Town and the City*, Peggy Coffey makes her appearance as the youngest Martin sister, Liz, who runs off with an aspiring jazz musician. She's painted as a passionately tenacious, tough-talking girl. "Listen you, why didn't you come tonight?" she says to her lover, whom she calls "big and foolish." Without much encouragement from him, she keeps projecting a future in which they'll surely end up married once he comes to his senses. "It was her first furious smothering love," Jack wrote.

Sebastian too sought an exclusive kind of relationship with Jack, even though he had sworn that he had no intention of displacing G.J. as Jack's closest male friend. Nonetheless, he was obsessed with the whole issue. Extending his own sphere of influence, Sebastian organized a kind of writers' group largely for Jack's benefit. One night a week, Jack, Sebastian, and four or five other serious young men, including John MacDonald, crowded into a booth at the Eight Ball Café (a bookie joint by day); there they wrote stories on the spot to read aloud to one another and discussed books like *U.S.A.* by John Dos Passos and James Joyce's *A Portrait of the Artist as a Young Man*. But Jack and Sammy had their best times together when they went off alone to wander around Boston, looking at the architecture, trying to meet girls, hanging out on Boston Common, where Jack would listen to Sebastian give soapbox speeches on brotherhood and his romantic conception of Leninism. (Under Sammy's influence, Jack began thinking of himself as a Communist.)

That summer, Jack tried to incorporate Sammy into his Pawtucketville gang. It was as if he felt the need to somehow bring the two sides of himself, poet and hoodlum (or "whoremaster," as he sometimes put it), together. But unity wasn't possible. Sammy disliked Scottie, and although he tried to convince himself that G.J. was, at heart, a fellow poet, he was unable to appreciate what Jack admired most about him—his "Rabelaisian" humor. When the boys got riotously drunk and went out trolling for sex, sharing the bodies of Filthy Mary or the girl they all coarsely referred to as "Layo," Sebastian had no desire to participate. In fact, he was profoundly troubled by the way Jack changed before his eyes when he was with his gang and by his new need to drink himself into oblivion.

On a trip they all took to Vermont, they drank whiskey around a swimming hole at a granite quarry. Totally drunk, Jack dived down to the bottom of the deep water; when he didn't surface, Sebastian dived in after him. "I popped up laughing," Jack recalled in *Vanity of Duluoz*. "He cried on the bank." That day Jack drank to the point where the Green Mountains swayed back and forth before his eyes. Sick on the drive back, he passed out on Sammy's lap, as Sammy wept for him.

Long after he'd left Lowell, Jack would still seek out his "roaring gangs"—putting them together from the flotsam and jetsam he met in bars if he wasn't out with friends. He would drink to the point where "everything exploded," as he put it once in a letter to me, and where he took no responsibility for anything that happened, simply giving himself over to the furious action—wherever it led him.

By the end of July, one of Jack's closest boyhood friends was thousands of miles away from Lowell on an army base in Manila. When he'd stopped over to say good-bye to Jack, Billy Chandler was in uniform. Billy had always wanted to see the tropics. Once when they'd been drawing cartoons together not long after they'd met in junior high, Billy had daydreamed aloud that if the two of them actually were cartoonists, they would be in the jungles of Guatemala together at that very moment.

Shaken by Billy's departure, Jack immediately felt nostalgic. In a piece he wrote in August to which he gave the title "Farewell Song, Sweet from My Trees," he recalled how "the sun shone on Bill's sandy hair one afternoon on the sandbank in the long-ago Summer gold" and how the two of them used to sit in the living room "turning out strip after strip of adventure serials, while my mother cooked some caramel pudding for us and while my father sat in the parlor listening to the negro singers with tears in his eyes." In his intense desire to hold on to his past, born out of all the leave-takings he had experienced since his early childhood, he was beginning to find an elegiac lyricism that was all his own.

Still hungrily absorbing the lessons of Thomas Wolfe, Jack was reading *You Can't Go Home Again* that summer. He must have been struck by this passage about the writings of its protagonist, George Webber: "In his effort to explore his experience, to extract the whole, essential truth of it . . . he sought to recapture every particle of the life he knew down to its minutest details. He spent weeks and months trying to put down on paper the exactitudes of countless fragments—what he called "the dry, caked colors of America." As Jack's own writing matured, "the exactitudes of countless fragments" would come to preoccupy him more and more.

Meanwhile, however, what he was clearly most infatuated with was Wolfe's rhapsodic prose, often addressed to the reader in long soliloquies with driving rhythmic sections in which image would be piled upon image in crescendoing catalog-like lists. Jack quickly adopted this construction and learned to use it with remarkable facility. In one 1941 piece where he declared himself "part of the American temper, the American temperament, the American tempo," he took the longest breath he'd taken in his writing so far, rolling out a two-hundred-word-long sentence about his love for America and jazz with a blaring extended crescendo about jitterbugs "who let their hair grow long and sleek, with a knockout dazzling wave; their wide-brimmed, low-crowned hats (3¼ inches); their pegged trousers with high belts, their swaggering walk, the way they smoke, the way they let you know about it, the way they click their shoe heels, the way they look around with a broad sweep and take in everything . . ." Although Wolfe had suggested the form of the sentence, the voice and the images are recognizably Kerouacian.

There is little in Jack's summer 1941 journals that suggests how much he was able to achieve in the Saroyanesque pieces he wrote around the same time. The journal voice tends to be excruciatingly self-conscious and inauthentic, tremendously concerned with its own importance. It's as if the uncertain part of the young writer still drawn to the false-literary is sequestered there. Apart from a reference to a hard wooden floor that kept Jack from achieving an orgasm during one of his sexual encounters, there is a notable absence of exactitude. Drink and sex are referred to euphemistically as "Bacchus" and "Venus." As Jack contemplates starting a novel, he thinks it will be an easy enough job, though he expects "the development" may give him some trouble. Rereading the journal in his forties, probably as he was about to write *The Vanity of Duluoz*, Kerouac found this pretentious young upstart insufferable. "No!" he scrawled next to every sentence he hated, including a cherished quote from *Of Time and the River* that had to do with "the tragic weft of life." The idea that this egotistical nineteen-year-old kid thought he could pull off a good novel got to him most of all.

———

Thinking about football that summer, Jack acknowledged his loss of interest in it, but expected he'd have a big football career all the same. He had come to view it as a job, better than most. A day spent shoveling gooey dough onto a conveyor belt at the Educator Cookie factory showed him exactly the kind of fate he was escaping by going to college. In an indignant piece called "Birth of a Socialist," he wrote, "And every time that I have fed the machine, I must return to the tub for more, because the machine is hungry and the apron keeps turning, and the factory is on full-time schedule, and we must hurry and produce for America." Jack looked at the recent high school graduates who worked there and thought they "should be reading Tolstoy or Whitman." After an exhausting eight-hour day that began at five A.M., he walked off the assembly line for good covered with cookie dough and went swimming. A ditch-digging job in New Hampshire in July was much more to his liking. He could report to work any time he felt like it and get a good tan in the bargain. Meanwhile, in the midst of his freedom at home, the prospect of resuming his life as a "boorish" Ivy League college boy made Jack feel so restless he hoped there would soon be a declaration of war. War was bound to provide him with the romantic adventure he craved. He had begun to think about joining the merchant marine and going to sea like Jack London.

In August, the last golden summer of Jack's youth ended abruptly. The Kerouacs had been forced to leave Lowell and move to New Haven, Connecticut, where Leo, who had been working only sporadically, had finally landed a steady job in a linotyping plant and found them an apartment.

Jack had been ready for change, but this one was wrenching. He put all his sadness into "Farewell Song, Sweet from My Trees," which turned out to be the strongest story he had written up to that point. "You see," he wrote, "I have to pull up my stakes and roll." In a way, what Jack chose to fictionalize is one of the most poignant things about this piece, for the youth who is narrating it the night before the moving van arrives is sitting on the porch of an old house where he has lived nearly all his life, saying good-bye to the trees that have been the constant companions of his boyhood. For Jack there had never been one tree-shaded house to call home. Home was Lowell and all the friends he had to leave behind. "Why couldn't I just simply turn back Time and begin all over again?" the narrator asks futilely. "Why?"

As their fortunes declined, the Kerouacs had lived in some pretty rundown tenement apartments, but the filthy living quarters Leo had rented for them, sight unseen, in a black neighborhood in New Haven were so far below their lowered standards that Gabrielle refused to spend even one night there. "Is that man crazy?" she asked her son, insisting they all go straight to a hotel. Just the sight of that "hole" had sickened her, Jack reported to Nin, who had decided to keep her job at Sullivan Printers and stay behind in Lowell on her own. Shaken by Leo's lack of judgment and Gabe's despair, Jack must have felt terrified that he would find himself responsible for looking after his parents.

Fortunately, they found a new home quickly through a French Canadian connection of Leo's, who rented them a five-room summer cottage in the seaside community of Sea Bluff. They moved into it on a blustery day. Jack escaped from the tension between Leo and Gabe by plunging immediately into the "mountainous" waves of Long Island Sound. As he enthusiastically wrote his sister shortly before he left for Columbia, he was "billowed high and then low" until he managed to climb into a rowboat anchored in the cove. "Boy, did I get a thrill when it dipped its bow way up at a 45 degree angle." Meanwhile his shell-shocked mother frantically tried to wave him in from the porch. After telling Nin about all the charms of the beach cottage, Jack begged his sister to give up her job and move in there with their parents to make sure that Gabe would not feel abandoned by her children. But Nin may have been harboring a secret longing to get far away from the family. Soon after the war began, she would enlist in the WAACs and be stationed down south.

THE ESCAPE

Jack arrived at Columbia a day late. A couple of Horace Mann friends had driven him from Sea Bluff directly to football practice at Baker Field, where he was received coldly by Lou Little, who saw that Jack was out of shape after a summer of hard drinking and his mother's heavy cooking. A few days later, Little told him he wasn't running so well. He made a remark about the heaviness of Jack's legs and said he thought he was going to make him a lineman. Even though Jack told him his legs were sore, Little kept ordering him to run faster. Kerouac was "tired," the coach would tell Jack's Lowell biographer Charles Jarvis.

Two weeks later Jack learned during Friday afternoon practice that Little did not plan to put him in the starting lineup when the team played Army that Sunday. He went back to the dorm and brooded. Because he'd counted on being able to settle a score with a former member of Lowell's varsity team who was now playing for Army, he felt particularly slighted. The following evening after dinner, he stuffed all his belongings into a suitcase and strode out of his dorm right past Lou Little, who was talking to another coach on the steps. Little stopped Jack to ask where he was going with that suitcase. Jack answered that he was taking his laundry to his stepgrandmother's house and intended to sleep there. After a few more questions, Lou Little ordered him to be back early the next morning for a warm-up before the Army game.

Jack dropped his suitcase off in Brooklyn. He told his relatives he had to go back to the campus, but instead he took the subway to the Greyhound bus terminal and bought a ticket that would take him as far south as he could afford to go. Sped along by the locomotive in his chest, he was in flight toward literature, toward his destiny as a writer.

It had been an "everything exploded," bridge-burning act, and as the bus rolled through Maryland, Jack felt "washed clean." His imagined destination was the "Southland," Thomas Wolfe country, but his ticket took him only as far as Washington, D.C. He killed a day wandering blindly around the capital in the midst of a stifling September heat wave, trying to interest himself in the tourist attractions, barely able to look at the Rembrandts at the National Gallery. By the time he checked into a bedbug-ridden hotel, the thought that his grand escape had been a disastrous mistake overwhelmed him. It was the most awful feeling he'd ever had. In tears he wrote letters to G.J. and Sebastian. He was "afraid to go home, too proud and sick" to see if Lou Little would take him back on the team. After a night of being attacked by bedbugs, he left the hotel and took refuge in a store that sold five-cent books. He walked out with a copy of Emerson's essays, then returned to the bus terminal, where he bought a ticket that would take him north to talk things over with his father.

Years later, when he was the unhappy prisoner of his own myth, Jack presented this episode in *Vanity of Duluoz* as his first joyous "on the road" experience, leaving out the panic he'd felt. He also skirted around the subject of his reception at home, first indicating that Jack Duluoz's father, Emil, received him with rage, but then quickly showing Emil agreeing that Jack's coach had given him a raw deal, depriving him of the chance to show what a great player he was. The novel did not go into what Jack Duluoz's mother said. A few pages on, the immediate crisis has passed and she's "gaily" frying the bacon for her son's breakfast. In his novels, Thomas Wolfe had excoriated his family for their inability to understand or support him; in his own published work, Jack could never bring himself to do so.

The day after his return, the contrite prodigal son found a job as a tire hemmer in a rubber factory. It was worse than working on the assembly line for Educator Cookies, an intolerable reminder of how far he had suddenly come down in the world. Jack quit at noon and didn't bother to collect his wages.

For Leo, this was evidently the last straw. In *Vanity of Duluoz*, Jack's vow to make his father proud someday with his writing only brings an explosion of all Emil Duluoz's accumulated bitterness down upon him. Emile reminds his son that since he's a Canuck he might as well forget that ridiculous notion. "No Duluoz was ever a great writer. . . . There never was such a name in the writing game." (Apart from considering most artists parasites, Leo Kerouac firmly believed that a literary career was ruled out for someone with a Franco-American background; only a real Frenchman like Victor Hugo could produce books that anyone would take seriously.)

Jack hopped a train to Hartford, where his old friend Mike Fournier was working in a service station that had an opening for a grease monkey at $27.50 a week. Jack took it. Then he bolted for New York, where, as he reported to Sebastian, he spent an "amazing" twenty-four hours, feverishly roaming the streets, sleeping in a church, letting a pimp treat him to a meal (for which Jack refused to repay him with sex). As he sat writing to Sammy, he was on a train bound back to Hartford, exhausted but able to see his life as a Wolfean poem. Outside was "the faint suggestion of mysterious and melancholy October." In *Of Time and the River*, which Jack was urging Sammy to read, Wolfe had written: "All things on earth point home in old October: sailors to sea, travelers to walls and fences, hunters to field and hollow and the long voice of the hounds, the lover to the love he has forsaken—all things that live upon this earth return, return: Father, will you not, too, come back again?"

For the moment there was a rift between Jack and his father, and although all things were pointing home, he, Jack, was traveling in the opposite direction. "Everyone goes home in October," he would write in *On the Road*, a novel concerned with homelessness and lost fathers.

Today, despite its glass towers, Hartford is a depressed shell of a city whose streets are deserted after dark, but in 1941, with the country on the verge of war and its aircraft factories humming, it had turned into a boomtown. Jack responded to its stepped-up rhythms with some attempted typewriter jazz of his own: "Step on the gas, toot the horn," he typed on the keys of the Underwood he'd rented as soon as he arrived, "whip through that intersection, you don't give a damn Hartford, you've money, women, drinks, you've got everything." Hartford was jumping at night, with workers off their shifts pouring into the restaurants and taverns on Main Street. It seemed a terrific place to be—until Jack went back to his room with its stained brown wallpaper.

He had rented it for $4.50 a week. His desk was a greasy table, his bed was lumpy, his window overlooked a garbage-filled backyard that stank of urine. When he turned on a light, roaches crawled out of the Underwood. But it was his own place. "I am happy," he wrote one night. He had bought a ream of yellow paper and was filling those sheets with solid blocks of words—typed single-spaced almost to the edge of the page. Maybe he wrote two hundred stories and sketches those eight weeks he was in Hartford, as he claims in *Vanity of Duluoz*; maybe he wrote sixty. They were all going to go into one book Jack was calling *Atop an Underwood*.

He ran out of money fast in October. As he waited to be paid in the middle of the month, he became, literally, the starving young writer Saroyan had written about. It was the first time Jack had ever gone hungry. One night he wrote himself a meal. It began with a "thick mushroom soup," served in a heavy white bowl. Then came a huge sirloin steak: "Through it runs a great bone, protruding at one end like the mighty hock of a beast. I grasp this bone and snarl into the steak, thrusting my mouth into the warm brown side of the meat. . . . O my God, but I eat." After a few days without food, Jack fainted at work. A guy he was friendly with at the service station took him home and had his mother give him a decent meal. Through all this, he never asked his family for help.

In a direct, intimate voice, still more influenced by Saroyan than Wolfe, he wrote about his swim in Long Island Sound: "Man, but I was a Breton that day! Man, but I was powerful. Man, but my mother looked heroic, ancient, great and mighty . . . looking out to sea at her son." He wrote about his grandfather Jean Baptiste Kerouac swinging his lantern in a storm, daring God to strike him down. As if to refute his father's belief that a Canuck lacked the proper language with which to become a writer, he celebrated *joual*: "The language called Canadian French is the strongest in the world when it comes to words of power. . . . It is too bad that one cannot study it in college, for it is one of the languagey languages in the world . . . it is the language of the tongue and not of the pen . . . it is a terrific, a huge language," and he used it deliberately in the story about his grandfather. In a curious poem that he composed, he canceled his father out entirely:

> I am my mother's son. All other identities
> are artificial and recent. Naked, basic, actually,
> I am my mother's son. I emerged from her womb
> and set out into the earth . . .

He was feeling his latent power as he sat up nights at the typewriter in his little room in Hartford, driving his stuff "home, Americanwise," feeling his connection to "Wolfe, Saroyan, Halper, Whitman and Joyce," discovering that he was "a writing machine with a store / of literature that is boundless, enormous, endless / and rich." As for what scholars or critics might think of his efforts: "they're cold, you're warm, you're / redhot, you can write all day."

On November 13, he had to give the rented typewriter back, so he wrote about how that felt too: "Hell they're taking everything away. Even myself." That morning he'd been down to his last four cents and couldn't even buy himself a nickel cup of coffee. He cheered himself up imagining a trip to California. First, of course, he'd want to go south, "where it is warm and where there are weeping willow trees with moss and old houses with ground-level porches" and where, like Eugene Gant, he would sun himself in New Orleans on the banks of the Mississippi. He called the story he was writing "a little legend about myself."

When he had money to buy stamps, he sent stories to *Harper's*, the *Atlantic Monthly*, and *Esquire*. He needed to justify to his parents the path he had taken, and the only way to do it was to sell some of his writing. The stories bounced back to him with rejection slips. On the one attached to "Farewell Song, Sweet from My Trees," which he had continued to revise that fall, there were brief comments from three readers at *Esquire*, one of which said, "Good—tho not for Esky."

Thanksgiving promised to be grim. Instead of eating his mother's lavish cooking, Jack had to stay in Hartford and work a five-hour shift. When he returned to his room, there was a knock on his door and there stood Sebastian, who had shown up to keep him company during the lonely holiday. In some ways, according to the account of it in *Vanity of Duluoz*, it was an awkward reunion. For Sebastian it was apparently full of romantic pathos "like a sad Burgess Meredith movie." It pained him to see Jack in what he considered a fallen condition in a desolate furnished room. In the novel Jack Duluoz cuts off Sabby Savakis's lamentations curtly, telling him that the conditions of his life right now are not important.

Tears were no good to him, tears could undermine his determination. What he badly needed was Sebastian's approval of the brave, seemingly foolhardy step he had taken in the service of art—something he hadn't heard from anyone. The two had blue plate turkey specials in a "sad lunchcart," after which they went to separate movies because they had each seen the one the other wanted to see. They ended their day together in a bar on Main Street, where Jack nearly got into a fight defending Mike Fournier.

A few days afterward, Jack got a postcard from his father. Leo had managed to find a job in Lowell, and the Kerouacs were moving back there. He wanted Jack to help them pack and then go home with them.

The sojourn in Hartford in which Jack had begun to learn "the techniques of suffering in the working world, which includes football and war" and the techniques of solitude was over.

For Jack, the trip back to Lowell at the end of November was blissful. As he sat in an armchair in the rear of the truck filled with his family's much moved belongings, he was overjoyed to see the first white birches of the familiar woodland outside Lowell. But his happiness faded quickly once the Kerouacs settled into the small flat in a Pawtucketville house on Crawford Street that Nin had found for them. With the parlor shut up for the winter to save on heat, their new quarters were very cramped, and for Jack, who had to share a room with his father while Nin slept in another with Gabe, there was no privacy, no escape from Leo's needling reminders that he had to find a job as soon as possible. Worst of all was Jack's feeling that he had returned to Lowell as a has-been and a failure like his father, back from "glittering Manhattan" to "the brick walls of the mills." It was obviously the wrong time to be reading Dostoevsky, but he buried himself in the pages of *Notes from the Underground*, which did nothing to improve the way he felt: "unaccountably" lethargic and "black-souled."

On the night of Sunday, December 7, Jack went downtown to see *Citizen Kane*. As he emerged from the theater filled with the exhilarating notion that he could become "a genius of poetry in film" himself, newsboys in Kearney Square were shouting: "Japs bomb Pearl Harbor." An era had crashed to an end as he watched Orson Welles on the screen. With a paper under his arm, Jack walked home in tears. Perhaps he was thinking about Billy Chandler, who was on a base in Manila. Later he would believe that a premonition about the oncoming catastrophe in the Pacific had been responsible for his days of unaccountable depression. Yet once he sat at his old desk staring at the headlines, he felt a stir of excitement. If some tremendous change in America had occurred, he wanted to take its measure right away. He put on his overcoat and went out bareheaded into the freezing cold, "looking for the War" in the streets of Pawtucketville. At a diner, he listened to some mill workers fresh from their night shifts casually talking about a friend being drafted in the "tormented, severed, twisted French" he had been hearing all his life. As the jukebox played, Jack felt an overwhelming "nostalgia" for all his old dreams, but devoured a hamburger with a hunger that was "exclusively and completely American." His search led him to a second diner, where he wolfed down another hamburger. A whore came in who shrugged fatalistically at the mention of Pearl Harbor: *"Ah ben, quesqu'on peut faire!"* Jack walked home thinking that "the eye of war had changed nothing, not even the people," but then he realized, as he wrote shortly afterward in a piece called "Search by Night," that the American people were taking the war "in their stride," that beneath their "false virility, false coarseness" was a kind of grace and courage in the face of danger and uncertainty.

He applied to the V-12 Navy College Training Program, which offered officer training on college campuses with a combined academic and military program. As he waited to take the examination, Jack felt in limbo, even though he had unexpectedly found a good job at the *Lowell Sun*, where Sammy's brother Charley now worked. On Sammy's suggestion, he had applied there to be a delivery boy but had instead been hired as a sports reporter for fifteen dollars a week because the owner remembered him as the football hero who'd landed a Columbia scholarship. Nothing could have made Leo prouder—several times he even set his son's articles in linotype. After Jack's long training as the sportswriter Jack Lewis, the job was a cinch. He pounded out his reportage with such facility and speed that he was usually finished with his duties by noon. Then, still managing to look busy, he'd sneak the pages of *Vanity of Duluoz*, the novel he was writing, into the typewriter. At nineteen, he was planning to write a Duluoz trilogy, no less, set between 1942 and 1943, ending with the protagonist going off to fight against the fascists and vanishing into what Jack saw as "the immense void" of the wartime period.

The name *Duluoz* was Jack's Frenchification of *Daoulas*, a name he had come across at the *Lowell Sun*. It happened to belong to a large and prominent Greek family, but with its three syllables and its dominant *oo* sound, it rang in Jack's ear like the Breton *Kerouac* and thus became the name for his fictional alter ego. He would use it over and over again throughout his career as a writer. He would have called himself Jack Duluoz in all his books if he had ever been able to realize his dream of conforming all the names in them and publishing them as one long saga of his life.

The novel owed a great deal to Jack's growing admiration for James Joyce and his recent reading of *Ulysses*, which led him to experiment for the first time with portraying the intense inner life of the protagonist he was basing upon himself. Like Jack, Michael Duluoz had just walked out on his college education and returned to his hometown, where he was working as a reporter. Some of Mike's soliloquies lapsed from third person into first person and were awkward attempts at stream-of-consciousness writing. As Joyce had portrayed twenty-four hours in Dublin, Jack intended to portray twenty-four hours in Lowell (which he was calling Galloway). He had no retrospective distance whatever from the episodes in his novel. Watching himself day by day, he wrote the scenes in his book as he lived them—putting in his father's bitter early morning words about "stinkhole" Lowell, a tortured discussion with Sebastian, a night of heavy drinking in a saloon full of noisy Canucks, his two groups of friends—the "Bacchic" ones versus the intellectuals of Sebastian's circle. The town is much grayer and grittier than the Galloway Jack later wrote about nostalgically in *The Town and the City*, though there are effective lyrical moments when he is able to see its beauty. For Mike Duluoz, it's a trap, a dead end—a place to escape from into lonely exile. Taking a walk in the woods, he prays to his dead brother for the spiritual guidance he no longer seeks inside a church. The depiction of Mike—disaffected, arrogant, half callous, half sensitive—is not very sympathetic.

The novel is imbued with Jack's depressed feelings and sexual confusion; there's a grim heaviness about it. The one time Mike Duluoz seems happy is in a bar scene with his "Bacchic" gang. Everyone is yelling, swearing, drinking furiously, with no women around as wet blankets of etiquette and morality to spoil the fun. In Duluoz's scenes with his best friend, Christopher Santos, referred to as "Sappho's belated brother," Jack opened up the subject of the sexual tension that underlay his relationship with Sebastian. Mike is distinctly uncomfortable with Christopher's demonstrative behavior, the embarrassing way he talks at the top of his voice in the street. He worries that people will think the two of them are queer. Christopher calls him a cold-blooded and aggressive Breton; Mike calls Christopher affected and self-dramatizing. When Christopher swears that he will stick with Mike to the end, Mike's response is to guiltily think to himself that he will always disappoint Christopher. There's a telling exchange in which Christopher asks Mike whether he wants truth and beauty and fine ideals or the "pseudo virility" of the philistines Mike drinks with. Mike bluntly answers that he wants both. If there's tenderness in Mike, it's reserved for his parents, whom he portrays as hapless innocents. The real subject of *Vanity of Duluoz* is Mike's struggle to work out what it means to be a man outside the conventional definitions of masculinity. Considering that Jack was writing *Vanity of Duluoz* at a time when few male writers had the courage to raise such an issue, the novel was ahead of its time.

During the first three months of 1942, Jack attempted to lead a disciplined life, centered around his writing, which he did in the newspaper office rather than at home, and a rigorous course of self-education. He seemed out to prove that he didn't need Columbia. With H. G. Wells's *Outline of History* as his guide, he was planning to work his way through the entire history of the planet, starting with the Mesozoic period. Each day he put in two sessions at the Lowell Public Library—one after work in the afternoon and one in the evening—where he read and looked up references in the *Encyclopaedia Britannica* until closing time. When he left, he would usually find Sebastian waiting for him. They spent more time together in those months than they ever would again. Destabilized by the war and perhaps as a gesture of solidarity with Jack, Sebastian had dropped out of Emerson College. He too was in limbo, although he had vague ideas of establishing himself as an actor as quickly as possible before he was drafted.

Having already imagined his departure from Lowell into Joycean exile, Jack felt restless by March. He was bored by his relationship with Peggy Coffey, who had taken him back once again, as well as by the newspaper job that his father thought was the beginning of a career in journalism for him. With no raise in pay and no byline, he was now grinding out most of the articles in the sports section. He lost the approval of the senior sportswriter George McGuane when McGuane discovered that he was using the afternoons to work on his novel. With his fantasy destination again the South, Jack began dreaming about escape.

Since January, he had been getting letters from G.J., who, while he waited to be drafted, had found a job in Washington as a typist for the

Office of Price Administration. With the outbreak of war, young workers had poured into the capital. Jobs were plentiful there and so, evidently, was sex, with twenty-five women to one man, as G.J. wrote Jack. Although drowning in girlfriends and alcohol, G.J. felt he had become a neurotic mess. The only time he felt good, he said, was when something struck him as funny. When Jack sent him some chapters of *Vanity of Duluoz*, G.J. admiringly read them over and over again, but this only added to his gloom. The novel reminded him of the feeling he'd had during his last visit to Lowell that the town had died. He wrote to Jack in March, urging him to join him in D.C.

One early April day, on his way to interview the baseball coach at the Textile Institute, Jack stopped off at home. Instead of going out again, he sat in his room all afternoon, immobilized by depression, staring at the wall; when his boss at the *Lowell Sun* called, he wouldn't go to the phone.

Leo fell into a rage when he came home from work and found that Jack hadn't bothered to go to the interview. The issue of Columbia came up in a bitter quarrel during which father and son rubbed salt into each other's wounds. In Jack's mature version of *Vanity of Duluoz*, which he wrote twenty-five years later, Emil Duluoz can't resist saying Columbia will never take Jack back, even though Jack has recently heard that the coach wants him to rejoin the team. After Jack asks his father if he wants company "rotting away in Lowell," Emil warns his wife that she will starve if she ever has to depend on her son and stomps out. "Don't listen," Mrs. Duluoz tells Jack. "He's jealous that you'll go out and make something of yourself."

Jack resolved the situation by leaving. He resigned from the *Sun* the following day and bought a bus ticket that would take him to Washington, D.C. He got off the bus in New York to hear Frank Sinatra sing to an audience of swooning bobby-soxers at the Paramount. Badly in need of solace, he looked up Norma Blickfelt—she was still on his mind although they hadn't seen each other for a while. Norma hadn't forgotten him either, although by now she was involved with someone else. She and Jack spent an intense and rapturous twelve hours together, singing to each other as they wandered through downtown Manhattan. After a romantic trip on the Staten Island Ferry, they ended up in a penthouse on Third Avenue borrowed from one of Norma's friends. It may have seemed to

Norma as if they were finally launching into a real love affair, and perhaps it also felt that way to Jack. But it didn't keep him in New York. After saying good-bye to her, he resumed his journey to Washington, where he woke G.J. up in the middle of the night. She heard nothing from him until late August.

In July, after his return to Lowell, Jack wrote Norma a love letter which he never mailed. It opened with a highly romanticized account of "the fine time" he'd had after they'd parted. He wanted Norma to think that he had taken a job on a construction crew that was building the Pentagon "simply to remain in the South and make a casual study" and wrote about the time he'd stopped what he was doing to follow a black workman who was "singing the loveliest blues I ever heard." He had also been able to explore the surrounding Virginia countryside after hitching a ride away from his work site. "But finally I was fired because the field boss could never find me."

The truth was that Jack's six weeks in Washington had hardly been a carefree period of "casual study." They had quickly turned into one unbroken binge after he heard from Sebastian that Billy Chandler had been killed during the siege of Bataan. In Lowell, Sebastian was crying his eyes out. What hurt him most, he wrote Jack, was that Billy had never really had a chance to live.

Jack's grief took the form of relentless drinking that even frightened G.J. The two of them spent their nights in barrooms, blindly picking up girls to have sex with. There were no brakes on their behavior; everything was permitted. Billy's death had brought home to them that they too could die young.

For the first time, Jack was drinking hard liquor rather than beer. When he went to his job as an apprentice sheet-metal worker in the mornings, he'd usually crawl into a hiding place on the site to sleep off his hangovers. After being fired, he found a job in a Northwest Washington lunch cart as a cook and soda jerk. There he met a brunette from Georgia who introduced herself by showing him a pack of pornographic cards, after which she invited Jack to live with her as long as he didn't lay black women and agreed to walk her poodle. (One thing that made a lasting impression upon him was how pervasive racial prejudice was in Washington.)

He managed to write home and also to Sebastian. He evidently told his father about his sexual exploits, because Leo wrote back blaming Jack's metamorphosis into a "gigolo" on Roosevelt. (This would never have happened if Lindbergh had been president.) Despite his own hard drinking, Leo exhorted his wayward boy to think and act "clean" and not to forget his mother on Mother's Day because of some girl—in the next breath joking lasciviously that Jack should send one of his cast-off "skoits"—preferably a redhead—to him.

In another letter, Leo was surprisingly supportive, telling Jack to stay away from Lowell and to experience as much as he could. Get everything in, he told the son he now considered "strange," but who, he said, was still as dear to him as he had been when he was little. After this expression of paternal affection, however, he made sure to give Jack his low opinion of that overrated "guttersnipe" Saroyan, who, in Leo's view, came from the wrong part of Europe. True culture resided with the French. Hitler's Germany had unfortunately "lost its momentum."

Without a clear sense of direction or purpose, Jack left Washington after the brunette from Georgia took up with a one-armed cabdriver. As he dreamily began heading toward New Orleans—to "drowse" on a river wharf "humming the blues," as he wrote Norma—he suddenly realized that since he wouldn't be drafted for another year, the responsible thing to do was to get off the bus and go home and try to get Columbia to readmit him.

Back in Lowell, with its fresh reminders of Billy Chandler, Jack sat up late in the flat on Crawford Street attempting to write about the impact of Billy's death. In tears, he addressed Billy's ghost, trying to pull him back from the dead, recalling their old dreams of travel and adventure, the fantasies they'd had of shipping out together and sailing to exotic ports; he ended sentimentally with the ghost saying comforting words to him about the immortality of youth. A second version was much closer to the bone. In it Jack admitted that what he really wanted to say was beyond words and even beyond tears. In fact, despite his sadness, he was dry-eyed as he wrote, listening to the midnight rain, with a sense of being split between the self that was writing about his lost friend and the "real" one he couldn't reach, hovering out in the dark on the other side of the window.

It was a split he had not explored before. Just as he had once been the "knower" of Gerard's death, his writing self, the one that couldn't weep the way Sebastian did, had become the "knower" of Billy's.

For two months Jack marked time—a period he later described as "incomprehensible, misty, guilt-stricken, haunted" as other boyhood friends of his vanished into the armed services. He didn't bother to find another steady job in Lowell, but halfheartedly set the wheels in motion to play football again for Columbia, resisting the urge to follow the example of the friends who had enlisted. With the war on, good players were scarce, and in June he had definite word that Lou Little would take him back in the fall. The only problem was that his scholarship would not be reinstated until he made up his F in chemistry. Meanwhile he had to find a way of raising four hundred dollars for tuition—a daunting sum in 1942. A chance meeting with a merchant seaman named George Murray, who had just earned two thousand dollars on a voyage across the Atlantic carrying weapons to Russia, inspired Jack with the idea of joining the merchant marine himself. Murray made the adventure sound irresistible.

When Leo heard about Jack's latest reckless plan, he wrote to him from Meriden, Connecticut, where he was working that July, admitting that he was feeling heavyhearted. He reminded Jack that he wasn't a flag-waving father who believed in this war, so he would feel no pride whatsoever if Jack got himself killed in it. He'd rather have him alive, despite all their battles. All he could offer in the way of moral support was the message that death was the reward for living—one of the very ideas that had kept Jack out of church since the age of fourteen.

"What a strange call I hear from the sea," Jack wrote in the July 15 letter to Norma that he never mailed. "Perhaps my ancients, Breton fisherman, stir in my blood." It was his belief in "the Brotherhood"—not the desire to kill anyone—he explained, that had made him want to participate in the war. Already he could imagine himself in the "Arctic mists," like a character in a Jack London novel, sharing dangers and hardships with his American and Russian brothers.

Meanwhile, however, Jack's efforts to get assigned to a ship had been futile. Reluctant at first to embark on this adventure alone, Jack had convinced Jim O'Dea, a Young Promethean, to ship out with him. Sebastian, who had his own dreams of being in Russia with Jack, was also determined to join them, even though Jack had apparently neither urged him to do so nor had the heart to discourage him. None of them had any luck with the National Maritime Union, however, and Sebastian, for some reason, couldn't even get his seaman's papers. Jack attributed this to his friend having the wrong look for a seaman—"like a curly-haired goatsherd from Sparta.") Finally giving up on their plan, Jack and Jim O'Dea walked into a Boston recruiting office together and joined the marines, after which Jack spent the night alone drinking in Scollay Square. The next day, on a tip from a seaman he'd met, he went back one more time to the union hall in Arlington. The SS *Dorchester* was about to sail to Greenland with a construction crew and a load of explosives. They were short one scullion, the highest-paid job for ordinary seamen. With absolutely no sense of obligation to the marines, Jack signed on.

He hitchhiked back to Lowell to pack a "seabag," which he stuffed with classical literature in small-print editions, and told Sebastian the news. It was a painful conversation. Sebastian was devastated that Jack was leaving without him and was even more hurt when Jack let him know that he needed and wanted to get away from him as well as from Lowell and everything else that reminded him of the chaos of the past year. Jack seemed to be hoping that the voyage would be a cleansing and transformative experience from which he would emerge renewed like a character in a novel. (It was a hope he would bring to most of the journeys he would take during his lifetime.) In *Vanity of Duluoz*, he tells Sebastian that this time he has to sail by himself and tries to console him by saying he's seen "flowers of death" in the eyes of his crewmates. "Don't you see the flowers of death in *my* eyes?" Sebastian asks him—he has begun to have a premonition that he, like Billy Chandler, will die young.

After another night of drinking in Boston, Jack passed out in a toilet in Scollay Square, where he lay helpless on the floor as sailors urinated and vomited on him. He walked down to the docks at dawn and jumped into the sea to wash himself clean before reporting for duty on the *Dorchester*. Six days later, on July 24, he was on his way to Greenland. Sebastian did not come to see him off.

PART FOUR

THE WAR

AT SEA

In those days, many of the men who chose to join the merchant marine were radicals and nonconformists and those who, like Jack, were temperamentally unsuited to accept military discipline. In fact, the leadership of the National Maritime Union was dominated by members of the Communist Party. At the time Jack shipped out, he was probably unaware that he had volunteered for the most dangerous kind of service. The waters off the Atlantic coast of the United States were teeming with German submarines and U-boats and dead American seamen kept washing up on the shores. Each week throughout 1942, the newspapers reported that two Allied ships had been sunk; in reality the loss was much greater. The real numbers of casualties were also being kept from the public, so that men would not be discouraged from signing up. By the end of the war, one out of every twenty-six merchant seamen had been killed in the line of duty.

The *Dorchester* was a former luxury liner that had been stripped of its amenities and hastily refitted to carry as many men as possible. There were eight hundred men aboard, five hundred of them the civilian workers who were going to build an airfield in Greenland. With its sister ship, the *Chatham*, a freighter called the USS *Alcoa Pilot*, and an old wooden ice cutter that had seen service with Admiral Byrd, the *Dorchester* left Boston harbor, thinly protected by a destroyer and a cruiser.

With sudden death a constant possibility, the men aboard obsessed themselves with gambling. In the diary Jack kept until August 12, which he would use in an unfinished novel called *Merchant Mariner*, he described "the tremendous card games and crap games" that went on every night in the huge dining room and often broke into fights. On July 25, asking himself how he felt about death as the ship neared the mouth of the St. Lawrence, an area that had become known as Torpedo Alley, Jack wrote that he had entered a state of dreamlike acceptance.

Gradually Jack made friends with a few of his crewmates. The one who made the strongest impression on him was Pat Reel, a veteran of the Lincoln Brigade in the Spanish Civil War. At twenty-nine, Reel had already led the kind of adventurous life Jack had been dreaming about. Reel, who had been kicked out of Columbia for "inciting students," had lived for a time on the Left Bank in Paris, and met Ernest Hemingway. An ardent Communist, he tried to convince Jack to join the party and strongly disapproved of Thomas Wolfe because he had sought crass worldly success. Jack also got to know an army gun crew who shared his love of popular music and had brought a phonograph aboard. By and large, however, the voyage was hardly the universal brotherhood experience he'd envisioned. He felt little kinship with the men who never stopped cursing and making fun of him for being a college boy and spending his leisure time in his bunk reading Thomas Mann and H. G. Wells.

Since he wasn't drinking, Jack must have been very quiet aboard that ship, drawn into himself in a way that others found disconcerting or even arrogant. "Well, at least being misunderstood," he observed, "is being like the hero in the movies." Years later, in his *Book of Dreams*, he painted an even lonelier picture than the one in his diary: "rough seamen who saw my child's soul in a grown-up body broke my spirit by spitting and cursing." Nonetheless, he felt eager to go on more voyages, especially if he had a friend with him. In late September, he wrote to Sebastian, suggesting that they "grab a tanker for Texas" or sail to Newport News or to South America or Russia together.

The worst part of being at sea was his job as a scullion, which made him feel like a slave in a "steel jail" and seemed more unbearable than factory work. He hated the steamy, heaving, foul-smelling galley, where he had to wash and scour enormous pots and pans and endlessly peel potatoes. The galley was largely run by a team of black cooks. There was a heavyset cook, known as Chef, who called Jack stupid and piled so much extra work on him that he complained to a superior officer. But others were kind to him. On July 28, a gay pastry cook, who had conducted a religious service on deck two days before, insisted Jack accept a leather jacket, a gift he couldn't turn down. (For the next nine years, he would wear it constantly.) And quickly Jack came to admire the chief cook, Glory, a towering, gentle, inscrutable man whom he considered a born leader. These were the first black Americans Jack had ever really known.

At the beginning of August, when he was assigned to night work, Jack's spirits lifted considerably. Finally he had time to write and think and to see with his own astonished eyes "the fantastic North of men's souls," where there were sunsets at midnight, "icebergs as big as hills," schools of porpoises "with their Mona Lisa smiles, disporting and diving in formation." He kept thinking of a phrase of Wolfe's: "Morning and new lands." On a fjord in Greenland, where Eskimos in kayaks came out to greet the ship, he traded his Horace Mann football sweater for a harpoon. In *The Town and the City*, he would proudly reflect that his adventure in the Arctic sea was unlike anything Melville had experienced.

The *Dorchester*, which had separated from the *Chatham*, dropped anchor off a location known as Bluie East No. 1, where the airfield was being built, remaining there to house the construction workers aboard until barracks were put up. It was a slow time, during which Jack made friends with a seaman called Duke Ford, who had barely survived being torpedoed and shipwrecked off Cape Hatteras. One day, Duke and Jack went ashore to climb a boulder-covered mountain that loomed over the flat Arctic landscape. It was the first time Jack had set foot on land in a month. On his shaky sea legs he managed to make it to the mountaintop, where he sat with Duke smoking cigarettes at the edge of a three-thousand-foot drop. On the way down, they were nearly killed when Jack misstepped and set off an avalanche of boulders that crashed around them. It took them so long to get back to the ship that they were declared AWOL.

Jack wrote to Norma Blickfelt again on August 25—this time it was a letter he actually sent—recalling their "wonderful time last April" and asking her to forgive his four months of mysterious silence. Of all the girls he had known since Mary Carney, she was the one who had the most powerful grip on his imagination. To feel a woman could be his soul mate and intellectual equal was a new experience for him. He told Norma he was in "a very beautiful and enchanted land" and would be calling her as soon as he got to New York, paying her the supreme compliment of asking, "Can there be such a thing as a 'female humanist'?" Jack wanted to convince Norma that he had put "aimlessness and paradoxical chaos" behind him. "I am either frank, or egotistical & vain, or all three," he went on, making a case for the intense self-involvement she might criticize but pointing out that none of the great writers he most admired—neither Whitman, Wolfe, Saroyan, nor Joyce—could possibly be considered "self-depreciating," not that he claimed to have a "higher mentality" himself. He didn't realize that he had hurt and puzzled Norma by his long unaccountable silence, made her feel that what she thought was love was a figment of her imagination.

Two days later, the *Chatham* was sunk by a U-boat off the coast of Labrador. Although only thirteen men actually died, Jack still believed when he worked on *Vanity of Duluoz* twenty-five years later that a thousand had perished. Refusing to go into the catastrophe in detail, he explained to his readers that there was far too much to tell. But perhaps the memory had remained too disturbing to revisit. In *The Town and the City*, Peter Martin actually witnesses the sinking of a torpedoed ship called the *Latham*, seeing a red glow far out at sea. After that, he begins keeping a razor blade in his watch pocket "for the time, the night, when he should find himself floating alone in these Arctic sea immensities" and having vivid "daydreams" about drowning, a death that apparently had a peculiar horror for Jack.

One morning not long afterward, in the Davis Strait off the Newfoundland coast, the *Dorchester* also came under attack. Jack heard depth charges being fired by one of the coast guard vessels that was escorting them as he fried hundreds of strips of bacon, wearing the heavy life jacket he kept on most of the time. Glory calmly informed him that they were under attack and told him to just keep working. Despite his own terror, Jack's mind flashed to the galley of the enemy submarine where a boy who was his blond German counterpart was surely drowning in the unstoppable flood that was engulfing "him and his stove and his humble breakfast." It was a realization he found unbearable. It made him a lifelong pacifist. He wondered why the American and German vessels couldn't just meet "and exchange prisoners and phony pleasantries."

Meanwhile there was general panic and confusion all aboard the *Dorchester* since many of the men had not been issued life jackets.

By the time his homeward-bound ship docked off the coal-mining port of Sydney, Nova Scotia, in late September, Jack found it unendurable to be left onboard cold sober and assigned to guard duty (a penalty for his mountain-climbing escapade) when the rest of the crew were allowed to have a day of liberty ashore. He walked away from his post, jumped ship, and went on a two-day bender with four shipmates. Downing all the alcohol they could hold, they staggered in and out of dance halls and clubs, found a brothel where they shared two Indian prostitutes, and mistakenly broke into a miner's home where they spent the night passed out in the parlor.

The following day, when two MPs arrested him, Jack could remember neither his name nor the name of his ship. After a nap in a cell, he managed to climb out a window and escape, begging money from strangers so that he could buy more drinks. By the time he miraculously got back to his ship, where $5.50 was deducted from his pay, he was one of the last seamen to come aboard. If he had been in the navy, the consequences would have been dire.

In the first week of October, the *Dorchester* steamed into New York Harbor, then turned around and headed for Boston. With a fistfight over gambling debts raging in the mess hall, Jack got off the ship and, to his amazement, was handed his pay of eight hundred dollars by none other than G.J. Apostolos, who had joined the coast guard. He also found Sebastian beside the gangplank, waiting to take him home right away, despite G.J.'s hurt feelings.

Jack had been invited to sail on the *Dorchester*'s next voyage, but in Lowell he found a telegram from Lou Little confirming that Columbia was ready to readmit him. After a day with his family, during which he presented his mother with his harpoon as well as three hundred dollars, leaving the rest of his pay with her for safekeeping, Jack took a train to New York with his father.

Once again, he had a disappointing reception from Lou Little, who immediately saw how much weight Jack had lost at sea and said he would now have to demote him to a guard. With less interest in football than he'd ever felt before, Jack was back to long hours of practice, sitting out games like a second-stringer, and having little time for his studies because he was back to washing dishes every night.

Four days after Jack settled into a routine at Columbia, Sebastian came to visit him. The letter Jack had written him in September had been unusually open and ardent about Jack's desire to be with him—Jack had even been fantasizing that before shipping out together, they would share an apartment in Greenwich Village. But although the two of them walked over the Brooklyn Bridge, went to look at Thomas Wolfe's house in Brooklyn Heights, and attended a talk by a Communist organizer at the National Maritime Union, Sebastian was disheartened, as he later told some of his Young Promethean friends, by Jack's self-destructive drinking on the nights they spent in Harlem with Seymour Wyse.

Writing to Sebastian in early November, Jack acknowledged that his time so far at Columbia had been "one huge debauchery," which he had thoroughly enjoyed, but now he had begun to feel foolish when he compared himself with someone like Pat Reel, who had seen the world. He had been looking into joining the Naval Reserve program on campus, but couldn't bear the thought of putting on a uniform although he did want to go back to sea, he wrote, "for the money, for the leisure and study, for the heart-rending romance, and for the pith of the moment," and this time he unequivocally wanted his "mad poet brother" with him. But Sebastian had stopped waiting to be with Jack. He had just joined the army and applied to be trained as a medic, so that he would not have to kill. He wrote Jack a melancholy letter about a nostalgic final visit to Pine Brook, where they had gone with Billy Chandler.

Despite the debauchery he bragged about, Jack had never worked so hard at his studies, putting particular effort into the famous course taught by the poet, critic, and Shakespeare scholar Mark Van Doren, who recognized something unusual in his writing and would remember him as a brilliant student and later help him find a publisher. Jack was studying as if he knew this would be his last shot at a college education, for as much as he was tempted to leave Columbia, he had never longed so much to stay. Ever since his arrival, however, he had been getting distressing letters from Gabe. The family was in danger of falling apart because Leo had had to accept a poor-paying job from the WPA that kept him out of town most of the time. There was so little money coming in, his mother worried she wouldn't be able to heat the house. Everywhere Jack looked he could find a reason to feel guilty about selfishly staying in college. When he'd written to Sebastian he had offhandedly raised the possibility that the two of them might die at sea, "but it would only be in homage to Billy Chandler."

In late October, Leo, in desperation, had come down to New York to demand that Lou Little make good on his old promise to find him a job. The interview had been a disaster, ending with Leo exploding in rage, calling Little a "wop," and threatening that Jack would walk away from Columbia if Little kept him out of the Army game, which was now about to take place. Leo had irreparably damaged Jack's relationship with his coach, but this time Jack knew that his father would be on his side if he decided to quit football.

Jack had spent the Army game on the bench. The following Monday he cut football practice, deciding he'd rather stay in his room and listen to Beethoven's Fifth Symphony. He dropped in on Jack Fitzgerald to listen to some jazz recordings and then went to see his new girlfriend, Edie Parker, who was living with her grandmother in an apartment a couple of blocks away. So far he'd told no one what he'd just made up his mind to do.

Twenty-year-old Edie Parker had grown up in a wealthy, socially prominent family in Grosse Pointe, Michigan. Too rebellious and wild to stay home, she had come to New York to study art at seventeen and had started dating Jack's old Horace Mann friend Henri Cru, who happened to live in her grandmother's building. Without any particular encouragement from Edie, who later compared their sexual relationship to "an appointment with the dentist," Henri considered her his fiancée, and in October had entrusted her to Jack's care before shipping out to the Mediterranean. "Well, he might as well have put an ice cream in my hand and told me not to eat it," Edie wrote in her memoir. She had been eyeing Jack for the last two years, noticing his "periwinkle blue eyes," the unruly black cowlick that fell over his forehead, the music in his voice, while he had taken note of Edie's perfect figure, her honey-colored hair, her small "squirrel-like" teeth, her girlish readiness to giggle. Soon after his return to Columbia, Jack had run into Edie on Amsterdam Avenue as she stood on a corner, feeding lumps of sugar to an old cart horse—acts of kindness to animals always had deep resonance for Jack, and the sight of Edie and the horse struck him as something straight out of Saroyan. He took her to a deli where she ate five hot dogs in a state of nervous excitement as they conversed with each other, then later to Minton's to hear Lester Young. The following day, according to Edie, Jack wrote her a "Shakespearean" love letter. At the time he was still pursuing the elusive Norma Blickfelt, but his new relationship with Edie had very quickly gotten "sticky," as Edie later put it, and they'd begun to spend a lot of time together.

Their romance was now about to be interrupted. After making love to Edie on her grandmother's couch that early November afternoon, Jack reduced her to tears when he announced he would soon be going back to Lowell to wait to be accepted into the Naval Air Force V-12 program. It would pay his way at Columbia for another term without his having to play football, and keep him from being drafted when he turned twenty-one.

Without telling his parents or any of his friends at home, Jack quit the team at the end of the month. (Leo would learn of it while reading his newspaper.) When he left New York in January after finishing his fall courses, Edie was certain she would never see him again.

In Lowell, Jack promptly came down with the German measles and had to postpone his V-12 interview. As he recuperated and waited for the navy to contact him again, he began working on a novel entitled *The Sea Is My Brother*. Rather than writing about himself directly, as he had done in *Vanity of Duluoz*, he split himself into two fictional characters, making them ten years older than he was. The loner Wesley Martin, who may have been inspired in part by Pat Reel, was an experienced seaman, whom Jack intended to have a kind of austere and poetic purity and whom he planned to tragically kill off. The jaded intellectual Bill Everhart, on the other hand, was "a son without a conscience—a lover without a wife! A prophet without confidence, a teacher without wisdom, a sorry mess of a man thereat." "I'm only going on vacation," Bill foolishly says as he prepares to leave behind his senseless and empty New York life. "Conviction," Jack wrote, "had led Wesley to the sea," whereas Everhart had been led there by "confusion." Unfortunately, Wesley Martin is a poor foil for Everhart in the novel because, due to Jack's awkward and inflated third-person narration and his failure to give his protagonists individual voices, the two alienated men often seem indistinguishable. (He had been on much firmer ground the year before in those directly autobiographical stories he wrote in Hartford in which he at times came remarkably close to his mature voice.) Leo Kerouac makes his appearance in the book as Bill's beaten-down, self-pitying father. Jack couldn't stop writing about Leo, even though his portrayal of him in *Vanity of Duluoz*, which Leo had read on the sly that fall as he'd gone through Jack's papers, had hurt his father's feelings considerably.

With Sebastian in boot camp in Pennsylvania, Jack turned to the remnants of the Young Prometheans—Cornelius Murphy, Ed Tully, and John MacDonald, who hadn't yet been drafted—as well as to a new Lowell friend for intellectual companionship. At the time Jack met Bill Ryan, he was studying engineering and had recently been inspired to become a writer after reading Thomas Wolfe. After Jack read the novel Bill was working on, he compared him to Sinclair Lewis and called him a true artist in the "lean, hardhitting" vein. (Two years later, Bill Ryan would die in the South Pacific.)

Jack still considered himself a Wolfean. While he was beginning to have some critical thoughts on the subject and thought he was "'outgrowing' the adolescent side of Wolfeanism: the stone, leaf-door pattern," he absolutely refused to discredit the master, who had written about "the essential and everlasting America." Reading Alfred Kazin's mostly very admiring essay on Wolfe in *On Native Grounds* the following month, Jack felt deeply offended by the criticisms it contained. Although Kazin believed Wolfe was "the most alert and brilliant novelist of Depression America," he also saw him as a naïve romantic egoist and pointed out that he had made himself "the least interesting character in his work." "I loathe critics," Jack wrote indignantly to Sebastian, calling them "art killers."

By then it was February and he still hadn't heard from the navy. On February 3, the *Dorchester* had been sunk by a German submarine off Labrador where the *Chatham* had gone down. Over six hundred men had perished in the icy sea, including many of Jack's former crewmates. Glory was gone, as well as the steward who hated him, and the pastry cook who had given him the leather jacket. Again, he had been left a survivor haunted by memories. That month when he was drinking coffee, his mother noticed that his hands were shaking. When Jack heard that Sebastian, now at Fort Lee in Virginia, had been hospitalized with an injury to his jaw that had caused unstoppable bleeding, he was terrified he might lose him too: "If you die," Jack wrote him, "how shall I do it alone?"

He worked on his sea novel fourteen hours a day as he waited for his own fate to be decided even though he'd had to take a job in a garage. Sometimes G.J. would visit him there. They tried to outdo each other in senseless macho behavior and pursued the same woman. But since the summer Jack had been feeling increasingly estranged from G.J. He felt he saw him now only because they'd known each other for so long. "He is not my friend, only a 'pal,' " Jack admitted to Sebastian, who finally seemed the decisive winner in the old contest for Jack's soul.

Announcing to Sebastian one night in early March that he was not only very drunk but in a very "Bohemian," "Baroque," "very GAY" frame of mind, Jack implored him to *"live."* "We must go to Paris and see that the revolution goes well! . . . We must go to Bataan and pick a flower." The feelings he expressed to Sebastian all through this period kept fluctuating between unguarded expressions of emotion and self-protective coldness, as if two different Jacks were writing to him.

Sebastian's adjustment to army life had been an excruciating test of his idealism. Hoping to find brotherhood, he had been shocked by the brutality of basic training and the coarse behavior of the other recruits, most of whom were white Southerners. His first camp, the Shenango Replacement Depot, had been a "hellhole" where there were frequent suicides. He wrote Jack that he felt he had been "cheated," advising him to steer clear of the military. The armed services were no place for a poet. The officers seemed like Hitlers. Yet Sebastian's courage and openness carried him through. During his hospitalization in Virginia, where he "dared" to speak and joke with black soldiers, his faith in humanity and in the war against fascism began to be restored. Soon he was able to see nobility even in the bigoted white Southerners he was serving with. Sebastian was growing up fast in the army, beginning to look at Jack more objectively without his eyes brimming with tears. When Jack criticized Sebastian for doing little before the war beyond being the organizer of the Young Prometheans and "moralizing," Sebastian was able to defend himself proudly.

All through that spring, they were having a running intellectual argument in their letters that sometimes threatened to divide them for good. Jack was moving away from the collectivism Sammy passionately believed in and asserting the primacy of the individual, especially the individual artist. But the outsider's position of "defying all mankind" had no appeal for Sebastian. He wrote Jack that he would continue to value him as a friend, "but I will not lead a blind life—I want mine to have a purpose in uplifting mankind."

Despite Sammy's exasperation with Jack, he sent him a recording, which arrived just before Jack's twenty-first birthday. He woke up one morning to the sound of Sebastian's voice reading Thomas Wolfe, accompanied by his mother's sobs. Gabe was convinced Sebastian was sounding his own death knell. "I hope this will convince you," Jack wrote him on March 15, "that my mother is essentially a great woman and that whatever rancor she may have held against you was not rancor, but something reflected from my father's profound theories on Sebastian Sampas." In the same letter he told Sammy that he had just failed the V-12 test. He was about to be sent to boot camp in Newport to become an ordinary "gob," which meant he had finally been "washed out" of his college education. The news was devastating to Jack for another reason—as a gob, he would have to surrender the remnants of personal freedom he could have held on to as an officer.

During his first days at the naval training camp in Newport, Rhode Island, Jack continued his political and philosophical argument with Sebastian, which he felt had grown to "delightfully large proportions." On March 25, he urged Sammy to be less Byronic and to take himself more seriously as a poet, while "observing the phenomena of living, with the patience and scrutiny of a scientist" rather than reacting in an oversensitive way. Recalling Pat Reel's intolerant party line attitudes, Jack was having second thoughts about the "working-class movement" to which Sammy felt so dedicated and thought he would prefer to become "a solitary radical" focused on one thing: "the exploitation of the masses." The army and navy, Jack had decided after only a day or two in the service, were the perfect example of exploitation. "Prisoners of war don't go through as much crap and slave labor as do the poor kids training to die an orderly and disciplined death." He ended by telling Sebastian he didn't think much of the Prometheans' latest idea—a farm where they would all live communally. He could see it as a place for a vacation, but "the *ennui* would be awful—an artist needs *life*."

The communal living at the training camp, where he was surrounded by boys just out of high school and found no one he could talk to, didn't appeal to Jack at all. From the moment he arrived, which was probably on March 23, he became uncontrollably resistant to the military discipline he considered absurd and enslaving, making no self-protective efforts to go along with the system. Assigned to do an inspection of the uniformed recruits in his barracks, he defiantly thought, "They can have their peckers hanging out for all I care." As a dentist worked on his teeth, Jack addressed him as "Doc" and told him to stop hurting him, ignoring the man's superior rank. Forbidden to smoke before breakfast, he socked the officer who had knocked a cigarette out of his mouth.

By March 30, Jack was under observation in the "nuthouse" section of the sick bay and was in danger of being court-martialed. During a rifle drill, he had suddenly laid his gun down on the ground and walked off. When the military police found him reading in the base library, he told them he was a field marshal and asked to be let out of the navy so that he could serve as a civilian in the merchant marine.

The navy psychiatrists suspected that Jack was pretending to be crazy, but didn't know what to make of him. The discovery that he had the highest IQ on the whole base created the preposterous suspicion that he was a Communist Party official. After studying the handwritten manuscript of *The Sea Is My Brother* that Jack had brought with him, a team of doctors, analyzing his handling of duality, tentatively diagnosed him as schizoid. Not wanting to alarm his mother, Jack wrote her from sick bay that he had been hospitalized because of the headaches he had been having, reminding her that she had recently noticed his shaking hands.

He may truly have reached a breaking point. The night before he left for Newport, Jack had felt overwhelmed by sadness, haunted by the ghosts of those he'd loved. He had written Sebastian that he'd wept from sheer loneliness and his brokenhearted vision of humanity. Once he turned himself over to the navy, he had not only found himself in a rigidly confining situation he was constitutionally unable to tolerate but had abruptly been deprived of the alcohol he had been growing dependent upon, as well as the hours he needed to devote to the writing that kept him in balance. By the time he was twenty-one, Jack seemed unable to cope with his life unless writing was at the center of it; without it he tended to become unmoored. In any case, he made no effort to convince the navy doctors that he was sane, answering their questions with deliberately nonsensical responses and creating the impression of sexual confusion. He told them he was an alcoholic and that he slept with whores and had never had a girlfriend and that his strongest attachments were to men. (There were grains of truth in everything he told them.) When he demanded a typewriter, they accused him of impersonating a writer.

Months later, in his diary, Jack admitted to himself that he had half played along with the psychiatrists. Yet on one occasion he was so despondent that the doctors were truly concerned about him. In Newport, a Dr. Conrad Tully submitted a diagnosis of "extreme preoccupation" and noted that anyone who could not conform to the military regimen was of no use to the navy.

Jack himself was having doubts about his actual sanity. On April 7, he wrote a painful letter to G.J. in which he tried to make sense of what had happened to him—a letter that showed how surprisingly well he knew himself, as young as he was. Believing that he was now paying the price for having a "malleable personality," he had concluded that there were two sides to him. One was the alienated, introverted "schizoid side" that was like Raskolnikov and Stephen Dedalus and his own Mike Duluoz character. The other was his "normal counterpart," the side he showed to G.J., "which recommends a broad rugged America" and which required "gutsy, redblooded associates." He had spent his entire youth, Jack wrote plaintively, futilely trying to bring together in one single knot "two ends of a rope." "Sebastian was at one end, you on the other, and beyond both of you lay the divergent worlds of my dual mind."

Confined to a ward with a manic-depressive, a patient known as Rodmo the Modmo who was kept in a wire cage, and a man who had shot himself in the head and survived, Jack might have become suicidal himself out of loneliness if he hadn't met William Holmes Hubbard, a tall Texan who had been put under observation because of his tendency to be too free with his fists. Bill Hubbard had bummed his way around the United States, working as a cowboy, an oil worker, and a merchant seaman. He had even played varsity football for Louisiana State. (In some ways he was a forerunner of Neal Cassady; as Bull Hubbard or Big Slim he would later keep appearing in Jack's fiction.)

To Jack, Hubbard immediately seemed the iconic "last hobo," exactly the kind of free and intransigent American who was vanishing now that war had brought about the end of the Depression. The encounter with Hubbard stirred up his persistent fantasies about the vagabond life and going out west. Soon Jack would weave him into a second draft of *The Sea Is My Brother*. By modeling himself on Bill, Jack found a way to survive on the ward. They slept in adjoining beds and stayed up talking after lights-out, trading stories of their adventures. Bill said he'd find a way to get them out.

Jack had visitors in Newport that spring. First came his father, who was very pleased with him for finding a way to opt out of active service in the navy. Flourishing his cigar, Leo ranted about the Roosevelts and the war that was being fought on behalf of the Marxist Jews.

Then at the beginning of May came Sebastian, on leave before being sent overseas, looking changed with his crew cut and his khaki army uniform, but still "sad, idealistic." Sammy had tried to see Jack once before, on Easter Sunday, but had been turned away. Now they were allowed only twenty minutes. There was everything to say and no time to say it. When Rodmo the Modmo started fixating on Sammy, they ducked into a toilet, where Jack reminded Sammy how he had once run along beside the train that was taking him back to prep school, singing "I'll See You Again." It was the last time they would ever be together.

Meanwhile, Bill Hubbard had dreamed up an escape plan for himself and Jack that was only half serious, in which they would make their getaway from Newport in true hobo fashion by hopping a freight train on the rail line that ran behind the base. The plan involved picking locks on the ward with the butter knives they had stolen and hidden under their pillows. When the knives were discovered, the two of them were put into straitjackets, locked into separate sleeping compartments on a train, and sent down to Bethesda Naval Hospital in the custody of three huge armed guards.

It was nearly summer. From a small barred window in Bethesda, Jack looked out upon the green world he had been shut away from, where an inviting path wound through the Maryland woods, disappearing into the distance. He and Bill had been incarcerated on a ward where there were men who howled "like coyotes" and had to be wrapped in wet sheets. Surrounded by what seemed like the suffering of mankind and identifying with Raskolnikov, the "schizoid," "Hamlet-like" intellectual who had destroyed his life with one gratuitous act in *Crime and Punishment*, Jack wrote to Sebastian that "Dostoevsky was one of ourselves."

"You are not a Slav," Sammy responded sternly on May 26. "It is beyond the capacity of your Breton soul to understand him." Sebastian saw Raskolnikov as an ego-driven "over-refined" product of the Western world. It was only through the process of suffering, he reminded Jack, that Raskolnikov "forgot himself," thus becoming a true Russian: "one with all his brothers," rather than being "lost and lonely in infinity" like Western man—or, as Sammy implied, like Jack.

Contemplating the possibility that he would die in the terrible war that seemed like the end of Western civilization, Sebastian had been reading Oswald Spengler's *Decline of the West*, a book that seemed prophetic to many young intellectuals of their generation. Now, as he was about to be shipped to a port of embarkation for an unknown destination, Sammy saw no future for art in the dark new world that was coming into being, where, as Spengler had said, it was the reality "of living, that is essential." The task for Western intellectuals, as Sammy saw it now, was not to create but to bring about a spiritual transformation that would "actualize the fullest possibilities" of what Spengler had called "the All-Soul." As he wrote, Sebastian's voice took on more and more urgency, as if he were making a last-ditch attempt to liberate Jack from the Western prison of the ego by passing along the vision he now embraced. He had grown pessimistic about Russia's future, but was convinced that in America "a primitive man, crude, raw, unfinished—superb—is shaping in the heart of our land. He does not seek for 'other.' The meaning he knows is life." It was in this Spenglerian "primitive man" that Sebastian now put his "hopes."

Only the year before, Sebastian, guarding his fragile inner sanctum of art and culture against the macho know-nothings of Lowell, would have regarded a man who was crude and unfinished the way he regarded G.J.—as a philistine. But his experiences in the army were starting to free him from his self-defensive elitism and make him see spiritual possibilities in men who were unlike himself. Jack's embrace of humanity had always been instinctively expansive, but Sebastian's words codified Jack's feelings. Four years later, soon after he met Neal Cassady, a westerner like Bill Hubbard, he would recognize in him the embodiment of Sebastian's prophecy.

EDIE PARKER

In June, Jack walked out of Bethesda Naval Hospital with just enough money in his pocket to buy a new set of civilian clothes and get himself home. After being interviewed by a Dr. Rosenburg, he had been granted an honorable discharge, but one that disqualified him from receiving a veteran's pension. The doctor, who had carefully read the manuscript of *The Sea Is My Brother*, had started by asking Jack who he thought he really was, to which Jack, still impersonating a schizophrenic, had answered, "Samuel Johnson." But after more questioning, he simply told Dr. Rosenburg the truth. He was willing to serve in the merchant marine but not the navy, because he was unable to submit to miltary discipline. The official diagnosis of his condition was "schizoid personality with angel tendencies," but the navy finally set him free on the grounds that he had an "indifferent character." Years later, Jack had some regrets about not serving in the navy, wondering whether the experience would have been good for his character. But his immediate response to his regained freedom was to drink with a marine he encountered in Washington until he passed out on a lawn. After another day of drinking, he headed home.

Home had shifted radically while Jack had been hospitalized. This time it was a walk-up apartment over a drugstore in Ozone Park, Queens, across the street from a tavern where you could bring a tea kettle and fill it up with beer. The Jamaica racetrack was within walking distance, which made it a convenient destination for Leo. The Kerouacs had made a decisive break with Lowell, dismantling Jack's boyhood world in the process, although the moment he walked into the crowded and chaotic new apartment, he found all the old, overstuffed furniture of his nightmares that had been moved and set up so many times before. Even a phosphorescent white crucifix that had terrified him as a child had pursued him to Ozone Park, to this home that didn't seem like home.

Nin was not part of the new Kerouac household—she was having the time of her life in the WAACs' training camp down south, where she would soon meet her future second husband. Jack's parents, reunited now that Leo would no longer be going out of town to work, were enjoying the novelty of their New York life, taking in the sights and entertainments of Manhattan. For the first time in a long while, they were getting along in a companionable way. When they'd first arrived, Leo and Gabe had felt lost, wondering whether leaving Lowell had been a bad mistake, but by the time Jack arrived, they had both settled into steady jobs that paid good wages—Gabe in a factory that was making shoes for the army, Leo at a print shop on Canal Street. In order to make a home for Jack in his chosen city, they had given up a community where there were family ties, where everyone knew them and spoke their language. Feelings of profound dislocation would gradually set in.

Jack hated Ozone Park on sight. It looked blighted and centerless to him with its gas tanks and traffic and ugly low redbrick buildings, like a "cancer" that had spread from New York. There were no trees on his block on Crossbay Boulevard like the ones at the end of Crawford Street in Lowell. Overhead were the tracks of the elevated subway that would take him into Manhattan. He immediately wanted to get away, but on his first morning home he felt better after eating the big breakfast his mother cooked for him, and that night he took his parents to a darkened Times Square swarming with servicemen on leave to see a prewar Jean Gabin film at the Apollo movie theater. The following day he went to the National Maritime Union in search of a job. After that, what he needed was a girl.

The one who immediately came to mind was Edie Parker, who had not heard one word from him since he'd left New York in January. In Lowell that winter, Jack had taken up for the last time with poor Peggy Coffey, who made one final attempt to hold on to him by assuring him that although she still loved him, she no longer expected him to feel the same. It was Norma Blickfelt, however, who had continued to dominate Jack's fantasies, despite the angry letter she'd written him in January. He could actually envision marrying her someday, if he didn't shoot himself at thirty-three, and even breeding "a brood of brats, all of whom shall be distinguished writers, humanists, satirists, essayists, critics, playwrights, poets and all Communists," as he'd written Sammy in February. By the time he got out of Bethesda, however, he'd accepted the fact that Norma wanted no part of him.

So there he was three days after his return to civilian life, walking into Edie Parker's apartment building across the street from Columbia, assuming he would find her exactly where he'd left her in January. She wasn't there. A doorman told him she had gone to her grandmother's summer house in Asbury Park. When Jack turned up there later that day, Edie was stunned—and thrilled, even though she had some very serious reasons to remain angry about what she called his conceitedness and "absentmindedness." She punished Jack by making him wear earrings and took him to the beach to show him off to her girlfriends. They thought he was a gypsy.

It was undoubtedly during that long weekend that Jack learned that he had probably made Edie pregnant. She had written him a letter while he was in the naval hospital informing him that she was three months along, although she didn't know whether Jack or Henri Cru was responsible for her condition. That letter apparently went astray, as did one she sent to Henri, who was away at sea. After waiting in vain for an answer from either of them, Edie had decided not to keep the baby. She was four months gone by the time her grandmother took her to the Bronx for an agonizing kitchen table abortion. The baby, according to her memoir, was a boy with black hair. Edie kept the abortion a secret for decades until she revealed it during a Women and the Beats panel discussion at the 1982 Kerouac festival at the Naropa Institute. Although Henri as well as Jack had black hair, by that time Edie was expressing certainty that Jack had been the father of her child. He had fallen into a terrible rage, she said, when she told him what had happened to their baby.

The abortion remained Jack's secret as well. It was something he would never have wanted his parents to know about, and there is no mention of it in any of his published works. In 1956, however, he dealt with it briefly and ambiguously in an abandoned novel about his homecoming from Bethesda. He opened that handwritten manuscript with an extended treatment of an episode he later covered in less than a page in *Vanity of Duluoz* in which Jack Duluoz learns that his father has been forced to drown a litter of newborn mice in the toilet of the new apartment, while his mother remarks upon the cuteness of those tiny victims. The horror Jack recalled feeling was profound. But, in writing about the drowned mice, he may have been indirectly expressing his emotional reaction to the killing of that baby who Edie said looked like him.

In the one paragraph about the abortion in the 1956 manuscript, Jack revealed that he had tried to get Edie pregnant again but that the operation had left her unable to bear children. In the next breath, however, he denied that the infant had been his in the first place, and claimed he was sterile. He also made a point of mentioning that it was Henri Cru who had paid for Edie's abortion. Even after this complete denial of responsibility, Jack may have felt he had said too much, for he crossed out not only that paragraph about Edie's abortion but also every page of the chapter about Edie in which it appeared. The subject must have been weighing on his mind, however, for his second wife, Joan Haverty, was pursuing him for child support. (Although Jack knew better, he claimed his five-year-old daughter Jan had been fathered by one of Joan's lovers.) In 1957, when Jack was living with me, he warned me not to even think about having a child by him, since to give birth to a baby was to bring death into the world. The association of birth with death that may have had its origins in the death of Gerard and Edie's abortion had by then become bound up with Jack's tormented interpretation of Buddhism, in which life itself was a void.

Despite her lonely ordeal, Edie was resilient. She had found a modeling job in Best's department store, had been dating a steady stream of V-12

officers in training, and had finally escaped from her grandmother's supervision into an apartment on West 118th Street, which she was sharing
with her new best friend, Joan Vollmer Adams, whom she'd met one
night in the West End bar. Joan, who was studying journalism, was one
of the neighborhood's "college widows." Although only nineteen, she had
already been married twice. Her first husband, a man with whom she'd
had an overwhelming sexual relationship, had abducted her while she
was at Barnard College and taken her to North Carolina. Her second husband, Paul Adams, a more stable law student, had soon been drafted into
the army, and Joan was making no particular effort to be faithful. If there
was a wartime shortage of men, neither young woman was experiencing
it. Although Edie was two years older, Joan was more advanced and sophisticated in her exploration of sex. She counseled Edie to get herself a
diaphragm to prevent further accidents.

The two were an attractive but unlikely duo. Edie made no bones about
not being an intellectual. "If I read a book at all," she later confessed, "it
was Thorne Smith or Zane Gray [sic]." She hadn't been at all offended the
previous year when Jack decided to make a project out of teaching her one
new word a day and in fact had readily accepted her role as his student.
Joan, on the other hand, who had entered Barnard when she was only fifteen, was universally considered brilliant. She would take long bubble
baths during which she would read Marx or Kafka or Proust and was not
shy about holding her own in discussions with men. A pretty, soft-
looking young woman with fine features in a heart-shaped face, she had
her own distinctive way of wearing silky clothes and wrapping colorful
scarves around her curly brown hair, which seemed glamorous and
Garbo-like to Edie. Edie liked to flirt and drink beer at the West End bar,
surrounded by loud young men. Joan preferred quiet, intense intellectual
discussions in a booth in Childs Restaurant, farther down on Broadway,
as she daintily sipped a glass of kummel. Edie had a raucous, earthy sense
of humor; Joan was witty and sardonic.

What the two of them had in common were their rebellions against
their staid, privileged backgrounds in defiance of their overly protective,
socially ambitious mothers who had raised them to marry husbands who
would give them placid, comfortable lives centered around suburban country clubs. Joan had grown up in Loudonville, just outside Albany, where

her father managed a manufacturing plant. She had come to New York to redefine herself, but instead mistakenly stumbled into marriage. Her status as a married woman, however, at least gave her the freedom to live on her own, and she was far more radical in her bohemianism than Edie, attracted to behavior that was not only unconventional but dangerous. Edie's bohemianism, a more superficial experiment without an intellectual base, was essentially a search for high-spirited fun and romance. "As a child," Edie wrote, "I was perfectly aware of a more carefree, fun-loving, roaring twenties side to life," in her case exemplified by the alcoholic playboy father she adored whom her pious mother had divorced and who physically resembled Jack.

Joan's stimulating presence during Jack's love affair with Edie may have been a factor in keeping that relationship alive over the next three years. Soon after his reunion with Edie, he started splitting his life between the apartment she was sharing with Joan, where he and Edie slept on a mattress on the living room floor, and his parents' apartment in Ozone Park—an arrangement that was interrupted for a couple of months when he shipped out in August. He left Edie with a black cocker spaniel he'd bought for her that they named Woofit.

The *George S. Weems*, a Liberty ship carrying a load of five-hundred-pound bombs to Liverpool across the U-boat-infested Atlantic, was a much smaller vessel than the *Dorchester*, with a crew of only forty-four men. This time Jack had signed on as an ordinary deckhand. He immediately made himself unpopular with the bosun by diving into New York Harbor for a cooling swim shortly before the *Weems* sailed.

Whether out of choice or out of the shyness that came over him in periods when he was sober, Jack spent most of his second voyage inside a shell of solitude, forming no friendships aboard the ship. What he liked best was his dreamy, meditative early morning watch when he had the whole vista of the sea to himself as he stood at the bow, keeping his eyes peeled for U-boats. Once he spotted a barrel-like object that proved to be a mine and saved the *Weems* from being blown up, although he was given little credit for it. In fact, he was disparagingly known by his shipmates as "the sleeping beauty," since he spent so much time lying in his bunk when he wasn't working. There he would read the twentieth-

century British novels he'd brought aboard, among them John Galsworthy's *Forsyte Saga*, which started him thinking that he might write
a family saga of his own. Ideas were germinating inside the silence his
shipmates found puzzling or infuriating. At night, using the purser's
typewriter, he would work on his new draft of *The Sea Is My Brother*,
although he was having second thoughts about its elevated, poetic style.
Unfortunately, he soon made an enemy of the dour first mate. Until the
union men aboard put a stop to it, the officer kept deliberately endangering Jack, needlessly sending him out in storms to climb the mast into
the crow's nest or to bail out the lifeboats lashed to the side of the ship.
At Jack's first sight of land, the green Ireland of James Joyce as well as
the Celts his Breton ancestors had descended from, his eyes filled with
tears.

On September 18, he sent Edie a V-letter from Liverpool, assuring her
that "strangely enough" he missed her and expressing concern that she
would foolishly get into trouble again while he was gone "like the Dostoevskian creature that you are." She had threatened to do so because she
was upset by his departure. But Jack had promised to live with her when
he returned from his "grim" voyage; as proof of his intentions, he reminded her to go with Joan to Ozone Park, introduce themselves to his
parents, and pick up his most prized possessions—his radio and his jazz
records.

The British fiction Jack read during the voyage had left him convinced
that Hemingway and Wolfe (and, potentially, Kerouac) were far better
twentieth-century novelists than writers like John Galsworthy or Hugh
Walpole. Although he admired Dickens, the nineteenth-century French
writers Victor Hugo and Balzac meant far more to him. Perhaps that was
why Jack's first sight of London did not excite him. He wandered into an
exhibit of avant-garde art and went to a Tchaikovsky concert at the Royal
Albert Hall, followed by a round of pubs in Piccadilly Circus and foggy
encounters with a couple of British whores, one of whom picked his
pocket. He had to borrow money for the train back to Liverpool.

On a rainy morning in late September, just as the *George S. Weems*
was preparing to embark upon its return trip to the Brooklyn Navy Yard,
Jack had one of those epiphanies that come to writers after periods of
seeming dormancy—an illumination in which he could see his entire

life's work stretch out before him. Rather than telling the stories of fictional characters, he was going to keep writing the saga of his own life as it unfolded over the years, putting into it everything he experienced and witnessed. It was going to be "a contemporary history record for future times" that would define an entire period. Over the next eight years, this idea of wrting a multivolume autobiographical novel would remain in the back of Jack's mind. Perhaps it had first occurred to him as he read the interrelated volumes of the *Comédie Humaine* in which Balzac portrayed both Parisian and provincial life. But the plan would not come to its full flowering until 1951, when Jack was obsessively reading Proust's *Remembrance of Things Past* as he began *Visions of Cody*. From that time on, he regarded each of his "true life," memory-based novels as part of one vast Duluoz Saga.

As Jack was about to make the voyage back to America, he already knew that a novel about Lowell entitled *Galloway* would be the first installment of his projected work. Like his unfinished *Vanity of Duluoz*, which he believed was the most important writing he'd done so far, it was going to be about himself and his father, about the profound change war would bring to America and to his hero, Peter Duluoz, who, unlike Thomas Wolfe's pessimistic George Webber, would return home with the realization that change, rather than being destructive, as Peter's father saw it, had led to "new life."

At twenty-two, Jack felt ready to dedicate himself to the task of writing this demanding book, realizing now that his writing was the only thing in his life that "contained" him. Only two issues, as Joan saw it, threatened to hold him back: the obligation he felt to help support his parents and the deep sense that he must share the tremendous wartime sacrifices made by his generation in order to be worthy of love.

In early October, the *George S. Weems* arrived in New York after some close encounters in the mid-Atlantic with German submarines. During the farewell party onboard, Jack astonished his shipmates by saying more than he'd said the entire voyage after a few drinks dissolved his silence. Then he hopped on a subway and headed for Edie in the sixth-floor, three-bedroom walkup at 281 West 118th Street, where she and Joan Adams had just moved to make room for him. "That was the time when you should have tried making love to *me*," Joan revealed to him long after. But Edie, who had her heart set on marriage, had already signed the lease as Mrs. Kerouac.

For the next nine months Jack enjoyed playing house with the "crazy happy" childlike girl he later nostalgically referred to as "the bride of my youth." They fought a lot over Jack's resistance to rushing into matrimony—but they always managed to make up in bed after one of their spats. Edie liked to fuss over Jack, knitting him Argyle socks, improving his wardrobe, making his favorite dishes—tomato aspic and cold asparagus; she spiced up their lovemaking with an oral technique, unheard of in Grosse Pointe, which worldly Joan had recommended. That fall they even added a cat, which Edie named Kitkat, to their little family. There were times when Jack definitely thought he was in love. During one romantic period, they even went to Tiffany's and used Edie's allowance to buy matching silver friendship rings.

In the mornings Jack would still be asleep after staying up all night writing, when Edie, who was doing her bit for the war effort, left for her job as a longshoreman on the Hoboken docks. He would get up at noon and put in a few hours synopsizing scripts for Columbia Pictures. (Jack had hopes this would lead to a career as a Hollywood screenwriter, which would enable him to support Gabe and Leo in style.) Then he would return to his work on *Galloway* or on one of the short stories Edie would send out for him to magazines like the *Saturday Evening Post*.

When Jack took Edie out they often headed for Minton's, where Dizzy Gillespie was appearing with phenomenal young musicians like Charlie Parker and Thelonious Monk. Standing at the bar, they became acquainted with a twenty-seven-year-old Columbia student named Jerry Newman, who sometimes did lip-synching comedy routines at the club and had been lugging recording equipment up there for the past two years. Now that Seymour Wyse was serving with the Canadian air force, Newman would become Jack's guide to bebop. He had entrée to the after-hours sessions where the most radical developments could be heard and had been making his own acetate disks of Parker, Monk, Gillespie, and Charley Christian, which he played on the Columbia radio station, WKCR, and presented to the musicians he had recorded. At first Jack didn't know what to make of the new sounds. He was taken aback one night when he heard Monk play a note on the piano that sounded "wooden" and "off key": "The strange note makes the trumpeter of the band lift an eyebrow. Dizzy is surprised for the first time that day. He puts the trumpet to his lips and blows a wet blur—

"'Hee ha ha!' laughs Charley Parker bending down to slap his ankle. He puts his alto to his mouth and says 'Didn't I tell you?'—with jazz of notes. . . . Talking eloquent like great poets of foreign languages singing in foreign countries with lyres by seas, and no one understands because the language isn't alive in the land yet." Perhaps the foreignness of these black artists reminded him of his own.

For Jack, their bebop language was one he would need time to absorb and make his. From Charlie Parker's dazzling saxophone cadenzas, his ear picked up a new kind of sentence, a surge of digression and variation spinning off the original subject and taken all the way to the end of breath— the kind of sentence he would be writing in eight years' time.

"Well, mind is bebop," Allen Ginsberg would later explain to an interviewer. "There was always a correlation between bop rhythm and speech. Between the note movement, the note flow, which was what Kerouac picked up on." Allen believed that in the "varying rhythms" of Parker and Monk Jack had found "a simulacrum of his own speech, which he had a really perfect ear for."

On one of Newman's historic recordings, there is a Dizzy Gillespie rendition of a standard tune that Newman retitled "Kerouac," so that he wouldn't have to pay a copyright fee. Dizzy didn't know the white kid who was Jerry's friend, but liked the way the strange name sounded.

Every weekend, Jack would leave Edie to her own devices and visit his parents in Ozone Park. He would pack up his notebooks and disappear into the subway and moodily return a few days later with his toothbrush in his pocket. It wasn't long before his parents began to suspect that he and Edie were living in sin, though as yet they had no real proof.

One night in late October Jack took a chance and brought Edie home with him. To his amazement, all seemed to go well. Like double-dating couples, they went out for beers and walked back on Crossbay Boulevard arm in arm. But Edie got worried when Jack told her that once they got married they would move in with his folks. She tried to think of Leo as sort of cute, but found him pompous—a paterfamilias who didn't want women to have opinions and was always ready to pick a fight with his son. She noticed Gabe's immaculate housekeeping—intimidating for a young prospective bride. And then there were the parents' Canuck accents, that ugly worn furniture, the class differences Edie didn't think about when she was alone with Jack, except when she was mad at him. She had a secret aversion to poor people.

Jack had a grudge against the rich passed down by Leo. For him the difference between his class status and Edie's was epitomized by the fact that Mrs. Parker owned a chain of shoe stores while his mother still had to work in shoe factories. In January, he had one of his worst fights with Edie after she showed him a letter from her mother, begging her daughter to break up with Jack and come home to Grosse Pointe, because Jack could never give her the wealth and social position her happiness depended on.

That month, he wrote about Edie scathingly in his journal, saying how much he despised her for pampering him, for responding to all his whims, for even offering to go to work after they were married to support him so that he could write. By treating him like a king, she turned herself into his "inferior." He blamed Edie for bringing out the worst parts of his character—laziness, cruelty, and egocentrism—by overprotecting him the way his mother did. When he looked at himself honestly, in fact, he had to wonder whether he was only feigning masculinity, for the truth was that for his entire life he had depended upon women, and if not upon them, upon certain close male friends who possessed what he called "a feminine kindness" and were willing to believe in his promise and talent and thus be taken in by him. (He must have been thinking guiltily of Sammy.) In his black mood, Jack accused himself of using the excuse that he was an artist to con those around him as a way of evading any kind of responsibility. In other words, he was a "neurotic" whose most negative characteristics attracted others—people who he secretly felt were very colorless and uninteresting compared to him—the way "flypaper attracted flies." The only way to justify his existence, he concluded, was to pursue his art with such devotion that it could not be considered his alibi for his sins.

On a couple of short trips Jack took Edie to Lowell, introducing her to G.J. and other old friends as his fiancée. He even fantasized to Edie about returning there with her to live, pointing out a cottage that would be just right for them. Accustomed to the bright lights of Manhattan, Edie thought Lowell was the darkest place she had ever seen. Although she managed to enjoy herself partying there, the Lowellites did not know what to make of the rich girl with peroxided hair who laughed too much and drank too much, cursed like a man, and had no shame about openly living in sin. Even that "whoremaster" of former times, G.J., who was having an affair with a divorcée himself, was disapproving. At the end of one long night of drinking, G.J. had to rescue Edie when she passed out and slid under a car parked on the ice behind a barroom. In the eyes of Jack's old crowd, including John MacDonald, whose opinion was still very important to him, Edie Parker was the kind of girl you might sleep with, but you wouldn't marry her.

In Lowell the double standard remained as unchanged as the Moody Street Bridge or the redbrick and neon of Kearney Square. Yet Jack felt like a ghost whose earthly presence had been erased on those trips back to his old town. So many from his generation had been swallowed up by the war, yet the familiar streets were more crowded than he had ever seen them. Like Hartford, Lowell was experiencing a boom. Thousands of newcomers were making munitions and sewing uniforms in the old cotton mills, filling the Royal Theater on Saturday nights, drinking coffee in the cafeteria where he used to meet Sebastian after his sessions at the library. It all left Jack with a bewildered sense of loss, of a "strange near-grief," a sense of what John Clellon Holmes, another young writer who had been marked by the war, would later call "a broken circuit."

To experience discontinuity, however, Jack did not have to travel all the way to Lowell. All he had to do was take the subway from Morningside Heights to Ozone Park. In his parents' crowded rooms, where all the old households of his childhood seemed preserved in amber, the talk went round and round on maddening, well-worn tracks—the evil forces that made it impossible for Leo to earn a good living, Gerard's saintly perfection, Jack's increasing failure to make his parents proud—until all he could think of was wanting to escape as he despaired of ever making up for his shortcomings. Sometimes he thought he actually was schizoid because when he was with his parents in Ozone Park, he could scarcely remember his life on 118th Street.

———

From undisclosed locations on the Italian front, where he was working with a unit that evacuated the wounded, Sebastian kept sending melancholy V-mails—messages that may have contributed to Jack's feelings of worthlessness, reminding him that despite the vow he'd taken at sea, he had made no further contributions to what his generation was sacrificing to the war. Sammy had been under fire and had taken care of dying men. As unsuited to military service as Jack was, deprived of books and intellectual companionship and haunted by a premonition that he would die with his promise unfulfilled, Sammy had found a kind of brave self-sufficiency in a world that seemed leached of all its beauty. In the midst of battle, he had managed to write poems that were being published in *Stars and Stripes,* and he had not lost his belief in the power of love. Now he even had kind words to say about G.J. All through their relationship, Sammy had been Jack's moral compass. Perhaps that was why it often took Jack a long time to write back to him, and when he did, he evidently said little about his embarrassingly soft life with Edie Parker.

In late February 1944, from a hospital bed in North Africa, Sebastian Sampas sent Jack his final message of love—a recording of his own barely audible voice beginning to recite Shelley's elegy: "I weep for Adonais—he is dead!" Then the poem broke off, followed by a series of farewells that poignantly faded away. Sebastian had been wounded during the invasion of Anzio, where he had been under constant fire. On March 2, he died.

Two weeks later, just as he had done after Billy Chandler's death, Jack wrote a letter addressed to Sammy. He began it in English, reminding Sammy of their song, "I'll See You Again," and plaintively asking him where that would be. But English must have seemed inadequate, for he kept lapsing into the French that was his most intimate language. Only in French was he able to express the feeling for Sammy he had never given a name to before. In another lost time, they had been two youths together—"*ensemble,*" a word Jack now called *"ce grand mot d'amour."* As if he suddenly felt he'd revealed too much, he ended the letter in hard-boiled English, swearing that he would never forgive Sammy for making him "a damned sentimentalist."

Sammy's death was so painful that Jack did not record it in the diary he was keeping at the time, an omission that shocked him years later when he reread the entries for the spring of 1944. In April, still dealing with his shock and grief, Jack gave up his Columbia Pictures job, kissed Edie good-bye, and headed south to New Orleans—the destination he had been fantasizing about for a long time. En route, he made a pilgrimage to Asheville, North Carolina, where by chance he met Thomas Wolfe's brother. Jack later remembered little about this trip, which suggests that he may have been drinking heavily all through it. In his diary, he noted only that he had his fill of the Southland. His real need was to find some deep level of companionship to replace what he had lost. Soon after his return to New York a few weeks later, he would start to fill the void inside him with new relationships.

PART FIVE

THE LIBERTINE CIRCLE

THE SEASON OF LUCIEN

In the fall of 1943, a newly arrived student from St. Louis named Lucien Carr had begun to attract a good deal of attention on the Columbia campus. A faun of a youth with a slender frame, tousled blond hair, and mischievous, slanting green eyes, Lucien was both blessed and cursed with extraordinary good looks. In a sea of necktied male students, soberly dressed in business suits and sports jackets, as was the custom of the day, Lucien, a sworn enemy of "MBC" (modern bourgeois culture), strolled sockless in dirty khaki pants and torn white shirts, provocatively disheveled. Expelled from Andover and three other top schools, with an unfinished year at the University of Chicago, he was dazzlingly well read, already under the influence of Yeats, Baudelaire, and Rimbaud, and took particular interest in questioning the social value of art. The "sole imperative" of the artist was self-expression and ego-satisfaction, argued Lucien, who derived many of his ideas from reading Nietzsche and was ready to stick a pin into any accepted value. His verbal brilliance impressed professors and led admirers to believe he might well become "another Rimbaud." At nineteen, he looked the part of *poète maudit*. "Who *is* that marvelous boy?" asked a French professor who happened to catch a glimpse of him listening to Brahms in a booth at the music library.

While Jack was in New Orleans, Lucien had appeared in a nighttime painting class Edie Parker was taking. At her first sight of him, she became "spellbound" as she watched him move through the room like "mercury over rocks" pausing at each easel and laconically commenting, "Great." When he came to hers, Lucien stood in enigmatic silence, sizing Edie up before offering her the cigarette that started their friendship. Soon he introduced her to his girlfriend, a Barnard student named Celine Young, who was almost as striking as he was with her long curly blond hair, blue eyes, and chiseled features. To Edie, they seemed the personification of "energy and fun," with the devil-may-care roaring twenties gaiety she admired, which sometimes took the form of bizarre pranks. One night Lucien took Edie, Celine, and John Kingsland, a sixteen-year-old aesthete from Brooklyn, to the ballet. There, after helping himself to someone's cape, Lucien used Celine's eyebrow pencil to make himself look like the Phantom of the Opera. The four of them crashed a party backstage where everyone was speaking Russian and drinking champagne, after which they exited the theater with a stolen vacuum cleaner, which they ceremoniously presented to Joan.

By the time Jack returned from New Orleans in late April, Lucien had gotten into the habit of dropping in on Edie and Joan to take showers or raid the refrigerator as well as to hide out from someone he said was pursuing him. Once he arrived via an open window, having climbed up the fire escape. Jack thought Lucien sounded like "a mischievous little prick," but when he met him one night in the West End, he too fell under his spell. They immediately engaged in the kind of intellectual sparring Jack had been starved for, and after the two of them had nearly drunk each other under the table, Lucien rolled Jack home in a beer barrel he found on Broadway.

Lucien Carr was one of Jack's "great, mad" people, an extrovert with an incandescent and dangerous wildness in him that went beyond the Rabelaisian buffoonery of G. J. Apostolos. Although he at first found Lucien brilliant but cold, Jack soon saw a beauty in him that was spiritual as well as physical. He later described him in *Vanity of Duluoz* as a golden-haloed "Shakespeare reborn almost." They quickly became inseparable, with Jack following wherever Lucien led. One night in the midst of a rainstorm the two of them sat in a puddle on Broadway pouring ink over each other's heads as they belted out folk songs.

One song Lucien often sang was "Violate me / In violent times / The vilest way that you know." Like Rimbaud, he had a Verlaine—an infatuated thirty-three-year-old man with red hair and a flowing beard, who, according to Jack, looked like the poet Swinburne. This obsessed individual, who had fallen in love with Lucien when he was eleven, showed up one night in the West End and acted unsettlingly possessive. David Kammerer had been Lucien's scoutmaster and had made a good impression upon Lucien's divorced and apparently clueless mother. He was from a socially prominent local family and had gone to Harvard, and was teaching physical education at the University of St. Louis. Mrs. Carr had been quite willing to let Kammerer become the man in her son's life and had even allowed Kammerer to take him to Mexico. There, fourteen-year-old Lucien had been forced to fend off his advances. Over the next few years, he had followed Lucien to his four prep schools, taking menial jobs in order to remain near him. When Kammerer pursued him to the University of Chicago, Lucien had tried to commit suicide. Now he had turned up in New York and found a dishwashing job in the Lion's Den right on the Columbia campus. In his small Greenwich Village apartment, the words "LU DAVE" were carved into the plaster wall above his bed.

Despite Lucien's aura of jaded worldliness, he had no idea how to cope with Dave Kammerer. Since he couldn't get rid of him, he introduced him to all his new Columbia acquaintances, treating him half like a friend, half like a slave to be ordered around with open contempt. No amount of humiliation seemed to discourage Kammerer, who was endlessly, masochistically ready to do Lucien's bidding. In a perverse way, Lucien was attached to him, deriving a sense of power from the awareness of his own fatal charm. Kammerer had, to an extent, created him, developed him intellectually, taught him how to be decadent in the manner of the French symbolists, sparked the rage that made him flamboyantly act out. At first Jack regarded Lucien's attempts to evade Kammerer whenever possible as "just a lot of fun." He rather liked Kammerer and could almost understand the way he felt about Lucien. He noticed that he too was somewhat obsessed with Lucien and often found himself wondering what he was up to and going in search of him. It had been different with Sebastian; there, Jack had been the one pursued.

One of Lucien's most passionate admirers was a nearsighted, gawky-looking scholarship student from Paterson, New Jersey, named Allen Ginsberg. Allen had met Lucien that winter shortly after Columbia had transferred him to a dorm room at Union Theological Seminary. One night not long before Christmas, hearing strains of an unfamiliar Brahms trio emanating from a room at the end of the corridor, Allen had shyly knocked. The two of them felt an immediate rapport.

On the surface, the two boys had little in common. At seventeen, intensely uncomfortable inside his own skin, shaken by homosexual desires he admitted only to his diary, Allen lacked the assurance and magnetism that later made him a compelling public figure. The son of Louis Ginsberg, a poet who taught in the Paterson public schools and whose rhyming, conventional poems regularly appeared in the *New York Times*, Allen was planning to study law and dedicate his life to the workers of America. (During his childhood, his mother, Naomi, had often taken him to meetings of the Communist Party.) Lucien discovered that Allen had also been been writing poetry—awkward attempts at rhymed quatrains inspired by A. E. Housman and Shakespeare.

Refusing to take Allen's ambition to become another Eugene Debs very seriously, Lucien sensed he had more interesting possibilities, more in line with his own predilections, and lent him his copy of *A Season in Hell*. Rimbaud had an electrifying effect upon Allen. He quickly embraced Rimbaud's dictum that a poet became a seer through "the derangement of all the senses," through experiencing "all shapes of love, suffering, madness," including criminality. Having barely survived a childhood decimated by his mother's mental illness, Allen knew a great deal about suffering and madness. Generous and compassionate, he saw the writing of a poem as a way of reaching "the hearts of others," as he told Lucien in one of their late-night discussions. Although dazzled by Lucien's brilliance, he couldn't swallow the idea that a poem was only an assertion of ego. "The artist may be a free spirit; artistry may be moral. Everybody's satisfied (and he wept a big tear . . .)," Allen wrote in his journal, where more and more of his entries had to do with his tormented need to be loved by Lucien Carr.

Amused by Allen's naïveté and his lack of experience with alcohol and women, Lucien considered him unusual enough intellectually to introduce him to the most brilliant man he knew, a Harvard classmate of Kammerer's named William Seward Burroughs, whose grandfather had invented the Burroughs adding machine. Burroughs, who like Lucien and Kammerer had grown up in St. Louis, had also recently moved to New York and was now living in the Village on a small remittance from his family plus a part-time job as a bartender. He was a tall, prematurely ageless man of thirty, who peered at the world through steel-rimmed glasses with an air of mysterious detachment. Everything about Burroughs was thin and precise—from his colorless hair to the straight line of his lips. What Allen responded to immediately was the dry, witty way he used language. Describing a lesbian named Louise, who lived in Kammerer's building, Burroughs called her "straightforward, manly and reliable." Bored by Lucien's account of a fight, Burroughs cut in with an apt quote from Shakespeare's *Troilus and Cressida*—" 'Tis too starved an argument for my sword"—that made Allen wonder who this "intelligent aristocrat" was.

In May, when he met Jack, Allen, desperately hoping to make a good impression, would resort to quoting Shakespeare himself. Lucien had given Allen the address of his new friend Kerouac, whom he described as a kind of Jack London, and told him to just drop by there. When Allen did so late one morning, he found a dark-haired young man, as striking in his own macho, working-class way as Lucien, sitting at a table in his undershirt, waiting to consume a breakfast of bacon and eggs that his blond girlfriend was cooking for him. After being temporarily at a loss when this "sensitive and intelligent" "big jock" offered him a beer he had no desire to drink at that hour, Allen refused it with the line "Discretion is the better part of valor." "Aww, where's my food?" Jack bawled at Edie, not taken at all with this foolish, skinny, big-eared Jewish kid whose devouring black eyes had an overly intense look and who spoke in a low, deep voice he hadn't yet grown into. Allen instantly reminded Jack of Sammy—another "Mediterranean type." Perhaps that—and Allen's intensity—initially made him uncomfortable. When Allen told him he intended to become a labor lawyer, Jack gruffly made the point that Allen obviously knew nothing about working in factories. "Go be a poet—you're too sensitive."

Their relationship didn't really blossom into friendship until the end of the month when they ran into each other in the neighborhood and Jack accompanied Allen to his room at Union Theological Seminary. Allen had to move out, and Jack helped him carry some boxes down the stairs. "We were talking," Allen later remembered, "about the phantomlike, ghostly nature of moving from place to place and saying farewell to old apartments and rooms," something both of them had experienced all too often during their painful childhoods. As they descended the seven flights, Allen began saying good-bye to each step of the building where he had fallen in love with Lucien, and Jack said, "Ah I do that, too, when I say goodbye to a place." As Allen later remembered that crucial exchange, "I suddenly realized that my own soul and his were akin, and that if I actually confessed the secret tendernesses of my soul he would understand nakedly who I was. And it was like I was already inside his body."

Allen regarded that epiphany as the beginning of what truly made him a poet, because he had suddenly come "into an area of intimate feelings that I wanted to begin articulating outwardly to communicate with him." He would futilely attempt to transfer the erotic feelings he had for both Jack and Lucien to his worship of Rimbaud.

Just before meeting Allen, Jack had also become acquainted with Burroughs, who came over one day, accompanied by Kammerer, ostensibly to ask Jack how to get papers to ship out, but really, as Jack later wrote, to make his own appraisal of this rough-trade Canuck merchant seaman Lucien had described to him. Soon afterward, Burroughs invited Jack to his apartment in the Village for a memorable lunch with Lucien and Kammerer. As they waited for Burroughs to emerge from the kitchen, Lucien bit off shards of his beer glass, with Kammerer following suit. Then Burroughs appeared bearing a tray of lightbulbs and razor blades, which he said were "delicacies" sent by his mother.

When Burroughs moved uptown in early summer to a friend's apartment on Riverside Drive, Jack and Allen decided to "pay him a formal visit" for the purpose of "examin[ing] his soul," because, as Allen put it, he seemed like some sort of "international spiritual man of distinction to us." Burroughs had a fascinating collection of books that he offered to lend his two younger visitors, including Spengler's *Decline of the West*, Korzybski's *Science and Sanity*, and Yeats's *A Vision*, as well as Cocteau's *Opium* and the works of Hart Crane, Kafka, Rimbaud, William Blake, and Louis-Ferdinand Céline. According to Allen, the first long conversation he and Jack had with Burroughs was probably about Korzybski's idea that words were not identical with "the things they represented."

Burroughs had actually studied with Korzybski in Chicago (during a period when he was working as a bedbug exterminator) and he remained deeply interested in general semantics. Another of his interests, Burroughs told them, was psychoanalysis, which had evolved into the study of "original mind . . . preconceptual primordial mind." In the late thirties, he had studied medicine in Vienna and had helped a Jewish refugee escape to America by marrying her. He must have seemed to Jack infinitely worldly wise—a fabulous individual who possessed an "evil" Faustian intelligence that Jack found riveting, even though it made him uneasy. There was still—and always would be—a lot of Lowell in his divided, skeptical soul. At the same time, he was ready to embrace all these extraordinary new players who, one by one, had stepped into his "future life," setting it in motion again just when he needed to escape from the shadow cast by Sebastian's death. That spring, he immersed himself in his new friendships as if he were resuming the late adolescence that had been interrupted by the war. Once again he was part of a gang, and this wild and brilliant New York one, which Allen called a "libertine circle," suited him to a T.

In the center of the action was Lucien, involving all his admirers, male and female, in the ongoing melodrama of his unresolvable relationship with Kammerer. Lucien's supporting cast participated willingly in the game of misdirecting Kammerer to various places where he futilely waited for his golden-haired protégé to appear. Kammerer had always been a determined and resourceful stalker, but now he had to compete with several others for Lucien's love. To add to his frustration, he had easily been able to form a friendship with Allen, whose self-appointed mentor he had become, while Lucien was making himself more and more scarce.

Kammerer soon became jealous in all directions—of Allen and Jack; and especially of Lucien's romance with Celine Young ("flaming youth," Burroughs drily called the young lovers), which had an infuriating adolescent intensity, despite the fact that Lucien had not yet "gone all the way" with her. For all Lucien's knowing talk of women—he referred to Celine as his "bourgeois kitten"—he apparently had had little actual sexual experience with girls.

It wasn't long before the apartment Jack shared with Edie and Joan, with John Kingsland renting the third bedroom, turned into what later generations would call a "pad," where the door was always open and where the bodies of the various young Columbia intellectuals who had slept over could be found on the living room floor in the morning, surrounded by ashtrays, beer bottles, pillows, and books, with Celine and Lucien still occupying the couch where they had worn themselves out in heavy necking. (Finding the two of them entwined there fast asleep late one afternoon, Kammerer indignantly commented to Burroughs that Lucien looked unusually pale because that blond vampire from Barnard College was draining his blood.) The group began trying out different drugs, and on one occasion, Jack became violently ill from drinking his own attempt to approximate absinthe—Rimbaud's favorite beverage—by mixing wormwood with Coca-Cola.

The cleaning up of the apartment was presumably left to Edie and Joan. Edie didn't participate much in the "arguments about the way the world was and how it got that way," which she considered "a very inactive kind of fun." Nor could she keep up with the ambitious reading of the others, despite some tutelage offered by Allen. Still working on the Hoboken docks, she fell asleep over Dos Passos and never went on to T. S. Eliot or Proust. She had residual Grosse Pointe housekeeping standards and resented having to deal with the household mess. But this companionable chaos, where there were always interesting people to talk to and stay up with until dawn, had soon become Jack's preferred way to live. His mother would have been horrified had she seen him nonchalantly wash a cockroach out of a glass and pour himself a morning drink of milk. Joan, who, unlike Edie, was able to participate in the intellectual discussions as one of the boys, may have welcomed the distraction from her own lonely drama, for one of her lovers had gotten her pregnant. (According to Ted Morgan, William Burroughs's biographer, Joan had feigned a mental breakdown in order to trick her husband, Paul Adams, into requesting an emergency leave from the army and had then given him reason to believe the child was his.) As she faced the prospect of being tied down by motherhood, Joan made a bitter observation about freedom: To her, the whole idea now seemed "truncated"—"an unintended caricature of human relations."

The freedom of the individual was one of the hotly debated issues that kept everyone up talking until their nihilistic brilliance ran out with the last of the cigarettes and the early morning clank of milk bottles just outside the door. Lucien's latest thoughts were often the focus of attention. After reading André Gide's *The Counterfeiters,* he had become fascinated by the notion of the gratuitous act, the idea that one could do something—even commit a crime—so arbitrary it could not be judged. He was also developing his earlier thinking about the role of the artist into what he called his "New Vision"—a conception of the artist as a transformative being with the potential to bring about "the ultimate artistic society." Lucien believed he had progressed beyond Nietzsche by envisioning a "post-human, post-intellectual," even, as Jack put it in a letter to Allen that fall, "a post-soul." Right now, as Lucien airily put it, they were merely in the "pre-ultimate" period, with nonartist leaders like Roosevelt and Churchill "work[ing] out the gory details of progress."

Although Jack thought Lucien had gone too far in rejecting his "humankindness," the New Vision may have reminded him of Sebastian's belief that it was up to Western intellectuals "to actualize the fullest possibilities of the All-Soul." But where Sebastian had despaired of the role of the artist in the future and seen him replaced by "primitive man," the New Vision restored the artist to primacy. As he struggled with his guilt about his "selfish" refusal to play a traditional male role, Jack was beginning to formulate an idea he would call "self-ultimacy"—a justification of the artist's egoism, whatever the cost, and of the absolute necessity for the artist to seek out the widest possible range of human experience. Meanwhile, experience—in an extreme form—was about to descend upon him and the "libertine circle" with a vengeance.

The new Tin Pan Alley hit "You Always Hurt the One You Love" was the song everyone would later associate with the summer of 1944. By then, Kammerer's need for exclusive possession of Lucien Carr had grown to proportions that could not be contained by the stratagems that had fended him off so far. Nor could Kammerer be neutralized by being treated like a friend. "Why is the perfect lover always jealous?" Allen wondered in his journal on July 28. "He sees his own love in everybody's eyes." Even Burroughs had begun to feel concerned about the situation and attempted to convince Kammerer to leave town, although it was his usual policy to watch with scientific detachment as the madness of those around him ran its course.

One afternoon Burroughs accompanied Kammerer when he insisted on going over to 118th Street to see if Lucien was there. When they let themselves into the apartment, no one was home but the cat Jack and Edie had added to the household. Kammerer caught Kitkat and, making a noose of Burroughs's necktie, attempted to hang him from a lamp. The cat was rescued by Burroughs (although one may wonder why he'd provided Kammerer with his necktie in the first place). When Jack learned about this incident from Bill, Jack felt like killing Kammerer, although up to this point, he had felt some sympathy for his misery. Cats were sacred to Jack—connected to his feelings about his mother and Gerard.

By the end of July, Allen was suffering intensely from his own unspoken longing for Lucien's love, yet he felt that if others knew the kind of love he craved, "I should have to commit suicide." (Although Allen always maintained that he did not lose his virginity until the following year, there are cryptic indications in his early journals, which were not published until 2006, after Lucien's death, that he may have had a few tentative sexual encounters with both Lucien and Kammerer.) In 1966, careful not to name Lucien, whose heterosexual reputation he had sworn to protect, he told an interviewer: "There was a kid I was in love with at Columbia, who even tried overtly to bring me out of my shell, seduce me. It was somebody I was really in love with and still am, a real deep, passionate, desirous adoration, but I was too locked in on myself to admit to and respond to him. He took me to his room and took off all his clothes and said, 'Get in *bed*,' and I sat there like a frightened creep."

Trying to look at Lucien with stern objectivity that summer, perhaps in the hope of loosening Lucien's hold on his feelings, Allen set himself the task of writing an "Essay in Character Analysis," in which he portrayed the sworn enemy of modern bourgeois culture as a pathetically "sterile" impostor whose "pathogenic dread of non-self-recognition and non-social recognition drives him to red shirts, wild songs, drink, women, queer shoes, loud talk, arrogance, infantilism on a high intellectual level." Allen avoided the subject of Lucien's ambiguous sexuality. Even so, some of his observations were devastating in their accuracy: "Unfortunately he has enough talent in him to encourage his hopes. Unfortunately, he has too little talent for him to realize himself in some artistic creation." Already possessing the rigor of a true artist, Allen had not been too infatuated to notice how Lucien used the excuse of perfectionism to avoid doing any actual creative work. (Blocked, even when he'd needed to write a story for freshman English, Lucien had borrowed one from Jack and gotten an A.)

Lucien had recently confided to Allen his growing desire to flee the Columbia scene, where the unbearable demands of others were preventing him from communing with his own soul. To Jack, however, Lucien appealed more directly: He had to find some means of putting distance between himself and Kammerer—perhaps running away to sea was the answer. In July, the two of them came up with a secret plan to ship out together as soon as possible on a vessel bound for the Second Front in France, where they would outdo Hemingway in a grand adventure, envisioned by Lucien, that would depend very much on Jack's fluency in French and Lucien's impersonation of a deaf mute. After jumping ship, the two of them would hitchhike to Paris, disguised as peasants (like the escaping war prisoners in the film classic *Grand Illusion*), arriving there in time for the imminent liberation of the city. Although Jack should have known better at the age of twenty-three, the prospect of this potentially fatal escapade was irresistible. They secretly went down to the National Maritime Union to begin the process of getting Lucien his seaman's papers.

It wasn't long before Kammerer found out what they were up to and joined the merchant marine himself, distraught at the thought that Lucien was planning to go off with Jack and leave him behind. On the night of August 11, he climbed up the fire escape of Warren Hall, the off-campus residence hotel both Allen and Lucien had moved into, and slipped into Lucien's room. After watching Lucien sleep for half an hour, without touching him, he left by the stairs and was stopped by a night clerk who called the police. Roused from his bed, Lucien had to vouch for Kammerer, supporting his claim that the two of them had been drinking together. To tell the police the truth, which would have raised mortifying questions about his own sexuality, was unthinkable.

On August 12, too frightened to sleep in his room, Lucien took refuge on the living room couch at 118th Street, where, as proof of his manhood, he had intercourse with Celine for the first time, telling her, according to Allen's journal, that her sexual satisfaction was more important than his. In the morning he and Celine were congratulated by Edie and Jack, but apparently the experience had been far less earthshaking than Celine had hoped; while Lucien was asleep, she had climbed into bed with John Kingsland, with whom she had started necking. All of this the bewildered Kingsland would shortly confide to Allen, swearing him to secrecy. But it was a secret Allen would keep only until he ran into Lucien at the West End bar on the night of August 13.

That evening Lucien had been looking for Allen and had gone to his room in Warren Hall. Noticing the journal lying on Allen's desk, he couldn't resist opening it, and there he had read the "Essay in Character Analysis" that portrayed him as a poseur who would never be a true artist. "I shed tears all over your book," Lucien told Allen sarcastically, allowing that the sketch had been "competent" enough to make him sweat "like a bitch." As if he had not inflicted sufficient pain upon the object of his unrequited love, Allen then proceeded to tell Lucien what he'd heard from Kingsland, sparing him none of the graphic details. Whatever was going on inside him, Lucien reacted only by informing Allen that he had finally "copulated" with Celine. "My face lit up," Allen claimed afterward in his journal. It could have been an episode from *The Counterfeiters*. There too the characters concealed the truth of their feelings about each other and a journal played a role in the unfolding of events.

Earlier that day, ironically, Lucien and Jack had almost succeeded in pulling off their escape to France. When they'd checked in at the National Maritime Union, they couldn't believe their luck when they found two openings on a Liberty ship about to sail for the Second Front on Sunday, August 14. They headed back to Morningside Heights to say good-bye to Celine and Edie and do some hasty packing, bumping into Kammerer only a block from the union hall, for he was bound there himself. He had an uncanny way of materializing wherever Lucien went, as if an invisible wire connected them.

Unfortunately, no one at the union hall had warned Jack and Lucien that they would be working under a chief mate who was believed to be a fascist and whose behavior to the crew had just caused a walkout. They learned this from the bosun after they boarded the ship that afternoon in Brooklyn, blithely singing sea chanteys. In fact, the bosun advised them not to sign on for the voyage. Reluctant to change their plans, they'd hung around and helped themselves to some roast beef sandwiches and milk from the refrigerator in the galley and were goofily enjoying themselves when the enraged mate, a big redheaded man who looked like Kammerer, caught them eating, accused them of stealing, and ordered them ashore. And that was that.

Kammerer had spent the rest of the day looking for Lucien. After accidentally running into Jack, who unthinkingly told him where Lucien could be found, he turned up in the West End around midnight just as Lucien started to angrily question John Kingsland about Celine, ignoring Allen's efforts to pull him away. Kammerer was in a particularly black mood. Sitting down with the three extremely tense youths, he kept kicking Allen under the table until Allen threatened to retaliate. Then Kammerer walked over to the bar, where Lucien had gone to get away from him. It looked to Allen as if they were having a bitter argument, but he lost track of them as he sat consoling Kingsland, who now blamed himself for trying to seduce Lucien's girl. Around one-thirty, Allen looked up and noticed that Kammerer and Lucien had vanished. He never saw Kammerer again.

Riverside Drive had an area down by the river where few people ventured in those days—a narrow, sparsely planted strip of grass separated from the rest of the park by the West Side Highway. That was where Lucien ended up with Kammerer after they left the bar, which was strange, since he had avoided being alone with Kammerer for weeks. It was a secluded place where two men might go to make love. They took a bottle along with them. No one ever knew exactly what happened there, especially what went on in Lucien's mind—not definitively. He was an unmasked Rimbaud who couldn't write poems, a nineteen-year-old with a lot of rage and hurt and alcohol in him who had found out too many things about himself in one day and had reasons to doubt his manhood. Quite possibly Lucien had been impotent with Celine, judging by his remark to her. But in Kammerer's eyes he was still a god.

Perhaps Lucien had never hated Kammerer more; perhaps he had never felt closer to yielding to him. Or perhaps what happened between them came close to the way Allen conceived it four months later, when he wrote a scene in his journal in which Kammerer takes Lucien's Boy Scout knife out of his pocket and hands it to him with the words "Choose to love me or to kill me," and Lucien raises it, feeling "the conflicting ecstasies of fear and desire, revulsion and attraction, hatred and love."

At dawn on August 14, Lucien woke Jack up by shaking his arm and whispering, "Well, I disposed of the old man." Edie woke up too but wasn't told what was going on. Lucien looked so awful she thought he had broken up with Celine, and later recalled hearing him say, "I disposed of the old lady."

Kammerer's heavy, bloody body was in the Hudson River, where Lucien had rolled and dragged it, tied up with shoelaces and strips torn from his white shirt, and weighed down with rocks stuffed into Kammerer's pockets. (It was drifting toward West Seventy-ninth Street, where it would surface in a couple of days.) Still carrying Kammerer's glasses, Lucien took them out and put them down on a table along with the Boy Scout knife with which he had stabbed Dave twice in the chest. He felt too dazed to get rid of those incriminating objects without Jack's help.

To Jack, Kammerer's death—which immediately seemed a fated outcome—was no surprise, but he still couldn't get his mind around Lucien's act and kept asking Lucien why he'd had to do it. Years later, in *Vanity of Duluoz*, still fictionalizing the killing the third and last time he wrote about it, he would obliquely express the full extent of the horror he'd felt by having Claude de Maubris stab Franz Mueller a dozen times. Kammerer had asked for it, according to Lucien. He had tried to force himself on Lucien, sworn he couldn't live without him, and threatened to kill himself, taking Lucien along with him. Lucien started to cry as he remembered his dying words: "So this is how Dave Kammerer ends." Only that made him tearful.

Without a thought of telling Lucien he didn't want to be involved, Jack got dressed and they left the house. They buried the glasses in Morningside Park; on 125th Street, Lucien, at Jack's suggestion, dropped his Scout knife down a subway grate, after which they had a beer. They spent an odd day together, playing hooky from the dire consequences of what had happened—a kind of dreamy schoolboys' holiday, despite Lucien's terror of being sent to the electric chair. First they stopped off at the office of Lucien's psychiatrist, where Lucien made a confession and borrowed five dollars. Then they went to see the movie *Four Feathers* on Forty-second Street and strolled uptown to the Museum of Modern Art, where Lucien took a farewell look at his favorite Modigliani—a portrait of Jean Cocteau. After wandering back to Forty-second Street for hot dogs, they rode downtown to make one last appearance together at the National Maritime Union. By then, it seemed time for Lucien to talk to his mother about getting a lawyer. (Burroughs, whom he had visited right after he had disposed of Kammerer's body, had advised him to plead self-defense, although he'd suspected the story was darker than that.) Just before saying "So long" to Jack, Lucien remembered that he was still wearing Kammerer's bloodstained leather vest, and dropped it in a gutter. As a criminal, he was a complete amateur.

It was only when Jack found himself standing alone in the street that the spell Lucien cast over him—even on that day—evaporated. As he wrote two years later, he had the leaden feeling that "everything was finished." In the middle of the following night, after a day in which he saw four movies with Edie, he was arrested by two detectives who ransacked the apartment and held him as a material witness. By then Lucien had turned himself in and confessed to killing David Kammerer as he fought off Kammerer's attempt to have sex with him.

The *Daily News* ran the front-page headline HONOR SLAYING. A striking photograph in the *Journal American* showed golden-haired Lucien clutching copies of *A Season in Hell* and W. B. Yeats's *A Vision* as he was led into the Tombs by the police. Soon Allen Ginsberg, who surprisingly showed no shyness in dealing with the media for the first time in his life, would be explaining to tabloid reporters the importance of the New Vision. During the pretrial hearings, Mark Van Doren and Lionel Trilling, the leading lights of Columbia's English department, would appear as character witnesses for Lucien, and the influence of literature upon the defendant would be brought up by the defense.

BIRTH OF A SYMBOLIST

With the shock of Kammerer's death, the libertine circle scattered like a flock of startled birds. Earlier in the summer, Joan Adams had returned to Loudonville to have her baby. Now Kingsland and Celine retreated from Morningside Heights to Brooklyn and Pelham, respectively, and the crowd of eager talkers who had sprawled on the floor of Joan and Edie's living room suddenly made themselves scarce.

Like Jack, Burroughs had been arrested as a material witness. He had flushed a piece of evidence down the toilet—a bloody pack of Kammerer's Lucky Strikes—after refusing a smoke Lucien offered him. His father came to New York to post a bond for his bail and took him back to St. Louis. Jack, however, spent nine long days in the Bronx House of Detention. When he'd asked Leo to put up one hundred dollars against a bail of five thousand for his release, Leo had adamantly refused to pay a dime. With the possibility that Lucien could be found guilty of first-degree murder, which would then make Jack an accessory after the fact, it was the worst trouble Jack had ever been in and a watershed in his relationship with his father.

Leo had always had his suspicions about Jack's friends and worried about their influence on his son. In the past he had felt free to read Jack's mail, hunting for signs of effeminacy even in G.J.'s letters. The one time Jack had brought Lucien to Ozone Park, Leo had pointedly refused to let the arrogant "young punk" pay for his own drinks—"I can buy a rich man's son a drink," he'd sneered. And then there was Jack's living arrangement with Edie, which offended Leo and Gabe so deeply that even Nin had gotten into the act, feeling it her sisterly duty to tell Jack how upset he'd made their parents and to warn him that living with a girl out of wedlock was not for "people like us." But now, with Jack's name in the papers, Leo was confronted with black-and-white proof of everything he'd most feared. Even after he calmed down and a certain amount of denial set in, he would never let Jack forget that he had utterly failed to be the good son he and Gabe deserved. A part of

Jack silently agreed with everything his father said about his closest friends.

As Lucien awaited judgment, Jack's future as well as the defendant's depended upon the ability of Lucien's lawyers to make the watertight argument, supported by witness after witness, that their young client did not have the slightest taint of homosexuality. All the tabloids seemed fixated on that question, as well as the mafiosi and members of Murder, Inc., who were Jack's fellow inmates up in the Bronx. They took a prurient interest in Lucien and felt no less entitled than the detectives to incessantly demand the lowdown on him. The detectives on the case had also asked Jack whether he was a "homo" himself. "Heterosexuality all the way," Lucien managed to mouth at him as they waited to be arraigned in a courtroom on Chambers Street on August 16.

Three days later, Jack was led into the basement morgue at Bellevue to identify Kammerer's nude, bloated body. It was a horrific sight. With his patriarchal red beard jutting straight up, he looked, Jack later recalled in *Vanity of Duluoz*, as if his "unimaginable spiritual torment" had caused his flesh to turn completely blue.

It was Edie Parker who came to Jack's rescue. She too had been brought in for questioning the night Jack was arrested. Proudly displaying her full bosom, Edie had retorted indignantly, "Are you nuts? Do I look like a boy to you?" when a detective asked her whether her boyfriend liked boys. Insinuating that the apartment on 118th Street was a "love nest" with ongoing orgies, they had then asked whether Jack was her pimp and whether Lucien had made her pregnant, while she continued to insist that Jack was her fiancé. All through her humiliating session with the police, Edie still had no idea what Lucien had done. In an answer to a question about Kammerer, she told them Kammerer was a "real pest" and that he had tried to kill Kitkat. Afraid that something awful had happened to Celine, she was relieved to find her alive and sipping iced tea when she got back to the apartment.

The two "widows" learned why their men had been been taken away from them and jailed only when they went out to a newsstand on Broadway late that night and saw the headline in the *Daily News*. Edie was immediately ready to use part of a recent inheritance from her grandfather to bail Jack out, but his will was still being probated in Detroit.

Celine advised her to call her family lawyer and see what he could do to help.

Although she and Jack had recently gone for their blood tests and Jack had talked about getting married as soon as he came back from his next voyage, Edie felt a little daunted when she learned that the probate judge would agree to advance the money for Jack's bond only if she and Jack got married beforehand. "How in the world can I do that?" she asked her lawyer.

She needn't have worried. Under the circumstances, Jack readily agreed to marriage when Edie was allowed to see him for fifteen minutes the following day. Whatever reluctance he may have felt he kept to himself.

Since Edie's lawyer happened to know the judge who was handling his case, arrangements were quickly made for Jack to be let out of jail for a few hours on August 22 for the purpose of matrimony. Favorably impressed by Jack's connection to the Parkers, the judge reduced his charge to "material witness," knocked twenty-five hundred dollars off the bail, and referred to Jack at his arraignment as a "misguided seaman."

As he languished in his cell in the Bronx over the next few days, smoking the cigarettes Edie brought him, trying to kill time by reading Somerset Maugham's *Cakes and Ale*, which she had taken out of the library for him at Joan's suggestion, Edie went shopping. At Best's department store, she found the perfect outfit for "a jailhouse wedding"—a cream-colored top with a low neckline and flaring peplum to be worn over a black knee-length skirt—and, since she and Jack were down to their last twenty-six dollars, defiantly charged it to her grandmother, who took a dim view of her intended husband. But Edie also wrote Jack a series of letters that betrayed some of her anxiety about the step they were about to take. Feeling obligated certainly wasn't the ideal reason for him to marry her, and she was afraid he might regret it afterward, despite some beautiful things he'd said when she visited him. In one letter, she begged Jack to promise "to make my mind as you want."

Writing to him on the night of August 21 from Pelham, where she had taken refuge with Celine after giving up the apartment, Edie painted a romantic picture of the future they would have together—full of "mountain lodges and fireplaces." (She had been trying to calm herself by reading the novels of Rose Franklyn about "happy married people in Connecticut with no problems.") The following day, with Jack handcuffed to a detective, she stood with him before a judge, who had asked that the prisoner be kept confined during the ceremony.

After Jack kissed the bride, things lightened up. In the corridor outside the judge's chambers, Detective McKeon removed Jack's handcuffs and suggested they all go for a drink. He had his eye on Celine, who had come along as Edie's bridesmaid and witness, wearing a little embroidered veil from Best's that matched Edie's over her long blond hair. Since she was desperate to find a way to see Lucien, who was being kept incommunicado, McKeon persuaded Celine to meet him later at the Roosevelt Hotel, promising he could get her a pass.

As he toasted the newlyweds in a pub, McKeon reminded them that he had a gun "if you're thinking about any funny stuff" and coarsely alluded to the fact that Edie wasn't exactly a virgin. Then the wedding party went on to O'Henry's steak house, where Edie at last felt "in heaven . . . with my love almost out of jail and the beer and the food." But with Jack locked up in a cell until Edie was able to pay his bond the following day, she spent her wedding night in Pelham alone, trying to read Dos Passos.

They honeymooned in Ozone Park, since Jack had patched things up with his parents. Leo and Gabe were "surprised" he'd actually married Edie Parker, but understood why he'd had to do it and had come around to thinking of him as an innocent victim of "decadent friendships." Or at least Gabe had. She was "tickled pink," as she told Edie, to have Jackie home with her again. Edie was not tickled pink—she was afraid of Leo and had dreaded running into him on her visits to Jack in jail.

For a week and a half, they all tried to be on their best behavior. To please Gabe, they went to Radio City Music Hall, to a Jean Gabin film Edie and Jack had already seen, and to a rathskeller on Forty-second Street, where the elder Kerouacs, louder than everyone in the room, boisterously sang along to the "Beer Barrel Polka." Gabe seemed insatiably curious about Edie, who knew not to protest when her new mother-in-law "looked in my closet and dresser drawers to see how I did things." Feeling that Jack's mother wanted any wife of Jack's to be "a mirror image of herself," Edie obliged by twisting her hair into a bun like Gabe's.

Leo, so drunk his nose looked as if it had caught fire, got through their ham and chicken wedding feast without blowing up at Jack and took them to the Belmont racetrack, where he apparently knew everyone who worked in the stables. At the Brass Rail Restaurant in Times Square, he asked Edie to dance, clutching her against his sweaty body. As soon as she could, she excused herself in a ladylike manner, though she was surprised to find him a far better dancer than his son. (In my own memory, Jack padded around a dance floor as if he were carrying a football.)

Nin came home for a weekend, on leave from the WAACs, to check out her new sister-in-law. "You married this big lug? Well good luck! Mom has spoiled him rotten." Through various sarcastic digs, Nin made it clear she had run out of patience with Jack's foolish ambitions. (Her attitude had changed a lot since the days when she'd looked up to her football hero brother.) Hearing Jack working at his typewriter in another room, she asked Edie, "Don't you wish that he was dedicated to a real job?" One morning Edie was present during a bitter argument between Nin and Gabe, who was demanding that Nin turn over her allotment check to her even though Nin needed it herself. Ever since she'd lost her savings in a bank collapse in Lowell, Jack's mother had been keeping the family's earnings in a blue teapot (apart from the emergency cash stashed in her corset). Gabe had gone to the teapot and doled out a little of Jack's money whenever he needed a few bucks of his own on his honeymoon, but Edie thought Jack should start holding on to the money he made so they would have it for their future rather giving it to Gabe. Jack got mad when Edie raised the issue. He would shrug impatiently when Gabe kissed him in front of Edie or ran her fingers through his hair, but no one could say a word to him about his mother.

If Edie was having some doubts about the marriage, Jack, now that the euphoria of being released from jail had worn off, was beginning to feel trapped. In a letter to Edie's mother, written on September 1, he tried to sound positive, but the best he could do was to say that although circumstances had "catapulted" them into a "badly timed union . . . a bad beginning might augur a successful ending." Perhaps he already had a speedy ending for himself in mind, because he was particularly anxious to work off his debt for the bail bond money, which had been advanced by Mrs.

Parker, as soon as possible. He said it weighed on him "like a scourge." Mrs. Parker wanted Edie to come home, since her younger daughter was leaving for college, and the plan was that Jack would go back to Grosse Pointe with his bride and they would both find well-paying jobs in defense factories. Despite his previous hatred of factory work, Jack vowed to Mrs. Parker that he was now willing to do anything. As if he felt an urgent need to put himself on some equal footing with his patrician mother-in-law, he described his father as a man of "conservative Republican New England vintage" and suggested that morally the two of them would have much in common.

By the time Jack and Edie left for Michigan on Labor Day, some open class warfare had broken out in Ozone Park. Snooping around in the young couple's bedroom, Leo had come upon a letter Edie was writing to Lucien, commiserating with him for being in jail with a bunch of bad-smelling poor people. Incensed by this, Leo had scrawled across it a nasty comment that Jack later quoted in *The Town and the City*: "You can always spray your nose with perfume, it will lessen your own odor!"

Jack lasted in Grosse Pointe just long enough to pay off his debt to Mrs. Parker from his earnings as a night watchman in the Fruehauf ball bearings factory. It was a job Edie's well-connected father had secured for him, which required him to do little more than show up, and left him plenty of time to write. The year before when Edie brought Jack home with her, her father had taken them out on his yacht on Lake St. Claire, introduced Jack to his mistress, and treated them to steak dinners. They'd gone to lavish house parties with yelling teenagers and an endless flow of beer. It was an America Jack had never seen—paradise in the affluent suburbs. But now that he was actually living there on the largesse of Edie's family, he felt like a fish out of water, even though Mrs. Parker had warmed to him and tried to engage him in conversations about the best-selling novelist Pearl Buck in order to demonstrate her sympathy for his literary aspirations.

Other Depression-raised writers—Cheever, Updike, Richard Yates—would find endless interest in the examination of suburban life; but Jack immediately wrote off Grosse Pointe as an inconceivable setting for "tragedy." "To me a home in the suburbs is a sort of isolated hell in which nothing happens," he would declare in a letter to Nin a few months later. Since the day he'd walked out of Columbia, he'd accumulated enough raw experience and been in enough deep trouble for three young men. Yet just when everyone expected him to settle down, he couldn't stand the whole idea of any safe and predictable life that wouldn't feed his fiction. An inability to tolerate the routine of a job or his marriage or any other kind of *ennui* was growing into more and more of a problem for him. By now, he had become hooked on the continuous "mad" action of his unrolling story, in whatever comic or tragic form it came. Like Peter Martin, the hero of the novel he was working on, which he now called *The Haunted Life* rather than *Galloway*, Jack was driven by the desire to be "everywhere at the same time."

Edie had been looking forward to the fun of showing off her brand-new husband. Instead Jack locked himself away from her to read Shakespeare in the bathroom and didn't respond when she spoke to him. He refused to put on the nice clothes she wanted him to wear and grudgingly escorted her to gatherings, unshaven, in the old leather jacket the cook on the *Dorchester* had given him. "Artist," he muttered when people asked him what he did, then clammed up. They had a few good times on her father's boat and in a bar Jack had discovered called the Rustic Cabin and even fantasized together about having a baby or running off to Montparnasse when the war was over. But without Jack's other friends around him, Edie wasn't enough for him and she knew it. Feeling a little desperate, she wrote to Allen and, swearing him to secrecy, asked for a list of books she should be reading—in return for which she promised not to reveal that he had climbed into bed with her one night while Jack was in jail and given her a lot of wet kisses she hadn't cared for. But then Edie discovered that Jack was sleeping with one of her Grosse Pointe girlfriends, and that was the last straw. When he told her he was going to leave and ship out again, she didn't attempt to persuade him to stay.

On September 15, Lucien Carr stood before a judge and pleaded guilty to first-degree manslaughter rather than face the uncertain outcome of a trial by jury. Ironically, he was sentenced to spend an indeterminate number of years at the New York State Reformatory in Elmira on the same day Paris was liberated, setting off the wild celebrations he and Jack had been hoping to participate in. The outcome of the case, however, had freed Jack of all charges against him for being Lucien's accessory.

As soon as he was back in New York, Jack sought out Allen, who had spent some intensely lonely weeks mourning the loss of Lucien and "wonderful, perverse Kammerer," twice drafting suicide notes in his journal. With Lucien gone—and being kept incommunicado—the relationship between Jack and Allen quickly deepened. Writing to Allen in September, Jack hailed him as a kindred spirit, seeking identity in the midst of "sprawling, nameless reality." The two of them were different from Lucien, Jack theorized, because Lucien hated his own "human-kindness."

The last they heard from Lucien for the next couple of years was a coded letter forwarded to Allen but addressed to *"Cher Breton,"* in which he wrote that he was undergoing some changes in prison that were leading him to wonder whether the power of the intellect was less important than the "spirit." His greatest regret, he told them, was his "betrayal" of "Bebe." Jack must have winced guiltily when he read that reference to Celine Young because he was in the grip of a feverish need to start a romance with her before sailing for Italy in mid-October on the SS *Robert Treat Paine.*

The night before the long voyage ahead of him, Jack, Allen, and a Columbia student named Grover Smith went drinking with Celine in the West End. As accustomed as she was to being a magnet for young men, as well as to charmingly deflecting their advances—Edie with some jealousy called her "a professional virgin"—Celine was unnerved by the intensity of Jack's sudden determination to sleep with her. "Why don't you actively help me seduce Celine?" Jack asked Allen in desperation as she turned her charms on two naval officers at the bar, who unfortunately decided she was being harassed by "queers." Although Jack hated fights and usually avoided them, he went out on the sidewalk with the two men to defend his honor. The officers overpowered him and were starting to bang his head against the asphalt, with Allen futilely trying to intervene, when Johnny, the West End bartender, broke up the fight and sent everyone home. Back in Allen's room in Warren Hall, Jack wept in Celine's arms as Allen tried to comfort him by reading him Shelley. When it appeared that Jack was about to have sex with Celine, Allen tiptoed out discreetly.

The following morning Jack boarded the *Paine*, where this time he had signed on as an able-bodied seaman, hoping to return in several months with a cleared mind and a couple of thousand dollars. The ship would be stopping in New Orleans on its way to Italy, but Jack made it only as far as Norfolk, Virginia. By then he had become convinced that the bosun, who persecuted him relentlessly and called him "baby face," intended to rape him. Unable to deal with the threatening situation, he jumped ship, took a bus back to New York—and was blacklisted by the NMU for the rest of the war, a disaster for his finances. Too ashamed to tell his parents what had happened or to write to Edie, who had not heard a word from him since he'd left Grosse Pointe, Jack took refuge with Allen in Warren Hall, sleeping on a mattress on Allen's floor. As far as Gabe and Leo knew, he was still bound for Italy.

Even at eighteen, Allen had a nurturing side to him. He had started taking care of his paranoid schizophrenic mother when he was only eleven, staying home from school to make sure she did no harm to herself and escorting her on harrowing journeys to mental hospitals. Now he took care of Jack, as he would often do in the years to come, making sure he had a place to stay, sharing bowls of soup with him at the West End, withdrawing the books Jack needed—the works of Nietzsche, Aldous Huxley, and Rimbaud—from the Columbia library. Perhaps it was the first time he realized Jack was fragile.

But Jack had counted on returning to Celine. On the night of October 26, he waited for her to join him in Flynn's, a gloomy Irish bar a few blocks away from the West End. Sitting there alone as it grew later and later, realizing she was not going to show up, Jack felt as if he were in *"l'enfer."* Reaching for a pen to fill the backs of a couple of menus with a frantic rush of words, he let his Frenchness overwhelm his English without stopping to translate the *joual* in his head into sentences that sounded American. His thoughts veered distractedly between his two languages, between pleas for love and beauty and cries for money, between self-flagellation and self-dramatizing adolescent grandiosity. He was a "weakling"—but, then, so was Rimbaud. He spent his life futilely waiting—but so had Pound and Milton. He was as penniless a poet as Edgar Allan Poe, but, like Thoreau, refused to make his living through work that wasn't "poetic." He thought about going to a movie to stave off the anguish of knowing he had been stood up, but then cried out to Celine to come and save him. For a while anyway.

Suddenly all this agony morphed into a novel Jack thought he could definitely write in three weeks' time—in which a "Self-Ultimatist" of great purity and talent would be driven mad by the "bourgeois caution" of a wealthy beauty. This cruel girl amuses herself briefly with her poet, then goes straight back to her empty conventional existence. Her victim, Michael Breton—fatally gauche as a lover (as gauche, perhaps, as Jack felt with Celine)—ruins his mind with alcohol and contemplates suicide. In the last scene, Jack planned to show him in a delirious state rummaging through a garbage can—a magnificent ending for a work that would surely make its author famous.

When a room became empty on the sixth floor of Warren Hall, Jack holed up there, possibly without the knowledge of the management, and immediately got down to work, writing by the light of a candle and isolating himself from everyone except Allen. In his new incarnation as a starving symbolist, Jack was reminded of his Saroyanesque months in Hartford, which he considered one of the most important periods in his development as a writer. Though he had not abandoned his "Joycean" *Galloway* novel, this "neo-Rimbaudean" one, *I Bid You Love Me*, took precedence. Deliberately cutting his hand one night with a penknife, he dipped his pen into the "blood of a poet" and wrote the word *Blood* on the title pages of both manuscripts. There was still enough of it to write a quotation from Nietzsche on a calling card—"Art is the highest task and proper metaphysical activity of this life"—which he tacked to his wall. By the end of the month, however, Jack started using his candle on a daily basis to burn what he had written. Giving up on the pursuit of worldly success, at least he could prove to himself that he was pursuing art for art's sake.

Forty pages of *I Bid You Love Me* survive. Jack gave up on it right after writing the scene in which the Self-Ultimatist slashes his hand (though there the poet does it by accident), since the whole melodramatic business was beginning to embarrass him. He now saw the absurdity of acting symbolically in order to be able to write about it, but for the moment the thought of returning to mere naturalism seemed like torture.

Only last summer, he had felt confident about his direction. When a girl had asked him what he was looking for in his writing, he had answered, "A new method!" Responding to Lucien's insistence that he must also seek a New Vision, Jack had answered that he already had a vision of his own. But now Lucien's influence seemed to overpower him as his search for a method continued.

He became excruciatingly self-critical during this period, believing that he could impregnate every sentence he wrote with "profundity" only through the slow process of rewriting. In a November workbook for *I Bid You Love Me,* he analyzed the effect of each phrase he used in a sentence about the effect of moonlight upon a red truck as it slowly moved out of, then back into, the darkness of the highway. He felt he had managed to write superb prose but wondered whether he could sustain it as the truck climbed an incline at the end of town. A few months later, he would find a term for what he'd been after in the composition of that sentence—"sense-thinking," which he felt was the essence of poetry, equivalent to the painter thinking with his eye or the musician thinking with his ear. Yet "sense-thinking" in the novel seemed hemmed in by rules Jack felt the writer could not ignore—from the immutable laws of English grammar to the need to supply necessary information and keep the narrative moving toward its final destination.

To complicate matters for him, despite the half million words he'd written since 1939, he did not yet feel fully at home in English. Determined to write his adopted language flawlessly, Jack took few liberties with it and was still trying to enlarge his vocabulary through reading the dictionary. A notebook contains a list of the new words Jack was trying to assimilate in November 1944: *ectogenic, dysphasia, calescent, surah.* (*Surah* would be put to use seven years later in a description of Mr. Groscorp's obscene face in *Visions of Gerard*—"sleek as surah"—as he watches Gerard's funeral from his window while stuffing himself with food.)

When William Burroughs returned to New York in December, moving into a small furnished room above Riordan's, an Irish bar near Columbus Circle, Jack and Allen immediately sought him out. "Eddify yer minds," he had said to them last summer in a cracker-barrel voice that sounded like W. C. Fields, presenting Allen with Hart Crane's poems and Jack with a two-volume edition of Spengler's *Decline of the West*, which he said was a Christmas present out of season. Jack understood that Burroughs, rather than Kammerer, had been Lucien's great teacher—and now he wanted the same education for himself. "Burroughs is the *authentic* devil," he told Allen.

Jack showed Burroughs some of his symbolist efforts, literally sitting at his feet upon a stool as Burroughs turned the pages. "Good, good," Burroughs said politely when pressed for his opinion, then quickly changed the subject. As soon as he'd come back, he'd pointed out the absurdity of attempting to suffer and starve in a symbolist manner and treated Jack to an excellent dinner at the Harvard Club.

Burroughs collected odd and disreputable characters, whom he studied with interest and amusement, but he had few close ties. "Burroughs was always a very *tender* person," Allen told Tom Clark in a 1965 interview, "but very dignified, shy and withdrawn." With Kammerer dead and Lucien gone, Burroughs's involvement with his two eager and brilliant young acolytes gave him a new sense of power and soon became the center of his life. When the two of them urged Burroughs to write himself, he revealed that while at Harvard he had collaborated on a story with his classmate Kells Elvins, entitled "So Proudly We Hail," about the barbaric rush to the lifeboats of the *Titanic*'s first-class passengers as the vessel was sinking and had afterward felt there was nothing more he would ever want to say about America. But now he found something infectious in Jack's passion for writing. In fact, he later thought Jack had been far more of an influence on him than vice versa.

By January, Burroughs began collaborating on a novel with Jack entitled *And the Hippos Were Boiled in Their Tanks*—a line Burroughs had picked up from a newscast about a fire in a St. Louis zoo. It had a surreally desensitized, deadpan quality—just the right tone, he felt, for a story based on the Lucien Carr/Dave Kammerer affair. The joint effort was written in a hard-boiled, Dashiell Hammett–like style, with its two authors contributing alternate chapters. The minimalistic *noir* prose came naturally to Burroughs, but even though Jack was a good mimic, it was apparently a struggle for him to write in a voice that was the antithesis of his own. Stifling his natural inclination toward lyricism and evocative texture, he gave it free rein only here and there in bits of physical description that stood out awkwardly in the text.

Although Jack and Burroughs had been careful to protect Lucien after his arrest by testifying to his heterosexuality, a definite ruthlessness took over now that they were writing about him under the cover of fiction. They made it clear that Philip Tourian (Lucien) kills Ramsay Allen (Kammerer) because he can't accept the fact that he is gay himself. Far from being a youth with a "Shakespearean" halo around him, Philip is mercilessly portrayed as a narcissistic young poseur, with a headful of halfbaked, pseudointellectual ideas. In fact, the deluded Ramsay Allen, whose love he brutally rejects, is the only relatively sympathetic character in the novel. By then Jack had begun to think that Kammerer's capacity to love without hope had made him "the true poet" of them all, if not a saint. But Burroughs had not a grain of such romanticism and it was his bleak vision that prevailed. He killed off Ramsay Allen by having Philip Tourian strike him on the forehead with an ax, his deadpan narrative making the murder seem as meaningless and absurd as all the other gratuitously nasty behavior recounted in the novel.

If Jack was consciously attempting to wean himself away from the temptation to turn himself into a symbolist, imitating Burroughs may have seemed a perfect corrective exercise, but not all Burroughs's lessons were literary, to say the least. In December he gave Jack his first shot of morphine—an experience Jack recorded, comparing it in a poem written under its influence to a soaring flight over a warm sea, from which he soon uneasily wanted to descend. Under Burroughs's tutelage, Allen went much further, experimenting not only with morphine but with a whole panoply of other drugs—NoDoz, phenobarbitol, codeine, Pantopon, and Benzedrine—taking each just once and methodically noting the effects upon his consciousness in his journal.

Now that Burroughs had released him from his self-imposed isolation, Jack reconnected with his parents. In mid-December he "broke down" and called his abandoned bride. Tactfully editing the truth, Celine had told Edie that Jack had unsuccessfully tried to seduce her in October. But despite all her grievances, Edie joined Jack in New York. Their feelings for each other during the first few days they spent together were both "real" and "primitive," Jack noted in his diary, and were heightened even more after Edie went through the windshield of a car when she went home for Christmas and was nearly killed. Jack rushed to Michigan to spend New Year's Eve at her bedside. He is said to have fainted when he arrived at her mother's front door in the midst of a blizzard and saw a wreath hanging there.

As soon as Edie came back to New York, the two of them moved into the six-room apartment Joan Adams had just found at 420 West 115th Street after returning to the city with her baby daughter. But Jack's major preoccupation by then, apart from his work, was his relationship with Burroughs, which left little room for the kind of reunion Edie had envisioned. It was Burroughs's company Jack was now "hungering" for in the same intense way he had hungered for Lucien's. In fact, 1945 would prove to be "a whole year of drug-taking and talking with [Burroughs] and meeting characters of the underworld I started to study as an *acte gratuite* of some kind." Jack became so caught up in all of this "low evil decadence" that by February, he told Edie they should have their marriage annulled. At the same time, however, he was writing a novella in which he explored his negative feelings about the path he had taken in his city life and projected the hope of a return to innocence.

In *Orpheus Emerged,* Jack dealt with his internal dividedness by splitting his protagonist into the young symbolist poet Michael ("the genius of imagination and art") and the penniless vagabond and "country bumpkin" Paul ("the genius of life and love"), who has come from "the road" to follow Michael to an urban university. The reader soon realizes that Paul and Michael are two halves of the same person. In "the North," they had both loved their Helen (whom Paul calls their queen), and there had been no physical separation between them, though now Michael keeps evading Paul and angrily trying to fend him off.

The corrupted, unhappy Michael is living as a matter of convenience with the shallow and bourgeois Maureen, described as "old enough to be his mother," although she is only in her late twenties. (As a matter of fact, all the young women in this book—even the ethereal Helen—are "strangely maternal," often calling their men "babies" and tucking them in for naps.) In addition to Maureen, Michael has a real mother who humiliates him by kissing and caressing him in public.

Michael and his crowd believe that to find "the ultimate, artistic society" envisioned by Nietzsche they must reject the "false . . . compromising society" all around them. Paul, on the other hand, sees this ascetic rejection of "life, happiness, naturalness" in the quest of some "false saintliness" as "the first step toward the disease of good and evil" and deplores the pretentious symbolist writing to which Michael dedicates himself like a priest. Why does Michael absolve himself of all responsibility? Paul asks, implicitly rejecting Nietzsche's belief that the artist is beyond good and evil.

Michael has rejected psychoanalysis, believing that it would rob him of "the dark secrets and nightmares and dualisms and thrilling conflicts" that make up his "poetic equipment." But when a friend compares him to Prometheus, who stole creative fire from the gods and brought it down to earth, Michael passionately declares that he would prefer to be Orpheus, "the *artist-man*"—unchained to a rock and unwounded. "In art I found halfness," Michael realizes. The only solution he sees for this condition is a "journey to new lands. I shall embark soon upon one of these. I shall sleep on the grass and eat fruit for breakfast."

Toward the end of this curious novella that seems philosophically at war with all Jack's recent influences, from Lucien and Burroughs to Nietzsche and Rimbaud, Michael nearly throws himself off a bridge after witnessing a barroom fight that results in a man's death (an echo of Kammerer's). Feeling desperate enough to seek out Paul, he immediately achieves the wholeness he yearns for. The two of them merge into Orpheus, the artist-man, who then vanishes on a mystical journey, accompanied by his Helen. Here was the healing fusion Jack could accomplish only through a flight into the symbolism he was about to reject. In *The Town and the City*, which he started writing in late 1946, he would divide himself into the three oldest Martin brothers—but without suggesting that the fragmented psyche of Jack Kerouac could ever be made whole.

APARTMENT 51

In *Orpheus Emerged*, Allen made his first appearance in Jack's fiction as a naïve and annoying kid named Leo, who is always avidly probing Paul/Michael with questions they'd prefer not to answer in order to get on intimate terms with them. But at eighteen, Allen was infinitely more formidable than that. If Lucien appeared to have the aura of a budding Rimbaud, it was Allen who was the real thing. Although it would take him another ten years to come into his full powers as a poet, there was ample evidence of Allen's precocious brilliance in a novel he had been forced to put aside in the fall that came dangerously close to the truth about what had really happened between Lucien and Kammerer.

Unfortunately, he had made the mistake of showing his first chapters to his Columbia adviser, Professor Richard Steeves. Horrified that Allen was openly writing about homosexuals as well as calling further attention to a shocking incident that had damaged the reputation of the university, Steeves dismissed the pages he'd read as "smutty" and reported the whole appalling matter to the dean, Nicholas MacKnight. During a conference with Allen's father, in which the dean implied that Allen was in danger of becoming "unsavory," as he euphemistically put it, all Louis Ginsberg could say in defense of his son was that Allen and his friends had been reading too much Gide for their own good and had succumbed to the notion "that even the abnormal was normal."

Threatened with the loss of his scholarship, Allen agreed to stop work on *Bloodsong* immediately, as well as to move back into the Columbia dorms. He was also advised to have nothing further to do with that "lout," Kerouac. But although Allen could give up his novel, he could not give up Jack. Despite the risk of further censure, Allen let Jack sleep over in his room in Hamilton Hall whenever he needed to after he had left Edie and moved back to Ozone Park.

On one of those cold February nights when Jack was camped out on a mattress on his floor, Allen summoned up all his courage. As they lay in the dark, he said, "Jack, you know, I love you and I want to sleep with you, and I really like men." It was a dangerous admission, but Allen was certain Jack "was going to accept my soul with all its throbbings and sweetness and worries and dark woes and sorrow and heartaches and joys and mad understandings of mortality." He heard a deep groan from Jack, "Ohh nooo," and with that the subject was dropped for the time being.

Over the next few months, however, all the references to Allen in Jack's journals implied that Allen was someone with ulterior motives, someone who was, as Jack put it, a "world-seeker" posing as a "soul-seeker." Even the compassion Jack had come to depend on seemed "crafty," as suspect as the "butterfly collector" way in which Allen would jot down information in his notebook about the poets people recommended to him. Yet by the summer, Jack was writing affectionate letters to Allen in which he called him his "little brother," and before the year ended, he did let Allen blow him a couple of times. Allen later attributed this to his own persistence and to Jack finally taking pity on him out of pure kindness. He never believed that Jack was gay, as he stated with increasing exasperation many times over the years to those who thought otherwise. On the other hand, he believed that in every man there was some degree of homosexuality.

In my own experience with Jack, he never gave me reason to think he was sexually attracted to men, though I realized he had his deepest relationships with his intimate circle of male friends. Our relationship ended because of his uncontrollable drinking and his womanizing, which went on very openly after he became famous, though he did try not to hurt me. His inability to make a commitment to any woman other than his mother took me a while to understand, because it seemed so bizarre. Besides our shared interest in writing, what kept us together for nearly two years (a long time for Jack) was a bond of friendship and affection—feelings that lasted on Jack's side as well as mine even after we stopped seeing each other, judging by what he wrote about our time together in *Desolation Angels*. In 1962, he sent my publisher a letter of praise for my first novel; ten years later, when I was working as an editor at McGraw-Hill, I was able to bring about something he had longed for but unfortunately never achieved while he was alive—the publication of the complete text of *Visions of Cody*.

To me it has always seemed a futile pursuit to try to affix labels of sexual identity to Jack. The more profound issue was that he did not know what to do with love—no matter whom it came from. To be loved was to be entrapped, and any open declaration, whether from Allen or a woman he desired, was particularly threatening. Yet there was love radiating *from* Jack all the same, and it expressed itself in the quality of the attention he gave to people, as if he were drinking in their souls, their "humankindness." When he was alone, however, the voice of the darker, judgmental, innately distrustful part of himself often spoke out harshly, arrogantly, and even cruelly in his journals.

Theo Van Gogh once observed that there were "two persons" in his brother Vincent. One of them was "marvelously gifted, delicate and tender, the other egotistical and hardhearted!" In Vincent Van Gogh (as in Jack and many another gifted male artist), these two different personae would "present themselves in turn." Perceiving this duality as a trait that led to isolation, Theo Van Gogh pointed out that his brother was "his own enemy, for he makes life hard, not only for others but for himself."

In Jack's relationship with Burroughs in 1945, it was Burroughs who had the upper hand. Awed by his intellect, Jack was a little afraid of him as well, although he saw in Burroughs "a perfection of attitude." Burroughs, in his own way, Jack thought, was more insatiable than either he or Allen. Always an avid listener to people's stories in anticipation of some "magic happenstance," Burroughs was driven by a curiosity that seemed boundless—as if he were searching for an "aperture" not only into life and death but into the afterlife.

Perhaps it was Burroughs's insatiable curiosity—compensating for the difficulty he had in achieving intimacy by other means—that led him to offer to "psychoanalyze" Jack and Allen. The Burroughs method of treatment, as Jack described it in a letter to Nin in March, was an operation upon the will employing free association to evoke early memories—not the poetic epiphanies of childhood that Jack and Allen took enormous delight in sharing with each other but primal material of a very disturbing nature, such as Allen's identification with his schizophrenic mother or Jack's ambivalent feelings about Gerard. Allen broke down in tears during one of these sessions, sobbing, "Nobody loves me." (He would later say that this "psychoanalysis" had left him "with a number of my defenses broken, but essentially unchanged, with nothing to replace the lost armor.")

Painfully, Jack tried to relive the circumstances surrounding the slap his brother had given him, hoping this would free him from his lifelong guilt about wishing Gerard would die. Gazing downward with his hands folded, Burroughs would listen as if deep in meditation, reminding Jack of a "medieval saint."

By March 14, when he wrote to Nin, Jack was still waiting for the healing flow of memories that would corroborate all that his mother had told him about the great forgotten love he and Gerard had felt for each other. Jack told Nin he was looking forward to the time when he would no longer continue to exercise his "destructive will" against himself in the "blind circles" of failure that his sister and parents attributed to his "aimlessness and laziness." Since Nin had once met Burroughs and come away dismayed by his coldness, Jack referred to him in his letter as "a psychoanalyst I recently met."

Two days later, however, Burroughs astutely touched upon the issue Jack least wanted to examine when he pointed out that Jack was bound too closely to his mother and needed to cut himself loose from her apron strings before it was too late. In fact, Burroughs believed that the "conclusion to which psychoanalysis leads" was the recognition that there should be no conflict between obligation and feeling and that "the only possible ethic is to do what one *wants* to do." Although this was a tenet Jack would later adhere to (in every relationship except the one with Gabe), he rushed away from this session distraught and went in search of Allen, who agreed completely with what Burroughs had told him.

That night, they talked for hours in Allen's room. After Jack listened to "The Long Voyage," an ambitious poem Allen had just written, inspired by Rimbaud's "Le Bateau Ivre," they both fell asleep from exhaustion, this time sharing Allen's bed. They were discovered there in the morning by the assistant dean, Ralph Furey, who had been one of Jack's football coaches, and who instantly jumped to the conclusion that they had been having sex. Jack bolted out of the room in his underwear and went back to sleep in an empty bed next door.

Furey had burst in because he was looking into a complaint from a cleaning woman that Allen had scrawled obscene graffiti into the grime on his window pane. Unfortunately, there in plain sight were the damning inscriptions "Fuck the Jews!" and "Butler has no balls!" (Butler was Columbia's revered president), plus crude drawings of a penis and a skull and crossbones. Allen's apologies and his excuse that he had only been trying to get the cleaning woman's attention were deemed insufficient.

An hour later, Allen was called down to the office of Dean MacKnight, whose first words to him were: "Mr. Ginsberg, I hope you understand the enormity of what you've done!" The word *enormity* seemed "incredible" to Allen, under the circumstances. "Watch out, he's a dangerous madman," Allen thought to himself, his mind flashing to a scene in *Journey to the End of the Night* where Louis-Ferdinand Céline's protagonist had a similar reaction as he looked at the officers urging their troops forward on a battleground filled with slaughtered men. It was a profoundly politicizing moment for Allen. He realized for the first time that there was a total disconnect between "private consciousness" and "official public consciousness," and felt further outrage when his father received a letter from Dean MacKnight referring to Jack as a person "unwelcome" on the campus. How could a *writer* be barred from a university? It seemed so stupid and "unacademic."

Suspended from classes until a psychiatrist could vouch for his mental rehabilitation, Allen moved into one of the empty bedrooms in Joan's apartment. Shortly afterward, Jack moved back to 115th Street himself, since he and Edie were having another try at marriage. The "libertine circle" was reconstituting itself in a new configuration.

Edie Parker had found a job at a Times Square nightclub called the Zanzibar, selling cigarettes in an abbreviated red costume six nights a week from seven P.M. to four A.M. She must have been seeing relatively little of Jack, but she needed every penny of the $27.50 she earned since her allowance from home had been cut drastically and she was now supporting Jack as well as herself. Sometimes he would drop in on her there with Burroughs, and she would manage to slip them a couple of steak dinners. Often joined by Allen, Jack was dedicating his nocturnal hours that spring to deep exploration of Forty-second Street with its floating society of thieves, pimps, muggers, and male and female hustlers, who drifted in and out of the Angle Bar on Eighth Avenue or a dive called the Pokerino or the seedy cafeterias filled with nodding junkies trying to make a well-sugared cup of coffee last till morning.

One night Jack and Allen turned up at the Zanzibar after hours with a new acquaintance of Burroughs named Herbert Huncke (known to the police as Creep), whom Burroughs had just introduced to Jack. A spectral wisp of a man with an eerily soft voice, a pallid, mimelike face, and elaborately courtly manners that came into full play when he was speaking to women, Huncke had once dreamed of becoming an actor, a dancer, or a writer. He supported his addiction to morphine by hustling and petty thievery and occasionally going to sea. Recently, Huncke had earned a few dollars acting as a guide for Dr. Alfred A. Kinsey, who had spent some illuminating weeks around Times Square conducting interviews for his groundbreaking study into the sexual behavior of the American male. (On Kinsey's next visit, Huncke would make sure he talked to Burroughs and his two naïve young friends.)

The first time he saw Jack, Huncke thought he was only seventeen or eighteen—he had an air of wonder about him that made Huncke think he was as "green obviously as the day was long." Burroughs he regarded as a weird kind of dilettante, eager to be instructed, for example, in the eso-teric art of picking pockets. But Huncke's first sight of Burroughs that past fall in his Chesterfield coat and black homburg had frozen him in his tracks; he had been positive Bill was a government agent. Fortunately, it turned out that Burroughs had only wanted to "unload" a sawed-off ma-chine gun that had come into his possession along with some morphine syrettes. When he heard that Burroughs had not yet tried them himself, Huncke gave him his first shot of morphine. Burroughs pronounced it "very interesting." It was Huncke's view later on that Bill's addiction to drugs was "principally the result of research."

Soon Huncke was flitting in and out of 115th Street on a regular basis. He liked the atmosphere, having always gravitated toward creative peo-ple. Like the members of the libertine circle, he too had once imagined that he was only collecting material for a book. He felt drawn to Allen, who struck him as a "starry-eyed" kid who didn't know whether he was "heterosexual, homosexual, autoerotic, or what." But Joan, the "college widow," was the one who impressed him most. Huncke thought he had never met a woman with such "inner beauty . . . so warm and so outgo-ing that it sort of swept one off one's feet." He quickly noticed that Joan admired Bill Burroughs "beyond words."

Now that he knew he was welcome uptown, Huncke would bring Forty-second Street—both its denizens and its argot—right into Joan's living room. "And so Huncke appeared to us and said, 'I'm beat,' with ra-diant light shining out of his despairing eyes," Jack would recall years later. He thought the term had originated "in some Midwest carnival or drunk cafeteria." In Jack's Catholic interpretation, *beat* implied a state beyond exhaustion or defeat—as if a plunge to the bottom of existence could, like martyrdom, result in the opening up of consciousness into a kind of beatitude. In a small spiral notebook, he wrote his latest definition of the artist: "evil saint," whose requisite range of experience included crimes and perversions. For him, Dostoevsky embodied that definition of sainthood.

One day Huncke showed up at the apartment with a tall glamorous redhead who called herself Vicki Russell. Vicki, who sold drugs and worked when necessary as a high-class call girl, was the daughter of a midwestern judge; over the next few years she would have an on and off, no-strings-attached sexual relationship with Jack. Vicki had some valuable tips to pass along about a cheap way to obtain Benzedrine. You didn't need to have a doctor's prescription, since the drug could be easily extracted from the paper wrappings of the inhalers sold to alleviate coughs at the corner drugstore. You could soak these bits of paper in coffee or Coca-Cola and then swallow them, as she demonstrated with Jack, giving him an overdose that immediately made him pass out.

Jack had been cautious about morphine, but now that he had discovered Benzedrine, he took to it the way he had taken to alcohol, using it just as indiscriminately. Despite the awful depression that came in its aftermath, Benzedrine seemed to provide Jack with a way of being "everywhere at once," giving him the endurance for marathons of writing or frenetic living, unbroken by meals or sleep, that sometimes lasted as long as thirty-five hours. He took so much in those first months after he met Vicki that he lost thirty pounds and his hair started falling out; he even took it as an antidote to the tedium of the days he spent in Ozone Park. Once Vicki, afraid of attracting the attention of the police, refused to let Jack get onto the subway with her unless he put Pan-Cake makeup on his face to disguise his wasted appearance. He had always been proud of his strong, athletic body, but now he watched it wither with strange hypnotized indifference, despite the appalled reactions of Edie and his parents.

Joan Adams also discovered that Benzedrine was the perfect drug. Married to a man she had barely seen over the past three years and imprisoned by motherhood at the age of twenty-two, with no outlet for her intellectual gifts beyond the incredibly perceptive conversation stoppers everyone gave her so much credit for, she had her own reasons for needing the heightened feeling Benzedrine gave her. Although Joan became enshrined in Jack's mind that year as the "heroine of the hip generation," he was becoming more and more aware of the helpless despair she tried to stave off with love affairs and narcotics, with her giggling insistence that everything was absurd—as if even her intelligence were working against her.

The only immediate cure for Joan at hand, however, was one more love affair—this one with Bill Burroughs, a matchmaking idea the entire household actively promoted. Both were witty, both were alone, more or less (though Joan had been sleeping with John Kingsland, whose mother had accused her of corrupting the morals of a minor), both were immersed in studying the Mayan codices. Joan kept telling Burroughs she was saving her best room—one equipped with bookshelves and a large desk—just for him. By the spring he finally took her up on her offer and moved into the room she had reserved for him. When she kept knocking on his door, fiercely determined to make him love her, he fitted her into a small compartment of his life. In Burroughs's first novel, *Junkie*, he would write, "What I look for in any relationship is contact on the non-verbal level of intuition and feeling, that is, telepathic communication." Apparently, Burroughs had found that with Allen and with Jack; despite his lack of attraction to women, he also found it with Joan. Their lovemaking was "dry," Jack noted in his journal, but Joan insisted, with pathetic bravado, that Bill made love to her "as well as any pimp."

That spring, noticing considerable tension between Jack and Edie, Huncke assumed that they too had a sexual problem. But money was the issue they were actually fighting about most in this final phase of their marriage. Only the year before, Edie had declared her willingness to support Jack, but now her constant refrain had become "If you loved me, you would get a job." Aside from the steaks she smuggled out of the Zanzibar and the meals Burroughs sometimes treated them to at the Harvard Club, they seemed to be living on mayonnaise sandwiches. She had never bargained for a life of poverty, and by this time she wasn't having any fun at all. In one of the bitter letters in which she berated Jack for his failings, Edie told him he was unworthy to have Sebastian's photograph. Forgetting that not so long ago he had regarded his first year with Edie as "the happiest time of my life," Jack described her in his journal as a selfish, hard-hearted, deceiving "little animal." By the time he portrayed her as Peter Martin's bride in *The Town and the City*, however, Jack had begun to miss her and thought of her with nostalgia. "Happy, crazy, childlike" Judie is like a "sister" to Peter Martin, but, as the narrator of the novel observes, it saddens Peter to have a wife who is his sister.

One of the visitors to the apartment on 115th Street in the spring of 1945 was Allan Temko, who was resuming his studies at Columbia after serving as a naval officer. He was horrified by the whole "Dostoevskian scene" that confronted him each time he walked in—by Burroughs, whom he considered "capable of killing someone"; by the drugs everyone was taking; by a "level of violence" in the discourse that Jack and Allen seemed to enjoy. "I felt that these people were very nineteenth-century and *Lower Depths*," he later recalled. "Very much like St. Petersburg in the under-thing of New York." Temko was made particularly indignant by the way these Morningside Heights Raskolnikovs, these intellectuals who hadn't played any part in the war, sounded off on its "absurdity." But Burroughs was undeniably brilliant, in a "reptilian" way, and Temko, an ardent devotee of Hemingway who was struggling with a novel himself, found much to talk about with Jack.

In Apartment 51, Temko heard for the first time the name of the writer Louis-Ferdinand Céline, whose autobiographical fiction would soon become an important influence upon postwar American writers. Céline's *Journey to the End of the Night*, based on his experiences during and after World War I, was regarded by young intellectuals of Jack's generation as a great antiwar novel. To read him, writes Morris Dickstein in *A Mirror in the Roadway*, was "to feel the impact of a blow: the shock of a dark, disillusioned, almost savage view of the human struggle." Little would be known in America until after 1945 about Céline's fascist sympathies and the virulent anti-Semitism that had made him notorious in France, as Dickstein points out. But even Jewish writers, from Alfred Kazin to Kurt Vonnegut, would continue to admire his work.

The violent talk that shocked Temko arose from the conscious effort of those who lived in Apartment 51 to bring about a communion of souls in which what Jack called "Ultimate Reality" could be explored. In their urgent, revelatory exchanges with one another, everything was out on the table—or rather out on the Oriental cover of Joan's big bed in the living

room, where they had taken to sprawling in an incestuous tangle of bodies, creating a zone where anything unmentionable could be mentioned
without shame. As Allen listened to his friends' stories—as they spoke of
"their faggishness, or their campiness, or their neurasthenia, or their solitude, or their goofiness, or even . . . their masculinity," he realized that
what he was hearing was everything left out of the literature and discourse sanctioned by the official culture. There was a profound difference
between the way they were talking to one another on Joan's bed, "heart
to heart," and the pronouncements of university professors or public figures for whom consciousness was only theoretical. Were they living in a
real America, Allen wondered, or "in the midst of a vast American hallucination" where a sensitive human being like Huncke was hounded by
the police and considered a criminal?

Burroughs had heightened everyone's awareness that America was
turning into a military-industrial complex with a profound disconnect
between public and private consciousness, a process accelerated by the
war. Disgusted by a speech of Harry Truman's, Bill remarked that if an
elephant had taken a shit right in front of him, the president wouldn't
have known about it.

By April, Jack was calling for revolution—"an inner revolution" led by
artists who marched to a "Marseillaise" by Bach and Beethoven. He ad-
vocated the complete elimination of "the American home"—a place of
emptiness, poisoned by incest. "Home" had to be replaced by groups of
children growing up together, free of the neurosis resulting from family
life. Perhaps the arrangement he envisioned was like Joan's apartment,
which was something like a commune but most of all like a new kind of
family of brothers and sisters. If there were erotic currents and entangle-
ments among the various siblings—between Burroughs and Allen, between Allen and Jack, between Jack and Joan, even, briefly, between
Huncke and Edie—they were played out very openly with no effort made
to conceal them.

By May, however, Jack was having second thoughts about his psychoanalysis. In his journal, he blamed Burroughs for not trying hard enough
to open the door of his "psychic cage" and for corrupting him in order to
feel less weak himself. Suddenly no longer idealizing Burroughs to the
degree he had before, Jack welcomed a new friendship with Haldon Chase,

a Columbia anthropology student who had just moved in and was sharing a room with Allen. In fact, Jack soon looked to Hal to restore the self-esteem he now blamed Burroughs for stripping away.

Hal Chase had grown up in Denver and had just gotten out of the army, where he'd served in the ski corps. Tall, lean, and blond, he physically reminded everyone of Lucien, and it surprised no one when Celine Young took up with him. Hal had a face that reminded Jack of a witch doctor's—it seemed perfectly in keeping with Hal's anthropological interest in prehistoric Indian culture—yet Jack also saw in him "the grace of a western hotshot who's danced in roadhouses and played a little football," and he found the western twang in his voice appealing.

In high school, Hal had amazed his friends by composing a dialogue between Nietzsche and Dostoevsky, and his precocious brilliance had come to the attention of a well-connected city official and retired high school teacher named Justin Brierly, who made it his mission, for whatever ambiguous sexual as well as philanthropic reasons (Jack called him "Gidean"), to take handsome and promising youths under his wing, introduce them to culture, and pave the way for them to go to Columbia, his alma mater. Jack and Allen would hear a lot from Hal about Brierly's most unusual protégé—a fabuluous, self-educated "jailkid" named Neal Cassady, who couldn't stop stealing cars and was reading his way through the Denver Public Library while Hal was studying in New York. Hal had also become one of Neal's mentors. In one of their most important conversations he had managed to persuade Neal, who at the time was immersed in Schopenhauer and was hoping to become a philosopher himself, that poetry was more important than philosophy. Feeling grateful that Hal had set him on the right course, Neal had introduced him to a fifteen-year-old girl willing to have sex. Neal, it seemed, seduced girls with the same guilt-free ease with which he helped himself to cars to go joyriding. When his awkwardly pretentious but interesting letters arrived, Hal would pass them around.

While Hal's unshakable heterosexuality disappointed Allen, who made some unsuccessful sexual overtures toward him, it meant a good deal to Jack in a household where his other adopted brothers were openly gay—one more thing that undermined his self-esteem. Hal Chase's western background, his love of mountains, his soulful introspective manner, and his admiration for Thomas Wolfe also made Jack gravitate toward him, although he couldn't help pulling back a little in his journal. There he reflected that Hal was less of a Nietzschean "New Man" than he imagined himself to be and that nothing important would ever really happen to him. Unlike Lucien, who had the strong will and the kind of personality that would always generate significant events, Hal could never be the hero of a story.

At first, Hal Chase succumbed to what he later called "the destructive fascination" of the scene on 115th Street, with its emphasis on "haughty self-indulgence" and "the proud aimlessness of madness." What appealed to him about Jack, however, was Jack's underlying innocence and goodheartedness. They were both wrestling with conflicting feelings about Christian morality—on the one hand, finding its rigid absolutism absurd; on the other, yearning for its stability and comfort. Neither of them had yet found a belief system to replace the religion of his childhood, but as Hal's initial fascination with decadence wore off, it seemed to him that what Burroughs and Joan, the "realists" of Apartment 51, were offering in their proselytizing way was "inhuman."

Jack was secretly beginning to agree with that assessment. In the midst of his love affair with decadence, he pulled himself together enough to look for a means of escape. In June, he applied to go to the University of California on the GI Bill—a continent away from Apartment 51 as well as from his family in Ozone Park. Besides, he had always wanted to go out west. He noted in his diary for that month that his father's health was failing.

The apartment started to empty out as the summer began. Joan went back to Loudonville for a couple of months with one-year-old Julie. She had been taking so much Benzedrine that she had sores all over her body. Her bourgeois parents were insistent that their daughter and grandchild remain with them and suggested that Joan look for a job in Albany. But Joan did not find that prospect "alluring." She had begun to submerge herself in her communion with Bill, with its challenges and its strangeness and the highs of perception that came with self-immolation, and that was where her sense of identity rested now.

Edie moved out for good at the beginning of July. She was fed up with being the only one in the household working for a paycheck, coming home after her exhausting shifts at the Zanzibar to find Jack and all the others idle and strung out. Perhaps because Jack was spending so much time with Hal, Edie focused some of her anger on him. Accusing Hal of stealing her food, she demanded that Joan put a lock on the refrigerator. When Edie's teeth went bad and she couldn't afford to see a dentist, that was the last straw. After a fight with Jack in which he told her they should abandon their marriage, she fled to her grandmother in Asbury Park—leaving so abruptly she didn't bother to pack.

With Edie no longer paying his share of the rent, Jack lost his base in Manhattan and retreated to the "mopey dullness" of Ozone Park. For two weeks he stayed away from his New York scene completely—"clear and lonely," he wrote in his diary. He broke his solitude in the middle of the month for a reunion with Burroughs, Hal, and Celine; Edie also joined them and took the opportunity to tear into Jack. After they went to a French film and were treated to dinner by Burroughs at the Café Brittany, where they picked up some naval ensigns and a couple of society girls, Jack got into a drunken argument about Proust in the West End bar and tried to set fire to his hand. The following day he couldn't account for his behavior. He went back to Ozone Park carrying a copy of *Journey to the End of the Night* that he had stolen when the group stopped by a Columbia student's apartment.

Perhaps the fight about Proust had touched upon the internal conflict that was frustrating Jack between wanting to write like an American and wanting to write like a European, while feeling like neither. It all seemed as difficult to resolve as the dualities in his own nature. Should he go back to the lyrical, Wolfean Galloway novel, which he now called *The Haunted Life*, or write in the stylized vein of his "Rimbaudean" *Orpheus Emerged*? Could there be a way to bring the organic and the stylized together?

That summer Jack felt a long way from finding his own method—his own voice. Yet he actually did find it briefly—without recognizing it—when he wrote some trial pages of an entirely new novel in his notebook. He had decided, for the first time, to write very openly about his Franco-American background—about being the American-born descendant of an immigrant family who bore the emotional scars of a long history of privation and hardship, whose austere Catholic morality was akin to Calvinism, and who did not really feel American even after decades in the United States. The few passages Jack wrote in July or August had a power and immediacy that were missing from the other work he produced that year—particularly some haunting paragraphs about the birth of Mike Daoulas (a name he was once again using for himself), announced by the sound of factory whistles, on a March afternoon at the end of winter when snow was dropping from the trees and the Merrimack falls were thundering in the distance. As the red light of the setting sun was flaming in the windows of the mills, a mother was standing on her porch calling to her children, wondering where they were in the "otherworldly" light. There would be similar descriptive passages in *The Town and the City*, and Jack would describe his redlit birth again, using many of the same details and in strikingly similar language, in the breakthrough letter he wrote to Neal Cassady in the winter of 1950 and in his 1952 novel *Dr. Sax.* For the time being, however, he abruptly turned away from his ethnic material and in fact rejected the whole idea of writing a directly autobiographical novel—the point of view was too limited, he decided, and many of the events in real life were not only trivial but occurred too randomly for his taste. In the rhythms and cadences of the paragraphs about Mike Daoulas's March birth, however, in the long, suspended breaths of the musical sentences with their rush of detail in short phrases pushing toward an ecstatic crescendo, Jack had actually achieved for a few pages the "sense-thinking" he had been striving for.

There is reason to believe that, to some degree at least, the sense-thinking inside Jack's head always went on in *joual* before it was transmuted into English. But at twenty-three, he had not yet found a way to *instinctively* make that transition from one language to another. A note in his journal that summer shows that it was still a process accompanied by a very conscious shifting of gears. First Jack had to remind himself that he was not writing in French; then he had to figure how to capture his "simultaneous impressions" in English, which often required using many more words than the more bluntly evocative French he had grown up speaking. Then he had to take care not to fall into the English literary tradition of distanced *"reporting"* on what the writer was sensing. Ideally, only the sense—the essence of all the writer was—would determine the words on the page. Perhaps the process of calling up his deepest sense memories of Lowell had briefly freed Jack from the self-consciousness about making literature that was holding him back in other writings from this period.

BENZEDRINE WEEKENDS

Apart from significant progress in his development as a writer, Jack seemed at a dead end during the summer of 1945, often in a state of such apathy that he didn't even care that it had been weeks since he'd had sex. In fact, he doubted that he would ever be capable of dedicating himself to any one person (which sadly proved to be correct), or that he would ever be loved or admired by his fellow human beings. All he had—and all he told himself he needed—were the riches of his lonely self-absorption; all he worshipped was Art—the only god he now recognized. While he craved human fellowship, by this time Jack had become convinced that love would only get in the way of his pursuit of greatness. Nonetheless, he made an attempt to get Edie back, but his trip at the end of July to Asbury Park, where he intruded upon a visit from Celine, went badly, with the two women ganging up to make fun of him and show him he was not wanted.

Having ruled out love, he wrote to Allen, who had offered it, coldly outlining what he saw as the major differences between them. The primary one was that Jack was a "romantic visionary"—while Allen, whom Jack now openly called "self-aggrandizing" in his search for self-fulfillment, was neither a visionary nor a romantic. Allen defused that judgment rather masterfully in a reply written around the beginning of August, not only agreeing with everything Jack had said but declaring that he now could accept those differences without shame since he saw them as a source of his own power. Well aware by this time of Jack's anti-Semitism, which he didn't take too seriously, Allen deliberately brought up another important difference Jack had left out, calling himself an "isolate" and "introspective" Jew, while Jack, like Lucien, had all the "natural grace" of a "participator" in America. (Like Jack's other New York friends, he seemed to have no understanding of how French Jack felt.) Admitting that he might seem devious and manipulative in his search for love, Allen assured Jack that "inwardly" he had always been sincere and predicted that they would again be brothers when they next saw each other. By now, Allen evidently realized that Jack's feelings about his friends were as volatile as his moods—a trait exacerbated that summer by Jack's heavy use of Benzedrine.

Jack noticed himself that he was on a weird kind of seesaw—veering from the heights of elation to depression within seconds, not that this stopped him from buying those inhalers at the drugstore. Because he couldn't tolerate any kind of external pressure, he kept losing whatever jobs he managed to find—from reading scripts again for Columbia Pictures to cleaning bathrooms at a resort in the Mohawk Valley, where he greatly resented the well-to-do patrons, who happened to be Jewish. When he returned from there to Ozone Park, he had to deal with the boiling rage of his ailing father and his mother's "cruel" and insatiable need for the kind of love it was beyond his capacity to give her. He was still waiting to hear if the University of California would accept him. For a couple of months, before his application was turned down due to the circumstances in which he'd left Columbia, his escape seemed just within reach.

All through the first weeks of August, as World War II drew to a close, preceded by the news that atomic bombs had been dropped on Nagasaki and Hiroshima, Jack was reading *Journey to the End of the Night,* with its savagely brilliant opening chapters, set on the front lines of the previous war. Céline saw war without glory, as a factory of death reducing a generation of young men to cattle senselessly sent to slaughter. Recovering from a minor wound in Paris, Céline's protagonist, Ferdinand Bardamu, either feigns madness or has been "driven mad by fear" just as he is about to be sent back into battle. Ironically, he can escape the "infernal lunacy" only by being put under observation in a military hospital—a solution that undoubtedly reminded Jack of his own escape from serving in the navy.

He read the last pages of the novel during the third week of August and came away from it knowing he'd had a transformative experience, comparable to his discovery of Thomas Wolfe five years earlier. In fact, he was convinced that Céline, the "arch pessimist," and Wolfe, "the so-called arch lyricist," had essentially the same dark view of humanity.

But, unlike Wolfe, Céline communicated with the reader in a frontal, outrageously comic way that was seemingly artless; his voice, which immediately reminded Jack of Rabelais, appeared to be the language of the streets, blunt and even understated, yet it was supercharged with the electricity of an unpredictable, cranky, vibrating sensibility—a consciousness that seemed almost physically present on the page. In fragmenting paragraphs, often composed of splintered sentences and phrases separated by ellipses (a mode of punctuation Jack immediately began to adopt in his letter writing), Céline's narrator leaped from one association to another with the speed of thought. Although Jack was not yet ready to abandon what he had absorbed from Wolfe, he caught a glimpse of the writer he wanted to become in the unlikely fusion of Wolfe and Céline, and it was the naturalism of Louis-Ferdinand Céline that finally liberated him from his floundering efforts to be a symbolist.

Jack had spent a year trying to turn himself into the American equivalent of the French writers Burroughs and Lucien had introduced him to. In one month alone, he had read Burroughs's entire bookshelf of symbolist poets, all of whom wrote in the classical French his father believed could never be mastered by a writer with a name like Kerouac. Céline, who had grown up like a weed in the foul-smelling back streets of Paris, may have seemed like a kinsman to Jack not only in his voice but in his vehement rejection of the exalted view the French had of their culture. "What you call a race," Ferdinand Bardamu rants, "is nothing but a collection of riffraff like me, bleary-eyed, flea-bitten, chilled to the bone. They came from the four corners of the earth, driven by hunger, plague, tumors and the cold and stopped here. They couldn't go any further because of the ocean. That's France, that's the French people."

But nothing in *Journey to the End of the Night* made a deeper impression on Jack than the way Céline explored duality by creating a darker alter ego for Bardamu—the mysterious Leon Robinson, whom Bardamu first encounters during the war and who subsequently turns up in Africa, New York, Detroit, and the slums of Paris. Older, more lawless, and more troubled than Bardamu and always several paces ahead of him, Robinson shares with him what Bardamu calls "my vice, my mania for running away from everywhere in search of God knows what, driven, I suppose, by my stupid pride, by a sense of some sort of superiority." The wholesale carnage they have seen on the battlefield has unhinged both men, but Bardamu, who becomes a failed doctor, unable to save his wretched patients, retains some elements of conscience and compassion, while the once sad and harmless Robinson, whom Bardamu calls a trickster—"We were all tricksters"—loses all ability to feel and becomes a killer consumed with the "idea of getting himself bumped off." Robinson also becomes Bardamu's great teacher, leading him on into the night, forcing him to open his eyes in the darkness, even when Bardamu lacks "the courage to really get to the bottom of things." While afraid of Robinson, Bardamu can't give him up: "We'd get to the end together, and then we'd know what we'd been looking for. That's what life is, a bit of light that ends in darkness. But, on the other hand, maybe we'd never know, maybe we wouldn't find anything. That's death." There would be more than one echo of Céline in the Sal Paradise/Dean Moriarty relationship in *On the Road.*

In his journal on August 21, Jack wrote that no writer had ever moved him as much as this "alien" and "madman," and he predicted—correctly, as it turned out—that the "gap" his reading of Céline had opened would eventually widen enough to allow him to release all that was pent up inside him. In an essay published by the *Paris Review* almost twenty years later, Jack equated Bardamu's pursuit of Robinson with Inspector Javert's obsession with the escaped prisoner Jean Valjean in *Les Misérables* and revealed that he had always thought of Céline's novel as "the story of the Shroud of Céline's self [Bardamu/Javert], pursuing the Shroud of Céline's non-self, Robinson."

Jack read the last pages of *Journey to the End of the Night* in the midst of a tremendous family crisis. On August 20, Leo Kerouac had been rushed to the hospital for an emergency operation to remove a tumor from his stomach. Following the operation, Jack noticed a great change in his father—as Leo confronted the possible end of his own journey through life, he seemed able to accept people simply for who they were, without the "nonsense" of racial prejudice. Nonetheless, on his first visit to Leo's bedside, Jack's stored-up anger at his father made him unable to locate his emotional response to Leo's suffering—unable even to bring himself to make the simple, loving gesture of touching his father's face.

On August 22, the Kerouacs were told that Leo had cancer of the spleen. As he talked to his mother and sister, Jack felt a powerful impulse to vanish, leaving all this sickness and dying behind him. He walked the streets of his neighborhood for hours filled with guilt, sorrow, and "patricidal" anger and felt despair when he could find no language for this welter of emotions. How could he fail to find the words to write about his dying father? But if the words that eluded Jack were the English equivalents of the language in which he was experiencing his inner turmoil, his tormenting writer's block may have had something to do with difficulties of translation as well as with the difference between what he *should* have felt and his ambivalence toward Leo.

Late that night, as Jack lay awake, an image came to him of his father walking past a streetlamp and disappearing into the darkness, and he was finally able to tell himself that Leo was a great man. The next day at the hospital, there was the welcome news that Leo had only been suffering from an enlarged spleen. To Jack, this seemed entirely in keeping with Leo's Céline-like anger at the world's injustice. He wrote that the two of them were having a tremendous reconciliation. And now that he was free to go off to California, he felt as if his own life had been handed back to him. By Labor Day, Leo seemed almost fully recovered.

The weather was cool and bright that holiday weekend, with a sky of crystalline blue and early turning leaves that reminded Jack of October. As he walked through the streets of Ozone Park, where people were out in their yards grilling hot dogs and drinking beer—undoubtedly in a particularly celebratory mood because the war had just ended—Jack felt surrounded by the richness of American life. He was seized by the exhilarating urge to understand all of it and make it the subject of one huge novel. Then, as if a cloud passed over him, he felt that he was "alien" to all this richness he saw around him, that "none of it could be mine, only to express." "All of this America," he wrote, "not for my likes, never." Certain that nothing could eradicate the "Breton bleakness" that kept him an outsider, he called himself "half-American" for the first time.

On the night of December 7, 1941, Jack had wandered through Lowell proudly identifying with American fortitude and good-heartedness. In the aftermath of the war, however, in the wake of the horrific carnage caused by the atom bomb, his allegiance had shifted to his own generation. Riding a bus late one Saturday night in the fall of 1945, he was struck by how many empty seats there were—seats that should have been filled by young men returning from their dates. He thought that his generation was not a lost one but the very last and in some ways the most interesting one, walking into the final destruction of Western civilization full of the "strange joy" he saw in his friends.

As the summer had ended, Jack had tried to capture that nihilistic energy in *I Wish I Were You*, his reworking of *And the Hippos Were Boiled in Their Tanks*, adopting the structure of its story and its fictionalizing devices, but writing it in his own way. Stylistically, in fact, the novel was a declaration of independence from the influence of Burroughs. In two successive drafts of the first one hundred pages, Jack put in all the textural detail that had been left out of *Hippos* and even returned with renewed confidence to the lyricism he had abandoned just the year before. It was really quite brilliant, the best prose he had written so far.

One of the great strengths of *I Wish I Were You* was its disillusioned first-person narrator, an unidentified player in the story, who reflects ruefully yet at the same time romantically upon the "eccentric little courage" of its characters. The novel embodies Jack's increasingly dark and now Céline-like vision of Manhattan as a magnetic "deathtrap" that draws its victims to it from everywhere in America. In some of the novel's most striking passages, a phantom haunts the streets of New York (as a phantom would later haunt the streets of Galloway in *Dr. Sax*), keeping its eye especially on Ramsay Allen, fated to die at the hands of Philip Tourian, and driving the other characters into senseless, self-destructive behavior.

Although he did not condone Lucien's act, Jack had never stopped believing that there was something "magnificent" and important in Lucien's all-out rebellion against society, and he restored some of Lucien's boyish grandeur to the Philip Tourian character as well as capturing his fatal mixture of decadence and adolescent naïveté. But the character who clearly fascinated Jack most was Dennison, based on Burroughs, who, like the phantom, seems to drive the action forward, always hovering presciently at the edge of things as the tragic outcome of the conflict between Ramsay Allen's pathetic obsession with Philip Tourian and Philip's intense desire to jettison his "inconvenient" worshipper becomes more and more inevitable. Dennison, Jack wrote, was "something tied on to a brain," a kind of scientist concerned with "facts," who studied the young people he influenced "under a shabby microscope."

I Wish I Were You shows what a remarkable leap forward Jack had made in his writing within a few weeks of his discovery of Céline, but he quickly lost interest in completing this new work of fiction, deciding, as he confided to Allen that fall, that it was too neurotic. In August, he had been working on three novels at once, but it was his Galloway novel that had begun to preoccupy him most, although he still hadn't figured out a form for it. Nonetheless, he showed the unfinished manuscript of *I Wish I Were You* to a literary agent at Ingersoll and Brennan, who liked it well enough to send it to Robert Linscott, the editor in chief at Random House. Linscott found the content so offensive that he told Jack's agent he would have a fight with the author if he ever met him. Still he recognized that this infuriating young writer had "an ability to put words together" and asked to see his future work.

Hungry for encouragement, Jack had so far found very little of it outside his circle of friends. His greatest champion was Allen Ginsberg. That spring Allen had shown the manuscript of *The Sea Is My Brother* to Raymond Weaver. Professor Weaver was a famous Melville scholar who had discovered the manuscript of *Billy Budd*; he had studied Buddhism and Gnosticism and in fact was the only teacher Allen had met in the Columbia English department whose interests lay outside the accepted literary canon. After reading the novel carefully and seeing in it an affinity to Melville's *Pierre*, Weaver had asked to meet with Jack and recommended that he and Allen read the Egyptian Gnostics, a suggestion the two of them followed up. Allen also talked Jack up to his mentor Lionel Trilling, but the distinguished critic took a dim view of Jack because of his involvement in the Kammerer affair.

Despite his tremendous belief in Jack's writing, Allen found himself siding with Burroughs during a passionate debate one night in September between the non-Wolfeans and the Wolfeans (Jack and Hal) when all four were high on Benzedrine. The battle was waged in the room Hal shared with Allen, with Jack and Bill sprawled on one bed and Hal and Allen on the other. The heterosexual Wolfeans, according to Hal, who was fed up with attempts by Allen and Burroughs to convince him that he too was gay, had an idealistic, lyrical love of America, while the Baudelairean non-Wolfeans (Jack called them the "Black Priests") looked toward Europe and tried to corrupt the innocent manly Americans. But as the discussion raged on, Allen became upset at the thought of any such divisions between them.

Although they all later joked about their differences, that night's debate was one more manifestation of the waning of Burroughs's influence upon Jack. Over the coming year, his increasing sense of independence from Burroughs would turn, for a time, into rancor and a feeling of profound disaffection.

With Jack's enrollment at the University of California no longer an option, he had no alternative but to go on living with his parents. His life settled into the pattern that it would essentially take from that point on, apart from the months he would later spend on his travels. His existence in Ozone Park was celibate, lonely, and largely devoted to his work, with the pall of his father's illness hanging over everything, since Leo's seeming recovery had been followed by the discovery that he indeed had stomach cancer. Jack's escapes to Manhattan to see his friends invariably turned into prolonged binges into which he tried to cram all his living before returning to Ozone Park drained and depressed to deal with his father's angry questions about the friends who were destroying him. The radical split in Jack's existence seemed to reinforce his sense of the duality inside him. He worried that even his writing had become as changeable as his mind, for he would start one novel only to drop it and start another. As an ending for his Galloway novel, Jack thought he might use one of his "Benzedrine weekends"—so much happened in each one of them that he would come away feeling there was nothing left to experience.

As soon as he'd moved into Apartment 51, Hal Chase had found the scene there an ongoing "psychodrama," but by late fall everything seemed on the verge of spinning out of control, and even he had stopped going to his classes. Burroughs was now addicted to morphine and was actively pursuing a life of crime, Huncke was more and more often in residence, and Joan was miserable because narcotics had killed Bill's interest in sex—whenever she hoped he was ready to make love, he would complain of a cramp in his foot. As Hal saw it, the two of them were engaged in a "life and death struggle." Meanwhile Joan had become obsessed with a couple who lived in the apartment next door, claiming she could hear their conversations through the wall and recounting them in clairvoyant detail. The couple were talking about reporting the suspicious goings-on in Apartment 51 to the police; the husband was violent and threatening to kill his wife (perhaps Joan's premonition of the outcome of her relationship with Bill). The apartment next door, however, was empty. Everyone around Joan was taking Benzedrine, but the amount that she was taking was causing hallucinations.

In November, Jack spent one of his typical Benzedrine weekends rushing frantically between 115th Street, the Angler Bar on Eighth Avenue, and the cold-water flat downtown on Henry Street where Burroughs had started to sell narcotics and house some of his underworld connections. There, fueled by his third "uppey" of the day plus marijuana, Jack stayed up talking with Huncke until seven-thirty in the morning before the long, weary subway ride back to 115th Street, where he found Hal, Allen, and Joan in states of benny depression and went to bed with Edie, who happened to be visiting Joan, in the middle of the afternoon. After a short nap—the only sleep he got the entire weekend—and another uppey, Jack went out to dinner with Hal to talk about Spengler. On his return to the apartment he was still high enough to feel thrilled as he read Nietzsche and to engage in a conversational marathon with Joan and the others that lasted until the next morning, when he fell into one of the inevitable black holes he had grown all too familiar with.

In his journal, Jack also mentioned that he was limping. In fact, his first stop in the city on the previous day had been at a veterans center, where he had been warned that he was in danger because he was suffering from phlebitis—a condition brought on, it was then believed, by excessive Benzedrine use. He had been feeling some uncertainty, as a matter of fact, about the "advisability" of continuing to live.

That theoretical question was put to the test the week before Christmas when after five sleepless days, Jack went walking with Hal and Allen over the Brooklyn Bridge. After crossing back into Manhattan and carrying Allen on his back for several blocks, Jack collapsed and was taken to a Queens veterans hospital in serious condition. For the next two weeks he lay in bed, his legs swaddled in compresses, while doctors debated whether or not to operate.

Separated from both his friends and his parents, Jack found the kind of solitude he had not experienced since he had been at sea, as if he were stranded above life, listening to the moans of suffering humanity far below him. Very soon he must have asked for the spiral notebook in which he wrote an account of his thoughts in the hospital in the alienated voice of "Claude Breton," an experimental alter ego in which he merged himself with Lucien. Claude finds nothing ennobling in suffering—to him, it is a "mockery" that does not even afford him the intellectual satisfaction of being able to interpret it existentially like his cynical, clever friends.

Then a second voice—"Michael's"—takes over. His attitude is the polar opposite of Claude's. In the quiet of the hospital, Michael is discovering an exhilaration that reminds him of how he feels on drugs or alcohol. In this state of mind, what suddenly matters to him most is to find a voice in writing that is all his own in every way—down to the exact sounds of his intonations.

Jack's strange exhilaration still prevailed on December 20, as he urged himself to move ahead fearlessly and buoyantly on his journey through life without being slowed down by the heavy baggage of problems he had so far been unable to resolve. He wrote that he wanted to learn to operate like Burroughs in a scientific "Cartesian" manner, taking things as they came, understanding them as the results of processes it was his duty to study and formulate.

But Burroughs had not only studied Jack. Through his version of psychoanalysis, he had actively tried to change him—to make him into *one* person, a skeptical Claude-like person, rather than being tormentedly split between a Michael and a Claude. Burroughs had put his finger on the most obvious *cause* of Jack's duality—his Oedipal feelings about his mother—then left him drifting right to the brink of self-destruction with that shameful knowledge eating away at him. In one entry in Jack's journal, even Claude was now having doubts about "B," though he could no more imagine cutting himself off from him than doing without the suspect empathy of "Goldstein."

In a sudden shift of feeling, Jack realized he must now cast Burroughs and all his dangerous teachings aside, for while he was lying in the hospital, his profound depression and his apathetic readiness to die had given way to an upsurge of a desire to live and be like Michael that had all the power of a religious conversion. In some ways, one might say that it was a "born again" Jack who went home to Ozone Park in early January, convinced he had completely turned away from the cynicism and nihilism that he felt had nearly killed him. But the vehemence of the hatred he was directing at what he now felt he must eradicate from his life was itself a kind of sickness.

Jack had also left the hospital determined to concentrate all his creative energy on one book, his huge and daunting Galloway novel, for after reading *The Brothers Karamazov* during his convalescence he'd finally seen a way to deal with his conflicting selves in fiction. He would create three separate characters—Joe, Francis, and Peter, the older brothers of the Martin family—each of whom would represent a different aspect of his psyche, as well as a spectrum of attitudes toward American culture— from Joe's full embrace of it to Francis's alienated rejection, with Peter Martin torn between the conflicting values of small-town America and urban life. The idea had crystallized with the onslaught of Jack's revulsion for all that New York represented and with the sudden birth in his mind of Francis Martin, whom he would make the embodiment of the hateful Claude-like side of himself in contrast to the sensitive idealist, Peter. At the end of *Galloway*, Jack could imagine Peter Martin crawling out of the "abyss of modern decadence" to walk unsteadily in the sun— just as he had come limping home to Gabe and Leo on bandaged legs. As he planned the new novel, he initially thought he would have Francis commit suicide—since that was the direction in which this inimical persona had been pushing him.

A FATHER'S DEATH

Although Jack would soon set about rejecting much of what Burroughs had taught him with the violent prosecutorial fervor of someone convinced he has seen the light, his dependence on Bill as his "analyst" was not so easy to break. In fact, soon after returning to Ozone Park, Jack wrote that he wished he could tell Burroughs about a disturbing dream in which he opened a closet and discovered the decomposing bodies of cats. In his dream he had heard his mother "mournfully" calling "Petit Minou [Kitten]," the same nickname, he now realized, that she had given Gerard and that she had subsequently transferred to him.

Shortly after this dream, however, Jack wrote his first attack upon Burroughs—a short piece, entitled "My Analyst and I," in which he depicted a Burroughs-like figure standing with his patient amid the rotting garbage of a city dump. The analyst, who had been counseling his patient to cast aside the "handicap" of self-respect, was now promising to lead him out of the very wasteland where he had, after all, ended up himself.

Nonetheless, Jack continued to remain in touch with Bill, staying on 115th Street whenever he needed to, but by February his behavior evidently became so disruptive that Burroughs kicked him out, telling him that he was instituting a "new regime" in the apartment. This "rectitude," which Jack found both insane and downright "upper-class," was something else for him to hold against Bill. For a few days Jack went into exile in a heatless room on Columbus Avenue, where, feeling very sorry for himself, for his lack of funds, for his "slimy" relationships, he wrote himself a letter of encouragement, signed Michael J. Daoulas, that reminded him never to forget Sebastian. Although Burroughs had little patience with people who rejected his ideas, he may have been unaware of the intensity of Jack's disaffection. In 1969 he would write: "During all those years I knew Kerouac, I can't remember ever seeing him really angry or hostile. It was the sort of smile he gave in reply to my demurrers, in a way you get from a priest who knows you will come to Jesus sooner or later."

Like Jack's other friends, Burroughs was evidently unacquainted with the hellfire preacher who would rage in Jack's journals over the rest of that year, in diatribes written with paranoid intensity, against the European writers who had helped to lead him down the path to destruction. "Prissy" and "lazy" André Gide now headed the list of those whom Jack despised as men, along with Goethe and Stendhal. By the following fall he would also turn against Rimbaud and even condemn James Joyce for advocating "silence, exile and cunning," finding nothing admirable in a black sheep who "hated life" and did not respect his father. Jack had always been an eclectic reader with wide-ranging enthusiasms, but his political and literary opinions throughout 1946—the grounds upon which he rejected certain works, his denunciations of decadence—were reminiscent of Leo Kerouac's ignorant pronouncements. Just as Jack had briefly become a symbolist under Burroughs's influence, now he was becoming infected with Leo's primitive hatreds. As Leo gradually succumbed to the process of dying, he was reclaiming his authority over his son.

As soon as Jack felt well enough, he took a night job in one of the dreary residence hotels near Columbia, so that he could contribute toward his father's medical expenses. By seven in the morning, he was back in Ozone Park—in time to spell his mother so that she could go to the shoe factory without leaving Leo unattended. He would brew a pot of coffee and he and Leo would talk. Having recently faced the possibility of his own death, Jack found his father's fierce desire to live inspiring—a stark contrast to the existentialist attitude of "despairist" intellectuals that life was absurd.

By the spring, Leo was often so weak he could barely stand, but he dealt with his condition with fortitude. He followed the races, smoked his pipe, fulminated against Roosevelt, and seemed almost content, Jack reported to Nin and her new husband, Paul Blake, who had just moved into a house in North Carolina. He advised his sister not to worry, since all they could do was accept the inevitable outcome of Leo's illness. But he would soon discover how unprepared he was to lose his father.

As he moved toward death, Leo was changing in Jack's mind into the "great man" Jack had always wanted him to be, the father who could be loved without reservation. He was astonished one day when Leo tenderly called him "my poor little boy" as he was tucking a blanket around his knees. It had been only a few months since Leo had jumped down his throat at every opportunity. They'd had one of their characteristically senseless arguments in November, when they'd been listening to Tchaikovsky. When Jack made an innocent remark about the tremendous loneliness of the great Russian composer, Leo had accused him of not caring about the loneliness of his own father and then had started yelling that he was trying to figure out how Jack and his "crazy gang" thought.

In his journal Jack had once called his father a bourgeois who had never found any effective use for his hatred. But now Leo was turning into George Martin, transformed in Jack's imagination into an exemplar of old-fashioned "American manliness" and morality, exactly the kind of patriarchal figure who would have flourished on the western frontier. Even Leo's extreme political views that had once been a source of embarrassment for Jack were now seen as the "America First" thinking that went along with George Martin's rugged individualism. In fact, Jack was beginning to embrace that ideology himself, forgetting that only last summer he had been advocating revolution and the abolition of the nuclear family.

Such left-wing ideas Jack now considered "European"—synonymous with *decadent*—and he congratulated himself on being at least "half-American" because he was certain he would have nothing to write about if he lived in Europe. He began to fill the pages of his notebook with essays about the superiority of American culture, even singing the praises of capitalism as the pure and natural expression of America's Dionysian energy and selfhood. Jack now categorized men like Burroughs and Allen as Apollonian—products of urban life and European influences. (Ironically, he was still thinking in Germanic, Nietzschean terms.)

He had soaked up *The Brothers Karamazov* in the hospital, coming to it at a time when he would have been most receptive to Dostoevsky's depiction of the dualities of Russian culture: the old values versus the influences of Western Europe; the spirituality of the Orthodox Church versus the materialism and skepticism of new thinking. In Dostoevsky's changing Russia Jack saw reflections of postwar America, of his own confusion and questioning and loss of faith. He had risen from his sickbed determined to take to heart Father Zossima's admonition to love life. But despite his admiration for Dostoevsky as well as Tolstoy, Jack's literary gods had, for the time being, become an all-American team: Emerson, Thoreau, Twain, and Whitman, with Thomas Wolfe fully restored to supremacy because of his tremendous effort to evoke the " 'unuttered' American tongue in the wilderness." (There was no room in Jack's pantheon for the "European" Edgar Allan Poe or Henry James.) But he noted that it was in jazz rather than in literature that he found the purest expression of the American spirit. He could see the reflection of American individualism in the supremacy of the improvising bop soloist who could drive a standard tune out to the farthest reaches of his musical imagination in a progression of variations and then come home again to the original melody. But Jack was not yet ready to bring to his own work the depth of concentration and sheer daring the creative act of a Charlie Parker or a Thelonious Monk required. It would be another half dozen years before his discovery of the method that would lead to what Allen Ginsberg would call Spontaneous Bop Prosody.

With his grueling schedule, Jack had little time to spare for his friends in early 1946. He apparently made few efforts to stay in touch with Allen, who, hoping to be readmitted to Columbia in the fall, was earning money toward his tuition by shipping out on freighters. The friend Jack sought out most was Hal, who was still living on 115th Street as the scene there steadily deteriorated around him.

In March, Jack spent one of his rare nights away from Ozone Park with Jack Fitzgerald, reviving their interrupted friendship. Unhinged by his wartime experiences, Fitz was back at Columbia studying anthropology and struggling with an anguished novel about the Battle of the Bulge. Warm, passionate, and a heavy drinker, Fitz was about to be married despite his profound restlessness and his appetite for sexual encounters. His devotion to jazz was almost religious. That night the two of them went to Minton's, where Fitz's consumption of alcohol apparently surpassed Jack's. Drunk as they were, Jack noted afterward, neither of them had felt in the slightest danger because of the intoxicating pleasure of feeling totally at ease among the black people in the club. Fitz was so caught up in the excitement of the music and the whole scene that he didn't even care that the woman he had picked up had probably robbed him. Nothing could deflate Fitz's "general ecstasy," Jack noted admiringly, as if rather than sharing it, he'd been the awed witness of another man's wild abandon. Echoing this insight in *The Town and the City*, he would define *ecstasy* as "a feeling of irresponsible wanderlust of the soul" when one went in "dizzy circles . . . responding to everything at the moment."

If there was a route to Jack's own unique portion of joy, it was most of all what he recognized in the young jazzmen soloing on their instruments—an absorption in their music that stopped time and kept thoughts of death at bay. For a few days after his night in Harlem, he contemplated getting an apartment there and even jotted down the particulars of a vacancy on 133rd Street. But nothing came of it. He had to stay home and help his father die. As Leo wasted away with a belly so swollen with fluid that a doctor had to stop by every two weeks for the agonizing process of draining it, Jack had risen to the task of nursing him as devotedly as if Leo had become his child.

During much of the spring, despite Leo's worsening condition, Jack was sustained by a kind of euphoria, with an accompanying sense of power and a feeling of certainty and mission about his writing and his developing ideas. But every few weeks darkness and doubt would overwhelm him. On April 23, he found himself in one of the worst depressions he had ever experienced. He had no idea what had caused it—was it perhaps some perverse craving for excitement?—but with this abrupt plummeting into deathly emptiness, his suicidal thoughts had returned. On May 3, he noted that he was again feeling joyful.

What was his greatest fear? Jack asked himself a few days later—and decided it was the seemingly limitless power of his own mind, which might lead him on and on into "vast" and endless "space" until he gave out from sheer exhaustion and died totally alone—like the dancer who couldn't stop dancing in the story "The Red Shoes." In some ways, this would prove to be a prophetic insight, but at the age of twenty-four, Jack mostly took pride in the insanity of his "genius." He believed he had the potential to become one of America's key transformative "Faustian" figures.

Although Jack had initially planned to conclude his book with Peter Martin staggering away from one of his decadent New York weekends, Leo's last months would inspire the concluding episodes of *The Town and the City*. In the novel, the father and son, who have been at odds with each other, seem to merge spiritually, as if they are of one mind: "Peter and his father," Jack would write, "by just looking painfully at one another seemed to understand that to question the uncertainties and pains of life and work was to question life itself." His two characters would share their love for life, along with the contradictory, traditional French Canadian view that human existence was "a poor miserable disconnected fragment of something . . . far greater."

The account of George Martin's last days in *The Town and the City* leaves out the argument Jack had with Leo on the morning of May 16, one of their tiresome disputes—this time about the proper way to brew coffee. Shortly afterward, Leo had one more agonizing session with the doctor who came by to drain his belly, and then he died in his chair right in front of Jack, who thought at first that his father had fallen asleep without realizing that the snores he was hearing were death rattles. As he stared at his dead father, Jack had the awful feeling that he had been "forsaken . . . left alone to take care of the 'rest,' whatever the rest is."

In 1951, Jack would write some opening pages of a possible sequel to *The Town and the City*. There, the death of the father is such an overwhelming event for the son that he immediately falls ill himself—his sickness having something to do with the "nerves" in the stomach, for which he is given a sedative, implying that he is having some kind of breakdown. Although there is no indication that Jack actually had such an extreme reaction, it suggests the profound impact on him of Leo's death, although in his journals he hardly touched upon it directly.

On June 23, he dealt with the loss of his father for the first time—but wrote from the perspective of Peter Martin, who realizes during George's funeral that his father's entire life had been composed of "infinite longing," a longing that was fulfilled only when he was laid to rest in the New England soil where he had asked to be buried. George's longing for his piece of the American dream is epitomized for his son Peter by a house Jack had seen when he went up to New Hampshire for Leo's burial in Nashua beside the grave of Gerard. The house had evidently been a white-framed classic New England dwelling surrounded by a big lawn, the kind of house the Kerouacs had never owned or lived in; nor had Leo been a classic New Englander like George Martin. His funeral had, in fact, been the occasion of Jack's reunion with a horde of French-speaking relatives, one of whom implied in typical mordant fashion that Leo's downfall had resulted from being "too ambitious and proud and crazy"—traits he could see in Jack as well. Perhaps Jack was mourning not only for Leo but for the idealized American father Leo had never been, though he found himself wishing he had his father's "longings"—so much simpler and less conflicted than his own.

It had weighed heavily on Leo's mind that he had never been able to give his wife her own house and had caused her such pain and hardship. Not long before he died, he charged Jack with the overwhelming duty of taking care of his mother and eventually installing her in a home of her own. When he finally became successful, Jack would buy Gabe not one but a series of houses in which the two of them, both alcoholics by then, would live in drunken and contentious seclusion. In effect, the promise he made to Leo at twenty-four would seal the fate Burroughs had warned him to avoid.

A couple of months after Leo's death, Jack had a dream in which he was wandering through a field carrying his father's remains in a potato sack, with a trickle of red sawdust seeping out. Was that red dust Leo Kerouac's unfinished business?

PART SIX

POSTWAR

ENTER NEAL CASSADY

Gabrielle Kerouac was only fifty-one when she was widowed, a woman filled with enough midlife energy to work in the shoe factory all day and come home at night to keep house for her son. Perhaps the two of them guiltily found themselves enjoying the peace that had fallen over the household now that Leo was gone. He had always been his son's harshest critic, while Gabe had always defended Jack and said she believed in him. Now she offered to support him while he gave his Galloway novel—the book they both hoped would bring him fame and prosperity—his full attention. It may have seemed to both of them like the old days in the house on Phoebe Avenue as Jack quietly worked away in his room and she fed him the favorite foods of his childhood. Although permanently scarred by her harrowing memories of being orphaned, Gabe had always been a spirited and gregarious woman. If she had still been living in Lowell, she would have been surrounded by a community of Franco-American friends and relatives, but in New York, her social isolation and lack of fluency in speaking English, and now her widowhood, intensified her dependence on the companionship Jack gave her. Her terror of losing him made her greedy. Increasingly unwilling to share her son with others, and especially threatened by young women or homosexual or Jewish friends who might lead Jack down the wrong path, she became the arbiter of his relationships, making it very clear who was welcome in her home and who was not. She would soon feel jealous of her daughter's husband and would increasingly make her two children vie for her affection, turning to Nin when Jack had fallen out of favor and vice versa, longing to be with whichever one she was separated from—something Nin would come to see more clearly than Jack.

Locked into an Oedipal marriage from which he had sworn not to extricate himself, Jack struggled to justify it—at least to himself. One way he found to look at the Oedipus complex was to regard it not as the psychological problem so troubling to decadent intellectuals like Burroughs but as the very basis of American dynamism. For wasn't the son's need to outdo his father for the sake of the mother he held in reverence responsible for that son's success? Wasn't it in fact the national Oedipus complex that had made America stronger than any other nation?

When he went into Manhattan and voiced some of his new ideas, they did not get a positive reception from the people he knew. One of them must have called him a reactionary, for he wrote indignantly in his journal that to be a reactionary simply meant that one was dealing with the realities of life. Someone else asked him why he was bothering to write about very ordinary people, to which he answered that the people he had lived with all his life were hardly "fence posts." When he sat in the Thalia, an Upper West Side art house, watching *Of Mice and Men*, it seemed to Jack that he was surrounded by the homosexual intelligentsia from the Midwest who had taken over American letters, and that he was the only one in the audience who appreciated the authentic humor of the scene in which a rancher and his son soaked their apple pie in milk then consumed it in big spoonfuls. The others didn't realize that only someone who loved American culture as much as he did could become the "universal American writer." Using the privacy of his journal as a place to test the outer limits of how provocative and offensive he dared to be, Jack declared himself one of the "great ravaged spirits" in a list that included Dostoevsky, Whitman, and Nietzsche—and ended defiantly with "even Hitler."

In the spring he had written episodes of his Galloway novel, which he would soon begin to call *The Town and the City*, as inspiration seized him. Now, fortified by the pep talks he gave himself, he struggled with the opening section of the book, which seemed to require constant painful revision and rethinking. But the grueling work made him feel he was earning his redemption, making up for the disappointment he had caused his parents and the damage he had done to his own soul and body in his hunger to experience every aspect of life. This novel would, he thought, "explain everything to everybody." He took heart from something Hal Chase had said to him: "How can you fail if you just don't want to?"

Jack missed Hal that summer, since Hal had gone home to Denver, thankful to have extricated himself from what he called "the dark horror of Apt. 51," and the "realists" who had kept pressuring him to come over to their side with their Freudian and anthropological arguments. Hal was going through a process similar to Jack's as he tried to find a way to recover from his fascination with "self-indulgence" but feared this might lead him into asceticism, and he wrote to Jack that he depended very much on his guidance. Convinced that Jack's wisdom might set Neal Cassady on the right path as a writer, Hal also wrote to Neal, urging him to find some way of getting to New York that fall and promising to introduce him to two professors who could help him get a scholarship to Columbia.

By late September, Joan Adams finally had to abandon Apartment 51. In April, Burroughs had been arrested for trying to obtain prescriptions for morphine, which he was selling in order to finance his heroin habit. Joan had immediately bailed him out of the Tombs, but in June, after a psychiatrist hired by Burroughs's parents interceded for him, Bill had been sentenced to spend the rest of the summer in St. Louis in their custody (the presiding judge drily called this the worst punishment he could think of). Utterly lost without Bill, Joan had let Huncke take over her life. He helped her out financially by selling the luggage he lifted from parked cars, and stole a car or two as well while he was at it. Unable to make any rational decisions for herself, Joan had let the empty rooms of the apartment become occupied, as she later wrote Edie, by "desperate characters" of Huncke's acquaintance who filled the place with hot merchandise and parked stolen vehicles right in front of the building. When her roomers started going to jail and she found herself unable to pay the rent, Joan was evicted. For a few weeks she lived in a grim series of Times Square hotel rooms with her one-year-old daughter and a dim-witted thief named Whitey, until Whitey was arrested for trying to steal a safe from a Howard Johnson's restaurant. Joan left her child with an aunt and tried to find Whitey a lawyer, but she had been taking so much Benzedrine that in mid-October she ended up in a mental ward in Bellevue. The life to which Burroughs and Huncke had introduced her was leading to her complete destruction.

Jack saw the apartment for the last time when he went there in late summer to meet Edie's younger sister, who was picking up some things

Edie had left behind. Edie had moved back to Grosse Pointe and had filed for an annulment, which became finalized that fall. Here was another sobering ending in Jack's life—one of the failures and mistakes he hoped his book would redeem. He had not been brought up to take the breakup of a marriage lightly.

He was in a troubled mood one afternoon in late August after he had spent the previous night looking through a family album—it seemed to him that nothing had ever taught him so much. In the city, he reflected gloomily, the people he knew felt threatened by what a family album represented. There was a widespread fear of the past, fear of what was disparagingly referred to as Victorianism, all of it leading to a future of "familial-societal disintegration" and ultimately the end of humanity.

Having had these anachronistic thoughts, he suddenly felt overwhelmingly lonely. Where could he find someone with an "earnest sensitivity" like Sebastian's, someone who would understand his kind of thinking instead of calling him a neofascist? Where were the boyhood friends he'd left behind in Lowell?

Proud of his "austere" way of life that others found incomprehensible, Jack rarely admitted that he needed anyone. In fact, it was when he left his work to mingle with other people that he felt empty, as if it had all been a waste of spirit, as if he should have stayed in Ozone Park and not interrupted his writing.

By nature, he was silent, and when he was sober, he probably kept most of his angry, unacceptable ideas to himself. When he was drunk enough, he would express them with the alcohol-ignited vehemence of someone dangerously certain that he alone sees the truth. Yet judging from their recollections, his friends remembered another side of him—open and kindhearted, wonderfully perceptive, at moments a little naïve. Jack may have felt that he had turned himself into an outcast, but in reality he was the one doing the wholesale rejecting—so secretly and privately, however, that few apparently realized it.

The year 1946 brought another influx of war veterans to Columbia— among them Ed White, a boyhood friend of Hal's from Denver who had emerged from the navy with an interest in architecture as well as literature, and Tom Livornese, an accomplished jazz pianist now buckling down to premed courses. Along with Hal, Allan Temko, and Jack Fitzgerald, it was these veteran friends Jack usually sought out whenever he succumbed to his need for companionship. Young men who had made the generational sacrifice he guiltily felt he had partially evaded, they had a gravitas that he was drawn to.

Coming back from the war and their intimate acquaintanceship with death, the old young men of Jack's generation pursued their intellectual development with the same seriousness with which they partied, drank, and womanized, attempting to make up for the lost years of their youth, for the unbearable, destabilizing memories they carried with them, for the guilt they felt over surviving lost comrades, and for what they had learned about the fragility of life. Accustomed to the heightened emotional intensity of living under the threat of sudden death, some found civilian life a tremendous letdown and were drawn to danger. Drinking problems were common among America's returned vets, and there were crack-ups and suicides. But in those days no one attributed such things to post-traumatic stress disorder.

Evoking the postwar mood in his brilliant essay "The Name of the Game," John Clellon Holmes, who became part of Jack's circle in 1948, writes of the shared feeling "of expectation without reasonable hope, of recklessness without motivation, of uniqueness seeking an image," of the arguments and jokes "about our own identity as an age group" that went on over drinks as well as in classrooms. While the majority of vets sought a fast entrée into good jobs and settled, bourgeois life, the group to which Holmes made an immediate, instinctive connection defined themselves by their "immediate attraction" to extremes of experience: "madness, drugs, religious ecstasies, dissipation and amorality." Here was where they found their sense of reality. Like Burroughs, Allen, and Jack, Holmes felt that if rationality had resulted in the carnage of the twentieth century, then "nothing rational" could provide a solution for the ills of civilization.

The new *noir* films that came out of Hollywood in the late forties captured the mood of existential alienation, and so did some of the art that was evolving in abandoned industrial lofts in lower Manhattan, where artists had begun turning away from the figure and the influence of European cubism toward a new kind of abstraction that looked like explosions of energy painted straight onto the canvas—work considered too "violent" or too "primitive" to hang in galleries or the living rooms of rich collectors. But most postwar novelists, even the acclaimed newcomer Norman Mailer, looked backward to the Lost Generation, as Holmes pointed out, framing their recent war experiences in the romanticized way Ernest Hemingway had framed his. It would take some years for this generation to find—or recognize—its authentic voice in literature.

Holmes's friendship with Jack, whom he would meet in 1948, would result in his discovery of bebop— an art form that "specifically separated us from the time just passed." Although bop would not transform the way Holmes wrote, it would become one of his subjects in his essays and his fiction. He ranked it as "a key conversion experience," after which one would "comprehend the difference between the confining intelligence and the soul directly recording its own drift." Not that his own conversion was instantaneous. The first time Jack made him listen to Dizzy Gillespie and Charlie Parker, Holmes found their music puzzling, despite his conviction that it was important. As Gertrude Stein once observed, "Everything new is ugly."

Jack's trips to New York, which involved a tedious journey on the elevated line that ran above Crossbay Boulevard followed by a long subway ride to Times Square or Columbia or Harlem, were often precipitated by his craving for bop. He shared his passion for the new sounds not only with Jack Fitzgerald but with Tom Livornese, who lived nearby in Lynbrook and who began dropping in on Jack on a regular basis. At Jack's neighborhood tavern on Crossbay Boulevard, they would fill a kettle with beer, then take this "bom" back across the street to Jack's apartment where they listened with mounting excitement to recordings of their two favorite pianists, Art Tatum and Lennie Tristano. Tom taught Jack some bop "changes" that he could play himself on the piano Gabe had brought down from Lowell. While stationed in Guam during the war, Tom had played in a band of servicemen that featured a Chicago musician who had done arrangements for Dizzy. He was the only friend Jack had who could talk about bop from the perspective of a practicing musician, and Jack kept trying to persuade him to give up the bourgeois idea of becoming a doctor and rededicate himself to jazz.

Another of Jack's frequent visitors was Allan Temko, who had grown up in the adjoining neighborhood of Richmond Hill and was still living there with his family, although he was planning to become an expatriate writer in Paris at the earliest opportunity, since he had fallen in love with France when he passed through there during the war. Temko relished the long walks he took with Jack beside the tracks of the Long Island Rail Road, discussing the novels they were both writing and Jack's strange inability since Edie's departure to find himself a girlfriend and the intriguing stories they'd both heard about Denver from Hal Chase and Ed White.

After serving out his summer "sentence" in St. Louis, Burroughs did not return to Morningside Heights that September, as everyone had expected. Instead, he headed for East Texas with his Harvard friend Kells Elvins—the plan was that the two of them would strike it rich by buying a farm and raising vegetables and citrus fruit. What also made the area attractive to Bill was that it was wild enough and remote enough for him to find land where he could raise a cash crop of marijuana.

Jack found himself thinking of Burroughs with a certain nostalgia. While he no longer considered himself one of Bill's disciples or regarded him as an important thinker, he had to admit that nothing compared to watching Bill star in his own extraordinary ongoing drama. Although only a short time ago he had written Burroughs off as a "life-hater," it now seemed to Jack that the opposite was true, for why would Burroughs live behind doors with three locks and keep a machine gun under the bed if he did not value life? In a short sketch with a distinctly elegiac tone, he recalled the time in the summer of 1944 when the two of them had first really bonded, when they had dressed up alike in dirty striped shirts, talking so loudly on the subway in Liverpool accents that they had attracted the attention of a cop. That was the same day Jack had asked Bill what he thought death was like and Bill had answered in his factual way that death was "just being dead." Jack wrote about all this now as if an infinite amount of time had elapsed since those days of his youth.

Up at dawn on September 24, after a night of writing, he reminded himself that Lucien was due to be released that day from the Elmira reformatory, after serving only two years of his twenty-year sentence. He wondered what that " 'pale criminal' " was thinking as he awoke to the same morning. Would Lucien accomplish the great things they had all expected of him now that he had paid for his crime? But it would be nearly three months before anyone heard from Lucien, who for a while tried to live very carefully and stay out of trouble.

Still obsessed with Lucien, Allen felt very hurt by his deliberate silence, which he interpreted as a rejection. It was a lonely time for Allen in general with Joan and Burroughs gone and Jack definitely giving him the cold shoulder. He felt caught between two warring factions—Hal and Jack on one side, Bill and Joan on the other. Although he sided with Bill and Joan intellectually, Allen still loved Jack. It made him unhappy to hear that Jack had come to Morningside Heights and spent his time with Ed White or with Hal, who did not conceal his distaste for Allen, and he would feel very hurt when Jack invited both of them to Ozone Park for Thanksgiving dinner and left him out.

After having his sanity evaluated by a university-appointed psychiatrist, Allen had finally been readmitted to Columbia, but his studies felt unimportant compared to his concerns about his writing and his sexuality. Unlike Jack, who was feeling filled with "phenomenal fire" as the pages of *The Town and the City* began to accumulate, Allen was undergoing a collapse of confidence in all directions. At his darkest moments he thought of taking a business course. After Burroughs had made him realize "that what I write is not me," he doubted he would ever be able to write poems. Yet Allen had lost some of his own absolute faith in Bill, and even Joan had pointed out to him that Burroughs had limited psychoanalytic powers. "I don't suppose he could really analyze anyone's sexual problems," she had said. "He'd be too discomfited or uneasy or embarrassed."

Although Burroughs returned to New York on October 25, five days before Joan was released from Bellevue, he did not intend to stay. In mid-November, he took Joan and her daughter, Julie, down to the farm he had bought in New Waverly, Texas, where Huncke soon joined them to help with the marijuana operation, completely forgetting to bring the seeds he'd promised Bill. Neither Joan nor Bill realized that Bill had made her pregnant during one of the rare occasions when they had sex. When Joan found out, she asked Bill whether he would let her have an abortion. Bill refused to consider it. He regarded abortion as murder.

On December 2, still suffering from being pointedly excluded from

Jack's Thanksgiving arrangements, Allen wandered into Riker's cafeteria on Broadway and 112th Street, which had once been a hangout for the libertine circle. Only two years ago, he would have headed there with a "sense of longing and juvenescence acquired from atmosphere of Carr. A terrible beauty is born," he lamented; "all is changed, changed, utterly." Soon, however, a new galvanizing male figure would enter Allen's life, as well as Jack's.

In the original draft of *On the Road*, Jack's first sight of Neal Cassady in December 1946 is the startling vision of Neal as unabashedly naked as a statue of Apollo as he opens the door of the East Harlem apartment where he is staying with his teenage bride, Luanne, glimpsed tantalizingly in the background as she scrambles off the couch where they have been having sex. In reality, their introduction took place less sensationally, with Neal and Luanne fully clothed, in the attic room in Columbia's Livingston Hall, which Hal Chase was sharing with Ed White.

Earlier that mid-December afternoon, Hal and Ed had taken the young couple to the West End, where they had run into Allen, who had then trailed along with everyone else to the dormitory, where Luanne had to be smuggled upstairs. Despite his unpopularity with Hal and Ed, Allen was determined to make a connection with Neal. One thing he must have noticed immediately was Neal's almost fraternal resemblance to Jack—both in his muscled physique and in the strong features of his face. Tom Livornese, Allan Temko, and a few other specially invited guests also dropped by that afternoon to make their own assessment of the Proust-reading "jailkid" whom Hal had been talking up—in fact, it was a little as if an inspection of some specimen of primitive man had been arranged. Temko saw nothing remarkable whatever about Neal and was repelled by his treatment of Luanne and his deplorable attitude toward women, as was Ed White.

By the time Jack arrived, Neal was engaged in an intense conversation with Allen that showed no signs of winding down. Although Allen had been described to Neal in withering terms by Hal Chase, who regarded him as someone "whose amazing mind had a germ of decay in it and whose sterility had produced a blasé and fascinating mask," Neal immediately saw in Allen everything he had come to New York longing to acquire—"intellectual polish, learning, subtlety of thought"—while Allen immediately felt that Neal was in possession of nothing less than "the secret of existence."

Jack, however, was more skeptical and guarded. What he saw before him that first day was "a young Gene Autry," who had a certain shiftiness, he thought. But Neal also reminded him of the tough boys in Lowell who hung out at the boxing matches he had gone to with Leo, boys who knew what it was to be poor and have no future but always managed to snag the prettiest girls. In fact, he found Neal's sideburns very French Canadian. He listened to Neal use big words and blather on about Schopenhauer and Nietzsche in the hope of impressing the confident young intellectuals in the room and understood his poignant culture-hunger, as his ear began picking up Neal's unique boplike way of speaking the American vernacular, veering off his initial subject or the narrative line of an anecdote into a series of riffs or even riffs upon riffs, punctuated by percussive exclamations. Like a testifying Dostoevskian character, he seemed to open up his soul in his rambling but intense monologues. "There was nothing clear about the things he said," Jack would write in *On the Road*, "but what he meant to say was something pure and simple."

It is doubtful, however, that Jack immediately began to mythologize Neal as a "western kinsman of the sun," as he would write in the final draft of *On the Road*, or to see him as the embodiment of Spengler's magnificent "primitive man," who would teach others the meaning of life. In fact, the naïvely written letters Hal had shown Jack had prepared him to find Neal somewhat boring, and he was relieved to learn that this was not the case. A few days later, when Jack saw Neal for a second time—in that apartment in Spanish Harlem described at the beginning of *On the Road*—he had an almost protective feeling for him, realizing how chaotic his existence was and how much he needed some friendly guidance. Neal seemed like a kid to him, yet he recognized something "severe" in his nature that he found remarkable.

Hal Chase had actually been feeling worried about Neal's reception in New York. Denver, in those days, was essentially a small town, somewhat like Lowell, as Jack would soon discover, where intersecting crowds of young people who knew each other from high school played pool together and hung out in the same few proletarian bars and eateries. Among them, Neal had been a star attraction, famous for his most questionable achievements—his prowess in stealing cars and seducing women—as well as thought to be some kind of autodidactic genius. Since Hal's New York friends were much less easily impressed, he had warned Neal that they wouldn't "go for" too much of his cockiness, as Luanne Henderson later confided to Allen.

Neal's exceptionally pretty child bride was a sweet sixteen. With her ringlets of golden hair, her big blue eyes, and her round innocent face, she looked like Shirley Temple dressed up in an older sister's clothes, and Jack, who saw her as a country girl, felt an immediate strong desire for her. He consulted Hal, who told him it was quite easy to get Luanne into bed, but advised Jack that if he wanted to make a move on her, he had better ask for Neal's permission.

Luanne was a waif like Neal. She had been only fourteen when Neal had first set eyes on her as she sat in the Walgreen's drugstore next to the pool hall he frequented. "I'm going to marry that girl," he had indiscreetly told his current thirteen-year-old steady, Jeannie. (Neal had been living with Jeannie and her mother and grandmother and in return had been bestowing his sexual favors upon all three members of the household.) Weeks of intense intrigue ensued, during which Neal attempted to juggle all these amorous relationships. By the end of that summer, he succeeded in marrying Luanne, whose divorced mother couldn't have cared less, and ran away with her to Nebraska. Since Luanne's Nebraska aunt and uncle refused to take them in, Luanne took a job keeping house for a blind lawyer and his wife, who gave the young couple a room. There Neal passed his time poring over his copies of Shakespeare and *Remembrance of Things Past*, explaining his favorite passages to Luanne at night.

The last straw had come that November when Neal came home during a blizzard and found Luanne turning blue as she scrubbed the porch floor. It was definitely the moment to head for New York, where he still planned to go to college and become a writer, though by then he had missed by two months the appointments Hal had gone to the trouble of setting up for him at Columbia. After stealing a car from Luanne's uncle along with three hundred dollars her aunt kept in a strongbox, they were on their way, ditching the hot car outside Chicago and traveling the rest of the way by bus. Their first stop in Manhattan was Times Square, where they gawked at the crowds and the billboards and the neon and were dazzled by the gleaming abundance of the pies and cream cakes in Hector's cafeteria (an experience Jack would later evoke in a virtuoso descriptive passage in *Visions of Cody*).

The young couple got along quite well at first on the kindness of strangers. A friend of Hal's let them stay for the first few days in his apartment in Spanish Harlem. Then a cousin of Allen's came up with another nearer Columbia, which they lost after infesting the place with crab lice. They moved to Bayonne, New Jersey, where Neal had found a job in a parking lot. Their tiny room had kitchen privileges, which finally allowed Luanne to feel like a real wife as she cooked Neal a meal for the first time. Thirty years later she still remembered some pathetic but hopeful drapes she'd made out of paper. Everything seemed wonderful, but perhaps that was the problem because very soon something made Luanne need to destroy the little bit of stability they were enjoying by lying to Neal, who had a tremendous fear of being incarcerated again, and telling him that the police had come looking for him. The two of them fled to New York City and for a week or so slept in parked cars they broke into until Luanne took a bus back to Denver alone in mid-January.

No sooner had she left town than Jack took Neal to a gathering at Vicki Russell's apartment, where Neal ran into Allen for a second time, and, as Allen saw it years later, recognized Allen's desperate need for love and generously provided it, although he was mainly attracted to women. After "a wild weekend of sexual drama" that left Allen shaken out of his feeling of isolation and a little frightened, his writing block melted and he found himself pouring out sonnets to his liberating new lover, who had more sexual experience than anyone he had ever met. Neal "had an element of faith," Allen later recalled, "in sexual intercourse and intimacy as an ultimate exchange of souls." The gospel he preached made a convert of Allen, who did not see that it was also the way Neal justified his sexual voraciousness.

Neal soon replaced Lucien as Allen's main love object. Allen had finally seen Lucien a few weeks earlier, but the longed-for reunion had not measured up to his fantasies. When Allen announced that he was homosexual, Lucien did not seem to feel the news was earth-shattering and proceeded to ask him questions Allen considered naïve. Then, after a New Year's party Jack took the whole crowd to at the home of one of his wealthy Horace Mann friends, Lucien had blown up at Jack for helping himself to a scarf and a hat—a prank that would hardly have troubled him in the old days. When Allen had sex with Lucien later that year, it would seem anticlimactic after his affair with Neal.

Not long before Christmas, Jack had begun to have doubts about all the work he'd done over the past few months and had shown his early draft of *The Town and the City* to Jack Fitzgerald. On December 23, Fitz wrote him a letter expressing the "amazement" he felt about the ambitious scope of the novel and the vividness of Jack's depictions of incidents and characters—all of which left him feeling abashed about his own efforts as a writer. But even Fitz's all-out enthusiasm did not restore Jack's confidence. On January 19, he put the draft aside and began the discouraging task of tackling the novel all over again, right from the beginning. Despite his growing interest in Neal Cassady, Jack stayed holed up in Ozone Park, unwilling to break his concentration.

One of the people who missed him most was Vicki Russell, who kept photographs of Jack on the walls of her small Upper West Side penthouse. Jack had recently given her reason to think she was going to be his girl, holding out the possibility—maybe even believing it himself—that they would start a new clean life together in California once he sold his novel. Vicki wrote to him in January, hoping he'd find a literary agent to make that happen soon and telling him how embarrassed she felt that she'd been entertaining one of her male clients the last time he'd dropped by. Her work as a call girl, she explained, was due to laziness, but she'd awakened that morning determined to get a self-respecting job in a factory, so that Jack could feel proud of her. All she could think about now was "us, and us. And us," she wrote him rapturously. But Jack's thoughts, which had rested on her briefly, were totally absorbed by the 380,000 words he would have to write before reaching his finish line.

The sensational romance of that winter was the one between Allen and Neal, which totally shocked Hal Chase and Ed White. For Allen the study of Neal became an education in sensibility. In the ability to understand the implications of every situation, he felt Neal was way ahead of him. Rather than indulging in the endless intellectual analyses of consciousness and emotion Allen had often engaged in with Bill and Joan, Neal seemed to exist in a state of *"complete* projection, feeling, identification with things" in which, as he would often remind Allen, "everything takes care of itself." As Neal's myriad unconscious associations rose to the surface, he was able to verbalize with "16 modifications," compared to Allen's paltry four. Without warning, he would also fall silent with complete lack of self-consciousness, retreating to such a depth inside himself that Allen would ask him anxiously, "Are you really down there?" and wonder whether his own "bewildered 'deep' thinking" constituted "true awareness." Sometimes he also wondered whether the vibrations Neal set off by his "16 deep" responses accounted for his uncanny success in conning people.

In fact, Neal's survival had always depended on his ability to psych out those who could provide him with what he needed. Wanting access to the riches of Allen's mind and spirit, he saw that the fastest route to winning Allen's devotion was through sex. He had discovered how you could con someone for love by turning yourself into everything they desired— until the time when your own priorities demanded that you abruptly take back your gift.

One night Jack had a surprise visitor in Ozone Park, when Neal simply turned up there, explaining he had come so that Jack could teach him how to write (he also had the ulterior motive of hoping Jack and his mother would provide him with a free bed to sleep in until he found another job). Gabe's pursed lips made it clear to Jack that she was suspicious of Neal's looks, so Jack quickly took him out to the tavern across the street. There, he offered Neal his only advice about writing: "You've got to stick to it with the energy of a benny addict."

Neal had naïvely hoped to get some quick tips to literary success, but even though Jack did not supply them, he kept coming back. Emitting the fervent "Yes's," "Wow's" and "That's right's" that often peppered his conversation, he read over Jack's shoulder as he labored on *The Town and the City*. Quickly intuiting that Jack was starved for affirmation, he told him, "Everything you do is good. Just do it, do it." That winter Jack often felt on the verge of giving up, since he had grown so dissatisfied with the heavy lyricism of the first half of the novel; he later thought that perhaps only his reluctance to disappoint Neal had kept him going. Neal also turned out to be a fellow Wolfean—he had read his first Thomas Wolfe novel at seventeen when Justin Brierly had sent it to him in the Colorado State Reformatory, where he was serving a two-year sentence for selling stolen tires. In the prison library, Neal had read his way through the Harvard Classics, developed an interest in philosophy (Plato and Santayana, in particular), and devoured the novels of Dostoevsky. His passion for self-education had a lot in common with Jack's. He had the kind of life story that seemed more fabulous than most fiction and planned to write it himself.

Jack was particularly captivated by Neal's accounts of his earliest experiences, which included hopping freight trains with his father. Before Neal's birth, Neal Sr. had been a respectable barber. Ruined by alcohol and the Depression, he had raised his small son in a Larimer Street flophouse on Denver's skid row after his wife left him, taking the older children. In *On the Road*, conflating Neal Sr.'s absence with Leo's death, Jack would make him "the father we never found," a recurring motif that runs all the way through the novel to the very last lines of the book. (In real life, Neal's hapless weak father never lost touch with his son, sending affectionate, muddled, childlike letters from wherever his wanderings took him.)

On one of Neal's visits to Jack, the two of them stayed up all night, with Neal lying on Leo's old bed reading aloud from a *Reader's Digest* account of the life of Jack London, so that Jack could hear the sound of a true western twang. Even by then, according to *Visions of Cody*, Jack still felt he did not actually *know* Neal, whom he felt was "serpentine," yet a deep intuitive understanding between them was already there on an "animal relationship" level. As they walked to the neighborhood library one unseasonably warm afternoon, they decided to hitchhike together to Denver that spring. After his long period of disillusionment, anger, estrangement, and solitude, Jack was more than willing to become infected with the excitement with which Neal embraced life and his "wild yea-saying overburst of American joy."

Like most of Neal's plans, that trip did not come off. Instead, very early in March, Neal abruptly decided to rejoin Luanne in Denver just as Allen was beginning to realize sadly that the more he and Neal understood each other, the less Neal seemed interested in having sex with him. Allen couldn't help having possessive feelings about Neal that Jack found uncomfortably Verlaine-like. "Why don't you take your damn hand off his thigh," he said sharply to Allen on one occasion when the three of them were together. Allen thought Jack sounded like his puritanical mother, but also wondered whether he was feeling jealous.

The night before Neal left town, he was indirectly responsible for breaking some of the ice between Allen and Jack. On March 3, as the three of them were having a farewell meal in a cafeteria near Columbia, Allen was suddenly able to talk to Jack "soberly (and severely) and straight and vibrant . . . à la Cassady—and it worked!" he jubilantly reported in his journal. Jack, however, still believed that Allen, like other Columbia intellectuals he knew, did not consider the Wolfean novel he was writing a work of any literary importance.

The following morning the two of them went to the Greyhound terminal on Forty-second Street to see Neal off on a bus that would take him as far as Chicago. He was unusually well dressed for his westward journey in a sharp pencil-striped zoot suit he had acquired in New York, by whatever means, and as he puffed on his cigar and patted his full belly, Jack was suddenly reminded of Leo. To kill some time, the three of them crowded into a booth and had their picture taken for a quarter, with Jack in the middle, one arm around each of them. They cut it into halves, which Neal and Allen solemnly placed in their wallets. The two of them were planning to meet in New Waverly, Texas, that summer, so that Allen could introduce Neal to Bill and Joan.

Exhausted from so much drinking and conversation and perhaps troubled by the sexual aspect of Neal's relationship with Allen, Jack went home to Ozone Park in very low spirits, with his usual feeling that New York was an "abyss" where the people he knew pursued little beyond their immediate gratification.

The two letters Neal sent back to New York during a stopover in Kansas City a couple of days later demonstrate his mastery of the art of being all things to all people. His letter to Allen, which he signed "love and kisses," enumerated some forty books (essentially the William S. Burroughs reading list combined with some Ginsbergian suggestions about modern poetry) that he intended to "digest" as soon as possible. Tactfully, the dedicated student of literature left out the racy story that was the center-piece of the letter received by Jack—an account of Neal's sleazy campaign to seduce a young girl he'd met on the bus between New York and Chicago by convincing her he could read her soul. Neal compared his intended conquest to Venus de Milo and had her swearing undying love, but since his efforts to bed her had been thwarted by her vigilant older sister, he'd had to console himself in Columbia, Missouri, with a virginal schoolteacher whom he screwed in the bushes and who just happened to be French Canadian. Though it was hardly great erotic writing, Jack dubbed this "The Great Sex Letter" in his answer to Neal. What struck him particularly was the very thing Neal found it necessary to apologize for—the completely uninhibited and rather disconnected way it was written, as if Neal (who was drunk at the time) had just jotted down anything that came into his head.

Although somewhat mystified by Jack's praise, Neal quickly seized the opportunity to play the role of his literary mentor. Three weeks later, in his next letter, typed on a purloined Underwood, he asked for nothing less than complete sincerity in their future correspondence, pointing out that some of the sentiments Jack expressed had sounded false to him in contrast to what Jack had written about the ridiculous ways he'd botched his attempt to take over Neal's job in a parking lot. He pronounced this account "very unstraight and complex and really blown out of all proportion," magnanimously adding, "but that's where we shine." Unfortunately, Neal's call for complete sincerity in language was somewhat compromised when he swore that Jack's continued struggle with *The Town and the City* was a source of "grief" for him and that he expected that he would "probably bawl" if Jack didn't "get that damn thing" off his chest.

Since his own confidence in the quality of what he was writing was so fragile, Jack interpreted Neal's hand-wringing as one more indication of his friends' lack of faith in what he was determined to accomplish—completing within one year this huge novel he had begun to feel he was writing with far too much care, given the time frame he had set himself.

He wrote back to Neal rather coolly in April, warning him not to make too much of an "issue" of the struggle he had been having and suggesting that Neal did not really understand him as well as he thought he did.

THE ROAD

Only a few hours after Neal's departure from New York, Jack decided to use his journal to record his fluctuations of mood day by day, in the hope of getting some insights into why the process of writing *The Town and the City* so often plunged him into depression. He went to sleep hoping to wake up with his almost religious belief in what he was doing restored to him. But he spent much of March in doubt and anguish, flagellating himself for the slowness with which he was working, although his average output of fifteen hundred words a day would have satisfied almost any other novelist. (The thought that Thomas Wolfe had managed to produce ten thousand words in one night tormented him.)

Although Jack recognized that his mood plummeted whenever he became bogged down in his writing, it never seemed to occur to him that he had set himself an inhuman goal in his determination to have half of his 380,000-word novel finished by the beginning of May, so that he could immediately try to get a contract for it. The rate of production this required ruled out almost all *life* in the interim, and Jack's "Mood Log" for March and April indicates that he left Ozone Park to go into Manhattan only three or four times. Each visit was a binge, followed by self-loathing and despair when he found himself unable to get right back to work the following day. One night, Jack drank himself into insensibility, downing beer, whiskey, vermouth, and whatever else he could get his hands on, wandering the streets in a daze, and waking up in the morning bruised and battered, unable to remember what had happened to him. It took him four days before he was able to write the next thousand words.

On his next trip into the city two weeks later, he met a beautiful red-head named Ginger Bailey, whom he called "Dark Eyes" in his journal, and immediately declared himself "in love." Ginger visited him in Ozone Park and they stayed up dancing to the Victrola and singing to each other through one romantic night without incurring Gabe's disapproval when she found Ginger there in the morning. But during the following days,

Jack sternly resisted the impulse to become distracted by this love affair, a decision he would later have reason to regret. Love, like everything else, would have to wait until his work was done, for the work was *everything*. In fact, there was so much riding on it that the thought of failure seemed a threat to his very existence. This monumental novel would surely prove to his family and all those who doubted him that he was a self-respecting male, able to support himself, his mother, and eventually a wife by his hard, honest labor, but more than that, Jack saw it as a "victory" over fear and death—even over the melancholy that lifted completely only every now and then when a sudden feeling of elation, usually unconnected to any cause, came over him. Meanwhile, however, the process of writing seemed to demand that he remain in an undisturbed state of solitary, brooding "gravity."

Only toward the end of March did Jack start to feel more confident. One night he wrote some pages that he actually considered amazing. By April 10, he could even feel that the end was in sight, with only 25,000 words to write in the next two weeks. A brief slump followed that terrified him, but by April 19, he realized that he had written 85,000 words during the past three months, which, combined with the 65,000 he had been able to salvage from the work he'd done in the fall, added up to 150,000. He went on a five-mile hike to celebrate.

When he came home, he started reading *The Oregon Trail* by Francis Parkman Jr., which he had recently taken out of the library. "My subject as a writer is of course America," he wrote to Hal Chase that night, "and simply I must know everything about it." He wanted to be like Balzac, who had written about every class of society in France from criminals to aristocrats and every aspect of Paris, the city he considered "the center of the world." Jack also noted that he felt he was undergoing a shift in his consciousness, cryptically describing it as "a new interest in things rather than ideas." Perhaps he was starting to recognize that the grandiose and condemnatory abstractions that had dominated his thinking since the winter of 1946 were a sign of malaise rather than proof of his brilliance. In 1951 he would start the first draft of *On the Road* with an allusion to "a serious illness that I won't bother to talk about except that it really had something to do with my father's death and my awful feeling that everything was dead."

As preoccupied as Jack still was with *The Town and the City*, the contours of another book were already forming in his mind as he read Parkman and devoured other books about the West and American history. Although he was briefly tempted to write a novel about George Washington after reading some biographies, Jack kept returning to the germ of an idea that had first occurred to him fourteen months earlier, when he'd written a thumbnail description in his journal of a book in which the protagonist would be driven by the passionate desire to live after his recovery from a debilitating illness. Fed up with pessimistic thinking, this character would take to the road, where he would meet an assortment of other wanderers, connected to one another only thematically, who would share his need for movement. Rereading that entry, perhaps around the time he wrote to Hal, Jack wrote a brief note under it commending himself for the "energy and earnestness" of this vision.

During the next weeks, he sent away for road maps of every state. Spreading them out on his mother's kitchen table, he spent hours going over their geographical features, dreaming the journey ahead of him that summer. A number of times during the past two years, Jack had been on the verge of setting out for the West Coast and had even considered hitchhiking all the way to Alaska and working on the Alaskan pipeline with his new brother-in-law, but his father's illness and then his complete absorption in *The Town and the City* had kept him grounded in Ozone Park. Now every thousand words he wrote moved him closer to an actual departure. While a stop-off in Denver to see Neal as well as Hal and Ed had recently become an essential part of the plan, it was by no means Jack's primary reason for his first trip west.

He reached his self-imposed finish line on May 5 after a grueling all-night marathon in which he wrote twenty-five hundred words. Delirious with joy, Jack acknowledged that the tremendous struggle he had been engaged in since January had probably taken ten years off his life. But now that it was time to live before tackling the daunting "City" half of the novel, which would include the story of Lucien and Kammerer, he realized that neither the town nor the city would ever be the right place for him. Fortunately, he had a new terrific idea, as clear and bright to him as that May morning—the idea of a farm (like the one Burroughs had just purchased), which he could buy with a loan from the Veterans Administration. There he would be his own boss, take care of his mother, and live with the "real woman" he was bound to meet someday and the children he would have with her. This idea was like the ancestral dream of owning land that the grandfather Jack was named for had futilely realized in Rivière-du-Loup before pulling up stakes and moving his family to America.

Jack waited a month to read his manuscript—from the symphonic opening with its brooding and tender evocation of the Merrimack River as it rushes through the town of Galloway still drowsy in the early morning light to the end of the section he had just completed, where, with the advent of the war, the Martin family starts to break apart. Although it already seemed to him "a veritable Niagara of a novel," he reluctantly decided it would be wise to complete it before trying to get it published, perhaps fearing that a string of rejections might tempt him to abandon it. "It's sorrowful to know," he wrote in his journal, "that this is not the age for such art." In the fall Jack had read *The Great Gatsby*; since then he had been painfully aware that it was the "leaver-outers" like F. Scott Fitzgerald and Hemingway who were now in vogue, rather than the great "putter-inners" like Wolfe, whose piled-on, Whitmanesque "catalogues"—the maximalist device Jack had embraced in his own writing— Temko had recently made fun of. Jack had also begun wishing he were narrating the story from only one point of view rather than going into the minds of so many different characters.

Looking for inspiration, he spent a good part of June 19 reading Tolstoy's moral essays, and decided there was "a lugubrious senility in morality which is devoid of real life." He felt far more affinity with Dostoevsky's "Karamazov Christ of lust and glees." A few days later, Jack sat down with the New Testament, which he felt he was suddenly absorbing as if he had never read it before. The teachings of Jesus, with their "confrontation" and "confoundment of the terrible enigma of human life," the inevitability of death, seemed to be speaking to him directly.

The teachings of Jesus were still very much on Jack's mind after a visit to Kinston, North Carolina, where Nin and her husband, Paul Blake, were fixing up a small house they had just moved into. A war veteran who had grown up in the South, Paul had some problems settling down to make a good living. His greatest interests, which Jack fully appreciated, were hound dogs, hunting, and roaming around in the backwoods. Jack had looked forward to going fishing with his new brother-in-law, but when they'd caught a bass, he'd been struck to the heart by its terrible death throes, which he equated with human suffering. "Oh God—this is all of us, it happens to all of us. What shall we do, where shall we go and why do we die like this?" Why had God made it so *"hard"* for men? he asked despairingly in his journal.

Despite such dark reflections, he had come back to Ozone Park with his appetite whetted for "getting around." Jesus had said, "My kingdom is not of this world." But his own kingdom *was* the world and now he felt the need to rush back into it. An unexpected visit from Henri Cru, who came sailing into New York on a freighter the first week in July and presented him with three outsized reefers he had picked up in Panama, provided Jack with guilt-free justification for a trip that would take him through the West all the way to the Pacific. Even more of a con artist than he'd been in prep school, Henri liked to make extravagant gifts and grandiose promises to friends he was trying to impress, for which he expected payback in abject gratitude and submissive behavior. He urged Jack to join him right away in Marin City, claiming the two of them would soon have cushy jobs on a luxurious ocean liner, where as chief electrician Henri could practically guarantee that Jack would be hired as his assistant. He repeated this offer, with some additional flourishes—fine wines and dining, etc.—in a letter sent from the Coast.

Here was the ideal way for Jack to make good money to repay Gabe for the year and a half she had been supporting him. When even she told him to go, Jack wrote Henri to expect him within ten days and left on the morning of July 19. According to the map he was using to plot his trip, the straight red line of Route 6 would take him almost as far as Denver, his first destination.

Three decades later, William Least Heat-Moon, a writer often compared to Kerouac, set out to explore the back roads of America in the white van he made famous in *Blue Highways*. The vehicle featured a bunk bed, a camping stove, and a portable toilet that Least Heat-Moon had installed;

he also took with him a typewriter, a tape recorder, and a very useful credit card. Jack, on the other hand, went on the road in a pair of flimsy huaraches, the favorite summer footwear of Greenwich Village bohemians; he was carrying a small knapsack containing a change of clothes and one of his spiral notebooks and had sixty dollars in his pocket. Except for the money, which had to last him all the way to the Coast, he was traveling as light as those freight hoppers and hobos who had captured his imagination in the films he saw in the thirties, and he never found that straight red line from here to there that he had been counting on.

The night of July 19 found him marooned in the rain somewhere near Bear Mountain, where Route 6 was headed north rather than west and where there was no passing traffic to pick him up. He had to take a bus back to New York in order to get another to Chicago—a detour that cost him a day and two-thirds of his cash. Two days later he finally connected with Route 6 just outside Joliet, Illinois, where he hitched a ride on a dynamite truck and felt the thrill of heading at last into the legendary West, a trip that had taken vivid shape in his imagination before he embarked on it.

Least Heat-Moon returned from the road with stacks of tapes to be transcribed. Jack would return to Ozone Park in the fall of 1947 with remarkably little down on paper in the form of notes on his recent adventures. Carolyn Cassady would later swear that she had seen him standing on Denver street corners jotting down everything he saw and heard—a "fact" that immediately made its way into Kerouac biography. But the truth is that apart from a paragraph listing the names of places he passed through, Jack recorded very little of what he saw and experienced during the course of his first trip to the West. As the changing American landscape kept unrolling before him, he was far too absorbed in what his eyes and memory were constantly taking in to be able to pull back from it to take out his pencil. Meanwhile, his mind must have had to make constant adjustments between what he'd imagined and what he actually saw.

Jack wrote no accounts of the moments when his western fantasies had to give way to postwar desecrations of what he'd expected to find intact—his first sight of the dry-bedded (and already polluted) Mississippi "with its big rank smell"; or his arrival in Council Bluffs, Iowa, where streets of "cute suburban cottages" obliterated the great gathering place of covered

wagons described by Parkman; or the first genuine cowboy he saw, walking along "like any Beat character," past the "bleak" meat warehouses of
Omaha; or the travesty of Wild West Week in Cheyenne. Left out as well
are the things that surpassed his dreams—the green smells of the prairie, the brightness of the stars over the Great Plains, the astonishing
"long flat wastelands of sand and sagebrush," the moment when the great
snow-covered Rockies finally loomed up before his eyes in Longmont,
Colorado, and he knew that one more ride would take him into smoky
Denver, where he was awaited by Neal and the whole Denver gang, plus
Allen, none of whose actual spoken words he would write down in his
notebooks, although he would evoke them with seemingly total recall in
On the Road. The trip Jack takes there, although it can be traced on a
map, is "a journey often through his own mind," as Lawrence Sterne's
travels in France were once described by Virginia Woolf.

Jack's notebooks contain no proof that he actually ran into every one of
that string of colorful western characters whose paths he crossed en route
to Denver. But when he wrote about them four years later, he certainly
used some of them symbolically and structurally, as had been his intention when he first thought about writing a road novel in 1946. Since duality was a theme he was far from done with, Jack would use the sneaky
behavior of hyperactive Montana Slim to evoke the trickster side of Dean
Moriarty's nature, while his portrayal of Mississippi Gene, who, like an
older brother tenderly looks after a sixteen-year-old runaway, would sig-
nal that Sal Paradise would find a guide and brother in Dean, despite
Dean's failings.

In one famous scene in the novel, Sal Paradise wakes up around sunset
in a trackside hotel room in Des Moines with the recognition that for the
first time in his life "I really didn't know who I was for about fifteen
strange seconds. . . . I was just somebody else, some stranger, and my
whole life was a haunted life, the life of a ghost." This disoriented awakening, often wrongly cited in biographies as the turning point in Jack's
perception of himself and his entire generation, was described in a piece
Jack wrote in November 1947 right after he returned home from his travels. But the reference to a "haunted life," which would later give it a generational significance, was not attached to it until 1951. It was an image
that had been with Jack ever since his friends started dying in World

War II, and he had even thought of using it as a title for his early Galloway novel. The red late-afternoon light Sal wakes up to in *On the Road* is
the same red light that suffuses Jack's "memory" of birth, which he first
described in a novel fragment in 1945 and would use again in *Dr. Sax*.
And that lost feeling of being "somebody else" had been set down on
paper for the first time in the poem "I Am My Mother's Son," which Jack
wrote at nineteen in his furnished room in Hartford when he also felt
very far from home:

> I woke up in the middle of the night
> and realized to my horror that I did
> not remember who I was.

It is clear that Jack brought the mind of a poet to his fiction rather than
the mind of a note-taking "reporter." "A poet . . ." W. B. Yeats once wrote,
paraphrasing his friend George Russell, "does not transmute into song
what he has learned in experience." Reversing "the order," the poet instead "first imagines" and then "later the imagination attracts its affinities."

Down to his last dollar and after surviving for a good part of his trip on
a starvation diet of apple pie and ice cream, as he cheerfully reported on a
card he sent his mother, Jack walked into the Denver bus terminal on
Larimer Street several days behind schedule. Hal Chase arrived there in
a car to take him home overnight, plunging Jack immediately into a
world of clean sheets, square meals, and bourgeois comforts. After a
good night's sleep under Hal's bust of Goethe, Jack was installed the following day in Ed White's pleasant apartment, already occupied by Ed's
summer houseguest, Allan Temko. Temporarily expatriated from New
York, Temko worked on his novel wearing a silk smoking jacket and
talked of French wines and his scorn for arty people. Both he and Hal
were loftily vague about the whereabouts of Neal Cassady and of Allen
Ginsberg, who was working as a stockboy in May's department store
after his visit with Bill and Joan.

In mid-April, Neal's letters to Jack had stopped abruptly and the last
one Neal had written gave no indication of the growing complications in

his love life since his return to Denver. Fully intending to return to Lu-anne while keeping his relationship with Allen alive on a more platonic basis, Neal had immediately become distracted by the challenging con-quest of a classy blond graduate of Bennington, four years older than he was, who was studying art and theater in Denver and dating his pool hall friend Bill Tomson. In a letter to Allen in June explaining why he was not going to join him in Texas, Neal had finally decided to mention Carolyn Robinson: "Her lack of cynicism, artificial sophistication and sterility in her creative make-up will recommend her to you. She is just a bit too straight for my temperament; however, that is the challenge." For Neal, whose mother had chosen to abandon him when he was four, Carolyn's maternal straightness—a quality that would hem him in a little, provide a structure to rebel against—may have been precisely what he craved. He told Allen that being with her gave him "a sense of peace," meanwhile swearing that he needed Allen "more than ever." As for Luanne—he de-clared that his only interest in her now was "fatherly," although, in point of fact, he was still secretly sleeping with her on the days he wasn't devot-ing to his so far chaste courtship of Carolyn.

Although Carolyn was spellbound by Neal's genius (nothing prompted her *not* to believe that he had been studying philosophy at Columbia), she was relieved that he didn't try to pressure her into having sex with him, since she had soon found out about Luanne. She was a young woman with a great craving for *attention*—a word that crops up frequently in her memoir *Off the Road*, and no one could be more attentive than Neal, once he put his mind to it. Her defenses had broken down considerably that spring when he presented her with a passionate declaration of love in the form of a sonnet that had actually been written to him by Allen, but the courtship remained mostly on the level of soul talk until the night in mid-June when Allen arrived on a bus from Texas and Neal brought him to Carolyn's hotel room to spend his first night in Denver on her couch. When Allen was presumed to be asleep, Neal climbed into bed with her. He shocked Carolyn by pumping away furiously without any prelimi-nary tender lovemaking until he had his orgasm and didn't seem to no-tice her pain and lack of response. She slipped out of bed to weep in the bathroom, but told herself that their sexual relationship was bound to get better. It apparently remained a terrible disappointment to her even after they were married. On a panel of Beat women fifty years later, Carolyn bluntly described Neal's approach to making love as "rape." Nonetheless, she had become hooked on Neal permanently. Once they were married she would accommodate his excesses and transgressions, until the evidence became too much to bear, by remaining in a state of denial as much she could, and after his death, she would find a kind of queenly, self-justifying pride in the religion she had made of her acceptance. "For me, he became the angel I wrestled with," she would write in 1981, "and, like Job, I did not let him go until he blessed me."

One of the bridges Neal had burned soon after his return to Denver was his relationship with Justin Brierly. Hoping to impress his former mentor with the progress he had made as a poet while he was away in New York, Neal had presented him with two of Allen's most ambitious poems, which he had laboriously copied out on his typewriter—Allen had let Neal have them expressly for this purpose. Brierly, whom Allen would afterward call "Dancing Master Death," immediately realized this was a scam, and had let his other Denver protégés know that this was the last straw. By the time Jack arrived on the scene, no one in Hal's crowd of young intellectuals from well-to-do families was talking to Allen or Neal. Temko, who had a tendency to be smug, told Jack that Neal was a "moron." The schism had an element of homophobia as well as class warfare. In Lowell Jack had gone back and forth between the Young Prometheans and his Pawtucketville gang; now, once again, he found himself caught in the middle, though his deepest bonds were with Allen and Neal.

Allen, who had been hoping to spend a "season" with Neal that would solidify their relationship as lovers, had moved into a dismal basement room. There he worked on a long poem of lamentation entitled "Denver Doldrums," and waited for Neal to fit him in between Neal's conscientious daily bedside visits to Luanne and to Carolyn (who despite her feelings of possessiveness could not have looked forward wholeheartedly to her share of lovemaking). Neal was operating on a very tight schedule. There wasn't much sex left over for Allen—in fact, practically none, although Allen's soul-to-soul conversations with Neal had taken on a frantic new intensity charged with his suffering. He seemed to Jack now like a "Russian saint," poised on the edge of revelation, but Jack thought that Allen's exchanges with Neal—their attempts to work out some ultimate psychic connection neither could articulate—might drive both of them mad. Allen's passion for Neal apparently no longer disturbed Jack, though just the year before he might have condemned it as decadent. Perhaps he even respected it, for he himself would never experience that consuming kind of love. He felt a little excluded, though, listening in on their private rapports, which they seemed to be conducting in their own bewildering language, and wished he could simply talk to Neal alone over a beer or two.

When Carolyn Robinson was finally introduced to Jack, she was certain he was very taken with her. He showed up once or twice to watch her rehearse in a play at the University of Denver. One night they danced together. According to Carolyn's memoir, Jack whispered his regret that Neal had seen her first and she felt somewhat sorry about that herself. But Jack had reservations about the new woman in Neal's life. In August, he commented to Neal: "A nice girl. But hardly your type—she's too pale and furtive." As if he sensed something was missing in their sexual relationship, he thought a girl like Edie, "giggling in the sheets at morning, not just smiling," would be more Neal's ticket.

Jack's unusual buoyancy of spirit that summer enabled him to move lightly in Denver between his two factions of friends without trying to reunite them or passing judgment. He wrote his mother that he was having fun, claiming that he had ten girlfriends (a far less threatening number for Gabe to think about than one), that he had been wined, dined, and taken up to the mountains, and had even seen an opera—a performance of *Fidelio*, whose dungeon scenes reminded him, four years later, of "the gloom, rising from the underground" of "a new beat generation that I was slowly joining." He mentioned Temko and Hal, but left out Allen and Neal. Assuring Gabe that he couldn't wait to be home with her again, he asked for a loan so that he could afford to take a bus to San Francisco. By then it was the end of July. When Gabe wired him fifty dollars a week later, Jack bought his ticket and headed for the Coast, still feeling disappointed that he'd seen so little of Neal.

REACHING CALIFORNIA

In 1935, at the height of his fame, Thomas Wolfe went all the way west for the first time in a first-class compartment on a Zephyr train and was lavishly feted in Hollywood when he reached California after a speaking engagement in Denver. "I have no words to tell you of the beauty, power and magnificence of this country," he wrote his editor Maxwell Perkins from the Coast. "Thank God that I have seen it at last—and I know that I did not lie about it." Twelve years later, on August 10, Jack staggered out of the Market Street bus station in San Francisco feeling like a "haggard ghost." Though he would soon call San Francisco "the queen of cities," his first impression was "long bleak streets" full of panhandlers, and even his first sight of the Pacific Ocean from the Golden Gate Bridge daunted him, since he expected to soon be out on its vast waters with Henri Cru. "It's the end of the land, babe," Jack wrote me in 1957 from Frisco, when he was about to give up on the place all over again. For him that city came to represent the end of expectation. Like all his dreamed-of destinations, it never gave him what he'd hoped to find. Within a week of Jack's arrival in August 1947, he would be writing a passage for his novel about Peter Martin's longing to return to New York. As he thought of decadent Manhattan from the western edge of the continent, he could suddenly see it as "Bethlehem" as well as "Babylon."

He found Henri Cru living with a sullen and petulant girlfriend in a little shack in Marin City, near a military installation where he had just been employed as a guard. Once Jack moved in, all three of them slept in the same room. The two soft ocean liner jobs with the fat paychecks that Henri had touted had gone up in smoke, if indeed they ever existed, and the girlfriend often gave vent to her fury, which mounted steadily after Jack's arrival, that Henri was not supporting her in the style to which her blond good looks entitled her. Fortunately for Jack, there was an opening for another barracks guard at forty-five dollars a week and he took it, sending thirty to his mother, scraping along on the remaining fifteen, and strapping a gun to his hip for the first time in his life. He wondered what Burroughs would think about his taking a job as a cop. While his Keystone Kop disguise was hilarious, it also made him uneasy.

Meanwhile Henri tried to run Jack's literary career. First of all, he ordered Jack to write about an old street vendor called the Banana King whom Henri considered the most unforgettable character he had ever met. He persisted and persisted, while Jack good-naturedly failed to comply. It was the madness of Henri Cru, not the Banana King, that interested him, and that was what he wrote about in his notebook. Then Henri decided Jack must write a screenplay, claiming the Hollywood contacts of his sister could practically guarantee an immediate sale whose proceeds they would share. This scheme Jack fell for, figuring his old connections with Columbia Pictures would help as well. On a typewriter that belonged to the military, he pounded out a ninety-nine-page script called *Christmas in New York* during the nights he was supposed to be standing guard over a barracks filled with brawling construction workers due to be shipped overseas.

To his California address came a bombardment of letters from Ozone Park—letters that must have kept him in a constant state of worry about his mother's loneliness, even though she maintained that his trip—including some limited contact with "cuties"—was "just what the doctor ordered" and made a point of telling her beloved boy she had never realized what a good son he truly was until he sent her that first thirty dollars. She wrote him that she was saving the money from his paychecks toward the purchase of a Frigidaire (the first refrigerator in the family, Jack would proudly note in *On the Road*) as she fought off the landlord's attempts to raise the rent, worked in the shoe factory where her hours were being cut, and came home at night to read her copy of the *Daily Mirror* as she ate her solitary dinner off a plate she rested on the piano stool. Gabe had only a fifth-grade education but she had narrative and descriptive powers. Sometimes Jack even compared her storytelling ability to Dostoevsky's. As she built up the picture of Jack's selfless little mother valiantly holding down the fort at home, weaving a rag rug for his return like Penelope waiting for Odysseus, Gabe had an excellent instinct for when to bring in the pathos in case he was enjoying himself too much—little touches like that plate on the piano stool or a line or two about how she had begun to talk to herself like the crazy people she saw on the street. Still there was no doubt she wanted those money orders to keep coming. While Jack was raiding the barracks' food supplies with Henri in order not to go hungry, Gabe bought some silver settings she felt Nin couldn't do without now that she was married. When Jack sent her a copy of *Christmas in New York*, she gave it her highest praise—it would make just the kind of movie Louella Parsons said America needed.

Gabe may have been flattered to discover that she was the kindly grandmother in her son's script, but she may also have read it with some pain. Although Jack rightly regarded it as a sentimental potboiler, his Christmas story was far too dark for Hollywood. At its center was a child artist who believes in angels and who dies of rheumatic fever, bringing together his estranged parents, a glamorous movie star and a merchant seaman. The little boy's last name was Fitzgerald, but his first name was Gerard.

Now that Jack was reunited with a typewriter, nothing gave him more pleasure, as he wrote to Neal Cassady on August 26, than writing down everything that occurred to him "with all sorts of silly little remarks and noises" as if he were conversing with Neal directly. This unguarded "scribbling-away" was becoming Jack's letter-writing mode and would eventually lead to the intimate tone and seemingly artless way in which he wrote his books, where, as the poet Clark Coolidge very perceptively put it in his *Village Voice* review of the first volume of Jack's letters, "The first person seems already a form of address, the I needing a you, if only imaginary, to tell it all out to, complete the energy jump." Although Jack did not yet consciously apply his new approach to letter writing to his fiction, his poetic urgency to communicate directly with the "you" of the reader could already be felt in *The Town and the City*, especially in passages that seem to insist that the feelings being described are universal:

A kind of lyrical ecstasy possesses certain young Americans in the springtime, a feeling of not belonging in any one place or in any one moment, a wild restless longing to be elsewhere, everywhere, right now!

But in Jack's first novel, the intended intimacy would often be undermined by the omniscient, generalizing voice of the third-person narrator.

———

In December, Neal Cassady, picking up on what he'd been absorbing from Jack, would attempt to apply some of Jack's casually framed thoughts about epistolary writing to more serious literary endeavors. In the inflated magisterial tone he still often fell into, mixed with some true eloquence, Neal would urge him to "forget all rules, literary styles and other such pretentions [*sic*]" and instead to "write, as nearly as possible, as if he were the first person on earth and was humbly and sincerely putting on paper that which he saw and experienced and loved and lost; what his passing thoughts were and his sorrows and desires." Having witnessed Jack's tremendous struggle to write like "the first person on earth," Neal was responding to the sense of mission that had awed him during his visits to Ozone Park; less than a year later, however, he was already beginning to fear that the "roots" of his own urge to write were not as deep as Jack's or Allen's.

Jack's August 26 letter to Neal was full of deep affection for him as well as for Allen, which Jack expressed with new openness. At the same time, he found some good tactful reasons to discourage Neal from joining him in California. He told Neal he was now planning to go to pursers' school in Frisco and suggested that a visit might derail his plan to ship out. He urged him to go to Texas with Allen instead so that Neal could form his own friendships with Burroughs and Joan and come back with interesting stories to tell him. Whenever Jack patiently explained to someone the benefits of not getting together with him, it was a sign that he actually didn't want company. In this case, he may have wanted to continue to be on his own without having his thoughts and experiences mediated by Neal's powerful presence. (So far his conception of the road novel he wanted to write involved the protagonist making a solitary journey.) There was also some deep part of himself that he preferred not to share and he expressed his resistance to Neal's pressure "to consistently lay myself before you." Yet Jack ended the letter by confessing one of his most painful secrets—the fact that he had once hated the very sight of his father's face and only realized too late that his hatred had been a "mad love." He asked Neal why human beings had to learn such things in an excruciating way, making harsh judgments instead of being happy with each other: "It were far better that, instead of perfecting our attitudes . . . we would spend time perfecting doubt, become saints, saints."

Jack was still in the grip of these ideas the following day when he answered a letter from Allen, who was asking whether he should now "close [his] heart," since he was suffering to the point of despair from Neal's continued unwillingness to have sex with him and from the insulting aloofness of Ed, Temko, and especially Hal, to whom he used to feel so close. Like a wise older brother, Jack counseled him to "doubt your disappointment in them . . . doubt their valuelessness, for they have value," and in other words to "Forgive everything." He gently criticized the poem "Denver Doldrums," which Allen had sent him, pointing out the places where Allen was passing off his sadness as "art," but assured Allen that he had the love of the "fallen angels" and that the life he was putting together for himself would be "wonderful." As Jack saw it, they were all walking around in temporary confusion like Shakespeare's mistaken lovers in the Edenic "Forest of Arden."

In the weeks since he had completed the first half of *The Town and the City* and left Ozone Park, Jack had begun to undergo a spiritual transformation that would affect much of his thinking as well as the tone of almost everything he wrote. It was as if through the process of looking backward to his boyhood in Lowell and writing about everything he most loved, he had somehow come out into the light as he had imagined Peter Martin doing at the end of the novel. As John Clellon Holmes would later tell him, the process of writing the novel had "brought life to you, while you were bringing life to it."

While Jack tried to bring the perfection of doubt to bear upon human relationships, the fights between Henri Cru and his girlfriend, Diane, were growing more and more vicious. When Diane was alone with Jack, she would embarrass him by excoriating Henri, but she had no use for Jack either and let him know that she considered him a freeloader (thinking that he would soon be going home to finish his novel, he was sending even more of his earnings to Gabe and trying to live on only five dollars a week). Meanwhile, Henri had pointedly started tacking grocery receipts to the wall. After Henri and Diane flew down to Hollywood with Jack's script and failed to interest the famous director whose Malibu party they crashed, after Henri lost all his money at the races, after a screaming fight during which Jack retreated to a corner as Diane and Henri clawed at each other and Diane tried to get her hands on Henri's gun, Jack realized he had stayed too long. The spectacle of such gnawing hatred between a man and a woman filled him with a "melancholy horror" he knew was very dangerous for him—perhaps the fight and his own helplessness during it reminded him of the old fights his parents used to have about Leo's gambling. He vowed to become an "idiot," like Dostoevsky's Myshkin, to suspend his tendency to judge others, and to forgive everything, as he had advised Allen to do, existing in a state of "dreamy thoughtfulness" as an example to other men. But the words he wrote in his journal on October 11 vibrated with his rage and disgust.

He stuck around long enough to get disgracefully drunk in a French restaurant where Henri Cru's efforts to make a good impression on his disdainful aristocratic father were completely undone. And he kept a promise to himself to climb Mount Tamalpais the following day, despite the hangover he must have had. But by October 14, he was gone, heading for L.A.—from there he planned to travel home by a southerly route that would take him through parts of America he had not yet seen.

For the time being, Jack was through with San Francisco. To him, the Queen of Cities now seemed a shallow, spiritually empty place, epitomized by some spoiled socialites he'd seen at the races wearing pretentious long gowns. After coming all the way west looking for Parkman's frontier, Jack had only been reminded of the exclusion of people like himself from the American dream.

He hitched as far south as Bakersfield, then decided to take a bus down the San Joaquin Valley the rest of the way. Just across the aisle sat one of those small, soulful-looking Mexican girls whose bodies reminded him of grapes. Acutely lonely, he did something he usually felt too shy to do—and approached her. After offering to let her use his raincoat as a pillow, he asked if he could sit with her, and she demurely agreed. They hit it off so well, in fact, that it wasn't long before they were holding hands and saying they were in love. Jack had a habit of "falling in love" all at once, captivated by the look of this woman or that one—certain types of women were vessels for his dreams. This was the dream of the pure, uncorrupted girl he hoped to find someday—in this case, a girl who also had Indian blood. Often founded solely upon fantasy, Jack's relationships with women were almost inevitably disappointing—like the trips he imagined before taking them. This one would be an exception.

The Mexican girl portrayed in *On the Road* is warm, simple, and fatalistically acquiescent, but Bea Franco, who had been deserted by her husband and had been picking grapes in the vineyards of Bakersfield, was far less archetypal. She had her own longings to go adventuring in the world, and Jack seemed to her, as she later wrote him, the most "unspoiled boy" she'd ever met. Hungry for a romantic interlude in her hard life, she went with Jack to a hotel room in L.A. There her uncomplicated willingness to go to bed with him, plus Jack's own gringolike assumptions about Mexican women, caused him to suspect that he'd picked up a hustler who would steal the remaining twenty dollars in his pocket—an ugly attack of paranoia he would later ruefully write about. But all Bea Franco actually wanted was a little of Jack's tenderness, and when she went out to buy food after they'd made love and he had fallen asleep, she used a page of his notebook to write him an IOU for fifty cents.

"She was going to be my girl in town," Jack quickly decides in *On the Road,* his mind leaping ahead to the "wild complexities" of a "new season" (always a code term for a new love) that would involve Neal and Luanne. Bea, who had always yearned to travel, was tempted to go with Jack when he proposed that she hitchhike to New York with him but she was tied down because she had a child, whom she had left for the time being with her mother. For the next forty-eight hours they wandered the streets of Los Angeles, spending what little money Jack had, a dollar of which went for marijuana. All around them Jack saw a "fantastic carnival of lights and wildness. Booted cops frisked people on practically every corner. The beatest characters in the country swarmed on the sidewalks— all of it under those soft southern California stars that are lost in the brown halo of the huge desert encampment L.A. really is." The flotsam and jetsam of lost Americans from everywhere looked to Jack as if they had all mistakenly come to Hollywood to be in the movies.

He had been in a hurry to get home, because he wanted to finish *The Town and the* City by his twenty-sixth birthday, but he made a quick decision to delay his trip and stay with his Mexican girl a few days longer, undoubtedly seeing that he had a rare chance to make a cultural detour into Bea Franco's fellaheen California. He was dark enough himself so that when he was with Bea everyone perceived him as a Mexican, rather than the American "college boy" Bea had noticed on the bus. *Anglais* white people treated him accordingly. "They thought I was a Mexican of course," Jack would later write, "and in a way I am."

As soon as they hitchhiked back up the Coast to the agricultural village of Selma, where Bea's relatives lived, Jack arranged for his exit from there, sending a penny postcard to Gabe asking for one last money order. After splurging the last of his cash on one night with Bea in a motel room, it became essential for him to find some work in Selma before his departure. They moved into a tent, where for a few days Jack shared the hopeless poverty of Bea and her people, a life he later evoked with a radiant intensity that spiritualized its harshness, just as Louis Hémon had found a devotional purity in the lives of the *habitants* in *Maria Chapdelaine*.

From the start Bea accepted that the "college boy" who treated her so gently could not possibly stay with her, and even told Jack that she envied his freedom. "I wish I were you, Jackie," she would often say, as she later reminded him. But unlike Jack, she could handle adversity with a true gaiety of spirit. Perhaps Jack's soul did begin getting all "mixed up" with hers, as he wrote in *On the Road*. When Bea's little son, Albert, joined them, Jack fantasized that the three of them were a family. But they were living on grapes and he was afraid they were all going to starve.

Shortly before he could start for home, he took one of the worst jobs in America— picking cotton. It seemed beautiful at first working under the blue California sky as he knelt on the warm brown soil—like his back-to-the-land dream of having a farm—but Bea and Albert, laboring in the field right beside him, were skilled enough to pick far more cotton than he did. For their combined efforts all they got was $1.50—enough for Bea to buy some canned spaghetti, which she heated up for them as Jack rested his aching back and took care of his blisters.

Meanwhile, the October weather had abruptly changed and the cold nights in the tent signaled to Bea that the time had come to take Albert and move back in with her mother, which she did just before Jack left. When he said good-bye to her after their last night of love, guilty about leaving her in circumstances he could do nothing to improve, he interpreted Bea's lack of anger as a lack of emotion. He left her with an invitation to join him and his mother for Christmas in New York, without realizing how seriously she took everything he said.

It had been a perfect little marriage, but Jack's sadness at ending it passed almost immediately. He was joyful at the thought of returning to his real life in the East. A cowboy fiddler, who might not have stopped for him if he'd been with Bea, took him to L.A., where he picked up his rejected script from Columbia Pictures. After buying a bus ticket that would take him as far as Pittsburgh and the ingredients for ten salami sandwiches, he had exactly one dollar in his pocket. Klieg lights streamed across the night sky as Jack spread mustard on his salami in the toilet of a parking lot, realizing he'd just had his "Hollywood career." "There was no end to the American sadness and the American madness," he would write in *On the Road.*

By the time Jack arrived home on October 29, the Frigidaire was due to be purchased. The rag rug, now completed, covered the spotless floor of his room. Stacked on his desk where he'd left it was the half-finished manuscript of his novel. He'd had his last meal in Columbus, Ohio, paid for by a girl he'd picked up on the bus. Faint with hunger and exhaustion during the last stretch of his journey, he'd hitchhiked all the way from Pittsburgh and had to ask a stranger in Times Square for the dime that got him to Ozone Park. His mother was shocked by his haggard condition.

After Gabe went to bed, he stared around his room, not yet fully believing that he actually had a home, that after living like a hobo, he was even "a gentleman." He had filled that small space with hundreds of pages of words, but it seemed to him now that he had only been "a boy writing." And he thought of that boy's arrogant ambition with a weary detachment.

As he felt his familiar depression descending upon him, Jack realized that on the road he had been "moodless," his mind totally absorbed in the struggle to survive. Out there, he thought, you could almost lose your sense of "humanity." It was hard to come back from that "half-animal" existence to the "decency and humility" of his life as a writer. He would always be happiest *between* his departures and arrivals.

———

When it appeared in the *Paris Review* in 1956, "The Mexican Girl" would change Jack's luck and result in *On the Road* finally getting published. I wonder how long it took for Bea Franco to find out Jack had written about her. In fiction, their love affair lasts nearly twice as long as it actually did and the reader never asks whether the young dreamer who has slipped so easily into the Mexican girl's alternate reality and wakes up from it so reluctantly, only when he realizes it is impossible for him to stay there, could possibly have had the ulterior motives of a writer.

Bea kept in touch with Jack until early December. The half dozen letters expressing her longing to be with him are filled with her sweetness, and she wrote them with a down-to-earth eloquence, making not one mistake in her English. Little Albert had come down with pneumonia soon after Jack left, and once he recovered, she'd had to move back alone into a tent, where she had to keep a gas plate going day and night. Still she was saving every penny toward her Christmas visit and couldn't wait to cook a Spanish dinner for Jack's mother, who she was sure was "just tops." She told Jack that he never would have gone hungry on his way home if he'd had her along with him. A number of her letters went unanswered before Jack wrote her that he was planning to ship out and had just signed on for three voyages. How long would those voyages take? Bea wondered. Then gently and proudly she let him off the hook. New York would be too cold for her; she'd only wanted to come because of him. "Jackie," she asked him, "why do you feel the way you do?"

OZONE PARK

On November 1, before he tried to reconnect with *The Town and the City*, Jack sat down at his typewriter and wrote twenty-five hundred words in the same compelling first-person voice that could be heard at times in his journals when he was calling up one of his memories. This memory was of very recent vintage—an encounter he'd had in Harrisburg, Pennsylvania, with an old hobo who had materialized in the dark like a ghost as Jack hiked along a desolate stretch of the Susquehanna River that made him feel like someone lost in an "Eastern wilderness." The old man, a World War I veteran who carried a broken cardboard suitcase and was full of indignation about the way America had treated him, was, Jack thought, a "professional" hobo (and ready-made symbolic figure) who had spent a lifetime on the road. Now he was heading for Canada—a final destination that he seemed to regard as "Eldorado," insisting over and over again that he knew a spot up in Batavia, New York, where he was going to "go right into her." On his way back from his own American journey, bound for the little Canada he shared with his mother, Jack may have felt he too was about to cross that border—which he called the darkest and "loneliest" one in the world. In the story he wrote on his third day at home, he introduced his "Ghost of the Susquehanna" memory with another—that strange awakening in Des Moines when he had been unable to locate his identity.

Two days later, he forced himself to go back to work on *The Town and the City*, fighting off a persistent daydream about running off to the gold rush in northwest Canada with Hal Chase. But on November 4, he gave in to his restlessness and spent a drunken night with Lucien Carr, "the daemonic one," during which they walked the rainy streets of Manhattan bashing each other on the head with Mozart records. After that, he returned to Ozone Park feeling more settled, ready to take his manuscript off the top of his desk and read it straight through.

Jack described the novel in his Mood Log entry of November 7 as an unfinished "cathedral" that now seemed far too elaborate. But he had committed himself to finishing this "monstrous edifice" and there was nothing to do but move forward. Grimly, he sat down to do just that, and to his surprise, wrote twenty-five hundred words almost effortlessly. By the time he got up from the typewriter, he felt an increasing sense of mastery—as if these latest pages were *"more myself."*

Jack's ideas about what he wanted to accomplish as a writer were very much in flux that fall. He was still searching for his "method." Yet, as the pages about the Ghost of the Susquehanna demonstrate, his mature, first-person voice was already well within his grasp, although it would take him another three years to embrace its power. He had been sensing something lacking in his writing for a while; in the spring of 1946, he had observed in his journal that so far he'd been the imitator of Wolfe and Dostoevsky, but thought he would have to find a way to "imitate" himself in order to become "great."

In late 1947, Jack's thinking kept moving back and forth between opposing concepts of fiction. In California, he'd made a crucial discovery when he realized that "mood" was the "living principle" of the literature that moved him most—that it was, in fact, the mood evoked by a writer that would remain in the reader's mind long after plot and characters had been forgotten. And he'd declared in his journal that what he burned to conjure up on the page in a wholly original way was the "presence" of life, its sheer fact and substance. It was this that filled him with wonder rather than the drama of the acts of men or the reasons why they behaved as they did. Predictably, he called Thomas Wolfe the supreme master of mood. Nonetheless, Wolfe's grip upon Jack was beginning to weaken. As he looked objectively at *The Town and the City*, Jack reminded himself to guard against an unbridled obsession with description. He could see that the novel demanded more "narrative power" and knew that he would have to discipline himself to "sing" less in his "lyrical-epic" prose.

Important new characters, based on Allen, Burroughs, Kammerer, Lucien, and Joan, were about to make their entrances, and despite his declared lack of interest in motivation, Jack was forced to think about what motivated them, even though the Carr/Kammerer affair was old material for him by now. He had romanticized his friends in *I Wish I Were You*, only to rail against their decadence a few months later. With his new forgiving outlook, he could see them more as Dostoevskian seekers whose inability to believe in right or wrong caused them to be fascinated by evil and driven by a need to find intensity in experience by any possible means. He had intended Peter Martin to be morally superior; now he asked himself whether Peter was the evil one, since Peter had participated in the decadence around him while retaining his moral sense. For the time being, Jack resolved this question by deciding that although Peter would give up decadence, he would not give up his friends. In his future novels, Jack decided, which he would write with a "moral fury," all his characters would be entirely fictional creations.

In early October, Jack's "City" section characters had returned to New York. First came Joan on a grueling train ride from Texas with her four-year-old daughter, Julie, and her two-and-a-half-month-old son, Bill Jr. Burroughs was meanwhile traveling separately in a jeep driven by Neal Cassady; the vehicle's backseat was so filled with bags containing Mason jars of pot that there was barely room for Huncke, who had helped with the harvest, to squeeze himself in. Although Neal drove almost nonstop, making the trip in only three days, Bill did not arrive in time to meet Joan at Grand Central Station. Picked up for loitering there and suspected of planning to abandon her two children, she had been taken to Bellevue for observation. After impressing the authorities with his membership in the University Club, Bill was able to get her out.

Neal had arrived in New Waverly with Allen on August 29. He had spent nearly six weeks on Burroughs's marijuana plantation, building a fence, laying a cement floor, making some routine attempts to seduce Joan (Huncke was quite indignant about that), and putting a strain on Bill's dwindling financial resources at time when Joan and Huncke were forced to reduce their consumption of Benzedrine. Allen, however, had cut his own visit very short. He'd been counting on winning back Neal's love once he got him away from Carolyn, who at one point had angrily suggested that Allen find himself a wife. In Oklahoma, he'd been able to persuade Neal to kneel down with him on a dusty roadside and exchange eternal vows of love and fidelity. But once they reached New Waverly, Neal had made it clear that he no longer had any "use" for Allen sexually.

After a few excruciating days, Allen wisely decided to give up and asked Neal to drive him to Houston, where he went straight to the National Maritime Union to line up a job. Unfortunately, he was unable to stop himself from extracting a promise from Neal to have sex with him one last time—an act Neal performed with devastating coldness and contempt, although he'd been too fond of Allen to say no.

On September 7, Allen departed from Houston aboard a coal freighter bound for Dakar. He wrote his father that he was going to spend some of his earnings on psychoanalysis. On the other hand, he asked himself defiantly, why should he try to change? For years, he had been thinking he was crazy. Now he could see it was "the usual slob hangup. I'm queer."

All through the voyage, Allen wrestled with the impulse to drown himself. About to throw himself into the sea just as the harbor lights of Dakar appeared against the night sky, he was saved only by his need to write a suicide note. As he searched for the most eloquent way to express his despair, Allen realized his dry spell had broken—he was writing a poem. By the time he returned to New York around the beginning of November, he had written enough "Dakar Doldrums" poems to fill a book. But awaiting him was another blow from Neal, who had gone west on October 27 to settle his women problems without waiting to see either Allen or Jack. With no tenderness at all, he'd written Allen to inform him that their sexual relationship was over.

In desperate need of affection, Allen rushed frantically from one friend to the other. High on bennies, he wrote to Neal that he no longer hoped for his love because "my own love is compounded of hostility and submission." He told him that he hated and feared him, at the same time promising to do anything that would get him back—"any indecencies any revelations any creations"—offering him the ultimate bribe: "you have never touched my intellect; I can teach you, really, what you want to know," and proudly declaring that Neal would someday learn "you have no existence outside of me." When the response was silence, Allen tried to accept the terms Neal had offered him in Texas. But a convoluted platonic love wasn't at all what he could imagine settling for.

In the midst of Allen's misery, a letter arrived from a doctor at Pilgrim State Hospital asking him to authorize a lobotomy for his mother. Since Allen's father had divorced Naomi, the hospital had first approached her older son, Eugene, who had found the decision too unbearable to make and left it up to his twenty-two-year-old brother. No one had ever protected Allen from his mother's madness. As a small child, he had looked on terrified as Naomi was taken away to mental hospitals for shock treatment. At eleven and thirteen, he had stayed home from school to make sure she didn't kill herself. At fifteen, he had accompanied her on a harrowing bus ride to a rest home. He had seen Naomi naked, seen her covered with blood after slashing her wrists. And he'd been the one responsible for her confinement in Pilgrim State after calling the police during one of her violent episodes. "Allen, don't die," he wrote in his journal on November 25, after seeing how pitifully blank the lobotomy had made her. He had agreed to the operation, hoping it might free his mother from her paranoid delusions. Over the next two years, his own psychic survival often seemed to hang by a thread.

Neither Allen nor Jack knew that Neal had proposed to Carolyn that summer. Despite some misgivings about their continuing sexual difficulties and about Neal's marital status, which Carolyn naïvely regarded as an "error" to be erased so that life could go on "anew," she was ready to become his bride. After stopping off in Denver to try to talk Luanne into agreeing to an annulment, Neal had joined Carolyn in San Francisco, reporting to Jack on November 5 that he now found her "enough" and mentioning, with deliberate offhandedness, that he had just received a "great letter" from Allen—"He calls me down plenty & I'm sure he's right." Neal seemed concerned, however, about what Jack might think of him after hearing Allen's side of the story.

Allen no longer seemed like a younger brother to Jack. In early December, one of the conversations they had astounded him, and he called Allen's vision of life "deeper" than his own "though not as grave. . . . A sorrow has come over him," he wrote, "and he speaks without intellectual guile." Seizing upon Jack's image of all the people they knew wandering around in the Forest of Arden tormented and confused by their thwarted attempts at love, Allen had claimed he found the whole comedy funny to watch. (Since boyhood he had always masked his pain by seeming gleeful.) "My vision," Jack reflected, "emphasizes the urge to brooding self-envelopment while all the love is going on." He thought Allen's was "more benign." If his own lack of a passionate involvement with someone was beginning to preoccupy him as the year ended, he did not admit it.

Jack was the only one who came without a girl to the New Year's Eve party at Tom Livornese's house. At midnight he stood brooding by the piano watching all the young couples kiss as he tapped out "Auld Lang Syne" with one finger. After that, the more riotous everything became, the better he felt, and it seemed to him, as he later reported to Allen, that he had even invented a new kind of jazz singing—some incredible combination of Sarah Vaughan and Lennie Tristano. The following morning he was still singing and drinking and yelling with Jack Fitzgerald, whom he took home with him so that the fun could continue. He made a point of noting in his journal that he and his mother had later had a great conversation.

He went into Manhattan a couple of days later and did something about his girl-lessness, spending the night with Ginger Bailey, whom he still called "Dark Eyes." Shortly after his return from California, they'd had a brief reunion, which had left him feeling "all confused." And Ginger had continued to pursue him, showing up again in Ozone Park, where Gabe found her one morning sitting with Jack on the rag rug in his room, as if the two of them were innocent children who had just stayed up all night to sing each other every song they knew. Ginger, Jack wrote to his sister enthusiastically, was the kind of girl who liked to put on her "ballet shorts" and dance all around the room. Unfortunately, although still strongly attracted to Jack, Ginger Bailey had given up on him in the spring and become involved with Hal. She had been living with Hal in Denver when Jack had passed through there, but in New York she had moved into a place of her own so that Hal could concentrate on his studies. Jack reported his affair with this "wrong woman" to Neal, worrying that what he and Ginger were doing could "shrivel" Hal's "soul right down to the roots," yet he also couldn't help feeling a small sense of triumph, since he had always envied the ease with which Hal attracted girls, starting with Celine Young. (Over the next few months, neither Jack's twinges of guilt nor Ginger's kept them from intermittently continuing their secret romance; meanwhile Jack, who had never felt closer to Hal, seemed to seek him out at every opportunity—another tangled subplot in the Forest of Arden.)

That winter Hal, who had bought himself a small car, would often drive out to Ozone Park with Ginger. Once Jack found the two of them waiting for him when he returned from a grim two-day binge in the city—"I was so glad to see them—more than they knew." They would take Jack along when they went to the movies (after seeing *The Treasure of the Sierra Madre*, Hal was so overwhelmed he could hardly speak) and the three of them talked about going on a trip together—to New Hampshire, perhaps, or to North Carolina to see Nin. On impulse, they drove up to Lowell on March 25, bringing Gabe along. After showing Hal and Ginger the scenes of his boyhood and introducing them to Mike Fournier, Jack wrote elatedly in his journal that now he knew his "premonitions about life" were not "illusory." He never expressed any jealousy of Hal's relationship with Ginger—feelings of possessiveness about women seemed foreign to him, almost unimaginable. He only feared that if Hal ever learned about the affair, he might see it as Jack's lack of respect for him.

———

Jack had planned to finish his novel by his twenty-sixth birthday, but March 12 found him still wrestling with the "City" section—which he considered the most "dangerous" part of the book. Both Hal and Ed White had been telling him that he was not making Peter Martin enough of a participant in the action. He couldn't wait to be done with the "sad, nightmarish world" of 1944–45. After a week of very uneven output, Jack celebrated the night before his birthday by producing forty-five hundred words, working until six-thirty in the morning. After this heroic marathon, Hal compared him to the frontiersman Jim Bridger emerging from his " 'prairie solitude.' " But he still had another thirty thousand words to go.

One of Jack's problems was the need to fictionalize the Lucien/Kammerer relationship far more than he had previously done. Now that he was free, Lucien feared the consequences of reviving interest in his case. He had asked that *And the Hippos Were Boiled in Their Tanks*, which had been accumulating rejection slips from publishers, be withdrawn from circulation and had made Jack promise to disguise the circumstances surrounding Kammerer's death as much as possible. But Jack was finding it hard to "create facts," and his substitutions were not very inspired. He had turned Lucien into Kenny Wood, an effete seaman whom Peter Martin had met during the war and then somehow reencountered in New York—a sketchily drawn character with none of the magnetism Jack had given Claude de Maubris in *I Wish I Were You*. Kammerer had become Waldo Meister, who had lost an arm in a car accident caused by fourteen-year-old Kenny and who, because of this, had become obsessed with him. His death was the result of a suicidal plunge from the window of Kenny's room. "Did I do that?" Kenny asks Peter Martin as they confront the horrifying sight of Waldo's mangled body in the morgue. "You didn't do *that* to him," Peter answers. "Oh yes I did—in my fashion."

The most striking character in the "City" section was Leon Levinsky. Here Allen had given Jack a free hand, and had even helped by showing Jack a short story he'd written in which he described his state of mind as he wandered through Times Square, high on Benzedrine, convinced that everyone he saw had been infected by the invisible "atomic disease" (Joan Adams had become obsessed with the idea that there was indeed such an epidemic). Allen's most vivid and comic pages, however, were based on a subway ride he had once taken with Jack during which the two of them had disconcerted their fellow passengers and then made them laugh by staring at them through the eye holes they cut in newspapers. In the novel, Leon Levinsky, described as having "the beady glittering eyes of a madman" performs this stunt solo as Peter Martin watches with fascination and embarrassment until the two of them can't help cracking up.

For Jack, *mad, madness,* and *madman* were seldom words of actual diagnosis—they were literary terms that suggested a certain awed admiration for the extremes of behavior. But there were times that winter when he felt very troubled by Allen's mental state. On January 11, Allen appeared on Jack's doorstep at four o'clock in the morning, convinced that he was truly going insane. "As usual," Jack wrote, "I was oblique with him but watchful." To take Allen's mind off the terror he was feeling, he read him some parts of *The Town and the City,* which Allen pronounced greater than Melville—a reaction Jack didn't trust under the circumstances. "He is so close to me," he reflected afterward, "that sometimes I can't see him." He really didn't know what to do for Allen, who couldn't decide whether he wanted to be "a monster" or "a God" and who accused him of finding his suffering "interesting" rather than "real." Visiting Allen in his room on West Twenty-seventh Street one night that winter, Jack, who had gotten high on Benzedrine, once again let Allen make love to him. Allen would always regard this as an act of compassion. But Jack did not continue their sexual relationship for very long.

Perhaps it was Allen Ginsberg's middle-of-the-night visit to Ozone Park that prompted Gabe to renew her warnings that Jack's friends were jealous of him and didn't wish him well. He listened to his mother in partial agreement. Though he resisted joining her in her "league against the rest of the world," the suspicions she was voicing reminded him of the unease he still often felt in the company of his Columbia friends—"a Canuck farmer among 'the eager young students.' "

Neal Cassady had stopped sending letters in early January and had not given anyone his address. In the void left by his unexplained disappearance, Allen's attachment to Jack became more intense. On March 16, as the two of them were returning from Paterson, where Jack had eaten Passover dinner with Allen's family, the thought that Jack was about to abandon him and spend the rest of the night with a girl was too much for Allen to bear. As they were parting company in the 125th Street subway station, he suddenly challenged Jack to beat him up. Appalled and disgusted, Jack walked away as Allen shouted after him that he was "turning away from the truth." Still shaken by this incident the following morning, Jack swore that he was done with the "daemonic foolishness" of people like Allen and Lucien and the rest of his old New York circle, doubting he'd ever liked any of them, apart from what they'd had to teach him. Two days later, however, he admitted, "But like the drunken Comanche, I'm glad I know them."

PART SEVEN

"WHITE AMBITIONS"

THE CONQUEST OF MANHATTAN

By May 1, Jack had completed the "City" section, and only the final chapters about George Martin's funeral and its aftermath remained to be written. It was eight months, however, since he had brought in any money and Gabe was insisting that he type up selections from the book to show to publishers before he wrote one more word. Managing to assemble three hundred hastily revised single-spaced pages, he dropped them off three days later at the wood-paneled Fifth Avenue office of Scribner's, the house that had published Wolfe as well as Hemingway and Fitzgerald. Jack walked away feeling he had reached a milestone. "This is the way a novel gets written," he reflected a few hours later in his journal, in the tone of an established writer long past his youthful struggles, "in ignorance, fear, madness, and a kind of psychotic happiness that serves as an incubator for the wonders being born."

Too restless to stay home the following day, he took his entire working draft into Manhattan with him, hoping to read parts of it to Hal and Jack Fitzgerald. Both of them, however, had women troubles they preferred to discuss. Jack had a moment of panic, wondering what everyone would think of him if by any chance the novel was rejected.

After a night's sleep, he felt confident again. Suddenly the idea of getting a cattle ranch in Colorado or Arizona with either his brother-in-law, Paul, or Mike Fournier as his partner seemed altogether feasible. It was time for him to live—to descend from "the peopled, fabulous moor of myself," and yet he knew that no companionship could equal the companionship of art.

A few days later, the fantasy bride he hoped to take to his fantasy ranch—a pretty eighteen-year-old brunette who reminded him of Mary Carney—materialized before him on a street in Queens. One look convinced him she had everything he wanted—seriousness, simplicity, the innocence of a little girl. He followed this ideal woman into a roller-skating rink, where he rented a pair of skates, fell flat on his face, and introduced himself, already visualizing her as the mother of six. Beverly Ann Gordon agreed to let him take her to dinner the following day at the Stockholm, a fancy Midtown restaurant where Jack presented her with a gardenia and left her in the middle of the meal to sprint to the nearby headquarters of United Press to borrow some cash for the check from Lucien, who had recently been hired there as a reporter.

This did not make a good impression on Beverly, who refused to be taken to meet Gabe. Four days later she told Jack that a man who didn't earn a living was not "good husband material," and didn't turn up for their next date. While it was true that they'd had little to talk about and that Beverly Ann Gordon had shown no appreciation of what it meant to be a writer, Jack was stunned by this rejection. Lucien's cynical comment afterward, "Everybody in the world is beautiful and sweet but dumb," was not much consolation—although the remark went straight into his novel.

Jack hated to think that only an intellectual girl might truly understand him. At nineteen he had been drawn to Norma Blickfelt's "humanist's mind"; now the kind of wife he thought he wanted was required to have the mind of a child. For a moment—and hardly the first time—he missed Edie. His sadness, however, passed quickly; in fact, it had a "soothing" quality that put him in the mood to write. He went back to the novel, finished the funeral chapter within the next few days, and began to tackle the last five thousand words.

Nothing had prepared him for his next disappointment—a form letter from Scribner's politely explaining that the company's decision to decline the novel had nothing to do with its literary merit, though probably whoever went through the pile of unsolicited manuscripts had taken no more than a glance at Jack's messy-looking submission. Jack fought off the black mood he began sinking into by going into Manhattan to see his friends. Saturday afternoon found him at the Polo Grounds watching the Giants play the Cubs with Lucien's United Press colleague, Tony Manocchio; Saturday night found him all dressed up in a borrowed suit and a clean shirt, provided by Ed White, fox-trotting with Tom Livornese's "starry-eyed" kid sister, Maria, at the Barnard College junior prom. Only hours before he had been walking around in his old leather jacket feeling suicidal. Now everything suddenly seemed more hopeful. Against all odds, he had managed to write his novel. Calmly, he realized that getting it published would also involve a struggle he had not foreseen. For a while longer, Jack's sustained engagement with the long process of writing *The Town and the City* would make him more resilient than he would ever be again.

Meanwhile it looked as though Allen's "Doldrum" poems might get published with the promised help of Mark Van Doren. Allen had been urging Jack to show Van Doren his novel, hoping he would have similar luck. But although Jack asked Allen to put in a word for him, he had failed to contact Van Doren himself, and by May 25, when he was ready to do so after a frantic fifteen hours of trying to make the manuscript more presentable, he learned that the professor had just gone away for the summer. Finally, Jack asked Allen to read his entire first draft, which looked to him now like "a vast confusing sprawl" of questionable merit.

"I'm *amazed*," Allen told him after reading the first few chapters in Jack's room in Ozone Park. Although he took that reaction with a grain of salt, Jack brought the rest of the book to him two days later, lugging his one thousand pages onto the subway in an old black leather doctor's bag Tom Livornese had given him. (Friends would remember Jack carrying that black bag everywhere he went during the coming months.)

It was the end of the academic year—a festive time for Columbia students, who had just finished their exams. Jack saw Hal and Ginger and Ed and almost everyone else he knew. Uptown and downtown, in the balmy weather, there were parties to go to, dinners, drinking sessions. Wherever Allen went with Jack, he spread the word that Jack was writing the great American novel.

All that spring Allen had barely been able to drag himself to classes after spending long sleepless nights in Greenwich Village, making the rounds of gay bars or drinking at the San Remo, an old Italian bar on MacDougal Street that had recently become the focal point of an exciting convergence of artists, hipsters, and rising young intellectuals. It was also one of the rare places in Manhattan where gay and straight people mingled very comfortably. There Allen had recently discovered Alan Harrington, Ed Stringham, and Alan Ansen—or perhaps it was they who had discovered him, quickly recognizing what a remarkable intelligence he had.

Harrington, an outgoing fellow who towered over the other habitués of the Remo like "a great auk with flapping wings," as he would later be described by his widow, Margo Burwell, had Burroughs-like interests in mind-altering drugs and psychopathology and was writing a satirical novel about a salesman. The elegant and witty Ed Stringham did editorial work at the *New Yorker* and spoke so eloquently about contemporary music and French literature that everyone wondered if it was Ed's unerring taste that kept him from attempting to write himself. Ansen was a brilliant eccentric who knew seventeen languages, wrote baffling poetry with classical rhyme schemes, and had the enviable job of being W. H. Auden's secretary. These three unusual men in their early thirties had all found one another at Harvard before the war.

Their friend Bill Cannastra was Jack's age and already a hopeless alcoholic. His flamboyant acting out, which at times approached the level of performance art, concealed a bottomless sadness and an essentially sweet and vulnerable nature. Everyone in the Remo was watching the riveting Bill Cannastra show the way they might be hypnotized by the spectacle of a clown playing Russian roulette. Somehow Cannastra had picked up a law degree from Harvard, but he didn't do anything with it—in fact, Cannastra didn't *do* anything apart from giving infamous parties that were the talk of the café for weeks afterward.

These four new acquaintances of Allen's would soon become important to Jack, and would quickly be woven into his ever-widening New York circle, but apart from Cannastra, whom Jack recognized immediately as "the fabulous mad star," they were a blur to him by the time he was introduced to them that weekend, and what impressed him most was their eagerness to buy him drinks and take him to dinner. This was fortunate because he'd left Ozone Park three days earlier with only two dollars in his pocket. You could live very high in New York, Jack reflected afterward as he was recuperating in Ozone Park, simply by making your friendliness "interesting" to a succession of "lonely generous people."

———

Meeting Allen's strikingly handsome friend Jack, who was so engaging and strangely naïve, had made Ed Stringham very curious about the novel Allen was so excited about. Stringham asked if he could read some of it too, and it was probably Allen who dropped off chapters 2 and 3, since Stringham's brownstone apartment was just around the corner from the West End bar.

When Jack picked up those two chapters on June 1, he was surprised by the warmth of Stringham's enthusiasm—and by Stringham's determination to find a way to have Alfred Kazin, one of the most respected and independent-minded scholars of American literature, meet Jack and take an interest in *The Town and the City*. Ironically, Kazin was the very critic who had prompted Jack at nineteen to denounce all literary criticism after reading Kazin's essay on Thomas Wolfe, where he had dubbed Jack's idol the "Tarzan of rhetoric" and suggested, despite his admiration for Wolfe's achievement, that Wolfe had never been able to mature. "Wolfe was always a boy," Kazin had written, "a very remarkable boy, and his significance as a writer is that he expanded his boyhood into a lifetime, made it exciting and important . . . without ever transcending the alienation and pain of his boyhood." But Jack was no longer looking at Wolfe as an extension of himself.

Later that day when Jack told Allen about Stringham's unexpected offer, Allen laughed and told him he had better learn that "society" could actually work *for* him. Allen, in fact, had just been writing to Lionel Trilling, telling him that Jack's novel was "monumental, profound, far, far finer than anything I had imagined." But he had been careful not to press Trilling to read it, "because you don't sympathize really," evidently hoping this offhanded approach would result in Trilling demanding to see this "great American novel under our noses." Trilling, however, did not take the bait. Frustrated by his own lack of talent when it came to writing fiction, he remarked in his journal, after reading Allen's letter, that he refused to believe "a criminal" like Kerouac could possibly write a good novel.

Ultimately, it was just as well that Lionel Trilling chose to ignore *The Town and the City* and that Jack was never taken up, at this stage in his development, by the other influential mandarins who ran the *Partisan*

Review. In its radical heyday during the 1930s the publication had made an important contribution to American letters, but by 1948, it was rapidly becoming the conservative literary voice of the cold war culture, and the incestuous world that had formed around it was an airless place inhospitable to creativity. A few ambitious hipster writers of Jack's generation, such as Seymour Krim, Anatole Broyard, and Chandler Brossard, all of whom also drank at the Remo, where they vied with one another for conversational dominance in discussions of Kierkegaard and Kafka, had been let into the exclusive *PR* circle and their criticism was starting to appear in the "right places," but the price of admission could be high. Neither Broyard nor Krim would ever write the novels everyone was waiting for them to produce.

As Seymour Krim would recall in an essay written two years after the publication of *On the Road*, a book he admired, "The phantom of great European-inspired ambition drove all of us in my group to the most miserable heights and voids of despair, like Hitlers in our own mad little Berchtesgadens. . . . With such standards running wild and demonic in our lusting heads, there can be little wonder that some of us cracked under the intense pressure." Krim, who, like Jack, had been inspired to write novels by the unmentionable Thomas Wolfe, felt he had lost his way in a literary "torture chamber" where "the entire notion of originality was drained out of explicitly creative writing and put into under-glass exegesis, where the critic could fly to the moon without risk or croon masturbatorially over the courage and demonism of a Dostoevsky but jump five feet if he met it in present-day life." Which was indeed exactly what would happen when *On the Road* came out, with the Columbia and *Partisan Review* intellectuals leading the hue and cry against the book and its author.

Jack had been pushing himself to finish his revision of *The Town and the City* by July 1, but the work went slowly and was interrupted completely on June 13 when he and his mother had to rush down to North Carolina, after Nin nearly died during the difficult delivery of a baby boy. Ten days later Jack returned to Ozone Park, leaving Gabe, whom her family now began to call Mémére, behind. It was the first time he had ever been alone in the apartment, but rather than enjoying his temporary freedom, he brooded over his mother's absence. A house should be filled with people, he thought. Daydreaming again about the ranch where, surrounded by friends and family, he would never be lonely, he shifted its ideal location to Mendocino, California, so that he could be within reach of San Francisco and Neal. There, Jack thought longingly, he could establish the base that would allow him to remain "my *childlike self forever.*"

THE SUMMER OF VISIONS AND PARTIES

On June 16, Neal Cassady broke his six-month silence, writing Jack that his trials and tribulations and "terrified stupidities" had at one point driven him to steal a gun with which he'd intended to shoot himself and that all his previous attempts to give an account of himself had been "overbalanced" and "incoherent" to the point of madness. Now the best he could do was to present "a chronological table of unimportant developments," which included his down payments on a couple of cars used for frantic drives between San Francisco (where Carolyn was demanding matrimony) and Denver (where Luanne was refusing to grant a divorce), his participation in a three-way sex orgy with a black couple, plus the details of his new job as a brakeman on the Southern Pacific Railroad, and—more briefly noted than any other item—his marriage to Carolyn Robinson on April 1. He alluded to being in agony and indicated that the reason for this was his persisting desire and need for Luanne, but didn't explain to Jack that Luanne had pursued him to San Francisco, where she had driven him to the point of suicide by taking up with another man. Despite all this, Neal claimed that Carolyn, who would be presenting him in August with the fifth child he had fathered since he was in his teens, now seemed "perfect."

In May, Jack had written Neal, inviting him to join him as a partner on his imaginary ranch. Now Neal seized that "beautiful" idea as if it were a life jacket, adding his own elaborate fantasies to it—an eight-room house where he and Jack would grow old together, a vision of Carolyn and Gabe harmoniously collaborating on its interior decoration, his pool room pals from Denver working as ranch hands. In a rush of feeling that was apparently sincere as well as somewhat calculated, he told Jack he regarded him as his "older blood brother."

Allen rushed over to read the letter that had arrived in Ozone Park, and stayed for a thirty-hour conversation, during which he and Jack consumed much beer and brought out their latest writings. Neal, of course, was their main topic. While Jack considered Neal's letter "stupendous," Allen felt devastated by the news it contained. Two weeks later, when he finally managed to write to Neal to express his "complete amused enthusiasm" for Neal's marriage and approaching fatherhood, Allen couldn't conceal his bitterness, although he hoped he was slowly reaching the point where he could accept Neal for what he was.

As for Jack, Neal's overabundance of women seemed to remind him of his failure to find just one of his own. The following weekend Ginger Bailey was awakened at six-thirty A.M. by Jack pounding on her door. Although Hal had just gone to Denver for the summer, their relationship had been growing more serious, and she did not receive Jack's insistence on getting back into her bed warmly. What did he need love for, Jack asked himself afterward, when it was "the *world*" that he needed? A "Goethean passion" was not for him. He thought about Leon Robinson's cold rejection of love in *Journey to the End of the Night*—" 'I'm busy enough trying to stay alive' "—then added to it his own words, "and enjoying it weirdly," since that was indeed the case at the moment, despite what had happened with Ginger.

In just a few weeks, Jack's Manhattan world had expanded greatly. With Stringham taking such an interest in his writing, he had instantly been folded into the group that drank at the Remo and went to Bill Cannastra's parties. On June 18, in fact, Stringham had arranged a gathering at his apartment mostly for Jack's benefit, although the ostensible reason was to have a group of friends listen to the recording of David Diamond's score for a new film. Diamond, a notorious gossip who had bragged to Stringham about his friendship with Alfred Kazin and who might be especially generous in advancing the career of such a good-looking young writer, was the contact Stringham had in mind. The meeting with Jack went almost better than Stringham could have predicted, with Diamond, who made no secret of the fact that he was gay, immediately dropping the names of Aaron Copland, Artie Shaw, Benny Goodman, and Lana Turner—to whom he might also be inclined to introduce Jack. At thirty-seven, the composer was at the height of his career and was able to live on the proceeds of prestigious grants. He had been unusually well connected even during his wild student days in Paris, where before the war he had known Igor Stravinsky, Maurice Ravel, and the choreographer Leonid Massine. At the art colony Yaddo, where he had met Kazin, Diamond had also become the intimate friend of the young novelist Carson McCullers—after going so far as to ask her to marry him, he had devastated her by running off with her handsome alcoholic husband, Reeves.

Diamond's illustrious connections were undeniably impressive to Jack, but his fascination with the possibility of having a more glamorous social life also made him uneasy and sent him back to dreaming of his ranch. On June 27 when he answered Neal's letter, he vowed that as soon as his book was sold, he and his mother would be starting their new life in San Francisco: "I want all the Shakespearian gamut of things in one tumultuous house. I don't want to be alone in a garret and I don't want to be an 'artiste.'"

When Stringham received a postcard from Jack after the evening with Diamond with the inscription *"C'est toujours un voyage au bout de la nuit,"* he laughed at Jack's absurd attempt to impress him with his knowledge of French literature, doubting that Jack had any familiarity with the works of Louis-Ferdinand Céline. Never quite at ease with Ed, who was charmed with him but regarded him as primitive, Jack felt on more comfortable terms with Alan Harrington, and was delighted when Harrington invited him to come to dinner along with Stringham on June 26.

Harrington, unlike Ansen and Stringham, was heterosexual. He had a wife, whom Jack found delightful, and an infant son and supported them by writing copy for a big advertising agency, where, like a spy, he observed the corporate mores he would mercilessly dissect a few years later in his book *The Crystal Palace*. (If Harrington seemed like a man in a gray flannel suit on the surface, some of his ideas, as well as his background, would have startled his Madison Avenue colleagues. Harrington believed, for example, that psychotic behavior would someday be accepted as normal, and that, through science, men would eventually become immortal; when he reluctantly died at the age of seventy-nine, the words

"Get me out of here" were engraved on his tombstone.) A strain of mysticism was interlaced with Harrington's atheism. His childhood had been upended when his mother, a young woman from an old Boston Brahmin family, had disappeared on a spiritual quest that led her into the jungles of Amazonia. It was years before she resurfaced in Arizona, married to a powerful southwestern tribal shaman, believed by his followers to have the power to transform himself into a wolf.

On Jack's first visit to Harrington's apartment in an old Yorkville tenement building, he dazzled Harrington by quoting entire passages from Dostoevsky. An intense discussion of Dostoevskian forgiveness was served up with dinner, with Harrington envisioning a time when there would no longer be a conception of responsibility and therefore no such thing as guilt. Jack had some doubts about the satirical novel his host was writing, thinking it would be better if Harrington concerned himself with the lives of real people rather than moral abstractions. Apart from that, he came away convinced that Harrington was his "kind of man."

If it was a good time for Jack, it was the beginning of a strange and disturbing one for Allen, who had the first of a series of awesome and terrifying mystical experiences right after receiving a letter from Neal, who had been hurt by Allen's dismissive reaction—"Everything you do is great, Pops"—to the news of his marriage. Returning Allen's sarcasm, Neal told Allen he should have been congratulated as if he were, "say, buying a car or some such impersonal object," at the same time admitting that both Carolyn and his approaching fatherhood were "secondary" in his gloomy thoughts, which were mostly concerned with his increasing doubt that he would ever do anything "great." But he didn't want Allen to rub salt into his wounds by encouraging him about his writing, which he was about to give up. In fact, he felt the only thing to do was to break off their correspondence.

For Allen, this was "a great mortal blow to all my tenderest hopes," as he later told Tom Clark in an interview for the *Paris Review,* and when it came, at the beginning of July, he was feeling hopeless in general, seeing "nothing but the world in front of me, and . . . not knowing what to do with *that*" as he looked toward a blank future after his approaching graduation from Columbia. Allen had been spending much of his time in complete solitude smoking a lot of marijuana and reading St. John of the Cross and William Blake in the East Harlem apartment he was subletting. He also haunted the basement of the Museum of Modern Art, where there was a show of Cézanne's watercolors that summer. Cézanne's juxtapositions of contrasting colors in his paintings fascinated Allen and he would later try to do the same thing with language, bringing together unlikely combinations of words, such as "hydrogen jukebox," in his poems. (Similar juxtapositions—often using one noun to modify another, as in "eternity dream"—would also become a feature of Jack's style.)

Lying on his bed in loneliness one afternoon, masturbating as he read Blake's "Ah, Sun-flower," Allen had the sudden realization that *he* was the "Sun-flower! Weary of time," and that *he* was "Seeking after that sweet golden clime," and that the "deep, earthen, grave voice" that was filling his room was William Blake's. When he turned his head to look out the window, he had the blissful sense that he was gazing into "the depths of the universe" and that this was the moment he had been born for—to see Blake's "golden clime" in the sky over the rooftops of East Harlem. Twice more Blake's voice sounded in the room as Allen read "The Sick Rose" and "The Little Girl Lost," and he felt certain that if he could only hear the "rhyme and rhythm" of those poems in his "inner inner ear," he too would achieve penetration into "the very secret core of the *entire* universe."

When the room was silent again, Allen got off the bed and crawled out onto his fire escape; rapping on the window of the apartment next door, he told the two startled women who lived there that he had just seen God. He had just had the most profound mystical experience of his life. Still under its spell and somewhat frightened, Allen felt a tremendous need to surround himself with people. Over the next few days, he began calling up everyone he knew to invite them to a party over the Fourth of July weekend.

By the time Jack arrived at Allen's apartment on July 3, it seemed to him that there were "millions" jamming the four small blue-painted rooms, spilling over into the stairwell, drinking and sweating together in the unbearably sultry July weather. One unexpected guest was Huncke, who,

perpetually broke, homeless, and in a state of Benzedrine depression always turned up wherever Allen was sooner or later with his knowledge of
suffering and terror (greater than Leon Robinson's, Jack thought) written
on his face. Huncke darkened the party for Jack when he told him that on
his way back from Texas, he had passed through Detroit, where he had
looked up Edie. With sudden anguish Jack asked himself whether he still
loved "the bride of his youth." In the harsh blue light, it seemed to him
that he and all the others were laughing and drinking at the bottom of an
ocean.

The following morning the party still had sparks of life, and in the afternoon, there was an influx of new arrivals, among them Alan Harrington, whom Jack ran into when he went out to the corner bodega to
buy beer. Harrington had brought with him a blond, round-faced, very
serious and ambitious young writer who had recently moved out of Harrington's building into an apartment farther downtown. John Clellon
Holmes had been hearing a lot of stories in recent weeks about the naïve
"poet and athlete" with the thousand-page manuscript. (It was partially
Jack's rough edges and his rugged appearance that seemed to fascinate
people.) The word from those who had seen some of Kerouac's novel
(spread by others in the Remo who hadn't read one sentence) was that the
book was "stunning," although too long, too lyrical, and truly in need of
restructuring.

Although he was only twenty-two, Holmes had begun to have his
poems published in places like *Poetry*, the *Saturday Review of Literature*,
and the *Partisan Review*. Due to Harrington's efforts, one of his essays
was about to appear in a new quarterly called *Neurotica*. But he was full
of uncertainty about the novel he was writing. It would have been natural
for Holmes to feel competitive with Jack, but as they chatted for the first
time on the corner of East 121st Street, what struck him immediately was
Jack's warmth, shyness, and odd dividedness—the way his "strangely tender" blue eyes "noted me as we spoke, but all the time I felt that he was
more keenly attuned to the tangled life of that street than to anything we
were saying." He had the sense that Jack was simultaneously "distracted
and somehow emptied" and immediately picked up something melancholy in his mood, but "above all there was that quietly impressive intensity of consciousness." Kerouac was, Holmes remembered after fifteen

years of the affectionate and at times rancorous friendship that began that night, "so evidently on his way toward some accomplishment, or some fate, that it was impossible not to warm to him immediately."

For Holmes, Allen Ginsberg's July Fourth party would be a landmark event—the moment when he realized that something important and culturally transformative was about to happen. All the details he afterward recorded carefully in his journal, as was his habit, seemed to point to imminent change—the bop records on the phonograph, the book-crammed orange crates that were the chief furnishings of the apartment, the look of the crowd, "wilder, poorer and less settled into job and girl" than most of those he knew, and his strange sense that all these people were somehow "younger" than he was. Holmes was struck by the intensity with which Allen Ginsberg talked about Kerouac, urging him to read *The Town and the City* so that he could understand its amazing importance, shamelessly trying to shake him down for any connections that could be of use, peppering him with personal questions aimed at immediately eradicating any distance between the two of them, until, suddenly sensing that the energy of the party was flagging, he rushed away from their conversation to go around the room setting off firecrackers in ashtrays—which Kerouac explained was typical behavior: Ginsberg always wanted to "get things going." Kerouac also made sure Holmes understood that Allen was a "big poet . . . all involved with visions and apocalypses." From all of this Holmes drew the impression that a new group was forming "independent of the established intellectual life of the city, and somehow more vital, more life-engaged for that very reason." It was a group that had not yet defined itself but Holmes could see its contours because he had been looking hard for something like it.

Standing on the roof of Allen's building that same night watching fireworks go off all over Harlem, Jack felt part of *nothing* around him and only wished he could be elsewhere, in some no longer existing American small town where the Fourth of July celebration would be "truer." Even the rockets seemed to light up the sky less brillliantly than the ones before the war. When he went downstairs, he saw, as if looking through a telescope, everybody "drinking, talking, sweating, staring, wondering, stumbling, living, dying," with Alan Harrington, who looked as if he'd landed at the wrong party for "the salt of the earth," smoking his pipe and that newcomer Holmes hungrily taking everything in with "his wild shrewd look."

July was a month of relentless heat and more parties given by Allen, who, as his visions continued to come, was beginning to fear that they were "rubbish" and that his mind was "crumbling, just like crackers." At one gathering, Jack met Seymour Lawrence, the editor of *Wake*, a literary magazine in Boston, who asked to see an excerpt of *The Town and the City*. At another, on July 24, he fell under the spell of a new "Goethean" love object—a "Parisian" waif of sixteen who sang, painted, and studied ballet and who was trying out her powers of attraction on various susceptible older males, including a South American poet friend of Jack's. For half a week, vivid mind movies starring the wise, sad child Jinny Baker pleasurably distracted Jack from his work. Convinced he had found the "girl who will *allow* me my soul," he was willing to tolerate her "Progressive, intellectual background," as well as the prints from Picasso's Blue Period with which she, like many other bohemian young women, "conspicuously" decorated her walls. He took his child bride to Paris and San Francisco—and of course to his ranch, where he imagined her kissing the brow of an old brown horse and kneeling with him on a hearth rug to swear eternal love—clichés he would never have put in a novel. What drew him to Jinny most, Jack later told Neal, was "the way she clung to my bared wrist in the subway."

The day after they met, they had one perfect day at the beach, followed by the requisite introduction to Gabe, and then she began to distinctly back away from him. By July 28, Jack realized Jinny was too young to marry him. After a furious exit from a gathering where she was flirting with someone else, he went home and tore up her snapshots. (Years later he pasted into his journal a newspaper photo of a dark-haired gamine who resembled her.) But the feeling of happiness Jack's fantasies had given him lingered, and he felt he was now ready for "the real thing." Within forty-eight hours he felt attracted to a forty-year-old woman Tom Livornese introduced him to, and imagined making her his Esther Jack, the character Thomas Wolfe had based on his older mistress, Aline Bernstein, in *The Web and the Rock*.

In desperate need of some emotional support, Allen unexpectedly dropped in on John Clellon Holmes one afternoon in late July, talking like a train that could not slow down to stop at its station about "God, emotions, Blake, corporeality, visions, Cézanne, transfigurations, madness, prophecy. Everything his eye lit on . . . instantly became a sinister symbol, a mystical clue, a further scrap of evidence." At any moment, Holmes uneasily felt, all that energy was going to gather "itself into a fist of maddened concentration."

Nor did Jack want to deal with this latest madness of Allen's. Unsympathetically he noted on July 25 that Allen had been in tears that evening because no one wanted to hear about his "new silence and transcendence visions," which Allen could not even find the words to describe. How could he interest himself in Allen's "eternal values," Jack asked himself, when what concerned him were "tattered moments" of reality, which piled up like snowflakes obscuring any possible "purity of understanding"—an intriguing line of thought he didn't pursue, preferring to continue daydreaming about little Jinny.

Since Jack closely guarded many of the secrets of his own soul, he found the spectacle of Allen feverishly attempting to reveal the inside of his brain to anyone who would listen repellent—"a geekish exposure of self for the sake of invidious distinction." But Jack may have had an additional reason for this harsh judgment: Like Burroughs, Allen had laughed at his notion that all people were "god like." It could only have angered Jack to have Allen now attacking him for his refusal to surrender his pride and ego in the "battle for the inner heart," which Allen was fervently insisting was "one with god, which is the same substance as everything else."

In August, as his infatuation with Jinny died down, Jack's overwhelming preoccupation was the slow progress of his revisions. His ear had changed so much that he felt far from satisfied with the Wolfean wordiness of the novel, and this must have complicated the process. A letter from Seymour Lawrence at *Wake* magazine—the first detailed editorial letter Jack had ever received—echoed some of his own misgivings. Acknowledging the "power and beauty" of the pages Jack had sent him about the death of George Martin and saying he'd be happy to see a revision, Lawrence urged Jack to ruthlessly cut away the "bad writing" and rhetorical "speeches to the moon" that did not contribute to the unfolding of the narrative. Rather than admitting he agreed in any way with Lawrence, Jack preferred to go by Lucien Carr's complete dismissal of his criticisms—"*What?* That little piss-ass?" Yet even the friends who were praising his manuscript gave him the feeling that despite their enthusiasm for the novel as a whole, they had reservations about the way he had written it.

There was nothing to do, however, but ignore all this and plunge forward, and he drove himself so hard in this final stretch that he felt he had completely disproved the notion that an artist "had all the leisure in the world to 'work.' Work is involved with time; you can't waste time building a house, or you'll never move in," Jack wrote on August 19, adding mysteriously that it wouldn't be long before he started a new novel.

Four days later, he described what he had in mind, a further development of the road novel he'd started thinking about in 1946. Now instead of being about one man's journey, this novel would, like *Journey to the End of the Night,* have two protagonists: "two guys hitchhiking to California in search of something they don't really find, and losing themselves on the road, and coming all the way back, hopeful of something else." He also was still thinking about taking an entirely new direction in the writing of this book, finding some means "of preserving the big rushing tremendousness in me and all poets," of capturing, before they evaporated, the swarm of inchoate thoughts and sounds and associations that accompanied the writing process. All summer long, as he worked in his old laborious self-critical way, this challenging new approach had tugged at him. By August 28, he even had a name for it: "True thoughts . . . the thoughts that come unannounced, unplanned, unforced, vividly *true* in their dazzling light" before the conscious mediations of the writer.

Jack completed his revisions of *The Town and the City* on September 9, the same day he received a rejection card from Macmillan, where he had sent some chapters at the suggestion of Lucien's girlfriend, Barbara Hale, who had put in a word for him with the editor in chief, James Putnam. "I'm getting more confident and angrier each time something like this happens," Jack wrote, deciding that *"the people themselves"* would like his book despite what the editors and critics of the "Upper White Collar class" had to say. He now understood that these were his enemies, rather than "poverty and obscurity," but he wasn't going to let them drive him back to Canada. Defiantly, he quoted the just-written, plain last sentence of his book, in which there wasn't a trace of rhetoric: " 'There were whoops and greetings and kisses and then everybody had supper in the kitchen.' . . . Or would it be better if I said, 'everybody had dinner in the dining room.' " And then he reminded himself that his work was truly done.

ENTER JOHN CLELLON HOLMES

The dream of the Mendocino ranch faded for the time being, as Jack realized it might take a long time for *The Town and the City* to find a publisher. Meanwhile he couldn't go on letting his mother support him and would have to find some way of bringing in money. But when he was offered Tony Manocchio's old job on the sports desk at United Press, Jack decided he preferred to remain a "disreputable" writer rather than enter the "economic system" like Lucien. Reluctantly, he registered for courses at the New School for Social Research, where, without having to take his class attendance too seriously, he could qualify for a GI Bill stipend of seventy-five dollars a month, most of which he'd turn over to Gabe.

He had advised his mother to stop "slaving" in the shoe factory and go south to live with Nin and Paul. But his sister and her husband were very hard-pressed financially, particularly now that they had become parents. Paul Blake worked as a telephone lineman, but had few prospects for getting ahead, though he had briefly considered trying for a football scholarship at Columbia. Hoping to make some quick cash in September, Paul was planning to convert his yard into a parking lot during a county fair, and when he wrote to Jack asking him to come down and help him with it, Jack seized the opportunity to escape from New York before his classes began. He had also been corresponding with a nurse whom he'd met on his last visit to the Blakes. Ann looked like Joan Fontaine and, aside from Jack's doubts that she could be "all things" to him, seemed the ideal potential wife—"beautiful, pliant, quiet, sensible, but ready for a good time," he wrote enthusiastically to Neal on October 2. Despite some passionate sessions on the Blakes' couch, however, Jack's efforts to get Ann to go all the way with him were as futile as Paul's attempts to establish a parking lot, which turned into a carless sea of mud during two weeks of rain. Jack hitchhiked home just as broke as he'd been when he'd left Ozone Park.

That fall, Hal Chase, back on the Columbia campus after his summer in Denver, answered none of the messages Jack left for him with Ginger. By October 19, feeling something was amiss, Jack sat down to write him a letter. Adopting the breezy, ingenuous tone usually reserved for letters to his family, he brought Hal up to date, dismissing the New School as a "terrible" place "where the restraint of the lady-students goes hand in hand with weary utterances from the front of the room," telling him he was already working on three new novels, and announcing his latest plan (one he hadn't mentioned to Neal Cassady) to join Ed White in Paris in February and use his GI Bill stipend for courses at the Sorbonne. It was only at the end of this letter that Jack let a note of anxiety creep in—it seemed "eerie" to him that Hal was nowhere to be found, even though he was sure he'd seen his car parked in front of Warren Hall.

Jack soon learned that Ginger had finally confessed to Hal that she and Jack had slept together. Outraged by this breach of trust, Hal, who would marry her the following summer, continued to take measures to cut Jack out of his life. Jack was genuinely stunned by this outcome. It was very difficult for him to accept that a trifling thing like a little fling with Hal's girl could possibly cause a breach in their friendship, when the whole melodrama, as he wrote Ed White, was "nothing but Pepsi-Cola." He went on leaving messages for Hal, and roaming the Columbia campus in the hope of running into him. The prospect of losing someone he'd loved like a brother saddened and bewildered him, and he blamed Ginger for scheming against him until he realized he missed her as well as Hal. By December, however, he was comparing Hal to one of his least favorite characters, Stendhal's ambitious Julian Sorel, who saw enemies even in friends.

Despite the painful break with Hal, which turned out to be permanent, Jack was surrounded that fall by old friends who were fond of him and new acquaintances who wanted to get to know him better. This fact did nothing for his black mood on October 10, when, after reading through a batch of old letters, including one where Edie remarked on his strange inability to kill flies, he concluded that everyone he knew wanted him to continue being "stupid and naïve" and probably resented his "coming out." But for the time being such moods seemed rare. In fact, as he came out of three years of seclusion and labor and plunged back into the Forest of Arden, Jack seemed filled with a kind of manic love for everyone he knew—lit up in a way that must have drawn people to him. His darker self—the one that in August had identified with the vanity of Dostoevsky's desperately insecure Underground Man, with whom he shared a secret, isolating feeling of superiority—had gone into retreat for the time being.

Writing to Allen on September 18, Jack attempted to draw him back from the "complete otherness of the other world" into the radiance of reality. ("I have seen beyond my life," Allen had alarmingly written him, "and I want to go there.") Rather than arguing with him, Jack evoked the afternoon he'd just idled away in Greenwich Village when everything around him seemed to glow with the green light of a Cézanne painting: the brilliantly clear sky over Washington Square, and the Pernods he drank with Lucien and Tom Livornese in a "Parisian" bar, the beauty of Lucien's face that still made strangers turn to stare at him. Allen had called life a "bitter mystery" the last time Jack had seen him, but the mystery, Jack insisted, was "beautiful"—as beautiful as Cézanne had painted it. Addressing Allen's fear that no one loved him, Jack wrote: "We continually worry about how we feel toward each other, whereas if we were God, we would know that we always feel love for each other, without deviation, only with variations of complicated obtrusion and inversion of intent." Without the experience of "apartness," there would be no love, he told Allen, just as there would be no green if everything were the same color. Recalling Allen's observations on Cézanne, Jack asked him, "How can we know happiness and closeness without contrasting them like lights?"

It was true that there had been some negative moments with women during Jack's green-lit afternoon in the Village, but not even a scolding from Barbara Hale for getting Lucien drunk the moment her back was turned or an ugly chance encounter with Jinny Baker, who had looked at

Jack with "loathing" and told him to stop calling her, had diminished his conviction that there was a "divineness" behind everything because all of it was "life." "And you know, Jack, it gets more and more joyous all the time," Lucien had said to him as he balanced drunkenly and precariously on the rim of the fountain in Washington Square Park.

"I've got to rediscover 'the humility of writing-life,'" Jack wrote on November 1, resuming his "diary-log" after a lull of six weeks. But the disciplined rhythm of the past three years had been completely disrupted now that he was going into Manhattan almost daily for his night courses at the New School—often merely signing in before escaping to hang out in the Village or Times Square and drink into the following dawn with his ever-expanding circle of friends.

The New School, which still retained a brilliant faculty of émigré intellectuals who had sought refuge in the United States before the war, was a vital center of intellectual life in New York. Its teachers during the forties, when Tennessee Williams, James Baldwin, William Styron, Grace Paley, and Marlon Brando were all students there, included the Frankfurt School philosophers Hannah Arendt and Theodor Adorno, the British poet W. H. Auden, and the famed German director Erwin Piscator. With his deep-seated prejudices, Jack found the place too European, too liberal, and too Jewish for his taste—a "seat of anemic revolutions" that had nothing to teach him. The real "revolutionary intelligentsia," as he saw it, could not be found in any "pale school" but "on all the Times Squares of America smoking hay, talking Reich, reading the papers, listening to bop."

Although Jack often absented himself from his courses in mythology, the Russian novel, and the music of Beethoven as well as from his writing workshop, Elbert Lenrow noticed him listening with particular intensity to his lectures on "The Twentieth-Century Novel." Soon Jack started bringing Allen to Lenrow's classes. One night Lenrow accompanied the two of them to a Sixth Avenue bar where a third unusual young man named Lucien was soon summoned to join them. It was very meaningful to Jack that Lenrow had known Thomas Wolfe, walked over the Brooklyn Bridge with him, gone to his apartment on First Avenue, and seen with his own eyes the legendary crates Wolfe had filled with thousands of typed pages.

David Diamond had kept his promise to introduce Jack to Alfred Kazin just before Jack started taking Kazin's course, "Five American Writers." By November 3, Kazin had read a few chapters of *The Town and the City*. That night he took Jack aside, and speaking "from that remote fury of himself," asked to see the whole manuscript, telling Jack he obviously had *"something* there." To celebrate, Jack went over to Diamond's apartment, where he had recently been given an open invitation to crash whenever he was in need of a bed, and was joined there by Lucien and Barbara Hale. Everything seemed fine while Diamond played some recent compositions for his guests, but then as the drinking continued and Lucien and Jack became uproarious, Jack could feel the chill of Diamond's disapproval—"sobriety around his mouth, a harsh tongue, crazy frustration (I think)." The only thing to do was to rush to a bar with Lucien and get even more "blotto." There they encountered Barbara's boss, James Putnam, the tipsy editor in chief of Macmillan, who had taken a liking to Jack even though he had turned down his novel.

After Putnam took them home for more drinks, Jack and Lucien staggered through the empty early morning streets to Barbara's neat apartment, picking up a discarded dresser along the way and stuffing its drawers with items from the streets, which they insisted upon dragging out to show her. It was like the old days on Morningside Heights, though in other ways Lucien seemed a shadow of his former self, with little trace of his yearning to write, as if he had lost a vital piece of himself in the Elmira reformatory. A few weeks later, after keeping pace with Lucien during another of his "Lucien-daemonic nights . . . fights, dances, pukings from balconies, fallings-down-stairs, shouts and final half-expirings from alcoholic surfeit," Jack observed sadly that Lucien, now a "newspaperman middleclass Huncke and a Rimbaud," was becoming an "angel of death."

In a small spiral notebook, Jack took very sketchy notes on the points made by his New School professors—usually about the characteristics of various writers that he felt he could identify with: Tolstoy's stingy use of

290 | *The Voice Is All*

paper, and his embarrassment about his prominent red nose that made him shy with women; Whitman's way of using in his poetry "spontaneous words from letters," his divided nature (Whitman had several minds, Jack thought, not simply two), his insistence upon healthiness (stemming, Jack was certain, from Whitman's secret feelings about the unhealthiness of his homosexuality). He noted Hawthorne's belief that "simple men" were deep and agreed with Alfred Kazin's remark that "Allegory doesn't creak so much as symbolism." Although Jack felt more comfortable with Elbert Lenrow, he regarded the fiercely brilliant, less approachable Kazin as head and shoulders above all the other New School teachers, and finally succeeded in getting him to go out for a couple of beers. " 'So you want to be a writer,' " Kazin joked that night "with knowing sorrow." Jack couldn't wait for him to see the rest of what he had already accomplished, but he had sent the only good typescript of the entire novel to Little, Brown.

"Kazin won't stand for your drinking," warned David Diamond, his infatuated, self-appointed mentor, who seemed bent upon teaching him manners and was getting fed up with Jack's four A.M. phone calls announcing he was coming by to pass out on the living room couch. Although he respected the composer as a fellow "spectral artist," Jack felt Diamond could learn some things from *him*. He took Diamond to hear Lennie Tristano, whom he admired above all bop pianists for his stunningly innovative, intellectual approach to music, and was sure he detected some "professional jealousy" in Diamond's lukewarm reaction. Meanwhile, Diamond regretted that he'd told Jack so much about his youthful indiscretions in Paris, since he had the very odd notion that Jack was trying to outdo him in wild and unacceptable behavior. Apparently, he would have felt less upset if he had only been able to get Jack into bed.

As his relationship with Diamond began fraying, Jack found a new "great friend, for me, the taker," in John Clellon Holmes. Impressed by Holmes's intelligence, Jack began to spend whole days with him talking about writing and about what he referred to mysteriously in his diary as the "One Prophecy rising, rising in the world now."

Although Holmes was four years younger than Jack, their age difference had been leveled by Holmes's wartime experiences. Drafted at eighteen after dropping out of high school in Chappaqua, New York, where his suburban classmates had bored him profoundly, Holmes had been sent to boot camp in San Diego. He had been joined there by his twenty-one-year-old bride, Marian, whom he had impetuously married while on leave. Holmes had never been in combat, but he'd had the shock of dealing with the wrecked minds and bodies that were the residue of war during six months that nearly broke him when he served as an orderly in a Long Island naval hospital. Discharged because of persistent migraines, he emerged into civilian life with a tremendous restlessness that extended to his marriage and the beginnings of a drinking problem. Holmes's next two years were spent at Columbia, where he managed to talk his way into graduate courses in philosophy and literature.

"I want to get out in the streets and live," he wrote in his journal in September 1948, expressing his need to "feel things . . . cleanly and hardly, before one has to knuckle down to the cold dark age that is ahead." The poems he was writing at twenty-two were Audenesque; the protagonist of his novel was a hired killer named Frankel who, consumed with "Dostoevskian angst," eventually murders his employer. He showed *Frankel* to Jack, who tactfully commented: "I never realized that the universe was such a horrible place to you, peeling damp walls, spiders everywhere, horror."

Holmes and Marian had recently moved into a walk-up apartment on Lexington Avenue and Fifty-sixth Street, which would soon become the scene of an ongoing literary salon and Jack's base in Manhattan. Its narrow, high-ceilinged, book-lined living room became jammed with young literati and their decorative women at the parties they started giving regularly that fall. There were two rented couches, suitable for crashing visitors—a fact that was not lost on Jack. Glennon's, a dive around the corner under the shadow of the Third Avenue el, soon became an extension of 681 Lexington—the place where Holmes and his guests ended up for their final drinks and ruthless dissections of the behavior of their friends.

Holmes's leisure to think, study, and write was supported, like Jack's, by a working woman. Sultry-looking and bright, Marian believed in John, although she did not share his intellectual interests. Having come from a large Italian family, she was looking forward to the time when she would be able to have a baby, a prospect that had no appeal for Holmes.

Early each morning, she would leave him to his writing and go to her clerical job; more and more often she would come home tired and find her husband and his new friends drinking and being geniuses together.

Holmes's precociously intellectual fifteen-year-old sister, Liz, was living upstairs in the same building with their divorced mother. In her memoir *681 Lexington Avenue*, Elizabeth Von Vogt remembers Jack's sudden materialization in her brother's living room that fall, after which he became a frequent presence, often turning up in the small hours to occupy one of the couches, continuing his sleep in the Holmes's bed after Marian had gone off to her job, then spending most of the day drinking, talking, roaming the streets, with Johnny. With Jack, bop entered their lives and came to stay—there was one particular 1947 record, "The Chase," that always seemed to be playing on the phonograph. The musical duel between two brilliant tenor men, Wardell Gray and Dexter Gordon, was often the counterpoint to the intense exchanges in Holmes's living room. Liz adored her big brother, whom she later credited with giving her a "Beat education," but immediately developed a more romantic crush on Jack.

"Oh, yes, Jack's eyes in those hot forties days—full of youth, vulnerable and asking for love and pain. Of course I loved him, having heard all about him—the genius writer, the shy manner devoid of wit and repartee—then seeing him and feeling that sensual kindness for all earth's creatures." With John's smart, shy kid sister, Jack was invariably "kind and patient." The Jack Liz never saw was "the demonic boozer" she only heard stories about. Once he was about to make a pass at her, but then, to her regret, thought better of it.

November was very much the honeymoon phase of Jack's relationship with Holmes. To Ed White, he reported that he had recently become friendly with a "fine couple," very different from his "Carr-Burroughs-Adams-Ginsberg crowd" in that "they try their best to be humanly good." Perhaps his growing rapport with John almost made up for the loss of Hal. Jack initially felt so much trust in Holmes that he lent him all his journals and Mood Logs from the past three years—a kind of soul baring that was unusual for him.

On November 30, Holmes wrote him a huge letter—the first of what would become a lifelong correspondence—that immediately cemented their friendship. Jack had found his perfect reader, a fellow novelist with an instinctive understanding and admiration for his work—as well as a rare acceptance of the contradictions in his nature.

Holmes gave Jack the supreme compliment of telling him he had found the journals superior to Thomas Wolfe's *The Story of a Novel*, a book that had been a bible for both of them. Wolfe had written it, as Holmes pointed out, "years after creation with perhaps the advantage of hindsight and pleasing reviews." Jack, on the other hand, had recorded his progress day by day "with the desperate joltiness of life."

With a novelist's keen interest in character, Holmes had been fascinated by the fluctuations in Jack's internal landscape. Realizing Jack had given him rare permission to "see someone from the outside and yet have a key to the inside as well," he assured Jack he "rejected none of it, even those early enthusiasms which found repudiation the next day."

What struck him particularly, since he was struggling with the remaining chapters of his own book, was "how you grew with the novel. It brought life to you, while you were bringing life to it." Astutely Holmes noted that every one of Jack's "previously arrived at ideas about life, etc. has changed when you finish *T and C*. Even the excoriations against 'homosexual intelligentsia,' against 'maturity,' against 'international Americanism' etc. has been muted by the experience your *novel* brought to *you*."

Meanwhile Holmes had also been discovering with mounting excitement how much Jack's thinking was in tune with his. Lately, for example, they had both been saying to themselves, "Where do I fit in? If this world rejects *me*, how can it be the best of all possible worlds?"—the underlying question of "most great American thinking and writing." More traditionally radical than Jack, Holmes believed that America was on the verge of "a kind of revolution that will one day have to become social if it will be successful." This last observation perhaps stayed with Jack as he began to reach toward a clear and ringing definition of his mysterious "One Prophecy," the cornerstone of which was the very thing on which he and Holmes most fervently agreed—the burning need for a sexual revolution.

Partially due to his warm relationship with Marian Holmes, Jack credited himself with an improvement in his attitude toward women. Previously he had regarded them as "sexual souls," but now he was coming around to thinking of them as his "sisters," if not "unequivocally fellow creatures." Unfortunately, Jack's old attitudes prevailed whenever alcohol wiped out the shyness that often inhibited him from approaching women he found attractive. As the new apostle of sexual freedom, he began telling women what he wanted from them, often getting straight to the point the first time he met them. Some women laughed at him or turned away insulted; others mistook his urgency—accompanied by that devastating sad tenderness in his blue eyes—for love at first sight. As Holmes's and Cannastra's parties became progressively wilder, he saw encouraging indications that the old conventions of male/female behavior were becoming unglued.

Meanwhile, Jack had resumed his old habit of working on more than one book at the same time. At first, *Dr. Sax,* the development of a story he'd written in 1943, was the novel that took precedence, since he thought it would be short enough to finish within two months. He had originally based the story on the fantasies he used to have about evil horror-movie characters taking over the abandoned gothic-looking mansion in Centralville, but now he was planning to bring a real boy into it as well as the Lowell flood of 1938. The boy's family would be Irish, Jack decided, although he intended to make them "Martin-like." In fact, he suddenly realized, coming back to an old idea, there would be connections between all the novels he was going to write from now on. But he put *Dr. Sax* aside soon after getting it started—it seemed "a hodgepodge" of old material, and perhaps because he was fictionalizing the real boy, he somehow didn't feel deeply engaged with it.

The novel Jack was calling *On the Road* exerted a much stronger pull upon his imagination. Like *The Sea Is My Brother,* it was concerned with duality and had two protagonists—one the alter ego of the other. Jack's admiration for *Journey to the End of the Night,* as well as a recent rereading of *Huckleberry Finn,* undoubtedly gave him new confidence in this idea—although neither Céline nor Twain inspired him at this point to allow himself to use a first-person narrator. The voice of this road novel was a toned-down version of the Wolfean voice in *The Town and the*

City. One can feel Jack reining himself in, unable to forget all the recent criticism of the excesses in his writing.

Deliberately, he held back from opening himself up to the word rushes that seemed to come out of nowhere when he was lost in a "trance of writing," though once, at least, the temptation was too much for him. "I've always been afraid of trying this—this may be it," Jack wrote on November 17. That day he felt on the verge of an almost frightening breakthrough into what Mark Van Doren had called in one of his lectures "easy or impossible" writing—writing that would float, as Allen had expressed it when they'd discussed this possibility, "lightly over an abyss, like a balloon, like reality." The following day he felt relieved to find himself writing less compulsively, to have regained the feeling of being in control. He'd have to look into these "pink bubbles," these "loomings" of his—but he wasn't quite ready for that yet.

A good deal of the lack of immediacy in the hundred pages Jack wrote of his initial attempt at *On the Road* stems from the fact that he was dividing his persona between the Irish Ray Smith and the French Warren Beauchamp far less convincingly than the way he had split himself into the five Martin brothers, who shared the kind of family background Jack completely understood. Ray was an awkward combination of Jack plus Neal, while Warren was intended to be Lucien plus Jack. Neither had a backstory that supported his character. Ray, who has been knocking around like an orphan but has family living in New Jersey, has come to New York from some vaguely imagined Kansas City. Warren, a young intellectual with juvenile delinquent tendencies, has very concocted upper-class parents who live in Saratoga. The two young men meet by chance when Ray decides to head for sunny California after the black woman he has been living with in Harlem kicks him out—on the very day he receives a letter from his mother imploring him to get a factory job. Following the exact route of Jack's 1947 departure from New York City, Ray Smith gets stranded in the rain miles from Route 6, and takes shelter in an abandoned gas station that Warren Beauchamp has just broken into. Carrying a bag that contains Whitman's poems, Goethe's *Faust*, and a pair of brass knuckles, Warren is also California-bound—to see a Vassar girl.

They feel an instantaneous sense of communion—symbolized when they strip off their wet clothes to warm themselves by a fire. Ray, who doesn't think much of Goethe, is delighted when Warren tosses his copy of *Faust* into the flames, telling him he doesn't "read much no more," then revealing that he used to haunt libraries, where he read Kant and Schopenhauer and once started a novel. Before long Warren will be calling Ray a genius, while it becomes clear to Ray that the younger, less experienced boy, with his beauty and his "mysterious inner drama," will be the one who leads the way in their relationship. (Interestingly enough, it is to Warren rather than to Ray that Jack gives the experience of waking up in a strange room, feeling he is merely "a shadow among shadows.") With an immediate loss of narrative momentum, they detour to Saratoga to pick up some money from Warren's alcoholic, disapproving father, then return to New York to wander aimlessly around Times Square. There, after Warren tells Ray Smith he lacks a soul, the words Ray uses to define himself are "beat" and "floppy-poppy"—the floppiness suggests that Ray will become whole only by merging with his alter ego. As Jack incorporated elements of Neal into "my Ray Smith," the character began to embody Jack's newly defined beat hero, whom he could imagine swinging down the sidewalk with "a certain sure prowl," finding ecstasy, like Dostoevsky's Prince Myshkin, in the midst of the chaos around him.

It had been more than a year and a half since Jack had last seen Neal, whose recent letters had sounded grim, despite the upbeat energetic tone Neal tried to sustain. He was having a hard time adjusting to his growing family responsibilities, to the grueling routines of his job as a brakeman, and to having to put aside his dream of becoming a writer. Even when it came to sex, Neal complained of feeling "sterile"—too frantically insatiable to be able to enjoy it.

Although Jack worried about Neal "going blank," the Neal Cassady who had been growing in his mind on the basis of half a dozen letters and increasingly idealized memories far transcended the beset, confused, at times suicidally despairing person on the other side of the continent. "I must learn indefatigable ways of fighting from you," Jack had written Neal in October, "and you must learn sadness from me," revealingly adding, "I think I'm almost ready to say I no longer 'care' what you think about me, now all that concerns me is what I think about you." But he did not tell Neal he was folding him into Ray Smith. After begging Neal rather pathetically to teach him to be "natural," Jack felt some anxiety about being mistaken for a "sissy" and made sure Neal understood that he regarded homosexuality as "a hostility, not a love."

Neal wrote back as if the letter had been a transparent film over feelings Jack would have preferred not to examine. As if sensing that the power he had over Jack's imagination had mysteriously swelled during their months of separation, he addressed Jack's unstated desire to merge with him, pointing out that in the past they had "failed at fusion" because they had formed their souls "without each other" and reminding him that they had "never gone into action as one," nor did they need to. Almost warningly Neal wrote, "We are not 'one,' we are just lovers"—a loaded term he must have known Jack would never have used for their relationship—"that are somewhat similar in our taste, etc."

"THE RUDENESS OF BEING"

By the end of November, Jack had managed to write 32,500 words of *On the Road*—words that gave him a queasy feeling of "emptiness + even falseness" when he looked them over rather than a sense of accomplishment. Meanwhile, there was complete silence from Little, Brown, where he had left the manuscript of *The Town and the City* two months earlier. With this weighing on his mind, he went walking in his neighborhood and had a "paranoic attack" in which he felt like shooting at every car that got in his way. Jack noted that it had been a long time since he had been in such a state—not since he had started having much more contact with people.

On December 1, he received the extraordinarily perceptive letter Holmes had written him about his diaries. He had been seeing Holmes constantly, "basking" in this companionship in which he felt unusually unself-conscious. John was "a guy who refuses to let life slip out of his hands—intense he is," Jack wrote, "and avid with interests." He approved of John's avidity, which reminded him of Allen's, but Holmes's eagerness to know everything about him also made him wary, and he wondered whether "two observant novelists observing each other" would create a "vacuum." Now that Holmes had been privy to his innermost thoughts, it seemed to him that Holmes was " 'watching' me and that 'I won't tell,' " forcing him to be dishonest. But Jack stopped himself from pursuing that line of thought. He wasn't going to damage a relationship that was giving him so much.

That evening he had an appointment to see David Diamond, who was ominously insisting the time had come for a serious talk. When Jack went over to Diamond's apartment after Kazin's class, he was greeted by a tirade of "insults," to which he listened in silence, proudly refusing to defend himself. He was told that he was regarded around the San Remo as a "dope addict" and a "maniac," that his self-destructive tendencies would prevent him from achieving greatness, that Diamond could no longer afford to associate with someone so disreputable, that even writing *The Town and the City* couldn't redeem him, since Diamond had known plenty of "immature kids" who were talented enough to conduct symphonies. He even threw in an attack upon Louis-Ferdinand Céline, whom of course he had known personally in Paris. Diamond's fury made Jack sad. He left after Diamond demanded they have sex: "I almost decided to clout him one, but I'm glad I didn't. Lucien later said D. would have loved that, and anyway, of course, one doesn't go around clouting composers of beautiful music."

But the strange, ugly night was not over, for when Jack told Lucien about Diamond's insult to his "manhood," it triggered something in Lucien that made him launch into the story of a mass murderer who had killed forty people in Tacoma. He went into the grisly details with such disturbing relish that Jack realized someone could find actual pleasure in the act of killing. It was impossible not to think of Kammerer and of Lucien's evasive answer when he had once asked him whether he was sorry he had killed Dave. Always susceptible to Lucien's moods, which he seemed to catch like colds, Jack took refuge in Times Square, where he sat in a Bickford's cafeteria for hours, feeling *he* was actually the murderer who was writing the gleeful confession of three killings on the lined pages of his New School notebook. He slept at a friend's house, murdering David Diamond in his dreams.

Immature was a word Jack was coming to loathe as offended individuals like Diamond and James Putnam applied it to him and his recent behavior—especially the way he carried on at parties where, as Jack admitted himself, he had taken to acting like a "caveman" with women. Meanwhile, the condition in which he usually came home after his endless nights in New York upset his mother to the point that she urged him to go to Paris, so that he could be under the influence of wholesome Ed White, who was planning a trip there, and Allan Temko, rather than his latest crazy gang of friends.

Perhaps thinking a story she'd read in the papers would be a useful object lesson for her wayward son, Gabe told him about a situation in Italy that horrified the pope. There, bands of lawless children, orphaned by the war, were living together in caves, pillaging the countryside for scraps of food and having babies at thirteen. Gabe thought the pope should do something to save those children, but it excited Jack to learn of their existence. He wrote in his notebook, "I want to go there!" The image of the "cave children of Italy" stayed with him, joining itself to other defiant thoughts he was having now that he was being accused right and left of acting like a child himself.

Even *The Town and the City* had been called "childish" by Jack's New School writing instructor, Brom Weber, who suggested that he save some parts of it for "future use" and throw away the rest. Jack attributed this particular attack to Weber's own "frustration," since critics could only be "destroyers," not "makers." But the truth was that he had always cared intensely about what people thought of him and dreaded having anyone criticize him. Beneath the phrasing of Diamond's "insults," he'd heard a message that struck at what little sense of belonging he had recently acquired—the implication that a Canuck like Jack Kerouac could never be welcomed into David Diamond's rarefied world of elegant and supposedly mature artists. Diamond had insulted his family, Jack felt, and even his God. Soon he was referring to Diamond as his "Faust."

Brooding over his accumulating losses, especially the most hurtful one—the loss of Hal—Jack tried to account for the behavior that kept destroying his relationships in a few paragraphs entitled "Exhaustion Thoughts." Strangely, he omitted any reference to the role played by his drinking, but otherwise he saw himself with uncanny clarity. Whenever he was interacting socially, he realized, he was two different people. One was the extremely quiet, self-effacing, accommodating fellow, who, like the "host" at a dinner party, tried to keep everyone satisfied until his troublemaking other half, summoned up by some internal excitement, knocked him out of the way. Yet it was the quiet fellow who mortified Jack. According to his equation, self-effacement equaled "tact" and tact equaled "non-being." In his fear of the "rudeness of being," which was after all no more than direct involvement with life, Jack compared himself to a child overwhelmed by his shyness. He saw no remedy for the way he seesawed between tact and rudeness, no conceivable middle ground. All he could do was to refuse to apologize. Apologies were "geekish" and too humiliating, Jack thought, worse than either shyness or rudeness.

The Town and the City came back in the morning mail on December 8, accompanied by a letter from a Little, Brown editor alluding to the prohibitive printing costs of publishing such a huge book by an unknown writer. Jack found the editor's tone "snotty," though he later tried to find the reason for the rejection complimentary. He took the returned manuscript to New York in his black bag and left it that evening with a porter in Alfred Kazin's building. He had the sinking feeling that nothing would come of this since he felt Kazin had cooled toward him after his blowout with Diamond. It seemed to Jack that everyone was angry that a person like him had dared to write a "big novel."

With increasing frequency, the word *beat* had been cropping up in Jack's writings, either in reference to Ray Smith or to his "City" section characters or used as a term to indicate his own existentially exhausted state of mind. The code word had been picked up very quickly by John Clellon Holmes, and had been acquiring an extended meaning the more they talked. If Jack arrived at his ideas, or what he soon began to call visions, through emotional responses that led to epiphanies, Holmes used what he absorbed to thoughtfully analyze the trends in the society around him and came up with syntheses of Jack's thoughts and his. They were a perfect team, with enough intellectual tension, good-natured rivalry, and shared excitement to turn each other on. They often discussed Dostoevsky, whom they familiarly called "Dusty," analyzing the actions of Kirilov and Myshkin as if those characters were as familiar to them as their circle of friends, whom they examined in a similar fashion. One afternoon in late November, they happened to be talking about the impact of the Lost Generation upon the thinking of the existentialists, and Jack interrupted Holmes to say, " 'You know this is really a Beat Generation,' " and Holmes "leapt up and said, 'That's it, that's right!' "

Although they both adopted the idea immediately, there were fundamental differences in the ways they thought about it. Holmes, who had never been in trouble with the law and came from an old respected New England family (the Civil War Union general George McClellan was one of his ancestors) would popularize the Beat Generation five years later in a widely read article in the *New York Times* that would open with the image of a fresh-faced midwestern teenager caught smoking marijuana. For Holmes, the Beat Generation signified a revolution in the mores, values, and sexual behavior of the children of the white middle class, who were searching for something to believe in and refusing to conform to a repressive cold war culture; this, he believed, was the only sane response to the possibility that the next world war, which he was fully convinced was coming, would annihilate mankind. For Jack, who had been born an outsider in America, the Beat Generation was a subterranean revolution quietly going on outside of politics. For a while longer, madmen would continue to run the world, while those who were already "stunned" by the atomic bomb would have to continue to exist "from the bottom of their minds outward," moving toward a future of "apocalyptic love" and the discovery of joy in a society free of guilt.

Writing to Allan Temko on December 14, Jack condemned the ideal of maturity as the source of everything that was warping people's minds, forcing them to adjust to intolerable conditions. He painted the picture of a rising generation of American "furtives," whose very existence was "illegal" and with whom he identified passionately now that he had never felt more like one of them after all his futile efforts to have an American success. Some of this generation were anarchists by nature and had already done jail time (here, the incarcerations of Neal, Lucien, and Huncke as well as his own must have come to mind); others were hipsters, coolly impervious to society's demands. In 1953, Holmes's Beat Generation would feature a disaffected adman slugging down martinis in a Third Avenue bar. Jack's had a crucial place in it for black people (unmentioned in Holmes's article), notably the young beboppers he kept running into, who told him how fed up they were feeling: Jack considered them the "avant garde." All these unacceptable outcast Americans, he thought, were just like the cave children of Italy.

Jack concluded his brief manifesto with an image that seemed to be the touchstone for what he now meant by "beat." Driving with Paul Blake one night in North Carolina, he had seen the face of a black man, who was walking alone, suddenly illuminated by the headlights of the car—a face that instead of showing terror as the car full of white men passed him in the dark had a mysterious look of ecstatic "gladness."

Before he sent his letter off to Temko, who was working on his novel in the Paris cafés once frequented by Hemingway and Fitzgerald, Jack carefully made a copy of the part of it that contained his new thoughts on the Beat Generation. It was the first time he had put them down on paper. He sent a second version of these notes to Alan Harrington, who was away in Tucson visiting his mother and stepfather. Harrington responded rather facetiously, asking, What *was* a guy like Herbert Huncke stunned about, if not the atomic bomb? As for the rest of Jack's prophecy, which Harrington thought merely a "lamentation": "More poetic than helpful."

In August 1957, just weeks before the publication of *On the Road,* Jack would write in his diary that what he really thought was that the Beat Generation had ceased to exist, as he had originally conceived it, after 1949, when the people who had inspired the idea began disappearing either into jails or into "houses," by which Jack meant domesticity and more settled lives. Soon to be crowned the King of the Beats by the media, he would find himself in the unhappy position of having to represent an old idea whose new meaning he didn't believe in, which was ironically inspiring widespread imitation as a superficially available lifestyle.

Jack's letter to Temko had been written in the midst of a deep depression, during which his progress on the Ray Smith novel had come to a standstill. A few days later his spirits were briefly lifted not only by a rereading of his manuscript, which for the moment seemed "amazingly alive," but by the great news that Neal would be in New York by New Year's Eve. Neal had phoned out of the blue to announce that he had just blown all his savings on a '49 Hudson, in which he was about to hit the road after one more week working on the railroad. He promised Jack a fast trip back to the Coast; then they would drive to Arizona, where Neal claimed he had lined up railroad jobs for them.

He had been forced to use the phone because his stolen typewriter was broken and he was afraid it would be traced if he tried to get it fixed. Meanwhile he wanted Jack to send fifty dollars to some mysterious mailing address. Jack wondered whether the Hudson had been stolen too, but the point was that Neal was finally coming east, as he kept deliriously repeating in his letter to Allen, who had temporarily moved back to Paterson that fall and was seeing a psychiatrist.

Allen was still hurt that neither Jack nor any of his other friends had extended a hand to him when he'd needed it most—"No one cares when a man goes mad" was the bitter first line of one of his newest poems. Lately, he had been getting on Jack's nerves by taking apart every sentence Jack wrote him like a censorious literary critic. "Why don't you die, give up, go mad for once?" Jack asked him in his letter, admitting a few lines later that no one but Allen would take such abuse from him.

"Don't you see we both suffer?" Allen wrote back, saying their mutual suffering was the basis of their friendship. As for Neal—"perhaps I really love him—basically we are all angels."

Jack's letter also informed Allen that he might soon be getting married—not for any positive reason, but because he felt he had gone mad and "given up." The wife he had in mind that month was a strikingly beautiful woman with honey-blond hair and an appealing air of innocence, whom he had ill-advisedly started seeing. Like Marian Holmes, Pauline came from an Italian working-class background. Married to a truck driver with a violent temper, who tormented her by showing interest in other women and slapping her around to keep her in line, Pauline had created a secret life for herself by going upstairs in the afternoons to model for Alan Wood-Thomas, a painter who lived in Harrington's building and had become friendly with him and Holmes. Jack had immediately been drawn to Wood-Thomas, who had grown up and studied art in France, and to the down-at-the heels charm of his Yorkville version of *la vie bohème*. The romance with Pauline was promoted by Wood-Thomas's wife, Annabelle, who, like a Parisian woman of the world, had made the unhappy young housewife a protégée and soon amusedly noticed the way she and Jack were eyeing each other whenever Jack dropped by. With some misgivings, Holmes had tipped Jack off that Pauline found him "mysterious and intriguing" and that according to the grapevine, she had never before been interested in an " 'other man.' " He said he could understand why Jack would find her attractive: "she is certainly something of a wonder." The brief, explosive affair that started soon afterward would become one of the subplots in *Go*, the novel Holmes would start writing the following year, and as a result, Jack would only allude to it in *On the Road* without going into details.

It began chastely when Jack invited Pauline to have coffee with him and they sat in a diner holding hands. They met a few more times in the Village, a safe distance from Pauline's neighborhood and dangerous husband. Pauline was horrified at first when Jack told her he knew of an apartment (Holmes's) where they could go to make love, but she went there with him anyway a few days later. A devout Catholic, Pauline did not take her act of adultery lightly, and it seemed to her that now that she had sinned, she and Jack belonged to each other for life. She was too naïve and too much in love to be skeptical when Jack told her he wanted to rescue her and her shy little daughter from her husband and mentioned marriage. Marian Holmes began to caution Jack that Pauline was desperate and breakable and that he had better treat her very carefully.

For a few weeks Jack truly thought of Pauline as "the finest woman I'll ever know," which did not prevent him from starting a hot affair with Adele Morales, a Latin beauty (later briefly and disastrously married to Norman Mailer) who reminded him of Mary Carney and who he hoped would be a more intellectual Bea Franco. Nor did he refrain from going to bed with a willing seventeen-year-old whom he met in Poughkeepsie that month when he visited Jack Fitzgerald, who had recently moved there to work for his father. While Jack's prospects for getting published looked dim at the moment, he had never been having so much success with women.

By the time he and his mother went down to Rocky Mount to spend Christmas with the Blakes, Jack had evidently begun to think twice about the promises he'd been making to Pauline, for the truth was that there was no room for marriage in his immediate plans and there never had been, despite his vivid passing fantasies. Jack wrote Pauline that Nin and

Paul were about to pull up stakes and join him and his mother in Ozone Park until the entire family could move from their cramped quarters to a farm they would be renting in New Jersey, where they were going to make money by raising alfalfa. (Jack's lackadaisical brother-in-law had evidently been gullible enough to agree to this impractical scheme, but since Gabe was dead set against it, it would come to nothing.) Although every dollar he earned would always be split fifty-fifty with his family, he told her he would start saving up in case she ever decided to get a divorce and marry a suddenly awfully vague "somebody." Meanwhile, what he wanted to do was stop dreaming about life and live "the crazy thing it-self." Or as he wrote her in a subsequent letter in January, "Nothing is true, but everything is real."

PART EIGHT

"RAIN AND RIVERS"

"WHITHER GOEST THOU IN THY SHINY CAR AT NIGHT?"

On Christmas Day in Rocky Mount, a dirt-caked maroon-and-gray Hudson pulled up in Paul Blake's driveway. Out of it climbed Neal Cassady, his Denver pool hall buddy Al Hinkle, and, to Jack's astonishment, Luanne, dressed like Neal's twin in a matching travel-stained white garage mechanic's jumpsuit—she had evidently been given little time to pack. Ten days earlier, Carolyn, sobbing and furious, had been abruptly left behind in San Francisco after Neal told her he needed a vacation and wanted to see Jack and walked out the door to the new car parked across the street. With no advance warning, Luanne had been picked up in Denver. "We're on our way to New York," Neal informed her, and she couldn't say no, despite the fact that she was now engaged to marry a merchant seaman she'd met in California. And there had originally been a fourth passenger, a straitlaced, down-to-earth young woman named Helen, who wore suits and had just rashly married Al Hinkle and whose honeymoon money had been used to finance the trip. They had finally jettisoned Helen, the female spoilsport of the expedition, leaving her penniless in New Orleans, clutching a slip of paper with Bill Burroughs's phone number. Bill and Joan, who took Helen in, had left Texas, where they were still growing marijuana, and were now farming and going broke in nearby Algiers.

Jack's three guests were ravenous and shivering in their thin clothes. Their last meal had been some fried half-rotten potatoes, and they had driven a good part of the way on stolen gas. To Luanne's surprise, they received a warm welcome from Jack's family, even from Jack's mother, whom she had been terrified of meeting after the stories she'd heard from Neal. After a night's sleep and a couple of decent meals, they were on the move again, this time joined by Jack, headed for Ozone Park, where Luanne and Al were going to stay while Jack and Neal rushed back to Rocky Mount to pick up Gabe and some of Nin's furniture. Gabe had developed a soft spot for Neal. She wasn't fazed when they were stopped for speeding on their way to New York. "Don't worry. I'm not a gun moll," she told the cop and calmly paid the fifteen-dollar fine that kept Neal out of jail. Neal promised to repay her, and did. About certain obligations, he was absolutely punctilious.

Holmes got his first fascinated look at Neal when Jack brought him over with Luanne so that the two of them could crash for a couple of nights on the living room couches before staying briefly with Stringham. He noticed right away that Neal had the capacity to make others feel "inauthentic"—as if compared to Neal everyone else was square. As a matter of fact, Holmes thought Neal made Jack feel inauthentic too, and perhaps that was one secret of his power. Neal offered a "trajectory out" to someone who suffered over "the rudeness of being." Like Luanne, Holmes never felt there was any sexual attraction between Jack and Neal.

Luanne thought the two men became excited kids when they were together, enthralled by their discoveries of how much they thought alike. But she also saw that they were jealous of each other—jealous of what one had that the other didn't. If Jack envied the way Neal eased himself through the world, Neal wished he had Jack's extraordinary talent and his discipline and ability to focus. Recently, he had decided to learn to play the saxophone rather than having to shut himself away with a typewriter. His mostly friendly rivalry with Jack would play out over the years in their sharing of women. As Luanne astutely understood, when Neal offered Jack the use of her body, he did so in order to prove he could get her back anytime he wanted to. Holmes thought Luanne was "one sweet cookie," but the cookie was much smarter than any of those men gave her credit for.

Pauline met Neal Cassady at one of the parties that brought in the New Year—parties where there was a sudden intensification of sexual energy, where the throb of the music never stopped, where more marijuana than anyone had ever seen (some of it acquired up in Harlem or around Times Square, a good deal of it homegrown by Burroughs and mailed to Allen in a red and yellow Lipton's tea box) was passed around very openly and smoked by those who, like Marian Holmes, had never previously dared to try it. Not that pot seriously diminished the drinking—in those days, every sector of American society was running on alcohol. The uninitiated who overenthusiastically combined booze and pot were in danger of waking up the next day with little memory of what had transpired in the small hours of the morning.

In the midst of the "migraine headed intellectuals" in their suits and ties and the pretty sophisticates in little black dresses, who to young Liz Holmes seemed impossibly confident, Neal Cassady danced with Luanne with an abandon that drew every eye, or could be heard drumming on any available flat surface, or yelling "Go! Go! Go!" at a Dizzy Gillespie recording as if beyond every riff was another more far out if Diz would only go the extra mile. No one had ever seen anyone so possessed by a need for constant motion. Neal was probably a psychopath, John Holmes thought, not that this subtracted from his charisma or from the spell he cast upon certain women subjected to the electrifying concentration of his need and attention. Other women were left cold, to say the least, worried about the effect Neal was having on their men.

Walking into one such party, Pauline, who had barely managed to sneak out of the house, frantically looked for the nearest exit like someone who had gotten off at the wrong station. The pot smoking horrified her, Neal horrified her, and what horrified her most was Jack, who seemed to be turning into his friend Neal and acted completely untroubled when Neal made a pass at her, as if he failed to remember that they now belonged to each other.

Allen had just moved back to New York and was renting a fifteen-dollar-a-month cold-water flat in Yorkville. Jack had given him the narrow bed in which Leo Kerouac had done much of his dying. Right after New Year's, when Neal, Luanne, and Al Hinkle all moved in with Allen, Luanne found herself squeezed into that bed with Allen as well as Neal. At first, it was a relatively happy household, but as the time approached when Neal would have to drive back to the Coast and placate his angry and distraught wife, Luanne and Allen began to feel depressed, which created a certain bond between them although they had once felt terribly jealous of each other. Jack also half moved in. After the Blakes' arrival, the apartment in Ozone Park had become so crowded, with his baby nephew sleeping in his room and his mother on a bed in the kitchen, he no longer had a place to write.

"We goofed all day," he wrote on January 10, after a visit to Allen's when they'd all had a fine time smoking marijuana, making each other laugh, pretending they were characters in B movies. Surely they were having "a great season." In a particularly upbeat mood because he had just heard that Alfred Kazin had given his novel to an editor at Harcourt Brace, Jack rejoiced that he was keeping a diary, if only to record that in the West End bar the night before he had said to Allen and Neal, "This life is our last chance to be honest," after which Allen had asked, "How did we get here, angels?" (It was rare for Jack to write down what anyone said.) He didn't seem too worried that he had failed to show up in the Village that afternoon for a date with Pauline. According to his journal, he had overslept after "balling Luanne" the night before. Jack had a feeling Pauline might not accept this excuse, even though—apart from deleting Luanne—he would be telling the absolute truth.

What Jack did not go into was that "balling Luanne" had been Neal's idea—in fact, he had been very insistent about it and had stayed in the room to watch. But even though he had persuaded Neal to wait in the kitchen, Jack had felt too self-conscious to go through with the sexual act. Shortly after that, he was in the kitchen as the odd man out listening to Neal and Luanne taking up where he'd left off. Neal had just shown Jack which of them was dominant, and demonstrated to Luanne how little she meant to him, when in reality he didn't want to let her go and felt distraught about her decision to marry her seafaring boyfriend as soon as he returned from his voyage.

Jack went home the following day, and found a letter admitting him to the Sorbonne, a plan he'd already had to put aside because he could not possibly afford to pay for his transatlantic passage. His family was upset that he was wasting his time with Neal and showing up so little at home. He stayed one night, then went right back to Allen's, where he was shocked to find Luanne covered with bruises from a beating Neal had given her. Later on when they all went out to hear bebop, Neal stole two dollars from Lucien Carr's wallet. "Everything is all right," Neal would always remind others, abolishing guilt the way he abolished time. But in

On the Road, the other running refrain would be "Everything was collapsing"; and the story would develop from the tension between those two points of view.

Rather than passing judgment on Neal's "savagery," Jack wrote that he found it interesting. In his own way, he too created havoc—not through direct hostile action but through a kind of forgetfulness that came over him when the attention he was giving to a relationship suddenly shifted elsewhere, leaving a black hole. In the case of Pauline, it almost had tragic consequences.

On January 15, the day before he took off for the Coast in Neal's Hudson, Jack received a scorching letter from her. Devastated by what she perceived as Jack's coldness and betrayal and by the guilt she had been feeling about sleeping with him, Pauline had told her husband everything. He had brutally struck back by attempting to push her face down against a gas burner and had demanded to know where he had to go in order to kill Jack. Pauline had lied and said she didn't know Jack's address, but she wanted Jack to know that she was through with him and that he "couldn't even polish" her husband's shoes. Aiming her blows where she knew they would hurt most, she ridiculed Jack for still being supported by his mother, said she was sick of hearing about "jerks like Dr. Sax and his rainy nights," and made it clear that she did not consider writing honest work worthy of a real man. She hoped Jack would burn in hell, or, better yet, be condemned to a lifetime of hard "Manual Labor," the only thing that might improve his character.

Jack preferred burning. After calling Pauline a "whore" in his journal, he wondered whether she was right about what even Lucien called his "loutishness." It was too late for him, though, to be like Myshkin and crawl on his knees to the husband begging for forgiveness. (It did not cross his mind to ask for Pauline's.) "You think I care?" he wrote the following day as he waited for Neal to come and pick him up in the Hudson. But his defiant tone indicated that another part of him cared.

Seen off by a gang of friends a few hours later, Jack and the "Western threesome," plus a girl named Rhoda who had taken up with Al, sped away from Manhattan heading south rather than westward, since their first destination was a visit to Burroughs and Joan. The time-suspending magic of the road—the "moodlessness" Jack had discovered on his first transcontinental trip—worked quickly upon all the passengers in Neal's car with their troubles, anxieties, and conflicts blowing away behind them in a cloud of exhaust. By dawn they were in Washington, where they said good-bye to Rhoda, and drove past a huge amassment of military armaments to be paraded before the public that very afternoon in honor of Harry S. Truman's inauguration. In Virginia they were stopped twice for questioning by the police. After paying a couple of fines, they were down to fifteen dollars. Taking turns at the wheel, they drove mostly without stopping and made it the rest of the way to Bill's farm on the gas Neal helped himself to whenever filling station attendants weren't looking. "Same old Kerouac," Joan Adams said drily when they pulled up in her yard. She had been standing on the back steps, staring fixedly at a distant fire.

There wasn't much left of the enchanting young woman who liked to wear silk and lounge in bubble baths reading Proust. Now, unable to sleep, she spent much of her time scrubbing down walls and raking lizards off a dead tree—the latter had become a kind of obsession. Her two children ran around naked, defecating in Revere Ware pots she afterward scrubbed out and used for cooking; little Julie had the terrible habit of biting herself, leaving scabs all up and down one arm. By this time, Joan had the worn-out face of a drug addict, "stony, red and gaunt," Jack observed. To stay on her feet, she required the contents of three Benzedrine inhalers a day. She was doing even more poorly than Bill, whose addiction to morphine had brought him to the point where he was actually contemplating returning to New York to check himself into the free treatment center on Rikers Island.

Helen Hinkle, a good deal less innocent than she'd been when she'd left on her "honeymoon," had been given the job of going to the drugstore each day to pick up Joan's "cough medicine." Impressed by Helen's wholesome appearance, the druggist finally offered her a twelve-day supply. Thinking Joan wouldn't be needing that much, she turned down the offer. Joan had understandably been quite upset. The accumulating capsules she'd emptied were all lined up on a mantelpiece and used by Bill for target practice with his air pistol.

According to Helen Hinkle, Bill was very glad to see Jack, whom he found "more sensible, more sure of himself" than he had ever been but was not pleased to be playing host to Neal a second time. In fact, as Bill wrote to Allen two weeks later, shortly after the departure of his guests, he was not only enraged by Neal but shocked by the way "decent, honest, well-meaning" Helen, whom he had found to be the "perfect guest," had been left high and dry by her husband. Despite the peculiarities of his household, Bill had standards of behavior—the same WASP rectitude that had once caused him to bar Jack from 115th Street—and he had pegged Neal as an out-and-out con artist, "ready to sacrifice family, friends, even his very car itself, to the necessity of moving from one place to another." He'd turned Neal down flat when Neal tried to hit him up for money for the rest of the trip, but gullible Jack had written home for twenty-five dollars and Neal was planning to stop in Tucson to extract more cash from Alan Harrington.

"Now, Dean, I want you to sit quiet for a moment and tell me what you're doing crossing the country like this," Bull Hubbard rather mildly asks Dean Moriarty in *On the Road*, where the vehemence of Burroughs's anti-Neal feelings has been left out in the interest of the valorization of Dean. In truth, Burroughs considered the whole trip "a voyage which for sheer compulsive pointlessness compares favorably with the mass migrations of the Mayans." In New York, even Allen had asked them, "Whither goest thou in thy shiny car at night?" a question whose deep philosphical meaning the passengers in the Hudson had explored together as they were driving through New Jersey. But for Jack, quite apart from his desire to deepen his understanding of Neal, the trip had a very definite purpose—the gathering of more experiences that he could draw upon for his writing. After showing his Ray Smith *On the Road* to Allen and Neal and getting unenthusiastic responses, he had decided to start again with different characters and more of a traditional western background. Traveling with Neal, he had been excited to discover that Neal had a memory equal to his: "The greatness of Neal is that he will always remember everything that happened . . . with significant personal connotation."

Leaving a chastened Al Hinkle, who had been forgiven and taken back by Helen, in New Orleans, Neal, Luanne, and Jack took off for the rest of their journey on January 28, crossing the Mississippi at Port Allen,

316 | *The Voice Is All*

Louisiana—"where the river's all rain and roses in a misty pinpoint darkness and where we swung around a circular drive in yellow foglight and
suddenly saw the great black body below a bridge and crossed eternity
again," Jack would later write in *On the Road,* transforming the "meaningless" trip into a poem.

By January 30, they were in San Francisco, where Jack planned to spend
five or six days before turning around and going home. In Neal's rapidly
deteriorating vehicle, they had driven through eerie swamps and sunk to
the car's hubcaps in the mud outside Houston. Neal said his mantra,
"Everything takes care of itself," as he turned the wheel over to Luanne
after he and Jack had dug them out. Hungry in Sonora, they'd filled their
empty stomachs with bread and cheese Jack stole from a store. En route
to El Paso on the Texas Plains, it grew so hot that the three of them
peeled off their clothes and sat in the front seat naked, startling passing
truck drivers. In Benson, Arizona, Jack had pawned his watch for a
dollar—enough for the gas that took them to Tucson, where Harrington,
who was quietly making progress on his novel but missing New York,
gave them the five bucks for gas that took them the rest of the way to
California.

Like Holmes, Harrington believed that Neal, with his need for constant motion, was a psychopath. "Just beyond the rim of the throbbing
present lies boredom—pursuing the psychopath and all who emulate
him," he would write in 1972. "Are saints bored?" Harrington would ask
sarcastically, taking issue with Jack's portrayal of Neal as a saint in *On
the Road.* Yet he also believed that the "middle-class greed and hypoc-
risy" of American life had produced a generation of people like Neal and
wondered whether that made the "direct-action psychopath . . . under
certain dramatic circumstances, a relatively well man."

Despite all the hardships of the journey with Neal, Jack had never been
attacked by an onslaught of ennui and in fact had hardly ever felt so jubilant. But once they arrived in San Francisco, his high faded fast after Neal
drove off to make peace with Carolyn, leaving him and Luanne forlornly
standing on O'Farrell Street with one dollar between them. It was like
the bleak anticlimax of the road novel he had originally intended to

write—his two young men would reach California only to find "nothing there." Neal's one gracious parting gesture was to present Jack with an empty notebook.

Perhaps Neal's abrupt lack of concern for the welfare of his two traveling companions had to do with his promise that at the end of the road Jack could take over Luanne and his growing suspicion that she might be looking forward to the switch. All through the trip Jack had been longing to sleep with her and had even proposed that they hitchhike back to New York together. Luanne had seemed just the kind of girl who could transfer her affections pretty easily. Yet even though Luanne knew Neal was "easing" her "off" on Jack, Jack noticed that she had not stopped looking at Neal the way Joan still looked at Bill—as if she could hardly believe such a marvel of a man actually existed. (Psychopaths, Harrington would drily note, often inspire intense devotion.)

Although Luanne had become truly fond of Jack, she found that Jack seemed to become a child once Neal had dumped them, expecting her, of all people, to take care of him and tell him what they should do. She led him to a rundown hotel where she knew the manager, who let them have a room on credit. For a couple of days, they lay in bed and talked—about whether or not Luanne should marry her seafaring boyfriend; about a weird book Jack was writing about a Dr. Sax. They lived on noodles that they heated up in cans of chicken soup on an electric iron while Jack waited for Gabe to wire him money. Before it arrived, Neal came to his rescue and, leaving Luanne to fend for herself, brought him home to the tiny apartment on Liberty Street that Carolyn had recently moved into. During his absence, when she had been reduced to applying for welfare, Carolyn had discovered that Neal was back with his first wife. She had told herself that she was through with Neal but once he appeared on her doorstep "all smiles and effervescence," as she described him in her memoir, she rapidly began to thaw, agreeing to let him stay with her until he found a job and to let Jack sleep on the floor, although she had said some bitter words to Neal about Jack, whom she partly blamed for her husband's disappearing act.

The night before Jack moved into Neal's tense household, his romance with Luanne came to a cold and abrupt ending. As he'd waited for her in a bar on Geary Street, he'd seen her climb into a car with an older man at the wheel and drive off with him. According to Luanne, she'd been promised a job in the man's bar, only to find that she was being set up to have sex with him. But Jack didn't believe her and felt he had been betrayed. "I saw what a whore she was," he wrote in *On the Road*, where Sal never gives her fictional counterpart the benefit of a doubt. "Now I had nothing and nobody."

This was the low point of his trip, and although Jack was not delirious with hunger, as Sal is in the novel, since he had just eaten a bowl of steamed clams, he was in such a wrought-up state as he walked back to Carolyn's apartment that he had an odd visionary experience when he caught a glimpse of an English-looking older woman behind the counter of a fish 'n' chips shop on Market Street. As if Gabe were appearing before him in another form in the midst of his pain and humiliation, Jack recognized this woman as his "Dickensian mother." As she stared back at him uneasily, he felt he was her wayward son who consorted with thieves and whores and lived in the shadow of the gallows and was "returning to cheat her" once again. "Depart," he heard his sorrowing "Dickensian mother" tell him. "Do not haunt my soul." A flood of memories of his previous existence as an eighteenth-century footpad came to him, and he stood transfixed on Market Street as time dissolved, filled with an ecstasy that entirely replaced his dark mood. A little later, as he climbed the front steps of Carolyn's building, San Francisco suddenly looked to him like Lowell and he was sure that he would someday live there himself.

On February 5, Jack left town on a Greyhound bus, choosing a route that would take him up into the Pacific Northwest as far as Spokane before heading eastward through Idaho, Montana, and North Dakota. Luanne and Neal—who had quickly become reentangled with each other and had spent the previous night with Jack at a jazz joint in Richmond—accompanied him to the bus terminal to see him off. But by now, suspecting they had been using him in some game, Jack was as furious with Neal as he was with Luanne, and he blamed himself for his habit of moving in on his friends' women. Sullenly, he parted from both of them, flatly refusing to give them any sandwiches from the fifteen he had prepared for his trip. He was sorry about this a few days later when he saw that five of his sandwiches had spoiled. By then he had begun to forgive his two friends and was a little ashamed of his own behavior.

As the bus rolled away from San Francisco, Jack's mood became buoyant again and he filled the pages of the notebook Neal had given him with memories of their trip to California mixed with descriptions of the magnificent landscapes he was now seeing through his window and of the towns where he was able to spend an hour or two during rest stops. As soon as he had received it, he had given this notebook a name, "Rain and Rivers," to separate it from the kind of diary he usually kept, and over the next two years, he would add to it other entries about his travels with Neal as well as about his solitary wanderings across America. Like the few notes he took on his first trip, it was more a record of Jack's ruminations and epiphanies and of what he had seen than of events or memorable conversations, and there were passages and images and recognitions in it that would later find their way, either verbatim or in an altered form, into the pages of *On the Road*. His "Dickensian mother" vision had been immediately recorded, along with a realization he'd had while he was staying with Neal and Carolyn that "The Secret of time is the moment, when ripples of high expectation run—or the actual moment of 'highness' itself when all is solved. We know time," he'd written, quoting Neal.

Jack's undated entries kept returning to the motif of rivers, which were as bound up for him as they'd been for Thomas Wolfe with his conception of time. He was writing not only about the Mississippi and the Columbia but about the Merrimack, as if all rivers were one, and he imagined the long journey a floating log might take before it reached the sea, and meditated about rain, the "rainy nights" on the roads he and Neal had traveled, the rain that eventually became part of rivers. "I have read the big elaborate manuscript of the night," he'd written in San Francisco. "And what is the Mississippi River? It is the movement of the night and the secret of sleep; and the emptier of American streams which bear, (as the log is borne) the story of our truer fury." Opening himself up to rushes of associational thought, he was able to write with a lyrical freedom in this notebook that far surpassed his more formal and conventional efforts when he turned to fiction. Although he could not yet sustain this voice for an entire book, it would be there in the notebook for him like a musical template when he reread these writings in the spring of 1951.

When the bus stopped in Butte, Montana, Jack stowed his bag in a locker and explored the town. It was a Sunday night and only drunks were out on the streets. In an old-fashioned gambling saloon, he was thrilled to find a tough crowd of Indians and whites who seemed like characters from all his fantasies of the old West. There he saw "one old professional house-gambler who tore my heart out" and suddenly knew that a lost gambler father would play a crucial role in his next attempt at *On the Road.*

By the time he reached Minnesota, he had fallen so much in love with the West that he was sorry he had not spent his entire life in Dickinson, North Dakota, where the bus had to be dug out of a snowbank by a gang of vigorous youths impervious to the forty-below temperature. Minnesota, filled with respectable citizens of the middle class, "which is ruining the entire nation anyway," felt like a distinct letdown. When the bus pulled into Toledo, Ohio, a "wild desire" came over him to see Edie and he rashly got off to hitchhike to Detroit, arriving there with only twenty-five cents in his pocket. He used a nickel to call Edie's mother, who coldly told him her daughter was not at home and refused to let him come over or lend him three dollars. After finding that he could still use his bus ticket to complete his journey, Jack spent a miserable night on the floor of the men's room in the terminal. "Life is so short!—we part, we wander, we *never* return. I die here," he lamented, feeling anguish all over again that he had parted from Neal with so much anger.

A CHANGE IN LUCK

In the middle of the night on February 11, Jack let himself into the apartment in Ozone Park, fried up all the bacon and eggs he could find in the refrigerator, and fell asleep exhausted but happy. The following evening he saw almost everyone he knew at an uproarious bon voyage party for Ed White, who was leaving for his year in Paris on the *Queen Mary* with his girlfriend, Beverly Burford, her brother, Bob, and another former Justin Brierly protégé, Frank Jeffries. It seemed to Jack that this gathering on "the Great Ship of the World" signaled the "end of another era." The truth was that his friends were all getting older and soon would begin to scatter, going their separate ways. Allen was there and had brought whiskey and his latest poems and so were the Holmeses, Tom Livornese, and even Stringham. Jack heard that Hal Chase and Ginger and Lucien were also somewhere aboard, as well as Truman Capote and Somerset Maugham. After downing a lot of Allen's whiskey, he was ready to accept Bob Burford's dare that he sail to France as a stowaway and hid himself in a closet in Burford's cabin. It was Marian Holmes, more sober and sensible than the men, who had to drag Jack down the gangplank back to reality—to another round of courses at the New School, to the overcrowded apartment in Ozone Park, to more waiting for someone to buy his novel, since nothing had been heard from Harcourt Brace during the weeks that he'd been gone. But Jack prolonged the party a while longer by playing imaginary football in the dark among the packing crates on the pier.

The Town and the City had been sent to Robert Giroux, an unusually gifted and sensitive editor at Harcourt whose authors included T. S. Eliot, Carl Sandburg, and Thomas Merton. When Jack had written Kazin in January asking for news, Kazin had advised him to be patient, reminding him that it would take a long time for an editor to read his twelve hundred pages. Meanwhile, Jack plunged back into *Dr. Sax*, which he now called "a description of darkness."

He also spent a couple of days very belatedly writing the second of the two papers assigned for Elbert Lenrow's course. His first, contrasting Theodore Dreiser with Sinclair Lewis, had demonstrated "critical powers" that impressed his teacher, but Jack had bailed out of Lenrow's final exam, given while Neal was in town, handing in a brief note in which he asked to be excused, "at least temporarily."

To keep his GI Bill stipend, Jack needed to get credit for Lenrow's course, but the paper he belatedly submitted, "The Minimization of Thomas Wolfe in His Own Time," meant more to him than the fulfillment of a requirement. As if he were anticipating the reasons *The Town and the City* might never be published, Jack's essay was as much a defense of his own work as it was of Wolfe's. Jack saw them both as metaphysical and Shakespearean writers, concerned with what Wolfe called "the river of time"; both writing during materialistic periods when the reading public, whose appetite for naturalism was served by market-oriented publishers, had turned away from spirituality. While he was now ready to admit that Wolfe had his rhetorical excesses, he felt this was unimportant compared to what Wolfe had achieved in his use of language. "The metaphysical intelligence," Jack wrote in his journal, working out the arguments he was about to use in his essay, "is concerned with the furthest possible reach of an idea or image, and the most basic, simple possible way of evoking this feeling on the edge of relative meaning." Thus, when Wolfe wrote the line " 'It was a place where great boats were blowing in the gulfs of night,' " he was able to suggest "Aeolus with puffed cheeks" as well as the sounds of a foghorn, which he would not have been able to do had he written that ships were "whistling in the harbor." Jack's essay contained a brilliant analysis of the sounds Wolfe used in that sentence, the "alliterative rhythm" of his long *o*'s, the "indecipherable mystique" of his *l*'s, as if they had "a dull light of their own."

As March arrived with no news from Harcourt Brace, Jack felt that his faith was being tested, though it was loneliness—the extreme loneliness he imagined Wolfe had felt in the late thirties—that was overwhelming him rather than despair. When two Lowell Prometheans, George Murray and Connie Murphy, came to town, he took them to one of Holmes's parties, feeling unusually detached that night, as if he were watching his New York friends "agitate furiously in the nothingness" from the eye of a storm as he wondered whether his calmness was real.

Allen was again urging him to have Mark Van Doren read the manuscript of *The Town and the City*. Van Doren had influence with Giroux, who as an undergraduate at Columbia had been one of his most brilliant students in a class that had included John Berryman and Thomas Merton. Van Doren had hoped Giroux would do graduate work at Cambridge, but Giroux, inspired by Raymond Weaver's thrilling discovery of the lost manuscript of *Billy Budd*, had opted for the discoveries an editor could make in publishing new writers.

When Jack sent Van Doren some excerpts from *The Town and the City* on March 9, he could not resist including the first two chapters of *Dr. Sax*, now subtitled *The Myth of the Rainy Night*, as well as an enthusiastic but rather incoherent synopsis of this new novel "about children and glee." Jack's allegorical story was going to include a river flood of almost biblical proportions and a gathering of evil forces at a "castle of life" (the abandoned mansion in Centralville that he had woven into the Dr. Malodorous fantasies of his boyhood), as well as the arrival of a "giant serpent" representing the dreaded "Second Coming," which threatened to bring about the end of the world until it was transformed into nothing but "a husk of doves" by the wizard Dr. Sax, whom the children knew in his disguise as the friendly football coach. The novel Jack had in mind at this point was plotted more elaborately and contained more pure fiction than his final 1952 version of *Dr. Sax,* which would offer a poetic portrayal of his Franco-American upbringing and Lowell boyhood and daringly combine these true-life recollections with the supernatural elements of the story. Apart from Allen, most of the people who heard Jack's descriptions of *Dr. Sax* did not know what to make of it, and neither would Van Doren or Kazin or Giroux.

News about the latest developments in San Francisco came to Allen from Neal, who was avoiding writing to Jack. "I'm listless without reason," he wrote to Allen dejectedly. "I sit as would Rodin's statue were his left arm dangling." Neal had put an end to his dream of playing the saxophone by giving Luanne such a blow to the head that he had severely fractured his thumb, where a steel pin had been inserted after he spent three days in excruciating pain. One reason he was so depressed was that Luanne was finally through with him. "You take him," she'd said to Carolyn after helping her bring Neal home from the hospital. "I'm getting married." And Carolyn had taken him back, although at the moment she was punishing him by making him feel he could only remain in the household for a little while longer.

In her 1990 memoir, Carolyn politely remembers to ask Luanne how her head is feeling, adding, "I can't believe Neal would do a thing like this." Evidently she couldn't and wouldn't. Above all, she'd wanted Neal to stay with her and for them to be a family, "even if only on the surface." Now that Luanne, the most "luscious girl" she'd ever seen, was finally out of the picture, she'd needed to put together a version of Neal that she could live with. Even in 1981, at the height of the women's liberation movement, Carolyn argued that Neal only hit "certain women in an obviously sexual connotation. None were ever seriously hurt and they were only the women who liked it, consciously or unconsciously."

On March 20, trying to make amends in a convoluted way, Jack wrote to Neal, reminding him of the night in San Francisco when they'd gone to hear Slim Gaillard together and had been so transported "into the realities of no-time" it had seemed an angel was about to carry them off. Bringing up the accursed sandwiches, Jack blamed the rift in their relationship on his "own folly."

That spring Allen was the friend Jack sought out most. They would take long walks together, or go to foreign movies or the Central Park zoo, high on the marijuana Burroughs kept sending. Allen had given Jack a key to the apartment in Yorkville, where Huncke had also been staying since February. After sixty days of incarceration on Rikers Island, he had been put back on the streets ill and completely destitute. One cold night he had turned up at Allen's door with his shoes filled with blood. Although he didn't want to live with Huncke, Allen felt guiltily responsible for his welfare and naïvely believed all Huncke needed was love. Soon Huncke was not only eating the food Allen bought on the thirty dollars a week he earned as a copy boy but also wearing Allen's clothes, and even taking over Allen's bed. He was cross with Allen for not providing Benzedrine as well and forcing him to fall back on smoking grass.

By mid-March, Allen's apartment was beginning to fill up with expensive overcoats and other property stolen by Huncke and his two accomplices, Vicki Russell and her new boyfriend. Jack Melody ("Little Jack") was an elfin-looking ex-con who had painted Vicki's portrait and helped her kick her heroin habit, and Allen had some wild metaphysical conversations with him. Trying to save up for a trip to New Orleans to see Bill, he'd agreed to let the couple sublet the apartment. They'd moved in with Vicki's terrific collection of Billie Holiday records. They also did some interior decoration. One day a fully stocked cigarette machine arrived, then some handsome carved furniture of dubious origin, which Allen couldn't help admiring, though Huncke preferred Chinese moderne. Get rid of these people before there's trouble, Lucien and Jack warned Allen, but he didn't have the heart to ask them to leave. Although he had begun to think of Huncke as "an actual damned soul already living in Hell," he still regarded him as a spiritual guide and even a father figure.

Jack was staying at the apartment on March 14 when a friend of Little Jack's came by to warn Allen that he was wanted by the FBI. Huncke went off into the night to check out the situation. Returning at dawn, he gave out no information and instead launched into a strange comic send-up of some lurid headlines in the *Daily News*. "I learned a law of drama," Jack coolly observed afterward. "Drama is mostly ambiguous danger interrupted by funny things." But like Lucien, he was becoming extremely worried that the police would raid the apartment and seize Allen's papers, which he knew were full of allusions to his own use of drugs as well as to Lucien's sexual relationship with Allen—revelations that could reopen the Kammerer case.

Allen seemed paralyzed, unable to come up with a plan. If he took his papers to Paterson, his father might read them. What about Ozone Park? he asked Jack, who was scared enough to tell him it would be too risky to keep them there. Allen, who had expected more, felt "somewhat disappointed."

During the last weekend in March, Jack escaped from the tensions in his New York life and visited Lowell. He walked past the house on Phoebe Avenue where he'd sat by the window when he was ten dreaming of Sax and his predecessor, Dr. Malodorous. Now he wondered whether "mystic, mad Allen G" was exerting too much influence upon his conception of the novel and whether the whole idea was too "loony" in the first place. The uncertainty about *The Town and the City* seemed to be undermining his confidence in *Dr. Sax,* and he had not yet been able to start writing a new version of *On the Road.*

When Jack returned to Ozone Park, he found a letter from Van Doren, who had read the sample chapters "with great interest and respect" and immediately called Robert Giroux to give his endorsement of the novel. During a meeting with Giroux on March 29, Jack learned that *The Town and the City* had finally found a publisher. Giroux had obviously come to his own decision even before he'd heard from Van Doren and had been showing the manuscript to the heads of Harcourt Brace while Jack was waiting for word. Despite his brilliant reputation, Giroux didn't always get the backing of the management. He'd had great success with George Orwell's *1984* and Thomas Merton's *The Seven Storey Mountain*, but a couple of years later Giroux would feel tremendously frustrated when Alfred Harcourt made him turn down *The Catcher in the Rye* on the grounds that Holden Caulfield was too "crazy." This time, fortunately, his instinctive response to an exciting new writer had prevailed.

From a business point of view, Giroux would have had reason to feel that *The Town and the City* had come along at exactly the right time. Only the year before, Ross Lockridge Jr.'s thousand-page first novel, *Raintree County*, had been a huge best seller for Houghton Mifflin. Like Jack, Lockridge had tried to grasp the essence of American life and owed a great deal to Thomas Wolfe, as well as to Joyce and Whitman. Despite the longueurs and the stylistic unevenness of the novel, which had the passion and fervor of a testament, some critics had hailed Lockridge as better than Wolfe—perhaps Giroux believed Jack would get a similar reception. But Lockridge, who had committed suicide three months after publication, would never write another novel, while Jack at twenty-seven seemed to have a lifetime of writing ahead of him.

Dazed and elated, Jack left the Midtown offices of Harcourt Brace and started walking, making his way uptown. After sitting alone in a Third Avenue cafeteria, still trying to take in the fact that he'd finally gotten what he'd always wanted, Jack had to tell someone and so he called Holmes. As luck would have it, Holmes walked into the cafeteria with his own news—he had just come from lunch with an editor at Knopf, who had halfheartedly praised *Frankel* and then offhandedly rejected it. It was a difficult moment for the two friends, with Holmes barely able to congratulate Jack, though he would normally have felt overjoyed for him, and Jack feeling he almost had to apologize for his triumph.

But Allen was exultant that Harcourt was taking Jack's novel and, in the midst of a time when his own life seemed to be collapsing around him, found hope for himself in Jack's luck. "You (Jack) are *it*," he wrote in his journal, "(Queen of the May), as all of us who follow in the circle of our lifetimes are chosen sooner or later to be it."

After hearing about Jack's great good fortune, Alan Harrington wrote him on April 2, predicting that he could very well become "an historic American writer"—if he could only organize and clarify his ideas. Still very down on Jack's notion that there was such a thing as a Beat Generation, Harrington couldn't resist telling him that it was time for him to go beyond marveling at "the street beggar" and, above all, to stop "pretending" he was a Republican. Bringing up Holmes's current state of discouragement, Harrington advised Jack to treat him like "a Cadillac with engine trouble."

The sale of *The Town and the City* instantly removed so much anxiety from Jack's life that he hardly felt like himself without it. Suddenly he had money—the one-thousand-dollar advance seemed like a huge sum to him—and all the choices he'd made over the past ten years that seemed unfathomable to others had been justified. In fact, Jack felt the novel had been his salvation. When the first excitement wore off, an unaccustomed calm settled over him—causing him to worry that he might never again feel things with the same intensity. But the feeling he had seemed to be happiness. He spent a small amount of his money on a pair of shoes and some new slacks and Arrow shirts consistent with the image of a rising young novelist and on April 27 dropped out of the New School.

For the time being, success had made Jack the head of his family—a position he must have relished. When he told his mother, his sister, and his brother-in-law the plan he now had in mind—that they would all go out to Denver in early summer and rent a house where they would live until their earnings and Jack's anticipated royalties would enable them to buy a ranch—he found them willing to go along with this scheme, rather than decamping to the alfalfa farm in Jersey. Gabe looked forward to being released from the shoe factory, while Paul Blake, still not putting much effort into finding a decent job, looked forward to the fishing out west. (By this time, Jack was resigned to the fact that he and his brother-in-law would never have much to talk about.) But Jack was also looking beyond Colorado. He wrote to Ed White and Bob Burford, who were urging him to join them in Paris, that he expected to be there the following year—and would probably bring Edie with him.

That spring, stimulated by his discussions with Allen Ginsberg and the poems Allen showed him, Jack was writing a lot of poetry himself. The two of them were even experimenting with collaborating on a poem of many stanzas, which would later appear in *Neurotica*. "Pull my daisy, / Tip my cup," Jack wrote, with Allen adding, "All my doors are open." It seemed to Allen that Jack had a real feeling for the "prophetic biblical" and the "prophetic joyful." He could envision Jack writing a "beautiful book someday which like Rabelais and Quixote and Boccaccio is filled with tales, poems, riddles, lyrics and secret phrases."

During one of their conversations they were both excited to discover they'd had strangely similar nightmares about a "shrouded stranger." In Jack's, an ominous "hooded wayfarer" had relentlessly pursued him, threatening to overtake him before he could reach "the Protective City." When Allen asked Jack who he thought this pursuer might be, Jack answered that he thought it was himself "wearing a shroud." In May, Allen would begin writing a series of poems about the "shroudy stranger of the night," whom he depicted as a corpselike bum haunting the streets and the dump, sleeping on railroad embankments—a horrifying yet vulnerable figure somewhat suggestive of Huncke.

In Allen's poem "Please Open the Window and Let Me In," he asked whether the "shroudy stranger" was:

> The double mummer in whose hooded gaze
> World has beckoned unto world once more?

Jack had evidently told him about the trance he'd fallen into a few hours after their talk on April 12, during which it was revealed to him "that there is definitely another world . . . in which we have our other existence, while dreaming," that although we lived in Heaven and would be buried there, we came from a "Shrouded Existence" in hell.

The fear of being pursued by some deathly apparition, very likely connected with Jack's conflicted feelings about Gerard, would continue to recur in his dreams, but only five days after that vision, his thoughts were turning in a more earthly direction—his pleasurable anticipation of spending many nights in May in Giroux's office as they worked together on the revisions of *The Town and the City* and shared a bottle of whiskey. The plan was that the manuscript would be fully edited before Jack left for Colorado. Jack felt very much at ease with his elegant, soft-spoken editor, who had read his manuscript "(it almost seems) with my eyes," as he excitedly wrote Ed White the day the book was accepted. "I've now found my father," he told Holmes, convinced that in Giroux he had found his own Maxwell Perkins, who would do for him what Perkins had done for Wolfe and Fitzgerald.

Giroux, who had prematurely gray hair that made him seem older than thirty-five, had grown up in a blue-collar family in Jersey City. He was not only a lapsed Catholic but partly French Canadian. The common ground they shared was reassuring for Jack, as well as the feeling Giroux gave him that he was important and that his first novel might well have a huge success. As for Giroux's feelings about Jack, Holmes wasn't the only one who would soon notice that Giroux "maybe even more than liked" his new author.

The third week in April, however, Jack's unaccustomed feeling that he had it made was abruptly shattered. "All my geniuses are in jail," he wrote to Alan Harrington on April 23. In New Orleans, Burroughs had just been arrested on a narcotics charge and threatened with the prospect of spending two to five years in the Angola penitentiary, while closer to home—only the day before Jack heard about Bill—Allen's three roommates and, worst of all, "innocent Ginsberg" had been locked into prison cells in Queens. All the New York newspapers were running articles about the weird AP copy boy and Columbia graduate who had "tied in" with a gang of thieves "to obtain 'realism' [*sic*] he needed to write a story." Stunned that all of this had happened at the very moment when his own life had been transformed, Jack told Harrington that he could no longer think of himself as "beat." "I am more *alone*," he lamented, "than when I 'lurked' on Times Square at 4 AM, or hitch-hiked penniless down the highways of the night." As if he again needed to disassociate himself from Allen and Bill, Jack insisted he'd never been a rebel himself, only an open-hearted "sheepish imbecile."

On April 20, Little Jack, Vicki, and Huncke had pulled off their most sensational haul—ten thousand dollars' worth of clothing, furs, and jewelry taken from a house in Astoria, half of which they left in Little Jack's stolen convertible. Terrified, Allen threw out all the narcotics in the apartment and gathered up his journals and letters; the following day he asked

Little Jack and Vicki to drive him and his papers to his brother's house in New Jersey. (He had already left all his poetry manuscripts with Holmes, who had told him he was planning to write a novel about Allen entitled *The Visionary*.) Unfortunately, Little Jack insisted on dropping in on his mother before taking Allen to Paterson. Driving around Bay Shore, Long Island, after this visit, Little Jack made a wrong turn onto a one-way street where a patrol car happened to be parked and frantically floored the accelerator. Minutes later, the car overturned, scattering Allen's papers all over the back seat. By the time Allen crawled out of the wreck, minus his broken glasses, Vicki and Little Jack had melted away. Clutching his 1943 notebook, with its entries about Lucien and Kammerer, Allen groped his way along Northern Boulevard until he came to a phone booth. He used the nickel he had in his pocket to leave a message for Vicki with Little Jack's relatives and waited there until she arrived in a cab to pick him up. By the time they got back to Yorkville, Huncke was making some ineffectual efforts to hide incriminating items, but it was only minutes before the arrival of two detectives. They had found Allen's address on an envelope that contained one of Bill's letters and had already traced his connection to Lucien.

Although Huncke, Vicki, and Little Jack all insisted that Allen had taken no part in their crime wave, Allen was held in jail along with them until Louis Ginsberg got him out with the aid of a lawyer and a character reference from Lionel Trilling. Until a hearing in June, where Allen was offered the option of checking himself into a mental institution, the threat of a prison sentence hung over him.

Jack lay low in Ozone Park, spending more time there than he had for months. On April 27, the day he quit the New School, he handwrote the opening pages of his new *On the Road*, in which his protagonist, Red Moultrie, is about to be released from jail, where he has been doing time on a narcotics charge, drawing upon memories of his own incarceration in 1944, which must have been very much on his mind. He didn't see Allen until the twenty-ninth, when they met in the late afternoon at Elbert Lenrow's apartment. Jack refused to "grieve" over Allen, though he found him "grievous." Nor did he have any feeling of closeness to Holmes, Stringham, and Tom Livornese when he saw them afterward. Psychically preparing for a break with the whole scene, he walked down to the Battery, where he stared at the river and felt ready to leave New York behind —just like Red Moultrie, in fact. He did not see Allen again before he headed for Denver on May 13, making up his mind to go very abruptly after a weekend in Poughkeepsie with Jack Fitzgerald. "Will go alone, hitch-hiking, in the red, red night."

"Where is Jack?" Allen had plaintively kept asking Holmes during the first weeks of May. "Do you think he's avoiding me?" He left phone numbers, but Jack didn't call him until the night he left. Others seemed to be making themselves scarce as well. "We can't understand Allen," fastidious Stringham told Holmes. "Our feelings in a similar situation would be entirely different." Holmes had to agree, but felt a little queasy about it, perhaps wondering whether some of his own stranger feelings would pass muster.

Stringham lived his own life with great care. In one compartment, he went to his job at the *New Yorker* and kept annotated, constantly updated lists of developments in the arts—an obsessive personal encyclopedia of the culture. In the other compartment was his sometimes violent relationship with his lover, George Wickstrom, his nocturnal explorations of Forty-second Street, and his secret bouts of drinking. Perhaps it was Allen's complete openness about his private life that was particularly disturbing to him.

Holmes, on the other hand, made it his business to keep up with all the developments in Allen's situation, and was hungry for every detail. He interviewed Allen in a professional way and took copious notes, thereby staking his claim on this sensational new material, even though he was evidently aware that Allen was thinking of writing an autobiographical novel of his own. Writing to Jack on May 10, Holmes shared a few juicy highlights of what Allen had told him—how at a meeting Allen's lawyer had set up with Mark Van Doren, Van Doren had sternly asked Allen, "Do you believe in this society?" When Allen answered in the affirmative, Van Doren had indicated that as long as Allen wasn't an anarchist he would back him up. "They treated me as though I were a communist!" Allen had commented in amazement.

Despite his support from Trilling and Van Doren and even Dean Carman, who would testify at his hearing, Allen was now considered a nonperson by his alma mater. An acquaintance of Holmes's who had an administrative job at Columbia told him that Allen's records had been put in the "dead file" as soon as the news came about his arraignment and that as far as Columbia was concerned, Allen Ginsberg—guilty or not—did not exist.

"I think he felt good being Lucien in their eyes," Holmes wrote to Jack, "but losing his own identity didn't please him much in the last analysis." His theory was that Allen "courted rejection, wishing that everyone should be confronted with their 'monster' in him."

CONTINENTAL DIVIDE

By May 22, Jack was camping out in a small house in Westwood, Colorado, just outside Denver, waiting for his relatives and all their furniture to arrive. At first, he felt very content with his solitude, with the view from his back steps—a vista of golden fields and mountains—and his quiet days of continuing to make notes on *On the Road*, cooking his own meals, and falling asleep at night after reading dime western novels. (He admired writers like Zane Grey for their "beautiful and authentic descriptions" of the landscape.) His house was near "the wrath of sources," he wrote Allen, "the Divide where rain and rivers are decided." With the exception of Justin Brierly, who helpfully drove him around, steered him through the formalities of becoming a renter, and flatteringly lionized him now that he was going to be a published author, none of Jack's friends were in Denver, and without a car it was hard to get into town. Despite its magnificent views, Westwood was a raw and isolated place—Gabe would soon be calling it a "lonely mud puddle."

Jack quickly became involved with a neighbor, a woman named Johnnie, who had been deserted by her husband. With Johnnie and her fourteen-year-old son, he went to an amusement park—so forlorn and "sinister" that he fell into a two-day depression afterward. Their next excursion, this time to a ranch, was more consistent with Jack's fantasies of the West—there he rode a strawberry roan in an alpine meadow and drank beers while still remaining upright in the saddle. He was so sore the next day that he had to stay home instead of riding in a rodeo, which he had been all set to do despite his total lack of experience as a bronco buster. By the end of May, however, Jack began to worry about losing contact with the literary life he'd built up for himself in New York. "After all," he wrote, "great art only flourishes in a *school*," even if his school was only his circle of close friends, plus Lenrow and Van Doren, whom he now regarded as supporters.

In Ozone Park, Gabe was packing up and writing him almost daily. In his mother's eyes, Jack was finally completely golden. She could hardly wait to get to the "cute little heaven" he had found for her retirement and to say good-bye to the "filth" in New York and the "rotten hole" of the shoe factory, where a strike was now imminent. Paul Blake, on the other hand, who hadn't worked since Jack's departure, was definitely in the doghouse as far as she was concerned, which must have created some tensions in Nin's marriage. By the last week in May, Gabe was counting the days before she could leave North Carolina, where her son-in-law had selfishly insisted on spending a week with his relatives before the long drive to Colorado.

By June 1, the night before his family arrived, Jack had run out of patience with the empty house, his lack of a typewriter, and his interminable waiting. To add to his edginess, the house had a defective well pump and he was almost out of money, since he had staked almost his entire advance on the move out west. He had been looking forward to hearing his mother rhapsodize about her new quarters—only the down payment on the promise he had made to his father—but he was about to have a tremendous disappointment. Gabe proved to be untransplantable. No sooner had the worn family furniture been set up in the rooms than she was missing Radio City and longing to be back not only in Ozone Park but in the shoe factory where by now she'd made friends with a number of the other women. She told Jack that she wasn't cut out for life on a farm and that she hated not having a job and earning her own keep. As for Paul Blake, he didn't see any good prospects for fishing and made no move to find employment in Colorado; only Nin managed to find work.

Writing to Elbert Lenrow on June 28, Jack tried to sound philosophical about the whole situation: "it is extremely interesting to learn," he observed, "that a man ought to get his own family instead of trying to surround himself with a second-hand synthetic one." He told Lenrow that in fact the experience had left him "a little freer than before" and that he and his family would simply regard their weeks out west as "a good vacation."

That Sunday, Gabe boarded a bus bound for New York, where her old job awaited her and where she was temporarily going to stay with friends. Jack thought his mother was a "trouper" for insisting on her independence, but it hurt him to see her temporarily reduced to a "poor vagabonding widow-woman." He promised to join her as soon as she'd found a new place for them to live. "The big American night keeps closing in, redder and darker all the time," he wrote in his journal. "There is no home." It was the end of the dream that had sustained him for the past three years. Perhaps some form of communal life would actually have worked for him—at least for periods before ennui inevitably set in. But Jack would never have his ranch, nor would he ever find the right balance between his need for solitude and his hunger for companionship. He had a gloomy picnic after Gabe's departure with Paul and Nin, who couldn't wait to save up enough money to leave as well. It was just a year after Allen's Fourth of July party. This time Jack found himself alone, listlessly watching fireworks in the sky over Denver in a stadium full of strangers, who seemed indifferent to the celebration.

One of the few bright spots in Jack's Denver summer was a three-day visit from Robert Giroux in mid-July—something they had planned before Jack left New York. For the first time he got a sense of the way Giroux would be editing *The Town and the City*—all in the interest of making it more of a conventionally "well made novel." Giroux was after all a businessman, Jack realized, as well as a "big intellectual Catholic N.Y. Ignu." He reported to Allen that Giroux had revised one of his favorite passages—"the child saying from a dark corner—'I see you . . . Peek-a-boo!' to just 'I see you.' I asked him if he knew what he was doing and he said, 'Of course.'" That fall, Jack would find himself reluctantly agreeing to other changes of more major proportions. Gently, Giroux tried to discourage Jack from continuing with *Dr. Sax*, pointing out that he should write about real people rather than imaginary wizards and warning him not to become obsessed with poetic image making, which he attributed to Allen's influence. For the moment Jack agreed with him and decided to put *Dr. Sax* aside. But an intense new focus on the allusive power of language plus the poets he had been reading that summer (T. S. Eliot, Hart Crane, Emily Dickinson, and Edward Arlington Robinson), and the poems he had been writing and sharing with Allen, were already changing his prose. He was consciously starting to bring a poet's ear to every prose sentence he wrote.

Before Giroux's arrival, Jack had been working on "The Rose of the Rainy Night," which he described to Allen as "a big Spenserian work of many cantos." Written in Elizabethan language, it opened:

So doth the rain blow down
Like melted lutes, their airs condenst,

Writing to Allen on July 5, Jack had admitted there was room for improvement in this experiment: "I merely put down what comes into my head, though not recklessly." So far his poetry, like Allen's, imitated the poetry of the past. It would not be until the mid-1950s that Jack would develop the distinctive voice that can be found in his *Mexico City Blues*. Oddly enough, that voice—which would have a profound effect on Allen's—would spring directly from the discoveries Jack had been making by then in his bop-influenced prose.

As he waited for his family to arrive in the summer of 1949, Jack had been filling a good part of a notebook with his "Private Philologies"— going into the derivations of various words and exploring what could be suggested, beyond their manifest meanings, by the way they sounded. In his letter to Allen he'd included a demonstration of how "the influence of pure preoccupations with language" could strengthen "the scaffolded exigencies of the reasonable and light-of-day prose sentence" by quoting two sentences he had just written for *On the Road* about the last night Red Moultrie spends in jail. The second sentence was marked by deliberate alliterative repetitions of the melancholy sound of the long *o*:

And by and by all the lights but one dim hall light were out, and the men were shrouded in May-night, preparing their minds to sleep. To his right Eddy Parry seemed to moan alone, to roll his own bones on the hard, hot pad; unless he moaned to someone in the next cell further.

A subtler example of his new poetic approach to language was a longer passage about what Red Moultrie could hear as he listened to the silence: "the great sea-roar of New York outside, the rumorous [*sic*] Saturday night stretching its tide far over the [wash?] of the vast eventful plain," with the echo of *sea-roar* in the word *rumorous*. An image in another phrase was particularly striking and unexpected: "the Jamaican reaches that guttered like altar waxes on the hooded horizon."

"Your prose has many more *bleak echoes* than before," Allen had written back enthusiastically, citing the "seriousness" of his and Jack's investigations into the expressive possibilities of language.

Giroux was evidently excited by the richness of the writing in the new pages of the Red Moultrie novel that Jack showed him during his visit. He was also enthusiastic about the book's western setting and sagalike story, which by this time had been worked out in detail. In order to get a feeling for the West, he gamely agreed to spend one day hitchhiking through the back country with Jack. By the time Giroux flew out of Denver, Jack was able to look forward to receiving another thousand-dollar check in December to finance his progress with the manuscript and was confident that he had forged a real friendship with his editor.

He also believed he could convince Giroux to publish Allen. After all, Giroux had published Robert Lowell, another mad poet, and had gone with him to visit Ezra Pound at St. Elizabeths psychiatric hospital. To whet Giroux's interest, he had shown him a long letter containing Allen's brilliant impressions of life on the psychiatric ward at Columbia Presbyterian, which Allen had voluntarily entered in late June after the hearing on his case. "There are no intellectuals in a madhouse," Allen had written Jack. "The rest of the people here see more visions in one day than I do in a year." He had gone into the hospital with actual relief, hoping to be cured of his madness, but what he seemed to be discovering was how sane he actually was compared to the others in the "Kafkian" world he had entered. As for the seersucker-suit-wearing liberal doctors who were supposed to help him and the other patients, Allen found them "absolute ghouls of mediocrity." He did meet one fellow intellectual, however. "I'm Kirilov," said Carl Solomon, a tall man with a booming voice and a surreal sense of humor, who walked up to him one day on the ward—to which Allen answered, "I'm Myshkin." (In 1956, Allen's ground-breaking poem "Howl" would be dedicated to Solomon.) Carl, who had a history of schizophrenia and would continue to need periods of hospitalization, was getting shock treatments at Presbyterian that summer. He immediately introduced Allen to the writings of Jean Genet, whom Allen now considered perhaps "greater than Céline," and to a "madman" surrealist "who had opened all doors" named Antonin Artaud. When Jack read these two French writers in 1951, it would be with similar excitement.

"Your stories of the madhouse are so actual that I feel again as I did in the Navy nuthouse—scared and seeing through heads," Jack wrote to Allen at the end of July, telling him to get a manuscript to Giroux as soon as possible and assuring him that "The world is only waiting for you to pitch sad silent love in the place of excrement."

On July 18, Jack was in a melancholy mood after accompanying Giroux to the Denver airport. After hitchhiking back to the center of the city, he wandered through Denver's "Negrotown," with his "white ambitions" very much on his mind, remembering the premonition he'd had during one of his conversations with Giroux that getting published would turn out to be "merely a sad affair." Looking at the people he passed in the black neighborhood, he realized that "the best the 'white world' had to offer was . . . not enough life, joy, kicks, darkness, music, not enough *night.*" When a young black woman warmly greeted him with "Hello Eddy," he would have given anything to be Eddy, anyone but himself—and it seemed to him again, as it had when he'd written his definition of the Beat Generation, that the "true-minded ecstatic Negroes of America," who weren't driven by ambitions like his, who weren't "pale" and "white collar," who hadn't shut themselves off from ordinary happiness to write books, knew more about joy than he would ever know. Watching a neighborhood softball game as he sat in the bleachers among a cheering black and Mexican crowd, Jack realized that the "white ambitions" he'd had since his boyhood had even prevented him from playing ball "in an innocent way" purely for the fun of it. "Down in Denver all I did was die anyway," he would write afterward.

———

Gabe had agreed to leave her furniture in Westwood, so that it would be in the house during Giroux's stay. Shortly after his departure, a truck came to pick it up and take it to the new apartment she had just rented in a two-family house in Richmond Hill, and the Blakes finally got in their car, took Jack's last thirty dollars, and headed there as well, since they had nowhere else to go. Gabe had expected Jack would ride back with the van full of furniture, but instead he stayed on for two more weeks in the house he had paid for, rattling around in the empty rooms that reminded him of how much money he had wasted. For one miserable day, he unloaded a boxcar of cantaloupes for a Denver market (a job Neal had in his teens) and walked away with thirteen dollars and change. Acutely lonely, Jack tried for a rapprochement with Hal Chase, who had just returned to Colorado to work on an archaeological dig, but although they had a long conversation on the phone, Hal refused to see him, since that would have meant breaking a promise he had made to Ginger. "Hal is really dead," Jack wrote Allen.

Ahead of him, though frustratingly out of reach for the time being, was his promising future as a famous novelist. Mentally, he splurged all of his next thousand dollars from Harcourt on a trip to Italy in the spring, which would be followed by a season in Paris financed by his royalties. He wanted Allen there with him as well as Burroughs and Neal—all of them "together before it is too late." And, in a new mood of defiance now that his family had let him down, he'd decided Edie would accompany him, no matter what his mother and sister thought. In June he had written to "the bride of his youth" to tell her he'd sold his novel. "When you're a Hollywood writer and live in a big mansion, I have first dibs for parasiting off you," she'd written back encouragingly. But Edie's response to his offer to sweep her off to Italy was wearier and more noncommittal than he was willing to recognize: "Maybe you and I are just a dream. I guess we'll always be night birds."

In the last days of July, Jack felt torn between three options—hitchhiking to Detroit to reunite with Edie, returning immediately to New York, or reconnecting with Neal in San Francisco. Earlier in the month, he'd sent Neal two more letters that had gone unanswered. On July 28, he finally received a long account of how Neal had been brought low—it had taken Neal three weeks to write it because of his painfully injured thumb, which had become infected after his operation and part of which was about to be amputated.

Grounded at home for much of the time, with Carolyn nursing him and watching him like a hawk, Neal had finally been able to concentrate long enough to write a four-page prologue to his intended book, but had done nothing more on it since June, when he'd taken a grueling job capping tires, despite the cast he was wearing. As he and Carolyn awaited the birth of their second child, Neal's life had never been grimmer or more respectable, yet Huncke's prison sentence and Allen's incarceration on a mental ward had reawakened all his terror of going back to jail himself. In contrast, there was Jack, who wasn't driven by such fears and who was about to be let into the "world of the big boys." Neal realized that Jack's own two incarcerations had never defined him: "your deep anchor has been this involvement with writing which unerringly threw you into the other camp." While he insisted he'd been "Glad, Glad, Glad" to hear that Jack sold his novel, the news had apparently made him see his own predicament in particularly stark terms, and his feeling that he was getting nowhere with his own writing had become excruciating.

Using up the last sheets of paper in the house, Jack responded immediately with an outpouring of more generosity than he'd ever shown anyone, swearing to Neal not only that their friendship would last forever but that "I even want to help you the rest of my life—that is, with money"—a portion of the huge royalties he was expecting to receive in the coming year. Through his "efforts & 'position,'" he wanted to liberate Neal from having to patch tires, so that he could make himself into a writer. "Of all the teachers you have had don't you think I'd be the hippest?" Jack asked, promising to show Neal "the way to what you somewhat sarcastically called the 'world of the big boys.' . . . But once in this world you need not fear the American Gestapo that hounds the American Dispossessed." It all came down to "playing the game," Jack thought. In fact, he advised Neal to change his appearance so that he "looked right" rather than like "a jailbird," at the same time assuring him, "Yours is the gaunt soul of a Dostoevsky." Jack's mounting offers to Neal included an invitation to join him and Edie, "my great mad chick," in Italy on that infinitely stretchable one thousand dollars he expected to receive from Harcourt in December when he turned in the first part of his new novel.

In all this extravagance, there was a desperation that went beyond Jack's urge to come to the aid of a friend. It was as if Neal's letter had reminded him that once again the fulfillment of his "white ambitions" could separate him from the people he felt closest to, even from his "blood brother." By offering to share the spoils of his success, by proclaiming his belief (based on very little evidence) in the potential greatness of Neal's writing, Jack was trying to erase the glaring difference between himself and Neal that Neal was already acutely aware of.

"I know I have nothing for you," Neal immediately responded abjectly. Then in no uncertain terms he demanded that Jack come to him: "*now* is when I need you." He was asking for two weeks of "talk and beer, cigars and smutty jokes, nights of crazy happenings." But most of all he needed Jack to help him decide "what can be done."

Without writing back, Jack packed up and rushed toward San Francisco the morning after a night spent with a sympathetic older woman Brierly had introduced him to. She gave him a hundred dollars to speed him on his way.

As far as Carolyn Cassady was concerned, nothing—with the possible exception of the reappearance of Luanne Henderson—could have been more unwelcome than a visit from Jack Kerouac. Around August 10, without any advance warning, there was a knock on the door in the middle of the night. Naked, Neal got out of bed to see who it was, and the next thing she knew she could hear Jack's unmistakable voice saying, "My God, man—what if it had been someone else?" followed by laughter and conspiratorial whispers, as if they were two schoolboys already planning mischief. With a feeling of panic, Carolyn pictured "a drawbridge between me and Neal being drawn up, enclosing them in their castle of delights and leaving me sitting wistfully on the opposite bank, filling the moat with tears." She had not forgiven Jack for luring Neal to New York, and now he was back, bringing chaos into her household just when she'd begun to hope Neal was settling into their marriage.

Although Jack spent only three days under Carolyn's roof, his visit, according to her memoir, dragged on interminably, for at least a week and a

half, with Neal and Jack always talking above her head in their maddening "diggings" of everything they saw and heard. As soon as they'd eaten
the dinner she'd cooked after her long day of working in a doctor's office,
off they'd go on their nocturnal adventures, leaving her with the dishes
and her baby daughter. What she hated most was her exclusion from their
enjoyment of each other's company—a recurring theme in their three-
way relationship. But Carolyn did not enjoy herself in the least on the one
occasion Neal and Jack invited her to join them. In search of marijuana,
they circled a black neighborhood in Fillmore for hours, and the night
ended in a seedy nightclub where Carolyn had to watch some "pathetic
strippers" while her husband flirted with a singer. An innocuous remark
of Neal's the following day threw her into such a rage that she ordered
him to get out and to take Jack with him—words she didn't really mean
and would very soon regret. "Liar, Liar, Liar," she sobbed in her bedroom
as Jack and Neal hastily stuffed clothing into their bags.

When the two men found themselves cast out on the street with no
idea where to go next, Jack realized it was up to him to take charge of
the situation. Again he urged Neal to join him in Italy, reminding him
he was willing to pay his way there, but first the two of them had to get
to New York on Jack's remaining eighty-three dollars. They postponed
their departure, however, for a few more nights of "kicks" in the Fillmore Street jazz clubs and were given shelter by long-suffering Helen
Hinkle, whose husband had run off again and left her. After watching
Neal, completely revved up by Jack's presence, cavorting around her
living room with his grimy bandage unraveling from the stump of his
thumb, she gave him a maternal scolding for leaving his family and told
him he'd better get serious and stop all this goofing. In *On the Road*, it
is then that Sal Paradise starts thinking of Dean as the "Holy Goof"
and the incarnation of "the ragged and ecstatic joy of pure being,"
though part of him agrees with everything he is hearing from Galatea
Dunkel.

Two days later, after a glorious mad night in the Fillmore Street jazz
clubs, which Jack would later evoke as if he could still hear every note and
modulation of an unknown tenor man's riffs on "Close Your Eyes," he
and Neal left San Francisco in a travel bureau Plymouth driven by a gay
man from Kansas who was taking them along for the gas money Jack

contributed and with whom Neal had businesslike sex in a hotel room in Sacramento in order to get some cash that was not forthcoming. Before leaving Frisco, Neal had dictated a note for Carolyn to Helen, in which he told his pregnant wife that this time she was rid of him for good. He enclosed three dollars and made it clear that this time he was *not* going back to Luanne. Although he was unable to write because of his injured thumb, Neal had no difficulty taking over the wheel of the Plymouth, which he drove one-handed most of the way to Denver with a speed and recklessness that terrified all the passengers in the car except Jack.

Into his new Red Moultrie novel, Jack was putting Neal as Red's half-brother, Vern Pomeray. Like a Leon Robinson, Vern would "come and go," in addition to a second Robinson-like alter ego—a demonic jazzman whom Red would keep encountering during his westward travels. There was a lot of doubling (too much for the good of the book) in the intricacies of the plot. Born to the same mother, who dies giving birth to Vern and vanishes from the story, Red and Vern have different fathers who also seem like two halves of the same coin—both have a disposition to drink, wander, and get lost in America. Vern Sr. is a morose alcoholic hobo who has been hired to work on the failing ranch Red's Leo-like father, Smiley, inherits after the death of his older brother. Although Vern Sr. runs off with Smiley's lonely wife, Mary, who has become fed up with her husband's gambling and absences from home, Smiley lets him return to the ranch with six-year-old Vern after Mary's death. He never speaks to Vern Sr. again, yet the two go on the road together during the Depression selling flyswatters (as Neal had done with his father). In the next generation, the love triangle configuration is repeated when Red and Vern Jr. fall in love with the same woman. The narrator of the novel observes that two male rivals who may want to kill each other can also be tied together by "strange confluences of love, or lovelikeness." (By now, Jack was acknowledging the recurring triangular pattern in his own love life and a "love-likeness" beween himself and Neal.)

As Jack reeled across the country with Neal, this time without a Luanne to distract them from the close attention they were paying to each other, Vern Pomeray was a presence who traveled with them, and Jack was both intensely *with* Neal and outside him, being him and committing him to memory.

The Plymouth took them to Denver, where Jack had planned that both of them would stay for a few days in the comfortable home of the woman who had given him traveling money, but she had been warned by Justin Brierly not to let Neal into her house. In fact, Neal had become persona non grata in his hometown, where he was no longer regarded as Brierly's diamond in the rough but as an incorrigible criminal. They both ended up staying in Westwood with Jack's former neighbor Johnnie, where the repercussions of Neal's womanizing and his compulsive theft of a series of cars seemed to invite the incarceration he feared so much. They got out of Denver one step ahead of the clutches of the law in a shiny Chicago-bound Cadillac limousine that the Denver travel bureau had found for them. By the time it reached its destination, battered and dented after being driven through the Midwest at speeds of 100 to 110 miles an hour, Neal had practically run it into the ground.

In Chicago they immediately went in search of kicks and found great jazz in a saloon where some young musicians, whom Jack would call "children of the great bop innovators," were playing and where George Shearing, the blind British pianist he worshipped almost as much as Lennie Tristano, made a surprise appearance. But it was all downhill from there when they took a bus to Detroit to see Edie. Jack had truly imagined he would be able to collect her the way Neal had collected Luanne and take her back to New York with them, but she was not the same wild, glamorous-looking girl he remembered. The twenty-seven-year-old woman who appeared before him dressed in overalls had put on a lot of weight and cut off her long hair. She had fortified herself against the potential pain of seeing him again with a candy bar in one hand and a bottle of beer in the other. As if pathetically trying to roll back the clock, Edie arrived with an entourage of teenagers. Like Neal's thumb, she reminded Jack of entropy—he had a very hard time dealing with anything that reminded him that his own youth was passing. (In *On the Road*, Sal flies into an irrational rage after Dean, who has had a hard lesson in physical damage, warns him that he is wearing out his body.) Jack immediately lost his yearning to go back to Edie, and was disgusted when she told him that the next time she lived with him he'd have to get her a maid. But neither marrying Jack again nor going to bed with him that night and reawakening all her old feelings was what Edie had in mind. She accompanied Jack and Neal to a bar, then slipped out the door and drove off with some of the teenagers. Jack concluded, wrongly, that she had become totally indifferent to him. It was the low point of his trip.

With no place to sleep, Jack and Neal spent a miserable night in a skid row movie theater where a singing cowboy in a western landscape alternated on the flickering screen with Peter Lorre and Sydney Greenstreet in Istanbul. They woke up blearily the next morning "permeated completely with the strange gray Myth of the West and the weird dark Myth of the East." Since they had to wait in Detroit to get their last travel bureau car, they went out with Edie one more time, and ended up in a police station after she was stopped for speeding through a red light. Invoking her socialite connections, Edie got them all released without fines, then yelled at Jack and Neal for looking like hoodlums and getting her into trouble. She helped them finish off the case of beer she'd brought along with her, then drove home alone. She would spend the rest of her life in Grosse Pointe, Michigan, thinking of her years with Jack in New York as the time when she'd felt most alive.

THE EDGE OF SUCCESS

Although Allen Ginsberg would later recall it as a "brown" and "gloomy" place, Gabe Kerouac regarded her new home in Queens on the second floor of a ramshackle Victorian house at 94-21 134th Street in Richmond Hill as a very lucky find, as she'd enthusiastically written her son. An old wooden staircase led up to Jack's room, which had a window overlooking a tree-shaded sidewalk, and there were more trees in the backyard where Gabe was able to hang her laundry. Jack's mother was thrilled with the four rooms that were larger than the ones in Ozone Park plus the storage attic and the venetian blinds and blue tile floor of her new kitchen. But the quiet small-town appearance of the street was deceptive, as Jack discovered when he and Neal arrived there in late August. All night long, the loudspeaker from the nearby Sheffield Milk Company could be intermittently heard, summoning workers to their shifts, while just around the corner, vehicles surged along the sunken highway of the Van Wyck Expressway, which brutally bisected the neighborhood.

Very grudgingly—as long as it wasn't for more than a few days— Gabe agreed to put Neal up, but in no time at all he found a far more comfortable berth on the Upper East Side of Manhattan after he went to one of Cannastra's parties and met Diana Hansen, a twenty-six-year-old fashion writer, recently divorced from her poet husband, who immediately succumbed to his sexual energy as if she had been struck by lightning. Diana, who cultivated a Lost Generation look with her flapper hairstyle and a ton of mascara, was, according to John Clellon Holmes, a glamorous fixture at literary gatherings. He later recalled seeing Neal having sex with her right in front of him and all the other guests that night. Such things were increasingly likely to happen at Cannastra's wild gatherings, which seemed to be a kind of petri dish for the sexual revolution. Cannastra had even drilled a peephole into his bathroom door, so that he could spy on the couplings that went on in there.

In his new quarters in Richmond Hill, Jack resumed work on his Red Moultrie novel, which he now retitled *The Hip Generation*. He reworked the opening, adding a reference to Dr. Malodorous to his depiction of Red's boyhood, but his efforts seemed "ragged" to him, and now that his travels were over he felt "very very ennuyée (in the French-Canadian sense, meaning unhappy and sick)." "But 'work saves all?'" he asked himself in his journal on August 29. "'The details are the life of it?'" The question marks reflected his lack of faith in what he was writing, although Giroux had arranged for him to get $250 on the new book to tide him over until Christmas. Perhaps the trouble was "merely that I no longer want to think down to the bottom of things."

His social life also seemed thin to him, with Allen focused on the misery of being "a poor broken spirit in a hospital," Edie absorbed in her makeshift life in Michigan, and Neal, immersed in his affair with Diana, acting as if he had forgotten the soul-to-soul understanding he and Jack had reached on the road. Even Leo's death no longer seemed so freighted with meaning, as if Leo had simply vanished "past the last streetlamp like Céline's people do." Jack felt a lack of seriousness among the people he knew, a pervasive indifference—a kind of cruelty in the way they all dissected one another's behavior—that made him feel he was "losing track" of his own "deepest feelings." If there was nothing left to write about but details, Jack thought, then he no longer cared to continue writing.

But the next day he felt connected again to his work. His dark mood had evoked the memory of the night in Denver when he'd walked along Welton Street brooding on his "white ambitions" after taking Giroux to the airport. As he recalled that night in his journal, all the details he remembered seemed precious to him, and he would incorporate most of them into his final version of *On the Road*.

That evening he went to Manhattan. Five days of drinking ensued, during which he stayed at Giroux's apartment, went out to hear bebop each night, and acquired a black girlfriend named Lee Nevels, whose hip glamour greatly impressed Liz Holmes. He returned to Richmond Hill admitting he felt much better, though doubting that happiness was good for his art.

Jack had little time in September to make progress on the Red Moultrie novel since Giroux had asked him for substantial revisions on *The Town and the City*. With the office of Alfred Harcourt, the head of Harcourt Brace, put at his disposal, Jack wrote a couple of long inserts in what he now called "T&C style," as if it were a voice he'd outgrown but still had to imitate, and entertained Lucien, who visited him there with his latest girlfriend, Sarah Yokely, a "honey brunette" from North Carolina who, like Lucien, was working as an editor at United Press, an impressive job at that time for a woman. Jack was immediately drawn to Sarah, who had an appealing way of asking what Holmes later called "close, concerned questions," who held her own intellectually, and who idolized Lucien and seemed able to put up with his outrageous behavior. That night Jack was feeling successful and expansive. When the three of them went out to a restaurant, he ordered them lobster dinners and blew all his money. Two days later he received a disapproving telegram from Lucien: "Without discipline Kerouac will be tiny. Stand man, don't wilt in these hobo enervating rose bushes."

The "rose bushes" were clearly a reference to Giroux, who was wining and dining Jack after their daily work sessions and introducing him to important people, like Carl Sandburg. To Jack's unpublished friends, who looked upon editors as the natural enemies of writers, Giroux represented the establishment. They seemed to feel that Jack was in danger of being co-opted by him, though there may well have been a little envy in their attitude. "Oh to be what everyone wants me to be," Jack wrote, weary of all the "unnecessary fuss."

Allan Temko had just come back from Paris with his completed first novel, and Jack immediately arranged to have him meet Giroux. Temko, characteristically disdainful, felt "there was something wrong with the whole scene." It seemed to him that Giroux "doted on Jack" and that Jack was making the most of it. But, then, he had met Kazin in Paris and hadn't thought much of him either. He immediately alienated Giroux by being unable to resist telling him that Kazin reminded him of "one of these guys who used to come up to Columbia on the subway with their corned beef sandwich in their briefcase."

Jack's evenings with his editor often required a rented tuxedo. In one of them, he accompanied Giroux to the Metropolitan Opera House (Giroux was on the board) to see the Ballet Russe de Monte Carlo, which they watched from the privileged vantage point of the wings. Ballet was an exotic new experience for Jack: "It is the most exquisite of all the arts—and one can die a strange little death after seeing it for the first time (although I did not die)." Afterward there was dinner at the Blue Angel with the leading male dancer, Leon Danielian, and a high-powered crowd of "strange balletomanes," including the actors Don Gaynor and Burgess Meredith, the successful young Broadway lyricist John Latouche, a somewhat predatory millionaire patron of the arts named John Kelly, who subsequently kept urging Jack to join him on his Virginia estate, and the novelist Gore Vidal, who came with his socialite mother. They all apparently made much of Giroux's handsome rising young literary star, and to Jack's bewilderment there was a flurry of invitations, which he found himself accepting. He could have gone out for cocktails with Vidal and John Kelly that very night. Instead he went home to Richmond Hill with a toothache and the thought that he had to avoid getting lost in an "all too swirling" social scene.

He and Giroux spent the last week of September finishing up the revisions of *The Town and the City*, which went to the printer on the twenty-eighth much shorter than the original manuscript. The following day, Jack sat down to work on *The Hip Generation* and felt panic when he came up empty. He was still determined to write imaginative fiction, but his resistance to using himself as the protagonist of the novel seemed to be the problem. He sensed he was coming dangerously close to direct autobiographical writing in his portrayal of Red Moultrie, but didn't know how to prevent it.

By October 3, beginning to come out of his slump, he sternly reminded himself that he was *none* of the characters in his novel, and that all he had to do with Red Moultrie was "stand back and scan" him, "describing evidential phenomena for the sake of my own personal salvation." Jack may have been remembering James Joyce's famous dictum in *A Portrait of the Artist as a Young Man* that "The artist, like the God of the creations, remains within or behind or beyond or above his handiwork, invisible, refined out of existence, indifferent, paring his fingernails." Perhaps Joyce had felt some of the same anxiety about being labeled a mere memoirist that Jack was now feeling. Yet it was Jack's self-conscious standing back—reflected in his distanced omniscient authorial voice and his fictional inventions that went far beyond the ones in *The Town and the City*—that was draining the energy from his new fiction.

By the following day when he registered once more at the New School, where he would again be taking courses in American literature with Kazin and Lenrow, he had racked up another thousand words. He spent the evening with Lucien and Sarah and with the Holmeses, and went to hear Lennie Tristano with Seymour Wyse, who had just returned from England and had quickly been absorbed into Jack's expanding circle. Jack seemed proud that this time his socializing had not included Giroux, noting in his journal that he had not come home through "the rose bushes." With his confidence and optimism temporarily restored, he looked ahead to October 1951, projecting his future life as a successful author. By then, he thought, he would have finished *On the Road* (he had just reinstated that title) as well as *Dr. Sax*, received a Guggenheim, traveled throughout Europe, bought a house and maybe even a car (although he still hated to drive), and would probably be married to one of the scores of beautiful women who would be dying to meet him. By then, he thought—because he knew himself—he would also have been "lonely, mad, pompous, and foolish." The only possibility Jack couldn't imagine was that he was riding for a fall.

By October 17, Jack was able to estimate that he had written twenty-five thousand words of his second novel, yet he continued to feel as if he had not yet truly gotten a grip on it. In his journal, he wrote a trial paragraph about his mother losing all her teeth after Gerard's death. These were the facts of real life. "This is what I want to write," he declared impatiently, "not *stylistic* crap." He seemed to be having an attack of what the novelist David Shields would call, sixty years later, "reality hunger."

He spent the next few days consuming book after book that might feed his writing. He read John Donne's sermons and Thomas Merton's *Seven Storey Mountain* and revisited *Ulysses*, Ahab's speeches in *Moby-Dick*, and Céline's *Death on the Installment Plan*. After studying *Hamlet* line by line, he began thinking about Red Moultrie (and possibly himself) as a "hitchhiking, penniless, mystical Hamlet."

Meanwhile, there were the weekend parties to distract him. Jack spent one of his happiest Saturday nights with Neal, Lucien, and Allen, who by now was allowed to spend his weekends away from the mental hospital. The four of them stopped off at a cocktail party at the elegant Hotel St. Moritz, went on to Lenrow's apartment for music and drinks, then woke up Sarah Yokely, who served them all roast beef at four o'clock in the morning. The following day Jack wrote in his journal that he would always love his three closest male friends, "each one & en masse." He had another fine time with Seymour Wyse and Holmes when the three of them dropped in on Jerry Newman and used Newman's equipment to make "some astounding 'prophetic' voice-music recordings" in the style of Lennie Tristano.

But nothing seemed to break Jack out of his state of "introspective paralysis" for very long, as he continued to reevaluate his approach to writing. In early November, he read the galleys of *The Town and the City* with numb detachment, rather than the excitement of finally seeing his work in print. As if he'd had nothing to do with the process himself, it seemed to Jack that Giroux, who had cut some of the very episodes and passages he'd once considered essential, "had done a splendid job of revision." Giroux had often told him he must write from his strengths. "It may be," Jack observed in a dispirited way, "that where a story like T&C

is concerned, the story is more important than the poetry." But he was far from convinced.

In late November, thanks to an attack of phlebitis, Jack had his first prolonged period of quiet since his return from the West Coast. As he lay in bed, a new thought came to him—"*It's not the words that count, but the rush of what is said*"—and he realized that in his recent writing he had become "wrapped in a shroud of words and arty thoughts." A couple of days later, he refined this new insight: "IT'S NOT THE WORDS THAT COUNT BUT THE RUSH OF TRUTH WHICH USES WORDS FOR ITS PURPOSES." The same held true of music, Jack thought, where it was "the melody of the bar" that was important, rather than any particular "combination of notes." This was an idea he would keep returning to, though he was not yet ready to act on it.

While Jack was distractedly trying to find an approach to *On the Road*, Holmes was doggedly forging ahead with his new novel, in which the pivotal figure would be closely based on Allen Ginsberg, whose visionary madness continued to fascinate him. Despite some ambivalent feelings, which he had expressed to Jack that summer, Allen had given Holmes what Holmes took to be his wholehearted cooperation, sending him a nine-and-a-half-page letter about his mystical experiences in Spanish Harlem in response to a series of Holmes's probing and perhaps at times intrusive questions about the relationships, fantasies, and ideas he associated with his visions. Ignoring Jack's warning that Allen's openness could be something of a pose, Holmes was convinced that Allen had revealed himself in an extraordinary way. Rather than relying upon his imagination to supply the details for his novel, as Jack kept urging him to do, Holmes was proceeding for the time being like a journalist on assignment, planning to use big pieces of Allen's letter as well as extracts from his own journals, which had become a detailed chronicle of the lives of his friends, filled with accounts of events and conversations he had transcribed while they were still fresh in his memory. Although he would change his time frame later on, Holmes initially planned to open the book with the Fourth of July party where he had met Jack and Allen and end it with the acceptance of Jack's novel and the rejection of his own. Of course the book was also going to be about himself—"the hesitant, overly intellectual skeptic" and "minor poet" who was observing everything. "I think there is a kind of form to that, what you might call 'deep form,'" Holmes had written Jack from Provincetown that summer. "Deep form"—how a story could take its shape from the contours of actual experience—was something Jack had started to think about more and more, but for another year and a half he would continue to struggle with densely plotted fiction.

Still hurting from the rejection of *Frankel*, although he had lost all his desire to ever write another novel of ideas, Holmes needed support—and he got a generous amount of it from Jack, who not only encouraged him to write "great canvases of the New York scene," but carefully read the latest portion of the new novel whenever he stayed at Holmes's apartment. He praised John, argued with him, offered what John called "strange creative hints," and challenged him in ways that opened up new insights. The two bleary-eyed friends would have intense discussions over the early morning coffee they drank to rouse them from their hangovers after Marian had gone to work and on the long walks they took together down Sixth Avenue, which in those days below Rockefeller Center turned into a seedy thoroughfare, where they were likely to run into jazz musicians and where they could stop in at secondhand record stores with tables of dusty .78s. Unlike Jack, Holmes was managing to write every day, despite his nightly consumption of alcohol and participation in the "Dostoevskian" social life that was furnishing him with material. He was living his novel as it unfolded around him, writing in the tensions that were beginning to destroy his marriage and his growing sense that he and everyone around him were somehow losing their way. "There is something nearly malignantly fascinating," he'd observed to Jack, "to watching people change before your eyes and looking suddenly, seeing yourself there as well, and to yourself, nearly unrecognizable."

It must have been an odd feeling for Jack to read about a moody, womanizing writer called Kerouac in Holmes's rapidly accumulating pages, where at first he was using actual names. Once Jack told Allen that Holmes hated people and was writing a "savage book"—a message Allen passed along. But when Holmes confronted Jack, he said diffidently, "Hell man, why do you think I know what I'm talking about?" By December, in fact, Jack gave him a supremely gratifying compliment: "You're doing

Ginsberg better than I ever did. He's really an unbelievable character the way you've done him." He even asked Holmes if he could show a chapter he particularly liked to Giroux. "All of which is soul balm to me," Holmes wrote Alan Harrington, who was still in Arizona.

Another of Holmes's characters, Neal Cassady, had also taken to dropping in on him, since Neal regarded Holmes as a seasoned novelist, compared to himself. He claimed he was working on a novel of his own, but when Neal came home to Diana Hansen after his days of parking cars at a Midtown lot, it was much more likely that he could be found smoking marijuana in Diana's red-lit living room, wearing a short silk kimono that didn't quite conceal his genitals, than pounding the keys of the discarded typewriter from Harcourt Brace that Jack had gotten for him.

As the new year began, the difficulties Jack was having with his own writing continued, and so did the rounds of parties. In a state of exhaustion, he wrote to Allen, predicting that an archangel would one night appear at Cannastra's in a "flash of white light," and that when it spoke, everyone would "see, hear and shudder." Like Holmes, who was intending to put Cannastra into his novel, where he would graphically portray him as a human wreck "talking from a nightmare through which he was making his way on sheer nerve," Jack had become fascinated with Cannastra and often visited him at his loft at 121 West Twenty-first Street, a cavernous derelict place that seemed to mirror Cannastra's state of mind. Randomly furnished with dilapidated items like an old car seat that Cannastra had picked up from the street, it was littered with shards of broken records, smashed bottles, and cast-off clothing. Stored out of sight were a collection of exquisite Japanese kimonos and several unused rolls of expensive Japanese drafting paper that Jack would find an important use for in the spring of 1951.

Cannastra's life had secret compartments. In one of them was a lovely-looking nineteen-year-old from Albany named Joan Haverty, whom he kept away from his decadent friends. She thought of herself as a "girl who had fallen from a star," and had the curious, somewhat proud belief that she was a "blank page," constitutionally incapable of feeling physical pain, sexual pleasure, or any deep emotions. Cannastra advised her to find the protection of a husband if she wanted to stay in New York. He mentioned Jack as a matrimonial possibility, but did not attempt to introduce them. Meanwhile Joan played Cathy Earnshaw to Cannastra's Heathcliff. Together they scaled fire escapes and took dangerous flights across rooftops, leaping from building to building. In special notebooks, they jotted down everything they'd seen when they peeped in people's windows. Once Allen came upon them out on Twenty-first Street dressed in identical outfits, shooting water pistols at each other.

When he wasn't with the girl, Cannastra played darker games. In waterfront bars, he'd walk up to a sailor or a longshoreman and plant a kiss on his lips. At his parties he'd smash wineglasses and dance on them in his bare feet. In the midst of one gathering, he stripped off all his clothes for a run around the block and got Jack to join him, though Jack kept his shorts on. Like Neal Cassady, Cannastra was another of the mad ones Jack felt impelled to imitate; the outrageous verve of his drive toward annihilation made him magnetic.

As Cannastra's disintegration visibly gathered momentum, Jack seemed headed for triumph. Among the early signs that *The Town and the City* was expected to be a hit was its printing of fifteen thousand copies—unusual during a time when first editions of one thousand were the norm for debut novels—and its sale in January, two months before its American publication, to the British publisher Eyre and Spottiswoode, a distinguished old house that had published Oliver Goldsmith and Samuel Johnson. In a postcard to Giroux, Jack's London editor, Frank Morley, wrote: "Please tell Kerouac he is in good company, and what is more, is worthy of it." Jack couldn't resist quoting that to Allen, marveling that "a beat American kid from a milltown, me," was now in the company of such classic writers. Perhaps he was also thinking how strange it was that a book by a French Canuck could find acceptance with the British.

Giroux had demonstrated his own belief in *The Town and the City* by sending out letters with advance copies to E. M. Forster, Thomas Mann, Lewis Mumford, and Carl Sandburg. Van Doren contributed a blurb, calling Jack a "mature and responsible" writer; Kazin found "enormous humanity" in the novel. If Jack had anxieties, they had more to do with the question of what had been lost during the editing process than the way the book would be received. The long, detailed letter Allen wrote him in early February, after spending an entire day and night reading the copy Jack had presented to him with a dedication poem, may have reassured him. While Allen admitted he had been "pessimistic" about Giroux's efforts, he now felt that most of the problematic overblown prose was gone and that the story unfolded from chapter to chapter in a clear and inevitable way. Although he wished certain "beautiful" things had not been taken out, especially in the section based on Kammerer's death, Allen was certain that the book would "make a big stir and get singing reviews." He told Jack he could see how "ripe" his power as a writer had become.

From Mexico City, where he and Joan Adams had been living since the fall and where they planned to settle permanently to avoid the dire consequences of Bill standing trial in Louisiana, Burroughs sent his drily understated compliment: "Frankly, it is a lot better than I expected," and asked when Jack was coming down to visit. Joan also sent a note to say that Jack's book had been the first she'd read in four years "since Benzedrine." (She was off the drug for the time being, since she'd been unable to find a source for the Glaxo and Kline inhalers, and was trying to compensate with thyroid medicine and tequila.) Like Bill, she liked the way Jack had portrayed their Times Square connections, but claimed she "deeply" resented being turned into Bill's sister.

In early February, Jack felt ready to tackle his Red Moultrie novel again. Trying to fire himself up, he wrote in his journal that *On the Road* would be the "vehicle with which as a lyric poet, as lay prophet, and as the possessor of a responsibility to my own personality (whatever it rages to do) I wish to evoke that indescribable sad music of the night in America"—as if the sacred duty to evoke the American night had been passed on to him by Louis-Ferdinand Céline. Jack's new prospectus for the book showed some striking similarities to his ultimate version of *On the Road*. With Red's half-brother, Vern (now called Wayne), substantially reduced in importance, a new character, Dean Pomeray, more closely based on Neal, would now dominate the second half of the novel, where a number of the episodes—Red's romance with a Mexican girl in L.A., his encounter with the Ghost of the Susquehanna, and a series of wild car trips back and forth across the United States with Dean and Dean's girlfriend Marylou—would obviously be drawn from Jack's experiences. In New York, Red's involvement with characters who resembled Huncke and Burroughs would lead to a year in prison, after which Red would embark upon his "Big Circling Trip in the Night," rejoining Dean and Marylou for more travels, finding his lost father in Butte, Montana, and making up with his abandoned (and very sketchily conceived) teenage bride, Laura. The book would end with Red settling down with Laura in Denver and "poor Dean" still on the road on a winter night with that "rock in his belly giving him no rest." The ending may have reflected Jack's new interest in leading a healthier, more respectable life, and a decision to distance himself from Neal, whom he had stayed away from since Neal's involvement with Diana.

Despite having this new plan for the novel, Jack seemed unable to give it his full concentration. He worked on it sporadically, along with *Dr. Sax*, a rewrite of an old football novel, and another idea he'd been mulling over. By February 18, he had finally laid Red Moultrie to rest and replaced him with Chad Gavin, a character more like himself. As he started all over again, Jack felt sick to his stomach, yet after a night of writing he was satisfied enough with the pages he'd written to ask himself whether he should put off the western trip he was contemplating so that he could present Harcourt Brace with fifty thousand "publishable words" in April, when Giroux returned from a month in Rome. Jack reminded himself that even though he was still walking around in a ragged coat, he might soon be "rich & famous," and decided that in his future travels, he would simply take buses instead of hitchhiking, sleep in interesting old run-down hotels, and try not to have people relate to him as a public figure. Now that he believed he was coming to the end of his "raggedness," he saw it as worth preserving—"a real means to joy & learning."

Perhaps some of Jack's friends felt he was getting too full of himself as he awaited the life-changing reception of *The Town and the City*. A few days later, he became the victim of a practical joke when a telegram informed him that Tom Livornese had just been killed in a car crash. Completely devastated, Jack rushed to the Livornese house to pay his respects after having a Mass said for his departed friend. Laughing his head off, Tom opened the front door.

Although Jack regarded the prank as "innocent," this reminder of the terrible fragility of life had almost undone him and he was still feeling "all turned upside down" two nights later as he tried to concentrate on the opening chapter of his Chad Gavin novel. In his troubled state of mind, he remembered something Kazin had said in one of his classes: "Relationship is the diamond upon which existence rests." Suddenly Jack understood his primary task as a novelist: "You establish relationships between the souls of all concerned, on all sides, and then use the naturalistic material for the purpose of placing said relationships in their earthly position." He felt he had discovered the secret of writing as well as the principle for all his future books.

He was still at his typewriter when the morning mail arrived. In it was the first article on *The Town and the City;* its glowing words had been written by Allan Temko for the *Rocky Mountain Herald* and forwarded by Justin Brierly. "I'm so happy, I'll go up in smoke," Jack wrote. It was February 24, only five days before publication.

THE FRENCH CANADIAN OLDER BROTHER

In October 1929, shortly before *Look Homeward, Angel* was published, Thomas Wolfe, who, unlike Jack, was in the grip of anticipatory "dreamlike terror," asked his editor what the outcome of all his labor would be. "All that I know," Maxwell Perkins answered, "is that they cannot let it go, they cannot ignore it. The book will find its way." Wolfe saw Perkins's prediction come true. There were some negative reviews but they were counterbalanced by ones that immediately established him as an important American writer, and the book started to sell with increasing success.

Two decades later, *The Town and the City* would have a different kind of reception. There were some positive reviews in important places along with negative ones, but the positive reviews did not suggest that Jack had written the great American novel of his generation. Like most first novels, *The Town and the City* would sink quickly and quietly, its publication more of a nonevent than a disaster.

The review in the daily *New York Times* by Charles Poore, which appeared on March 2, was generally enthusiastic with some caveats having to do with the influence of Thomas Wolfe. At first, it seemed auspicious as Jack listened to Lucien read it to him over the phone. It was midnight as he stood there holding the receiver, excited to be at that important moment in the home of Artie Shaw. He and Frank Morley had serendipitously run into the famous jazz clarinetist as they were getting "blotto" in the bar of the Chatham Hotel.

Less than twenty-four hours later, however, Jack was indignantly lamenting in his journal, "That I spent 4 years abandoning the joys of normal youthful life, to make a serious contribution to American literature, and the result is treated like a cheap first novel." His "commuter-middle-class-reviewers," Jack felt with some justice, would only regard a "portrait of themselves" as "significant." They saw characters like Leon Levinsky and Alexander Panos (whom he had based on Sebastian) as "useless nuts," while "my Job-like Father" had been reduced to a "death-of-a-salesman-tearful-lamentation." How could the "miserable hitchhiking boy" he intended to write about in *On the Road* possibly have any meaning for someone like Howard Mumford Jones, the Harvard professor who had panned *The Town and the City* in the middlebrow pages of the *Saturday Review of Literature*, attacking it as much for its author's ambition as for its execution: "It belongs to the category of the 'big' novel," Jones had sarcastically commented, "the lengthy book, in which a prodigious splashing about, general emotional appeals in the 'lost, lost, lost' cadence of Thomas Wolfe, and a rather simple notion of what constitutes fictional characters are supposed to compensate for radical deficiencies in structure and style."

The larger problem was that even sympathetic critics like the novelist John Brooks, whose review appeared in the Sunday *Times Book Review*, wrote about Jack as if he were still serving his apprenticeship, rather than as a novelist in full possession of his powers. Calling Jack's novel "a rough diamond of a book," Brooks made the point that "the author grew spiritually and improved technically while writing" it, in other words implying that a good portion of the first part of the novel was weak: "The early scenes in Massachusetts tend to be overly idyllic in content and word, even ungrammatical, in presentation. On the other hand, Mr. Kerouac's somewhat Dostoevskian view of New York City is certainly exaggerated in another direction, but it is powerful and disturbing." Even the praise with which Brooks ended his review was tempered:

> Like Wolfe, to whom he seems to owe much, Mr. Kerouac tends to over-write. Admirably, however, he avoids imposing a false thematic frame-work on his material, pinning everything by force to "lostness" or "loneliness." His is the kind of novel that lets life lead where it will. More often than not, the depth and breadth of his vision triumph deci-sively over his technical weakness.

Although *Newsweek* called Jack "the best and most promising" of the new novelists, the reception of *The Town and the City* left Jack grimly feeling he had to write a better book. It also showed him how much tastes had changed since the heyday of Thomas Wolfe and that to be compared to him was a real liability. He celebrated his very low-key publication day with a shot of bourbon in a bookstore with a Harcourt salesman, followed by a gloomy little afternoon gathering at Holmes's apartment, "hidden from the sun."

What saved him from feeling totally crushed was "a Woman . . . of beauty unsurpassable." The woman was Sarah Yokely, whose heart had just been smashed to bits when Lucien coldly terminated their relation-ship and went back to Barbara Hale. Desperately needing to talk out her pain, Sarah turned to Jack, who was ready to listen and explain Lucien to her. He took her to dinner the day after Holmes's gathering; the follow-ing night he went to her apartment with a bottle of Cognac and inevitably the two of them landed in bed. The morning after, Jack found a tender note Sarah had left him along with a fresh pot of coffee before she went to her job. In its last line, she'd written something he very much wanted to believe: "I know I am going to love you more than I love Lucien."

He had been seeing Adele Morales again, as well as another woman, but Sarah seemed to be the wife/companion he'd been looking for—someone too real to him for a relationship based on his usual fantasies. She had that quality that always attracted him to certain people—a hunger for a life of emotional intensity. She'd come to New York six years earlier to find it and had ended up with a string of failed love affairs, though she maintained she still wasn't ready to get married. "Hold onto Sarah," Holmes advised him, "because she is warm inside her heart." But Sarah's continued obsession with Lucien made Jack uneasy in the midst of his happiness. "I want the truth," he wrote in his journal, "but not in women." From the start, he found the diamond of this relationship "fibrous" even though he had soon begun suggesting marriage to Sarah.

On March 11, he left her for a few days to go to Boston and Lowell to publicize his book. He arrived in Lowell just as an abridged serialized version of the novel started running in the *Lowell Sun*, introduced by an article written by Charles Sampas that identified the Lowell characters and praised Jack for his determination to keep writing despite all odds. But apart from old friends like Father Morrissette, G.J., John MacDonald, and Roland Salvas, Jack's appearance at the Bon Marche Bookshop to sign copies was sparsely attended, and a review of the book that also appeared in the *Sun* that week found his portrayal of Lowell ugly rather than idyllic and condemned the morals of his "Greenwich Village queers" and loose women. When Jack returned to New York, he wrote to Sebastian's sister Stella that he wished he had arrived in his hometown disguised by a beard and a slouch hat.

"BOOK NOT SELLING MUCH," he wrote in his journal on April 3. By then, there was apparently a new complication in his relationship with Sarah: Lucien, who still saw his former girlfriend every day at work, had temporarily changed his mind about letting go of her and Jack once again found himself "squaring off a triangle." But Sarah had stirred up unusually passionate and possessive feelings in him, and the tug of war between Jack and Lucien was threatening to end their friendship. "You'd be awful easy to forget," Lucien said to him contemptuously during a bitter quarrel in which Jack had issued him an ultimatum.

Giroux had finally returned from his month in Rome—too late to use his clout to get Harcourt to support *The Town and the City*. A seventy-five-hundred-dollar advertising budget had originally been allocated to the book, but the promised ads did not run, and it soon seemed to Jack that he was being coldly received on his visits to Harcourt. Giroux, however, still desired his company at cocktail parties and the opera—elegant occasions that only made Jack, brooding in his rented tuxedo, all the more aware of what lean times lay ahead of him now that his book had failed to put him on his feet. He began to feel that Giroux had betrayed him and that at heart Giroux was a "businessman" pretending to have finer values, while demanding pity because he was "rich and sad" and professing to envy the freedom Jack had despite his poverty. He wrote to Kazin about his tremendous disappointment, and received a brusque note weeks later asking him how he could possibly have imagined that "one month" would change his life.

With no more income expected from *The Town and the City* until he had earned out his advance, Jack worked on a story Giroux had offered to help him sell, using material he planned to later put into his Chad Gavin novel. Taking an image from *Dr. Sax* that haunted him, he gave the story a poetic title, "The Flower That Blows in the Night," which, on Giroux's recommendation, he changed to "Go! Go! Go!" The story shows Chad Gavin and Dean Pomeray arriving in a small "hip" town on the West Coast. Certain they're about to find kicks there, Dean immediately winds himself up into a manic state of tremendous verbal excitement. It was one of Jack's first attempts to capture the way Neal spoke, with his hyperenergy, explosive exclamations, and comical W. C. Fields–like elaborations. Having tapped into Neal's voice so successfully, Jack let Dean Pomeray speak as if an unstoppable gusher had been turned on—with Chad, to whom he allowed very few words, submerged to the point where he almost vanishes from the reader's consciousness. Although Jack was still keeping his distance from the real Neal, who seemed so sadly diminished in his role as Diana Hansen's lover, his imagination was on fire with a larger, more mythic character. On "Rain Street," Dean and Chad run into a hip black guide who recognizes them at once as kindred spirits and leads them to a wild jazz joint, where they find the ultimate tenor man— he has the "it" they have been searching for, and the third-person narrator's account of the climactic jazz session that follows is very close to the famous Slim Gaillard passage in *On the Road* that would demonstrate to Jack's future readers how brilliantly he could write about jazz. His voice wasn't quite there yet—rather than being in the thick of the action in the first person, his omniscient narrator hovers above it at a remove that drains away some immediacy—but he was getting close to finding the literary equivalent of "it." One is almost prompted to reach into the past and whisper in his ear, "Please let Chad tell this."

A large part of "Go! Go! Go!" may have been written in Sarah Yokely's apartment, where Jack was living during much of April. In fact, he accompanied Sarah to the Easter Parade, which she had been assigned to cover for United Press. They'd had a brief period of separation, but now she was determined not to get reinvolved with Lucien. When John and Marian Holmes visited them toward the end of the month, they felt Jack and Sarah had become very much a couple, although Holmes was troubled by Jack's dark silences and wondered whether he and his wife had "broken in on something." He attributed Jack's mood, however, to what he often found himself worrying about lately—some resentment or suspicion of him that Jack may have been harboring—and assured Jack at the end of the enormous letter he wrote him on the twenty-fifth that he wanted nothing more than his happiness.

Three days later Holmes wrote again, this time agitated by an article in the chic new magazine *Flair*, where it seemed to him that the critics of the establishment were already "trying to divide the 'beat' against themselves." Although the term "beat" had still not surfaced outside their immediate circle, Holmes was upset by the distinction being made between "the 'cool man' of this year, and the hipster of last. They call bop, and those who follow it, a 'cult,'" he complained, "and compare it to an intellectual, and artistic, movement in Europe called 'miserabilism.'" Looking forward to the time when his own novel and Jack's *On the Road* would be published, he worried that university professors and "New Bohemian" dilettantes might disregard the spirituality and real significance of their message and say that the two of them were merely writing about "lunatics" and "juvenile delinquents"—an accurate forecast of what would actually happen seven years later.

Holmes told Jack that they had better start thinking about "our material." To write about someone like Neal, who was seeking "the deepest, realest PANG of life," seemed the answer, Holmes felt, for Neal's pang was essentially "a great affirmation of simple creatureliness, with all the intimations of mortality and transiency that that word possesses." He quoted back to Jack the saying "Everything is 'tomic,'" which Jack had heard uttered by "a seedy little Negro hipster, named Cleo during a recent weekend with Fitz in Poughkeepsie. Because they were spending so much time together discussing the same people and ideas and books, Holmes often seemed to forget where Jack's mind left off and his own began—until he felt a sudden twinge of proprietary anxiety: "You and I must understand the 'why' of beatness," he wrote. "It is the escape from the trap. But it is not mere whistling in the haunted wood. It is for these reasons that such ideas as 'the end of the night' and 'bottom of the lake' have occurred to me. And 'the forest of Arden' to you." ("The end of the night," in this instance, had been an intrinsic part of Jack's imagery ever since he first read Céline.)

In his previous letter, which Jack had not answered, Holmes had brought up a very awkward moment at Sarah's, when Marian had picked up Sarah's wallet to look at a photo of Jack and said "Oops!" as she pulled out a photo of Lucien concealed beneath it—concrete evidence of the difficulties Jack and Sarah were having. Holmes had advised Jack to relax about the whole issue and have patience, but Jack was in real pain. The fact that Sarah was still deeply drawn to Lucien, whom Jack now called "the archangel of death," was making her turn away from Jack sexually and pull back into her own anguished thoughts. Now when he was with her, he often felt "dulled" and canceled out, as he confessed to Holmes in a letter he wrote at the beginning of May. For this particular "pang of life," escape seemed the solution, and he was thinking about disappearing from New York's Forest of Arden until the fall. His destination was up in the air—he might go to Hollywood and look for a screenwriting job or to Mexico to see Bill.

Although he complimented Holmes on his "brilliant" and "profound" second letter, Jack felt too low to respond to it point by point. He warned Holmes, however, not to compensate for his rejection of the *Partisan Review* assessment of their generation by going overboard in his faith in the "kids," whom Holmes believed constituted a latent mass Beat movement. And in a postscript, he offered Holmes some "corrections" for his own good, pointing out that at times Holmes's eagerness to expound on his own ideas caused him to misinterpret the sayings he picked up from others. Jack urged him to be more than "a chronicler of bleats."

In mid-May, Sarah Yokely went down to North Carolina to think things over and visit her family. When she wrote to Jack, her distance from him enabled her to reveal her tormented state of mind with unusual frankness. The truth was that the craving for Lucien that was splitting her in two wouldn't leave her, and she confessed to having a perverse need for a "love seasoned with idolatry." There may have been other reasons why Sarah was unhappy with Jack, but he had valued her and tried to be patient. Perversely, she warned him not to be "too good" to her and begged him to make her wait on him and to silence her and to become her "intellectual god," so that she could sit at his feet—as if only being put in her place could make her feel like a real woman. Her intelligence and independence seemed to be burdens she wanted to be rid of. Then came a short typed note in which she apologized for deceiving him by "pretending to be your dame." Whatever the cost, Sarah wrote, she was resigned to the fact that she was unable to love anyone but Lucien, though she thanked Jack for trying to change her.

"She was too haughty for my kind," Jack wrote in his journal on May 19, reflecting that if this love affair hadn't failed, there would be no need for him to go off on any journey. He had shown Sarah the best side of himself, and it hadn't been enough. Her rejection of him sexually had been humiliating, and it must have seemed more bearable to attribute their breakup to class differences. "I really travel because I'm loveless. I'm going to another life by dying like this." In *On the Road*, he would write only one line about this excruciating affair with "a woman who fed me lobsters, mushroom-on-toast, and Spring asparagus in the middle of the night but gave me a bad time otherwise."

The loss of Sarah, combined with the collapse of his other "white ambitions," stirred up Jack's recurring preoccupation with the question of what it meant to be his "kind." During the breakup, he'd had a marijuana-induced vision in which he was visited by a "French-Canadian older brother" whom Jack believed represented the return of his "original self." The older brother knew Jack's travels would be futile and provide no solution for him. Sarah, he told Jack, should have been "slapped down," Lucien was a "silly ass," Neal was basically all right but *"un excite."* He advised Jack to get married to a French woman, have children, and become a man.

Not only did the older brother direct Jack to go back to church, he advised him to return to either Lowell or Canada, stop trying to "defrench" himself, and, above all, to "shut up." For the moment Jack interpreted this to mean he had been writing in the wrong language, and considered "Anglicizing my Frenchness or Frenchifying my English." "Se dur pour mué parle l'Angla," he typed at the top of a page. He wrote a paragraph about his decision to write in French, then translated it into correct English, and followed that with an attempt to find the English equivalent of the *joual* sound. He referred to his inner translator as someone "on the other side."

In early June, an autographing party in the book department of the Denver Dry Goods Company that had been set up by Justin Brierly gave Jack a way to leave town with Harcourt footing the bill. From Denver, he planned to hitchhike to Mexico City and stay there until his money ran out. With the $120 Harcourt gave him for a train ticket, he bought a bus ticket instead and pocketed the change.

Just before Jack's departure, he spent some time with Neal again and found him unusually subdued, entrapped by his relationship with Diana, who had recently discovered she was going to have a baby—one more adult responsibility for him to deal with. ("You can't go all around the country having babies like that," Sal's aunt says to shamefaced Dean in *On the Road* when she hears the news.) Meanwhile, on the other side of the country, Carolyn, whom Neal was required to support with a portion of his earnings from parking cars, had given birth to their second daughter. Paralyzed for the moment, Neal told Jack it was going to feel strange to be left behind in New York without him.

Jack showed up in Denver with a sinister kid named George Glass, who had boarded the bus in Terre Haute, fresh from his release from reform school. Their first stop was Larimer Street, where Jack tried unsuccessfully to help George pawn his telltale penitentiary-allotted clothing. He then took George to a bar that used to be a hangout of Neal's, and called Ed White, who had just reluctantly come back from Paris and arrived shortly afterward with Frank Jeffries. A round of nonstop partying began, during which Jack found himself treated like a visiting celebrity with many occasions to wear the suit he had packed in New York. There, his book was already forgotten; in Denver, it was a one-week wonder and everyone wanted to meet the author. Jack introduced George Glass to his Denver gang. They received him much more warmly than they did Neal, who, after impulsively speeding all the way west in a 1936 Ford, unexpectedly walked into a party in Jack's honor given by Ed's older sister, and announced he had come to take Jack to Mexico. There he intended to get divorced from Carolyn so that he could marry Diana and legitimize their child. Once that was taken care of, Neal planned to return to Carolyn, remarry her, and have Diana move to California and set up a second household. Neal's former friends, Ed White, Justin Brierly, and Bob Burford, made it clear they wanted nothing to do with him. Perhaps Jack himself almost wished Neal hadn't come—he would later describe him as "the Shrouded Stranger on the plain, bearing down on me." But as usual, he found Neal an irresistible force. Within days, he and Frank Jeffries were climbing into Neal's Ford. Frank had impulsively decided to go on the road with Neal and Jack and study in Mexico City on the GI Bill.

Bob Burford could never figure out why Jack was so fascinated by Neal Cassady or why he saw any similarity between himself and Neal. "I think that Jack just picked up the wrong hero in Neal," he told Barry Gifford and Lawrence Lee. "There was a character treatment, and then he exaggerated it, and he blew it out of all proportion to anything that was real." Like many others, Burford didn't understand that for Jack verisimilitude was never the objective, and that what Jack imagined about someone was as real to him on the level of his art as "reality."

It was the last long trip Jack would take with Neal, to whom he had just given full mythologizing treatment in the pages of "Go! Go! Go!" As they drove the nineteen hundred miles that took them through New Mexico and Texas straight to the Mexican border, Jack bounced on the busted front seat of Neal's jalopy, listening to the rattle of the unhinged right-hand door and the stories they told each other to keep whoever was at the wheel from going off the road. Perhaps he felt he was living out an extension of his story about Dean and Chad. The "it" they were looking for this time was the crossing in Laredo that would take them into the "Magic South," where, if the car didn't disintegrate under them, their journey ahead could be infinite—the "dying" away from the past that he was seeking.

He made no notes on this trip and would later re-create it, heightening his memories to build up the ecstatic series of epiphanies that would bring the denouement of On the Road to a climax. In the moodlessness of constant movement, he found temporary escape from the depression that was dogging him like the Shrouded Stranger and would catch up with him very soon in Mexico City.

Meanwhile, everything he was about to see would be new and different and distinctly fellaheen. There were intimations of Mexico even in the raw back streets of San Antonio, and once they drove through "sinister Laredo" and crossed the bridge over the Rio Grande, they instantly found themselves in a country that looked amazingly like the way Jack had always pictured it and at the same time seemed like the first truly foreign place he had ever visited—a permissive paradise of "lazy and tender" officials, ten-cent beers, and six-cent packs of cigarettes, with sweet, smiling purveyors of marijuana, which everyone was smoking openly, and dance halls throbbing with the beat of mambo where alluring teenage girls were selling their bodies at prices even Jack and Neal could afford. "There's no *suspicion* here," Jack has Dean Moriarty say wonderingly in *On the Road* as they arrive in a peasant village after crossing a desert. "Everybody's cool, everybody looks at you with such straight brown eyes and they don't say anything, just *look* and in that look all of the human qualities are soft and subdued and still there." But these words sound so thematically apropos, one might suspect Jack was translating his own thoughts into Dean's voice.

PART NINE

THE "RUSH OF TRUTH"

THE UNWRITABLE ROAD NOVEL

In Mexico City, which he saw as "one vast Bohemian camp" and the "great and final wild uninhibited Fellahin-childlike city that we knew we would find at the end of the road," Jack immediately came down with a terrible case of dysentery. In the original April 1951 Scroll version of *On the Road*, Neal stays just long enough to obtain his Mexican divorce, before heading to New York to marry Diana, leaving Jack moaning and half conscious in a hotel room (in the 1957 Viking Press version, which had been much revised and edited, Dean leaves Sal with some stranger named Stan). In reality Neal left Jack in the care of Burroughs and Joan, but the exigencies of fiction required Sal to feel abandoned (a feeling Jack probably remembered actually having) and Dean's ratlike betrayal of Sal Paradise's trust. The Leon Robinson con-man side of Dean Moriarty had to counterbalance the "prophet" Jack had portrayed just a few pages earlier in Dean's encounters with Mexican peasants, so that Sal Paradise could find enough forgiveness and largeness of spirit to say gently, "Okay, old Dean, I'll say nothing." It was a brilliant stroke—without it, the conclusion Jack was building toward would have had considerably less poignance and depth.

In 1982, in an essay entitled "Danger: Unexploded Myth," Carolyn Cassady would attempt to change the public's impression that her husband and Dean Moriarty were identical by warning Kerouac readers that "while Jack had captured the pattern of Neal's speech or physical appearance in action, the ideas, the thoughts are almost entirely Jack's, or Jack's deduction of Neal's meaning or intent." But it was too late. By that time neither the Cassady myth nor the Kerouac myth could be shattered. Not only did the public adhere to the misperception that everything in Kerouac's confessional writing must be true, but the pioneering and most influential Kerouac scholar, Ann Charters, persisted in regarding and dealing with his books as "thinly disguised memoirs," despite the numerous instances where interviews had revealed to her that "The way Kerouac portrays the people in his books isn't necessarily the way other people saw them or the way the characters saw themselves." Nonetheless, Charters went so far as to write in the same year Carolyn's essay appeared that "There never was a novelist who trusted his imagination so little."

Academicians and critics of Charters's generation, as well as Jack's, tended to have rigid conceptions of what constituted a novel and what did not and to feel a distinct prejudice against autobiographically-based fiction. (Alfred Kazin, who had written a memoir, *A Walker in the City*, was one of the exceptions.) Until 1951, Jack's awareness of this bias undoubtedly contributed to his frustrating efforts to fictionalize his own story as much as possible. Once the publicity and media attention surrounding *On the Road* had established the Kerouac myth, he would often find himself called a "reporter," contributing to the impression that he had simply jotted down and then typed up everything that had happened to him, and he would even be hailed as "the father of new journalism" by Seymour Krim. While Jack insisted that he told the truth in what he wrote, it should be noted he never used the word *memoir* to describe his work. His own term for *On the Road* and the books that came after it was "true life novels."

Jack's true life novels do contain much verifiable fact, but by the second half of 1951 the truths he would seek to recapture above all would be the texture of his experiences, the feelings associated with them, the Proustian epiphanies he'd had, rather than the precise factual details surrounding each event. The crucial element in his work would not be the invention of plot or the creation of composite characters but the alchemy that turned his memories into art, shaping, altering, and refining the raw material he worked from—all toward arriving at what Wolfe had called "a life completely digested in my spirit."

In the summer of 1950, however, Jack still could not see his way forward as a writer with any clarity. In *The Town and the City*, he had avoided the issue of writing directly autobiographical fiction. But nothing had come of his dreams of producing the sweeping, best-selling great

American novel, as it was conventionally defined. Instead he had been left with the daunting recognition that he was free to take his work in any direction he chose—with poverty and obscurity as the probable result. With increasing panic and little hope, and this time with the aid of drugs, which could be obtained effortlessly in the rapidly deteriorating Burroughs household, he would try to come up with an entirely new approach to the road novel he had been unable to carry forward in the adventures of Chad Gavin and Dean Pomeray.

In Mexico, Joan Adams had become an alcoholic; her steady consumption of forty-cent bottles of tequila began at eight in the morning. By some miracle, she managed to keep house and live with the knowledge that Bill was picking up boys (forty cents a boy) in a local bar. She wrote Allen, who knew that Bill's lack of sexual interest in her had become a form of ongoing torture, that she had "infinite patience." Burroughs was studying Mayan culture at the University of Mexico—the GI Bill supplement that he received when added to his two-hundred-dollar monthly stipend from his family was enough to take care of all his needs now that he was no longer in the States. Besides boys, Bill had an endless supply of morphine, and his obsession with guns had only increased. He drilled Jack on how to draw a weapon and engaged him in target practice. Recently Burroughs had also started writing—he called his manuscript, which he hoped to sell for additional cash, a "novel about junk."

On the marijuana that could be had so cheaply, Jack stayed continually high for the next month and a half; he also began to develop a taste for Bill's morphine, a drug he had previously resisted. Through his exploration of narcotics, Jack was hoping to take his mind to a deeper level, where "inescapably true subconscious subjects" could be brought up to "the light of objective clarity." He wrote Ed White that he felt like a "scientist." On marijuana, he believed, he could once again see "the light" he had bathed in when he was a child who had been able to love everything. In fact, Mexico City, with its Catholic churches and its streets filled with the poor, seemed strangely familiar to him. "It so wondrously reminded me (in its simplicity, straightness)," he would recall in Visions of Cody, "of Lowell (and French Canadians)." He told Ed White that "Something is bound to happen, some revelation is about to appear to me soon," and that one day, in a pile of orange bricks, he had sensed the presence of God. Obeying his inner older brother, he started praying for a full return of his faith.

One reason Jack was feeling so preoccupied with Lowell may have been an insightful review of *The Town and the City* his mother had forwarded to him. Written by Yvonne Le Maître, a formidable Franco-American intellectual who during the 1930s had been the Paris correspondent for the *New Yorker*, it had appeared that spring in *Le Travailleur*, a Worcester, Massachusetts, newspaper devoted to "the promotion of Franco-American cultural activities." While Le Maître recognized Jack as a writer of *"talent considerable,"* she labeled his novel *"un livre curieux,"* comparing it to a sturdy tree that had been planted without roots and without regard to the makeup of the soil. Like a reproachful relative, Le Maître took Jack to task for failing to portray the true ethnic composition of Lowell—an American *"melting pot"* whose elements were very imperfectly blended—as well as for using only one French phrase in the entire novel and mentioning only one work of French literature, André Gide's *The Counterfeiters*. Although she allowed that Jack had been trying to avoid the pitfalls of the ethnic novel, she found that a feeling of unreality haunted the entire book. Jack must have read the review with shame and with the sinking feeling that Yvonne Le Maître was right. She had exposed him to his own people as a dishonest writer and as a young Franco-American who had betrayed the ideals of *la survivance*.

By castigating Giroux—the editor who had tried to keep him from writing in *Dr. Sax* about his original French Canadian child self, "what I *really* know"—Jack tried to displace some of his guilt. From now on, he decided, he would reject all of Giroux's suspect advice, which also meant that he would make his writing as "wild" and lyrical as he wished, structuring his stories on a "rack" of poetic imagery.

But his rebellion only intensified his terror about his future. Why hadn't he been able to make thousands like a "proud" F. Scott Fitzgerald? Why was his only option a return to the lonely asceticism of the years when he worked on *The Town and the City*? Jack felt he could never go back to that way of being. In fact, what he now craved was "uninterrupted rapture"—something he found only in the passing moments when he was listening to jazz, reading Shakespeare or Dostoevsky, having sex, or getting drunk or high. This was Jack's first expression of a need that would be impossible to fulfill. He was losing not only his capacity to tolerate periods of unheightened existence but his ability to concentrate on his work, which, rather than being a source of bliss, was becoming a kind of torment for him.

Although Jack didn't admit it to Ed White, he had found no rapture in starting yet another novel on the flimsy lined pages of the fat notebook he'd bought himself. In this one, as if it were written as a response to Le Maître's objections, his protagonist and narrator was a fifteen-year-old Franco-American boy from New Hampshire named Wilfred (Freddie) Boncoeur, who goes on the road in search of his reprobate of a father, who had disappeared into the West when he was two. Since he could hardly write this book in French if he expected to get it published, Jack gave Freddie full command of the English language, but he did have a phantomlike companion named Cousin, a word that in *joual* often meant "my kind," who would be uncorrupted by "English silliness" and would frequently have to set Freddie straight, warning him at the outset of their journey that the two of them would have to walk every step of the way and reminding him that "the world is nothing" and that everywhere they went the dead would be buried under their feet. To his cast of characters, Jack added Dean Pomeray, again based on Neal, plus a half-brother of Freddie's and a walking "hipster saint" named Pictorial Review Jackson, who would stand by the side of the road asking the drivers of passing cars, "Whither goest thou?" In the Wilfred Boncoeur road novel, Jack had returned to the kind of poetic imagery he had used in *Dr. Sax*, with "the flower that blows in the wind" becoming "the rose of the rainy night." At Freddie's window a bird with a rose in its beak would appear, then fly off over the river and turn into a bat. Jack was calling this desperate composite of two different novels *Gone on the Road*, and he decided to dedicate it to John Clellon Holmes, who, after hearing about Jack's continuing high and the visions he was having and that his mind was "cracking open" as well as flowering, assumed he had fallen into complete despair about his writing, and sent him a long, concerned brotherly letter.

It wasn't long before Jack felt deep frustration with the elaborately plotted adventures of Freddie Boncoeur. Owning up to the fact that Freddie was really himself, he wondered what was holding him back from simply writing straight autobiography. Nonetheless, he kept writing, and, fully aware that it was exactly the kind of novel Giroux didn't want from him, typed up enough pages to submit to Harcourt Brace before he left Mexico in the third week of July. He crossed the border into the United States with a kilo of marijuana hidden in a silk scarf tied around his waist.

As could have been predicted, Giroux rejected *Gone on the Road*, thus giving Jack an excuse to break with him. "But your best writing is when you don't know it, your narration," Giroux wearily insisted. At Holmes's suggestion, Jack gave the manuscript to Rae Everitt, who was now working in the new literary department of the talent agency MCA. Over the next several months, she kept sending it out with no success.

For the rest of the summer Jack holed up in Richmond Hill. He smoked the marijuana he'd brought back with him and went into New York very seldom. In the living room was the big oak rolltop desk his sister had gotten him for his twenty-eighth birthday that spring and sent up from the South with Paul—a reminder of the faith his family had had in him only recently. He dragged himself over to it to start a second version of *Gone on the Road*, but felt too listless and discouraged to keep a writing log or a journal.

It was not until he had been home for nearly a month that he wrote a letter to Yvonne Le Maître. By this time he had digested her review thoroughly and seemed grateful for its sternness, despite the pain it had caused him. He told Le Maître that because she had understood him so well, like "a very aunt of mine," it was the best review he'd gotten.

Portraying himself as someone who had never found a true home in America or in the language of his people, and giving his phrasing, consciously or not, a decidedly French sound, Jack vowed to never "English" himself again and to write a book about his true New England background in the "most rudimentary" French, which was all he had been able to master.

His frank explanation of how he had lost a good deal of his fluency in *joual* in the course of developing his complicated relationship with English was probably something Yvonne Le Maître understood. But she may not have had much sympathy for the literary ambition that had led

Jack's decision to make the Martins a "universal" American family. Although he urged her to write back, he evidently never received a reply.

No one saw much of Jack that fall as he holed up in Richmond Hill and smoked his way through his kilo of grass. In September, worried about the torpor he'd fallen into and fearing that he'd developed a drug habit, he wrote to Burroughs and received a stern, commonsensical response: "You are a strong healthy man with no habits and I cannot understand why you are not more active." Burroughs's parting advice was to return to Mexico to live as soon as possible. As for himself, he couldn't "see the States now at all." In July, the Korean War had broken out, threatening to involve America in another wide and deadly conflict. Meanwhile, as Joan saw it, the fear of radiation from the continued testing of atomic bombs had become a sinister means of governmental mind control, and Bill was beginning to think she had a point.

It took Jack until November to start to come out of his depression, and when Allen first saw him, it seemed to him that Jack had changed. "He has been strangely out of town the last several months, in retirement and brooding on T [marijuana] alone," Allen would report to Neal, "and when he rejoined N.Y. society he seemed to be more settled in reality, more sober." He reminded Allen now of an "F. Scott Fitzgerald after the party of ego was over."

THE GIRL WITH THE
INNOCENT AND PURE EYES

One ongoing New York party ended tragically in mid-October—the one at Cannastra's. Cannastra had been barred from the San Remo for a while, but had recently been reinstated. On October 10, Allen had a long talk with him there, in which Cannastra, in despair over an unconsummated love affair with a woman, spoke about "coming to an end." Love, he said, meant "touching people, though he loathed the touch of flesh." Allen realized Cannastra was admitting he was homosexual. Two days later, Cannastra was killed in horrifying circumstances. He was on his way to meet Lucien with a small group of people and had just boarded a subway train at the West Fourth Street station in Greenwich Village.

Suddenly, as if he were about to play one of his usual pranks, Cannastra said he was getting out to go to the Bleecker Street tavern. Since the train had just closed its doors and was already moving, he started to climb out a window. As his friends frantically tried to drag him to safety, his head was crushed against a pillar at the opening of the tunnel and he fell onto the tracks.

Was it an accident or a suicide? Allen did not think Cannastra understood "what it really meant to die," but everyone had different theories when they gathered the night afterward in Cannastra's loft. "Weeklong drunks" followed; "everybody's pride was beaten for a week," as Allen reported to Neal. One thing that soon changed was the ending of Holmes's novel, where Cannastra's death replaced the sale of Jack's novel as a much more dramatic concluding episode.

The girl from Albany, Joan Haverty, who had not been seen on Twenty-first Street that fall, reappeared to help Cannastra's mother and sister clear out the loft. When the relatives had taken the little they wanted to keep—in Schenectady they would burn Bill's collection of silk kimonos—Joan decided to move into the loft herself and maintain it as a shrine to Cannastra's memory, even though he had angrily terminated their relationship the day she had proudly announced to him that she had let a physics student named Herb awaken her libido. She washed the floor, arranged the car seats around Bill's makeshift coffee table, and thought about changing the position of one painting. At night she worked at her sewing machine and waited for something else to happen to her. Noticing that she was back, Allen thought about making her his girlfriend, since an affair with an older woman that summer had temporarily convinced him he wasn't gay, but he rejected the idea because Joan did not seem bright enough for him—a verdict Allen tended to pass on women.

Inevitably people started giving parties again, and one of the first to do so at the beginning of November was Lucien. As Jack walked down Twenty-first Street on his way there, he saw a light in Cannastra's loft, where he'd heard that Cannastra's girl was living. Hearing a shout from the street, Joan Haverty looked down, heard his name, and invited him up for hot chocolate, throwing him a key. When he'd climbed up the stairs, Jack saw a slender brunette with the kind of Mary Carney looks that always made him spin his fantasies. Joan Haverty was in the midst of a quarrel with her physicist ex-boyfriend, whom she had infuriated that evening by asking whether rocks had "any kind of awareness or consciousness." As she stood at the stove heating milk, she was stabbed to the heart to hear him say "Nope" when Jack asked him if she was his girl.

Via the fire escape that connected Cannastra's building with Lucien's, Jack took them both to Lucien's party. At first, he'd seemed awkward, even foolish, to Joan—with "coarse features" that saved him from being "pretty." But he seemed to light up as he kept drinking and she saw how his friends gathered around him and how "captivating," warm, and funny he could be with people he knew.

Over the next few days Jack kept dropping by to see her. The third time he appeared, he told her he loved her and asked her to be his bride. By then she had tried to read *The Town and the City* and had been left cold. His plan for the two of them was that as soon as he finished his new book, they would head to California in an old truck to live near some couple he knew and start having lots of babies.

A year later, in *Visions of Cody*, Jack would attribute his impulsive and disastrous proposal to the amount of marijuana he was smoking at the time and the dark mood that nothing seemed to dislodge. Perhaps he was still suffering over the loss of Sarah, but suddenly all he wanted was a feeling of security, and here was a pretty face he thought he could marry. He even made a bet with Lucien that Joan would accept him. Besides the face, it seemed to augur well that the unformed person who went with it worked as a seamstress and that Cannastra had once told him she was a great cook. How many other women in his circle knew how to cook and sew? In fact, he told Haverty that she filled the bill for exactly the "sweet little home-type girl" he'd once described to Cannastra as his ideal wife: "Not witty or wise, not worldly or jaded." So how about it? he asked her. And she said she'd think it over.

Two weeks later Joan said yes, primarily because she was frightened of being on her own in New York, where men constantly tried to prey on her (she had recently narrowly escaped being raped by a man who had followed her into the loft building), and marriage to someone like Jack seemed "the least of a number of evils." She also believed Cannastra would have found this marriage "propitious."

On November 18, Allen reported to Neal that he and Lucien had just been best men at a ceremony in a judge's apartment where Jack had married "a tall, dumb, darkhaired girl just made for him," though without Jack's "largeness of spirit." A huge party had followed at Cannastra's loft with the whole crowd there until three A.M., plus a horde of crashers from the San Remo, one of whom asked Joan who the bride was. "I believe in Jack and Joan," shouted Holmes as he toasted them with a bottle of champagne. But Allen sensed there was something missing. "I did not feel passionate or exultant that night but dead, as did [Lucien] and I think Jack," Allen wrote, "as we were all too old and weary to exult over anything but was new and outwidening into unknown joys beyond control, and this was not exactly like that."

"The first evil," Jack would write a year later, "was not putting her down when I first realized I didn't love her or like her at all," which was a week before their wedding.

According to Haverty, she told him the day she became his bride that he need not bother making declarations of love to her. Perhaps this was one reason he drank so much at the party that he passed out before Joan got into her "diaphanous" nightgown and slipped into bed beside him. The following day he moved his rolltop desk into the loft, set it next to the bed despite her objections, and got down to work. He told Joan he liked to watch her sleep while he wrote. After all, despite her coldness, she still had the face—the high cheekbones that he told her made her look like an Apache. He insisted on making a number of other changes in the loft, since Joan made him feel they were sharing it with Cannastra's ghost. She agreed he was right, but in general felt resistance to whatever he had to say and didn't like him ordering her around. Ordering people around was not Jack's style, but he may have been futilely attempting to turn his unresponsive young bride into his French Canadian wife—to "make her mind," just as the "older brother" he'd dreamed about had advised him to treat Sarah Yokely. "My women never understand," he would cluelessly lament the following year. "I want them to wear housedresses all the time," forgetting that his real need was the kind of love and rapport he'd hoped to find with Sarah.

Joan Haverty wrote *Nobody's Wife* in the last ten years of her life. Found under her bed in fragments by Jan Kerouac, the daughter she had by Jack, it was pieced together, and partially rewritten, by a professional editor who was able to mimic Joan's voice. The book contains the telltale evidence of fictionalization with its long stretches of "recalled" dialogue and was to some degree an act of vengeance, directed at tearing away at Jack's image—especially to bring his masculinity into question by emphasizing the point that he was rarely motivated to make love to her during the six months of their marriage. (It should be noted, however, that Jack wrote the number 150 next to Haverty's name in the curious record he kept of his sex life with Joan and other women from 1939 to 1963.) Haverty gave a more sentimental account of their marriage in 1978, when she was interviewed by Gerald Nicosia, but perhaps what she told Nicosia should also be taken with a grain of salt:

> Joan was learning to love Jack. She saw much good in him, much sensitivity, and the fact that he wanted to care for his mother just enhanced his "nice-boy" image. He was, besides, her "Angel Bunny," who amused her when she got too serious. Once when all his boyish charm failed to draw a smile, he stood on his head on a busy sidewalk.

Unwilling to admit to Neal that he had picked the wrong woman to marry, Jack portrayed her on November 21, as the "great 20 yr. old girl" who was bringing him back to life. A few weeks later, since he remained very proud of her looks, he sent Neal snapshots of his cold young bride. In late December, after infuriating Joan by reading her diary without her consent, he reported to Neal that she had the kind of natural talent for writing most women lacked and hailed her as "a new writer on this old horizon."

In *Nobody's Wife*, however, Haverty claims that Jack brutally dismissed her literary aspirations. "I can't stand women who think they can write," he warns her. "It's all just so much sentimental bullshit." (In my own case, Jack, unlike other male artists I knew during the deplorably misogynist fifties, surprised me by completely encouraging my efforts to write. Although he predicted I would probably settle for just having babies, he kept urging me to quit my secretarial job and, following his example, sacrifice everything to my work.)

By the beginning of December, after spending less than two weeks with his bride in the loft on Twenty-first Street, Jack abruptly decided they should give the place up and move in with his mother in Richmond Hill because they had run through too much money to pay the rent. Joan took her sewing machine with her. Jack took his desk as well as all of Cannastra's Japanese drafting paper. Perhaps he discovered those five rolls when they were packing and had been reminded of something Melville had written to Hawthorne a hundred years earlier:

> If the world was entirely made up of Magians, I'll tell you what I should do. I should have a paper-mill established at one end of the house, and so have an endless riband of foolscap rolling in upon my desk; and upon that endless riband I should write a thousand—a million—billion thoughts all under the form of a letter to you.

Meanwhile such fluidity continued to elude him as he remained torn between writing a road novel with western characters and one with a cast of French Canadians like Freddie Boncoeur and Cousin. In his plan for each book, he incorporated a character directly based on Neal, but he could not settle on the identity of his protagonist, or the voice in which to write his second novel. He had nothing to show for two years of work but a humiliating pile of abandoned novel starts.

"THE VOICE IS ALL"

In August, Freddie Boncoeur had been supplanted by Cook Smith, a young Red Moultrie–like wanderer from Denver, who recounts his adventures in a strained, overly heightened voice. The thirty-two-page manuscript, a brief return to symbolism, again attempted to combine *On the Road* with *Dr. Sax*. Smith woke up on its opening page in a dreary room near the Des Moines freight yards with the feeling that he had forgotten who he was (it was the third time Jack had written this scene that would become a defining moment for Sal Paradise in *On the Road*). Another familiar element was the pursuing shrouded stranger who haunted Cook Smith's thoughts.

In October, Freddie and Cousin made a reappearance, though Jack's conception of these two characters had changed. He now saw Cousin, who had been "born bleak" and gloomily pessimistic, as the alter ego of warm little Freddie, obviously intending to have them express the two sides of his own personality. He hand-printed two alternate openings for this novel in columns on soft gray construction paper, creating front pages for an imaginary newspaper called *American Times*, perhaps hoping to recapture the pure pleasure writing had given him when he used to play at being Jack Lewis. The following month, by merging Freddie with Cook Smith, Jack came up with Ben Baloon, a multiethnic poet/bum, part English, French, and Comanche ("every kind of everyone he met"), before turning his thoughts to a set of all-American characters, based on Ed White, Hal Chase, and Justin Brierly, for a novel about a search for a lost father. Frantically recombining and recycling old characters, motifs, and plot elements, and unable to sustain any idea for very long, Jack was in danger of completely wearing out the material that meant the most to him.

Standing back from his fruitless struggle, he pretended the *Reader's Digest* had asked him to write an article on the challenges of writing a second novel. Adopting the confident persona of a successful author, he wrote a credo for himself to follow. The important thing, he declared, was to write for yourself and for God and to put down only what you really meant to say, staying as faithful as possible to the language in which your thoughts first came. In this way, the writer could experience the "joy" of Shakespeare or Rabelais with no need to engage in elaborate plotting, while never losing the intense exhilaration he'd felt at the first conception of his book. By now Jack was coming to believe that nothing was worse for a novel than an intricate, carefully worked-out plot. He managed to deal calmly with the increasingly worrying problem of his own distraction and indecision. Acknowledging the way his interest in facilely invented characters was apt to evaporate in a matter of weeks, he tried to accept the speeded-up flux of his "mental life" as something entirely natural and even positive, rather than being driven to despair by the intrusions of a "new spiteful self" that kept undermining whatever he produced. "Working is just waiting," he told himself. But the difficulties he was having may have been due in part to the cumulative effects of alcohol and narcotics on his brain chemistry.

———

In mid-December, while Jack continued to "wait," Neal Cassady was seized by enough inspiration to sit still for five days of writing. His unusual ability to concentrate may have been partially due to the fact that he had finally chosen to limit himself to only one wife—Carolyn, although he had promised Diana, after her disappointing attempt to rejoin him in California, that he would return to New York in February to see their newborn son. He had also been motivated by the urge to compete with John Clellon Holmes, who had sent him a "whoop-de-do" of a letter in late November that included ten pages of graphic detail about a sexual encounter he'd had in his adolescence. Neal envied the effortlessness with which he thought Holmes had tossed this off without the "20 man hours of sweat" that would have discouraged him from sitting down to write something in a similar vein. Two weeks later, however, with the aid of Benzedrine, Neal managed to produce in three days a twelve-thousand-word account of two overlapping affairs he'd had in his late teens—one with a young woman named Joan Anderson, to whom he paid a hospital call after a suicide attempt; the other with an oversexed sixteen-year-old girl he called Cherry Mary.

Although the iconic "Joan Anderson letter" would epitomize to Jack and Allen what could be achieved with spontaneous writing, its literary effect was not actually what Neal aimed at and the process that went into it was hardly fluid. As Neal would explain to Allen a few months later, he would start with the outline of the memories that had prompted him to write, proceed from sentence to sentence, and then "get hopelessly involved in words to contain the increasing number of ideas" and the effort to express himself grammatically—to the point where his narrative would bog down with a total loss of "clarity."

Judging by the five-thousand-word fragment that survives, Neal had made progress since 1946. He was now writing with less grandiosity but he still overreached himself whenever he strived for some literary effect. In one of his most ambitious passages, Neal redundantly described Joan Anderson as a "white waxed mummy. White is the absence of all color; she was white, all white, unless beneath the covers whose top caressed her breasts, was still hidden a speck of pink." At moments of peak emotion, he inserted melodramatic exclamations: "Oh, unhappy mind; trickster! O fatal practicality!" A roast beef dinner with Cherry Mary was described thus: "Over the prosperous supper on which we soon pounced hung an air of excitement." Apart from problems of style, Neal's Joan Anderson tale lacked a point. What it undeniably had, however, was a voracious comic energy that propelled it forward as it swept up every detail, relevant or not, in its zigzagging path.

When he sent his enormous handwritten letter to Jack on December 22, Neal apologized for his inability to create fictional "composite" characters, as Wolfe and Proust had been able to do, then asked the very question that had been weighing on Jack's mind: "But how for one [character] as just straight case-history?"

The letter arrived in the morning mail on December 27, just as Jack was leaving the house to go into Manhattan; he read it on the subway with growing excitement, reread it more carefully in a cafeteria, then rushed it over to Holmes's apartment to show to Holmes and Harrington. To his surprise neither of them was bowled over by the writing Jack was comparing to the works of his literary gods, from Dostoevsky to Céline, Joyce, and Proust. Jack praised the Joan Anderson story immoderately as "the exact stuff upon which American Lit is still to be founded" when he wrote to Neal later that day, urging him to keep writing "only what kicks you and keeps you overtime awake from sheer mad joy." Extolling the very disorder and lack of selectivity that Neal did not have enough discipline to deal with, Jack assured Neal that every one of his "poolhall musings" and "excruciating details" was "painfully necessary" and advised him not to "undervalue" any of them, even such irrelevant oddities as "the heights of trees." Flooded with a full return of his own confidence, Jack predicted that within twenty years, "You and I will be the two most important writers in America."

For Jack, Neal's letter was like a mirror. Looking into it, he could suddenly see where his own power truly lay—in his extraordinarily acute memory, which he had been muffling with his fictional disguises, and in the images, associations, and language swirling around his own recollections, which he could begin to capture only if he wrote as himself rather than as a Freddie Boncoeur, Chad Gavin, or Red Moultrie.

There had been signs that all Jack's remaining resistance to autobiographical writing was about to crumble even before he heard from Neal. Just the week before, without changing his own name or any other identifying details, he had begun to write about Neal's first visit to him in Ozone Park. His long opening sentence about the sun going down over America contained much of the imagery and language he would use a few months later in the extraordinary concluding paragraph of *On the Road*. Jack had also been thinking for the first time about a novel that would deal with his relationship with Gerard. In preparation, he had made two lists—of early childhood memories and the moments he had felt the presence of God—and had written a short story depicting Gerard as a child saint rescuing a mouse from a trap.

Into the confessional outpouring Jack began writing two days after receiving Neal's Joan Anderson letter he put all the tangled emotions he had left out of his story about his brother only one week before. Born from that urgency of inspiration Jack now knew was essential to his art, it was a stunning piece of prose—a dazzling leap toward the height of his powers.

In three more installments, written during the first ten days of January 1951, he continued to pour out his memories, as if he and Neal were in the same room. On December 28, he had related events in an orderly chronological way. On January 8, he had decided this approach bored him and gave himself complete freedom to digress wherever his thoughts took him. "Let's tear time up," he proposed. Rather than continuing to write about the immediate aftermath of Gerard's death, as he had been doing five days earlier, he allowed himself an abrupt shift to 1947 and his Market Street vision of his Dickensian mother. On the ninth, Jack backtracked to his childhood, but as he wrote about the ironing board his mother had mistaken for Gerard's ghost, he was reminded of the thoughts he'd had about "the Catholic myth" as he was sitting in St. Patrick's Cathedral earlier that day watching a succession of young women kneel before the statue of the Virgin Mary. The devout young women made him think of his wife saying that she sometimes felt like a "frog" when they were having sex.

Not everything in Jack's confessions to Neal that winter was the truth. Apart from quoting Joan's caustic remark about their sex life, he went to great pains to maintain Neal's impression that he was happy with her. Either on her own initiative or Jack's urging, Joan wrote to Neal herself as "your buddy's buddy," expressing her own excitement about his writing. In a misguided attempt to sound hip, she claimed that she was completely willing to let Jack continue to have his kicks, although she would rather not know about the sexual ones, and flirtatiously offered Jack's much married friend a gift—an introduction to a "mad, wild blond gal" who was studying art in San Francisco and with whom she supposed he'd "inevitably" have an affair. For a brief time she was evidently pinning her hopes on having her life improve once she and Jack had saved enough money to extricate themselves from Gabe and join Neal, whom she was lining up as an ally, on the other side of the continent. (Apparently, the feelings of Carolyn Cassady did not enter into Joan's consideration.)

Meanwhile in Richmond Hill, where Gabe supervised her and Jack as if they were children, Joan's drab and isolated existence was unmitigated by any feeling of connection to her husband, any pleasure in his company or belief in his writing, which she felt—or professed to feel in her memoir—did not compare to Neal's. She did get along much better with Gabe than Edie had, appreciating Gabe's efforts to make her feel comfortable by turning the storage room into a sewing room for her and acknowledging Gabe's superior wisdom on how much dish detergent to use or how to make pie crusts, but she had come to New York to escape from her own domineering mother, not to acquire another one. Every morning her mother-in-law would tiptoe into the big bedroom she had given up to the newlyweds with a glass of freshly squeezed orange juice for her pampered son. Jack would go back to sleep until around three P.M. and would then need to be fed before going to his typewriter. Since Joan had quit her job and Jack had no income, Gabe was supporting the entire household. One night, after hearing that Joan needed comfortable shoes for job hunting, she presented her with a hideous thick-soled pair in fake red suede that had been made in her factory. When Jack started laughing, he got swatted with his mother's dish towel. "Ti-Jeanne, don't listen to Jackie," she would say. "He ees *fou.*" Gabe apparently realized that Joan did not love her son, but did not seem to hold it against her. For Gabe the most important thing was that Jackie was back after leaving her for only two weeks. She was willing to be martyred, Joan thought, if that would keep him with her.

Late one afternoon in early February, Neal Cassady showed up in Richmond Hill without warning when Joan was alone in the house and proceeded to charm her completely. "No matter how faithful the reproduction," she wrote in *Nobody's Wife*, taking an indirect swipe at *On the Road*, "I was sure text could never capture the vitality and intensity of the voice I now heard." When they were joined by Jack, Joan noticed at once an immediate change in the glum personality of her husband— "the difference between the brooding Ti-Jean and the laughing, charming Jack I had seen at Lucien's party." There was another big change as well. Normally, Jack became enraged if another man so much as looked at her. That night, however, he interrupted Joan as she was making dinner so that he could tell her something in the bedroom. With some embarrassment, according to Haverty's account, he brought up the mutual attraction he thought he had detected, and then gave Joan his permission to sleep with Neal, explaining that he and Neal always "shared everything." When Joan told him that he and Neal could go into New York with her permission and share some other girl instead, Jack yelled at her and remained silent and angry all through dinner. Although Neal was naturally "disappointed," he gallantly advised Jack to appreciate the devotion of "such a sweet girl." That night Joan listened in fascination as the two men talked. Despite Jack's unforgivable proposal in the bedroom, somehow Neal succeeded in making her unloved husband seem "more interesting."

This time Neal's visit to New York, which would shortly provide a concluding episode for *On the Road* that resembled the way Jack had planned to end the Red Moultrie novel, was a very short one. After spending ten days with Diana Hansen, who had agreed to let him divorce her in June after establishing the legitimacy of their son, Neal went back to Carolyn, whom he had impregnated for the third time, and to his grueling job on the Southern Pacific Railway. He said good-bye to Jack and Joan, waving at the receding back window of a borrowed Cadillac that Henri Cru had adamantly refused to let him ride in. Landing in town loaded with cash after months at sea, Henri was obnoxiously intent on making a big splash by taking Jack and his bride and a girlfriend to a Dizzy Gillespie concert at Carnegie Hall. He wasn't about to share Jack with a loser in a moth-eaten secondhand overcoat.

Around the time of Neal's departure, Joan began thinking about her own. After one fight too many with Jack, she retreated to their bed and refused to eat for several days until Gabe and Jack forced chicken soup down her throat. "First you eat. Then you die," Gabe said. Ignoring their insistence that she get a job in the neighborhood in order to save on carfare, she quickly found one in Manhattan waiting on tables at Stouffer's restaurant. To avoid having meals with Jack and her mother-in-law, she worked the afternoon and evening shifts and started putting money aside toward getting an apartment in which she planned to live alone. In mid-February, Joan rented a studio in Chelsea on the second floor of an old brick rooming house at 454 West Twentieth Street and made secret arrangements to have all her belongings picked up and moved there while Gabe was at work. The following day she went to meet the truck—and found Jack standing on the sidewalk next to his rolltop desk. "I'm your husband," he reminded her. Perhaps he hoped they would be less unhappy together if they had their own home. In any case, Joan's dramatic departure from Richmond Hill had given him a good excuse to break away from his mother, which he may have been longing to do, although he told Gabe Joan had insisted on the move.

Writing to Alfred Kazin on February 20, Jack pleaded for a recommendation for a Guggenheim Fellowship on the grounds that his life depended on getting enough money to spend three years in Mexico. He depicted himself as entrapped in an "American Tragedy rooming-house newlywed marriage all soaked in dolors" that could have come out of the pages of Theodore Dreiser, and included a melancholy passage from an abandoned version of On the Road in which the protagonist realizes that the road he is wearily trudging will only lead him to a life of inevitable disappointment.

Joan had agreed to go on with the marriage under certain conditions. One was that they would never move in again with Gabe; the other was that Jack would contribute to paying the expenses of the household. Since January, he'd had been synopsizing scripts for Twentieth Century-Fox, the work he'd done when he'd lived with Edie. Three synopses a week netted him a pittance but left him with time. He hadn't been forced to find any kind of job for the last couple of years, since he'd been able to scrape by on the GI Bill. But those days were over.

The menial jobs he'd had to take when he was young—and might have to take in the future—were on Jack's mind as he settled down to work in the new apartment. The street of handsome rundown town houses set back from tiny yards with iron railings had an air of nineteenth-century gentility that ended abruptly at raw Tenth Avenue. The one room of the studio was large and bright, quiet when Joan wasn't around, and conducive to writing. He liked the shutters on the windows, which looked out on the grounds of the old red Theological Seminary across the street. The Hudson River, a short walk away through a rough waterfront no-man's-land, was close enough to smell. Occasionally a train rattled by on an elevated high line bound for the meat markets on Fourteenth Street.

In January, when he'd discontinued his memoir, he'd tried an experiment—writing the first chapter of a sequel to *The Town and the City* in *joual*, using Peter Martin as the narrator. Struggling to maintain the literary quality of Peter Martin's voice in the language of blunt, plainspoken people who were not given to nuance or imagery, he'd kept falling back on words and expressions in English—even for a phrase like "the feeling of tears." Now something impelled him to try this experiment another way. It was as if he felt the need to start over again as a writer—to strip away his youthful dreams of greatness, his determined acquisition of an extensive English vocabulary and the mastery of its "fancy" words, his ten years of striving after lyricism, epic structures, a prose style modeled on Melville or Wolfe. It was time to write in the language he had started losing when he was six years old, the language in which he nevertheless dreamed and brooded and which he now began setting down on the page with simplicity and directness. This time the voice flowed naturally because the narrator was himself, despite the fictitious name he'd given him. The book had an honest matter-of-fact title, *Les Travaux* [jobs] *de Michel Bretagne*, as well as the poetic one he added directly underneath: *La Nuit Est Ma Femme*.

The opening paragraphs got right to the point, with Michel Bretagne telling the reader he did not care for his life, explaining that he used his sadness in order to think and that he did not have a language of his own, in case anyone was wondering about his imperfect French. He was a French Canadian writer, dependent on his relatives and women for support. He had worked on a book for four years, received little for it, and had been unable to publish or complete anything else, but predicted (correctly, as time would prove) that in the future others would make money from his writings that should have come to him. If Michel Bretagne didn't like a job, he quickly left it. On the other hand, if he was writing, he could work forty hours at a stretch—much longer than most people, to the point of being "hung up *et fatigué*." He had always slept later than everyone else, but could get up early when there was something he really wanted to do.

He was a man alone in a room, overtaken by the need to account for himself. Jack gave Michel the view from his window on Twentieth Street. It was winter; the trees on the seminary grounds were bare. At the Tenth Avenue end of the block, two old black hoboes were warming themselves over a fire—they were "shroudy strangers" (this phrase implied that they had followed Michel here, and suggested his ultimate fate) who had come out of the darkness, the *"noirceur."* They wore large-brimmed hats they'd gotten in North Dakota down by the railroad tracks. I do not like my life, Michel Bretagne repeated; what he loved was *"le Coeur du monde."*

In this manuscript, Jack wrote about his lifelong insoluble dilemma— the conflict between what a man had to do in order to survive and the dreams of immortality that kept him an artist/child, preventing him from making the compromises others made out of necessity. He wrote about the mill whistles he used to hear in Lowell as he lay in bed and the people flowing toward the factories with their pathetic lunch pails and his fear that he could end up as one of them that had made him get scholarships and start writing, and how the die was cast once he'd discovered the classic American writers, Twain, Melville, Thoreau, and Wolfe, who wrote what he called "unknown, unsoundable *books*" in a passage that he subsequently translated into English: "I wanted to write in a large form which was free and magnificent like that, a form which would give me a chance to go out the window and not stay in the room all the time with old ladies like Henry James and his European sisters."

He wrote about Michel Bretagne's fast escapes from the series of absurd and demeaning jobs he'd had when he was young and how he'd run away from Columbia as well in order to find his soul, ending up in a dismal room in Washington staring at the little pieces of paper for which he'd turned his life upside down. Although the narrator's development is clearly delineated, he does not tell his story in a continuous way. Instead the narrative hangs loosely upon what Jack had for a while been calling a "rack"—the various jobs Michel had—with much connecting expository material left out. In similar fashion a few weeks later, Jack would build *On the Road* upon a rack of trips—the one he took by himself in 1947, then the three he took with Neal as their relationship deepened—reaching a natural climax in their trip to Mexico.

By the middle of March, when Jack put the manuscript aside, he'd written fifty-seven pages of something that was neither novella nor memoir, but contained some of the most eloquent prose he had ever written. His French voice was plainer than the more fluidly associative one he'd used in his letters to Neal, but its bluntness and emotional openness gave it a particular immediacy and intimacy. That plainness and concreteness was what he was after now—the way thoughts came to him before he changed them by turning them into English or tried to make them literary in ways that embellished them too much. As he translated some passages, discovering how to capture the rhythmic patterns and music of his narrator's broodings, he struck out a simile from the original opening that seemed out of character in which Michel had compared his *tristesse* to the sadness of an old dog with big wet eyes. Describing the *"grands formes"* of American literature, the word *unsoundable* came to him as a more forceful equivalent of *insondable* than *unfathomable*, which had more syllables and would have been weaker rhythmically. When Jack sat down to write *On the Road* a month later, he would keep the ingenuous-sounding forthrightness of the Michel Bretagne voice as well as the overtones of its cadences and the tinge of melancholy that washes through it even at the moments when its energies seem highest:

> . . . they rushed down the street together digging everything in the early way they had which has later now become so much sadder and perceptive . . . but then they danced down the street like dingledodies and I shambled after as usual as I've been doing all my life after people that

interest me, because the only people that interest me are the mad ones, the ones who are mad to live, mad to talk, desirous of everything at the same time, the ones that never yawn or say a commonplace thing, but burn, burn, burn like roman candles across the night.

It was a voice that would seem to his future readers as American as apple pie but it had been born in French.

Apart from *La Nuit Est Ma Femme,* which he never transcribed from his notebook and has unfortunately never been published, Jack never wrote about this period on Twentieth Street. The writer in the room seems entirely alone, despite his mention of a *"petite femme"* whom he loves. He has a mother who has the kindness of an angel, but she is living with his married sister, which by mid-March was the case with Gabe. She had been devastated when Jack left her—not just for a trip to California but for what must have seemed forever. Terrified by the first weekend in her empty home, Gabe had written the two young people who had deserted her, begging them to return. She reminded Jack of the promise he had made to his father, and pitifully asked Joan what she had done wrong. Should she have said nothing about turning off the lights or putting more detergent in the dishwater? When the letter did not succeed in bringing Jack and Joan back to her, Gabe decided to live with Nin and Paul. In March, she had Jack take her down to Kinston, leaving most of her belongings, including her beloved TV set, stored in Richmond Hill, in case she changed her mind. It was the outcome Nin had been dreading, fearing it would destroy her marriage. With only little Paul for company most of the day and deprived of the TV shows she watched incessantly and her New York papers, Gabe felt even lonelier in Kinston than she had in Richmond Hill and soon began to complain to Jack about the hard work of child care and the way she was being mistreated by Nin, whom she suspected was reading her mail. By April, Gabe declared herself ready to be "buried" somewhere if she couldn't return to New York and get her old job back.

The letters from North Carolina were constant reminders to Jack of the terrible thing he had done to the person who loved him most. Writing about G.J. and his widowed Greek mother in *La Nuit Est Ma Femme,* he called his old friend the most unhappy man he had ever known and Oedipus's descendant—grimly adding that he was their cousin.

During March, Jack had made no real headway with his road novel, but during his brief visit to Kinston, he did write a brilliant essay that pointed the way to how he would approach his writing in the near future—possibilities he would only begin to explore in *On the Road*. Driving through the North Carolina countryside on a moonlit night, he had listened to the cacophony of voices coming in over the car radio and marveled that the hillbilly twang, which could be heard less and less in daily life, could still be picked up by an antenna. He imagined the mind as a kind of antenna as well, picking up the signals streaming in from the "waking consciousness," some so faint they could only be sensed rather than registered. While most writers made no use of them, Jack believed that within these overlooked sensory perceptions one could discover "the natural story" that was of far more importance than any plotted tale. How to capture them was the problem. (A reference to a "rental recording machine" suggests that Jack was reminded of the wire recorder Neal Cassady had recently acquired, which he was dying to try out.) But there was no mechanical device with enough "subtlety" for the task he was thinking about. For the writer, it would require "an enormous trancelike discipline."

THE ROAD OPENS UP

As far as John Clellon Holmes could tell in the early spring of 1951, Jack remained hopelessly bogged down in his writing, no further along than that day in late December when he'd brought over Neal's Joan Anderson letter and flung himself down on the couch, admitting he was at a "creative loss." In fact, after Jack had gone home, Holmes had written him a letter attempting to buck him up a little:

> Go back to the moment (if this can be done) when "On the Road" came to you out of nowhere. Go back to that instant, and remember it in all the naked excitement it possessed then. . . . Start writing some night in this reverent mood and go on.

He had urged Jack to portray the events in his book in their "natural order" and not to try to be too deep. "Fill your book with everyone who lives in your head, make them live and readers will commend you and buy." It was good, practical, implicitly disheartening advice—of the kind one gives to a writer who has just about given up. Writing *La Nuit Est Ma Femme*, an effort he may not have mentioned to anyone, Jack may have remembered it.

Meanwhile, Holmes had been steadily plowing ahead with his own novel, which Jack had continued to read as it progressed. Despite the closeness between the two men, who at times saw each other almost daily, they were in an unacknowledged race, and on March 3, when Holmes handed Jack his just completed concluding chapter, there was no doubt which of them had come out ahead. After reading Holmes's concluding pages about the aftermath of Cannastra's death, Jack got up and, without speaking, walked over to the window, finally saying tersely, "It's very moving," although Holmes had expected to hear much more from him.

A few days later, Holmes received a letter that did not succeed in concealing Jack's ambivalence. He told Holmes that he had finally turned into a "fullblown artist," and that the book, like his own first novel, had "touches of greatness." He offered him a "gone" title, "The Beat Ones," though it may have hurt to think that Holmes would probably be the one who would be credited with originating the concept of the Beat Generation. Without overtly attacking the book, Jack brought up the things that troubled him about it: the characterization of the novelist now called Eugene Pasternak, whom he felt was not at all like him (according to Holmes, Jack was especially troubled by the depiction of Pasternak's sex life, which he was afraid his mother and sister might read), as well as the harshness with which Holmes had portrayed the lives they were all living, everything depicted as corrupt and doomed without one note of optimism. With veiled sarcasm, Jack assured Holmes that Harrington would love this grim point of view, and so would everyone else. Jack had seen Holmes earlier that day when he'd dropped off yet another possible opening for *On the Road*, and had evidently come away freshly upset. He said he was writing the letter with "trembling hands," but attributed that to an attack of the flu. The following week when he had a party on Twentieth Street to celebrate his twenty-ninth birthday, which coincided with Holmes's twenty-fifth, he did not invite John and Marian. Very upset at being excluded, Holmes may have remembered the eagerness with which Allen, always a purveyor of gossip in the name of full disclosure, had told him a few weeks earlier that Jack felt "you had no right to write a book about everybody's private lives."

This was a right that Jack had taken for himself when he wrote *The Town and the City*. Undoubtedly, he felt conflicted about this issue—one no writer can ever resolve comfortably. The nature of the work requires a certain ruthlessness, which Jack, like Holmes, definitely possessed. With Neal, with whom he was not in competition, Jack seemed to find no problem in urging his "blood brother" to write the story of his life while openly planning to use him and parts of his life story in fiction. But his relationship with Holmes brought both sides of his dual nature into play. On the one hand, he was vitally engaged in giving Holmes suggestions for his book; on the other, he regarded him as an opportunistic latecomer to his intimate circle who was trespassing upon the very territory he had staked out for himself as a novelist.

By using up certain key episodes and subject matter, Holmes had indeed limited Jack's conception of what would go into his own work. Jack would never describe Allen's visions in East Harlem or the episode of Allen's arrest or Cannastra's subway death, or even write about the day his own book was accepted or his disastrous affair with Pauline, both of which Holmes covered in detail. In fact, Jack would leave out of *On the Road* most of the experiences he'd had in New York between 1948 and 1951, giving only a rapid-fire impression of the whole scene, with Holmes, Cannastra, Stringham, Harrington, Pauline, and others very lightly sketched in. Holmes had even scooped him when it came to writing about Neal. There was a scene in Holmes's novel in which Neal hit Luanne and broke his thumb, an event either Jack or Neal had described to him and which Holmes had transplanted to New York. Proud of the way he'd handled it, Holmes had felt fiercely possessive, yet nervous. "These are *my* characters and only vaguely anyone we know," he'd written Jack in July, referring in the same paragraph to "*my* Ginsberg."

Still there was a strong bond between these two men and this first rupture lasted only a week. By late March, they were again taking their long, ruminative walks together. On April 2, according to Holmes's journal, Jack led him through the dangerous western edges of the Chelsea neighborhood along the docks on the Hudson and the streets of the meat market district, a desolate milieu deserted by everyone after dark but the whores, drunks, beggars, and waterfront hoods who emerged from the shadows. To Holmes, it seemed an end-of-the-night wasteland, analogous to their own damaged lives.

In the essay Jack had written only two weeks earlier, he'd remarked that the "greatest perceptions" usually came when the writer was away from his desk, or when traveling. Perhaps during the walk with Holmes he suddenly saw how *On the Road* could be written in one long sustained trance—as if it were a poem, composed before the initial epiphany or burst of inspiration ran out. Holmes later remembered Jack saying around this time that he was going to put a roll of shelf paper in his typewriter "and just write it down as fast as I can, exactly like it happened, all in a rush, the hell with these phony architectures—and worry about it later."

"Went fast because road is fast," Jack would tell Neal in May, explaining that on April 2, he'd written twelve thousand words and hadn't stopped working until April 22, averaging six thousand words a day. Using Cannastra's rolls of Japanese paper, carefully trimmed with a ruler to an eleven-inch width that would fit into his typewriter, he'd eliminated the moments it took to feed in fresh sheets. Once Jack taped the rolls together, the completed 125,000-word manuscript was one unbroken flow of words— the physical proof that he'd found a way to overcome his great enemy, distraction.

If we are to believe Joan Haverty, however, it was she who finally told Jack how to get the book off his chest after he returned from his walk with Holmes. According to the story she tells in her memoir, she came home from work and found Jack still stymied sitting gloomily at his typewriter (a sight that probably annoyed her profoundly after a hard night of waitressing). She claimed that, tired of hearing about his difficulties, she gave him advice similar to what Holmes had told him—to just write about what had really happened during his road trips as if he were telling the whole story directly to her. Then, like a man magically freed from an evil spell, Jack immediately started typing "with accelerating speed" after hearing her stream of questions about "Neal, Neal, Neal, and

Neal." But he would not have been able to do so if he had not been over-whelmingly ready.

In 1958, right after *On the Road* was published, Allen Ginsberg would call Jack's method of writing "spontaneous bop prosody," a term that caught on quickly and would prove to be misleading. "He just spewed his words on paper!" misinformed Kerouac admirers like the singer Patti Smith exclaim enthusiastically to this day. But if the words had merely been spewed, we would not be reading them now. With unfortunate consequences for Jack's literary reputation, the idea of spontaneous writing suggested the process was easy, leaving out the immense discipline that went into it, the extraor-dinary verbal sensitivity Jack had acquired by existing between two lan-guages, the instinctive and learned aesthetic judgments that shaped the writing, and all the rehearsals that preceded Jack's seemingly effortless high-wire act, enabling him to finally leap "out the window" into the vast-ness of the American landscape and uncharted territory in fiction. Whereas Holmes had set his novel in rooms where his beat characters talked and talked and talked like actors in an existential comedy of manners, Jack would follow transcontinental highways, cross rivers and deserts, and watch the sun go down in western skies. He would celebrate the energies and mystery of his characters with the underlying sadness of knowing they are mortal and that time is passing and turn Neal Cassady into a new kind of American hero, con man and prophet, destroying angel and life force.

Jack made a list of events and people he wanted to include in the book and kept it beside his typewriter, but didn't follow it to the letter. He stayed off Benzedrine and marijuana and was proud that he'd kept going on innumerable cups of black coffee—something he advised Neal to try for "real mental power kicks." The typing all by itself—pounding the keys of a rusty old L. C. Smith with a worn ribbon, hauling the heavy carriage all the way right then left for each new line—was grueling. Sometimes he stopped to look at a passage in his "Rain & Rivers" note-book or an abandoned manuscript or a letter, but much of what he took from his papers was subtly but crucially altered so that it fitted seam-lessly into the new novel in prose that matched the voice he had created for the narrator. For the most part, Jack worked from what he remem-bered—but his memories were transfigured by the power of his imagination and the demands of the unfolding story. Memory alone does not account for his brilliant evocations of the jazz sessions he'd heard a few years earlier, or the way Neal drove and talked. Although Jack captured Neal's physical dynamism and constant motion, he created him most of all through the sound of his voice and the supercharged rhythms of his language, giving him more electricity and urgent poetic fluency than he possessed in real life.

The Neal in *On the Road*, never at a loss for words despite his reformatory education, has a memorable way of getting to the heart of the matter despite some circling around it:

> "And of course now no one can tell us that there is no God. We've passed through all forms. You remember, Jack, when I first came to New York and I wanted Hal Chase to teach me about Nietzsche. You see how long ago? Everything is fine. God exists, we know time. Everything since the Greeks has been predicted wrong. You can't make it with geometry and geometrical systems of thinking. It's all THIS!"

As Hart Kennedy in Holmes's novel *Go*, Neal loses his charisma. Although he too was fascinated by Neal, Holmes had listened to him more coldly and skeptically than Jack did. Working from his attempts to approximate what he'd heard Neal say, he captured his repetitiousness, his vagueness, and his tiresome insistence that his listeners *understand:*

> "You get what I mean? Everything's really true, I mean, the same as everything else. Now on benny or psychology or something like that, you get hungup on one thing, you don't just escape everything anymore. You know, you get compulsive like with those cars! Why man, that isn't getting your kicks and having your life! . . . Now on tea, everything slows down, everything's interesting and real profound, and you realize that everyone really *knows* everything but just doesn't see it, you understand. . . . See, you and I *know*, really, that everyone's the same; I mean, they know the same things that we do actually, about life!"

Following this rambling speech, Holmes took care to indicate that to his autobiographical protagonist, Paul Hobbes, " 'everything' was not really true." He made his Hart Kennedy an unusual oddball character, but he lacked the riveting urgency of a messenger of truth and the capacity to become mythic.

"Story deals with you and me and the road," Jack wrote Neal on May 22, telling him that their parting on a Seventh Avenue street corner in January had provided him with an ending. "Plot, if any, is devoted to your development from young jailkid of early days to later (present) W. C. Fields saintliness." It was as if, unlike Red Moultrie, Red Smith, Chad Gavin, Freddie Boncoeur, etc., the character now called Jack was of secondary importance in this novel, although it is the voice of that narrator and his developing point of view that gives profound meaning to what would have otherwise been only a series of vivid anecdotes.

Perhaps Jack was already beginning to feel dissatisfied with the way he had portrayed his own fictional counterpart. Although he hadn't given him an invented life story, he'd left a good deal of complexity and dividedness out of his nature. Once again, despite the promises he'd made to Yvonne Le Maître, he'd obscured this character's ethnic identity in the interest of writing a universal American novel. The narrator of *On the Road* does not identify himself as "half-American" despite his feeling of identification with fellaheen people like the Mexican Girl for which no specific reason, such as his ancestry, is given. He is a writer but his work is not the central focus of his life. He has less sexual confidence than Neal, but he is not racked by ambivalent feelings about women. When he goes on the road it is not with the intention of writing a book about it but out of the need to heal himself spiritually. He is a relatively healthy Jack, less afflicted by depression, with a more constant appreciation of life. The Neal Cassady he keeps seeking is his missing Dionysiac half—the side of himself that must have ecstasy at all costs and is drawn toward death. Once again, Jack was dealing with his duality by splitting himself into two characters. In a revealing passage that appears in the original version of *On the Road* and was later cut along with the whole Detroit episode in which it appears, Jack wrote:

> We got on a trolley and rode to downtown Detroit, and suddenly I remembered that Louis Ferdinand Céline had once rode on the same trolley with his friend Robinson, whoever Robinson was if not likely

Céline himself; and Neal was like myself, for I'd had a dream of Neal the night before in the hotel, and Neal was me. In any case he was my brother.

When the fictional Jack finds the ideal "girl with the innocent and pure eyes" (the Laura ingenue of various abandoned manuscripts superimposed upon Joan) at the end of the road, he is able to regretfully let Neal fade out of his life as he settles down into maturity and domesticity. Although their parting scene is poignantly written, it is not a convincing resolution of the narrator's duality and is a curiously conventional conclusion for such an unconventional novel. "I AM GOING TO BE MYSELF," Jack would vow in his August 1951 journal, full of second thoughts about the book he had finished with so much confidence and exhilaration on April 22.

Robert Giroux had been in his office that spring day when Jack phoned him shortly before noon to announce that he had just written the last sentences of *On the Road* and wanted to bring it right over. A half hour later Giroux looked up from his desk and saw him standing in the doorway with a roll of what looked like shelf paper under his arm. "He was in a very funny state," Giroux told me in 2007. "I was too dumb to realize he was drunk or on drugs."

The strangeness Giroux attributed to drugs may have been another kind of high entirely—the dream/trance in which Jack had just written his last lines, from which he had not yet emerged. Unfurling the scroll, he "tossed it across the office like a piece of celebration confetti. 'And here it is!'" Giroux remembered him saying. "'The Holy Ghost wrote it.'"

As he stared in disbelief at the yards of single-spaced typescript lying all over his carpet, the first thought that came into Giroux's mind, which he made the mistake of voicing to Jack, was that no editor or printer could possibly work from such a manuscript. "He was celebrating," Giroux told me ruefully, "and I was making a problem out of it when I should have said, 'This is great. Let's go out and have a drink.'"

In a rage, Jack yelled that Giroux had to either take the book exactly as it was or leave it and that not a word could be changed. "Are you trying to say you can't publish this?" After calling Giroux some insulting names, he rolled up the scroll and stormed out. Soon after this, Giroux received a very short note: "You have offended the Holy Ghost."

That week, Jack gave the scroll to Holmes, who spent eight hours glued to the black typescript unreeling before him, which he read nonstop, swept along to its last line, "I think of Neal Cassady." Exhausted, he staggered out to meet Marian at a movie theater, but found himself too "troubled and elated" to focus on the screen. The material was wonderful, he thought. The writing had all the "lyric power" he'd always admired so much in Jack's work, yet the Wolfean verbiage had been cleared away. But Holmes felt shaken. He could see how Jack's "melancholy had darkened and toughened" since he'd written *The Town and the City*. "I caught my first glimpse of the Kerouac to come," he would write in *Nothing More to Declare*, "a Kerouac for whom I was oddly unprepared; a lonely, self-communing, mind-stormed man," a man who was "immeasurably old in his soul," despite his hunger to live.

On April 27, Holmes dropped by Twentieth Street to return the manuscript and went out with Jack to a waterfront bar. Afterward, the two of them sat on the pilings of a pier, watching an ocean liner, lit up in the darkness, majestically moving out of the harbor. He conveyed to Jack all his excitement about the novel, but confessed he was too involved with its conception and most of the people in it to be objective about it. "You know, kid," Jack said to him that night, "your book and mine constitute a new trend in American literature."

By the middle of May, Jack had patched things up with Giroux and resigned himself to the idea of having him read the manuscript in an acceptable format. Still drained from the work he'd done in April, he started retyping *On the Road* on 8 x 11 inch paper and making minor revisions. Although he felt his uninterrupted stream of words was the perfect typographical form for the book he had written, he reluctantly broke the text up into paragraphs and created chapters. Using Benzedrine to keep up his stamina, he drenched his T-shirts with sweat as he labored on.

By this time, other friends who had come over to read the scroll had weighed in with their reactions. In a letter to Neal, Allen called the writing "dewlike, everything happens as it really is with the same juvenescent feeling of spring: the hero is you." But as Allen tried to superimpose the real Neal upon the fictional one, he was troubled by the ways they didn't match up. He thought Jack needed Neal's help "to understand last true longings of [Neal's] soul," and suggested that Neal write him "a serious self-prophetic letter foretelling your future in fate, so that he can have courage to finish his paean in a proper apotheosis or grinding of brakes." He apparently was unhappy about the pathetic diminishment of Neal at the end of the novel. Without having read a word of *On the Road*, Neal offered Allen the opinion that its theme was too "trivial" for an entire novel and should be either forgotten or enlarged. Lucien said the book was "shit," though only a few months later he would be comparing Jack to Faulkner.

At a kitchen table hidden behind a screen, Jack kept typing while Joan slept. Although they were often visited by Jack's friends now that they had moved back to the city, it wasn't much of a life for her, coming home from her new waitressing job at the Brass Rail to a husband so absorbed in his work, he barely acknowledged her presence unless he asked for something. One night in May, he awakened her demanding they have sex right then and there, too impatient to wait for Joan to get her diaphragm out of the bedside drawer. The next morning, wondering what had suddenly aroused Jack's passion, she went over to his typewriter and found he had been typing a tender passage about Bea Franco. As far as she could tell, it was inertia that was keeping them together, and she was thinking again about escaping from the marriage.

It was the season of breakups in Jack's crowd, where the women were finding it impossible to sustain their relationships with their difficult men, even when they felt real love for them. Liz Lehrman, Lucien's twenty-year-old girlfriend, had just left him after returning from a very lonely trip to Chicago where she'd had the frightening experience of getting an illegal abortion in a strange city. The night she returned, expecting to find Lucien waiting for her at Penn Station, he wasn't there. When she got home to their loft, she found him obliviously drinking with his buddies. All through their relationship, he'd paid far more attention to Allen Ginsberg, who was always hanging around, than to Liz, and had made her miserable by rarely having sex with her.

Joan spent an evening with Marian Holmes when Jack went down to North Carolina in late May to see his mother. Although they usually saw each other only when they were with their men, the two young women were becoming friendly, and their growing discontent with their marriages gave them a lot to talk about.

Marian was fighting with John more and more, always about the same issues—his excessive drinking, his poorly disguised interest in other women. She was getting tired of supporting him, fed up with the chaos she came home to each night. One of the few inventions in her husband's novel was a brief affair between her and Jack. Perhaps Marian had been brooding about the injustice of that and wondering how John came by the idea, for although she was fond of Jack, she made a nasty reference to him that evening after she'd had a few drinks—calling him a "minute man," according to Haverty.

Since the two of them were letting their hair down, Joan revealed her new ambition—to go to City College and study genetics, which Marian said was exactly what she should do. According to Haverty, Jack had told her it would be more to the point if she studied home economics. As he'd retyped *On the Road*, he'd been talking about the two of them moving very soon to a cheap pad in Mexico City on the advance he was going to get from Giroux after he gave him the manuscript in acceptable form.

By the beginning of June, Jack had to finish his typing in Lucien's loft, where Lucien's dog, Potchy, attacked the scroll and ate the original ending. It had to be reconstructed for the new draft, which also included a small amount of other rewriting, but that was the least of his problems because he'd had a tremendous falling out with his wife. Joan had discovered she was going to have a child and was refusing to consider having an abortion, like Liz Lehrman. She had felt not the least grain of sympathy when Jack told her there was no way he could stop writing to support a wife and child. (Her memoir would make it clear that she regarded Jack's single-minded dedication to his work as a kind of egotistical self-indulgence.) They were at an impasse, and there was no love or understanding on either side to get them through it.

By June 10, when Jack wrote Neal, Joan was with her mother in Albany and he was spending his last hours in the apartment on Twentieth

Street as he packed his belongings. Panic-stricken and hardly able to focus his thoughts, he confessed to feeling at a total loss. The completion of his book was his only consolation. The retyped and somewhat revised draft was now in Giroux's hands and Jack was pinning all his hopes on hearing some good news. In addition to everything else, he had a swollen left foot—the sign of an oncoming attack of phlebitis. Jack didn't mention Joan's pregnancy to Neal. Perhaps he felt ashamed to admit that he couldn't rise to the responsibilities of fatherhood, even though having children of his own had always figured in his fantasies. The day after the wedding night he'd slept through, he'd boasted to Neal that Joan could already be pregnant.

Jack had told her a baby was out of the question, but by the time she returned to New York to pack her things, he may have been starting to change his mind. He asked her to meet him on the rooftop of Lucien's building. She had assumed they would be talking about a divorce, but instead Jack surprised her by demanding, "What if I said you could have the baby? What then?" When she told him she didn't need or want his permission, he turned away as if he had been slapped and went downstairs, and she heard him yelling to Lucien that he was not responsible for her kid and never wanted to hear about it again. Joan was so sure of Jack's indifference that she didn't realize or care that she'd given him a devastating blow. He was a man who'd had a dream of family, whose own child would be a stranger to him. Although Jack had never had the kind of feelings for Joan that he'd had for Sarah Yokely, their relationship had given him something he needed badly. For a brief time during their months on Twentieth Street he had almost found a way to live with a degree of normalcy between the stark polarities of solitude and binge. The utter failure of this marriage would end his attempts to find that balance in his daily life.

Concerned about Jack's state of mind, Neal sent him a telegram on June 19, ordering him to come to California at once, following it up the next day with one of his warmest and most affectionate letters. Suggesting that a Cassady/Kerouac living arrangement would someday be regarded as historically important as the households shared by Van Gogh and Gauguin and Wagner and Nietzsche, he offered Jack a "magnificent attic" where he could stay and write as long as he needed to. The attic in

San Francisco came not only with free laundry and coffee and the use of Neal's tape recorder, but with the promise that Carolyn would be Jack's surrogate mama. Neal swore his wife now wanted to make up for throwing Jack out of the house the last time she'd seen him, and might even, he jokingly hinted, be open to orgies.

But just before Neal's letter arrived, Jack had had another blow he had not seen coming when *On the Road* came back to him in the mail. Giroux hadn't even shown Jack's new typescript to the Harcourt management, since he'd been positive they'd refuse to let him publish a book with such daring content. He told Jack the novel was "like Dostoevsky," but that was very cold comfort. Despite Giroux's stated reason for rejecting the novel, his response immediately undermined Jack's feeling of accomplishment and left him wondering how he would manage to survive without the infusion of money he'd been counting on. Jack wrote Neal that now he couldn't afford to come to California and that even if he got there, he'd only have to find a job. He also seemed reluctant to be around when Carolyn's new baby arrived in the fall and told Neal he thought he'd be in the way. For the time being there was only one option—to join Gabe down in Kinston and try to pull himself together. But he was about to have his worst attack of phlebitis since 1946.

DEEP FORM

Trapped in the sweltering heat of Nin's house with his swollen left foot propped up on a chair, unable to disappear into the woods for long walks the way he usually did, Jack must have had to answer a lot of questions from his relatives about why his marriage had broken up. He had told his mother a great deal, but had left out the baby, mistakenly thinking he was protecting Gabe from pain. If she'd known she was going to have another grandchild, she would never have stopped futilely insisting he get back together with Joan. For the same reason, Joan was also choosing to keep her pregnancy a secret from her mother-in-law. She'd called Gabe up, but all she'd told her was that she and Jack hadn't been getting along. Perhaps because the baby could not be mentioned, it began to seem less and less real to Jack, yet denying its existence must only have intensified his guilt about his mother's loneliness and his awful feeling that he had somehow done irreparable damage to himself by failing to take on the responsibilities of a man.

Also weighing on Jack's mind were all his new doubts about *On the Road*—he knew how much of the truth about himself he'd left out of it and had also begun to feel he hadn't penetrated the mystery of Neal's character. To add to his loss of confidence in the book, he received news from Allen that Rae Everitt was willing to act as agent for it, but was urging him to cut 150 pages of what she considered nonessential material (such as the sections about Henri Cru and the romance with the Mexican girl) in order to keep a sustained focus on Neal that would make the book more attractive to publishers. Although Jack decided to do some cutting as well as to put in some new sections about Neal's boyhood, the idea of trying to simplify *On the Road* to make it more marketable was distasteful to him. What he was really intent on doing now, as he wrote to Holmes on July 14, was to find a form that would combine what he considered the two "conflicting" sides of his writing—his intensified dedication to relating "the truth" and his "lyric-alto knowing of" America. Now the question of how to achieve "deep form" pressed upon him.

After two weeks with his relatives, Jack climbed onto a bus with his leg still swollen and returned to New York with the idea of joining Allen and Lucien, who were about to drive down to Mexico to visit lonely Joan Adams. (Bill had gone to Ecuador that summer, accompanied by a young American student he was infatuated with.) By the time Jack arrived in Manhattan, however, he was in too much pain to travel with them. He later thought it had been lucky he'd stayed behind, since the frantic drinking and drug taking he would undoubtedly have indulged in might have finished him off. He stuck it out alone for a while in Lucien's loft, then checked himself into the Kingsbridge Veterans Hospital in August. By then his thrombosis was so severe that he was confined to bed for almost a month.

In the journal Jack started keeping at Kingsbridge, he expressed no desire to reenter the world. It was a relief to him to be immobilized, to submit to the orderly routines of the hospital, to have his life taken out of his hands. In daily entries he tracked his progress as a patient the way he tracked his word counts, recording the fluctuations of his weight and his intake of calories. He also noted his winnings and losses from the bets he was placing on horses. Strangely, he was making more money in the hospital than he'd been able to make outside it.

Meanwhile, Jack's doubts about *On the Road* were deepening and he was steadily losing interest in doing more work on it. By this time, what had begun to trouble him most was the way he had dealt with his duality in his portrayal of his relationship with Neal.

Like his hospitalization in 1946, the month and a half in Kingsbridge was an important time of retreat and reflection for him. With his mind drifting as he lay in bed, Jack had intense waking dreams of episodes in his boyhood with every detail radiantly clear to him—visions that restored his soul, he later believed. He'd wasted three years in what he now considered senseless self-destructive behavior. Once he recovered, he promised himself, he'd go back to the healthy, ascetic life he'd led while he was writing *The Town and the City*. He'd move in with his mother again, be content with solitude, humbly increase his daily pile of words.

Jack had been reading Melville's *Pierre* and Malcolm Lowry's *Under the Volcano*, works he considered flawed but very illuminating. He admired Lowry's stream-of-consciousness prose and probably also Lowry's portrayal of Mexico and his alcoholic protagonist, but *Pierre*, written with Melville's vast "soul-sorrow," was more of an inspiration. Part gothic romance combined with realism, part philosophical treatise, it was a novel that made him suddenly want to return to *Dr. Sax*, also a book in which he would have to combine genres. One element in Melville's tale, Pierre's marriagelike relationship with his monstrously possessive mother, whom Pierre calls "Sister," seems to have struck close to home.

On August 28, after reading the introduction to *Pierre* by the psychoanalyst Henry A. Murray, Jack thought about portraying his family without idealizing them. Two of the words he chose for Gabe— "madwoman" and "gravedigger"—were the harshest ones he had ever voiced. Though he had not forgotten that in many ways his mother had remained a frightened child, he blamed her now for having "castrated" his father. Gerard he compared for the first time to the great serpent in *Dr. Sax*, who after threatening to destroy the world turns into a dove. In his copy of *Pierre*, Jack underlined Dr. Murray's observation that "Melville was not writing autobiography in the usual sense, but from first to last, the biography of his self-image." Later that same day, he felt a moment's panic rather than relief when he was told that he was now well enough to start walking again. It was as if he knew he needed protection from himself.

On August 31, Jack tried again to decide what to do about *On the Road*. He considered giving his two main characters fictional names, Sal Paradise and Dean Pomeray, but he couldn't settle on the name for himself—Peter Martin? Victor Duchamp? In fiction, nothing was fixed, anything could be altered; he was appalled, in fact, by the "malleability" of what his imagination came up with and the degree to which he had lied about himself in his first novel.

Three days later, Jack had another of his peculiarly intense visions. He saw Neal plain as day in the Hudson he'd driven in '47—and suddenly started writing as if he would never stop. Afterward he told himself that his own life had enough richness to provide him with all the plots he would ever need and vowed that from now on he would only write the truth. To do this he would have to portray himself as he really was, hiding and distorting nothing, without resorting to subterfuges like splitting himself up into different characters. Jack wrestled briefly with the tormenting question of whether truth required him to write in French, before reminding himself that during his boyhood he'd imagined the racetrack world of Jack Lewis entirely in English and that at twelve, when his parents had taken him to Montreal, he'd felt quite "homesick" for the English language. For the time being, he impatiently put aside his "Canadian dualism."

By September 8, Jack was well enough to spend the morning playing baseball with other patients and to go to Yankee Stadium in the afternoon. Exhilarated by the clarity of the late summer light that deepened the blue of the sky, he watched the Yanks play Washington and drank ten beers, the first time he'd gotten drunk in weeks. It was a "strange big day," he would write afterward. When he got back to the hospital, he picked up a newspaper, saw the name Burroughs in a headline, and learned Joan Adams was dead, the way he'd learned about Cannastra the year before. The newspaper called it a "William Tell" shooting. Bill and

Joan had been drinking with friends in Mexico City when Bill evidently had an urge to demonstrate his marksmanship. He suggested that Joan put a glass of champagne on her head, and she'd complied. Although he was a perfect shot, he'd taken aim at it and missed, and had been arrested. Lucien Carr, who had been working the night desk at United Press, had deliberately kept the story out of the morning papers, hoping to reach Jack and give him the news before he read it.

On his way back to New York, Allen was stopping over in Galveston when he too saw the story in the paper. With the two disturbing weeks he and Lucien had just spent with Joan running through his mind, he wrote a terse letter to Neal, recalling terrifying drives to Guadalajara and Mazatlán when Joan and Lucien had played "games of chance with drunken driving, egging each other on suicidally." Bill had still been in South America with his lover and although Joan didn't complain, her drinking had become a match for Lucien's. In fact, the two of them had had a strange rapport, almost like a love affair. In Allen's last sight of her, Joan was standing forlornly at a bus stop holding Billy Jr.'s hand as they drove away and left her. Lucien had almost impulsively asked her to come with them. "My imagination of the scene & psyches in Mexico is too limited to comprehend the vast misery & absurdity and sense of dream that must exist in Bill's mind now," Allen wrote.

In Kingsbridge, Jack thought numbly about the complete indifference Joan and Bill must have felt toward what happened to them. Only a few days earlier, he had written in his journal, "Bill don't die," after a vivid dream about Mexico. His mind tried to recapture the beauty of the September day that had just passed, but the blue sky and the deeper blue of the Hudson were irretrievable and his thoughts were about dying and his horror of growing older and families grieving for their lost children.

He forced himself to make his usual notes on the calories he'd consumed that day and the $510 that was now in his bankroll, but he spent a sleepless night. The next morning, he saw that his weight had ominously risen to 171½, the heaviest he'd ever been in his life. He had only four more days in the hospital—four more days to decide on the direction of his "life's work." Pursued by the shadow of Joan's death, he took his books and papers out into the sunlight.

Once again, passing through an emotional crisis seemed to open Jack to new insights. Two days later, he knew what he'd been searching for—a "vast subjective form"—and was flooded with thoughts that came in almost maddening profusion of what he could write and what he probably never would. Lately, he had been having more and more of these "visionary tics," each accompanied by a kind of mental ecstasy, but suddenly they seemed to frighten him, for he called them "epileptic." He drank whiskey that night with his dinner even though he had been warned not to start drinking again.

By September 12, when he left the hospital, Jack was convinced he had undergone a profound change—an acceptance of the beauty of life, despite any tragedy or difficulty he was facing. He went home to Gabe determined to create an "American mythology." It would be based on the lives of the people he knew with a magnificent "Protean" lying narrator.

PART TEN

INTERIOR MUSIC

VISIONS OF NEAL

In August, Gabe had moved back to their old address in Richmond Hill, but they had lost their spacious second-floor apartment. Their new one was small and dark and in the basement, crowded with unpacked boxes of their belongings. Above them the occupants of their comfortable old quarters moved noisily about.

Filled with the energy of coming back to life, Jack paid scarcely any attention to his dismal new surroundings, apart from what he needed to get right down to work. He immediately arranged to have his rolltop desk picked up from Lucien's loft and, too impatient to wait, retrieved his L. C. Smith, lugging it through the subway and across a field in Richmond Hill, after a night when he'd had a wonderful conversation with Holmes and talked with Allen by candlelight until three A.M. He'd been joyfully rediscovering all his friends. At his first drunken reunion the day after he got home, he was surprised to find himself on the verge of tears.

But trouble awaited Jack in Richmond Hill. In August, while he was in the hospital, his wife had telephoned his mother, demanding to be told his whereabouts. On September 18, he was awakened by a commotion outside the house. Joan Haverty and her lawyer were unsuccessfully trying to force their way in. Still, not even this brought him down, because he was so sure he'd gotten back his soul. He went for a long walk through a black and Italian neighborhood that still had lunch cart diners like the ones in Lowell and old-fashioned stores that sold penny candy. That night he wrote about Neal's reentry into Denver when he was fresh from the reformatory and no one knew anything about him.

"Around the poolhalls of Denver during World War II a strange looking boy began to be noticeable to the characters who frequented the places day and night," were the opening words of a sentence that seemed written in one great held breath, building up tension with every added detail

413

about the restless crowd that flowed from the back door of one smoky Glenarm Street poolroom into another, until the name Neal Pomeray was finally exhaled, as if heralding the arrival of a mythic hero. The long passages that followed, which Jack would write over the next few weeks, would eventually become incorporated into the second section of *Visions of Cody*. Feeling a surge of new power, Jack wished he could tell everything he knew in one great rush.

When he woke up the next day, he must have expected to continue writing, but instead he was served with a summons and taken to the Tombs on White Street, which was known in those days as the alimony jail. He was locked up for only ten minutes and was released when he agreed to start making weekly five-dollar support payments to Joan immediately. He made the first payment and a few more that fall and then had to stop, since he had hardly ever been so broke in his life. Until *On the Road* was published six years later, his vulnerability to being incarcerated at Joan's demand would haunt him, darken his outlook on women, make him feel he was a hunted man with an implacable enemy who wanted to steal what little money he was able to earn and keep him from his work.

Two days later, he tried to regain the fragile sense of well-being he'd brought home from the hospital and managed to write a thousand words about Dean's birth before being interrupted by a visit from Ed White, who had just returned from a summer in Paris, and Tom Livornese. They drove Jack into Manhattan, where the three of them went to a party with John and Marian Holmes. That day New York seemed no less fabulous to Jack than the Paris of the *Comédie Humaine*, though whenever he thought of Joan Haverty, hatred and fear overwhelmed him. In the hospital his feelings about his wife had sometimes been generous. Before he heard that she had called his mother, Jack even fantasized that once he became successful, he would set up a large trust fund for Joan and the child, in addition to the ones for his mother and sister and Neal. (Despite his denials of responsibility, he knew he was the baby's father.)

Exiled from the spacious quarters upstairs, Jack found the new apartment more and more oppressive, and it became hard for him to spend much time there. His cell-like room had so little daylight, he sometimes wrote in the backyard. As he began drinking his way through the early fall, Jack soon realized he'd lost the fragile sense of composure he'd found at the hospital, just as he always lost everything. One day, after picking up a book to synopsize from Twentieth Century-Fox, he migrated like a lost soul from one friend to another, ashamed of his dirty clothing and beer-drenched briefcase. After getting progressively drunker at each of his stops, he went to an elegant cocktail party where he hid out thumbing through books. His last stop was the back room of a jazz record shop on Greenwich Avenue that had become one of his regular destinations. The store belonged to his old friend Jerry Newman, who by then had begun to produce the pioneering recordings he'd made at Minton's in the early forties under the label Esoteric Records. Bop musicians and jazz critics like Barry Ulanov often dropped in on Newman, whose recordings of Thelonious Monk, Dizzy Gillespie, and Charlie Parker were making him a legendary figure in the jazz world. A heavy drinker himself, Newman kept a reliable supply of alcohol and marijuana in his back room for his visitors. As Jack drank the gin Jerry was always willing to provide, he listened to his "lonely voice" doing a word jazz improvisation on a tape recording Jerry had made in the spring when he'd briefly felt so hopeful after finishing *On the Road.*

When his desk finally arrived in Richmond Hill on September 28 along with his radio, his papers, and a box of his clothing, Jack once again felt ready to plunge into his work, but then his sister and her family arrived, clamorously crowding into the small apartment, depriving him of the quiet and solitude he needed and driving him out of the house. But by October 4, even though the Blakes were still there, he was able to concentrate well enough to add two new episodes to *On the Road,* taking off imaginatively on stories he'd heard from Neal. One was about a hunch-backed pool genius named Tom Watson, who had befriended Neal when he got out of reform school at fifteen and given him the first suit he ever had; the other was about Neal and his father selling homemade flyswatters door to door in Nebraska, accompanied by a fictional character named Old Bull Lewis, a composite of W. C. Fields and Bill Hubbard, who had kept cropping up in Jack's fiction over the last few years.

Through much of the fall, Jack continued to work on episodes that he would never have been able to successfully incorporate into the manuscript he'd completed in the spring because the new voice that had emerged in his writing was so rich and different in the way it sounded. In *On the Road* he had acquiesced to the idea of setting down his adventures with Neal in simple, direct language that would avoid poetic excesses. Six months later a wilder, more complex book was being born, coming from a deeper place in Jack's consciousness and exploring his darkening conception of both Neal and himself as tragic American figures who had enough energy, courage, and potential to rise above the conditions they'd been born into—only to discover that the promises America held out to them had as little substance as the gleam of red neon that transfigured an impenetrable brick wall.

"I accept lostness forever," Jack would declare in mid-November, adding a line in the small spiral notebook he was using—"Everything belongs to me because I am poor"—which he then crossed out, though he would restore it to the final text of *Visions of Cody*. Through evoking Neal's boyhood "greatness," which reminded him of his own, he seemed to be reaching for a way to recharge himself. But he was aware that the hero of his novel had also become a victim of time. "My mind is entirely empty," Neal had written Jack in September, with a plaintive postscript from Carolyn, who had just given birth to their third child, begging him to visit: "I need your help in order to make life worthwhile for Neal."

Although the foreword Jack would later write for *Visions of Cody* called the book one huge "character study" of the real Dean Moriarty, it was from the very start, whether he realized it or not, the "autobiography of a self-image." By late November he would be openly revealing in his manuscript that he and Neal, whose name had just reverted to Dean Pomeray again, "have the same soul." Passionate identification drove Jack's new writing about Neal—as if their two lives had always flowed into one stream, as if they shared the same consciousness and experience that had made them outcasts in America as well as the same futile dreams of glory absorbed from the B movies they'd both watched during their Depression childhoods. Denver and Lowell, Larimer Street and Moody Street, melted into each other in Jack's mind, as if both he and Neal had come from a place and a time that were steadily vanishing from the American psyche. In 1972, when *Visions of Cody* was posthumously published, Allen Ginsberg would write that Jack had succeeded in preserving the last vestiges of the Depression landscape of "mortal America": "disappearing Elevateds, diners, iceboxes, dusty hat racks." Jack painted Neal's Denver with the brownness and red brick of Lowell and the same tantalizing red neons of downtown that, like Hollywood, created illusions for naïve youths that excitement and glamour were just within reach. With a face that looked as if it had been shaped by being "pressed against iron bars," Jack's Dean Pomeray was no less long-suffering and heroic in the narrator's imagination than archetypal American figures such as Robert E. Lee and Walt Whitman.

As he allowed his mind new freedom to work its alchemy upon Neal's life story, Jack heightened the drama of Neal's transcendence over his Dickensian childhood, not only inventing episodes and giving Neal some of his own boyhood perceptions but charging even the smallest physical details with an urgency that suggested the narrator was possessed by these visions of another man's life in the way the narrator of *Swann's Way* is possessed by the details of Monsieur Swann's. Like Proust, whom Jack was reading obsessively that fall, carrying the Modern Library volumes of *Remembrance of Things Past* around in his battered, beer-stained briefcase, he was becoming a writer more interested in following the expanding ripples of meaning and association that certain images generated in his mind than in relating events. Although his need to get published had never been more desperate, he would soon be in the grip of an unstoppable rebellion against the conventions of fiction that would threaten the marketability of his work and his ability to survive.

TRANCED FIXATIONS

On October 7, after a gloomy Sunday in Richmond Hill when he again seemed to be making no progress with improving *On the Road*, Jack went to Birdland to hear the alto saxophonist Lee Konitz, a student of Lennie Tristano's who had come into his own as a leading innovator of cool jazz. During Konitz's solo in "I Remember April," which he played as if it were "the room he lived in," his music sounded "so profoundly interior" to Jack that he was sure very few people would understand it. In fact, he compared Konitz's extended phrases to the sentences he was writing lately, sentences whose direction seemed mysterious until the "solution" was suddenly unveiled in a way that shed light backward on everything that had preceded it. Admiring Konitz for refusing to make the concessions that would gain him a wider audience, Jack saw that both he and the musician were essentially doing the same thing—attempting to communicate "the unspeakable visions of the individual." Grabbing a pencil, he scribbled a reminder to himself: "BLOW AS DEEP AS YOU WANT TO BLOW." It was a rule he would start to follow in his work, despite his continued brooding about his lost career and his tormenting inability to finish his second novel. Even Gabe was beginning to have something to say about that—she told her son that it was a waste of time to write about Neal, who wasn't a big enough subject for him.

When Jack wasn't writing in his cell-like room, he often roamed the streets of Jamaica and Richmond Hill, where one day he saw a crowd gathered in an empty lot. A bloody miscarried fetus had been found there, dumped into the weeds in a paper bag. Shaken, he returned home, his reeling thoughts terrifying him, for it seemed he could hold on to none of them, making him wonder about the effect alcohol was having on his brain. If his mind was going, how could he ever finish *On the Road*? Unable to calm himself, he broke down into a prayer for forgiveness. The dead baby apparently reminded him of his guilty role in the conception of the one Joan was carrying. Within a month he would describe the scene in the lot, where even the maroon-colored roots of torn-up weeds seemed obscene. Putting Dean Pomeray there in his place, he used Dean's point of view to express his own horror over the transformation of sperm into "decayable flesh." Even the look Jack had been unable to prevent himself from taking at the red flesh of the fetus seemed to contribute to his guilt. He spent the next couple of days convinced he was being punished for his sins by losing the ability to write.

On October 15, Jack was still in a state of panic when he met Ed White for dinner at the Shanghai Café on 124th Street and Broadway. Although Ed assured him his block was only temporary, this did nothing to improve Jack's mood. Changing the subject to his own work, Ed showed Jack the pocket sketchbook in which he had been making drawings of buildings around New York that interested him. This led him to an idea he thought Jack should try out—a way for him to ease back into writing.

"Why don't you sketch in the street like a painter, but with words?" Ed proposed.

As an experiment in which nothing was really at stake, "sketching" immediately gave Jack what he most needed—the freedom to write his "interior music" just as it came to him, removing the inhibiting presence in his mind of the editor or reader whose needs and conventional expectations must always be taken into consideration. He was about to discover what he had been looking for—a way to write passages in which he would seize the peak moment of initial inspiration and ride it through to the end, without interrupting the flow of imagery. Sketching would dissolve the barrier between poetry and prose and lead to what Jack later believed was "a whole new movement of American Literature (spontaneous prose and poetry)."

The day after seeing Ed, Jack took a notebook and walked to Sutphin Boulevard, a skid-row-like area in working-class Jamaica, where he sketched two places that had a time-stopped feeling about them. The first was an old railroad-car diner permeated by a brown "FOODY" smell that reminded him in a Proustian way of the aroma of countless American diners, of parochial school and hospital kitchens, of greasy hamburger pans soaking in sinks—"makes the guts of men curl in October." The next scene he colored in shades of gray, a dilapidated B-movie theater, adjoined by a filthy hot-dog stand with its surrounding pavement littered with cigarette butts and chewing gum. No sign of entropy escaped Jack's eye—he searched out the broken bulbs behind the holes in the glass facing of the Capricio Theater's marquee, saw how the diner's scarred wood counter resembled "the bottoms of old courtroom benches." Without knowing it, Jack had just written the opening of *Visions of Cody*. Somehow he'd been able to induce in himself an exceptional state of awareness that gave his portrayals of these scenes a heightened immediacy that went beyond realism.

The following day found him on Forty-second Street in Hector's cafeteria, which in 1946 had dazzled Neal during his first hours in Manhattan. Jack's exuberant description of the pyramids of sweets heaped on the glass counters—a gleaming display of limitless American abundance—was infused with his own hunger and sense of deprivation, like the tantalizing loaves of bread the vagabond poet François Villon had glimpsed only in windows in fifteenth-century Paris.

The act of writing requires entry into a meditative state, different from normal concentration, in which the tension between what the writer knows or feels and the peculiar need to put it into words upon a page can be resolved. But sketching demanded something more from Jack—abandonment to a "tranced fixation" on the object, a deeper way of dreaming upon what he saw. "Everything activates in front of you in myriad profusion," he would explain to Allen the following spring. "You just have to purify your mind and let it pour the words (which effortless angels of the vision fly when you stand in front of reality) and write with 100% personal honesty both psychic and social, etc. and slap it all down shameless, willy-nilly, rapidly until sometimes I got so inspired I lost consciousness I was writing."

There were times when the bliss of these tranced fixations took Jack back to his boyhood absorption in the imaginary world of The Turf, but there seemed to be an inherent danger for him in becoming what W. B. Yeats once called in an essay about modernist, stream-of-consciousness writers "a man helpless before the contents of his own mind." Jack would emerge from complete immersion in one of his visionary states and find himself standing on a grim corner of the Bowery feeling diminished and alone. The more sketching he did over the next couple of months, the more he felt the need to drink when he wasn't writing. It wasn't long before it took only three beers for his thirst to become bottomless. He'd go for days without sleeping until he passed out on someone's couch. In his fall 1951 writings, especially in his journals, there began to be a palpable tension between his deepening melancholy and the addictive exhilaration the intensification of his creative energy was giving him.

Over the next half year, Jack would find ways to dive deeper and deeper into his consciousness. In a section of *Visions of Cody* written in the spring of 1952, he would find himself working with sound in a new, utterly free way, diving down to the level where words were just beginning to take form, like the roar of a foreign language in the ears of a small boy in a movie theater. On June 3, 1952, writing to Holmes from Mexico City, where he had recently finished both *Cody* and *Dr. Sax*, Jack would announce his discovery of what he called "wild form": something that was taking him "beyond the novel and beyond the arbitrary confines of the story into realms of revealed picture." He felt filled with "an irrational lust to set down everything I know—in narrowing circles around the core of my last writing." But without going into detail, Jack indicated that this development had come at a very heavy price: "I love the world . . . but at this time in my life I'm making myself sick to find the wild form that can grow with my wild heart." Four years later, in *Visions of Gerard*, he would admit tersely, "I've grown sick in my papers." By then, writing, instead of being a source of balance for him, had become a destabilizing act. He was using it, just as he did alcohol, drugs, and sex, to find the ecstasy that could ward off ennui. But no one can have ecstasy or epiphanies all the time. One must always contend with what Virginia Woolf called "the nondescript cotton wool" of ordinary life. When the ecstasy of writing began to run out on Jack after the publication of *On the Road*, he would feel more lost than ever, drinking, as he admitted to himself in 1962, like a "mental patient," unable to cope with the inevitable boredom, depression, and self-imposed isolation of attempting to remain sober.

Two days after Jack started sketching, he returned to the sections he'd been adding to *On the Road* with a new feeling of confidence. In one afternoon when his prowess astonished him, he wrote a brilliantly comic scene in which fifteen-year-old Neal, delivering his first circuitous con man speech, offers to teach Tom Watson philosophy as well as psychology and "metafisicks" in return for instruction in pool and to "establish a blood brother loyalty of our souls, if you wish to use clitchay expressions." He also wrote a football scene—played in a lot next to a highway against the backdrop of a red Colorado sunset, with a savage horizontal flying pass in the gathering dark that establishes Neal as the leader of the pool hall gang. In his estimation it surpassed the account of the Thanksgiving 1938 game in *The Town and the City*, which he considered one of his proudest achievements.

The following night at Birdland, Jack felt his mind ratcheting up in an alarmingly overexcited way as he listened to the new "apocalyptic" bop that had recently caused Seymour Wyse to declare that jazz was dead. The club was his last stop after a very bad day in the city. A friend of Jerry

Newman's had criticized him for sponging off Jerry and he'd found no warmth during a visit to Holmes, whose marriage to Marian was acrimoniously falling apart and whose living room couches were occupied by drunken strangers. As a sensational young musician named Terry Gibbs attacked the vibraphone, the old frantic feeling of wanting to be everywhere at once swept over Jack, along with the terrifying recognition that apart from his mother, there was nothing "solid" to hold on to except writing. The next morning, as he fought off the despair that accompanied his hangover, he made a fresh resolution to cut down on his drinking that lasted until the weekend, when he again went on a binge. Someone told him he'd be dead within a couple of years, as if he were the new doomed Cannastra whom everyone was watching now.

Meanwhile, not even alcohol could hold back the discoveries that were transforming his writing. On October 25, perhaps after spending the night at Holmes's apartment just around the corner, he went to sketch the old Forty-seventh Street el station, one of the disappearing brown places in Manhattan that still had its stained-glass window and cast-iron potbellied stove. In the men's room, the way the yellow-painted walls contrasted with the dark brown woodwork and stamped tin ceiling summoned up a picture in Jack's mind of the imitation wainscotting he'd noticed in flophouses out west. When he returned to Richmond Hill after taking a long walk down the Bowery to Chinatown, he was able to resume his sketching without the need to fix his eyes on anything, evoking images of what he'd seen during his walk with no loss of intensity. Tapping again the following day into all the associations summoned up by the contrast of brown and yellow paint, he took off from there into a three-hundred-word sentence about cowboylike bums wearing big slouched hats that suggested the great distances they'd traveled, recalling the look he'd seen of "grave, careful adventurous sorrow" on the faces of a group of them standing against a wall in an alley with their "drink wet mouths glistening in the moonlight in a lunar Bowery." He had described such slouch-hatted bums before in *La Nuit Est Ma Femme* but felt he'd never written anything better than that free-rolling sentence, which he stopped with a dash before the images spinning out of him went on forever. That night he was sure that the sketches in his notebook were far superior to all the "oil" painting he'd been doing for *On the Road,* and that he'd just had the "greatest" of all his Octobers.

In an unusually upbeat spirit the next day, he put on his red lumberjack shirt and went off to visit Jack Fitzgerald in Poughkeepsie with Allen Ginsberg and Dusty Morland, a young woman who had escaped to Greenwich Village from Lusk, Wyoming, to become a painter. She had become Allen's girlfriend over the past year, and Allen had even considered marrying her, but he encouraged Dusty, who was sexually adventurous, to sleep with all his friends. Jack was in the mood for the five-day binge that followed. Although he wrote afterward that his wild lovemaking with Dusty had reminded him that it was actually possible to have a good time with a girl, the sketch he brought back with him from "the town of Poke" was of "applepie wives" in housecoats and "backyards with wash hung out as far as the eye could see," backyards he called "gardens of silence." When he used it in *Visions of Cody,* it would seem perfectly placed, its sunlit white sheets deepening the somber tones of the writing that surrounded it.

In 1958, attempting to describe the still unpublished book he considered his "great one" to Elbert Lenrow, Jack would write:

> *Visions of Neal* is tears of gray rain, American mountains of used tires, mist, the West, snow and gray. It's Neal (you know old Neal). It includes 150 pages of tape-recorded dialog of Neal talking to me his not-caring about machine and of parties etc. then it has a 30 page stretch IMITAT- ING the sound of the tape, a la Joyce or e.e. Cummings of EIMI, and ends up with tears.

Visions of Cody had turned out to be collagelike in structure, with each of its five sections approached in a distinctly different way, adding up to what Jack still called a "vertical portrait" of Neal, though it was just as much a portrait of himself. Although written without a road map, all of it flowed from a sense of form that operated on an unconscious level. Even Jack's choices of what to sketch cannot be regarded as random, for they all related to the *other* book he thought he was writing about Neal that fall and were connected to it in a musical way and through a web of recurring imagery. The browns, grays, and reds of Lowell, Denver, and New York; the narrator's obsession with the Bowery; the allusions to films, movie queens, and comedians of the thirties and forties, would eventually run through the entire book like repeating motifs in a symphony. Apart from certain omissions, the order of the sketches included in *Cody's* first section is surprisingly close to the order in which they appeared in Jack's notebooks, and the chronological timeline—the brilliant "sugar-cured" skies of early October fading into autumnal gray and a darkening November—is kept very clear. While Jack provided no transitional passages per se, subtle thematic filaments link each sketch to the one that follows.

Although Neal was indeed very much on Jack's mind, since he had been writing about him all through September, the original sketches were written with far fewer of the references to thinking about Neal (and to the narrator's growing need to go on the road again) than Jack would put in afterward—practically the only concessions he made to future readers, who would be drawn immediately into the psychic space of the nameless narrator of the sketches, but would be challenged to piece together fragmentary impressions of his life story without the least help from expository passages. They would come to know him instead principally through his voice, his *sound*—this man with the agonized yet tender need to take in everything, so profoundly and alertly alone that he can imagine no one with whom he can share what he sees, apart from the one friend on the other side of the continent. They would feel permeated by the mood—the element Jack once identified as the most important one in writing—his voice created.

In the self-portrait the narrator projects, he has reached the point where his New York relationships are no longer enough to sustain him and where emptiness descends upon him immediately after the transitory feeling of absolute connection—the "Go"—that can be reached in orgasmic explosions of communal energy by those "who make the mad night all the way." Such "it" moments could be retrieved only when "the old file cards of the soul" were shuffled "in demented hallucinated sleep," Jack reflected in the letdown that followed his weekend in Poughkeepsie.

In *Visions of Cody*, the act of sketching only seems to increase the narrator's sense of isolation. While his extraordinary eye is able to capture the infinitely complex and mysterious "confusion" of flashing headlights and red neon in a mirror affixed to the frame of a rooming house window, no contact is possible between him and the city dwellers he also observes with such brooding attention. Spotting Lee Konitz on Sixth Avenue, he follows him into Manny's music store and listens in on his conversation with the proprietor but does not attempt to approach him. In a cafeteria, his eye has a love affair with a dark-haired girl daintily eating her solitary meal as she reads a Modern Library book—"She'd melt for me in two minutes." But he watches her get up and go "beautifully" away, just as "everything goes away" from him—"girls, visions, anything, just in the same way and forever."

Despite his deep knowledge of the city, Jack's narrator feels as lost and far from home in it as his old French Canadian aunts, "raw creatures of time and earth," would feel if they left Maine and landed in the middle of Sixth Avenue wondering where to eat a meal that would typify the experience of being in New York. Without proclaiming his "raw" Franco-American identity, Jack was finally openly inhabiting it in his sketches, as he would do more and more in the books he wrote next, addressing the feelings of shame and exclusion it gave him without using a fictional character like Freddie Boncoeur as a mask, and even starting to bring words from his own language into the text—the dreams his narrator has are called *rêves*, for example, in the first section of *Visions of Cody*. In a later section of the book, he would finally dare to write entire passages in *joual*, set alongside their translations. (In 1958, Jack would still be searching for the best way to capture in English the French music of his characters' speech as he struggled to write his never completed *Memory Babe*, in which he intended to tell the story of Jean Baptiste Kerouac and his New England descendants.)

A few days after his visit to Jack Fitzgerald, Jack was seized by the impulse to put his present work aside and hitchhike to the Coast with "mad" Dusty Morland, who was now intent upon completing her sexual education by meeting Neal. Perhaps she was trying to find a way to bind Allen to her by sleeping with all the men he was in love with—during the summer she had also gone to bed with Lucien. She kept pressing Jack to let her be his road trip companion. For a day or so the idea of secretly taking notes on an adventure with Dusty for a book drawn directly from whatever unfolded along the way excited him. But his sudden longing for flight may have been connected to an entirely different development—Allen had just come up with a way to get *On the Road* published with Carl Solomon as Jack's editor.

After being released from the mental ward of Columbia Presbyterian, Carl had been hired by his uncle, A. A. Wyn, the publisher of Ace Books, a line of cheap paperbacks with lurid covers that could be found on racks in drugstores. Undeterred by the company's complete lack of literary *cachet*, Allen envisioned taking the house over, working through Carl to turn it into a kind of Beat New Directions that would publish all the unknown but important writers he knew, including Burroughs, Cassady, and Holmes. More and more Allen was taking on the role of impresario for his friends' books, though the only one Ace Books would actually bring out would be Burroughs's first novel, *Junkie*.

Despite Allen's enthusiasm for the whole scheme, Jack felt wary. It would be a comedown to be published by Ace Books, and he was reluctant to risk exposing his latest writing to possible rejection. Carl's mental equilibrium remained fragile and he could be brutally tactless. As a reader, his tastes ran to surrealist literature and avant-garde Europeans like Antonin Artaud, Jean Genet, and Henri Michaux, but now that he was an editor, hoping to please his uncle, Carl's decisions about what to publish would prove to be more cautious and conservative than Allen could have expected. Perhaps jealous of Allen's devotion to Jack, Carl had developed a condescending view of him, which he was not shy about expressing with barbed words, referring, for example, to "the problem of The Brilliant Young Punk's Second Book." But even before Allen persuaded Carl to think seriously about signing Jack up, Jack's relationship with Ace had gotten off to an unpromising start earlier that fall when he brought in the scroll of *On the Road*, which was getting rather shopworn looking by then, to show Carl and his uncle. A. A. Wyn had not been impressed. He'd warned his nephew that this book had obviously been turned down everywhere it had been sent, and that Jack was trying to put something over on him. "And now you're taking *me* in," he'd said to Carl.

Jack took a day to think over the possible deal with Ace before overcoming his misgivings and deciding to delay his travels and try to get Carl and his uncle to give him a contract. He desperately needed the one-thousand-dollar advance Carl had mentioned. His October royalty statement from Harcourt Brace had arrived without a check. There was nothing between him and the kind of destitution he was seeing on the Bowery but the very small sums he received for synopsizing scripts and the roof over his head still provided by his mother. When Holmes ran into Jack right after his return from Poughkeepsie, he was shocked by his "terrible no-overcoat poverty. He goes around the city in these gray autumn days shivering, looking for a few dollars from 20th Century Fox, and reading the labels on delicacies in the windows of delicatessens."

Hoping to show Carl how "professional" he could be if he set his mind to it, Jack decided to add another three thousand words about Neal to his manuscript immediately. Before he sat down at his typewriter, however, he took a walk, searching the back streets of the neighborhood for the kind of rundown house Neal and his gang of friends would find on the border of Wyoming when they arrived there to see two girls on a Saturday night. The house in his mind stood by railroad tracks. The one he chose to sketch stood beside a water tank and had the kind of calamitous yard filled with castoffs—an old dresser, the corpse of a car, a sack of rotting potatoes—that could be seen in declining neighborhoods all over America. The scene had the iconography that was running through all his recent writing. He had filled *On the Road* with wide-open vistas, mountains, and plains, the grandeur of the Mississippi. But in his new work, which he would soon no longer think of as "inserts for *On the Road*," he was keeping his eye at ground level, noting such things as "the forlorn tufts of bunchgrass" flashing by in Neal's headlights, or the "old cellophane, old bus transfer tickets, the strange corrugated cardboard from egg crates" in the lot where he now had Dean see the dead fetus. While he still saw his sketching and *On the Road* as two separate entities, the sketching was beginning to feed the novel.

That night Jack made the football episode he'd written even more powerful by focusing his tranced fixation upon the pictures in his imagination, something he had not tried before. Writing fiction had never seemed so natural and unself-conscious. He felt like a kid making things up, totally *interested* in what his mind had the power to create. The following day he realized that what mattered to him most were "the things that haunt *me*." The mastery he'd been working toward for so many years was suddenly coming to him with a feeling of lightness.

Two days later he brought his new three thousand words to Carl—and was stunned when Carl asked him to write a synopsis of the entire book that could be shown to his uncle. How could he say where *On the Road* was headed? How could he explain to Carl's uncle, the pulp fiction publisher, that his intent was to be "vertical" and "metaphysical" rather than conventionally "horizontal"? Carl and his wife, Olive, invited him to stay for a meal. Sitting down with a pencil and paper in Carl's apartment, Jack tried to come up with some adequate description of what he would be writing. Dejectedly, he left there, having failed to perform. Instead of going home, he went to find Allen and Dusty and went on one of the worst drunks of his life, frightening himself into thinking afterward that he should never have another drop of alcohol again.

Trying to recover in Richmond Hill that Monday, Jack shuddered at the memory of himself yelling at Allen that God no longer interested him and stripping off his shirt as he danced to Stravinsky's *The Rite of Spring* in Dusty's living room. He remembered how he had horrified the two of them by losing control of his bowels. He had begun to think himself a little in love with Dusty, but now that he had humiliated himself in front of her, he felt that she had wronged him.

On Tuesday, he saw Carl, who gave him encouraging news. After reading the new pages, and especially the football scene, Carl was thinking in very definite terms about publishing Jack's new novel. What particularly attracted him to Jack's writing, however, was that he saw it as essentially visual, which suggested that he might not appreciate Jack's deeper purpose—to go into the mind so deeply that the "unspeakable visions of the individual" would be revealed. Although the two of them had a better rapport than usual, and Carl even told him about the time he'd seen the poet Antonin Artaud in the full grip of his mania screaming on the streets of Paris, Jack left their meeting depressed, wondering what he should be writing about now that he was going to be paid for it and have Carl and his uncle peering over his shoulder.

In Richmond Hill, he pulled out his old manuscript of *Vanity of Duluoz* and wept as he read it. It seemed to him that he had been only two people when he was nineteen, but now he felt split into five and feared this could be a sign that his mind, like Artaud's, was deteriorating. Years ago after the head injury he'd received in the car crash in Vermont, his mother had been convinced he had not come back to her as the same person. Now he asked himself whether she'd been right. Then, thinking about the thousands of times he used the word *I* in his journals, Jack wondered whether his real trouble came from being too obsessed with himself.

That night he had planned to continue writing about Neal's visit to the two girls in Wyoming. Instead, what interested him far more was his memory of what he'd noticed as he sat in Stewart's cafeteria—the refracted, crisscrossing reflections of red neon in the corner windows of an office across the street—but this had absolutely nothing to do with his narrative. Avoiding the issue of what he should be writing, he synopsized a script. He was still up several hours later when he recalled an early memory of a shoe repair shop in Lowell that had come to him that day as one of his visual "tics" and suddenly felt a resurgence of the joy that had deserted him, which swept him back into his work. By four A.M., as he experimented with a scene in his novel, he felt another enormous discovery coming that would revolutionize not only his own writing but all writing, he thought. The following evening, despite a complete lack of sleep, he was still so keyed up that he went into Manhattan to sit in Stewart's again, where he sketched the people who walked by in the downpour outside and those neon reflections further amplified and complicated by the rain. Back home at one A.M., too restless and excited to sit at his typewriter, he went out for a long walk.

But the discovery he'd been expecting did not come to him that night. Instead the trouble he was having writing about the two Wyoming girls brought him down into complete gloom. After describing them as Neal would have sized them up—the older, plainer one whose prim manner concealed her appetite for sex; the soft little blonde whom boys found frightening because she looked so much like their "Coca-Cola" ad fantasies—after even going into what the girls felt about the boys, he gave up. Although the water tank house was real to him, the two alluring teenagers he placed inside it were pure concoctions. Once again he felt defeated by the troubling fictionality—the *lie*—of fiction. He tackled the boys' arrivals all over again, adding new details about the girls, putting more emphasis on the theme of all this writing—the power of sexual fantasy—and once again impatiently broke off, never delivering the sex scene he seemed to be building toward. In *Visions of Cody*, where these two false starts are left in, they not only appear to rebelliously disregard all the rules of how to write but seem as much the deliberate statement of a new aesthetic as the drips abstract expressionists like Jackson Pollock were beginning to leave on their canvases, as vestiges of the furious experimental energy of the process.

On November 15, worn out from his forty-eight-hour struggle with his manuscript, Jack assessed himself as a complete failure, looking with disgust at his sweaty clothing, his uncut hair, his alcohol-swollen belly, his unending lack of money. He could also feel a burning nerve in one of his legs—a warning sign of phlebitis. As he continued to write in his journal, however, his mind cleared and he was able to recognize that his instinctive resistance to the idea of accepting money from A. A. Wyn for this work in progress had been hanging him up since his conversation with Carl. He was finally seeing that this indescribable, still unrevealed book he was being driven to write would be something entirely separate from the original *On the Road*. Was it "fiction" or something else? He had some doubts it was even "literature." Apart from "sketching," he had no name for this new departure in his work, but he had discovered the way he would write from now on.

RÊVES

On his forays into Manhattan that fall, Jack kept searching for the old feeling of excitement that had once led him and John Clellon Holmes to believe that the fifties would be a "decade of parties" where "the door would always be open, the lights would always be on, the music would always play." Instead he felt that now everything was repeating itself but in a much less interesting way, so that in effect nothing was happening at all. Nothing outside himself gave him the ecstasy he was finding in his explorations of his inner world. Sometimes he thought this was why he was turning into an alcoholic, frantically rushing from one group of people to the next as if he had a Neal-like mission to keep the lights from going out.

In his sleep he lived his other life, the one that never lost intensity—an alternate biography that scrambled all the places, symbols, periods, and remixed them, so that the path through the woods behind Bethesda Naval Hospital became the sandy path down by the Merrimack leading on and on toward Greenland; so that Neal turned up in the brick alley behind the Keith Theater where he'd been playing poker with Leo and his gang or materialized in some eatery that seemed Mexican, back from the dead, pleading for Jack's protection: "You have to keep me from being lonely." Gasping for breath, his limbs twitching, Jack would wake up in his room just before falling through the terrifying railings of the third-floor porch on Moody Street where they used to put his bed in the summers.

One unusual dream about a week before Thanksgiving opened an aperture through which he could glimpse the future where a big cocktail party was going on in the respectable precincts of the Yale Club. He'd been brought there wearing his shabby leather jacket but wasn't embarrassed, in fact felt rather stylish and avant-garde until he noticed that everyone was wearing jackets like his and that they were all smoking marijuana quite openly. He was surrounded by people who looked like hipsters and who seemed to represent an "anarchy" that would come to America, taking the form of a new "virility" that would be "sadomasochistic" and "bisexual"—an anarchy that would resemble his original idea of the Beat Generation only in a superficial way. He wouldn't participate—he knew that already. Or if he did, one side of him would be fighting the other, for he admitted he was "inconceivably old-fashioned." Yet the dream heartened him. It reminded Jack of everything he still believed he could teach the world.

For the past three months, Jack had paid little attention to his mother's needs, apart from his helpless awareness that he was failing her in every way. In fact, he spent much of his time escaping from Gabe's misery, walling himself off from it with his writing even when he could hear her moving about in the next room, carrying dishes to the sink, changing the channels on the television set that she kept playing constantly—for TV had only brought her a new way of being lonely. Sometimes when he was wandering around the city, he'd see a sign in an upstairs window and think about moving into the furnished room it advertised, but then he'd remind himself he'd be breaking the promise he'd made to his father. Yet he was hardly taking care of Gabe, and the truth was that the home she provided for him was about all the security he had.

Perhaps he was partly relieved when she told him that she was going down to North Carolina to spend Thanksgiving with Nin. For once she wasn't cooking him a feast and he'd have to fend for himself. He didn't realize it was a sign that Gabe was making up her mind to give up on him for a while and that she was about to act swiftly. Within a few weeks he would be putting his belongings in boxes—saying good-bye to his rolltop desk, Leo's old L. C. Smith, the room that had seemed too small and mean to contain him but now felt precious—as his mother prepared to move south and live with Nin. Although she would briefly return in 1952, years of uprootedness, of weary circular travels like the peregrinations of the Ghost of the Susquehanna, nightmares of railroad tracks and desolate hotels, lay ahead of him.

With Gabe gone from Richmond Hill, Jack avoided the empty apartment by spending the four days before Thanksgiving with Allen and Dusty Morland, indulging in what he'd recently called in one of his sketches "dissipation for the sake of dissipation," as he and Allen took their turns in Dusty's bed. By now her eagerness to have sex with changing partners made Jack think she must be trying to imitate Neal.

Fitz arrived from Poughkeepsie, contributing a second girl. To keep the excitement going, Jack went out for reinforcements and returned with a black guitarist, a piano player, and a third woman. For a couple of hours, everything turned into a "jungle," with Jack rushing from Dusty's piano to pound a bongo drum and the three women dancing without their tops.

On Thursday, Dusty had sufficent stamina left to roast a turkey big enough to feed a crowd of twelve. At the last minute, Allen and Jack had called around, collecting people who for one reason or another had been left with no place to spend Thanksgiving. Among the invited guests were Lucien Carr, Carl Solomon, Jerry Newman, Alan Ansen, and Jack's old flame and former enemy Ginger Bailey, who had unexpectedly just come back to New York and was singing folk songs at the Village Vanguard.

Dusty set the table, perhaps the way her family did in Lusk, even putting out some expensive wineglasses she'd bought, which would be the first casualties of the evening—deliberately smashed by Lucien Carr in a Cannastra-like gesture. Not to be outdone, Dusty joined in by pitching a glass or two over her shoulder. She seemed intent on becoming the next "heroine of the hip generation." Six months later, when her cat died, she would have a nervous breakdown.

When Lucien was in his Rimbaud period, his nihilistic acts had seemed meaningful and had only contributed to his charisma. But time had passed and they all had seen too much broken glass. Within a year, there had been two violent deaths—Cannastra's and Joan's. Now Lucien was acting like his might be next. Yet recently he had startled everyone (and devastated Allen) by announcing that he had become engaged to Francesca von Hartz, the daughter of a prominent editor of the *New York Times*.

Enraged by Lucien's desecration of Thanksgiving, Jack leaped forward to tackle him as Allen implored him to remember Lucien was too weak to fight back. Sprawled on the floor, too drunk to resist, Lucien went rigid as Jack held him and then seemed to be having a seizure. With his mortified future bride gripping his arm, he was finally escorted out the door, reviving just enough to knock down a lamp in the hallway that belonged to Dusty's landlady. The whole performance, conducted before the eyes of Francesca von Hartz, may have been connected to Lucien's ambivalent feelings about his approaching marriage. After futilely hoping Lucien would eventually return his love, Allen considered the marriage a travesty as well as a desertion, even though he had reluctantly agreed to be best man at the wedding. "I feel like Baudelaire in his damnation," Allen would write after Thanksgiving, "and yet he had great joyful moments of staring into space, looking into the middle distance, contemplating his image in eternity."

For the rest of that evening, Jack, whose rage hadn't left him, devoted himself to getting as high as possible on Jerry Newman's Mexican grass. He was sickened by the drunken, egotistical, "exhibitional" behavior of everyone at this party and he included himself among those he was fed up with. Not even a fascinating conversation about Jean Genet with the poet Alan Ansen, who reminded him of Leopold Bloom, lifted him out of his dark mood. The following morning, he woke up in such terrible shape that he presented himself at the emergency room of St. Vincent's Hospital before taking the subway back to Richmond Hill.

Although Ginger Bailey had come as Jack's date, he'd lost track of her as he got higher and drunker and she'd finally left him at Dusty's and gone home. A few days earlier, they'd been astonished to run into each other on Forty-second Street. After discovering they no longer felt any rancor and were simply very glad to see each other again, they'd spent the night talking and singing to each other, just as they'd done the summer they fell in love, before Hal took over and everything got complicated. No longer married to Hal, who'd left her for a woman he met in Mexico, Ginger had limped back to New York as confused and sad as everyone else Jack knew. Hal felt lost now too, she'd told him.

The "dominant note" of the fifties, John Clellon Holmes would observe when he was forty, was "the mysterious process of dispersal, the quiet weakening of cohesiveness," yet he couldn't say exactly what had broken up the magnetic sense of "vivid conjunction" that had immediately drawn him into the group of people he met in 1948 at Allen's Fourth of July party in East Harlem. Change occurs, he thought, when "some dissatisfaction, longing, or despair seizes everyone at the same time."

Jack went home to write to Neal, who he suddenly felt was the only real friend he had. It had been a long time since he'd sent Neal a letter—not since October 9, when, along with a short note congratulating him on the birth of a son Neal had named Jack Allen, he'd enclosed three new pages of his book "to show you that 'Dean Pomeray' is a vision" and heard nothing back. Too weighed down by his burdens to frame his thoughts into coherent sentences, it may have been painful for Neal to see how Jack had transfigured the story he seemed unable to write himself.

"I dig like you did," Jack wrote him. "I dig jazz, a 1000 things in America, even the rubbish in the weeds of an empty lot." He told Neal that now he too had come to value Joyce and Proust above all other writers, and "I dig *you* as together we dig the lostness and the fact of course nothing's ever gained but death." In Jack's repeated insistence that there was no difference between himself and Neal, the "you" and the "I" seem as nearly interchangeable as the intertwining of Dean Pomeray with Jack Duluoz in his vision. To separate his self-image from the Neal in his mind, he would have to go to California and listen to tapes of the two of them having the real conversations he intended to transcribe and use in his book. Between them for now was a year of separation and a nether-world of fiction.

"I'm completely your friend, your 'lover,' he who loves you and digs your greatness completely—haunted in the mind by you." In his desperate reach for a feeling of connection, Jack used Neal's word *lover* for the first time. But was it Dean Pomeray whom he loved in the way one loves what one has created, which can also haunt the mind?

He had begun the letter as if he'd merely intended to rap out the news that would be most interesting to its reader. The possibility that Dusty would accompany him to Frisco, her boundless appetite for sex, the three girls dancing topless to his conga beat which only proved that "you and I could be great jazz musicians *among* jazz musicians." Effortlessly he'd adopted Neal's uninflected way of telegraphing what happened as if it were only meaningful as a manifestation of energy. But darker tones, interjections of grief and abject need, began to break through. A plea for Neal not to give up on him abruptly interrupted Jack's account of the Thanksgiving gathering, before he attributed his low spirits to "no more than a hangover," and went back to relating the latest developments—the reappearance of Ginger, the brawl with Lucien, the Indian girl Hal had taken up with in Mexico.

But he had come home from the city with a premonition of dying and finally could not hold back an utterly desolate admission: "I feel like I've done wrong, to myself the most wrong, I'm throwing away something that I can't even find in the incredible clutter of my being." After castigating himself for all the time he'd lost, for even wasting 1949, the year he should have been happy, Jack again attempted to raise himself up from the dust by assuring Neal that everything was fine "because I've won." But the secret victory in his work he cryptically alluded to wasn't enough to turn his thoughts away from death. From so much despair another trip to California seemed the only means of escape.

Once Jack was able to imagine himself arriving on Neal's doorstep, a magic carpet landed him instantly on the Embarcadero, where, with his notebook in pocket, he saw himself strolling along, taking everything in—"the neons, the mad neons, the soft, soft night, secret chopsueys in the air." Yet even in this dream of flight, uncertainty—the likelihood of finding no answers at all—invaded his feeling of elation. Advancing more slowly now in his dream steps, almost fearfully approaching Neal's front door, he felt caught up again in one of the mind movies he used to play in which he was a lost desert traveler nearly dying of thirst before being rescued by an Arab chieftain who will demand total surrender in return for a single glass of water.

When the letter was done, Jack typed a copy to send to Neal, keeping the original, for it would come right after the sketches he'd written that fall, all of which had somehow been leading to it like streams feeding into a river. He had finally become the book he was writing. "I'm lost, but my work is found," he wrote that day on the next-to-last page of his journal.

ACKNOWLEDGMENTS

I am grateful to my editor, Paul Slovak, and my agent, Irene Skolnick, for their support of my first venture into biography and to Leon Friedman for his helpful clarification of legal issues. My friends and fellow Kerouac experts Ann Douglas, Regina Weinreich, David Amram, and John and Mellon Tytell were always ready to offer their thoughts and knowledge; Helen Weaver, Hassan Melehy, and Paul Maher very generously shared material they had gathered during their own research; and Howard Norman, Kate Blackwell, and Judith Dunford gave me some much appreciated feedback. For two particularly valuable insights I am indebted to the Yeats scholar Anita Feldman.

Most of all, I am grateful to my superb research assistant, Brittney Inman Canty, who helped me search through so many files in the Kerouac Archive and always seemed to know what would interest me, and to Isaac Gewirtz, Ann Garner, and Steven Crook, the gracious and dedicated guardians of the Berg Collection at the New York Public Library.

I also wish to thank Elizabeth Von Vogt for allowing me to quote from the papers of John Clellon Holmes, Kerouac's steadfast friend and fellow novelist.

NOTES

Abbreviations

Jack Kerouac: JK
Allen Ginsberg: AG
Neal Cassady: NC
William S. Burroughs: WSB
John Clellon Holmes: JCH
Sebastian Sampas: SS
On the Road: OTR
Desolation Angels: DA
Lonesome Traveler: LT
Mexico City Blues: MC
The Town and the City: T&C
Vanity of Duluoz: VD
Visions of Gerard: VG
Visions of Cody: VC
Dr. Sax: DS
Good Blonde & Others: GB
Windblown World: WW
Atop an Underwood: AU
Jack Kerouac: Selected Letters, 1940–1956: SL
The Book of Martyrdom and Artifice: BMA
Nothing More to Declare: NMD
You'll Be Okay: YBO
The Letters of William S. Burroughs, 1945–59: WSBL
Neal Cassady: Collected Letters, 1944–1967: NCL
Jack Kerouac and Allen Ginsberg: The Letters: JKAGL

Introduction

xviii: is **"not so much concerned with events"**: JCH, *Nothing More to Declare* (New York: E. P. Dutton, 1967), p. 69.

xviii: had to be a **"poem,"** *and* **"a breath separation of the mind"**: The Paris Review, *Beat Writers at Work*, edited by George Plimpton (New York: Modern Library, 1999), pp. 14–16.

xix: **"Poor Leecie"**: JK, *Desolation Angels* (New York: Riverhead Books, 1995), p. 334.

PART ONE: FRANCO-AMERICAN GHOSTS

The Lost Brother

3: **"He's still taking care of us"**: JK, *The Town and the City* (New York: Harcourt Brace, 1983), p. 20.

3: **"burn savagely"**: Ibid., p. 25.

5: **"I had me a companion there"**: JK, *Desolation Angels* (New York: Riverhead Books, 1995), p. 328.

5: **"When the little kitty"**: JK, *Visions of Gerard* (New York: Penguin Books, 1991), p. 107.

6: **"the voice is all"**: JK to NC, October 6, 1950, *Jack Kerouac: Selected Letters, 1940–1956*, edited by Ann Charters (New York: Viking, 1995), p. 232.

6: **"fiction and fear"**: JK to NC, December 28, 1950, ibid., p. 248.

6: **"red as fire"**: Ibid., p. 249.

6: **"the agonized cock of the matter"**: Ibid., p. 252.

6: **"My brother was a saint"**: Ibid., p. 253.

6: Having set himself the task: Ibid.

7: From his mother's grief: Ibid.

7: **"I know now I imitated him through life"**: Ibid., p. 252.

7: In fact, Jack's last memory of Gerard: Ibid., p. 259.

8: What particularly disturbed him: Ibid., p. 256.

8: As Jack continued his confession: JK to NC, January 3, 1951, ibid., p. 270.

8: the **"knower"** of his brother's death: Ibid., p. 272.

8: He could recall: Ibid., p. 257.

8: His father—groaning: Ibid.

8: **"a conspiracy between my mother and brother"**: Ibid.

8: **"But my triumph was my loss"**: JK to NC, January 9, 1951, ibid., p. 281.

8: **"Judas was me"**: Ibid., p. 282.

8–9: **Death-haunted childhoods** *through* **"into the graveyard"**: Stephen Edington, *Kerouac's Nashua Connection* (Nashua, N.H.: Edington, 1999), pp. 28–32.

9: **"a snarling pack of cubs"**: JK, *Atop an Underwood: Early Stories and Other Writings*, edited by Paul Marion (New York: Viking, 1999), p. 145.

9: Louis Lévesque married when she was eight: Edington, *Kerouac's Nashua Connection*, pp. 35–38.

10: **"inborn terror"**: Caroline Kerouac to JK, July 22, 1959, Kerouac Archive, box 67.

10: Whenever he looked: JK, *SL*, p. 259.

11: Gabe came apart: Ibid., p. 261.

11: the example of Marie Rose Ferron *through* victim soul: Victor-Lévy Beaulieu, *Jack Kerouac: A chicken-essay*, translated by Sheila Fischman (Toronto: The Coach House Press, 1979), pp. 25–26.

12: **"Gerard est mort!"** JK, *Visions of Gerard* (New York: Penguin, 1991), p. 109.

12: The small boy was certain: JK, *SL*, p. 260.

12: like **"a wave of dark light"**: Ibid., p. 261.

12: He had felt his first doubts: Ibid.

13: **"moan for man"**: JK, *On the Road* (New York: Penguin Books, 2005), p. 303.

13: **"to save me, as it were"**: JK, *SL*, p. 281.

13: **"thin, sallow, weary child"**: Ibid., p. 261.

13: **"the subtle and dishonest soul I am today"**: Ibid., p. 262.

13: **"I bow ... to the mystery"**: Ibid., pp. 261–262.

13: After Gabe learned: Ibid., p. 306.

13: **"nothing there"** at all: JK, *VG*, p. 27.

Jean-Louis Kerouac

14: **"to hide their real sources"**: JK to Yvonne Le Maître, September 8, 1950, *Jack Kerouac: Selected Letters, 1940–1956*, edited by Ann Charters (New York: Viking, 1995), p. 229.

14: **"the silent minority"**: Susan Pinette, "Jack Kerouac: L'Ecriture et l'Identité Franco-Américaine," *Francophonies d'Amerique* 17, 2004, 35–43.

14: **"French Canadian older brother"**: JK, May 19, 1950, *Windblown World: The Journals of Jack Kerouac 1947–1954*, edited by Douglas Brinkley (New York: Penguin Books, 2004), pp. 258–259.

16: **To them, everything about Jack's books:** Ibid.

16: **"To the end"** *through* **Kerouac remained faithful:** Armand Chartier, quoted by Pinette, "Jack Kerouac: L'Ecriture."

16: **Kerouac's novels "including *On the Road"*:** David Plante, *American Ghosts* (Boston: Beacon Press, 2005), pp. 147–148.

16: **"the best documentation we possess"**: Victor-Lévy Beaulieu, *Jack Kerouac: A chicken-essay*, translated by Sheila Fischman (Toronto: The Coach House Press, 1979), p. 27.

16: **"it was enough for him"**: Ibid., pp. 31–32.

17: **In the spring of 1957:** Paul Maher, *Kerouac: His Life and Work* (New York: Taylor Trade Publishing, 2007), pp. 450–451.

18: **"I would not have been able to stick to that"**: Louis Hémon, *Maria Chapdelaine*, translated by William Hume Blake (New York: Modern Library, 1934), p. 51.

17: **"If I should stay in here"**: JK, *Atop an Underwood: Early Stories and Other Writings*, edited by Paul Marion (New York: Viking, 1999), p. 89.

18: **"Saturday avidities of reading"**: JK, *Dr. Sax* (New York: Grove Press, 2007), p. 183.

18: **Louis Hémon was a romantic figure** *through* **as it rounded the bend:** Hugh Eayrs, Introduction to Hémon, *Maria Chapdelaine*.

19: **"beyond what is reasonable and right"**: Hémon, *Maria Chapdelaine*, p. 179.

19: **"pleasing in the sight of God"**: Ibid., p. 181.

19: **"Country folk do not die for love"**: Ibid., p. 175.

19: **Although Hémon was criticized** *through* **"superb carelessness"**: Ibid., Introduction.

20: **"to abide in that Province"**: Ibid., p. 283.

20: **"it was a time of great poverty"**: Beaulieu, *Jack Kerouac*, p. 15.

21: **"Canada brooded in the air"**: JK, *SL*, p. 260.

21: **Believing that factory jobs:** William Moran, *The Belles of New England: The Women of the Textile Mills and the Families Whose Lives They Wove* (New York: St. Martin's Press, 2002), pp. 111–140.

22–35: **In 1912** *through* **white niggers:** Ibid., pp. 171–224.

23: **"many centuries hence"**: Hémon, *Maria Chapdelaine*, p. 283.

23: **For Jack, whose attachment:** "1945 Journals" (1), July 24, 1945–November 6, 1945, Kerouac Archive, box 53, folder 5.

PART TWO: A HALF-AMERICAN BOYHOOD

La Salle de Mort

27: **"a catastrophe of their hearts"**: JK, *The Town and the City* (New York: Harcourt Brace, 1983), p. 239.

27: **"Our house is our corner"** *through* **value as images:** Gaston Bachelard, *The Poetics of Space*, translated by Maria Jolas (Boston: Beacon Press, 1994), pp. 4–6.

28: **"unreal estate"**: Vladimir Nabokov, *Speak Memory* (New York: Vintage Books, 1989), p. 40.

28: **"the horrible dream of the rattling red living room"**: JK, *Dr. Sax* (New York: Grove Press, 2007), p. 5.

28: **"All dreams," he would later write:** JK to NC, January 3, 1951, *Jack Kerouac: Selected Letters, 1940–1956*, edited by Ann Charters (New York: Viking, 1995), p. 268.

28: **"morbid child"** *through* **"not [to] be born"**: JK, *Atop an Underwood: Early Stories and Other Writings*, edited by Paul Marion (New York: Viking, 1999), p. 98.

28: **At twenty-eight, he still recalled:** JK to NC, January 9, 1951, *SL*, p. 283.

29: **"the deliberate beginning of forgetfulness"**: JK to NC, January 3, 1951, ibid., p. 270.

29: *"Les morts sont dans le maison!"* *through* **ironing board:** JK to NC, January 9, 1951, ibid., pp. 283–284.

29: **"that I was alive and could do things on my own":** Ibid., p. 284.

29: **In the void of his brother's absence** *through* **who had done that to him:** JK to NC, January 10, 1951, ibid., pp. 293–294.

30: **Jack would remember riding:** JK, *Visions of Cody* (New York: Penguin Books, 1993), p. 118.

31: **"A completely honest man":** JK, *Lonesome Traveler* (New York: Grove Press, 1960), p. vii.

31: **"Eat or be eaten":** JK, *Visions of Gerard* (New York: Penguin, 1991), p. 21.

33: **At Spotlite Print he watched:** JK, *VC*, p. 265.

33: **"a vigorous Canuckois"** *through* **"Don't call me a cow, dog!"** JK, *VG*, pp. 80–81.

34: **"I had a beautiful childhood":** JK, *LT*, p. vi.

34: **"moments of being":** Virginia Woolf, *Moments of Being* (New York: Harcourt Brace, 1976), p. 70.

34: **"the day I was born"** *through* **to the universe:** JK, *AU*, pp. 182–183.

A Catholic Education

34: **"little black stockings":** JK, *Dr. Sax* (New York: Grove Press, 2007), p. 34.

35: **drip-pipe water from the** *pissoir:* JK, ibid., p. 65.

35: **The long school day** *through* **their students:** Gerard J. Brault, *The French-Canadian Heritage in New England* (Hanover, N.H.: University Press of New England, 1986), pp. 93–96, pp. 47–50.

36: **that lost "French continent":** David Plante, *American Ghosts* (Boston: Beacon Press, 2005), p. 8.

36: **"so much the language of our religion"** *through* **"my English could not fulfill that promise":** Ibid., pp. 58–59.

36: **"I cannot write my native language"** *through* **"French images":** JK to Yvonne Le Maître, September 8, 1950, *Jack Kerouac: Selected Letters, 1940–1956*, edited by Ann Charters (New York: Viking, 1995), p. 228.

37: **"All my knowledge":** Ibid., p. 229.

37: **"AH BWA! AH BWAH!"** JK, *Visions of Gerard* (New York: Penguin Books, 1991), p. 106.

37: **the somber French readers** *through* **unfavorable light:** Brault, *The French-Canadian Heritage,* pp. 93–96.

37: **"The earth is an Indian thing":** JK, *Vanity of Duluoz* (London: Quartet Books, 1975), p. 91.

37: **"little death-haunted"** *through* **"also boredom":** JK, *Visions of Cody* (New York: Penguin Books, 1993), pp. 29–30.

38: **"When I got to public schools":** JK, *Good Blonde & Others* (San Francisco: Grey Fox Press, 1996), p. 93.

38: *"Mon pauvre ti loup":* JK, *VG*, p. 2.

38: **"the tremendous little kick"** *through* **"his wrath was postponed":** JK to NC, January 10, 1951, *SL*, p. 300.

38: **The comeuppance came** *through* **of his innocence:** JK, *Maggie Cassidy* (New York: Penguin Books, 1993), p. 43.

39: **"I was the first crazy person / I'd known":** JK, *Mexico City Blues* (New York: Grove Press, 1981), p. 88.

39: **In the home they moved into:** JK, *Book of Dreams* (San Francisco: City Lights Books, 1961), p. 98.

39: **"to ease my horrors":** JK, *DS*, p. 66.

39: **His father slept in his own "tragic bedroom":** Ibid., p. 102.

40: **"Nosferatu is an evil name":** JK, *GB*, p. 119.

40: **At ten** *through* **in Centralville:** "Ray Smith Novel of Fall 1948," Kerouac Archive, box 24, folder 5.

40–56: **By third grade** *through* **never gave them back:** JK, *Heaven & Other Poems* (Bolinas, Calif.: Gray Fox Press, 1977), p. 51.

40: **At Jack's age** *through* **in Gerard's place:** JK, *VG*, p. 28.

41: **The river fascinated him** *through* **into the sea:** JK, *The Town and the City* (New York: Harcourt Brace, 1983), p. 5.

41: **The two of them** *through* **Leo's son:** JK, *DS*, pp. 64–65; *VC*, p. 26.

41: **One Saturday in May** *through* **relieved fathers:** JK, *T&C*, pp. 26–34.

41: **Due to the deepening of the Depression:** Tom Clark, *Jack Kerouac* (New York: Thunder's Mouth Press, 1984), p. 88.

41: At the cottage on West Street: JK, *DS*, pp. 61–63.

42: All through much of **1931** *through* boxers and wrestlers: JK, "In the Ring," *GB*, pp. 137–144; Clark, *Jack Kerouac*, p. 16.

42: On another trip *through* Wichenden, Maine: JK, *VC*, p. 22.

42–43: There was a lot of the impresario *through* "the poetry of it all": JK, *GB*, pp. 137–141.

Pawtucketville

43–44: Badly needing a second job *through* around midnight: JK, *Dr. Sax* (New York: Grove Press, 2007), p. 40.

44: One boy skated up *through* "in Pawtucketville": Ibid., pp. 41–43.

44: Jack's closest new acquaintance *through* "raving maniacs": Ibid., p. 42.

44: "Everything hurt the guy": Barry Gifford and Lawrence Lee, *Jack's Book* (New York: St. Martin's Press, 1978), p. 9.

45: "Greekly tragic" *through* "worse for it": JK, *DS*, pp. 40–41.

45: Freddie, a thin handsome boy *through* his hand up her skirt: Ibid., pp. 39–40.

45: frequented "her purple doorways": Ibid., p. 70.

45: A fifth boy *through* "life wasn't black": Ibid., pp. 36–38.

45: Jack sang in the choir *through* did not effect a miracle: Ibid., p. 73.

46: That year an unusual idea *through* everything that happened: "Memory Babe," Chapters I–IV, Kerouac Archive, box 52, folder 6.

46: "It's a vast ethereal movie": JK, *Visions of Gerard* (New York: Penguin Books, 1991), p. 127.

46: Deeply depressed *through* so "cruel": Diary #6, "Mexico 1957 Summer," August 1957, Kerouac Archive, box 56, folder 6.

46: It seems metaphorically appropriate: JK, *DS*, pp. 63, 122.

46–47: As he walked across it *through* stared at nothing: Ibid., pp. 127–129.

47: He seems to have had *through* "fantasies of life": Ibid., p. 148.

47: Each day *through* afford to buy them: "Memory Babe."

47: At Bartlett, he felt so embarrassed *through* armload of books: Tom Clark, *Jack Kerouac* (New York: Thunder's Mouth Press, 1984), p. 21.

47–48: He read in that blind, indiscriminate way *through* The Last of the Mohicans: Ibid.

48: But he still stopped *through* "the penny after": "Memory Babe."

49: "those goddamn thrilling novels": JK, *DS*, p. 50.

49: "Those dime novels" *through* "sanctumed laugh": JK, *Atop an Underwood: Early Stories and Other Writings,* edited by Paul Marion (New York: Viking, 1999), p. 107.

49: The novel Jack wrote at eleven: JK, *Visions of Cody* (New York: Penguin Books, 1993), p. 267.

49: One provider of new material *through* every dollar: JK, *DS*, p. 97.

50: According to Jack's first diary *through* Mr. Micawber: Holograph notebook, childhood diary, 1934–1935, Kerouac Archive, box 56.

51: He was partial *through* belonged to his brother: "Memory Babe."

51: To make the races *through* put down: JK, *DS*, pp. 101, 84–85, 90–91.

51: the game had been born: JK, *VC*, p. 27.

51: But The Turf: JK, *DS*, pp. 75–76.

Football Hero

51–52: In November **1935** *through* "*mon maudit crève faim*": JK, *Vanity of Duluoz* (London: Quartet Books, 1975), p. 4.

52: All that year *through* real worlds together: JK, *Dr. Sax* (New York: Grove Press, 2007), pp. 52–54.

52–53: Over the next few years *through* "innocent ambition": JK, *VD*, pp. 7–8.

53: Until Jack was twelve: Barry Miles, *Jack Kerouac: King of the Beats* (New York: Henry Holt, 1998), p. 12.

53: On the slightest pretext *through* in his direction: JK, *DS*, p. 84.

53–54: In Jack's memories *through* "smiling, nice": Ibid.

54: In a 1954 poem: JK, *Mexico City Blues* (New York: Grove Press, 1981), p. 149.

54: By his late teens: Barry Gifford and Lawrence Lee, *Jack's Book* (New York: St. Martin's Press, 1978), p. 9.

54: On March **12, 1936** *through* "gloomy newsreel of 1930's": JK, *DS*, p. 164.

54: Early the next day *through* to jump off: Ibid., pp. 165–170.

54–55: It took a while *through* Sarah Avenue: Ibid., pp. 172–175.

55: Their rundown building *through* "wrinkly tar sidewalk": Ibid., p. 13.

55–56: Not long after the flood *through* didn't mind disappointments: Miles, *Jack Kerouac*, p. 21.

56: But when he told his father: JK, *Visions of Gerard* (New York: Penguin Books, 1991), p 49.

56: It would no longer be the game *through* "white ambitions": *Windblown World: The Journals of Jack Kerouac 1947–1954*, edited by Douglas Brinkley (New York: Penguin Books, 2004), p. 215.

56–57: With the Dracut Tigers *through* on the bench: JK, *VD*, pp. 8–9.

57: "Stinktown on the Merrimack": Ibid., p. 8.

57: Jack's chance *through* end of the game: Ibid., p. 9.

57: "No one could run as hard": Charles E. Jarvis, *Visions of Kerouac* (Lowell, Mass.: Ithaca Press, 1974), p. 43.

57–58: At sixteen *through* for the game: JK, *Atop an Underwood: Early Stories and Other Writings*, edited by Paul Marion (New York: Viking, 1999), pp. 14–16.

58: Because the two teams were well matched: JK, *VD*, p. 13.

59: When a bus *through* "silence and praise": JK, *The Town and the City* (New York: Harcourt Brace, 1983), p. 82.

59–60: The choice should have been his *through* take Jack with him: JK, *VD*, pp. 16–17.

60: Gabe had another motive: Ibid., p. 16.

60: Jack deferred his decision: Ibid.

First Love

61: The exception that spring was English *through* about himself: JK, *Vanity of Duluoz* (London: Quartet Books, 1975), p. 15.

61: "As for myself": *Faust*, translated by Barker Fairley, in *Johann Wolfgang von Goethe: Selected Works* (New York: Everyman's Library, 1999), p. 766.

61: "all that is given to humanity": Ibid., p. 789.

62: "the funniest guy in the world": JK to JCH, June 24, 1949, *Jack Kerouac: Selected Letters, 1940–1956*, edited by Ann Charters (New York: Viking, 1995), p. 198.

62: "my mother was sick": JK, *Atop an Underwood: Early Stories and Other Writings*, edited by Paul Marion (New York: Viking, 1999), p. 20.

62: After a sordid sexual encounter: George J. Apostolos to JK, 1939, Kerouac Archive, box 63, folder 9.

62: "roman candles": JK, *On the Road* (New York: Penguin Books, 2005), p. 6.

62: He later relished *through* eyes popping: JK to JCH, June 24, 1949, *SL*, p. 198.

63: "the terror and death": JK, *AU*, p. 38.

63–64: He had met her *through* "devourous lips": JK, *Mexico City Blues* (New York: Grove Press, 1981), pp. 27–29.

64: G.J. looked upon girls: Apostolos to JK, 1939.

64: For the next eight months *through* both of them: JK, *MC*, p. 37.

64: "that queer era": JK, *Good Blonde & Others* (San Francisco: Grey Fox Press, 1996), p. 99.

64–65: As insurance *through* hurt him: Mary Carney to JK, undated 1939, Kerouac Archive, box 64, folder 2.

65: "listened in the silence": JK, *MC*, p. 43.

65: Mary suggested one obvious way *through* "unknown suicides of weddings and honeymoons": Ibid., p. 150.

65: Meanwhile Gabe *through* "no good": Ibid., p. 47.

65: "Don't let no broad get you": Ibid., p. 51.

66: Decades later *through* "his imagination": Barry Gifford and Lawrence Lee, *Jack's Book* (New York: St. Martin's Press, 1978), pp. 15–16.

66: "She was a wench": JK to John MacDonald, 1943, *SL*, p. 57.

66: "How I loved": JK to JCH, October 12, 1952, *SL*, p. 382.

66: "Never dreaming was I": JK, *MC*, p. 26.

67: "There was something": Gifford and Lee, *Jack's Book*, p. 15.

67: a very different person after the accident: "1951/Journals/More Notes," November 12–November 13, 1951, August 28, 1951–November 25, 1951, Kerouac Archive, box 55, folder 6.

67: "Now Jack's going": Gifford and Lee, *Jack's Book*, p. 18.

PART THREE: AN UPROOTING

Manhattan

71: **"That black sweater":** JK to Joyce Glassman, January 13, 1958, Joyce Johnson and JK, *Door Wide Open* (New York: Viking, 2001), p. 119.

71–72: **Early the following morning** *through* **for the time being:** "Journal, Fall, 1939," September 21–25, Kerouac Archive, box 5, folder 10.

73: **To give the team a fighting chance:** JK, *VD*, p. 20.

73: **In fact, he had enough empathy:** Ibid.

73: **Leo despised President Roosevelt:** Leo Kerouac to JK, 1940–1943, Kerouac Archive, box 68, folder 9.

73: **The novelist Thomas Wolfe** *through* **blame him a bit:** Elizabeth Nowell, *Thomas Wolfe* (Garden City, N.Y.: Doubleday, 1966), pp. 409–410.

73: **His Uncle Nick** *through* **Father Charles Coughlin:** JK, *VD*, p. 18.

74: **his weekly diatribes** *through* **young street toughs:** Richard Sanders, "Father Charles Coughlin," http://coat.ncf.ca/our_magazine/links/53/coughlin.html.

74: **"Incunabular Milton Berles":** JK, *VD*, p. 37.

74: **The chief wit Eddie Gilbert** *through* **fleeing to Brazil:** JK, *Good Blonde & Others* (San Francisco: Grey Fox Press, 1996), pp. 78, 99.

74: **He wasn't much of a student:** JK, *VD*, p. 21.

75: **Jack's closest friend:** Ibid., p. 23.

75: **On the football team:** Ibid., p. 25.

75: **had anything against Jews:** Ibid., p. 29.

75: **He wrestled with such envious feelings:** Ibid., p. 22.

76: **At Pete Gordon's** *through* **"a Spartan":** Ibid.

76: **Jack kept G.J. informed:** Barry Gifford and Lawrence Lee, *Jack's Book* (New York: St. Martin's Press, 1978), p. 18.

76: **One letter of Jack's** *through* **very sensitive.** George J. Apostolos to JK, November 25, 1939, 1939–1962, fall 1939, Kerouac Archive, box 63, folder 9.

76–77: **Leo Kerouac had come down** *through* **high roller:** JK, *VD*, pp. 32–33.

77: **The street seemed to him like one vast "room":** JK, *Lonesome Traveler* (New York: Grove Press, 1960), p. 111.

77: **"Outside in the street":** JK, *Atop an Underwood: Early Stories and Other Writings*, edited by Paul Marion (New York: Viking, 1999), p. 61.

77: **In the history of jazz** *through* **"a revolution in culture":** Ralph Ellison, "Minton's," in *Reading Jazz*, edited by Robert Gottlieb (New York: Vintage Books, 1996), p. 546.

77: **the "Depression began to crack":** JK, *GB*, p. 117.

77–78: **The swing bands** *through* **"white musicians":** Ellison, *Reading Jazz*, pp. 553–554.

78: **"You only have so many notes":** Dizzy Gillespie, "Minton's Playhouse," *Reading Jazz*, p. 561.

78: **For Seymour Wyse** *through* **in his head:** JK, *GB*, p. 115.

78: **"Count Basie's swing arrangements":** JK, *AU*, p. 21.

79: **"real jazz" was:** JK, "Real Solid Drop Beat Riffs, *Horace Mann Record*, quoted in Tom Clark, *Jack Kerouac* (New York: Thunder's Mouth Press, 1984), p. 41.

79: **He felt he was surrounded** *through* **made G.J. laugh hysterically:** George J. Apostolos to JK.

79–80: **In early November** *through* **real "heartbreaker":** Mary Carney to JK, November 1939, Kerouac Archive, box 54, folder 2; JK, *Mexico City Blues* (New York: Grove Press, 1981), pp. 172–173.

80: **He hitchhiked home:** JK, *MC*, pp. 173–174.

80: **the attraction of Mary's "physical assets":** George J. Apostolos to JK, November 25, 1939.

80: **The first woman he ever slept with:** JK, *MC*, p. 176.

81: **because of his "manly beauty":** George J. Apostolos to Jack Kerouac, fall 1939.

81: **What broke up Jack's relationship:** JK, *MC*, pp. 179–182.

81: **When the weekend was over:** Ibid., p. 187.

81: **At the Horace Mann graduation exercises:** JK, *VD*, pp. 39–40.

82: **When he went to a reunion:** JK, *GB*, p. 100.

82: Heading back to Lowell: JK, *AU*, p. 59.
82: That summer, however: JK, *VD*, p. 41.

The Summer of Sebastian

83: A writer can have, ultimately, one of two styles: William Saroyan, *The Daring Young Man on the Flying Trapeze* (New York: New Directions, 1997), p. 12.
83: The precepts he offered: Ibid., pp. 10–13.
84: In the journal: "The Journal of an Egotist," fall–winter 1940, Kerouac Archive, box 4, folder 3.
84: "Une Veille de Noel": "Une Veille de Noel," 1939, *The Horace Mann Quarterly*, Summer, 1940, Kerouac Archive, box 5, folder 16.
85: For eighteen-year-old Sebastian: JK, *Vanity of Duluoz* (London: Quartet Books, 1975), pp. 42–44.
86: With his "flashing dark eyes": JK, *The Town and the City* (New York: Harcourt Brace, 1983), p. 132.
86: Jack, who would marry: Ibid., p. 131.
86: He had been marked as a target: Charles E. Jarvis, *Visions of Kerouac* (Lowell, Mass.: Ithaca Press, 1974), p. 55.
87: Sebastian had never forgotten him: JK, *VD*, p. 42.
87: "the brotherhood of man": Saroyan, *The Daring Young Man*, p. 32.
87–88: "that crazy bastart" *through* "poetry and truth": JK, *T&C*, pp. 132–134.
88: "a comrade, a confidante": Ibid., p. 131.
88: "Without Gerard what would have happened to Ti Jean?" JK, *Visions of Gerard* (New York: Penguin Books, 1991), p. 116.
88: Reunited with his Pawtucketville gang: JK, *VD*, p. 44.
88: The first time Jack and his friends: Ibid., p. 46.
89: During one night of drinking: Gerard Nicosia, *Memory Babe* (Berkeley: University of California Press, 1994), p. 73.
89: "The Spirit of '14": JK, *Atop an Underwood: Early Stories and Other Writings*, edited by Paul Marion (New York: Viking, 1999), pp. 46–48.
89: In "We Thronged": Ibid., pp. 33–34.
90: Before he left for Columbia. Ibid., pp. 24–40.
90: "I try to think hard and imagine myself nothing": Ibid., p. 26.
90: He went back to the rose-covered cottage: Ibid., p. 25.

Columbia

91: "At 18, I suddenly discovered": JK, *Atop an Underwood: Early Stories and Other Writings*, edited by Paul Marion (New York: Viking, 1999), p. 118.
91: His rebellion began: JK, *Vanity of Duluoz* (London: Quartet Books, 1975), pp. 48–50.
92: Lou Little put him into the first half: Ibid., pp. 50–53.
92: the campus hero he'd longed to be: Ibid., p. 55.
92: *Mon pitou*: Gabrielle Kerouac to JK, 1939–1941, September 1940–November 1940, Kerouac Archive, box 67, folder 1.
92: Leo had just lost another job: Leo Kerouac to JK, October 21, 1940, 1940–1943, Kerouac Archive, box 68, folder 9.
93: he went back to the journal: "The Journal of an Egotist," October 12, 1940, fall–winter 1940, Kerouac Archive, box 4, folder 3.
93: "O lost, and by the wind grieved": Thomas Wolfe, *Look Homeward Angel*, epigraph (New York: Scribner, 2000).
93: Jubilant the day he broke his record: Elizabeth Nowell, *Thomas Wolfe* (Garden City, N.Y.: Doubleday, 1966), p. 300.
94: he sequestered himself: Ibid., p. 194.
94: "in a more than ordinary degree": Ibid., p. 169.
94: "see it instantly just the way it was": Ibid.
94: "almost literally autobiographical": Ibid., p. xxii.
94: "as a life completely digested in my spirit": Ibid., p.112.
94: "Fiction is not fact": Ibid., p. 143.

95: **"put in more long, sober, grueling hours":** Ibid., p. 12.

95: **On November 27, 1940:** "Journal of an Egotist."

97: **He went home for Christmas:** JK, *VD,* p. 57.

97: **When she mentioned this to their parents:** Caroline Kerouac to JK, February 1, 1941, 1940–1961, *Jack Kerouac: Selected Letters, 1940–1956,* edited by Ann Charters (New York: Viking, 1995).

97: **When they were growing up together:** "Memory Babe," Chapters I-IV, Kerouac Archive, box 52, folder 6.

97: **Ten years later:** JK, *Book of Dreams* (San Francisco: City Lights Books, 1961), pp. 31–32.

97: **What he really liked best about the frat house:** JK, *VD,* p. 58.

98: **Although Jack was considered very popular:** Ibid., p. 57.

98: **Ellis Amburn makes much of an incident:** Ellis Amburn, *Subterranean Kerouac* (New York: St. Martin's Press, 1999), p. 54.

98: **He alluded to the gay-bashing incident:** JK, *The Subterraneans* (New York: Grove Press, 1958), pp. 7–8.

98: **That spring** *through* **Jack explored his complicated feelings:** JK, *AU,* pp. 76–77.

99: **In early June, Jack hitchhiked back to Lowell:** JK, *VD,* pp. 61–62.

99: **now he was calling himself a poet:** JK, *AU,* pp. 122–123.

99: **His latest literary influence was Albert Halper:** Ibid., 82–83.

99: **It may have been Sebastian:** SS to JK, January 20, 1940, Kerouac Archive, box 71, folder 28.

100: **The deep rapport between the two youths:** Ibid., October 1940.

100: **a feeling of "substance":** "Jack Kerouac:—Diary—beginning June 1, 1941," Kerouac Archive, box 6, folder 2.

100: **In** *Vanity of Duluoz:* JK, *VD,* p. 63.

101: **In** *The Town and the City:* JK, *The Town and the City* (New York: Harcourt Brace, 1983), p. 221.

101: **when they went off alone to wander around Boston:** JK, *VD,* p. 63.

101: **his "Rabelaisian" humor:** "Jack Kerouac:—Diary—beginning June 1, 1941."

102: **Totally drunk, Jack dived:** JK, *VD,* p. 62.

102: **"everything exploded":** Joyce Johnson and JK, *Door Wide Open: A Beat Love Affair in Letters, 1957–1958* (New York: Viking, 2001), p. 40.

102: **In a piece he wrote in August:** JK, *AU,* p. 108–111.

102: **"In his effort to explore his experience":** Thomas Wolfe, *You Can't Go Home Again* (New York: Perennial Books, 1998), p. 389.

103: **In one 1941 piece:** JK, *AU,* p. 114.

103: **Apart from a reference:** "Journal—(stupid)," November 26–December 15, 1941, Kerouac Archive, box 6, folder 7.

104: **A day spent shoveling gooey dough:** JK, "The Birth of a Socialist," *AU,* pp. 85–92.

104: **the prospect of resuming his life as a "boorish" Ivy League college boy:** "Jack Kerouac:—Diary—beginning June 1, 1941."

104: **He put all his sadness:** JK, *AU,* pp. 105–106.

105: **"Is that man crazy?"** JK, *VD,* p. 66.

105: **Just the sight of that "hole":** JK to Caroline Kerouac, late summer 1941, *SL,* pp. 12–15.

105: **Jack escaped from the tension:** Ibid., p. 14.

The Escape

105: **Jack arrived at Columbia a day late:** JK, *Vanity of Duluoz* (London: Quartet Books, 1975), pp. 69–70.

106: **He killed a day wandering blindly around the capital:** Typescript short stories and story fragments, "Washington in 1941," Kerouac Archive, box 32, folder 3.

106: **He was "afraid to go home":** JK to SS, mid-September 1941, *Jack Kerouac: Selected Letters, 1940–1956,* edited by Ann Charters (New York: Viking, 1995), p. 16.

107: **He also skirted around the subject:** JK, *VD,* p. 71.

107: **she's "gaily" frying the bacon:** Ibid., p. 72.

107: **For Leo, this was evidently the last straw:** Ibid.

107: **Then he bolted for New York:** JK to SS, late September 1941, *SL,* p. 17.

108: **"All things on earth point home in old October:** Thomas Wolfe, *Of Time and the River* (New York: Scribners, 1935), pp. 332–333.

108: "Everyone goes home in October": JK, *On the Road* (New York: Penguin Books, 2005), p. 103.

108: "Step on the gas": JK, *Atop an Underwood: Early Stories and Other Writings*, edited by Paul Marion (New York: Viking, 1999), p. 143.

108: Hartford was jumping at night: Ibid., p. 144.

108: "I am happy": Ibid., p. 165.

108: One night he wrote himself a meal: Ibid., pp. 156–157.

109: "Man, but I was a Breton that day!": Ibid., p. 141.

109: "The language called Canadian French": Ibid., p. 151.

109: I am my mother's son: Ibid., p. 162.

109: driving his stuff "home, Americanwise": Ibid., pp. 153–154.

109: On November 13, he had to give the rented typewriter back: Ibid., pp. 167–168.

110: there were brief comments from three readers at *Esquire*: Ibid., p. 104.

110: Thanksgiving promised to be grim: JK, *VD*, pp. 74–75.

111: The sojourn in Hartford: Ibid., p. 76.

111: For Jack, the trip back to Lowell: Ibid., p. 77.

111: Worst of all was Jack's feeling: Ibid., pp. 77–78.

111: As he emerged from the theater: JK, *AU*, pp. 170–171.

111: He put on his overcoat: Ibid., pp. 171–176.

112: As he waited to take the examination: JK, *VD*, pp. 79–80.

112: At nineteen, he was planning: "1944 'Galloway' Novel, 'Michael Daoulas—' a later re-doing of 'Vanity of Duluoz' of '42," Kerouac Archive, box 22, folder 2.

114: He seemed out to prove: Gerard Nicosia, *Memory Babe* (Berkeley: University of California Press, 1994), pp. 93–94; JK, *VD*, pp. 79–81.

114: Since January, he had been getting letters from G.J.: George J. Apostolos to JK, 1943, Kerouac Archive, box 63, folder 13.

115: Leo fell into a rage: JK, *VD*, pp. 83–84.

115: Jack resolved the situation by leaving: Ibid., pp. 84–85.

116: In July, after his return to Lowell: JK to Norma Blickfelt, July 15, 1942, *SL*, pp. 21–22.

116: In Lowell, Sebastian was crying his eyes out: SS to JK, April 1942, February 1942–December, 1942, Kerouac Archive, box 71, folder 31.

117: He evidently told his father about his sexual exploits: Leo Kerouac to JK, spring 1942, 1940–1943, Kerouac Archive, box 68, folder 9.

117: As he dreamily began heading toward New Orleans: *SL*, pp. 21–22.

117: In tears, he addressed Billy's ghost: "To a soldier killed in Bataan," Kerouac Archive, box 7, folder 8.

117: A second version was much closer to the bone: "Letter to Bill," Kerouac Archive, box 5, folder 74.

118: For two months Jack marked time: : JK, *The Town and the City* (New York: Harcourt Brace, 1983), p. 295.

118: A chance meeting with a merchant seaman: *SL*, p. 22.

118: When Leo heard about Jack's latest reckless plan: Leo Kerouac to JK, July 1, 1942, 1940–1943.

118: "What a strange call I hear from the sea": *SL*, pp. 22–23.

119: "like a curly-haired goatsherd": JK, *VD*, p. 88.

PART FOUR: THE WAR

At Sea

123: In the diary Jack kept until August 12: JK, *Vanity of Duluoz* (London: Quartet Books, 1975), p. 124.

123: Asking himself how he felt about death: "Voyage to Greenland/1942/Growing Pains or a Monument to Adolescence," Kerouac Archive, box 47, folder 10.

124: The one who made the strongest impression on him was Pat Reel: Ibid.

124: He felt little kinship: JK, *VD*, p. 90.

124: "rough seamen who saw my child's soul": JK, *Book of Dreams* (San Francisco: City Lights Books, 1961), p. 47.

124: **In late September, he wrote to Sebastian:** JK to SS, September 20, 1942, *Jack Kerouac: Selected Letters, 1940–1956*, edited by Ann Charters (New York: Viking, 1995), p. 28.

124: **The worst part of being at sea:** JK, *VD*, p. 101.

124: **There was a heavyset cook, known as Chef:** "Voyage to Greenland."

125: **"the fantastic North of men's souls":** JK, *The Town and the City* (New York: Harcourt Brace, 1983), pp. 304–305.

125: **He kept thinking of a phrase of Wolfe's:** JK, *VD*, p. 101.

125: **Jack wrote to Norma Blickfelt again:** JK to Norma Blickfelt, August 25, 1942, *SL*, pp. 26–28.

126. **He didn't realize:** Norma Blickfelt to JK, January 7, 1943, Kerouac Archive, box 63, folder 39.

126: **Although only thirteen men actually died:** JK, *VD*, p. 141.

126: **Peter Martin actually witnesses the sinking:** JK, *T&C*, p. 308.

126: **Jack heard depth charges being fired:** JK, *VD*, p. 134.

127: **Downing all the alcohol they could hold:** Ibid., p. 142.

128: **The letter Jack had written him in September:** JK to SS, September 26, 1942, *SL*, p. 29.

128: **"one huge debauchery":** JK to SS, November 1942, *SL*, p. 31.

129: **"but it would only be in homage to Billy Chandler":** Ibid.

129: **without any particular encouragement from Edie:** Edie Parker, *You'll Be Okay* (San Francisco: City Lights Books, 2007), p. 57.

129: **"Well, he might as well have put an ice cream in my hand":** Ibid., p. 66.

129: **the unruly black cowlick:** Ibid., p. 61.

129: **"squirrel-like" teeth:** Holograph draft novel, untitled, 1956, Kerouac Archive, box 18, folder 21.

129. **Soon after his return to Columbia, Jack had run into Edie:** Ibid.

130: **Jack wrote her a "Shakespearean" love letter:** Parker, *YBO*, p. 65.

130: **The loner Wesley Martin:** JK, *Atop an Underwood: Early Stories and Other Writings*, edited by Paul Marion (New York: Viking, 1999), pp. 212, 220.

131: **After Jack read the novel Bill was working on:** JK to Bill Ryan, January 10, 1943, *SL*, p. 35.

131: **Jack still considered himself a Wolfean:** Ibid., p. 37.

131: **Reading Alfred Kazin's mostly very admiring essay:** Alfred Kazin, *On Native Grounds* (New York: Harcourt Brace, 1995), pp. 479–480.

131: **"I loathe critics":** JK to SS, February 1943, *SL*, p. 42.

132: **When Jack heard:** Ibid., p. 39.

132: **"He is not my friend":** JK to SS, February 16, 1943, Kerouac Archive, box 75.

132: **Announcing to Sebastian:** JK to SS, early March 1943, *SL*, p. 44.

132: **Hoping to find brotherhood:** SS to JK, 1943, Kerouac Archive, box 71, folder 36.

133: **But the outsider's position:** SS to JK, March 15, 1943, *SL*, p. 46.

133: **"I hope this will convince you":** JK to SS, March 15, 1943, *SL*, p. 47.

133: **He was about to be sent to boot camp:** JK, *VD*, p. 153.

133: **Jack continued his political and philosophical argument:** JK to SS, March 25, 1943, *SL*, pp. 50–54.

134: **Assigned to do an inspection:** Ibid., p. 54.

134: **By March 30, Jack was under observation:** JK, *VD*, p. 156.

134: **The discovery that he had the highest IQ:** Ibid., p. 157.

134–35: **The night before he left for Newport:** Holograph fragment, notes and sketches, March 24, 1943, March–October, 1943, Kerouac Archive, box 8, folder 21.

135: **He had written Sebastian:** JK to SS, March 25, 1943, Kerouac Archive, box 75, folder 20.

135: **Jack admitted to himself that he had half played along:** Holograph fragment, March 24, 1943.

135: **In Newport, a Dr. Conrad Tully submitted a diagnosis:** Paul Maher, *Kerouac: His Life and Work* (New York: Taylor Trade Publishing, 2007), p. 110.

135: **Jack himself was having doubts:** JK to George J. Apostolos, April 7, 1943, *SL*, pp. 60–61.

136: **Bill Hubbard had bummed his way around the United States:** JK, *AU*, p. 206.

136: **Bill said he'd find a way to get them out:** Holograph draft novel, 1956.

136: **Jack had visitors in Newport that spring:** JK, *VD*, p. 163.

136: **Then at the beginning of May came Sebastian:** Ibid., p. 165.

137: **From a small barred window in Bethesda:** Ibid., p. 166.

137: **"Dostoevsky was one of ourselves":** JK to SS; SS to JK, May 26, 1943, *SL*, p. 65.

137: **"You are not a Slav":** SS to JK, May 26, 1943, *SL*, pp. 65–69.

Edie Parker

138: **After being interviewed by a Dr. Rosenburg:** JK, *Vanity of Duluoz* (London: Quartet Books, 1975), pp. 166–167.

138: **Years later, Jack had some regrets:** Ibid., p. 171.

139: **The Kerouacs had made a decisive break:** Holograph draft novel, untitled, 1956, Kerouac Archive, box 18, folder 21.

139: **they were getting along in a companionable way:** JK, *VD*, p. 173.

139: **Jack hated Ozone Park on sight:** Holograph draft novel, 1956.

140: **In Lowell that winter:** Margaret Coffey to JK, Collection of Love Letters to Jack Kerouac (1), 1947–1949, Kerouac Archive, box 73, folder 11.

140: **He could actually envision:** JK to SS, February 1943, *Jack Kerouac: Selected Letters, 1940–1956,* edited by Ann Charters (New York: Viking, 1995), p. 41.

140: **A doorman told him:** Edie Parker, *You'll Be Okay* (San Francisco: City Lights Books, 2007), pp. 67–68.

140: **She had written him a letter:** Ibid.

141: **He opened that handwritten manuscript:** Holograph draft novel, 1956; JK, *VD*, p. 174.

142: **Joan, who was studying journalism:** Holograph notebook [The/Spiral], "1945," Kerouac Archive, box 53, folder 4.

142: **"If I read a book at all":** Parker, *YBO*, p. 65.

143: **"As a child," Edie wrote:** Ibid., p. 41.

143: **This time Jack had signed on as an ordinary deckhand:** JK, *VD*, pp. 133–140.

144: **"strangely enough" he missed her:** JK to Edie Parker, September 18, 1943, *SL*, pp. 70–71.

144: **The British fiction Jack read during the voyage:** Ibid.

144: **He wandered into an exhibit of avant-garde art:** JK, *VD*, pp. 145–146.

144: **Jack had one of those epiphanies:** Ibid., p. 195.

145: **From that time on:** JK, *Visions of Cody* (New York: Penguin Books, 1993), Foreword.

145: **Like his unfinished *Vanity of Duluoz*:** Holograph "Liverpool Testament '43," Kerouac Archive, box 47, folder 3.

145: **At twenty-two, Jack felt ready to dedicate himself:** Holograph fragment, notes and sketches, August 1943, March–October 1943, Kerouac Archive, box 8, folder 21.

145: **"That was the time":** "1951/Journals/More Notes," August 28, 1951–November 25, 1951, Kerouac Archive, box 55, folder 6.

146: **the "crazy happy" childlike girl:** JK, *The Town and the City* (New York: Harcourt Brace, 1983), p. 388.

146: **Standing at the bar:** Robin D. G. Kelley, *Thelonious Monk: The Life and Times of an American Original* (New York: Free Press, 2009), pp. 70–71.

146: **At first Jack didn't know what to make of the new sounds:** JK, *Good Blonde & Others* (San Francisco: Grey Fox Press, 1996), p. 114.

147: **"Well, mind is bebop":** AG, *Spontaneous Mind* (New York: Harper, 2002), p. 373.

147: **On one of Newman's historic recordings:** Kelley, *Thelonious Monk*, p. 72.

148: **Jack had a grudge against the rich:** "1943–?44 Journals," Kerouac Archive, box 53, folder 2.

148–49: **He even fantasized to Edie about returning there:** Parker, *YBO*, pp. 58–65.

149: **So many from his generation:** JK, *T&C*, p. 359.

149: **a "strange neargrief":** Ibid.

149: **"a broken circuit":** JCH, *Nothing More to Declare* (New York: E. P. Dutton, 1967).

149: **Sometimes he thought he actually was schizoid:** "1943–?44 Journals."

150: **He began it in English:** JK to SS, February 12, 1944, *SL*, p. 75.

151: **Jack later remembered little about this trip:** "1943–?44 Journals."

PART FIVE: THE LIBERTINE CIRCLE

The Season of Lucien

155: **In a sea of necktied male students:** Author interview with Ed Gold, one of Carr's classmates.

155: **The "sole imperative" of the artist:** AG, *The Book of Martyrdom and Artifice: First Journals and Poems 1937–1952* (New York: Da Capo Press, 2006), pp. 39–41.

155: **At her first sight of him, she became "spellbound"**: Edie Parker, *You'll Be Okay* (San Francisco: City Lights Books, 2007), pp. 118–119.

156: **One night Lucien took Edie**: Ibid., p. 123.

156: **Jack thought Lucien sounded like "a mischievous little prick"**: JK, *Vanity of Duluoz* (London: Quartet Books, 1975), p. 153.

156: **"Shakespeare reborn almost"**: Ibid., p. 154.

156: **One song Lucien often sang**: AG, *BMA*, p. 26.

157: **At first Jack regarded**: JK, *VD*, p. 202.

157: **He noticed that he too was somewhat obsessed**: Ibid., p. 220.

158: **Rimbaud had an electrifying effect on Allen**: Barry Miles, *Ginsberg* (New York: Harper Perennial, 1990), p. 43.

158: **reaching "the hearts of others"**: AG, *BMA*, p. 43.

158: **Amused by Allen's naïveté**: Miles, *Ginsberg*, p. 41.

159: **What Allen responded to immediately**: Barry Gifford and Lawrence Lee, *Jack's Book* (New York: St. Martin's Press, 1978), p. 36.

159: **In May, when he met Jack**: Ibid., p. 35.

159: **"Aww, where's my food?"** JK, *VD*, p. 218.

159: **When Allen told him he intended to become a labor lawyer**: AG, *Allen Verbatim: Lectures on Poetry, Politics, Consciousness*, edited by Gordon Ball (New York: McGraw-Hill, 1973), p. 103.

159: **"We were talking"**: Gifford and Lee, *Jack's Book*, p. 35.

160: **"I suddenly realized that my own soul and his"**: AG, *Allen Verbatim*, p. 103.

160: **"into an area of intimate feelings"**: Ibid., p. 111.

160: **to make his own appraisal of this rough-trade**: JK, *VD*, p. 156.

160: **a memorable lunch with Lucien and Kammerer**: Ibid., p. 158.

160: **Jack and Allen decided to "pay him a formal visit"**: Gifford and Lee, *Jack's Book*, p. 36.

161: **"original mind"**: Ibid.

161: **"flaming youth"**: JK, *VD*, p. 215.

161: **It wasn't long before the apartment**: "I Wish I Were You (1945) Philip Tourian story," Kerouac Archive, box 15, folder 19.

162: **Finding the two of them entwined**: JK, *VD*, p. 166.

162: **on one occasion, Jack became violently ill**: Bill Morgan, *I Celebrate Myself: The Somewhat Private Life of Allen Ginsberg* (New York: Viking, 2006), p. 47.

162: **Edie didn't participate much**: Parker, *YBO*, p. 160.

162: **His mother would have been horrified**: JK and WSB, *And the Hippos Were Boiled in Their Tanks* (New York: Grove Press, 2008), p. 57.

162: **To her, the whole idea now seemed "truncated"**: "1943–?44 Journals," December 27, 1943, Kerouac Archive, box 53, folder 2.

163: **Lucien's latest thoughts were often the focus of attention**: "I Wish I Were You."

163: **Lucien believed he had progressed**: JK to AG, September 1944, *Jack Kerouac and Allen Ginsberg: The Letters* (New York: Viking, 2010), p. 5.

163: **the "pre-ultimate" period**: JK and WSB, *And the Hippos*, p. 41.

163: **"to actualize the fullest possibilities of the All-Soul"**: *Jack Kerouac: Selected Letters, 1940–1956*, edited by Ann Charters (New York: Viking, 1995), p. 68.

163: **"Why is the perfect lover always jealous?"**: AG, *BMA*, p. 46.

164: **One afternoon Burroughs accompanied Kammerer**: JK, *VD*, p. 166.

164: **"I should have to commit suicide"**: AG, *BMA*, p. 51.

164: **"There was a kid I was in love with"**: AG, *Spontaneous Mind* (New York: Harper, 2002), p. 56.

164: **Trying to look at Lucien**: AG, *BMA*, p. 48.

165: **Lucien had recently confided to Allen**: Ibid., p. 50.

165: **In July, the two of them came up with a secret plan**: JK, *VD*, p. 168.

165: **It wasn't long before Kammerer found out**: Ibid., p. 169.

165: **On the night of August 11**: Ibid., p. 170.

165: **On August 12, too frightened to sleep in his room**: AG, *BMA*, p. 59.

166: **That evening Lucien had been looking for Allen**: Ibid., p. 58.

166: **As if he had not inflicted sufficient pain**: Ibid., p. 59.

166: **When they'd checked in at the National Maritime Union**: JK, *VD*, pp. 171–173.

167: **Kammerer was in a particularly black mood**: AG, *BMA*, pp. 60–61.

168: Or perhaps what happened between them: Ibid., p. 114.

168: "Well, I disposed of the old man": JK, *VD*, p. 217.

168: Still carrying Kammerer's glasses: Ibid., p. 175.

168: Years later, in *Vanity of Duluoz*: Ibid., p. 176.

169: They buried the glasses: Ibid., pp. 177–178.

169: As he wrote two years later: JK and WSB, *And the Hippos*, p. 178.

Birth of a Symbolist

170: "young punk": JK, *Vanity of Duluoz* (London: Quartet Books, 1975), pp. 170–171.

170: "people like us": Caroline Kerouac to JK, 1944, Kerouac Archive, box 67, folder 1.

171: "Heterosexuality all the way": JK, *VD*, pp. 238–239.

171: "unimaginable spiritual torment": Ibid., p. 244.

171: "Are you nuts?": Edie Parker, *You'll Be Okay* (San Francisco: City Lights Books, 2007), pp. 146–149.

172: "How in the world can I do that?": Ibid., p. 154.

172: "a jailhouse wedding": Ibid., p. 173.

172: "to make my mind as you want": Edie (Edith) Parker to JK, 1944–1969, August 1944, Kerouac Archive, box 71, folder 6.

172: "mountain lodges and fireplaces": Parker, *YBO*, p. 180.

173: "if you're thinking about any funny stuff" *through* "and the food": Ibid., pp. 193–197.

173: "decadent friendships": JK, *VD*, p. 196.

173: "looked in my closet": Parker, *YBO*, p. 214.

174: Leo, so drunk: Ibid., pp. 213–219, 231–232.

174: "You married this big lug?" *through* "Don't you wish": Ibid. pp. 228–230.

174–75: a "badly timed union" *through* "conservative Republican": JK to Mrs. Parker, September 1, 1944, *Jack Kerouac: Selected Letters, 1940–1956*, edited by Ann Charters (New York: Viking, 1995), pp. 76–77.

175: "You can always spray your nose": Leo Kerouac to Edie (Edith) Parker, August 1944; JK, *The Town and the City* (New York: Harcourt Brace, 1983), p. 429.

175: "a home in the suburbs is a sort of isolated hell": JK to Caroline Kerouac, March 14, 1945, *SL*, p. 88.

176: "everywhere at the same time": Holograph notes, 1943?, Kerouac Archive, box 8, folder 44.

177: "wonderful, perverse Kammerer": AG, *The Book of Martyrdom and Artifice: First Journals and Poems 1937–1952* (New York: Da Capo Press, 2006), p. 63.

177: "sprawling, nameless reality": JK to AG, September 1944, *Jack Kerouac and Allen Ginsberg: The Letters* (New York: Viking, 2010), pp. 4–5.

177: addressed to "*Cher Breton*": AG, *BMA*, pp. 74–76.

177: "Why don't you actively help": Ibid., p. 80.

178: His thoughts veered distractedly: "Waiting for Celene in Flynn's Bar on Broadway, Oct. 26, 1944," Kerouac Archive, box 47, folder 11.

179: Suddenly all this agony *through* He now saw the absurdity: "The/Spiral/Composition/Book," Kerouac Archive, box 53, folder 3; "I Bid You Love Me," November 1944, Kerouac Archive, box 43, folder 6.

180: "A new method!": "1943–?44 Journals," August 21–September 3, 1944, Kerouac Archive, box 53, folder 2.

180: He became excruciatingly self-critical: "1944 Book of Symbols," Kerouac Archive, box 39, folder 6; "I bid you love me—workbook," "The/Spiral/Composition/Book."

180: "sense-thinking": Short story, "God's Daughter," 1945, "The 'God's Daughter' Method," Kerouac Archive, box 43, folder 16.

180: A notebook contains: "The/Spiral/Composition/Book."

180: "sleek as surah": JK, *Visions of Gerard* (New York: Penguin Books, 1991), p. 122.

180–81: "Eddify yer minds" *through* "the *authentic* devil": AG, *BMA*, p. 82.

181: "Burroughs was always a very *tender* person": AG, *Spontaneous Mind* (New York: Harper, 2002), p. 21.

181: When the two of them urged Burroughs to write: AG, *BMA*, p. 82.

182: an experience Jack recorded: Two holograph poems "Morphinea," December 1944, Kerouac Archive, box 80, folder 60.

182: Allen went much further: AG, *BMA*, pp. 83–84.

182: **In mid-December he "broke down":** "1943–?44 Journals."

183: **"a whole year of drug-taking":** JK, *VD*, p. 269.

183: **"the genius of imagination and art":** JK, *Orpheus Emerged* (New York: ibooks, 2000), p. 155.

183: **"strangely maternal":** Ibid., p. 34.

184: **"false . . . compromising society":** Ibid., p. 84.

184: **"the dark secrets":** Ibid., p. 62.

184: **"the *artist-man*":** Ibid.

184: **"In art I found halfness":** Ibid., p. 99.

184: a **"journey to new lands":** Ibid., p. 87.

Apartment 51

185: **Steeves dismissed the pages:** Bill Morgan, *I Celebrate Myself: The Somewhat Private Life of Allen Ginsberg* (New York: Viking, 2006), pp. 58, 88.

185: **"Jack, you know, I love you":** AG, *Spontaneous Mind* (New York: Harper, 2002), pp. 306–307.

185–86: **"world-seeker" posing as a "soul-seeker":** Notebook [The/Spiral] "1945," Kerouac Archive, box 53, folder 4.

187: **Theo Van Gogh pointed out:** John Rewald, *Post-Impressionism: From Van Gogh to Gaughin* (New York: Museum of Modern Art, 1962), p. 42.

187: **"a perfection of attitude":** Holograph notes "On Galloway," notes "On Bill," 1944, Kerouac Archive, box 43, folder 11.

187: **"magic happpenstance":** Ibid.

187: **The Burroughs method of treatment:** JK to Caroline Kerouac, March 14, 1945, *Jack Kerouac: Selected Letters, 1940–1956*, edited by Ann Charters (New York: Viking, 1995), pp. 87–88; Barry Gifford and Lawrence Lee, *Jack's Book* (New York: St. Martin's Press, 1978), p. 47.

187: **"with a number of my defenses broken":** Barry Miles, *Ginsberg* (New York: Harper Perennial, 1990), p. 96.

187: a **"medieval saint":** Holograph essay, "A Portrait of Burroughs as a Critic," 1945, Kerouac Archive, box 43, folder 15.

188: **"destructive will":** JK to Caroline Kerouac, March 14, 1945, *SL*, pp. 87–88.

188: **In fact, Burroughs believed:** WSB to JK, March 15, 1949, *The Letters of William S. Burroughs, 1945–59* (New York: Penguin Books, 1994), p. 42.

188: **"Mr. Ginsberg, I hope you understand":** AG, *Spontaneous Mind*, pp. 283–285.

190: as **"green obviously as the day was long":** Herbert Huncke, excerpt from *Guilty of Everything* (New York: Paragon House, 1990), in *Kerouac and the Beats*, edited by Arthur and Kit Knight (New York: Marlowe, 1994), p. 72.

190: **"starry-eyed" kid:** Ibid., p. 74.

190: **"inner beauty":** Gifford and Lee, *Jack's Book*, p. 55.

190: **"And so Huncke appeared to us":** JK, "The Origins of the Beat Generation," *Playboy*, June 1959.

191: **"evil saint":** Holograph notebook [The/Spiral] "1945," Kerouac Archive, box 53, folder 4.

192: the **"heroine of the hip generation":** Ibid., box 9, folder 25.

192: **"What I look for in any relationship":** WSB, *Word Virus: The William S. Burroughs Reader*, edited by James Grauerholz and Ira Silverberg (New York: Grove Press, 1998), p. 70.

192: **Their lovemaking was "dry":** Holograph notebook [The/Spiral] "1945," Kerouac Archive, box 9, folder 25.

193: **deceiving "little animal":** Ibid.

193: **Judie is like a "sister":** JK, *The Town and the City* (New York: Harcourt Brace, 1983), p. 388.

193: **the whole "Dostoevskian scene":** Gifford and Lee, *Jack's Book*, pp. 62–63.

193: **"to feel the impact of a blow":** Morris Dickstein, *A Mirror in the Roadway* (Princeton: Princeton University Press, 2005), p. 153.

194: **"their faggishness, or their campiness":** AG, *Spontaneous Mind*, p. 24.

194: **There was a profound difference:** Ibid., pp. 281–282.

194: **"in the midst of a vast American hallucination":** Ibid., p. 283.

194: **Disgusted by a speech:** Ibid.

194: **"an inner revolution":** Holograph notebook [The/Spiral], "1945," Kerouac Archive, box 53, folder 4.

194: **"psychic cage":** Ibid.

195: **"the grace of a western hotshot":** Holograph notes "Fate-natures" (of Hal Chase and Lucien Carr), 1945, Kerouac Archive, box 9, folder 25.

196: **less of a Nietzschean:** Ibid.

196: **"the destructive fascination":** Hal Chase to Jack Kerouac, September 6, 1946, 1946–1949, Kerouac Archive, box 64, folder 11.

196: **Her bourgeois parents were insistent:** Holograph notebook [The/Spiral] "1945," Kerouac Archive, box 53, folder 4.

197: **"mopey dullness":** JK to Caroline Kerouac, March 24, 1945, *SL*, p. 89.

197: **For two weeks he stayed away:** "1945 Journals," July 24, 1945–November 6, 1945, Kerouac Archive, box 53, folder 5.

197–98: **He had decided** *through* **"otherworldly" light:** Ibid.

198: **the point of view was too limited:** Ibid.

198: **First Jack had to remind himself:** Ibid.

Benzedrine Weekends

199: **While he craved human fellowship:** "1945 Journals," September 5, 1945, July 24, 1945–November 6, 1945, Kerouac Archive, box 53, folder 5.

199: **"romantic visionary":** JK to AG, July 1945, unpublished.

199: **an "isolate" and "introspective" Jew:** AG to JK, August 1945, unpublished.

200: **Jack noticed himself:** "1945 Journals."

200: **"driven mad by fear":** Louis-Ferdinand Céline, *Journey to the End of the Night*, translated by Ralph Manheim (New York: New Directions, 1960), p. 49.

200: **In fact, he was convinced:** "1945 Journals."

201: **"What you call a race":** Céline, *Journey to the End*, pp. 3–4.

201: **"my vice, my mania":** Ibid., p. 197.

202: **"We were all tricksters":** Ibid.

202: **the "idea of getting himself bumped off":** Ibid.

202: **"the courage to really get to the bottom":** Ibid., p. 271.

202: **"We'd get to the end together":** Ibid., p. 294.

202: **the "gap" his reading of Céline had opened:** "Diary (August 21–September 3)," 1945, Kerouac Archive, box 9, folder 20.

202: **"the story of the Shroud of Céline's self":** "Facsimile of Letter from Jack Kerouac on Céline," *Paris Review*, No. 31, Winter–Spring 1964.

202: **Following the operation:** "Diary (August 21–September 3)," August 22, 1945.

203: **The next day at the hospital:** Ibid., August 23, 1945.

203: **Jack felt surrounded by the richness of American life:** Ibid., September 3, 1945.

204: **Riding a bus late one Saturday night:** Ibid., November 11, 1945.

204: **"eccentric little courage":** "I Wish I Were You (1945) Philip Tourian story," Kerouac Archive, box 15, folder 19.

204: **there was something "magnificent":** "1945 Journals," September 24, 1946.

205: **"inconvenient" worshipper:** "I Wish I Were You."

205: **Linscott found the content so offensive:** Robert N. Linscott (Random House) to Madeline Brennan (Ingersoll and Brennan), October 17, 1945, Kerouac Archive, box 9, folder 30.

205: **The battle was waged:** Gerard Nicosia, *Memory Babe* (Berkeley: University of California Press, 1994), pp. 137–138.

206: **As an ending for his Galloway novel:** "1945 Journals."

206: **Burroughs was now addicted:** WSB, *Word Virus: The William S. Burroughs Reader*, edited by James Grauerholz and Ira Silverberg (New York: Grove Press, 1998).

207: **a "life and death struggle":** Ibid.

207: **In November, Jack spent:** "1945 Journals."

208: **Separated from both his friends and his parents:** Ibid.

209: **In a sudden shift of feeling:** "1946 Journals" (1), February 25, 1946–May 2, 1946. Kerouac Archive, box 53, folder 7.

209: **He would create three separate characters:** Ibid., February 25, 1946.

209: **the "abyss of modern decadence":** "1946 Journals."

A Father's Death

210: **In his dream:** "1946 Journals" (1), February 25, 1946–May 2, 1946, Kerouac Archive, box 53, folder 7.

210: **the "handicap" of self-respect:** "My analyst and I," January 1946, Kerouac Archive, box 20, folder 6.

210: **a "new regime" in the apartment:** "1946 Journals," February 25.

210: **where, feeling very sorry for himself:** From JK to himself, February 25, 1946, Kerouac Archive, box 20, folder 5.

210: **"During all those years I knew Kerouac":** WSB, *Word Virus: The William S. Burroughs Reader,* edited by James Grauerholz and Ira Silverberg (New York: Grove Press, 1998), p. 323.

210: **"Prissy" and "lazy" André Gide:** "1946 Journals."

210–11: **By the following fall:** "1946 Journals" (3), September 3, 1946–October 9, 1946, Kerouac Archive, box 53, folder 9.

211: **"despairist" intellectuals:** "1946 Journals" (1).

211: **He followed the races:** JK to Caroline and Paul Blake, March 22, 1946, Kerouac Archive, box 20, folder 4.

211: **When Jack made an innocent remark:** "1946 Journals" (2), May 6, 1946–July 21, 1946, Kerouac Archive, box 53, folder 8.

212: **In his journal:** "1946 Journals" (1).

213: **"a feeling of irresponsible wanderlust":** JK, *The Town and the City* (New York: Harcourt Brace, 1983), p. 89.

214: **On April 23, he found himself:** "1946 Journals" (4), from May 1946. Kerouac Archive, box 53, folder 10.

214–15: **"Peter and his father":** JK, *T&C,* p. 472.

215: **"forsaken . . . left alone":** JK, *Vanity of Duluoz* (London: Quartet Books, 1975), p. 212.

215: **There, the death of the father:** Typescript fragment, revised, 1951, Kerouac Archive, box 3, folder 4.

215: **"infinite longing":** "1946 Journals" (4), June 23.

216: **"too ambitious and proud and crazy":** JK, *VD,* p. 213.

216: **A couple of months after Leo's death:** "1946 Journals" (4).

PART SIX: POSTWAR

Enter Neal Cassady

219–20: **One way he found to look at the Oedipus complex:** "1946 Journals" (4), May 12, 1946, from May 1946, Kerouac Archive, box 53, folder 10.

220: **When he went into Manhattan:** Ibid., June 3, 1946.

220: **one of the "great ravaged spirits":** Ibid.

220: **"explain everything to everybody":** JK, *Vanity of Duluoz* (London: Quartet Books, 1975), p. 212.

220: **"the dark horror":** Hal Chase to JK, September 6, 1946, 1946–1949, Kerouac Archive, box 64, folder 11.

221: **Unable to make any rational decisions:** Joan Adams to Edie Parker, December 29, 1946, quoted in WSB, *Word Virus: The William S. Burroughs Reader,* edited by James Grauerholz and Ira Silverberg (New York: Grove Press, 1998).

222: **He was in a troubled mood:** "1946 Journals" (4), August.

222: **Proud of his "austere" way of life:** Ibid., October 3.

223: **"of expectation without reasonable hope":** JCH, *Nothing More to Declare* (New York: E. P. Dutton, 1967), p. 104.

223: **Like Burroughs, Allen, and Jack:** Ibid., p. 215.

224: **that "specifically separated us":** Ibid., pp. 104–105.

224: **He shared his passion for the new sounds:** Patrick Fenton, "The Wizard of Ozone Park," *Dharma Beat,* 1997; Gerard Nicosia, *Memory Babe* (Berkeley: University of California Press, 1994), p. 167.

224: **Another of Jack's frequent visitors:** Ibid., p. 168.

225: **Although only a short time ago:** "1946 Journals" (3), September 3, 1946–October 9, 1946, Kerouac Archive, box 53, folder 9.

225: **Lucien was due to be released:** Ibid., September 24, 1946.
226: **"phenomenal fire":** Ibid.
226: **a collapse of confidence in all directions:** AG, *The Book of Martyrdom and Artifice: First Journals and Poems 1937–1952* (New York: Da Capo Press, 2006), pp. 148–149.
226: **Although Burroughs returned to New York:** WSB, *Word Virus*.
227: **Only two years ago:** AG, *BMA*, p. 155.
227: **Earlier that mid-December afternoon:** Nicosia, *Memory Babe*, pp. 173–175.
227: **"whose amazing mind had a germ of decay":** William Plummer, *The Holy Goof* (New York: Thunder's Mouth Press, 1997), p. 36.
228: **"intellectual polish, learning":** AG, *BMA*, p. 169.
228: **"a young Gene Autry":** JK, *On the Road: The Original Scroll* (New York: Viking, 2007), p. 110.
228: **But Neal also reminded him:** JK, *Visions of Cody* (New York: Penguin Books, 1993), p. 339.
228: **"There was nothing clear":** JK, *Scroll*, p. 222.
228: **"western kinsman of the sun":** JK, *On the Road* (New York: Penguin Books, 2005), p. 8.
228: **"primitive man":** *Jack Kerouac: Selected Letters, 1940–1956*, edited by Ann Charters (New York: Viking, 1995), p. 69.
228: **In fact, the naïvely written letters:** JK, *VC*, p. 338.
228: **Neal seemed like a kid to him:** Ibid., p. 340.
229: **he had warned Neal:** AG, *BMA*, p. 205.
229: **She had been only fourteen:** Barry Gifford and Lawrence Lee, *Jack's Book* (New York: St. Martin's Press, 1978), pp. 98–105.
230: **The young couple got along:** Ibid., pp. 105–106.
230: **"a wild weekend of sexual drama":** AG, *BMA*, pp. 170–171.
230: **Neal "had an element of faith":** AG, *Spontaneous Mind* (New York: Harper, 2002), p. 293.
231: **Fitz wrote him a letter:** Jack Fitzgerald to JK, December 23, 1946, 1946–1961, Kerouac Archive, box 85, folder 18.
231: **Vicki wrote to him in January:** Vicki Russell to JK, January 1947. Collection of Love Letters to Jack Kerouac (1), 1947–1949, Kerouac Archive, box 73, folder 12.
232: **"*complete* projection":** AG, *BMA*, pp. 177–179.
232: **"You've got to stick to it":** JK, *Scroll*, p. 111.
232: **"Everything you do is good":** "1947 Journals," March 16, February 24–May 5, 1947, Kerouac Archive, box 54, folder 1.
233: **"the father we never found":** JK, *OTR*, p. 307.
233: **whom he felt was "serpentine":** JK, *VC*, p. 339.
233: **his "wild yea-saying overburst":** JK, *OTR*, p. 7.
234: **Allen couldn't help having:** JK, *VC*, p. 345.
234: **The night before Neal left town:** AG, *BMA*, pp. 182–184.
234: **Jack, however, still believed:** "1947 Journals," March 4, 1947.
234: **He was unusually well dressed:** JK, *VC*, pp. 343–344.
234: **New York was an "abyss":** "1947 Journals," March 4, 1947.
234: **His letter to Allen:** NC to AG, March 6, 1947, *Neal Cassady Collected Letters, 1944–1967*, edited by Dave Moore (New York: Penguin Books, 2004), pp. 13–16.
235: **Neal compared his intended conquest:** VC to JK, March 7, 1947, ibid., pp. 17–18.
235: **"The Great Sex Letter":** Nicosia, *Memory Babe*, p. 183.
235: **he asked for nothing less:** NC to JK, March 27, 1947, *Cassady, Collected Letters*, pp. 27–29.
235: **Jack interpreted Neal's hand-wringing:** "1947 Journals," April 10, 1947.
236: **not to make too much of an "issue":** NC to JK, April, 15, 1947, *NCL*, p. 41.

The Road

236: **Jack decided to use his journal:** "1947 Journals" (1), March 3, February 24–May 5, 1947, Kerouac Archive, box 54, folder 1.
236: **On his next trip into the city:** Ibid., March 22 and March 23, 1947.
237: **"My subject as a writer":** JK to Hal Chase, April 19, 1947, *Jack Kerouac: Selected Letters, 1940–1956*, edited by Ann Charters (New York: Viking, 1995), pp. 106–108.
237: **"a serious illness":** JK, *On the Road: The Original Scroll* (New York: Viking, 2007), p. 109.

238: **Although he was briefly tempted:** "1946 Journals" (2), February 6, 1946, May 6, 1946–July 21, 1946, Kerouac Archive, box 53, folder 8.

238: **"Fortunately, he had a new terrific idea:** "1947 Journals," May 5.

239: **"a veritable Niagara of a novel":** June 16, 1947, journal entry, *Windblown World: The Journals of Jack Kerouac 1947–1954,* edited by Douglas Brinkley (New York: Penguin Books, 2004), p. 7.

239: **the "leaver-outers":** Ibid.

239: **"a lugubrious senility":** Ibid., June 19, 1947, p. 9.

239: **their "confrontation" and "confoundment":** Ibid., June 27, 1947, p. 15.

240: **"Oh God—this is all of us":** Ibid., July 1947, p. 19.

240: **Despite such dark reflections:** Ibid., pp. 16–17.

241: **postwar desecrations of what he'd expected to find:** JK, *Scroll,* p. 118, pp. 122–129.

242: **"a journey often through his own mind":** Virginia Woolf, *The Common Reader* (New York: Harcourt Brace, 1960), p. 70.

242: **"I really didn't know who I was":** JK, *Scroll,* p. 110.

243: **I woke up in the middle of the night:** JK, *Atop an Underwood: Early Stories and Other Writings,* edited by Paul Marion (New York: Viking, 1999), p. 162.

243: **"A poet," W. B. Yeats once wrote:** William Butler Yeats, "My Friend's Book," 1932.

244: **"Her lack of cynicism":** NC to AG, June 1947, *Neal Cassady, Collected Letters, 1944–1967* (New York: Penguin, 2004), p. 48.

244: **Her defenses had broken down considerably:** Caroline Cassady, *Off the Road: My Years with Cassady, Kerouac, and Ginsberg* (New York: Penguin Books, 1991), pp. 18–19.

245: **"For me, he became the angel":** Caroline Cassady, "Danger: Unexploded Myth," *Beat Angels,* edited by Arthur and Kit Knight (California, Pa.: Unspeakable Visions of the Individual, 1982), p. 103.

246: **a "Russian saint":** JK, *Scroll,* p. 150.

246: **wished he could simply talk to Neal:** JK to NC, August 26, 1947, *SL,* p. 116.

246: **"A nice girl":** Ibid., p. 119.

246: **He wrote his mother:** JK to Gabrielle Kerouac, July 29, 1947, *SL,* pp. 111–112.

246: **"the gloom, rising":** JK, *Scroll,* p. 156.

Reaching California

247: **"I have no words":** Elizabeth Nowell, *Thomas Wolfe* (Garden City, N.Y.: Doubleday, 1966), p. 290.

247: **"haggard ghost":** JK, *On the Road: The Original Scroll* (New York: Viking, 2007), p. 162.

247: **"the queen of cities":** "1947 Journals" (2), "Sept. 1947–Oct., Notes written in California," Kerouac Archive, box 54, folder 3.

247: **"It's the end of the land, babe":** Joyce Johnson and JK, *Door Wide Open: A Beat Love Affair in Letters, 1957–1958* (New York: Viking, 2001), p. 29.

247: **Within a week of Jack's arrival:** Holograph notebook ("The Champion Line") dated "Aug. 10, '47/California," Kerouac Archive, box 54, folder 2.

248: **including some limited contact with "cuties":** Gabrielle Kerouac to JK, August and September 1947, 1947–1949, Kerouac Archive, box 67, folder 4.

249: **Now that Jack was reunited with a typewriter:** JK to NC, August 26, 1947, *SL,* p. 113.

249: **"The first person seems":** Clark Coolidge, "Jack," *Village Voice Literary Supplement,* April 1995.

249: **A kind of lyrical ecstasy:** JK, *The Town and the City* (New York: Harcourt Brace, 1983), p. 89.

250: **"forget all rules":** NC to JK, January 7, 1948, *NCL,* pp. 69–70.

250: **He told Neal he was now planning:** JK to NC, August 26, 1947, *SL,* pp. 115–118.

251: **"doubt your disappointment in them":** JK to AG, August 26, 1947, *SL,* pp. 123–124.

251: **"brought life to you":** JCH to JK, November 30, 1948, *The Beat Diary,* edited by Arthur and Kit Knight (California, Pa.: Unspeakable Visions of the Individual, 1977), pp. 116–119.

252: **"melancholy horror":** "California Swan Song Oct. 11, 1947," Kerouac Archive, box 54, folder 4.

252: **a shallow, spiritually empty place:** JK to Caroline Kerouac, September 25, 1947, *SL,* p. 131.

253: **the most "unspoiled boy":** Bea Franco letters, fall 1947, Collection of Love Letters to Jack Kerouac (1), Kerouac Archive, box 73, folder 10.

253: **"She was going to be my girl in town":** JK, *On the Road* (New York: Penguin Books, 2005), p. 86.

253: **"fantastic carnival of lights":** Ibid., pp. 86–87.

254: **"They thought I was a Mexican":** Ibid., p. 98.

254: **"I wish I were you, Jackie":** Bea Franco to JK, Collection of Love Letters to Jack Kerouac (1).

255: **he'd just had his "Hollywood career":** JK, *OTR*, p. 102.

255: **After Gabe went to bed:** "Winter journal, Winter 1947–1948, New York (Ozone Park)," Kerouac Archive, box 4, folder 51.

256: **Bea kept in touch with Jack:** Bea Franco to JK, fall 1947, Collection of Love Letters to Jack Kerouac (1).

Ozone Park

256: **an encounter he'd had:** "Winter journal, Winter 1947–1948, New York (Ozone Park)," "The Ghost of the Susquehanna," Kerouac Archive, box 4, folder 51.

257: **"the daemonic one":** November 4, 1947, *Windblown World: The Journals of Jack Kerouac 1947–1954,* edited by Douglas Brinkley (New York: Penguin Books, 2004), p. 24.

257: **an unfinished "cathedral":** "Winter Journal," "Gratitude," November 7, 1947.

257: ***"more myself"*:** November 7, 1947, *WW*, p. 25.

257: **so far he'd been the imitator:** "1946 Journals" (1), February 25, 1946–May 2, 1946. Kerouac Archive, box 53, folder 7.

258: **"mood" was the "living principle":** "1947 Journals" (2), "Sept. 1947–Oct., Notes written in California," Kerouac Archive, box 54, folder 3.

258: **He had intended Peter Martin:** "Winter Journal," "Prospectus for "City Episode of T and C, November 1947."

259: **Allen, however, had cut his own visit:** AG, *The Book of Martyrdom and Artifice: First Journals and Poems, 1937–1952* (New York: Da Capo Press, 2006), p. 229.

259: **He wrote his father:** Ibid., p. 227.

259: **"the usual slob hangup":** Ibid., p. 229.

259: **All through the voyage:** Bill Morgan, *I Celebrate Myself: The Somewhat Private Life of Allen Ginsberg* (New York: Viking, 2006), pp. 95–97.

260: **"my own love is compounded":** AG to NC, undated fall 1947, *As Ever: The Collected Correspondence of Allen Ginsberg & Neal Cassady* (Berkeley, Calif.: Creative Arts Book Company, 1977), pp. 27–29.

260: **"Allen, don't die":** AG, *BMA*, p. 239.

260: **Despite some misgivings:** Caroline Cassady, *Off the Road: My Years with Cassady, Kerouac, and Ginsberg* (New York: Penguin Books, 1991), p. 27.

261: **he now found her "enough":** NC to JK, November 5, 1947, *Neal Cassady, Collected Letters, 1944–1967* (New York: Penguin Books, 2004), p. 59.

261: **"deeper" than his own:** December 5, 1947, *WW*, p. 35.

261: **Jack was the only one:** December 31, 1947, ibid., p. 40; JK to AG, January 2, 1948, *Jack Kerouac: Selected Letters, 1940–1956,* edited by Ann Charters (New York: Viking, 1995), p. 141.

261: **Shortly after his return from California:** November 11–November 24, 1947, *WW*, pp. 26–30.

262: **Ginger, Jack wrote:** JK to Caroline Kerouac, Kerouac Archive, box 74, folder 23.

262: **"wrong woman":** January 5, 1948, *WW*, p. 41; NC to JK, January 8, 1948, *NCL*, p. 74.

262: **"I was so glad to see them":** March 7, 1948, *WW*, p. 58.

262: **"premonitions about life":** March 29, 1948, ibid., p. 63.

263: **Jack had planned:** February 25–March 2, 1948, ibid., pp. 58–59.

263: **After this heroic marathon:** March 12, 1948, ibid., p. 59.

263: **"Did I do that?":** JK, *The Town and the City* (New York: Harcourt Brace, 1983), pp. 434–435.

264: **"the beady glittering eyes of a madman":** Ibid., p. 378.

264: **"As usual," Jack wrote:** January 11, 1948, *WW*, pp. 43–44.

264: **her "league against the rest of the world":** January 30, 1948, ibid., p. 49.

264: **In the void left:** Barry Miles, *Ginsberg* (New York: Harper Perennial, 1990), p. 98.

265: **Still shaken by this incident:** April 17 and April 19, 1948, *WW*, pp. 67–69.

PART SEVEN: "WHITE AMBITIONS"

The Conquest of Manhattan

269: **"This is the way a novel gets written":** May 2–May 4, 1948, *Windblown World: The Journals of Jack Kerouac 1947–1954,* edited by Douglas Brinkley (New York: Penguin Books, 2004), pp. 71–72.

269: **"the peopled, fabulous moor of myself":** May 6, 1948, ibid., p. 73.

269: **One look convinced him:** May 11, 1948, ibid., p. 75.

270: **Four days later:** May 15, 1948, ibid., pp. 77–80.

270: **Jack hated to think:** Ibid.

270: **Saturday afternoon found him:** May 33, 1948, ibid., p. 84.

271: **"a vast confusing sprawl":** Ibid.

272 **"the fabulous mad star":** May 27, 1948, ibid., pp. 85–86.

273: **the "Tarzan of rhetoric":** Alfred Kazin, *On Native Grounds* (New York: Harcourt Brace, 1995), pp. 470–480.

273: **Allen laughed and told him:** June 1, 1948, WW, p. 87.

273: **But he had been careful:** AG to Lionel Trilling, June 1, 1948, *The Letters of Allen Ginsberg,* edited by Bill Morgan (New York: Da Capo Press, 2008), pp. 23–24.

273: **"a criminal" like Kerouac:** Louis Menand, "Regrets Only," *New Yorker,* September 29, 2008.

274: **"The phantom of great European-inspired ambition":** Seymour Krim, *Views of a Near-Sighted Cannoneer* (New York: E. P. Dutton, 1968), pp. 17–18.

274: **a literary "torture chamber":** Ibid., pp. 31–32.

275: **A house should be filled with people:** June 14–June 15, 1948, WW, pp. 90–91.

The Summer of Visions and Parties

275: **On June 16, Neal Cassady broke:** NC to JK, June 16, 1948, *Neal Cassady, Collected Letters, 1944–1967* (New York: Penguin Books, 2004), pp. 76–77.

276: **While Jack considered Neal's letter "stupendous":** AG to NC, late June 1948, NCL, pp. 81–82.

276: **"complete amused enthusiasm":** Ibid.

276: **What did he need love for:** June 26, 1948, *Windblown World: The Journals of Jack Kerouac 1947–1954,* edited by Douglas Brinkley (New York: Penguin Books, 2004), pp. 97–98.

276: **The meeting with Jack:** June 19, 1948, ibid., p. 95.

277: **He had been unusually well connected:** Sherill Tippins, *February House* (Boston: Houghton Mifflin, 2005), pp. 204–205, 223–224.

277: **"I want all the Shakespearean gamut":** JK to NC, June 27, 1948, *Jack Kerouac: Selected Letters, 1940–1956,* edited by Ann Charters (New York: Viking, 1995), p. 356.

277: **When Stringham received a postcard:** Gerard Nicosia, *Memory Babe* (Berkeley: University of California Press, 1994), p. 223.

278: **On Jack's first visit to Harrington's apartment:** June 26, 1948, WW, p. 97.

278: **"Everything you do is great, Pops":** AG to NC, July 1948, NCL, p. 82.

278: **Returning Allen's sarcasm:** NC to AG, July 1948, ibid., pp. 89–91.

278: **"a great mortal blow":** The Paris Review, *Beat Writers at Work,* edited by George Plimpton (New York: Modern Library, 1999), p. 52.

279: **unlikely combinations of words:** Ibid., p. 44.

279: **Allen had the sudden realization:** Ibid., p. 53.

279: **it seemed to him that there were "millions":** July 3, 1948, WW, pp. 100–101.

280: **the way his "strangely tender":** JCH, *Nothing More to Declare* (New York: E. P. Dutton, 1967), pp. 48-49.

281: **"so evidently on his way":** Ibid., p. 49.

281: **"wilder, poorer and less settled":** Ibid., pp. 49–51.

281: **Standing on the roof of Allen's building:** July 4, 1948, WW, p. 101.

282: **they were "rubbish":** AG to JK, late summer 1948, *Jack Kerouac and Allen Ginsberg: The Letters* (New York: Viking, 2010), p. 41.

282: **a "Parisian" waif of sixteen:** July 24, 1948, WW, p. 106.

282: **the "girl who will *allow* me my soul":** July 25–July 29, 1948, ibid., pp. 110–111.

282: "the way she clung": JK to NC, August 14, 1948, Kerouac Archive, box 74, folder 6.

282: After a furious exit: August 7–August 14, 1948, *WW*, pp. 116–118.

283: "God, emotions, Blake": JCH, *NMD*, p. 54.

283: Unsympathetically he noted: July 25–July 26, 1948, *WW*, pp. 106–107.

283: "a geekish exposure of self": August 28, 1948, ibid., p. 125.

283: Like Burroughs, Allen had laughed at his notion: JK to AG, December 16, 1948, *JKAGL*, p. 83.

283: the "battle for the inner heart": AG to JK, summer 1948, ibid., p. 40.

283: the "power and beauty": Seymour Lawrence to JK, August 20, 1948, Kerouac Archive, box 68, folder 4; August 21, 1948, *WW*, p. 121.

284: "*What*? That little piss-ass?" August 20, 1948, ibid..

284: an artist "had all the leisure": August 19, 1948, *WW*, p. 120.

284: "two guys hitchhiking to California": August 23, 1948, ibid., p. 123.

284: "of preserving the big rushing tremendousness": June 18, 1948, ibid., p. 95.

284: "True thoughts": August 28, 1948, ibid., p. 125.

284: "I'm getting more confident": September 9, 1948, ibid., pp. 129–130.

Enter John Clellon Holmes

285: he preferred to remain a "disreputable" writer: JK to AG, September 18, 1948, *Jack Kerouac and Allen Ginsberg: The Letters* (New York: Viking, 2010), p. 43.

285: He had advised his mother: August 23, 1948, *Windblown World: The Journals of Jack Kerouac 1947–1954*, edited by Douglas Brinkley (New York: Penguin Books, 2004), p. 122.

285: "beautiful, pliant, quiet": JK to NC, October 2, 1948, *Jack Kerouac: Selected Letters, 1940–1956*, edited by Ann Charters (New York: Viking, 1995), p. 168.

286: dismissing the New School: JK to Hal Chase, October 19, 1948, *SL*, pp. 179–180.

286: "nothing but Pepsi-Cola": JK to Ed White, October 29 and November 30, 1948, "Letters from Jack Kerouac to Ed White, 1947–68," *Missouri Review*, vol. XVII, number 3, 1994, p. 116.

286: Stendhal's ambitious Julian Sorel: JK to AG, December 16, 1948, *JKAGL*, p. 53.

287: to continue being "stupid and naïve": "For 'On the Road,'" October 10, 1948, Kerouac Archive, box 4, folder 20.

287: "complete otherness of the other world": AG to JK, summer 1948, *JKAGL*, p. 39.

287: Rather than arguing with him: JK to AG, September 19, 1948, *JKAGL*, pp. 42–43.

288: "I've got to rediscover the 'humility' ": November 1, 1948, *WW*, p. 159.

288: With his deep-seated prejudices: November 11 and November 13, 1948, ibid., pp. 166–167.

288: Elbert Lenrow noticed him listening: Elbert Lenrow, "Memoir: The Young Kerouac," *Narrative*, Ohio State University Press, vol. 2, no. 1, 1994.

289: "from that remote fury of himself" *through* dragging out to show her: November 3, 1948, *WW*, p. 161.

289: "Lucien-daemonic nights": November 23, 1948, ibid., p. 170.

289–90: Tolstoy's stingy use of paper *through* "so much as symbolism": Holograph notebook "1948" (1), Kerouac Archive, box 54, folder 9.

290: " 'So you want to be a writer' ": November 10, 1948, *WW*, p. 165.

290: "Kazin won't stand for your drinking": David Diamond to JK, November 2, 1948, *WW*, p. 163.

290: a fellow "spectral artist": Holograph notebook "1948" (2), Kerouac Archive, box 54, folder 19.

290: Meanwhile, Diamond regretted: David Diamond to JK, November 1948, 1948–1950, Kerouac Archive, box 65, folder 3.

290: a new "great friend, for me, the taker": November 13, 1948, *WW*, p. 162.

290: the "One Prophecy": Ibid.

291: "I want to get out in the streets and live": JCH, *NMD*, p. 195.

291: "Dostoevskian angst": Elizabeth Von Vogt, *681 Lexington Avenue: A Beat Education in New York City, 1947–1954* (Wooster, Ohio: Ten O'Clock Press, 2008), p. 31.

291: "I never realized": JCH, *NMD*, p. 194.

291: Its narrow, high-ceilinged: Von Vogt, *681 Lexington Avenue*, p. 4.

292: "Oh, yes, Jack's eyes": Ibid., pp. 34–35.

292: **a "fine couple":** JK to Ed White, November 30, 1948, *Letters from Jack Kerouac to Ed White 1947–1968* (Columbia, Mo.: *Missouri Review*, 1994), p. 119.

293: **Holmes gave Jack the supreme compliment:** JCH to JK, November 30, 1948, *The Beat Diary*, edited by Arthur and Kit Knight (California, Pa.: Unspeakable Visions of the Individual, 1977), pp. 116–119.

294: **"sexual souls":** November 15, 1948, *WW*, p. 168.

294: **The boy's family would be Irish:** November 2, 1948, ibid., p. 160.

295: **Deliberately, he held back.** November 17, 1948, ibid., pp. 169–170.

295: **A good deal of the lack of immediacy:** "Ray Smith Novel of Fall 1948," Kerouac Archive, box 24, folder 5.

296: **"my Ray Smith":** "Notes from a letter (to Temko, Dec. 13, '48)," Kerouac Archive, box 4, folder 70.

296: **He was having a hard time:** NC to AG, September 7, 1948, *Neal Cassady, Collected Letters, 1944–1967* (New York: Penguin Books, 2004), p. 102.

296: **"I must learn indefatigable ways":** JK to NC, October 3, 1948, *SL*, p. 166.

297: **"failed at fusion":** NC to JK, October 7, 1948, *NCL*, pp. 108–109.

"The Rudeness of Being"

297: **"emptiness + even falseness":** November 29, 1948, *Windblown World: The Journals of Jack Kerouac 1947–1954*, edited by Douglas Brinkley (New York: Penguin Books, 2004), p. 377.

297: **With this weighing on his mind:** November 30, 1948, ibid., pp. 377–378.

297: **He had been seeing Holmes constantly:** December 1, 1948, ibid., p. 399.

298: **a tirade of "insults":** Ibid., pp. 380–384.

298: **feeling *he* was actually the murderer:** Holograph notebook "1948" (2), Kerouac Archive, box 54, folder 19.

299: **like a "caveman" with women:** December 1, 1948, *WW*, p. 385.

299: **There, bands of lawless children:** Ibid.

299: **Even *The Town and the City*:** Ibid., pp. 382–383.

299: **Whenever he was interacting socially:** Ibid, "Exhaustion Thoughts."

300: **Jack found the editor's tone:** JK to NC, December 8, 1948, *Jack Kerouac: Selected Letters, 1940–1956*, edited by Ann Charters (New York: Viking, 1995), pp. 171–172.

300: **He took the returned manuscript:** December 8, 1948, *WW*, p. 388.

301: **"You know this is really a Beat Generation":** JK, "The Origins of the Beat Generation," *Playboy*, June 1959.

301: **Holmes, who had never been in trouble with the law:** JCH, "This Is the Beat Generation," 1952, *NMD*, pp.109–115.

301: **For Jack, who had been born an outsider:** "Notes from a letter (to Temko, Dec. 13, '48)," Kerouac Archive, box 4, folder 70.

302: **Harrington responded rather facetiously:** Alan Harrington to JK, December 1948, 1948–1966, Kerouac Archive, box 66, folder 9.

302: **In August 1957:** Diary #6, "Mexico 1957 Summer," Kerouac Archive, box 56, folder 6.

302: **Neal had phoned out of the blue:** JK to AG, December, 15, 1948, *SL*, pp. 176–178.

303: **"Why don't you die":** JK to AG, December 16, 1948, ibid., pp. 51–55.

303: **"Don't you see we both suffer?"** AG to JK, undated from December 1948, ibid., pp. 58–60.

304: **"mysterious and intriguing":** JCH to JK (1), December, 7, 1948.

304: **It began chastely:** Pauline to JK. January 15, 1949, Collection of Love Letters to Jack Kerouac (2), Kerouac Archive, box 73, folder 12.

304: **"the finest woman I'll ever know":** December 1, 1948, *WW*, p. 386.

305: **Jack wrote Pauline:** JK to Pauline, undated, Kerouac Archive, box 75, file 56.

305: **Although every dollar:** Ibid.

305: **"Nothing is true":** January 10, 1949, *WW*, p. 395.

PART EIGHT: "RAIN AND RIVERS"

"Whither Goest Thou in Thy Shiny Car at Night?"

309: **"We're on our way to New York":** Barry Gifford and Lawrence Lee, *Jack's Book* (New York: St. Martin's Press, 1978), pp. 124–125.

310: **She wasn't fazed:** JK, *On the Road* (New York: Penguin Books, 2005), p. 122.

310: **He noticed right away:** Gifford and Lee, *Jack's Book*, pp. 126–129.

310: **Luanne thought the two men:** Ibid., pp. 125–126, 141.

311: **Neal was probably a psychopath:** Ibid., p. 125.

311: **Walking into one such party:** Pauline to JK, January 15, 1949, Collection of Love Letters to Jack Kerouac (3), Kerouac Archive, box 73, folder 12.

311: **Luanne found herself squeezed into that bed:** Gifford and Lee, *Jack's Book*, p. 130.

312: **"We goofed all day":** January 10, 1949, *Windblown World: The Journals of Jack Kerouac 1947–1954*, edited by Douglas Brinkley (New York: Penguin Books, 2004), p. 395.

312: **What Jack did not go into:** JK, *OTR*, pp. 130–132; Gifford and Lee, *Jack's Book*, pp. 138–139.

312: **He stayed one night:** January 12, 1949, *WW*, p. 198.

313: **Devastated by what she perceived:** Pauline to JK, January 15, 1949.

313: **Jack preferred burning:** January 15, 1949, *WW*, pp. 398–399.

313: **Seen off by a gang of friends:** JK, *OTR*, pp. 132–137.

314: **"Same old Kerouac":** Ibid., p. 142.

314: **Now, unable to sleep:** Gifford and Lee, *Jack's Book*, pp. 133–134.

314: **"stony, red and gaunt":** JK, *OTR*, p. 142.

315: **"more sensible, more sure of himself":** WSB to AG, January 16, 1949, *The Letters of William S. Burroughs, 1945–59* (New York: Penguin Books, 1994), p. 35.

315: **"Now, Dean, I want you to sit quiet":** JK, *OTR*, p. 146.

315: **"a voyage which for sheer compulsive pointlessness":** WSB to AG, January 30, 1949, *WSBL*, p. 37.

315: **"Whither goest thou":** *WW*, p. 285, undated entry, 1949.

315: **"The greatness of Neal":** Ibid., p. 286.

316: **"where the river's all rain and roses":** JK, *OTR*, p. 156.

316: **"Everything takes care of itself":** Ibid., p. 158.

316: **"Just beyond the rim of the throbbing present":** Alan Harrington, *Psychopaths* (New York: Simon and Schuster, 1972), pp. 241–242, 23.

317: **Yet even though Luanne knew:** Gifford and Lee, *Jack's Book*, pp. 138–139.

317: **Jack seemed to become a child:** Ibid., p. 140.

317: **She had told herself that she was through:** Caroline Cassady, *Off the Road: My Years with Cassady, Kerouac, and Ginsberg* (New York: Penguin Books, 1991), pp. 83–85.

318: **According to Luanne:** Gifford and Lee, *Jack's Book*, pp. 139–140.

318: **"I saw what a whore she was":** JK, *OTR*, p. 172.

318: **he had an odd visionary experience:** *WW*, pp. 290–292, undated entry, 1949; JK, *OTR*, pp. 172–173.

318: **On February 5:** *WW*, pp. 290–291, 296, 298, undated entry, 1949; JK, *OTR*, p. 178.

319: **"The Secret of time is the moment":** *WW*, p. 295, undated entry, 1949.

319: **"I have read the big elaborate manuscript of the night":** Ibid., p. 289.

320: **"one old professional house-gambler":** Ibid., p. 304.

320: **"which is ruining the entire nation anyway":** Ibid., p. 311.

320: **a "wild desire":** Ibid., p. 313.

320: **"Life is so short!":** Ibid., p. 314.

A Change in Luck

320: **"the Great Ship of the World":** JK, *On the Road: The Original Scroll* (New York: Viking, 2007), p. 279; February 11, 1949, *Windblown World: The Journals of Jack Kerouac 1947–1954*, edited by Douglas Brinkley (New York: Penguin Books, 2004), p. 399.

321: **"a description of darkness":** *WW*, p. 400, February 20–21, 1949.

321: **His first, contrasting Theodore Dreiser with Sinclair Lewis:** Elbert Lenrow, "Memoir: The Young Kerouac," *Narrative*, Ohio State University Press, vol. 2, no. 1, 1994; JK to Elbert Lenrow, February 7, 1949, quoted in Lenrow; *WW*, p. 401.

321: **As if he were anticipating the reasons:** JK, "The Minimization of Thomas Wolfe in His Own Time," quoted in Lenrow; *WW*, p. 401.

322: **When two Lowell Prometheans:** *WW*, p. 406, undated entry, 1949.

322–23: **"about children and glee":** JK to Mark Van Doren, March 9, 1949, *Jack Kerouac: Selected Letters, 1940–1956*, edited by Ann Charters (New York: Viking, 1995), pp. 184–185.

323: **"I'm listless without reason":** NC to AG, March 15, 1949, *Neal Cassady, Collected Letters, 1944–1967* (New York: Penguin, 2004), p. 117.

323: **"You take him":** Caroline Cassady, *Off the Road: My Years with Cassady, Kerouac, and Ginsberg* (New York: Penguin Books, 1991), pp. 88–91.

323: **only hit "certain women":** Caroline Cassady, "Danger: Unexploded Myth," *Beat Angels*, edited by Arthur and Kit Knight (California, Pa.: Unspeakable Visions of the Individual, 1982), pp. 98–99.

324: **"into the realities of no-time":** JK to NC (2), March 20, 1949, Kerouac Archive, box 74, folder 7.

324: **After sixty days of incarceration:** AG, *The Book of Martyrdom and Artifice: First Journals and Poems, 1937–1952* (New York: Da Capo Press, 2006), pp. 284–289.

325: **"I learned a law of drama":** *WW*, p. 315, undated entry, 1949.

325: **If he took his papers to Paterson:** AG, *BMA*, p. 304.

325: **He walked past the house on Phoebe Avenue:** March 25, 1949, *WW*, pp. 410–411.

325: **"with great interest and respect":** Mark Van Doren to JK, March 23, 1949, Kerouac Archive, box 72, folder 31.

326: **As luck would have it:** JCH, *Go* (1952; Mamaroneck, N.Y.: Paul P. Appel, 1977), pp. 250–254.

326: **"You (Jack) are it":** AG, *BMA*, p. 262.

326: **"an historic American writer":** Alan Harrington to JK, April 2, 1949, 1948–1968, Kerouac Archive, box 66, folder 9.

327: **the novel had been his salvation:** *WW*, p. 412.

328: **"Pull my daisy":** AG to JK, May 15, 1949, *Jack Kerouac and Allen Ginsberg: The Letters* (New York: Viking, 2010), pp. 71–72.

328: **the "prophetic biblical":** Ibid.

328: **During one of their conversations:** *WW*, pp. 319–320.

328: **In May, Allen would begin writing:** AG, "Please Open the Window and Let Me In" *Collected Poems, 1947–1980* (New York: Harper Perennial, 1984), p. 31.

328: **"that there is definitely another world":** *WW*, pp. 319–324.

329: **"(it almost seems) with my eyes":** JK to Ed White, March 29, 1949, *SL*, pp. 185–186.

329: **"I've now found my father":** Barry Gifford and Lawrence Lee, *Jack's Book* (New York: St. Martin's Press, 1978), pp. 79–80.

329: **"All my geniuses are in jail":** JK to Alan Harrington, April 23, 1949, *SL*, pp. 188–189.

329: **"tied in" with a gang of thieves:** *New York Times*, April 23, 1949.

329: **Terrified, Allen threw out:** AG, *BMA*, pp. 307–313.

330: **Jack refused to "grieve":** April 29, 1949, *WW*, pp. 185–186.

331: **"Will go alone, hitch-hiking":** May 11, 1949, ibid., p. 190.

331: **"Where is Jack?":** JCH to JK, May 10, 1949, November 23, 1948–November 28, 1950, Kerouac Archive, box 66, folder 14.

Continental Divide

332: **"the wrath of sources":** JK to AG, May 23, 1949, *Jack Kerouac and Allen Ginsberg: The Letters* (New York: Viking, 2010), p. 73.

332: **a "lonely mud puddle":** Gabrielle Kerouac to JK, Summer 1949, 1947–1949, Kerouac Archive, box 67, folder 4.

332: **Jack quickly became involved:** May 22–May 30, 1949, *Windblown World: The Journals of Jack Kerouac 1947–1954*, edited by Douglas Brinkley (New York: Penguin Books, 2004), pp. 193–198.

333: **In Ozone Park:** Gabrielle Kerouac to JK, Summer 1949.

333: **Gabe proved to be untransplantable:** JK to Elbert Lenrow, June 29, 1949, *Jack Kerouac: Selected Letters, 1940–1956*, edited by Ann Charters (New York: Viking, 1995), pp. 201–202.

334: **Jack thought his mother was a "trouper":** July 4, 1949, *WW*, pp. 201–202.

334: **For the first time he got a sense:** JK to AG, July 26, 1949, *JKAGL*, pp.107–108.

334: **Gently, Giroux tried to discourage Jack:** JK to NC, July 28, 1949, *SL*, p. 212.

335: "a big Spenserian work": JK to AG, July 4, 1949, *JKAGL*, pp. 94–98.
336: "Your prose has many more *bleak echoes*": AG to JK, July 13–July 14, 1949, ibid., p. 100.
336: He also believed: JK to AG, July 26, 1949, ibid., pp. 107–108.
336: "There are no intellectuals in a madhouse": AG to JK, July 14, 1949, ibid., pp. 98–103.
337: "Your stories of the madhouse": JK to AG, July 26, 1949, ibid., p. 107.
337: After hitchhiking back: *WW*, pp. 215–217, undated entry.
338: "Hal is really dead": JK to AG, July 26, 1949, *JKAGL*, p. 108.
338: Mentally, he splurged: Ibid., p. 109.
338: "When you're a Hollywood writer": Edie Parker quoted by JK to AG, July 5, 1949, ibid., p. 94.
338: "Maybe you and I are just a dream": Edie Parker quoted by JK to AG, July 26, 1949, ibid., p. 109.
339: Grounded at home: NC to JK, July 3–July 26, 1949, *Neal Cassady, Collected Letters, 1944–1967* (New York: Penguin, 2004), pp. 118–119.
339: "I even want to help you": JK to NC, July 28, 1949, *SL*, pp. 213–215.
340: "I know I have nothing for you": NC to JK, late July 1949, *NCL*, pp. 127–128.
340: Around August 10: Caroline Cassady, *Off the Road: My Years with Cassady, Kerouac, and Ginsberg* (New York: Penguin Books, 1991), p. 100.
340: Although Jack spent only three days: Ibid., pp. 100–102.
341: In *On the Road*, it is then: JK, *On the Road: The Original Scroll* (New York: Viking, 2007), pp. 292–294.
341: Two days later, after a glorious mad night: Ibid., p. 307.
342: Vern would "come and go": JK to NC (2), July 10, 1949, Kerouac Archive, box 74, folder 7.
342: There was a lot of doubling: "Ray Smith Novel of Fall 1948," Kerouac Archive, box 24, folder 5.
343: "children of the great bop innovators": JK, *Scroll*, p. 337.
343: But it was all downhill from there: Ibid., pp. 342–344.
344: "permeated completely with the strange gray Myth": Ibid., pp. 343–346.
344: Since they had to wait in Detroit: Ibid., pp. 347–348.

The Edge of Success

344: Jack's mother was thrilled: Gabrielle Kerouac to JK, August 1949, 1947–1949, Kerouac Archive, box 67, folder 4.
344: But the quiet small-town appearance: Patrick Fenton, "The Wizard of Ozone Park," *Dharma Beat*, 1997.
345: a glamorous fixture: Barry Gifford and Lawrence Lee, *Jack's Book* (New York: St. Martin's Press, 1978), pp. 149–150.
345: but his efforts seemed "ragged": August 29, 1949, *Windblown World: The Journals of Jack Kerouac 1947–1954*, edited by Douglas Brinkley (New York: Penguin Books, 2004), pp. 204–205.
346: His dark mood: August 30, 1949, ibid., p. 214.
346: Jack had little time in September: Ibid., p. 220.
346: "close, concerned questions": JCH to JK, April 25, 1950, November 23, 1948–November 28, 1950, Kerouac Archive, box 66, folder 14.
346: "Without discipline": September 18, 1949, *WW*, p. 220.
347: "Oh to be what everyone wants me to be": September 21, 1949, ibid., p. 221.
347: felt "there was something wrong": Gifford and Lee, *Jack's Book*, p. 148.
347: Jack's evenings with his editor: September 21, 1949, *WW*, pp. 221–222.
348: By October 3: Ibid., p. 223.
348: Jack seemed proud: October 4, 1949, ibid., pp. 224–225.
349: "This is what I want to write": October 17, 1949, ibid., p. 237.
349: After studying *Hamlet*: October 24–October 26, 1949, ibid., p. 239.
349: Meanwhile, there were the weekend parties: October 9, 1949, ibid., pp. 233–235.
349: He had another fine time: October 20–October 23, 1949, ibid., p. 237.
349: his state of "introspective paralysis": November 2–November 6, 1949, ibid., pp. 244–245.
350: "It's not the words that count": November 30–December 2, 1949, ibid., p. 252.
350: Holmes was doggedly forging ahead: Ann Charters and Samuel Charters, *Brother-Souls: John Clellon Holmes, Jack Kerouac, and the Beat Generation* (Jackson, Miss.: University Press of Mississippi, 2010), pp. 146–149.

350–51: **"the hesitant, overly intellectual skeptic":** JCH to JK, July 3, 1949, November 23, 1948–November 3, 1950, Kerouac Archive, box 66, folder 14.

351: **"great canvases of the New York scene":** Charters, *Brother-Souls*, p. 148.

351: **"There is something nearly malignantly fascinating":** JCH to JK, November 3, 1950, Kerouac Archive, box 66, folder 14.

351: **Once Jack told Allen that Holmes hated people:** Charters, *Brother-Souls*, p. 176.

352: **"All of which is soul balm to me":** JCH to Alan Harrington, 1950, ibid., p. 155.

352: **In a state of exhaustion:** JK to AG, January 13, 1950, *Jack Kerouac and Allen Ginsberg: The Letters* (New York: Viking, 2010), p. 114.

352: **"talking from a nightmare":** JCH, *Go* (1952; Mamaroneck, N.Y.: Paul P. Appel, 1977), p. 73.

352: **Randomly furnished with dilapidated items:** Ibid., p. 71.

352: **Stored out of sight:** Liza Williams, "Another Pretty Face," *The Rolling Stone Book of the Beats*, edited by Holly George-Warren (New York: Hyperion, 1999), p. 304.

352: **She thought of herself:** Joan Haverty, *Nobody's Wife: The Smart Aleck and the King of Beats* (Berkeley, Calif.: Creative Arts Book Company, 1990), p. 16.

353: **"Please tell Kerouac he is in good company":** JK to AG, January 13, 1950, JKAGL, pp. 113–114.

353: **Jack couldn't resist quoting that:** Ibid.

354: **The long, detailed letter Allen wrote him:** AG to JK, February 1950, JKAGL, pp. 117–119.

354: **"Frankly, it is a lot better than I expected":** WSB to JK, March 10, 1950, *The Letters of William S. Burroughs, 1945–59* (New York: Penguin Books, 1994), p. 65.

354: **Joan also sent a note:** Joan Adams to JK, February 28, 1950, February 28, 1950–July 26, 1951, Kerouac Archive, box 63, folder 1.

354: **Trying to fire himself up:** February 1950, WW, p. 262.

354: **Jack's new prospectus for the book:** "On The Road 'Prospectus,' " February 15, 1950, Kerouac Archive, box 1, folder 33.

355: **As he started all over again:** February 18, 1950, WW, p. 460.

356: **Although Jack regarded the prank as "innocent":** February 21–February 24, 1950, ibid., pp. 268–269.

The French Canadian Older Brother

356: **anticipatory "dreamlike terror":** Thomas Wolfe, *The Story of a Novel* (New York: Scribners, 1964), pp. 12–13.

357: **"That I spent 4 years abandoning the joys":** March 2, 1950, *Windblown World: The Journals of Jack Kerouac 1947–1954*, edited by Douglas Brinkley (New York: Penguin Books, 2004), p. 276.

357: **"It belongs to the category of the 'big' novel":** Howard Mumford Jones, "Back to Merrimack," *Saturday Review of Literature*, March 11, 1950.

357: **"a rough diamond of a book":** John Brooks, "Of Growth and Decay," *New York Times Book Review*, March 5, 1950.

358: **"hidden from the sun":** March 2, 1950, WW, p. 277.

358: **"I know I am going to love you":** Sarah Yokely to JK, Kerouac Archive, box 11, folder 35.

358–59: **"Hold onto Sarah":** JCH to JK, April 25, 1950, November 23, 1948–November 28, 1950, Kerouac Archive, box 66, folder 14.

359: **"I want the truth":** March 8, 1950, WW, pp. 278–279.

359: **He arrived in Lowell:** Paul Maher, *Kerouac: His Life and Work* (New York: Taylor Trade Publishing, 2007), p. 211.

359: **"BOOK NOT SELLING MUCH":** April, 3, 1950, WW, p. 279.

359: **"You'd be awful easy to forget":** Gerard Nicosia, *Memory Babe* (Berkeley: University of California Press, 1994), p. 326.

359–60: **He began to feel that Giroux had betrayed him:** Holograph and typescript fragments and notes, revised, untitled, "The publishers show grave concern for one of their hacks," Kerouac Archive, box 2, folder 10.

360: **that "one month" would change his life:** Alfred Kazin to JK, May 5, 1950, 1949–1954, Kerouac Archive, box 66, folder 35.

360: **The story shows:** "Flower that blows in the night," Kerouac Archive, box 1, folder 36.

361: **When John and Marian Holmes:** JCH to JK, April 25, 1950, Kerouac Archive, box 66, folder 14.

361: **"trying to divide the 'beat'"**: JCH to JK, April 28, 1950, Kerouac Archive, box 66, folder 14.
362: **Holmes had brought up a very awkward moment:** JCH to JK, April 25, 1950, Kerouac Archive, box 66, folder 14.
362: **he often felt "dulled":** JK to JCH, May 1–May 3, 1950, Berg Collection m.b. Kerouac a.l.s. to Holmes, 1948.
363: **a "love seasoned with idolatry":** Sarah Yokely to JK, Spring 1950, Collection of Love Letters to Jack Kerouac, Kerouac Archive, box 73, folder 12.
363: **"She was too haughty for my kind":** May 19, 1950, *WW*, p. 259.
363: **"who fed me lobsters":** JK, *On the Road: The Original Scroll* (New York: Viking, 2007), p. 350.
363: **a "French-Canadian older brother":** May 19, 1950, *WW*, pp. 258–259.
363–64: **"Se dur pour mué parla l'Angla":** Typescript fragment, revised, Kerouac Archive, box 1, folder 24.
364: **Just before Jack's departure:** JK, *Scroll*, pp. 350–354.
364: **"You can't go all around the country":** Ibid., p. 354.
365: **"the Shrouded Stranger on the plain":** Ibid., p. 360.
365: **"I think that Jack just picked up the wrong hero":** Barry Gifford and Lawrence Lee, *Jack's Book* (New York: St. Martin's Press, 1978), p. 152.
366: **There were intimations of Mexico:** JK, *Scroll*, p. 379.
366: **"There's no *suspicion* here":** Ibid.

PART NINE: THE "RUSH OF TRUTH"

The Unwritable Road Novel

369: **"one vast Bohemian camp":** JK, *On the Road* (New York: Penguin Books, 2005), p. 301.
369: **"Okay, old Dean:** Ibid., p. 302.
369: **"while Jack had captured the pattern":** Caroline Cassady, "Danger: Unexploded Myth," *Beat Angels*, edited by Arthur and Kit Knight (California, Pa.: Unspeakable Visions of the Individual, 1982), p. 99.
370: **"thinly disguised memoirs":** Ann Charters and Samuel Charters, *Brother-Souls: John Clellon Holmes, Jack Kerouac, and the Beat Generation* (Jackson, Miss.: University Press of Mississippi, 2010), p. 21.
370: **"The way Kerouac portrays":** Ann Charters, "Reading, Writing, and Teaching Kerouac in 1982," *Beats at Naropa*, edited by Anne Waldman (Minneapolis, Minn.: Coffee House Press, 2009), p. 89.
371: **She wrote Allen:** March 24, 1950, WSB, *Word Virus: The William S. Burroughs Reader*, edited by James Grauerholz and Ira Silverberg (New York: Grove Press, 1998).
371: **a "novel about junk":** WSB to AG, May 1, 1950, *The Letters of William S. Burroughs, 1945–59* (New York: Penguin Books, 1994), p. 70.
371: **"inescapably true subconscious subjects":** "JK to Ed White, July 5, 1950, *Letters from Jack Kerouac to Ed White, 1947–1968* (Columbia, Mo.: *Missouri Review*, 1994), p. 137.
371: **"It so wondrously reminded me":** JK, *Visions of Cody* (New York: Penguin Books, 1993), p. 88.
371: **"Something is bound to happen":** JK to Ed White, July 5, 1950, *Letters from Jack Kerouac to Ed White*, p. 137.
372: **"talent considerable":** Yvonne Le Maître, review of *The Town and the City*, Le Travailleur, Worcester, Massachusetts, March 23, 1950.
372: **"what I really know":** "Road" workbook, Mexico City, July 1950, Kerouac Archive, box 2, folder 13.
373: **Since he could hardly write this book in French:** July 5, 1950, *Letters from Jack Kerouac to Ed White*.
373: **his mind was "cracking open":** JK to JCH, July 1950, Berg Collection m.b. Kerouac a.l.s. to Holmes, 1948.
374: **"But your best writing":** October 18, 1951, *Windblown World: The Journals of Jack Kerouac 1947–1954*, edited by Douglas Brinkley (New York: Penguin Books, 2004), p. 272.
374: **By this time he had digested:** JK to Yvonne Le Maître, September 8, 1950, *Jack Kerouac: Selected Letters, 1940–1956*, edited by Ann Charters (New York: Viking, 1995), pp. 227–229.
375: **"You are a strong healthy man":** WSB to JK, September 18, 1950, *WSBL*, p. 71.
375: **"He has been strangely out of town":** AG to NC, November 18, 1950, *As Ever: The Collected*

Correspondence of Allen Ginsberg & Neal Cassady (Berkeley, Calif.: Creative Arts Book Company, 1977), p. 81.

The Girl with the Innocent and Pure Eyes

375: **"coming to an end":** AG to Helen Parker, October 12, 1950, AG, *The Letters of Allen Ginsberg,* edited by Bill Morgan (New York: Da Capo Press, 2008), p. 61.

376: **"Weeklong drunks" followed:** AG to NC, October 31, 1950, *As Ever: The Collected Correspondence of Allen Ginsberg & Neal Cassady* (Berkeley, Calif.: Creative Arts Book Company, 1977), p. 71.

376: **When the relatives had taken:** Liza Williams, "Another Pretty Face," *The Rolling Stone Book of the Beats,* edited by Holly George-Warren (New York: Hyperion, 1999), p. 305.

376: **Joan Haverty looked down:** Joan Haverty, *Nobody's Wife: The Smart Aleck and the King of Beats* (Berkeley, Calif.: Creative Arts Book Company, 1990), pp. 69–75, 92–97.

377: **A year later, in** *Visions of Cody:* JK, *Visions of Cody* (New York: Penguin Books, 1993), p. 24.

377: **In fact, he told Haverty:** Haverty, *Nobody's Wife,* p. 94.

377: **Two weeks later Joan said yes:** Ibid., p. 129.

378: **"a tall, dumb, darkhaired girl":** AG to NC, November 18, 1950, *As Ever,* pp. 81–82.

378: **"The first evil":** JK, *VC,* p. 93.

378: **According to Haverty:** Haverty, *Nobody's Wife,* p. 129.

378: **to "make her mind":** May 19, 1950, *Windblown World: The Journals of Jack Kerouac 1947–1954,* edited by Douglas Brinkley (New York: Penguin Books, 2004), pp. 258–259.

378: **"My women never understand":** October 22, 1951, *WW,* p. 46.

379: **"Joan was learning to love Jack":** Gerard Nicosia, *Memory Babe* (Berkeley: University of California Press, 1994), p. 359.

379: **"great 20 yr. old girl":** JK to NC, November 21, 1950, *Jack Kerouac: Selected Letters, 1940–1956,* edited by Ann Charters (New York: Viking, 1995), p. 236.

379: **"I can't stand women":** Haverty, *Nobody's Wife,* p. 146.

380: **"If the world was entirely made up of Magians":** Herman Melville to Nathaniel Hawthorne, November 17, 1851, Melville.org.

"The Voice Is All"

380: **The thirty-two-page manuscript:** "Private MS of Gone on the Road, complete first treatment and with minor artistic corrections," Kerouac Archive, box 1, folder 37.

380: **In October, Freddie and Cousin:** "American Times," John Kerouac, Oct. 2, 3, 4. Titled: "On the Road I, II, III," Kerouac Archive, box 1, folder 3.

381: **"every kind of everyone he met":** "Whither goest thou, America, in thy shiny car at night?," Kerouac Archive, box 1, folder 30.

381: **Standing back from his fruitless struggle:** "Reader's Digest article, "autobiography of a second novelist," Kerouac Archive, box 11, folder 46.

382: **He had also been motivated:** NC to JCH, December 7, 1950, *Neal Cassady, Collected Letters, 1944–1967* (New York: Penguin Books, 2004), p. 232; Ann Charters and Samuel Charters, *Brother-Souls: John Clellon Holmes, Jack Kerouac, and the Beat Generation* (Jackson, Miss.: University Press of Mississippi, 2010), p. 179.

382: **As Neal would explain to Allen:** NC to AG, May 15, 1951, *NCL,* pp. 289–292.

382: **Judging by the five-thousand-word fragment:** NC to JK, December 17, 1950, *NCL,* pp. 244–245.

383: **To his surprise neither of them:** JK to NC, December 27, 1950, *Jack Kerouac: Selected Letters, 1940–1956,* edited by Ann Charters (New York: Viking, 1995), pp. 242–243.

383: **Jack praised the Joan Anderson story immoderately:** Ibid.

384: **Jack had also been thinking:** "Souls on the Road," December 13, 1950, Kerouac Archive, box 1, folder 5.

384: **"Let's tear time up":** JK to NC, January 8, 1951, *SL,* p. 274.

384: **"the Catholic myth":** JK to NC, January 9, 1951, ibid., pp. 287–290.

385: **Either on her own initiative:** Joan Haverty to NC, December 27, 1950.

385–86: **She did get along much better with Gabe** *through* **if that would keep him with her:** Joan Haverty, *Nobody's Wife: The Smart Aleck and the King of Beats* (Berkeley, Calif.: Creative Arts Book Company, 1990), pp. 151–170.

386: "No matter how faithful the reproduction": Ibid., p. 176.

386: "the difference between the brooding Ti-Jean": Ibid., p. 183.

386: That night, however: Ibid., pp. 179–184.

386: He said good-bye to Jack and Joan: JK, *On the Road: The Original Scroll* (New York: Viking, 2007), p. 408; Haverty, *Nobody's Wife*, pp. 185–186.

387: Around the time of Neal's departure: Haverty, *Nobody's Wife*, pp. 190–192.

387: Writing to Alfred Kazin: JK to Alfred Kazin, February 20, 1951, *SL*, pp. 312–314.

388: The menial jobs he'd had to take: "La Nuit Est Ma Femme—Winter/Spring 1951," Kerouac Archive, box 15, folder 20.

388: Struggling to maintain the literary quality: "On the Road, écrit en Francais," January 19, 1951, Kerouac Archive, box 2, folder 41.

388: The opening paragraphs: "La Nuit Est Ma Femme."

389: "unknown, unsoundable *books*": Kerouac Archive, box 15, folder 21; quoted in Isaac Gewirtz, *Beatific Soul* (New York: New York Public Library, 2007), p. 101.

390: As he translated some passages: Ibid.

390: "they rushed down the street": JK, *Scroll*, p 113.

391: Terrified by the first weekend: Gabrielle Kerouac to JK, 1951, Kerouac Archive, box 67, folder 6.

391: Writing about G.J.: "La Nuit Est Ma Femme."

392: Driving through the North Carolina countryside: Untitled holograph essay, March 13, 1951, Kerouac Archive, box 15, folder 25.

The Road Opens Up

392: As far as John Clellon Holmes could tell: Ann Charters and Samuel Charters, *Brother-Souls: John Clellon Holmes, Jack Kerouac, and the Beat Generation* (Jackson, Miss.: University Press of Mississippi, 2010), pp. 180–181.

392: "Go back to the moment": JCH to JK (2), December 23, 1950–May 25, 1956, Kerouac Archive, box 66, folder 16, quoted in Charters, *Brother-Souls*, pp. 180–182.

393: "It's very moving": Ibid., p. 184.

393: a "fullblown artist": JK to JCH (2), March 7, 1951, Berg Coll m.b. Kerouac a.l.s. to Holmes 1948.

394: "you had no right": JCH to Roger Lyndon, January 29, 1951, quoted in Charters, *Brother-Souls*, p. 176.

394: "These are *my* characters": JCH to JK, July 10, 1950, Kerouac Archive, box 66, folder 14.

395: On April 2: Charters, *Brother-Souls*, pp. 189–190.

395: In the essay Jack had written: Untitled holograph essay, March 13, 1951, Kerouac Archive, box 15, folder 25.

395: Holmes later remembered Jack saying: Ann Charters, *Kerouac* (San Francisco: Straight Arrow Books, 1972), p. 133.

395: "Went fast because road is fast": JK to NC, May 22, 1951, *Jack Kerouac: Selected Letters, 1940–1956*, edited by Ann Charters (New York: Viking, 1995), p. 315.

395: According to the story she tells: Joan Haverty, *Nobody's Wife: The Smart Aleck and the King of Beats* (Berkeley, Calif.: Creative Arts Book Company, 1990), pp. 201–202.

396: "spontaneous bop prosody": AG, review of *Dharma Bums*, *Village Voice*, November 12, 1958.

396: "real mental power kicks": JK to NC, June 10, 1951, *SL*, p. 318.

397: "And of course now": JK, *On the Road: The Original Scroll* (New York: Viking, 2007), p. 221.

397: "You get what I mean?": JCH, *Go* (1952; Mamaroneck, N.Y.: Paul P. Appel, 1977), pp. 144–145.

398: "Story deals with you and me and the road": JK to NC, May 22, 1951, *SL*, p. 315.

398: We got on a trolley: JK, *Scroll*, p. 345.

399: the ideal "girl with the innocent and pure eyes": Ibid., p. 318.

399: "I AM GOING TO BE MYSELF": "1951/Journals/More Notes," August 28, 1951–November 25, 1951, Kerouac Archive, box 55, folder 6.

399: Robert Giroux had been in his office: Author interview with Robert Giroux, spring 2007.

400: Exhausted, he staggered out: JCH unpublished journals, April 27, 1951, Charters, *Brother-Souls*, pp. 194–195.

400: "I caught my first glimpse": JCH, *Nothing More to Declare* (New York: E. P. Dutton, 1967), p. 79.

400: **On April 27, Holmes dropped by:** JCH unpublished journals, April 27, 1951, Charters, *Brother-Souls*, p. 195.

401: **"dewlike, everything happens":** AG to NC, May 7, 1951, *As Ever: The Collected Correspondence of Allen Ginsberg & Neal Cassady* (Berkeley, Calif.: Creative Arts Book Company, 1977), pp. 106–107.

401: **Without having read a word:** NC to AG, May 10, 1951, *Neal Cassady Collected Letters, 1944–1967*, edited by Dave Moore (New York: Penguin Books, 2004), p. 293.

401: **Lucien said the book was "shit":** JK to NC, June 24, 1951, *SL*, p. 320.

401: **Liz Lehrman, Lucien's twenty-year-old girlfriend:** Liza Williams, "Another Pretty Face," *The Rolling Stone Book of the Beats*, edited by Holly George-Warren (New York: Hyperion, 1999), pp. 304–305.

402: **When Jack went down:** Haverty, *Nobody's Wife*, pp. 201–202.

403: **Panic-stricken and hardly able to focus his thoughts:** JK to NC, June 10, 1951, *SL*, pp. 318–319.

403: **The day after the wedding night:** JK to NC , November 21, 1950, ibid., p. 236.

403: **She had assumed they would be talking about a divorce:** Haverty, *Nobody's Wife*, pp. 207–208.

403: **a "magnificent attic":** NC to JK, June 20, 1951, *NCL*, pp. 295–298.

404: **Jack wrote Neal:** JK to NC, June 24, 1951, *SL*, pp. 320–321.

Deep Form

404: **He had told his mother a great deal:** Joan Haverty, *Nobody's Wife: The Smart Aleck and the King of Beats* (Berkeley, Calif.: Creative Arts Book Company, 1990), pp. 209–210.

405: **What he was really intent on doing:** JK to JCH, July 14, 1951, Kerouac Archive, quoted in Tim Hunt, *Kerouac's Crooked Road* (Carbondale, Ill.: Southern Illinois University Press, 2010), pp. 115–117.

405: **He later thought:** JK, *Visions of Cody* (New York: Penguin Books, 1993), p. 42.

406: **Meanwhile, Jack's doubts:** "1951/Journals/More Notes," August 29, 1951, August 28, 1951–November 25, 1951, Kerouac Archive, box 55, folder 6.

406: **He'd wasted three years:** August 28, 1951, ibid.

406: **Jack had been reading:** Ibid.

407: **On August 31:** August 31, 1951, ibid.

407: **Exhilarated by the clarity:** September 9, 1951, ibid.

408: **On his way back to New York:** AG to NC, September 7, 1951, *As Ever: The Collected Correspondence of Allen Ginsberg & Neal Cassady* (Berkeley, Calif.: Creative Arts Book Company, 1977), p. 114.

408: **In Kingsbridge, Jack thought:** September 9, 1951, "1951/Journals/More Notes."

409: **Once again, passing through:** September 10, 1951, ibid.

409: **He went home to Gabe:** September 12, 1951, ibid.

PART TEN: INTERIOR MUSIC

Visions of Neal

413: **Filled with the energy of coming back to life:** "1951/Journals/More Notes," September 16–September 17, 1951, August 28, 1951–November 25, 1951, Kerouac Archive, box 55, folder 6.

413: **On September 18, he was awakened:** September 18, 1951, ibid.

413: **"Around the poolhalls of Denver":** JK, *Visions of Cody* (New York: Penguin Books, 1993), p. 47.

414: **When he woke up the next day:** September 19, 1951, "1951/Journals/More Notes."

414: **They drove Jack into Manhattan:** September 21, 1951, ibid.

414: **Before he heard:** August 20, 1951, ibid.

415: **One day, after picking up a book:** September 27, 1951, ibid.

416: **"I accept lostness forever":** JK, *VC*, p. 33.

416: **"My mind is entirely empty":** NC to JK, September 7, 1951, *Neal Cassady Collected Letters, 1944–1967*, edited by Dave Moore (New York: Penguin Books, 2004), pp. 306–307.

416: **Although the foreword:** JK, *VC*, Foreword.
416: **"have the same soul":** Ibid., p. 75.
416: **In 1972, when *Visions of Cody*:** AG, "Visions of the Great Rememberer," in JK, *VC*, p. 403.
417: **With a face that looked:** JK, *VC*, p. 416.

Tranced Fixations

417: **as if it were "the room he lived in":** JK, *Visions of Cody* (New York: Penguin Books, 1993), p. 23; "1951/Journals/More Notes," October 8, 1951, August 28, 1951–November 25, 1951, Kerouac Archive, box 55, folder 6.
417: **"so profoundly interior":** October 8, 1951, "1951/Journals/More Notes."
418: **"BLOW AS DEEP AS YOU WANT TO BLOW":** Ibid.; "Jack Kerouac: Belief & Technique for Modern Prose," *The Portable Beat Reader*, edited by Ann Charters (New York: Penguin Books, 1992), p. 59.
418: **A bloody miscarried fetus:** October 10, 1951, "1951/Journals/More Notes."
418: **Putting Dean Pomeray there:** JK, *Visions of Cody* (New York: Penguin Books, 1993), p. 70.
419: **"Why don't you sketch in the street":** JK to AG, May 18, 1952, *Jack Kerouac and Allen Ginsberg: The Letters* (New York: Viking, 2010), p. 174; October 16, 1951, "1951/Journals/More Notes."
419: **"a whole new movement":** JK to Ed White, April 28, 1957, *Jack Kerouac: Selected Letters, 1957–1969*, edited by Ann Charters (New York: Penguin Books, 1999), p. 34.
419: **The first was an old railroad-car diner:** JK, *VC*, pp. 3–4.
419: **a gleaming display of limitless American abundance:** Ibid., pp. 10–11.
420: **abandonment to a "tranced fixation":** November 14, 1951, "1951/Journals/More Notes."
420: **"Everything activates in front of you":** JK to AG, May 18, 1952, *JKAGL*, p. 174.
420: **There were times when the bliss:** November 14, 1951, "1951/Journals/More Notes."
420: **"wild form":** JK to JCH, June 5, 1952, *SL*, p. 371.
421: **"I've grown sick in my papers":** JK, *Visions of Gerard* (New York: Penguin Books, 1991), p. 112.
421: **"the nondescript cotton wool":** Virginia Woolf, *Moments of Being* (New York: Harcourt Brace, 1976), p. 70.
421: **one afternoon when his prowess astonished him:** October 18, 1951, "1951/Journals/More Notes"; JK, *VC*, pp. 59–61.
421: **The following night at Birdland:** October 19–October 22, 1951, "1951/Journals/More Notes."
422: **one of the disappearing brown places:** JK, *VC*, pp. 6–7.
422: **When he returned to Richmond Hill:** October 25–October 26, 1951, "1951/Journals/More Notes"; JK, *VC*, pp. 7–8.
423: **Although he wrote afterward:** JK, *VC*, p. 14.
423: **attempting to describe:** JK to Elbert Lenrow, January 13, 1958, *SL*, p. 118.
424: **the brilliant "sugar-cured" skies:** JK, *VC*, p. 14.
424: **In the self-portrait:** Ibid., pp.17–18.
425: **"She'd melt for me":** Ibid., p. 33.
425: **"raw creatures of time and earth":** Ibid., p. 22.
426: **Perhaps jealous of Allen's devotion:** Gerard Nicosia, *Memory Babe* (Berkeley: University of California Press, 1994), p. 357.
426: **He'd warned his nephew:** Barry Miles, *Jack Kerouac: King of the Beats* (New York: Henry Holt, 1998), p. 150.
427: **his "terrible no-overcoat poverty":** JCH unpublished journals, October 26, 1951, quoted in Ann Charters and Samuel Charters, *Brother-Souls: John Clellon Holmes, Jack Kerouac, and the Beat Generation* (Jackson, Miss.: University Press of Mississippi, 2010), p. 206.
427: **Hoping to show Carl:** November 5, 1951, "1951/Journals/More Notes."
427: **"the forlorn tufts of bunchgrass":** JK, *VC*, p. 71.
427: **"old cellophane, old bus transfer tickets":** Ibid., p. 70.
427: **He felt like a kid:** November 6, 1951, "1951/Journals/More Notes."
428: **Two days later he brought his new three thousand words:** November 8, 1951, ibid.
428: **his intent was to be "vertical":** JK, *VC*, Introduction.

428: **Trying to recover in Richmond Hill:** November 12–November 13, 1951, "1951/Journals/ More Notes."

428–29: **After reading the new pages** *through* **but all writing:** November 13, 1951, ibid.

429: **Back home at one** A.M.**:** November 14, 1951, ibid.

430: **On November 15, worn out:** November 15, 1951, ibid.

Rêves

430: **a "decade of parties":** JCH, *Nothing More to Declare* (New York : E. P. Dutton, 1967), p. 217.

431: **In his sleep:** JK, *Visions of Cody* (New York: Penguin Books, 1993), pp. 34–35.

431: **One unusual dream:** "1951/Journals/More Notes," November 17, 1951, August 28, 1951–November 25, 1951, Kerouac Archive, box 55, folder 6.

432: **Sometimes when he was wandering:** JK, *VC*, p. 23.

432: **"dissipation for the sake of dissipation":** Ibid., p.15.

432: **Fitz arrived from Poughkeepsie:** Ibid., p. 38–39.

433: **Allen implored him:** Ibid., p. 41.

433: **"I feel like Baudelaire":** November 28, 1951, AG, *The Book of Martyrdom and Artifice: First Journals and Poems, 1937–1952* (New York: Da Capo Press, 2006), p. 345.

433: **He was sickened:** Ibid.

434: **After discovering they no longer felt any rancor:** November 20, 1951, "1951/Journals/ More Notes."

434: **The "dominant note" of the fifties:** JCH, *NMD*, p. 217.

434: **It had been a long time since he'd sent Neal a letter:** JK to NC, October 9, 1951, *Jack Kerouac: Selected Letters, 1940–1956*, edited by Ann Charters (New York: Viking, 1995), p. 326.

434: **"I dig like you did":** JK, *VC*, p. 40

435: **He had begun the letter:** Ibid., pp 38–42.

436: **"I'm lost, but my work is found":** November 23, 1951, "1951/Journals/More Notes."

INDEX